ORIGINS OF THE AMERICAN
REVOLUTION

BOOKS BY

JOHN C. MILLER

❧ ❧ ❧

SAM ADAMS, *Pioneer in Propaganda*

ORIGINS OF THE AMERICAN REVOLUTION

ORIGINS
of the
AMERICAN REVOLUTION

✿✿✿✿✿✿✿✿✿✿✿✿✿✿✿✿✿✿✿✿✿✿✿✿✿✿✿✿✿✿✿

JOHN C. MILLER
With a New Introduction and a Bibliography

DECORATIVE DRAWINGS BY ERIC M. SIMON

✿✿✿✿✿✿✿✿✿✿✿✿✿✿✿✿✿✿✿✿✿✿✿✿✿✿✿✿✿✿✿

STANFORD UNIVERSITY PRESS
STANFORD, CALIFORNIA

TO GAY

This book owes much to the Society of Fellows of Harvard University, who made it possible for me to continue my research in American History; and to Mr. Ellery Sedgwick, who has given me a wealth of wise counsel.

CHRONOLOGY

1760
Accession of George III.

1761
James Otis's Speech against the Writs of Assistance.

1763
The Peace of Paris (end of the Seven Years' War).
The Ministry of George Grenville.
Pontiac's Rebellion.
Proclamation of 1763.
Patrick Henry's Speech on the Parson's Cause.

1764
The Sugar Act.
The Colonial Currency Act.

1765
The Stamp Act.
May. Passage of the Virginia Resolves.
June. Calling of the Stamp Act Congress.
July. Fall of George Grenville's Ministry; formation of the Ministry of the Marquis of Rockingham.
October. Meeting of the Stamp Act Congress.

1766
Repeal of the Stamp Act; passage of the Declaratory Act.
The Ministry of Lord Chatham (1766–1768).

1767
The Townshend Acts.

1768

Massachusetts Circular Letter; publication of the *Farmer's Letters*.
June. The "Liberty Riot" in Boston.
August. Adoption of the Nonimportation Agreement.
September. The Massachusetts Convention.
October. Arrival of British troops in Boston.

1768–1770

The Grafton Ministry.

1770

The Ministry of Lord North.
March. The Boston Massacre. Partial Repeal of the Townshend duties by Parliament.
August. Break-up of the Nonimportation Agreement.

1772

Burning of the *Gaspee*.
Organization of the Committees of Correspondence in Massachusetts by Sam Adams.

1773

Appointment by the Virginia House of Burgesses of a Provincial Committee of Correspondence.
The Tea Act.
December. The Boston Tea Party.

1774

March. The Coercive Acts.
June. The Quebec Act.
September. The Suffolk Resolves. Assembling of the First Continental Congress.
October. Adoption of the Continental Association.

1775

February. Lord North's Conciliatory Propositions.
April. Battles of Lexington and Concord.
May. Assembling of the Second Continental Congress. New England Troops Around Boston Adopted by the Continental Congress

June. George Washington appointed Commander in Chief. Battle of Bunker Hill.

July (to *March* 1776). Siege of Boston.

October. Invasion of Canada.

December. Repulse of Arnold and Montgomery at Quebec.

1776

January. Publication of *Common Sense.*

May. Virginia Convention instructed Virginia delegates in Congress to propose independence.

June. Resolution of Richard Henry Lee of Virginia that "these United Colonies are and of right ought to be free and independent States."

July 2. Independence voted by Congress.

July 4. Adoption by Congress of the Declaration of Independence.

Introduction

THE American Revolution was a struggle between two peoples who spoke the same language, hated arbitrary government with equal fervor, and proclaimed the ideal of liberty under law. It occurred in the empire distinguished above all others in the eighteenth century by the large measure of political, religious, and economic freedom it allowed its colonists overseas. It was mainly directed against the acts of a Parliament which has become renowned as "the Mother of Parliaments." It took place during the reign of a monarch who scrupulously observed the constitutional limits set by Parliament upon the royal power. And it happened at a time when European philosophers were looking to enlightened despots, rather than to the people, to usher in the new age of progress and reform.

"Origins of the American Revolution" attempts to explain why the American colonists rose in rebellion against a government whose authority, less than fifteen years before the Declaration of Independence, they had helped to extend over a large part of the North American continent. It seeks to chart the course of that radical alteration in the American mind—the transformation of the prevailing attitude toward Great Britain which preceded the War of Independence and which John Adams called the real American Revolution. "Origins of the American Revolution" does not account for the dissolution of the First British Empire by reference to any all-embracing single cause; rather, it emphasizes the complexity, the hesitancy, and the questioning which marked the colonists' progress toward independence.

Since "Origins" was written in 1943, new material relating to this phase of the American Revolution has come to light and, although the events of this period cannot yet compare to the Civil War in popular interest, in recent years historical scholarship has brought the struggle for independence measurably closer to the foreground of our consciousness of our past. The reader of this new edition of "Origins" may well inquire, therefore, in what respects our historical perspective has been altered by the new factual material that has been unearthed and by the course of events since World War II.

As comports with an ideological age, historians today emphasize the clash of ideas between Englishmen and Americans that preceded the War of Independence. "Origins of the American Revolution" was written at a time when the United States was engaged in a war for survival against two imperialisms which sought to conquer by ideas as well as by guns. As a result, "Origins" reflects the preoccupation of contemporary historians with the ideas generated by the upheaval in the American colonies. Here the Revolution is portrayed fundamentally as a conflict between the "English Mind" and the "American Mind."

As might be expected in a period of unexampled prosperity in which the Marxian interpretation of history has fallen into disrepute, the crass "economic interpretation" of the American Revolution, widely accepted in the depression-ridden thirties, has today few adherents. In *The Coming of the Revolution* Lawrence H. Gipson [1] chooses to emphasize the reciprocal benefits conferred by the Laws of Trade and Navigation and the very considerable amount of economic freedom permitted Americans. He finds no evidence of any design on the part of the British government to exploit the colonists for the benefit of privileged groups in the mother country. "The British mercantilist system," he observes, "was evolved not to lay tribute upon the colonies but to provide a system of protection along imperial lines for all those great interests that were sources of material wealth and power." Oliver M. Dickerson [2] contends that the evasion of the Acts of Trade and Navigation was not widespread; that after the middle of the eighteenth century smuggling was confined almost wholly to molasses and tea; and that after 1776, when the duty of molasses was reduced to one penny per gallon, the illegal importation of this commodity practically ceased. Professor Dickerson has demonstrated that the custom house officers, particularly the American Board of Commissioners of the Customs, deliberately fleeced American merchants by taking advantage of legal technicalities. Thus John Hancock and other merchants who complained of the actions of the custom house officers were actually the victims of waterfront racketeering.

The rejection of the economic interpretation of the causes of the American Revolution has been so thorough as to raise the question whether the reaction from the point of view espoused by Charles Beard and his followers has not been carried too far. "Origins of the

[1] Lawrence H. Gipson, *The Coming of the Revolution*, New York, 1954.

[2] Oliver M. Dickerson, *The Navigation Acts and the American Revolution*, Philadelphia, 1951.

American Revolution" does not wholly repudiate the idea that there was an economic conflict between Americans and Englishmen which had profound bearing upon the events of 1763-1776. However, the view here expressed is that the sharpest divergence was not between American and British merchants but between Southern planters and British merchants and manufacturers and between the American continental colonies and the West India "interest." In the context of the American Revolution, the psychological side effects of mercantilism seem almost as important as its economic results. Virtually all Englishmen believed that they rightfully possessed a monopoly of colonial trade and the power to regulate colonial economic activity as they saw fit. The preamble of the Acts of Navigation supposed no right in colonies to trade at all except with the parent country: any relaxations of that principle were a matter of mere favor and indulgence. In consequence of the restraints upon colonial manufacturing, said Adam Smith, Americans had "impertinent badges of slavery imposed upon them, without any sufficient reason, by the groundless jealousy of the merchants and manufacturers of the mother country." When their passions are aroused, men rarely weigh judiciously the good and evil of an economic system or even give precedence to the dictates of self-interest. As Lawrence Harper has observed in *The English Navigation Laws*,[3] there was no altruism in British imperialism, and many Americans believed themselves victimized by British businessmen. The enumeration of tobacco may have been of real economic advantage to the Southern planters inasmuch as it afforded them a protected market for their crops; but compulsion of any kind—even the very idea of subordination—was resented by men who thought that they were being so overreached by British merchants and manufacturers that they had become, in Jefferson's words, "a species of property annexed to certain mercantile houses in London." The credit advanced by British merchants to the colonists contributed to making England the most advantageous market for the sale of American raw products and the purchase of manufactured goods, but the interest rate (usually incorporated in the price of the goods sold) amounted to between fifteen and thirty per cent.

Living in an age of rapid democratic advance, it is natural that we should re-examine the American Revolution as a "Democratic Movement." A tendency to disparage the democratic achievements of the Revolution has recently been evinced. So little seems to have been

[3] Lawrence A. Harper, *The English Navigation Laws*, New York, 1939.

done—and always the comparison with our own day is implicit in this judgment—toward democratizing American institutions and in assailing privilege and vested interests. Were not Americans obliged to wait for the election of Andrew Jackson to the presidency before they experienced the "Rise of the Common Man?"

In his book, *Middle-Class Democracy and the Revolution in Massachusetts, 1691-1780*, Professor Robert E. Brown [4] has supplied an answer to this anomaly. It is Professor Brown's contention that since almost all adult males in Massachusetts enjoyed the right to vote—property qualifications being of little import among a people the great majority of whom were landowners—the American Revolution as a democratic movement was finished before it began. Americans had already achieved democracy, and the Revolution was fought merely in order to preserve what they already possessed.

Professor Brown makes an exact equation between democracy and the right to vote. But in eighteenth-century Massachusetts there existed a tradition of aristocratic and ministerial leadership which helped to establish the dominance of the "ruling families" of the province. It was against the rule of this "oligarchy" that Sam Adams and James Otis protested, for the most part unsuccessfully until the Stamp Act crisis enabled them to associate the Hutchinson and Oliver families with British "tyranny." That Massachusetts was not truly a "democracy" immediately after the Revolution is demonstrated by the fact that lands were taxed regardless of value or quality, that forty per cent of the revenue of the state was collected by poll taxes, the burden of which fell most heavily upon the poor, and that, partly because the state senate successfully resisted the popular demand for paper money, Massachusetts became the scene of an armed uprising of farmers. Moreover, the extensive use of the franchise by a qualified electorate in the United States waited upon the emergence of political parties, the improvement of communications, and the establishment of partisan newspapers.

"Origins of the American Revolution" gives only qualified acceptance to the doctrine that the American Revolution was "not an innovating upheaval, but a conservative restoration of colonial rights." It was not the American rebels but the Loyalists who sought to preserve things as they were in the colonies. The patriots were striving to enlarge the .area of self-government; the colonial assemblies, far

[4] Robert E. Brown, *Middle-Class Democracy and the Revolution in Massachusetts,* Cornell, 1955.

from being content with the gains they had already made, were bent upon changing the empire into a federation of self-governing commonwealths.

True, Americans protested against Acts of Parliament as innovations subversive of the British Constitution, but this was the British Constitution *as interpreted by Americans*—an interpretation which, from the British point of view, represented a revolutionary departure from the establishment. What the Americans called conservatism was such in fact only if their restrictions upon the exercise of parliamentary sovereignty were constitutional. It is significant that the government of the United States is not willing to abdicate the right of taxation, contenting itself with the exercise of an ill-defined right of supervision. Yet this was precisely what Americans demanded of the British government from 1765 to 1775.

While the American revolutionaries were conservative in the sense that they did not attempt to make a break with the American past, they left no doubt that they intended to make a break with the European past. It is when the American Revolution is viewed through the eyes of an eighteenth-century European that its revolutionary implications become most apparent. It was a revolution against Europe—against monarchy, imperialistic wars, feudalism, colonialism, mercantilism, established churches, the oppression of the many by the few. In this sense, the United States declared itself independent in 1776 not only of Great Britain but of Europe. Moreover, in its long-range effects, the American Revolution was intended to remake Europe in America's image. A few years after the United States had won its independence, Alexander Hamilton said that "the world may politically, as well as geographically, be divided into four parts, each having a distinct set of interests. Unhappily for the other three, Europe, by her arms and by her negotiations, by force and by fraud, has, in different degrees, extended her dominion over them all. Africa, Asia, and America, have successively felt her dominion. The superiority she has long maintained has tempted her to plume herself as the mistress of the World, and to consider the rest of mankind as created for her benefit.... It belongs to us to vindicate the honor of the human race, and to teach that assuming brother, moderation."

The American Revolution and the Declaration of Independence are not simply pale reflections of the European Enlightenment. Thomas Paine came much closer to the truth when he said that "great scenes inspire great ideas. The Nature of America expands the mind, and it partakes of the greatness it contemplates." At the time it was proclaimed, American independence seemed to be a desperate adventure, a gamble against heavy odds. For that reason it enlisted the support of the most sanguine, the most daring, and the most resolute part of the community, while the cautious and content tried to avoid involvement or, in many cases, openly supported Great Britain. The Revolution was the work of a minority, but it was the kind of a minority that has stamped its impress deeply upon the entire course of American history, not merely upon the revolutionary era.

One of the postulates of "Origins of the American Revolution" is that the revolution is still a continuing force in the world. With good reason, the American patriots believed that the outcome of the great adventure upon which they had embarked would determine the course of history for centuries to come, not only in the United States but in the world as a whole. They judged rightly: the success of the United States has been one of the most decisive events in modern history. But this material success is only one aspect of the continuing American Revolution, for, as Albert Camus has observed, "revolution originates in the realm of ideas—it is an attempt to shape actions to ideas, to fit the world into a theoretic frame." Within this definition, the American Revolution has not yet run its course. Indeed, its effect upon colonial peoples has never been greater than at the present time.

The Declaration of Independence is not merely an indictment of tyranny, nor does it confine itself to enumerating the liberties of Englishmen as the birthright of Americans. On the contrary, it lays down a program of action for the guidance of future generations of Americans. It makes clear that Americans, far from being satisfied with the freedom they already possessed, wanted liberation from restraints, the establishment of a truly competitive society in which individual creativity would be given free play. The English sought to maintain economic, social, and political boundaries in the interests of order and stability, and these boundaries tended to become hardened by usage and tradition. Implicit in the Declaration of Independence is the idea that freedom can exist only when these artificial boundaries have been removed. No man, the Declaration says in effect, is born with the right of ruling others, and there can be no reliance upon the wisdom of any class. The best way to achieve happiness, it is implied, is to give every individual the right to pursue it.

In contrast to the great revolutions that have marked the twentieth century, the American Revolution succeeded in accomplishing what it set out to do—to give men more liberty than they had previously possessed. This happy outcome was made possible by the fact that Americans had been trained in self-government under British rule; that they upheld the tradition of individual liberty, representative government, and the common law; that they never departed from their conviction that government, even the government of the people, must be subject to checks and controls; that they did not seek to establish Utopia overnight; that they had already achieved a greater degree of social, political, and economic equality than any other people; that they were, unlike the French, not obliged to overthrow feudalism; and that they never suffered the extreme oppression which is connotated in the twentieth century by the word "tyranny." As Tocqueville said, the great advantage enjoyed by Americans consisted in the fact that they were not obliged "to endure a democratic revolution." The foundations of a free society had been securely laid by 1776, and the superstructure was built gradually. The separation from Great Britain enabled Americans to carry on at an accelerated pace a social, political, and economic revolution that was already under way by 1776.

The leaders of the American Revolution did not simply assert the right of rebellion when government became oppressive. They were concerned with the kind of government and society that would emerge from the upheaval: a revolution, they said, was to be judged by its fruits. By their reckoning, no revolution could be accounted good unless it liberated the individual from oppression in all the protean forms it was capable of assuming. This aspect of the American Revolution was best expressed by Thomas Jefferson when he declared: "I have sworn upon the altar of God eternal hostility against every form of tyranny over the minds of men." At no time in history has this freedom of the mind been more essential to the welfare of mankind than at the present day. And at no time has it stood in greater jeopardy.

CONTENTS

CHAPTER ONE

The Economic Background

GEORGE III
King of England

IN 1763, Great Britain attained a height of power and dominion which led many Englishmen to conclude that a new Roman Empire had been brought into being through the genius of William Pitt and the valor of British arms. France and Spain, united by the Family Compact, had been decisively defeated and a large part of North America and India had been brought under British control. A period of "prosperity and glory unknown to any former age" seemed to be opening for Great Britain and her colonies. Yet those Englishmen who in 1763 regarded themselves as the heirs of Rome soon perceived a new and highly disquieting resemblance between Britain and Rome: the British Empire seemed about to go the way of the Roman Empire. It appeared probable that the same generation of Englishmen which saw the empire reach its highest point of grandeur would be the witness of its decline and fall. So swiftly did fortune turn that William Pitt, who had brought Great Britain to the zenith, died in the House of Lords fifteen years later in one of England's darkest hours.

The Englishmen who lost the American colonies were not solely responsible for the catastrophe which overtook the empire, although George III and his ministers must bear a large share of the blame. Because Americans were such good Englishmen — in the seventeenth-century mold — and held fast to the liberal traditions of English history, they made uncommonly troublesome subjects from the point of view of British imperialists. Eighteenth-century Englishmen found Americans "of a disposition haughty and insolent, impatient of rule, disdaining subjection, and by all means affecting independence" — in sharp contrast to "the remarkably pliant and submissive disposition" of the inhabitants of Bengal.[1] As a result, the British Empire was at best, in Benjamin Franklin's words, a fragile Chinese vase which required far more delicate

[1] *The Importance of the British Dominion in India Compared with that in America*, London, 1770, 58–60.

handling than George III and his baggage-smashing ministers gave it. Yet it is true that if the Englishmen of George III's reign blundered and muddled, their failure was partly owing to the fact that they had inherited a traditional conception of the relationship between mother country and colonies which proved, in the crisis, an utterly false set of rules for preserving a great empire. Many of the seeds of the American Revolution existed in the British Empire almost from its beginning. George III and his advisers ripened them and planted a new crop of grievances of their own in the colonies. They harvested the bitter fruit in 1776.

The British Empire of which George III became sovereign in 1760 was shaped largely by the principles of mercantilism. The goal of mercantilism — today it would be called economic nationalism — was the creation of a self-sufficient empire from which foreign trade and commerce were excluded; the domination of vital trade routes; and the acquisition of abundant stores of gold and silver by the mother country. Mercantilism was designed to gird a nation for war by recruiting its economic strength and crippling that of its rivals. Inevitably, mercantilism itself bred war: as the nations sought to bring vital trade routes under their control and to seize choice spots of the earth's surface and then bolt the door against foreigners, national rivalries were brought to white heat. George III's empire had not been created by the exercise of the virtues of faith, hope, and charity. Sterner stuff was required of empire-builders and the English had it in abundance. They struck down the Dutch in a series of bitterly fought naval wars; and in 1763 they succeeded in attaining a hard-won, "true, national felicity upon the ruins of the House of Bourbon."

The Laws of .Trade and Navigation or Navigation Acts enacted by the English Parliament during the seventeenth century were mercantilism translated into statute law. Although these acts were only a part of English mercantilism, they were its most important expression and formed the basis of British colonial policy long after the American Revolution had demonstrated their inadequacy. By mercantilist theory, the function of colonies was to produce raw materials for the use of the mother country, to consume its manufactures and to foster its shipping; and the purpose of the Laws of Trade and Navigation was to ensure that the English colonies fulfilled these ends. This implied, as mercantilists readily admitted, that the colonies were to remain dependent agricultural regions, closely tied to the economy of an industrialized mother country. No mercantilist saw any impropriety in consigning the Western Hemisphere to a position of perpetual economic inferiority.

In a larger sense, the purpose of the Navigation Acts was to enable England, by augmenting her national strength, to triumph over France, Spain, and Holland in the struggle for world power. In the seventeenth and eighteenth centuries, a self-sufficient mercantilist empire was thought essential to national greatness and to victory over aggrandizing rival states. The Act of 1651 — the first of the Navigation Acts — was directed mainly against the Dutch who by dint of sharpness in trade, financial resources which permitted them to give more liberal credit than the English, and the quality of the merchandise they purveyed, had been able to get the better of English merchants not merely in world trade but in the English colonies themselves. To cripple Dutch competition and lay the menace of the Dutch state to England's maritime supremacy, the English Parliament declared in 1651 that no goods the growth of Asia, Africa, and America could be carried to England, Ireland, the English colonies, except in English, Irish, or colonial ships, manned by sailors "for the most part" subjects of the Commonwealth. Dutch shipping was further discriminated against by the provision that goods from Europe could enter England, Ireland, and the colonies only if they were transported in the ships of the country "in which the said goods are the growth, production, or manufacture."

But the Navigation Act of 1651, however successful in barring Dutch and other foreign ships from trade with the English colonies, fell far short of erecting a mercantilist empire. Under its provisions, the colonists were able to send their products to any foreign market and to buy manufactured goods wherever they pleased — and Americans took full advantage of this privilege. After the restoration of Charles II in 1660, the English Parliament quickly set about closing the breaches in the mercantilist walls which remained after the Act of 1651. The Navigation Act of 1660 — the so-called "great Palladium" or Magna Carta of English commerce — went far towards making the English Empire truly mercantilistic. This measure prescribed that no foreign ships could engage in trade with the English colonies or import any of their products into England — a re-enactment of the Act of 1651. To guard further against the intrusion of foreign competition, all foreign merchants were excluded from the colonies. At the same time, England made clear its intention of concentrating control of the resources of her colonies in her own hands. It was ordered that certain commodities were to be "enumerated" — that is, that they could be sent only to England, Ireland and Wales, and — after the Act of Union — to Scotland. Despite the fact that it was greatly to the convenience and profit of the colonists to ship these products directly to the European market, the English government insisted that they must first pass through England, Ireland, or Wales, although from thence they might be re-exported to the European continent.

The commodities thus singled out for the mother country's monopolization were those generally regarded as essential to the wealth and power of the state which were not produced in the British Isles themselves: sugar, tobacco, cotton, indigo, and dye woods — the oil, rubber, and steel of modern imperialism. No country could hope to attain self-sufficiency without an ample supply of these semitropical products; and by enumerating them England hoped to relieve herself of dependence upon France and Holland and, ultimately, to oblige those powers to buy from her.

Although many important products of the American colonies were not enumerated — fish, hides, and flour, for example, were never monopolized by Great Britain — and might, therefore, be carried directly to European markets, this latitude permitted colonial trade was steadily narrowed during the eighteenth century. Great Britain adopted the practice of enumerating whatever commodities strengthened her trading position in world markets, benefited British manufacturers and merchants, or added revenue to the customs. This policy led to the enumeration of rice, molasses, naval stores, and furs prior to 1764. In that year, George Grenville, the British Chancellor of the Exchequer, in his efforts to raise a colonial revenue and strengthen the mercantile system added more colonial commodities to the list than had been enumerated during the entire period since the passage of the Navigation Act of 1660.

In 1663, the structure of English mercantilism was completed with the passage by Parliament of the so-called Staple Act. This law prohibited the importation of goods direct from Europe to England's American colonies: with few exceptions, notably wine from Madeira and the Azores, European goods were required to be first carried to England, where, after payment of duties, they might be reshipped to the colonies — if Americans were still willing to pay the cost, now greatly enhanced by duties and handling charges. Thus, in their completed form, the Navigation Acts required the colonists to send many of their most important raw products to Britain and to purchase almost all their manufactured goods in the same market. As a result, British merchants and manufacturers were placed in a position to determine the prices of what Americans bought and sold. Although the sharp edge of this pincers aimed at colonial producers was blunted by the fact that British capitalism was becoming increasingly competitive and, in consequence, probably few price-fixing agreements were entered into by British merchants or manufacturers, we shall see that many colonists raised the cry that they were being cruelly exploited by the system erected by the Laws of Trade.

In this manner, British colonial policy came to be dominated by the mercantilist principle that "all plantations endamage their mother kingdom, where the trades of such plantations are not confined to the mother kingdom by good laws and severe execution of them." For the remainder of the colonial period, the British government sought to tighten the screws of commercial monopoly upon the colonists and to devise means of more strictly enforcing the Laws of Trade. Even after 1764 when the British government turned its attention to raising a revenue in the provinces, it did not lose sight of the necessity of maintaining control of colonial commerce and trade. The Acts of Trade and Navigation were upheld to the last, and even the staunchest defenders of colonial liberty in England, including William Pitt, insisted upon keeping the colonies in economic leading-strings. The monopolization of colonial trade was held to be the *raison d'être* of the empire: "If we allow France and Holland to supply them with fabric," an Englishman said, "we may just as well give up all ideas of having colonies at all." [2] During the revolutionary period, English propagandists learned that nothing succeeded in incensing Englishmen against the colonists as did the charge that Americans were seeking to throw off the restraints of the Navigation Acts and to establish free trade with the world. [3]

Because British imperialism was primarily commercial, the British merchants and manufacturers regarded the empire as very nearly the best of all possible empires. Until 1764, at least, the govern-

---

[2] *Morning Post and Daily Advertiser*, London, January 5, 1775.
[3] James Macpherson, *The Rights of Great Britain Asserted*, London, 1776, 56.

ment carefully consulted the interests of British businessmen in formulating its colonial policy. During this period, British merchants and manufacturers found the American colonists rapidly becoming their best customers. Trade with the colonies grew steadily: in 1772, the exports of Great Britain to the colonies alone almost equaled her entire exports in 1704.[4] On the eve of the American Revolution, one third of the shipping of the British Empire was engaged in the colonial trade. "The vast cities along the coast of England and Scotland," it was said, ". . . are sprung from contemptible villages only by the American trade." [5] "The American," observed an Englishman, "is apparelled from head to foot in our manufactures . . . he scarcely drinks, sits, moves, labours or recreates himself, without contributing to the emolument of the mother country." [6] In 1774, it was estimated that in the province of New York eleven out of twelve inhabitants wore clothing of British manufacture.[7]

The spice to this feast was the fact that, thanks to the Navigation Acts, the expanding colonial market was protected from the competition of Dutch, French, Spaniards, and all other interlopers. As a result, the colonies helped cushion Great Britain against postwar depressions: when peace brought a revival of European manufacturing — with consequent loss to British businessmen who had profited hugely from the destruction of European industry — the colonies offered a market relatively free from competition. Here the merchants and manufacturers might charge what the traffic would bear, although their monopoly was tempered by American smuggling and by the reluctance of Americans to pay their debts to their British creditors. Nevertheless, British businessmen had their hands deep in Americans' pockets, and as long as the mercantilist system should endure, they looked forward to engrossing "all the money our colonists should ever possess." [8]

[4] David Ramsay, *The History of the American Revolution*, Trenton, 1811, I, 70.

[5] *The Necessity of Repealing the American Stamp Act Demonstrated*, London, 1766, 39, 43.

[6] *The London Magazine*, London, 1766, XXXV, 34.

[7] *Documents relative to the Colonial History of the State of New York*, Albany, 1857, VIII, 446. Matthew Robinson, *Considerations on the Measures carrying on with respect to the British Colonies in North America*, London, 1774, 134. *The Importance of the British Plantations in America to this Kingdom*, London, 1739, 108. *The Political Register*, London, 1768, III, 289.

[8] *Ibid.*

This trade was financed in large part by credit advanced by British merchants to their colonial customers, whether Northern merchants or Southern planters. "Credit," observed an Englishman early in the eighteenth century, "is a profitable plant that yields more fruit to our trade than the whole specie of the kingdom." Indeed, trade between Great Britain and the colonies could scarcely have been carried on without credit, for the operating capital of American planters and merchants came mainly from this source. Northern merchants in turn were enabled to extend credit to colonial farmers and thereby push forward the area of settlement; but throughout the colonial period the base of the pyramid of debt rested upon the shoulders of British merchants and manufacturers. In consequence, the capitalists of the mother country soon acquired a huge financial stake in the American colonies. By 1760, the value of British exports to the colonies was estimated to total £2,000,000 a year; but British merchants carried over £4,000,000 of American debts on their ledgers. In the case of Southern planters, they depended largely upon the sale of future crops for repayment; as regards Northern merchants, British creditors relied upon the colonists' ability to gather enough cash from the African slave trade, the fisheries, and the West Indies to pay their debts. In both cases, the merchants could ill afford to see colonial prosperity undermined by unwise restrictions, but on the other hand they felt obliged to maintain close watch over American affairs lest the colonists evade the laws upon which the monopoly of the mother country rested or seek to make themselves unwelcome competitors of British merchants in the markets of the empire.

The imposition of the mercantilist system exacted heavy sacrifices from the American colonists during the seventeenth century. Instead of the freedom of trade with the world which they had largely enjoyed prior to 1651, they were now confined for the most part to the markets of the mother country and other parts of the empire; and the colonial consumer was delivered over to the English merchant and manufacturer. From a free-trade area, the British Empire was transformed into a highly protected market closed to foreign competition. The losses in liberty and material prosperity attendant upon this economic reorganization of the empire were borne chiefly by the colonists; from the beginning, whether mercantilism appeared beneficent or oppressive depended largely from what side of the Atlantic it was viewed.

But as the mercantilists frequently pointed out, Americans were compensated for the restrictions imposed by the mother country upon their trade and commerce. Mercantilists did not advocate the exploitation by the mother country of the colonies: their ideal was rather an empire in which every part contributed to the best of its ability toward the goal of self-sufficiency; and they insisted that the good of the whole be made the guiding principle of the mother country's colonial policy. Accordingly, in exchange for the monopoly enjoyed by the mother country in the colonies, a virtual monopoly of the English market was given the producers of certain colonial commodities. All foreign tobacco, for example, was excluded from England (although this restriction was later modified to permit the importation of some Portuguese and Spanish tobacco) and Englishmen were forbidden to plant tobacco in England — a law which was consistently violated until at the end of the seventeenth century the price of tobacco became so low that it was no longer profitable to grow it there. Moreover, tariff protection was given by the mother country to sugar, cotton, and indigo grown in the British colonies — thus placing a burden on the English consumer who, in an open market, undoubtedly could have bought cheaper. At the same time, bounties were given upon the production of naval stores, pitch, silk, and wine in the colonies — in the hope that the empire would become self-sufficient in these commodities and that Americans, if encouraged to produce raw materials, would be diverted from manufacturing for themselves.[9]

Yet despite the benefits of mercantilism, Americans surrendered their economic liberties grudgingly. They lamented that the Dutch traders who in the seventeenth century sold goods at one-third the price charged by English merchants came among them no longer and that in their stead appeared Englishmen who, as the governor of Virginia said, would "faine bring us to the same poverty, wherein the Dutch found and relieved us." Bacon's Rebellion was caused in part by the depression that struck Virginia in the wake of the Acts of Trade. The Massachusetts General Court declared in the seventeenth century that it would not obey the Navigation Acts because the people of Massachusetts were not represented in the

[9] *The Trade and Navigation of Great Britain Considered*, London, 1730, 79–80. *The Importance of the British Dominion in India Compared with that in America*, 13–14. Philip W. Buck, *The Politics of Mercantilism*, New York, 1942, 15.

English Parliament and because "the lawes of England are bounded within the fower seas, and do not reach America" — a more sweeping assertion of colonial rights than was made by Americans until 1776.

As Great Britain became increasingly industrialized during the eighteenth century, the chorus of complaint in the colonies against high-priced British goods subsided, although the Southern planters remained unreconciled to British monopoly. In general, the price of British manufactures declined and the quality improved to such a degree that it is doubtful if the colonists could have bought cheaper from their old friends the Dutch. This was not true, however, of India goods, of which large quantities were purchased by Americans, a substantial part being smuggled from Holland. But even so there was considerable foundation for the claim made by Englishmen in the eighteenth century that the Acts of Trade could not justly be regarded as a hardship by Americans inasmuch as they procured cheaper and better goods in England than could have been bought in France or Holland. Later, after the United States had achieved its independence, Lord Sheffield was to elaborate this argument into the theory — and win the British government to his view — that the young republic was so inextricably bound to English economy that it could not break its bonds regardless of how inconsiderately it was treated by Great Britain.

New England did not readily fit into the mercantilists' scheme of a rightly ordered empire. Instead of busying themselves at home producing necessities for the mother country and exchanging them for English manufactures, the Puritans took to the sea with such vigor that it was said their commerce smelled as strongly of fish as their theology did of brimstone. Except for timber and masts, New England lacked valuable staples required by the mother country. And so New Englanders derived little advantage, in contrast to the Southern colonists, from English bounties: "A Cargo of any of them [bountied commodities] will be returned to us in a few Trunks of Fripperies," they said, "and we should be Bankrupt to Great Britain every Ten Years." [10]

The Puritans found that their salvation lay in manufacturing on their own and in pursuing that "coy mistress, trade" over a large

[10] *Providence Gazette and Country Journal*, February 9, 1765.

part of the world in order to scrape together enough cash to pay for the goods they imported from Great Britain. During the colonial period, the exports of the Northern colonies to Great Britain were far less than their imports from her; but the merchants prospered despite this adverse balance of trade. By engaging in the slave trade, making rum, exploiting the fisheries, manufacturing for the Middle and Southern colonies as well as for their own use, and acting as middlemen between land-bound colonists and English businessmen, they found profitable outlet for their energy and capital. The freightage, commissions, and charges for services and credits paid by the colonial consumer helped build the American seaports and laid the foundations for many of the early American fortunes. Herein the colonial merchants came into collision with the British merchants, who, by virtue of their vast financial resources, enjoyed a considerable advantage over their American rivals. But the colonists were by no means outclassed: ships could be built cheaper in New England than elsewhere in the British Empire; New Englanders possessed a canniness in trade that staggered even the Scotch; and they were masters of the art of slipping a cargo of contraband past the inefficient and undermanned colonial customhouse.

Under these circumstances, the American merchants found little quarrel with the Laws of Trade as they were actually enforced; they grew up under the system and — except for restrictions upon their trade with the foreign West Indies — were not unduly hampered by British commercial laws. The British Empire, they learned, was, in the main, big enough to hold both themselves and the British merchants, and so long as the mother country did not begrudge them a profit or too strictly enforce its laws they were in general well content. Given the lax enforcement of the Acts of Trade — by which the door was left ajar for highly profitable smuggling — and the advantages of carrying on business within the British Empire — one of the greatest trading areas in the world — it is not probable that the Navigation Acts alone would have produced a revolutionary spirit among American businessmen. On the contrary, the conviction was strongly established among many colonists that their economic well-being depended upon remaining within the empire and enjoying the benefits of its highly protected markets.[11]

In the Middle colonies, where a far more even balance prevailed

[11] For an opposing view see L. M. Hacker, "The First American Revolution," *Columbia University Quarterly*, September 1935, XXVII.

between agriculture and commerce than in New England, the Acts of Trade inflicted little appreciable hardship. These provinces exported large quantities of cereals and lumber to the European continent and the West Indies. It is important to observe in this connection that their trade with the West Indies, like that of the New England colonies, was not restricted to the British West Indies; the most profitable branch of their commerce was with the French, Dutch, and Spanish islands. Although this trade was not prohibited by the Navigation Acts, it ran counter to every principle of mercantilism and in 1733 was virtually prohibited by an act of Parliament which, as will be seen, proved unenforceable. In studying the origins of the American Revolution, it ought to be borne in mind that the prosperity of New England and the Middle colonies depended in a large measure upon a trade which had been built up outside the walls which mercantilists sought to erect around the empire.

Neither New England nor the Middle colonies were as intimately tied to the British market as were the staple colonies of the North American continent and the West Indies. Whereas the Northern colonies failed to produce vital raw materials required by the mother country and so fell short of the mercantilists' ideal, the Southern colonies fulfilled their highest expectations. These provinces constituted a rich agricultural area which supplied the mother country with such valuable products as tobacco, naval stores, rice, indigo, cotton, and sugar — the chief staples of commerce — and received in exchange British-manufactured goods. These commodities were enumerated and the planters themselves had little opportunity to supplement their incomes by smuggling. Moreover, they were excellent customers of British merchants and manufacturers. While it is true that all the American colonies depended largely upon imports of manufactured articles from Great Britain to maintain a European living standard in the New World, the Southern staple colonies were so lacking in local industries that they were compelled to look to the mother country for virtually all their manufactured goods.

Mercantilists rejoiced in the Southern staple colonies as the jewels of the empire; but many planters found that the shoe of mercantilism pinched acutely. The tightness of the squeeze differed considerably, however, among the various kinds of planters. Although they were all more or less at the mercy of the British merchants and manufacturers who sold them goods and advanced them credit, some planters had secured preferential treatment from the mother country. In 1730, for example, the British government partially met the demands of the Carolina rice growers by permitting them to export rice — which had been enumerated by the British government in 1704 — to southern Europe, although they were still forbidden to import manufactures except through Great Britain. In 1739, the sugar planters of the West Indies were likewise given the privilege of exporting sugar directly to Europe although they produced barely enough to supply the needs of the British Empire alone. This concession was won largely because of the presence in the British Parliament of a powerful bloc of absentee West India planters aided by a lobby of West India merchants.[12] As a result, during the eighteenth century, the sugar colonies were in little danger of finding their interests sacrificed to those of the mother country or of the Northern colonies; on the contrary, the Northern colonists and the British consumer were in dire danger of being made the victims of West Indian cupidity.

No such advantages were enjoyed by the tobacco growers of Virginia and Maryland. Certainly as regards tobacco, Great Britain was not in any sense "the natural entrepôt for the American trade with the continent" which the Laws of Trade sought to make it — rather, it was a bottleneck through which the British government attempted to force colonial trade. Of the 96,000 hogsheads of tobacco sent by Maryland and Virginia to England each year, 82,000 were re-exported to the continent, competing there with Spanish tobacco; and this re-exported tobacco paid double freight, insurance, commissions, and handling charges. Daniel Dulany of Maryland estimated that the Southern tobacco growers would have received £3 more for every hogshead they sent abroad had they been permitted to ship direct to the continent instead of through England.[13] In addition, the British government insisted upon its pound of flesh from the planters. A heavy duty was imposed upon all tobacco imported into Great Britain; and from this source the government drew a revenue of almost £400,000 a year. The planters complained that this duty was levied upon them rather than upon

[12] F. W. Pitman, *The Development of the British West Indies*, New Haven, 1917, 182–188.
[13] Daniel Dulany, *Considerations on the Propriety of Imposing Taxes on the British Colonies*, London, 1766, 73–76. Adam Smith, *The Wealth of Nations*, New York, 1937, 568–569.

the British consumer and that they were thereby more heavily taxed than even the British squires.[14]

The reason why the planters, more than other Americans, found their lot galling under British mercantilism was partly owing to their practice of pledging future crops in exchange for credits advanced them by British businessmen. In order to protect themselves against loss, the British merchants charged the planters high prices and high interest rates. Of the £4,000,000 owing British merchants by Americans in 1760, over half had been incurred by Southern planters. It is not surprising, therefore, that from the point of view of the tobacco growers, the Acts of Trade seemed designed chiefly for the better exploitation of American producers. The American colonies were the West of the British Empire and the Southern gentry, despite their great landed estates, slaves, and aristocratic manners, maintained an attitude toward British merchants not far removed from that of a Dakota dirt farmer toward a Wall Street banker. They were resentful toward their creditors, whom they blamed bitterly for having loaned them money. Thomas Jefferson believed that the British merchants conspired to get planters in debt by at first paying good prices and offering easy credit; then, when the planter was securely in their toils, cutting prices until he was inextricably in debt. Thus, said Jefferson, did Virginia planters become "a species of property annexed to certain mercantile houses in London."[15] Washington complained that British merchants had beaten down the price of tobacco until its cultivation was no longer profitable, and turned to wheat to free himself from their stranglehold. The Southern growers also grumbled that British middlemen devoured the lion's share of the profits, leaving only a few well-picked bones for the hapless producers. They declared that "they send their produce home, which is sold by the merchants at their own price, and aded to this Considerable Charges, there was but little Comeing to the poor planter, and Even that litle was sent out to him in some necessary furniture which cost him as Dear in proportion as his tobaco was sold Cheap. thus the Inhabitants of america were allways from hand to mouth."[16] To the planters, almost every class in England seemed to be thrusting

---

[14] *The True Interest of Great Britain, with respect to her American Colonies Stated and Impartially Considered*, London, 1766, 25, 42.

[15] *The Writings of Thomas Jefferson*, edited by Paul Leicester Ford, New York, 1894, IV, 155.

[16] *American Historical Review*, October 1921, XXVII, 74.

its hand into their pockets: "the Factors, the Carriers, the Shop-keepers, the Merchants, the Brokers, the Porters, the Watermen, the Mariners, and others," all fattened upon them. They declared that they were paying from 25 to 40 per cent more for manu-factured goods than if they had enjoyed free trade with Europe: and Daniel Dulany calculated that "the Artificial Value of a Bale of English Cloth arising from Taxes, Monopolies and ill-judged Laws" was over 50 per cent of its original worth.[17]

Besides fleecing the planters by these methods, the merchants were accused by Marylanders and Virginians of abusing their privilege of monopolizing colonial trade by making the colonies a dumping ground for shopworn, unsalable merchandise; cheating on weights and measures; and, what perhaps was most unforgivable of all to many Southerners, sending them goods which were not "genteel, well manufactured, and fashionable."[18]

No doubt the planters were less than just to their English cred-itors: there was no conspiracy to depress prices — in fact, the com-petition furnished by the Scotch merchants who were attempting to break into the tobacco trade tended to raise the prices of to-bacco — and no convincing evidence was ever presented that the British merchants were cheating on weights. Nevertheless, the fact that the Southern planters believed themselves the victims of price-rigging and scale-juggling is significant in accounting for the hostility which they displayed toward the British government after 1765. The planters' debts, observed the governor of Virginia, made them "uneasy, peevish and ready to murmur at every Oc-currence"; and Jonathan Boucher, a Church of England clergyman, concluded that the Southern gentry, despite their breeding and expensive tastes, were like conspirators and revolutionaries the world over: they were deeply in debt and eager to be free from their creditors.[19]

The low price of tobacco of which the planters complained was

[17] Dulany, 35, 73–76. *The American Gazette*, London, 1768–1769, 41. *Letters and Papers relating chiefly to the Provincial History of Pennsylvania*, Phila-delphia, 1855, 213–214.

[18] *Proceedings and Debates of the British Parliament respecting North America*, edited by L. F. Stock, Washington, 1937, IV, 221. Essex Institute, *Historical Collections*, January 1927, LXIII, 28. *Principles and Acts of the Revolution*, edited by H. Niles, Boston, 1817, 67, note.

[19] *Governor Fauquier to the Earl of Halifax*, June 14, 1765, P.R.O., C.O., Class 5, 1345. Jonathan Boucher, *A View of the Causes and Consequences of the American Revolution*, London, 1797, xliii (preface).

owing to circumstances over which the British merchants had no control. Tobacco consumption in England was leveling off after a long rise: it was said "multitudes have left off taking it" and that it had almost been cast out of "polite company." [20] The result was that tobacco prices fell but the planters refused to adjust their scale of living to new conditions: they continued to order luxuries from British merchants as usual and thus sank even more deeply into debt. Their contempt for trade likewise proved injurious to their interests. Disdaining commerce as unworthy of a gentleman, the planters were obliged to deal through resident Scottish and English representatives of the great British mercantile houses. These factors or merchants, particularly the Scotch, were regarded as an alien breed — money-grabbers and cheats who lived by defrauding the planters. Colonel Chiswell of Virginia called Robert Routledge, a merchant of Prince Edward County, a "fugitive rebel, a villain who came to Virginia to cheat and defraud men of their property, and a Presbyterian fellow." Whereupon the Colonel ran Routledge through with his sword, declaring as he applied the *coup de grâce*, "He deserves his fate, damn him; I aimed at his heart, and I have hit it." After which, "he called for a bowl of toddy, and drank it very freely." [21] Virginians complained that the Scotch merchants trading in America had raised Glasgow "from being a poor, small, petty Port, to one of the richest Towns and trading Ports in his Majesty's Dominions, and all by Fawning, Flattery, and outwitting the indolent and thoughtless Planters." It is significant that of the Tory property confiscated by Virginians during the Revolutionary War, one third belonged to the hated Scotch merchants of Norfolk. [22]

The repeated intervention by the British government on behalf of the English and Scottish merchants certainly gave the planters no cause to love British imperialism. It was the home government which thwarted their attempts to pass laws making lands and Negroes freehold and therefore not liable to seizure as satisfaction

[20] Dulany, 34. It is also clear that "soil exhaustion and the mounting burden of fixed charges and debt" contributed to the plight of colonial tobacco growers. A thorough discussion of this subject may be found in Curtis P. Nettels, *The Roots of American Civilization*, New York, 1938, 416–424.

[21] *Virginia Gazette* (Purdie and Dixon), July 18, 1766.

[22] *A New and Impartial Collection of Interesting Letters*, London, 1767, II, 131. *William and Mary College Quarterly*, April 1925, Second Series, 165. *Pennsylvania Evening Post*, May 14, 1776.

for debts due British merchants. Again, it was the British government that disallowed their stay laws, moratoriums, and laws prohibiting the importation of slaves — thus preferring, as the colonists saw it, "the immediate advantage of a few African corsairs, to the lasting interests of the American states, and to the rights of human nature." [23]

It became increasingly clear to Americans during the eighteenth century that the British Empire was not, as the mercantilists envisaged, a government of King, Lords, and Commons in which the welfare of the whole empire was the chief concern of imperial legislation, but a government of British merchants and manufacturers who pursued their own interests even at the expense of the colonists. The prohibition of paper money as legal tender in the colonies forcibly brought home this conviction to many Americans. Undoubtedly, the colonists had abused their privilege of issuing paper money and the British merchants had been the principal sufferers thereby. With considerable justification, the merchants complained that they found "more security, and better, & more speedy Justice in the most distant Provinces of the Ottoman Dominions from their Bashaws, than they do in some of the American Colonies, tho' under the Dominion of their own Prince." It became a proverb among the merchants that "if a Man goes over never so honest to the Plantations, yet the very Air there does change him in a short time." [24] In particular, it seemed to dispose him to pay his English creditors in depreciated paper money. Only the vigilance of the colonial governors and the Privy Council in disallowing colonial laws of this nature saved the merchants from ruin. Parliament was obliged to intervene repeatedly in their behalf: in particular, the act of the reign of George II which made lands and Negroes in the colonies subject to the payment of English debts was hailed as "the grand Palladium of Colony credit, and the English merchants' grand security." Nevertheless, the merchants insisted upon more drastic measures to prevent the colonists from wriggling out of their debts. They clamored above all for the prohibition of the colonial paper money with which they had

[23] *Massachusetts Spy*, November 10, 1774. The Virginia planters attempted to prohibit the importation of Negro slaves into the colony largely because they feared that Virginia would cease to be "a white man's country" if the blacks were not kept out.

[24] Additional MS. 27382, British Museum, folio 191.

repeatedly burned their fingers. The colonial creditor class joined in the chorus and in 1751 Parliament responded by passing an act which declared paper money illegal in New England; and in 1764 the issuance of paper money as legal tender was forbidden in all the colonies.[25]

Although this prohibition "hushed the complaints of a few arrogant merchants," it added materially to the burdens of the colonists.[26] The exportation of specie from the mother country to the colonies was not permitted because mercantilism dictated that gold and silver be kept at home — and in consequence a severe money scarcity prevailed in the colonies after 1764. The combination of the lack of a circulating medium and the threat of high taxes helped create the conditions from which the radical spirit in America sprang. It was widely recognized in Great Britain that by virtually stripping the colonies of paper money they had been left in an intolerable position; but Parliament was unable to bring itself to take any steps toward remedying the damage it had wrought. Constructive statesmanship was sadly lacking in the England of George III; and Parliament was content to rest with prohibitions and let Americans find their salvation if they could. Although Benjamin Franklin worked assiduously in England to persuade the government to relieve the money shortage, his arguments made little impression; too often Englishmen acted upon the principle that whatever the friends of the colonies wanted must be wrong and was certainly to the detriment of the mother country.[27]

Most of the colonies repeatedly petitioned the British government to relax its restrictions upon paper money. The American merchants were torn between their desire for an adequate supply of money and their fear that if Parliament let the bars down the debtor classes would flood the provinces with depreciated paper

[25] *The Interests of the Merchants and Manufacturers of Great Britain in the present Contest with the Colonies Stated and Considered*, London, 1774, 38. This legislation did not entirely suppress colonial paper money. A loophole was found in the issuance of treasury notes, which, not being legal tender, were redeemed after a short period by money derived from taxation. Also the notes of loan banks continued to circulate after 1764. About $12,000,000 were in circulation in the colonies in 1774. (Davis Rich Dewey, *Financial History of the United States*, New York, 1931, 29–30.)

[26] *Junius Americanus*, London, 1770, 4–5.

[27] *Pennsylvania Journal and Weekly Advertiser*, September 14, 1769. *Pennsylvania Chronicle*, March 13, 1769. *Colonial Records of North Carolina*, VIII, 10–11; IX, 79. *New York Gazette and Weekly Mercury*, June 4, 1770.

money. After 1764, however, the financial stringency became so acute that the merchants were driven to the conclusion that paper money was essential to their prosperity. Specie was quickly drained off to England. The fact that the colonies bought £500,000 of goods from Great Britain and sold only £300,000 in return made it inevitable, as Washington said, that the specie and wealth accumulated by Americans would "centre in Great Britain, as certain as the Needle will settle to the Poles." [28] One of the first acts of Parliament to be overthrown by the American revolutionaries after the calling of the Continental Congress was the prohibition upon paper money. The colonies began to print paper money in 1775; and it was decreed that anyone who refused to accept this or who spoke disrespectfully of it was to be treated as an enemy of the country.

By 1763, it had been made painfully evident to Americans that whenever a colonial commodity became important it was enumerated; and whenever colonial enterprise competed with powerful British interest it was struck down by an act of Parliament. To protect the monopoly of British manufactures, Parliament forbade Americans to export colonial wool, woolens, and hats from one colony to another on pain of seizure of ship and cargo; and in 1750 the erection of plating or slitting mills was prohibited. These acts were not part of the Laws of Trade but they were a significant manifestation of mercantilism. They were the work of British manufacturers who believed that colonial manufacturing was responsible for the hard times that had befallen these industries in Old England. Mercantilists warmly espoused the cause of the distressed English manufacturers: the colonists, they contended, must be prevented from rivaling the mother country since the very reason for their existence was to increase her wealth, not to compete with her industries. It is noteworthy, however, that Americans made little protest against these restraints upon their economic freedom. Subservience to unpopular laws merely out of respect for the majesty of the British King and Parliament was never an American characteristic; but so long as there was no effective enforcement of

---

[28] *The Writings of George Washington*, edited by J. C. Fitzpatrick, Washington, 1931, II, 466. *The Importance of the British Plantations in America to this Kingdom*, London, 1739, 108. *Political Register*, London, 1768, III, 289. *The Scots Magazine*, Edinburgh, 1766, XXVII, 49. *Pennsylvania Chronicle*, July 4, 1768.

the laws against colonial manufacturing, Americans were not greatly concerned over their existence upon the statute books. Even if the acts had been rigorously enforced, the damage to colonial economy would have been negligible — in contrast to the economy of Ireland, where the destruction of the woolen industry by Parliament did great injury. No important trade in woolens existed in the colonies; and the prohibition of the hat trade and the curtailing of the manufacture of iron and steel utensils did not cause serious distress. These articles could be imported from England as cheaply as they could be manufactured in America and unemployed workers could always be absorbed by agriculture or other trades. Moreover, only a small part of colonial manufacturing came within the purview of these acts of Parliament; and even in most of the industries affected the colonists were not prohibited from making articles for their own use — it was merely provided that hats, wool, and woolen goods could not be exported from one colony to another. The most important branches of colonial manufacturing were not touched. New England engaged in a considerable traffic with the other colonies in shoes (Lynn, Massachusetts, even in the seventeenth century was a center of shoemaking), soap, candles, coaches, leather goods, chariots, and chaises — but Parliament made no effort to interfere with this trade.

The law of 1750 prohibiting the erection of slitting mills was likewise not regarded as a grievance at the time of its passage. Americans "took no Notice of it as it was insignificant and did not hurt them." The act did not destroy the existing mills; it simply froze the industry, and did no injury to entrepreneurs already in the field. Although the law required American ironmasters to send their iron to England to be slitted and returned to the colonies in manufactured form, they found that they could still enjoy "a Very Pretty Profitt upon it." [29] A far more serious blow was the enumeration of iron in 1767. William Allen of Philadelphia, one of the leading iron producers, declared that his business had been "knocked in the head." He was obliged to shut down half his ironworks and run the remainder at a loss. Most of the forges in Pennsylvania, despite the abundance of cheap ore, were closed or converted into bloomeries. Indeed, the result of this legislation was to make iron manu-

[29] *The Trade and Navigation of Great Britain Considered*, London, 1730, 80–81. *The Importance of the British Plantations in America to this Kingdom*, London, 1739, 75–77, 107. Additional MS. 33030, folio 117.

facturers objects of charity: in 1771, Governor John Penn appointed to the customhouse at Philadelphia one Lardner, a bankrupt ironmaster who had lost his fortune, "as," said the governor, "has been the case with most people who of late Years have engaged in that sort of business." [30]

Americans were tardy in discovering the tyranny of these restrictions. It was not until after the passage of the Stamp Act that their real menace was perceived; and then they became rich grist indeed for the propaganda mills of the patriots. "When all this black roll of impositions is view'd together," exclaimed an American in 1776, "what a shocking series of partial, tyrannic oppression do they present." [31] The true significance of these acts lies in their effect not so much upon colonial economy as upon colonial psychology: they helped to establish the conviction in the minds of many Americans that Great Britain regarded the growth of the colonies with implacable jealousy and hostility. She seemed determined to check their progress lest they grow too strong for her control; therefore, exclaimed an American, she had adopted this "Ottoman policy, by strangling us in infancy." [32] So "jealous of our rising Glory" did Great Britain appear that the colonists began to believe that "if the extent of our commerce should draw into our hands the wealth of all the Indies," Parliament would "provide ways and means for conveying the whole into the treasury of England" — leaving Americans to find "another vacant world" beyond the reach of British authority. These evils, it is true, were merely in the breeze, but they were not for that reason less real to Americans after 1765. Charles Carroll of Carrollton believed that the British government might prohibit all household manufactures in America. "Ye severity of ye weather," said Carroll, "would pinch to death thousands of poor naked Americans. . . . England would then have nothing to fear from our numbers." [33] Carroll regarded

[30] A. C. Bining, *Pennsylvania Iron Manufacture in the Eighteenth Century*, Publications of the Pennsylvania Historical Commission, Harrisburg, IV, 38. William Allen to Thomas Penn, September 23, 1768, and October 8, 1767; John Penn to Henry Wilmot, January ?, 1771, Penn. MSS., *Official Correspondence*, X, Historical Society of Pennsylvania.

[31] *Pennsylvania Packet*, May 13, 1776.

[32] *Political Register*, London, 1768, II, 289, 292. Reverend Jacob Duché, *The Duty of Standing Fast in our Spiritual and Temporal Liberties*, Philadelphia, 1775, 15.

[33] *The Life and Correspondence of Joseph Reed*, edited by William B. Reed, Philadelphia, 1847, I, 31. *Unpublished Letters of Charles Carroll of Carrollton*,

the acts restraining colonial manufacturing as more inimical than the Stamp Act itself; they opened the door for illimitable oppression by Parliament and might be converted into a dangerous form of taxation. "If I am to be fleeced, an American might say," remarked Carroll, "if my money is to be taken from me without my consent, it is immaterial to me what manner this is effected." [34] Carroll's fears were shared by George Washington and other Virginians who believed that Virginia could never become a great center of manufacturing as long as this threat of annihilation by act of Parliament hung over the head of colonial enterprise.[35]

These restraints upon American economic liberty revealed, moreover, that a handful of English capitalists carried more weight at Westminster than the welfare of millions of Americans. "A colonist cannot make a button, horse-shoe, nor a hob-nail," exclaimed a Bostonian, "but some sooty ironmonger or respectable button-maker of Britain shall bawl and squal that his honors worship is most egregiously maltreated, injured, cheated and robb'd by the rascally American republicans." [36] "Britain," said Benjamin Franklin, "would, if she could, manufacture & trade for all the World; — England for all Britain; — London for all England; — and every Londoner for all London." Englishmen were given American soil and mines, and sometimes they refused, as in the case of the Louisbourg coal mines, either to develop them or to allow Americans to do so. By this means, it was contended, the British government made "an abridgment of the common bounties of Heaven"; "the water is not permitted to flow, or the earth to produce," lamented a colonist, "for the same beneficial purposes to the American as for the Briton." [37]

Thus these laws, in the hands of American propagandists, helped to establish the conviction that imperial policy was being perverted

---

edited by T. M. Field. The U. S. Catholic Historical Society, Monographs, Series I, New York, 1902, 139–140; 148–149.

[34] *Ibid.*, 139–140.

[35] *The Writings of George Washington*, edited by John C. Fitzpatrick, II, 502. *Virginia Gazette* (Rind's), July 6, 1769. *Providence Gazette and Country Journal*, March 12, 1766. *Pennsylvania Gazette*, February 22, 1775. *Boston Gazette*, April 29, 1765. *An Appeal to the Justice and Interest of the People of Great Britain in the present Disputes with America. By an old Member of Parliament*. London, 1776, 37.

[36] *Boston Gazette*, April 29, 1765. *Virginia Gazette*, December 3, 1772.

[37] *The Writings of Benjamin Franklin*, edited by A. H. Smyth, New York, 1906, IV, 244–245. *Pennsylvania Gazette*, February 22, 1775. Ramsay, I, 62.

to the enrichment of British monopolists. Americans seemed to be the sheep and British merchants and manufacturers the shearers. The colonists were not easily reconciled to exploitation: they did not believe that God had intended the American continent to be the property of English "merchant tailors and woolen drapers" nor was it ordained that Englishmen should have an "indefeasable right to the agonies, toils, and bloody sweat of the inhabitants of this land, and to the profits and products of all their labors." [38] Parliament had no right to "crush their native talents and to keep them in a constant state of inferiority." [39] Rather, God and nature had decreed that America was to be a "Great Empire" and the center of the arts and sciences. From this point of view, British efforts to prevent Americans from fully utilizing the riches with which nature had endowed them were an attempt to thwart God's plans for the Western Hemisphere.

It cannot be denied that there was widespread discontent among the colonists, particularly among the Southern planters, with the workings of British mercantilism. Certainly, they regarded a larger measure of economic freedom as one of the most desirable results of the revolutionary agitation of 1765–1776. The closing of certain channels of trade essential to the well-being of the Northern colonies and the efforts of the mother country to enforce the Acts of Trade after 1764 brought Northern merchants to see British mercantilism eye to eye with the Southern tobacco growers. In the correspondence of colonial merchants and planters there is a growing volume of complaint that they were risking their capital and expending their energy for the enrichment of British merchants and manufacturers. They chafed under a system which bottled up initiative and confined trade to channels prescribed by the British government, which, as was well known, frequently acted at the behest of powerful British commercial and manufacturing interests. We shall find that as Americans progressively enlarged their demands for liberty after 1765, the Acts of Trade and the entire system of British mercantilism came to be included within their definition of tyranny. Without doubt, underlying the resounding phrases and ideals of the American Revolution, there was a solid foundation of economic grievances which played an important part

[38] *Boston Gazette*, April 29, 1765.
[39] *Pennsylvania Packet and General Advertiser*, July 4, 1774.

in determining the course taken by both the Northern merchants and the Southern planters.

Yet it cannot be said that Americans were driven to rebellion by intolerable economic oppression. In general, after the postwar depression of 1763–1765, the revolutionary period was an era of growth and prosperity for the colonies. The British "tyranny" against which Americans rebelled did little to impede their material development; on the contrary, the population continued to double every generation by natural means and the demand for British manufactures increased apace. In many New England towns it was difficult to find a man not in easy circumstances. The colonial seaports continued to hum with business: in 1762 New York had 477 vessels; by 1772, the number had increased to 709.[40]

The immediate threat to American liberty and well-being after 1765 came not from the restrictions imposed upon colonial trade and manufacturing but from Parliament's efforts to raise a revenue in the colonies. It was the invasion of Americans' political rights by Parliament after the Peace of Paris which precipitated the struggle between the mother country and colonies and inspired the ideals and slogans of the American Revolution. Economic grievances played a secondary part in the patriots' propaganda; from 1765 to 1776, political issues were kept uppermost. This was in accord with the tenor of American history. Throughout the colonial period, the rights and privileges of the assemblies were regarded as the first line of defense of American liberty, both political and economic. If they were overthrown, the colonists believed themselves destined to become as "errant slaves as any in Turkey." Thus, so long as the colonists remained British subjects, they threw their full strength into the struggle to maintain the rights of their assemblies, firmly convinced that the success or failure of their efforts would determine whether liberty or slavery was to prevail in America.

[40] David Ramsay, *The History of the Revolution in South Carolina*, Trenton, 1785, I, 7–8. *Documents relative to the Colonial History of the State of New York*, Albany, 1857, VIII, 446.

CHAPTER   TWO

The Political Background

William Pitt,
First Earl of Chatham

I

HE LOVE of liberty and the hatred of arbitrary government that blazed so fiercely in the colonies during the revolutionary period had been present since their settlement. This spirit sprang chiefly from the character of the colonists themselves: the desire for a free and more abundant life and for a refuge from oppression which had led many settlers to leave the Old World was in itself a powerful barrier to the success of the plans of the British government after 1765. It is also true that the mother country itself did much during the period of "salutary neglect" to encourage the growth of self-reliance and love of freedom in its subjects overseas. The influence of the frontier and the vast expanse of ocean separating the colonies from Great Britain — which from the beginning tended to make the British Empire a federation of self-governing provinces — was never effectively counteracted by British authority. Consequently, the empire was at no time a closely integrated whole directed by skilled administrators in the mother country and sustained by obedient, loyal subjects in the colonies. Almost from the beginning of English settlement, the government permitted the tradition of local liberty to take such firm root in America that Alexander Hamilton could say in 1775 that "the rights we now claim are coeval with the original settlement of these colonies." [1]

Many of these rights were won despite the opposition of the English government. Finding that New Englanders were growing utterly out of hand, the government of Charles I was about to apply the rod to the Puritans overseas when the outbreak of the Civil Wars obliged the King to turn to the more pressing business of saving his Crown and later his head from the Puritans at home. In consequence, the New Englanders were happily preserved from punishment and encouraged to regard themselves as outside the pale of

---

[1] *The Works of Alexander Hamilton*, edited by Henry Cabot Lodge, New York, 1904, I, 172.

English authority. Indeed, while Cavaliers and Roundheads battled up and down the countryside, the power of the mother country over the colonies almost vanished. Freed from the supervision of the English government, the colonists began to think of themselves as beyond the mother country's control, trading wherever they pleased and conducting their affairs much in the manner of independent states. New Englanders in particular gave full rein to the notion that they were a separate and sanctified people: they loved "noe Government that is not like their owne," wryly observed Edward Randolph after he had run full tilt against the solid granite of New England intransigence.[2] Even on the eve of the American Revolution it was said that in Connecticut and Rhode Island, the King and Parliament had "as much influence . . . as in the wilds of Tartary."[3]

Precedents were established during this period which the colonists later flung at the English government when it attempted to restore its authority in America. The patriot leaders of the revolutionary period pointed to the liberties enjoyed by the colonies from 1640 to 1660 to justify their claims of extensive rights of self-government. During the "wise and righteous administration" of Oliver Cromwell, it was contended, the colonies had been treated as the equals of the mother country.[4] Although Englishmen protested that Americans were seeking to "establish into an inherent right what was actually an indulgence," the colonists remained unshaken in their conviction that the privileges which they had then enjoyed were theirs by law and right and that the subsequent acts of the British government were usurpations.[5]

Of equal significance in laying the foundations for the American Revolution was the policy adopted by the English government of establishing representative institutions in the colonies. Except for the brief interlude of the Dominion of New England (1686–1689) in which the assemblies were abolished and rule by an appointed governor and council instituted, the home government insisted upon the creation of a popularly elected assembly as soon as there were a sufficient number of Englishmen in the province to war-

[2] Additional MS. 28089 British Museum, Report of Edward Randolph, October 12, 1676.
[3] John Mein, *Sagittarius's Letters and Political Speculations*, Boston, 1775, 20.
[4] *Newport Mercury*, March 22, 1773.
[5] Macpherson, 33.

rant its existence. When, for example, it was learned in London that Nova Scotia was being ruled by the governor and council alone, the home authorities ordered that a popular assembly be elected despite the governor's protest that there were hardly enough Englishmen in the province to elect two representatives. This practice was intended to encourage emigration to the colonies by assuring prospective settlers that they would carry the "rights of Englishmen" with them overseas and to permit the more expeditious handling of local affairs. It proved, however, ill preparation for the efforts of George III's ministers to centralize control of colonial affairs inasmuch as it provided the basis for American claims to home rule. Thanks to the British government, the English colonies that revolted in 1776, however great their differences, had this in common: they all possessed representative assemblies and this institutional affinity laid the foundations for the concerted resistance without which the American Revolution would have been impossible.

It was largely because of what the British government did not do that Americans came to believe that the principle of no taxation without representation was the established rule of the empire. It was generally admitted by the mother country itself that the Crown could not tax the colonies. In 1724, Sir Philip Yorke, the Solicitor General, handed down a decision that a colony of English subjects could not be taxed except by a representative body of their own choosing or by the British Parliament. But because Parliament did not undertake to exercise this power directly until 1764, Americans were led to regard the levying of taxes as the privilege of their representative assemblies alone. When, therefore, Parliament began to tax the colonies directly in 1765, its action came as a shock to a people who had grown to believe themselves secure from parliamentary impositions and even that Parliament had no constitutional right to tax them. The decision of Parliament to hold its hand until after the colonies had become sufficiently strong to offer successful resistance proved one of the cardinal mistakes of British colonial policy.

In all other respects the British government sought to assert its authority and to restrict narrowly the rights of the colonial assemblies. Instead of treating them as local legislatures with wide powers of self-government, it required them to submit to the strict supervision of the mother country. Despite the government's concern that representative assemblies be established in the colonies, it had no intention of weakening the system of government by "royal grace and favor." In the eyes of English administrators, the most important elements of the colonial constitutions were the commissions and instructions given the royal governor by the King. It was held that there could be no appeal from the Crown's instructions: the assemblies must regard them as a mandate from a higher authority. Thus the King's prerogative — the royal will — became the supreme law of British America. The colonial legislatures were regarded as the King's creations; and it was assumed that what the King brought into being he could destroy at pleasure. By this means, the rights and privileges of the colonial legislatures were made dependent upon the King's will; with the Privy Council, he was the legislator of the colonies and his instructions to the colonial governors were the law of the land. To buttress further this system of centralized authority, the royal governor was given the power of vetoing bills passed by the assemblies and all laws approved by the governor were required to be sent to England where the Privy Council exercised the right of allowing or disallowing them.[6]

The mother country sought to make good its sweeping claims of authority by means of the royal type of colonial government. The reassertion of British authority over the colonies in the latter part of the seventeenth and the early eighteenth century took the form of supplanting charter and proprietary governments by royal governments. In 1685, there were only two provinces so governed: by 1763, eight of the twelve continental British colonies were royal. By that date, Pennsylvania and Maryland were the only remaining proprietary governments; Connecticut and Rhode Island were the only chartered colonies with elected governors.

From the fondness of the mother country for the royal form of government, it might be supposed that it was highly successful in achieving the purposes of British imperialists. It was not. The governmental machinery of a royal colony consisted of a governor and council appointed by the Crown and an assembly elected by the people. No form of government is more certain to produce friction and contention than this combination of a popularly elected assembly and an appointed governor and council. Yet in concentrat-

---

[6] Leonard Woods Labaree, *Royal Government in America*, Yale Historical Publication Series, VI, New Haven, 1930. *Proceedings of the American Antiquarian Society*, Worcester, Mass., 1924, New Series, XXXIV, 233, 244-246.

ing authority in the hands of British administrators, it was an improvement over the proprietary and charter types of colonies and for this reason enjoyed the favor of the home government.

The chief instruments employed by the mother country to make "government by instruction" effective in the colonies were the royal governor and council. Probably no more difficult assignment existed in the empire than that of governor of one of the more contentious North American colonies. Reconciling the colonists to the exercise of English authority was a task requiring vast ability in diplomacy. But the government never recognized the importance of choosing qualified men for colonial governorships: "Whenever we find ourselves encumbered with a needy Court-Dangler," exclaimed an indignant Englishman, "whom, on Account of Connections, we must not kick down Stairs, we kick him up into an American Government." [7] Americans themselves complained that their governors were raw youths, broken-down rakes, and bankrupt plungers who came to the colonies to escape their creditors and recoup their fortunes. The governor of Maryland, for example, was described as "a hearty, rattling, wild young Dog of an officer"; and at least one royal governor was pronounced to be "fitter for a bedlam, or other hospital, than to be set over a respectable province." [8] But in general, colonial governors were simply dull, commonplace Englishmen who badly needed a job but who ought to have been given a clerkship instead of a governorship. And, despite Americans' complaints, it may be questioned whether they would have been more endeared to the British government had first-rate men been sent to the colonies. Indeed, one of the principal advantages enjoyed by Americans in their struggle with the home government was the fact that the men upon whom it relied to carry out its orders were often nonentities who could be easily wound round the fingers of colonial politicians.

The position of a royal governor was the unhappy one of a man obliged to placate two jealous mistresses at once: the people and the King. Only the most adroit were able to retain the good will of the people and at the same time execute the royal instructions; most of the governors found themselves compelled to choose between arousing the resentment of the people by strictly upholding royal

[7] *Public Advertiser*, January 25, 1770.
[8] *Maryland Historical Magazine*, Baltimore, 1913, VIII, 172. *Newport Mercury*, March 22, 1773.

authority and incurring the disfavor of the home government by negligence and inaction. Governor Bernard of Massachusetts expressed the quandary in which every royal governor sooner or later found himself when he told the Massachusetts General Court in 1765: "If I could have dispensed with my duty, perhaps I might have pleased you; but then I must have condemned myself, and been condemned by my Royal Master. I cannot purchase your favor at so dear a rate."[9]

Next to the governor, the council was the most important cog in the governmental machinery of a royal colony. It was the governor's advisory board, the highest court of appeals in the colony, and the upper house of the legislature. In this last capacity it was expected to check the House of Representatives and to restrain "the Madness of popular fury." Without the support of the council, the governor found himself almost helpless because in many instances his instructions prevented him from acting without its advice and consent; the efficiency of the royal government depended in large measure, therefore, upon the willingness of the council to co-operate with the governor. It was necessary to exercise great care in selecting councilors lest there be admitted to the board "a fool who will not only be troublesome & Impertinent but will Blabb everything he knows" or a demagogue who would attempt to bring the council over to the camp of the popular party in the province.[10] Appointments to the council were commonly used as "a feather wherewith to Tickle the Vanity" of colonial merchants and planters and to ensure their support for the policies of the British government. Nevertheless, the council proved to be the weakest link in the chain of British authority: under the blows of the patriots it gave way early in the revolutionary struggle and left the British government weakened and discredited in the colonies.[11] The assemblies revealed themselves to be "the vortex which swallows all the power"; the royal council little more than "a mere *Tub* to the Whale, to sport and play with."[12]

[9] Bradford's *Massachusetts State Papers*, 57.

[10] Archives of Maryland, *Correspondence of Governor Horatio Sharpe*, III, 2.

[11] Sir Egerton Leigh, *Considerations on Certain Political Transactions*, London, 1774, 65, 72. Lord Dunmore to Lord Dartmouth, June 25, 1775, P.R.O., C.O. 5, 1533, Library of Congress Transcript. *Colonial Records of North Carolina*, IX, 973.

[12] Leigh, 60–62.

Indeed, it was apparent long before the outbreak of the Revolution that the royal governor and council had failed to establish government by prerogative in British America. The colonists refused to submit to royal instructions or to accept the premises upon which the prerogative was exercised; instead, they asserted the principle of government by the consent of the governed and denied that royal authority could be employed except for the welfare of the community. They contended that the King's power was limited to doing good: if he sought to invade the liberties of his subjects, he violated the compact upon which his authority reposed. In their eyes, royal instructions were merely rules laid down by the Crown for the guidance of the governors and therefore they could be dispensed with as occasion required. "To say that a royal instruction to a governor for his own particular conduct is to have the force and validity of a law and must be obeyed without reserve," said Richard Bland of Virginia, "is at once to strip us of all the rights and privileges of British subjects and to put us under the despotic power of a French or Turkish government." [13]

But far from experiencing such tyranny, Americans enjoyed during the colonial period a large and ever-increasing measure of political liberty. The most notable political development in the empire during the eighteenth century was the extension of the powers of the provincial assemblies at the expense of the royal authority. The colonial assemblies gained the undisputed right after 1680 of initiating all colonial laws, thus limiting the powers of the royal governor to approving or rejecting such bills as were laid before him. They gained control of provincial finance by winning the right not merely to appropriate money but to define the uses to which it was to be put, and to supervise its expenditure through an official elected by the lower house. Many administrative officers came to be appointed by the assemblies, despite the governor's contention that the right of appointment belonged to him alone. Only in their failure to permit judges to hold office during good behavior rather than during the King's pleasure did the assemblies meet defeat.

The bitterest struggle between the colonial assemblies and the Crown centered around the government's effort to create a civil list in the colonies. By royal instructions, the assemblies were directed

[13] *William and Mary College Quarterly*, January 1931, Second Series, XI, 23.

to grant permanent salaries to governors and judges, thus rendering them independent of the people's support and therefore of their control. Confronted with this peril, the colonial assemblies clung to their control of the purse as firmly as did the English House of Commons in its struggle with the Stuarts. For the most part, the British government suffered failure in its efforts to induce the colonial assemblies to settle permanent revenues upon Crown Officers and provide for the administration of the colonies by standing grants. Americans insisted upon making yearly grants and doling out funds with an eye to extracting the utmost advantage from each shilling. They believed it highly salutary that their governors be kept broke, or at least upon the edge of insolvency; in their eyes, the only good governor was a financially embarrassed one. Virginia alone settled a permanent salary upon its governor. After 1680, the governor of Virginia was paid from the funds raised by an export duty upon tobacco. This led to absenteeism: the appointed governor, sure of a comfortable living, usually remained in England and conferred the duties of administration upon a deputy resident in Virginia. But this system did not measurably strengthen the authority of the British government in Virginia; the House of Burgesses still retained the power of paralyzing the administration by withholding supplies and it made frequent use of this device to score victories over the Crown.

England's failure to create a civil list in the colonies weakened the colonial governors in their struggles with the assemblies. Without the patronage made possible by a civil list, the governors were deprived of one of the strongest weapons of the executive authority. The governor of Maryland declared that the clamor raised by colonial politicians could be silenced only by "throwing out a Sop in a proper manner to these Noisy Animals" and keeping them contented with jobs and offices until they were "tame enough to bear Stroking & tractable enough to follow any directions." [14] Repeatedly the royal governors lamented their powerlessness to buy off opposition to British authority with such grants. The governor of Virginia declared that he did not have "the disposal of one Single place of Consequence in the Government"; and Governor Bernard of Massachusetts pronounced "the Root of the American

[14] Archives of Maryland, *Correspondence of Governor Horatio Sharpe,* III, 3.

Disorders" to be "the Want of a certain and adequate civil List to each Colony." [15]

The British government accepted defeat at the hands of the colonial assemblies with remarkable composure. It did not employ force against recalcitrant colonies nor did it seek to deprive Americans of the legislatures with which they defied British authority. The mother country seems to have remained long in that state of absent-mindedness in which it acquired its colonies; in any event, it was content to see the colonists assert their rights and to win, point by point, the rights of Englishmen. This was owing to the want of sufficient power in the Board of Trade and Plantations, which exercised general supervision over the colonies, to carry its policies into execution, and to the jealousy with which the Crown and Parliament regarded the extension of each other's authority. Parliament sought to curtail the prerogative in the colonies; on the other hand, the Privy Council, in Franklin's words, was "afraid the Parliament would establish more Liberty in the Colonies than is proper or necessary and therefore do not care the Parliament should meddle at all with the Government of the Colonies; they rather chuse to carry every Thing there by the Weight of *Prerogative*." With the Crown and Parliament at cross purposes, the colonial legislatures were able to enlarge their powers despite the efforts of the Privy Council to clip "the Wings of Assemblies in their Claims of all the Privileges of a House of Commons." [16]

The cause of colonial liberty was also forwarded by the policy of "salutary neglect" adopted by Sir Robert Walpole, whose long tenure of power lasted from 1721 to 1742. Walpole applied to the American colonies his practice of letting sleeping dogs lie. He refused to be drawn into schemes to tax them, remarking that he would leave that to a man bolder and less friendly than himself to the interests of British commerce. He left colonial affairs to his Secretary of State, the Duke of Newcastle, who, in turn, seems to have entrusted them to Providence. Newcastle was chiefly a broker in boroughs whose life was spent in marshaling Whig majorities in the Commons by all means foul or fair. Gossip said that

[15] Lord Dunmore to Lord Hillsborough, May 2, 1772, P.R.O., C.O. 5, 1350, Library of Congress Transcript. Governor Bernard to John Pownall, April 23, 1769, *Bernard Papers*, VIII, Harvard University Library.

[16] *Proceedings of the American Antiquarian Society*, Worcester, 1934, New Series, XXXIV, 247.

he was so preoccupied with his borough-mongering that his closet was jammed with colonial dispatches, none of which had been opened. The noble lord's peace of mind was untroubled by colonial concerns: he knew nothing of them. But at least the Duke of Newcastle was shrewd enough not to tamper with something he did not understand: after Walpole's downfall, Newcastle, who retained office, refused to entertain suggestions that the colonies be taxed by Parliament.[17]

Although after Americans had risen in rebellion Englishmen looked back upon the period before 1763 as an era of good feelings in imperial relations — "Our prime minister's grey-goose-quill," it was said, "governed them [the colonies], 'till that fatal hour in which the evil Genius of *Britain* whispered in the ear of George Grenville, 'George! erect thyself into a great financier'" — in fact the colonial assemblies and the Crown had waged during the colonial period an almost uninterrupted struggle for supremacy.[18] By 1763, Americans could point to a long list of victories over royal authority. They had already rebelled against British despotism: Bacon's Rebellion in 1676, Leisler's Rebellion in 1690, and the uprising in New England against the Dominion of New England in 1689 revealed the temper of Americans when confronted with tyranny. The power of the royal governors was declining and the royal council was being stripped of its powers and, "like a turnip, squeezed between two trenchers" — the governor and the assembly.[19] The assemblies were making good their claims of extensive powers and successfully contesting the authority of the Crown. Each success increased their sense of self-importance and lowered the prestige of the royal government. Clearly, the balance of power in the colonies was shifting from the Crown to the popularly elected assemblies.

It was not until British authority had shrunk to this small measure and it was apparent that the royal prerogative alone was not capable of keeping the colonies in the subjection which British imperialists believed essential that the British Parliament cast its full weight into the scales. Having successfully withstood the attacks made upon their liberty by the prerogative, Americans were suddenly faced

---

[17] Horace Walpole, *Memoirs of the Reign of King George the Third*, London, 1845, II, 68–69. Philip C. Yorke, *The Life and Correspondence of Philip Yorke, Earl of Hardwicke*, Cambridge, 1913, II, 8–9.

[18] James Burgh, *Political Disquisitions*, London, 1774, II, 323.

[19] *Collections of the Massachusetts Historical Society*, Boston, 1858, Fourth Series, IV, 438.

with a far graver danger than any they had yet encountered. They rose to this emergency by resisting Parliament as stoutly as they had the Crown, largely because their experience during a century and a half had taught them that they could successfully challenge the authority of the mother country. The long struggle against the prerogative had kept liberty in the forefront; it had rarely ceased to engross the colonial mind. The British government had given Americans no opportunity to lapse into indifference; and as a result they had been thoroughly schooled in practical politics as well as political thought. Had the British statesmen who regarded Americans as unlettered "peasants" and "boors" traveled in the colonies instead of making the grand tour they might have been less eager to begin a quarrel with their cousins overseas.

II

THE most sweeping of the victories of the colonies over the Crown were gained by the assemblies during the Seven Years' War. From 1756 to 1763, they seemed far more eager to win their long-standing quarrel with the royal government than to come to grips with the French and Indians. Had they made war upon the French with half the enthusiasm with which they sought to take the political scalps of their governors and cripple royal government in the provinces, the early part of the war might have been less disastrous to British arms. Instead, they made the authority of the Crown one of the casualties of the war. The assemblies greatly strengthened their claim to exclusive control of the purse and succeeded in gaining the right to oversee expenditures. When they granted money, they often prescribed in detail the purposes to which the money was to be put; they interfered in the command of military forces in the conduct of military operations, and they even removed officers they considered incompetent. Americans appeared to be greater politicians than warriors: some of the most important triumphs of the war were won on the floor of their legislative chambers. The Maryland Assembly, declared Governor Sharpe, was determined to usurp all the powers of government, judicial, executive, and legislative, and would be content with nothing less than the powers of the British House of Commons. No supplies could be voted because the upper and lower houses of the Maryland Legislature were deadlocked; to crown her obstinacy, Maryland refused to co-operate with Virginia in sending an expedition against the French and Indians. Contrary to the orders of the Crown, the Maryland Assembly flooded the country with depreciated paper money. By its actions during the Seven Years' War, Marylanders acquired the distinction later held by New Englanders of being the most ill-humored, quarrelsome, and republican of His Majesty's American subjects. They were, complained their governor, "Levellers in their Principles & impatient of Rule"; "full of their own opinions, & entirely deaf to Arguments & reason." [20]

The success of the assemblies was owing to their practice of taking advantage of the critical position of the British government, hard-pressed by war in Europe, America, and India. While the French and Indians were pillaging and massacring on the frontiers, the assemblies refused to grant supplies until the governor had yielded to their demands. The governors, faced with the alternative of violating their instructions or permitting the enemy to overrun the provinces, often chose to run the risk of rebuke from the mother country rather than court destruction at the hands of the French. The New York Assembly attempted during the war to carry its point that colonial judges hold office during good behavior instead of at the pleasure of the Crown. In Maryland and Pennsylvania, the war was secondary to the dispute which raged between the people and the proprietors over the question of taxing proprietary lands.

While the colonies were engaged in dispossessing the Crown of its powers, they watched each other closely lest they contribute more than their share toward winning the war. To make sure that they did not do more than their neighbors, some colonies adopted the expedient of doing nothing at all despite royal requisitions for men and supplies. Only those colonies in immediate danger of attack obeyed requisitions with alacrity: and even they insisted that their grants were a free gift, similar to those made by the House

[20] *The Correspondence of William Pitt*, edited by G. S. Kimball, New York, 1906, II, 119, 134. Archives of Maryland, *The Correspondence of Governor Horatio Sharpe*, Baltimore, I, 96, 97; II, 124, 177, 373, 440.

of Commons, and not a compliance with a royal command. Requisitions were theoretically a command by the King to the assemblies for grants of supplies and men which admitted of no refusal or delay. But the requisition system was a standing affront to the colonists' conviction that their assemblies were local parliaments and entitled to most of the privileges and rights of the British Parliament – hence their determination to uproot the system even at the risk of making the French masters of North America.

Even the most loyal colonies refused to subordinate their long-standing disputes with the British government to the winning of the war. Although Virginia made important contributions in men and supplies, the struggle for provincial liberty was by no means forgotten. The disallowing of colonial laws by the Privy Council had long been regarded as a grievance in Virginia where the burgesses had been prevented by means of the royal disallowance from stopping the importation of slaves and impeding the collection of British debts. These differences were pushed into the background, however, by a dispute known as the Parson's Cause. By Virginia law, èvery Anglican clergyman in the colony was entitled to a salary of seventeen thousand pounds of tobacco a year. In the 1750's, there occurred several consecutive failures of the tobacco crop which led to a sharp rise in price. While Virginians valued the services of the men of God in the colony, they did not propose to overpay them and thereby lead them to endanger their souls with worldly goods; therefore the Virginia Assembly in 1755 and 1758 passed the Two-Penny Acts which commuted the salaries of clergymen into cash at the rate of twopence for each pound of tobacco – considerably below the market price. By these acts, the burgesses proposed to advance the interests of religion by keeping the clergy in apostolic poverty and, not incidentally, to save themselves money. But the clergy – most of whom had been born and educated in England – raised the cry of fraud against their parishioners and appealed to the Crown for justice. The Privy Council responded by disallowing the Two-Penny Act of 1758, whereupon the clergy instituted suit for the unpaid balance of their salaries. The Reverend Mr. James Maury brought suit in Hanover Court in 1763 where the judges, bound by the decision of the Privy Council, declared the Two-Penny Act null and void.

The clergy seemed to have been saved by the timely action of the British government when a jury was summoned to determine the

amount due the Reverend Mr. Maury. Patrick Henry, a mere
fledgling in the law (he was only twenty-four years old), was appointed to manage the defense. Henry was in 1763 a lively young
blade from the West, adept in dancing and music and regarded as
a wit. His uncouth frontier ways set him apart, however, from the
young aristocrats with whom he frolicked. Like Sam Adams, Henry
was a failure in business: when Jefferson first met him in 1759, he
had just "broken up his store — or, rather, it had broken him up."
Few Westerners were long cast down by failure; they quickly
turned to other ways of making their fortunes. Henry took up law
and six weeks after beginning his studies he presented himself
before the judges at Williamsburg for examination. With some
misgivings, the judges granted him a license. Despite his inexperience
and wide gaps in his knowledge of law — probably most crossroads
lawyers in Virginia knew more law than he — Henry made a
brilliant defense for his clients at the Hanover Court. His speech
to the jury evaded the question at issue: he chose, rather, to
denounce the clergy as unpatriotic ingrates and "enemies of the
community" who deserved to be punished rather than to be awarded
damages. The clergy, he declared, were ready to throw the colony
into turmoil rather than obey the laws of their "country." More
significantly, he pronounced the action of the British government
in disallowing the Two-Penny Act a high-handed encroachment
upon colony liberty. Henry declared that "a King, by disallowing
Acts of this salutary nature, from being the father of his people,
degenerated into a Tyrant, and forfeits all rights to his subjects'
obedience." Here Henry was greeted with shouts of "Treason!
Treason!" from some of the spectators, but because the judge made
no effort to interfere he went on with his speech; and the Reverend
Mr. Maury observed that one juryman "every now and then gave
the traitorous declaimer a nod of approbation." His argument
visibly affected the jury's verdict: Maury received one penny
damages. After the trial Henry apologized to Maury for the violence
of his language, assuring him that he intended nothing personal
and that he was merely attempting to make himself popular. "The
ready road to popularity here," remarked the outraged divine, "is to
trample under foot the interests of religion, the rights of the church,
and the prerogative of the Crown." [21]

In general, during the early part of the war, most of the colonies

[21] Ann Maury, *Memoirs of a Huguenot Family*, New York, 1872, 421–423.

— with the notable exception of Virginia and Massachusetts — were niggardly in their aid. Pennsylvanians were reluctant to transport supplies for Braddock's army; but they kept the French and hostile Indians supplied with powder and stores. The colonies quarreled over quartering British soldiers; refused to allow their troops to serve outside the boundaries of the province or to enact effective militia laws; insisted upon maintaining exclusive control by the assembly of colonial troops; and thwarted British efforts to create a colonial military union under Lord Loudon. Indeed, Lord Loudon, dispatched to America as commander in chief to unite the colonies, found himself obliged to spend more time in trying to persuade colonists to work in harness than in fighting the French and Indians. During the darkest days of the war, Americans abated not a whit of their dread of a standing army and centralized government. They were so firmly determined to maintain freedom and liberty at home that they refused to make the sacrifices of liberty which the successful prosecution of the war demanded.

The inability of the colonies to unite against the French and Indians was placed in high relief in 1754–1755 by their rejection of the "Albany Plan" of union. Drawn up by Benjamin Franklin and adopted by the Albany Congress (where delegates from seven provinces met in 1754 at the request of the British government to take steps to conciliate the Iroquois and win their support against the French) the plan proposed a federal union of the colonies under "one general government." The Crown was to appoint a President General to act as executive officer; the people or their representatives were to appoint members of a Grand Council of Delegates. This central government was to control Indian affairs, declare war and make peace, raise and equip soldiers and levy taxes.[22] The British government, however, objected to the scheme because it was believed to entrench upon the prerogative: the colonies rejected it because it curbed their freedom of action. "Every Body cries, a Union is absolutely necessary," exclaimed Franklin when it became apparent that his plan was doomed by shortsighted provincial isolationism; "but when they come to the Manner and Form of the Union, their weak Noddles are perfectly distracted. So if ever there be an Union, it must be form'd at home by the Ministry and Parliament." [23]

[22] *The Writings of Benjamin Franklin*, III, 197–226.
[23] *Ibid.*, 242.

Had it not been for British aid, it seemed likely that the British colonists in America would be driven off the continent, by an enemy which they outnumbered ten to one. Even in the face of disaster they displayed "a peevish reluctance to associate and unite"; and, in the eyes of British officials, they glorified their bad temper, unneighborliness, and niggardliness by calling them love of liberty. Royal governors were appalled by the colonists' preoccupation with petty provincial politics while the French and Indians ravaged the frontier; "I never was among People," wrote Governor Dinwiddie of Virginia, "y't have so little regard to their own safety, or the protection of their religious and civil Rights." Threats were of no avail; the obstinacy of the assemblies was beyond browbeating. General Forbes asked the Maryland Legislature if it imagined "that a great nation drained to the last in the protection and Defence of those Provinces and Collonys will forgive and forgett the being abandoned by any of them, in this critical time of public Calamity and distress." [24] The Maryland Assembly remained unmoved and left the disagreeable business of fighting the war to more exposed colonies.

After Pitt came into power in 1758, the British government dropped the plan it had adopted in 1756 of creating a colonial military union and ceased to try to persuade the American assemblies to shoulder their share of the expenses of the war. Lord Loudon was recalled by Pitt and the colonies were promised reimbursement for their war expenditures. As soon as it was clear that they were not spending their own money, the Americans entered heartily into the prosecution of the war. Knowing that the bills would be paid by Great Britain, they granted lavish bounties to encourage enlistment and threw economy to the winds in equipping and supplying their troops. For these services, the colonies received almost one million pounds in compensation. It was not merely humiliating for Great Britain to stoop to her colonies in order to conquer France: it increased the public debt and added materially to the cost of the most expensive war Englishmen had ever waged. It enabled the colonies, moreover, to emerge from the war with comparatively low public debts. This contrast between the heavily burdened mother country and the relatively debt-free colonies — for which Pitt's policy was partly responsible — became one of the chief reasons why the British government attempted to tax the American colonies.

The colony which most distinguished itself during the war was Massachusetts. Pitt declared that this "Loyal Province" had fulfilled his highest hopes. Required to raise 2300 troops, Massachusetts actually raised 7000, besides maintaining a twenty-gun ship of war and an armed sloop; and the colony even offered to send several thousand men to England to prevent a French invasion of the mother country. But, on the other hand, Massachusetts was one of the worst offenders on the score of smuggling and trading with the enemy.

If Americans angered the British government by doling out aid to British armies during the Seven Years' War, they sealed their infamy by largely nullifying the British blockade of the French and Spanish West Indies by supplying them with provisions and carrying away their sugar and molasses. Americans had always been fertile in expedients for violating British laws; and Yankee ingenuity was seen at its best — or worst, in the eyes of Englishmen — in devising ways and means of running the blockade of the foreign sugar islands. They persuaded the colonial governors to sell them flags of truce which enabled them to go to the foreign West Indies to release British captives. The governors were wrought upon by means of "pitiful Stories of Relations laying in French Dungeons" to grant the flags of truce; but the ships that sailed under this dispensation were observed to return far more heavily laden with molasses and sugar than with relations.[25] Other ships set sail for Jamaica with provisions but discharged their cargo at a beleaguered French island and returned with a hold bulging with contraband. William Pitt, a staunch friend of the colonies, was deeply angered when he learned how American merchants were setting profits above patriotism; other Englishmen, less well-disposed, were eager to make Americans pay dearly for having protracted the war in the West Indies.[26] Lord Chief Justice Mansfield, for instance, urged in 1763 that the colonies be punished for their transgressions during the war by depriving them of most of their time-honored liberties.

[25] *Records of the Colony of Rhode Island*, Providence, 1861, VI, 264. Archives of Maryland, *The Correspondence of Governor Horatio Sharpe*, Baltimore, II, 442. *Documents relative to the Colonial History of the State of New York*, VII, 117, 162.

[26] *The Correspondence of William Pitt*, edited by G. S. Kimball, New York, 1906, II, 320, 350.

Massachusetts, like Virginia, chose to pick a quarrel with the British government during the Seven Years' War. In 1755, the British government ordered the use of writs of assistance in Massachusetts to help suppress smuggling. These writs enabled customhouse officers to call upon constables and other provincial officers to assist them in the exercise of their duties and permitted the customs officers to enter private warehouses and homes in search of contraband. In 1760, these officers, armed with writs of assistance, began to seize illicit cargoes in Boston on a large scale; one huge shipment from Holland, worth over £ 10,000, fell into their hands. This unwonted activity on the part of the customhouse struck dismay among the Boston merchants, who blamed Governor Pownall since, as governor, he profited by the seizures. No doubt this explains why Pownall, when he left Massachusetts in 1760, was roundly cursed by the merchants and denied the honors usually accorded departing governors. In any event, the attack upon the writs of assistance launched soon thereafter by the Boston merchants was occasioned by the efforts of the British government to suppress their highly profitable but illicit trade.

The grievance of the Boston merchants was not merely that British commercial laws were being enforced with greater severity: they believed themselves unfairly treated inasmuch as the laws were not executed generally in the colonies. Rhode Island, a notorious smugglers' nest, was permitted to carry on illegal trade without the hindrance of writs of assistance or prying customhouse officers. The spectacle of Rhode Islanders piling up fortunes by methods denied Boston traders and cutting into Boston's share of illicit trade caused acute suffering among the Saints: rather than suffer this unjust discrimination, the Boston merchants went so far as to declare their willingness to submit to the laws provided they were enforced everywhere in the colonies. "Let no Indulgences be given any where," they said, "and we are content without them. We want nothing but to be as free as others are, or that others should be restrained as well as we." Although the merchants hired James Otis to plead their cause, they were unable to relieve themselves of the writs of assistance; but the British government did oblige them to the extent of making the use of writs general throughout the colonies.[27]

The practice of employing writs of assistance in the war against

[27] John C. Miller, *Sam Adams, Pioneer in Propaganda,* Boston, 1936, 31-34.

smuggling became a standing grievance of Americans during the revolutionary period. By attempting to procure general writs to give the customhouse officers blanket authority to enter and search whenever and wherever they desired, the British government stirred up a hornets' nest. The colonial judges refused to grant general writs on the ground that they were unconstitutional, and although the home government pressed the issue the judges stood their ground. On the other hand, the judges offered no opposition to granting writs in special cases. These writs were widely used in the colonies, but after 1764 writs of assistance were thrust into the background by new and more menacing dangers to American liberty.

During the Seven Years' War, the friction between British officers and American troops left soreness and resentment on both sides of the Atlantic. Few British officers could conceal their disdain of American troops: in their eyes, the colonists were low, blustering, cowardly fellows. General Wolfe swore that Americans were "in general the dirtiest, most contemptible cowardly dogs that you can conceive. There is no depending on them in action. They fall down dead in their own dirt and desert by battalions, officers and all. Such rascals as those are rather an encumbrance than any real strength to an army." Although he later modified this harsh judgment, British officers were anything but good-will ambassadors. Their manners were certainly not calculated to strengthen affection between the mother country and colonies: "with Airs of as much Consequence as a Turkish Bassa, and with as much Arrogance as a Captain in the Navy," it was remarked, the military man regarded himself "as a BEING which resembles the GODS." [28] These high-and-mighty airs soured the temper of the colonists. Daniel Dulany declared that during General Braddock's stay in Maryland, the colonists were "treated as slaves, and as arrogance unchecked knows no bounds, the military soon silenced the civil power, property became dependent on the moderation of a licentious soldiery, triumphing over the sanction of laws, and the authority of magistracy." [29] The British officers, on the other hand, insisted that their patience was exhausted by American "boors." Brigadier General Henry Bouquet declared that he was obliged to deal with "the insulting rudeness of an Assembly-man (of Pennsylvania) who,

[28] *The True Interest of Great-Britain, In Regard to the Trade and Government of Canada, Newfoundland, and the Coast of Labrador*, London, 1767, 30.
[29] *Pennsylvania Magazine of History and Biography*, 1879, III, 14.

picked up from a dunghill, thinks himself raised to a Being of Superior nature." [30] Colonial democracy thus became a stench in the nostrils of aristocratic British officers; and at the same time Americans were coming to recognize that, in the eyes of true-born Englishmen, they were distinctly an inferior breed.

Despite Americans' preoccupation in safeguarding their freedom from the British government, the century-long struggle between France and England for control of the North American continent which was brought to an end in 1763 partook of the character of a religious crusade. Protestant England confronted Roman Catholic France in the New World; and the English colonists regarded their victory over France as a smashing blow at "Popery and idolatry." But it was more than a triumph for Protestantism: it was a victory over absolutistic government as well as priestcraft. The Reverend Mr. Mayhew of Boston declared that "Popery" and civil liberty were irreconcilable: hence Roman Catholicism must be destroyed in order to make the New World safe for the rights of man. To the American colonists, the result of the Seven Years' War represented the triumph of Protestantism, free government, and liberty — the expansion of the frontiers of freedom. This was the wrong schooling for a people who were about to feel the smart of British "tyranny." American principles worked against George III as well as Louis XV; there was no room in America for absolutism, whether French or British.

The reorganization of the empire was clearly dictated by the weaknesses revealed by the Seven Years' War. Although the British Empire had been victorious, the failure of the colonies to work together and their refusal to throw their resources into the war until the mother country had promised them reimbursement might prove fatal in another war. The requisition system was now seen to be an anachronism preserved from the era of "salutary neglect." It hung like a millstone about the neck of British colonial policy, obliging the colonies to move, as in a convoy, no faster than the slowest. It presented formidable difficulties to the efficient management of colonial affairs from Whitehall for it obliged the Ministry "to procure a Majority in each of about thirty wrangling Assemblies." "Shall it depend upon the resolutions of a Philadelphian assembly," asked an indignant Englishman, "whether our fellow-

[30] *Ibid.*, 142.

subjects shall arm in defence of liberty and property? . . . Does the fate of a whole continent bear any proportion to an almost imperceptible encroachment upon the important privilege of an American, deliberating for a year or two, whether he will pay six-pence in the pound, to save himself and family from perdition?" [31] The final absurdity of the system seemed to have been attained when the Massachusetts General Court protested against parliamentary taxation to maintain troops in America on the ground that the colonies were always willing to raise troops by royal requisition, yet refused, in the same session, to obey the royal requisition to supply General Gage with seven hundred men to help suppress Pontiac's rebellion.[32]

To damn further the requisition system in Englishmen's eyes, it was held responsible for prolonging the war and adding millions of pounds to its cost. While these "little Rump Parliaments" in the colonies debated and fretted to determine "whether if Virginia was over-run by Indians, it would not be better for them," Great Britain had been compelled to strain every resource to keep the French at bay. Furthermore, Parliament was eager to scrap the requisition system because it seemed to endanger the House of Commons' control of the purse. "That Doctrine of Requis[itio]n," exclaimed George Grenville, "may one day put the King out of the power of Parl[iamen]t." [33] English parliamentarians were well aware that the destruction of the requisition system would leave only one method of effectively raising a colonial revenue — taxation by the British Parliament itself.

[31] Thomas Crowley, *Letters and Dissertations on Various Subjects*, London, 1776, 247. *An Application of Political Rules to Great Britain, Ireland, and America*, London, 1766, 78. *Gazetteer and New Daily Advertiser*, April 10, 1766; October 26, 1768.

[32] Governor Bernard to Richard Jackson, February 2, 1764, Bernard MSS., Harvard University Library.

[33] *American Historical Review*, April 1912, XVII, 567, 572. Earl of Abingdon, *Thoughts on the Letter of Edmund Burke, Esq. to the Sheriffs of Bristol on the Affairs of America*, Oxford, 1777, 62.

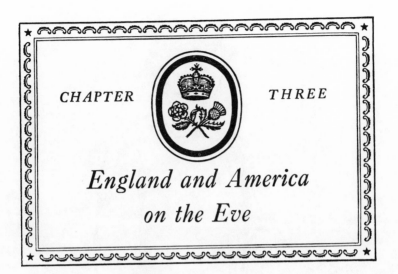

CHAPTER THREE

England and America

on the Eve

James Otis

IN 1763, the British colonies upon the mainland of North America which revolted from the mother country in 1776 contained a population of approximately 2,500,000 whites and blacks. Since there were about 8,000,000 people in Great Britain at this period, the War of American Independence — until the French Alliance in 1778 — was fought by Americans against odds of over three to one, not including the mercenaries engaged by Great Britain to fight in her behalf. The population of the colonies was largely English in origin but many thousand Scotch-Irish, Germans, and French Huguenots leavened the Anglo-Saxon mass. Partly because New England was not friendly toward the Scotch-Irish Presbyterians and New York had a bad name among the Germans, these peoples went to western Pennsylvania in large numbers, from whence they streamed southward along the frontier line into western Virginia, the Carolinas, and Georgia. The settlers of English descent — largely Anglican in religion — tended to remain in the lowland sections of these provinces and so was created a division between east and west along lines of nationality and religion as well as economics and politics.

Americans in 1763 were overwhelmingly rural in character — the typical American of this period was the substantial yeoman farmer whose life was invitingly pictured by St. John de Crèvecoeur in his *Letters from an American Farmer*. Although perhaps few American farmers experienced the poetic bliss of Crèvecoeur in contemplating the American scene and comparing it with the strife-torn world across the Atlantic, it was true that extreme poverty was almost completely unknown in the colonies and that the common man, travel the world over as he might, would find no country in which he met with greater opportunities to better his condition through the exercise of the virtues praised by Poor Richard. Hard work, thrift, and diligence brought their reward in the American colonies in the form of well-stocked farms, large families, and all the comforts of home. There can be little doubt that these virtues were practised as well as preached by Americans; and because of the almost illimitable opportunities presented to the average man, a far greater equality of wealth prevailed here than in the Old World. The population of the British North American provinces was in 1763 confined to the strip of land between the Appalachians and the sea: the frontier line had not yet crossed the mountains. Along the Atlantic Coast from which the settlements had crept westward for a century and a half were to be found the seaport towns, the most important of which were Boston, New York, Philadelphia, and Charleston, South Carolina. The towns redeemed the colonies from utter rusticity: they were the chief link between the Old World and the New — windows opening upon the cultured world of Europe that the colonists had left behind. Most of the intellectual activity of British America centered in the towns; and within this urban society were generated many of the forces that moved Americans during the revolutionary period. Indeed, it is not too much to say that unrest and revolutionary ideas spread from the towns over the country in an ever-widening arc. There was, moreover, far less equality in the towns than in the country; and among the discontented urban laborers the democratic ideas which were to play a large part in the history of the American Revolution found fertile soil.

The culture of the colonies was derivative, but in spite of the fact that the energies of Americans were largely taken up in the business of making a living and subjugating a wilderness, this culture compared favorably with that of the provincial towns of England. The Atlantic was not then — nor is it today — a barrier to ideas; it was rather a highway along which they passed with ease and dispatch. For example, Deism was carried across the Atlantic, where it enjoyed great vogue among the upper classes and even reached and converted frontiersmen like Ethan Allen. Americans did not live in splendid isolation either mental or material — and what is more, they knew it. Their outlook was in some respects less provincial than that of many Americans in the twentieth century. They recognized that they were part of a North Atlantic world, and were well aware that they were certain to be drawn into every war in which Great Britain became involved. Great Britain they looked upon as "home" and rejoiced in her victories and sorrowed in her misfortunes. Even their obstructionism during the Seven Years' War was designed to establish English liberties in

America. There was little sense of remoteness from the world's affairs and no desire to cut the ties that united them to the markets and culture of Europe. Far from wishing to live unto themselves, American merchants sought to range the world in search of markets, and the colonists in general, particularly the townspeople, attempted to identify themselves as closely as possible with the thought and life of Europe.

Although the colonial assemblies steadily extended their authority during the eighteenth century and restricted that of the Crown, this did not necessarily mean that the provinces were becoming democracies. On the contrary, in many colonies it was growing increasingly difficult for the common man to vote. The manhood suffrage that had prevailed in some of them during the seventeenth century gave way in the eighteenth to property qualifications for voting; and these requirements were steadily raised until the masses had been effectively debarred from the franchise. In Pennsylvania, for example, only 8 per cent of the rural population enjoyed the suffrage, and only 2 per cent of the population of Philadelphia possessed sufficient property to vote.[1] " 'Tis true they have a house of Assembly: but who do they represent?" asked Josiah Quincy, of the South Carolina Assembly. "The laborer, the mechanic, the tradesman, the farmer, husbandman or yeoman? No. The representatives are almost if not wholly rich planters. The Planting interest is therefore represented, but I conceive nothing else (as it ought to be)."[2] The royal governor of New York urged the Crown to put an end to the system that prevailed in that province whereby "any one or two families should be able to return so large a proportion of the Members of our assembly."[3] The victories of the assemblies over the Crown were essential in preparing the way for democracy; but it was yet far from certain that America was to be a democracy.

Indeed, the upper class had almost everywhere entrenched itself so firmly in power that aristocracy rather than democracy seemed likely to be the coming order in America. By means of the favoritism of royal governors and the ability or good fortune of the more ener-

---

[1] A. E. McKinley, *The Suffrage Franchise in the English Colonies in America*, Philadelphia, 1905.

[2] *Proceedings of the Massachusetts Historical Society*, XLIX, 454.

[3] *Documents relative to the Colonial History of the State of New York*, VIII, 565.

getic colonists, vast estates had passed into the hands of speculators
and landed gentry: Virginia was ruled by the great planters of the
tidewater; in New York, the patroon system concentrated owner-
ship of the best lands in a few wealthy families; and in New
England the old aristocracy of learning and godliness had been
supplanted by an aristocracy of merchants and traders. It was this
wealthy minority which profited chiefly from the ascendancy
gained by the colonial assemblies. The merchants and planters
dominated the assemblies and although they carried on the struggle
for home rule in the name of popular liberty, they had no intention
of making the people sovereign. They sought, rather, to transfer
power from the Crown to themselves without furthering the cause
of democracy, much as had the English aristocracy in the "glorious
revolution" of 1688.

Closely allied with this ruling class were the lawyers. Although
lawyers furnished a large share of the leadership of the revolutionary movement, many of them, radical as they were regarding
the rights of colonial assemblies against the British government, were
extremely conservative with respect to the rights of the common
people at home. The Whig lawyers of New England were more
reactionary than the Tories themselves in their insistence upon the
perpetuation of primogeniture in entailed estates, and they consistently upheld the harsh English code of punishment for crimes
against property. The rule of lawyers was as objectionable to
American democrats as was the rule of British imperialists. Their
exorbitant fees and overweening power led to repeated outbreaks
of mob violence against them in the Carolinas and New Jersey. In
New Jersey they were denounced as "Serpents, seven times more
devouring than the first [the Stamp Act], who in their daily Practice are as Private Leaches, sucking out our very Hearts Blood."
In the Carolinas, their exactions precipitated the armed revolt in
1770 of the Western farmers known as the "Regulators' movement." [4]

Although the common people did not submit without a struggle
to the domination of the planter-merchant aristocracy and its
lawyer allies, with scarcely an exception they went down to defeat

[4] *Quarterly Journal of the New York State Historical Association,* October
1932, XIII, 366, 369. *Documents relative to the Colonial History of the State
of New Jersey,* Newark, 1886, X, 148-149, note, 172-173. Richard B. Morris,
"Legalism versus Revolutionary Doctrines in New England," *New England
Quarterly,* 1931, VI, 203, 207.

at its hands. The chief bone of contention between rich and poor in colonial America was the currency, and this, in turn, centered upon the issue of inflation versus sound money. This conflict culminated in the attempt by the debt-ridden farmers and town artisans of Massachusetts to inflate the currency by establishing a Land Bank to issue paper money backed only by land. The scheme excited the hostility of the New England merchants, with the result that in 1741 the British Parliament, in response to the pleas of the hard-pressed conservatives in Massachusetts, struck down the Land Bank. The sound-money views of the merchants were ultimately imposed upon the colonies by Parliament and the inflationist farmers and artisans were completely routed. Thus the aristocracy seemed to be strengthening its position in colonial life, and the forces of democracy, even in America, could make little headway against the aristocratic ideal of the eighteenth century.

From among the colonial aristocracy, there was recruited a small group of office-holding patricians who, because of the British government's practice of concentrating offices in their hands, seemed likely to attain a "perpetuity in office" and to exclude many aristocrats as well as the common people from the most prized political jobs. Offices were bestowed upon influential colonists by the Crown to reward services rendered to the government or to buy off opposition. Although, to the regret of many British administrators, these positions fell far short of the English House of Lords in point of honor and prestige, they helped create a colonial oligarchy by placing power in the hands of a few favored American families.[5]

But unhappily for the mother country there were never a sufficient number of offices at the disposal of the Crown to purchase the good will of the entire colonial aristocracy; and there were numerous upper-class Americans who refused to surrender their principles in order to gain the favor of royal governors. In consequence, not all colonial aristocrats were oligarchs; particularly after 1765, a large number were proscribed from appointive offices by the British government because they had resisted the authority of the mother country. Many of the gentry found themselves in the plight of Richard Henry Lee of Virginia, a tidewater aristocrat who possessed a small estate, "a teaming little Wife," and a large family. Lee was an assiduous office-seeker and he repeatedly urged

[5] *Correspondence of "First Citizen," Charles Carroll of Carrollton, and "Antilon," Daniel Dulany, Junior,* edited by E. S. Riley, Baltimore, 1902, 46, 50.

his brother Arthur Lee in England to procure him a place which would at least permit his income to keep pace with his wife's fruitfulness. He met only with rebuffs. There was no possibility of appointment to any office in the gift of the Crown, wrote Arthur Lee, because "real merit or virtue" did not receive its just reward in the British Empire. On the other hand, the home government was ready to lavish emoluments and jobs upon those who would "prove themselves the most active instruments of oppression" — which no colonial patriot could consent to do.[6] Only by truckling to the British government could a colonial aristocrat hope to become a member of the oligarchy that owed its offices and power to the favoritism of the Crown. As a result, the colonial aristocracy was divided against itself — and this division was to have far-reaching influence upon the history of the American Revolution.

In Massachusetts a handful of "oligarchs" had succeeded in monopolizing the choicest political jobs. Composed of such wealthy and interrelated families as the Olivers and the Hutchinsons, these blue-blooded merchants, judges, and administrators were led by Thomas Hutchinson, the ablest member of the New England oligarchy. Hutchinson wished to make the American social and political system a replica of that of Great Britain: hence he urged the creation of an American aristocracy modeled upon that of the mother country. "An order of Patricians or Esquires," composed of men of estates and fortune, would, he observed, do much to redress the balance in the colonies between democracy and aristocracy. He proposed to make a seat upon an American council an approximation in dignity and honor to a place in the British House of Lords. At all times, he combated the "loose, false, and absurd Notion of the Nature of Government" by which the colonies were rendered virtually independent of the mother country and sought to oppose British authority to the democratic, leveling tendencies of the American frontier.[7] In one of his confidential letters to an English friend, he declared that there must be "an abridgement of what are called English liberties" in America in order to keep the colonies in subjection to the mother country. With good cause, the New England democrats regarded Hutchinson as their worst enemy:

[6] Arthur Lee to Richard Henry Lee, October 20, 1770, Lee MSS., American Philosophical Society. *Letters of Richard Henry Lee,* edited by J. C. Ballagh, New York, 1911, I, 72, 78.

[7] Thomas Hutchinson to ?, January 22, 1771, P.R.O., C.O. 5, 246, Library of Congress Transcript.

his triumph, it is clear, would have meant the victory of the au-
thoritarian, conservative views that from the beginning of our
history have struggled for mastery with the democratic, liberal
ideals which were to find expression in the Declaration of Independence.

Many colonists who had caught a vision of a democratic America
in which the common man should be master of his own destiny
watched with foreboding the rise of oligarchy. Long before the
outbreak of the revolutionary movement, the lines had been drawn
for a struggle between the oligarchs and the popular leaders, and
the common people had been made aware that they had enemies at
home as well as abroad. Led by James Otis, Jr., and Sam Adams, the
popular party had attained formidable proportions in Massachusetts
by 1763. Hutchinson, who as lieutenant governor of the province,
Chief Justice, president of the Massachusetts Council, and captain
of Castle William, was the chief target for the barbs of Otis and
Adams, declared that his enemies were merely disappointed office-
seekers — "canker-worms of the State" — whose concern for popular
liberty masked their ambition of ruling the province.[8] Some conservatives believed, indeed, that James Otis was so rancorous and
jealous of his betters that he would "burst like a Toad with his own
Venom." But Otis and Adams answered that they were not
actuated by envy or ambition but by solicitude for the welfare of
the people. The concentration of political power, they pointed out,
might lead to the concentration of wealth in the hands of these
same oligarchs — "a cruel yoke on a people who are so near to the
state of original equality." Otis declared that he was seeking to
overthrow "some who have no natural or divine right to be
above me and chiefly owe their grandeur and honors, to grinding
the faces of the poor, and other acts of ill gotten gain and power."[9]

During the revolutionary period, the popular leaders in the colonies did not cease to wage war upon two fronts: against the British
government and the colonial oligarchy. Both, it was clear, must be
overthrown if the colonies were to achieve home rule. Although
not all the Whig leaders wished to tear down the oligarchy in
order to open the door of political preferment to the common people, they were united in opposition to the system whereby only
those who were willing to sacrifice their popularity at home by

[8] *Boston Evening Post*, September 21, 1767.
[9] *Boston Gazette*, January 11, 1762, Supplement.

serving the interests of the British government were given the high political offices in the gift of the Crown. They found it intolerable that the road to political favor in the colonies lay in thwarting the wishes of the people. Whether or not these patriots realized it, the success of their efforts was destined to carry the colonies far in the direction of democracy.

The social cleavage in the colonies gave the British government an opportunity to rule British America by pursuing a policy of *Divide et Impera*. The disunion of the colonies made the task still easier: to ensure British rule, all that seemed necessary was "a Machiavel to take advantage of those feuds and jealousies" that divided them. The colonies, it may be said, were more intimately aware of their connection with Great Britain and their dependence upon her than they were of each other. They rejoiced in their community with the mother country; towards each other, they were apt to exhibit the jealousy of small children vying for the favor of a parent. Indeed, the most striking weakness of Americans — the best guarantee of British dominion — was their provincial isolationism. By dividing British America into comparatively small jurisdictions, the mother country seemed unwittingly to have followed the best method of keeping its overseas subjects from making themselves formidable to its sovereignty. The divergent economic interests of the colonies together with their social and religious differences had created two distinct ways of life and seemingly raised an insuperable barrier to union. Fire and water, observed Andrew Burnaby, an English traveler, were not more distinct than the Northern Calvinistic commercial colonies and the Southern Anglican planting colonies. Certainly, vigorous sectional prejudice barred co-operation between them: New Englanders with their "Kill-Devil" rum were regarded by the Southerners as sharpers and canting rascals; the planters of the South appeared to Northern farmers and merchants to be scandalous loose-livers and debauchees. In 1774, a young New Jerseyman summarized the reasons against going to live among the gay Virginians: "That the People there are profane, and exceeding wicked — " he noted. "That I shall read there no Calvinistic Books, nor hear any Presbyterian Sermons — That I must keep much Company, and therefore spend as much, very probably much more Money than my Salary." [10] Anglican

[10] *The Journal and Letters of Philip Vickers Fithian,* edited by John Rogers Williams, Princeton, 1934, 81.

churchgoers, on the other hand, were troubled by the menace to Church and State created by the subversive ideals of New England; far from a land of steady habits, Connecticut seemed to be "little more than a mere democracy, and most of them upon a level, and each man thinking himself an able divine and politician." [11]

Boundary disputes embittered colony against colony and occasionally led to fighting and bloodshed; it was found far easier "to incense a Marylander against a Virginian, or any one colonist against another, to such a degree that they would decide their differences by fighting, than to stimulate any of them to fight with an Englishman." New Englanders hated the citizens of Albany because they sold guns and ammunition to the Indians, who used them against the New England frontier; it was believed in Boston that even "the cloaths of some of our people, butchered by them [the Indians] have been amicably sold at Albany, *with the blood upon them.*" [12] The isolation of the Southern from the Northern colonies tended to bring them closer to the mother country with whom their trade was principally carried on; it was said that a South Carolinian, Georgian, or Floridan had a hundred opportunities to communicate with England to one with New York or New England. It was customary for Southern merchants and planters to send their children to England for their education; but, as Englishmen soon learned, even "genteel" education in the mother country did not prevent them from heading a revolt against its authority.

The colonies were further weakened by sectional conflicts within their own borders. The East sought to keep under its domination the more rapidly growing and more democratic West, leading to racking struggles of the antagonistic sections. In Pennsylvania, for example, the Quaker oligarchy of the east ruled the province by denying the western counties — peopled largely by Scotch-Irish and Germans — proportionate representation in the assembly with the Quaker-dominated counties despite the provision of the Pennsylvania charter that each county was to send at least four representatives to the legislature. [13] Quaker domination meant tyr-

[11] *Documents relative to the Colonial History of the State of New York,* VII, 440.

[12] Jonathan Mayhew, *Observations on the Character and Conduct of the Society for the Propagation of the Gospel in Foreign Parts,* Boston, 1763, 167.

[13] John Penn to Thomas Penn, March 17, 1764; William Peters to Thomas Penn, June 4, 1764; Richard Hockley to Thomas Penn, May 23, 1766, Penn MSS., *Official Correspondence,* X, Historical Society of Pennsylvania.

anny to westerners because the Friends refused to give adequate protection to the frontier against the Indians; they were accused, indeed, by frontiersmen of being in league with the Indians and even of supplying the tomahawks and guns with which they murdered the settlers. "For God's sake," exclaimed a westerner, "are we always to be slaves, must we groan for ever beneath the yoke of three Quaker counties; are we ever to bleed by the hatchet of an enemy that we feed and cloath?" [14] This conflict finally erupted in 1764 in the march of the frontiersmen — called "Paxton Boys" — upon Philadelphia to coerce the Quaker-dominated assembly to take up arms against the Indians. The Paxton or "Black" Boys "complained of grievances and sufferings," observed a contemporary, "that would have drawn tears from stones" — but the Quakers remained unmoved. The westerners declared that they were "loyal subjects, and had fought the King's battles since Braddock's defeat, and would not do what looked like rebellion; though they thought it exceedingly hard, that they should be obliged to pay taxes to maintain their enemies." [15] But outbreaks such as the Paxton riots failed to destroy the Quaker oligarchy; despite the storms that roared out of the west, the Quakers remained masters of the province.

The struggle between the Quakers and the Scotch Irish, who with the artisans of Philadelphia were the principal enemies of the Friends' regime, was intensified by Quaker efforts to change Pennsylvania from a proprietary to a royal colony. The Penns, having abjured their faith for that of the Church of England, no longer enjoyed any particular sanctity in the eyes of the Pennsylvania Quakers; and their refusal to permit the Pennsylvania Assembly to tax their lands alienated what little affection remained. The Quakers ...ised the cry that they were being made "slaves to the usurped and arbitrary Power of private Subjects" and urged that Pennsylvania be made a royal colony and thereby be placed under a king who was "justly celebrated for his tender Regard to the constitutional Rights of *Englishmen*." [16] Benjamin Franklin was the darling of the Quakers, who spoke of him as "that great *Patriot*." In espousing the

[14] Hugh Williamson, *The Plain Dealer*, Philadelphia, 1764, III, 22. *The Scots Magazine*, Edinburgh, 1764, XXVI, 22.

[15] *Ibid.*, 570–571.

[16] *Pennsylvania Gazette*, March 29, 1764. John Penn to Thomas Penn, September 22, 1764, Penn MSS., *Official Correspondence*, X, Historical Society of Pennsylvania.

cause of the Friends, Franklin was allying himself with the vested interests of the colony and opposing the more democratic west which threw its support behind the proprietors of Pennsylvania. During this period of his career, however, Franklin chose to ignore the oppression exercised by the east over the west and to concentrate his attention upon making Pennsylvania a royal province.

Because the balance of power in Pennsylvania politics was held by the Germans, Franklin and the proprietarians engaged in heated rivalry for their votes. Even Governor Franklin of New Jersey, Benjamin's natural son, canvassed among the Pennsylvania Germans in his father's behalf.[17] Germans by the hundreds were rushed to naturalization offices by contending politicians: "I have out of my own pocket spent some money for giting some people naterlized to git some votes more, who had no mind to be naterlized as a thing of not much benefit to them," wrote one of the proprietarians from the field. Poll watchers — "every man provided with a good shillelah" — were appointed to crack the pates of repeaters and other illegal voters.[18] Out of this rough-and-tumble fray, Franklin emerged in 1764 as colony agent and was sent to England armed with a petition that the province be placed under the direct jurisdiction of the King.

The revolutionary movement, instead of creating a united front in Pennsylvania against the mother country, merely fanned the flames of class and sectional hostility. In consequence, throughout the struggle with Great Britain Pennsylvania played a part incommensurate with its power and importance. The internal struggle between the Scotch Irish and the Quakers absorbed the greater part of the people's energy; even while a British army was in their midst, Pennsylvanians showed far more enthusiasm for quarreling among themselves than for fighting the redcoats. One of the principal reasons why Massachusetts took a position of leadership in the struggle against Great Britain was that the Bay Colony had achieved a high degree of unity and was comparatively free of the internal discord that rent Pennsylvania. Far from dominating its colony politically, as did Philadelphia, Boston possessed only

[17] *Ibid.*, October 19, 1764. *Correspondence*, X, Historical Society of Pennsylvania.

[18] William Young to Thomas Penn, December 14, 1765, *Ibid.*, *Private Correspondence. Letters and Papers relating chiefly to the Provincial History of Pennsylvania*, Philadelphia, 1856, 209, 211.

four votes in the Massachusetts General Court out of a total of over a hundred. Political power in Massachusetts resided with the yeomen; in Pennsylvania it rested precariously in the hands of an oligarchy of Quakers which ruled a population largely hostile to its domination. Moreover, the Massachusetts oligarchy stood upon a far narrower base than that of Pennsylvania: it consisted merely of a few families and was for that reason far more easily overthrown.

Englishmen, surveying the petty jealousies and bickerings of the colonies and the sectional conflicts within the provinces themselves, concluded that there was nothing to fear from an American union. Since the provincials had been unable to unite against the French and Indians while they were devastating the frontiers, it seemed highly unlikely that they could unite against the mother country. The colonies appeared to be so irreconcilably divided that their union was deemed "a silly Utopian fancy, which never can be midwifed into existence"; "it would not be more absurd," it was said, "to place two of his Majesty's beef eaters to watch an infant in the cradle that it don't rise to cut its father's throat, than to guard these weak infant colonies to prevent their shaking off the British yoke." [19]

It was made clear after 1765 that Englishmen had exaggerated the strength of colonial particularism and the security it afforded British sovereignty. Unperceived by the mother country, the foundation was being laid during the eighteenth century for the colonial union later called into being by the Stamp Act. By means of the colonial post office erected by the home government early in the century, Americans were becoming increasingly aware of each other's existence. Clubs of learned men corresponded across provincial lines; merchants established business connections; and newspapers circulated from one colony to another — all by means of the colonial post. Highways had been constructed to connect the principal cities along which passed a steady flow of stages and other vehicles. "The great roads leading from one government to another," reported a traveler, "exhibit in every circumstance rather the appearance of a thriving old country than a new one." [20]

Certainly the division among Americans was no guarantee against the consequences of British misrule. Englishmen failed to heed

[19] Jeremiah Dummer, *Defence of the New England Charters*, London, 1765, 72.

[20] *Reflections on the American Contest*, London, 1776, 5-6.

Franklin's warning: "When I say such an union of the colonies is impossible I mean without the most grievous tyranny and oppression." George III and his ministers, unmindful of the danger, weakened the most powerful guarantees of British rule in the colonies: the affection of the colonists for the mother country, their provincial isolation and their sectional discords. By 1765, as a result, the British government was confronted with what Englishmen had believed impossible: a union of the colonies against the mother country. This revolutionary change in the American colonies was the outcome to a great degree of the overturn in English politics — which it is now necessary to review — which took place after the accession of George III in 1760.

II

GEORGE III, the young monarch who ascended the throne in 1760, was determined to arrest the process that was making figureheads of the Kings of England. Rather than submit to the "Venetian oligarchy" of the Whigs, George proposed to govern as well as to reign — "to be a King" after the pattern that his mother and his tutor, the Earl of Bute, had designed for him. He set out, therefore, to redress the balance in favor of monarchy and to end the rule of the Whig lords by which "ministers were kings" in England. Ministers were created, young George believed, to do the bidding of kings and to regard the sovereign as the source from which all blessings flowed, including political office and parliamentary majorities.[21]

To achieve his ambition of governing England, George III did not make the mistake of adopting the policy of the Stuarts, who, by attempting to rule by prerogative, had lost the throne. Instead, he copied the example of the Tudors, who, having brought Parliament securely under their control, ruled England through it. George III believed that he could be a King without violating the constitution or attempting to extend the prerogative: if he could

[21] *The Correspondence of King George the Third*, edited by Sir John Fortescue, London, 1927, I, 174.

bring Parliament under tutelage, the game was already won. He attempted, therefore, not to change existing political machinery of England but rather to transfer authority from the hands of the Whig magnates into his own. He became a politician — a sort of crowned Duke of Newcastle — who dispensed patronage, managed the voting in Parliament, and made and unmade ministries by means of his position in the House of Commons.[22] George III, it is clear, went to school under the Whigs and, as was said of a later American politician, he ended by stealing the textbooks. When the Whigs denounced the frauds and corruption practised by the King's henchmen, they were silenced by the observation that it was "the greatest absurdity for a Whiggish champion to endeavour to make the Tories odious, for pursuing measures which the Whigs themselves were the first to promote and practice." [23]

The Whigs were caught off guard by George III's strategy. They were prepared to fight the Crown upon the ancient battlefield of the prerogative; but George III gave them no opportunity to take their stand upon this familiar ground. England had scarcely seen a King more self-denying in the exercise of this privilege than George III. His ministers actually declaimed against the prerogative: in 1775, Lord North opposed royal requisitions because "he could not see the difference betwixt such a requisition and the demand by Charles I of ship-money." Indeed, it was the Whig Camden who often defended the prerogative against the attack of the Tories; and in 1767, Lord Chatham's government unsuccessfully attempted to suspend an act of Parliament by the exercise of the power.[24] But as prerogative lost its terrors, there sprang up that "irresistible hydra, court influence," which made Parliament "a mere instrument of regal administration." [25] Burke exclaimed that "the power of the crown, almost dead and rotten as Prerogative, has grown up anew, with much more strength, and far less odium, under the name of Influence." [26] Against this menace the Whigs fought a losing battle; they, as well as the American colonists, experienced the force of Tom Paine's remark: "The fate of

[22] Brian Tunstall, *William Pitt*, London, 1938, 396.
[23] *London Chronicle*, January 7, 1764.
[24] *Parliamentary History*, London, 1813, XVI, 274, 283; XVIII, 572. Lord Fitzmaurice, *Life of William Earl of Shelburne*, London, 1912, I, 290.
[25] Catherine Macaulay, *Observations on a Pamphlet Entitled, Thoughts on the Cause of the Present Discontents*, London, 1770, 10.
[26] *The Works of Edmund Burke*, Boston, 1826, I, 259.

Charles the first hath only made kings more subtle — not more just."

After having made himself secure in the House of Commons, the King's first act was to overthrow the government of the "great Colossus Pitt" and to proscribe the Whigs from office. Pitt's fall from power was probably fortunate for his reputation: the glory of the conquests remained his, the bills had to be presented and collected by his successors. But the Whigs could not be consoled by such reflections; the grief of the Duke of Newcastle, in particular, was beyond healing by philosophy. The greatest borough manager in England found that his every relative, friend, or dependent was purged: even doorkeepers who owed their office to him were dismissed. The Duke himself was stripped of his offices and even his Lord Lieutenancies were taken from him. "There never was such an instance of cruelty and barbarity," he cried out in anguish; "never was man who had it in his power to serve, to make, to choose so great a part of the members of both Houses, so abandoned as I am at present." [27] The long reign of the Whigs was over; the King was at last free from the "Aristocratic Faction" which sought to "lead the Monarchy in chains." The fall of Pitt marks the beginning of a new chapter of English history in which England was governed by men who held their positions at the pleasure of a King who was master of Parliament.

The fact that George III governed England during the period of the American Revolution makes him responsible for the acts of the British government which led to the destruction of the first British Empire. George III attained the power he sought: he became a king — and lost an empire. But any indictment of him must be tempered by the admission that he ruled England at a time when the financial condition of the mother country made new sources of revenue imperative and when the necessity for a thoroughgoing reorganization of the empire had become visibly evident to Englishmen.

To ensure the continuance of his personal rule, George III sought to destroy the party system in England. To extirpate party, to unite all Englishmen in support of the Crown, became his goal.

[27] *Memoirs of the Marquis of Rockingham*, edited by George Thomas, Earl of Albemarle, London, 1852, I, 145, 152. George Harris, *The Life of Lord Chancellor Hardwicke*, London, 1768, III, 334. *London Chronicle*, January 20, 1763.

At the beginning of his reign, the prospects of success seemed bright: the party system had disintegrated during the rule of the Whigs; and English politics had for many years consisted of a factional struggle within the ruling party which took the form of a scramble for office without dignity, ideals, or honor. But ironically enough, George III succeeded in reviving the party system in England just when it seemed about to expire. All the King's horses and all the King's men could not scramble the Tories with the Whigs. As early as 1762, William Pitt declared that the names Whig and Tory were beginning to be heard again; and an alarmed Englishman remarked that his countrymen seemed to be "falling into and renewing the ridiculous squabbles, and nonsensical Jingo that disturbed the noodles and distracted the brains (if they had any) of our forefathers."[28]

The King's supporters declared that in seeking to destroy party, George III was merely trying to be a King over all his people and "to equally admit to favour and power, worthy, honest, and able men, not regarding whether they had received their education at Cambridge or Oxford."[29] Actually, he showed a weakness for gentlemen who had received their education at Edinburgh. In particular, he fell under the influence of the Earl of Bute, who, although he had been educated in England, was the most hated man in the kingdom.

Lord Bute was a heavy-handed Scotchman whose talents admirably fitted him, as did those of George III, for the life of a country squire. His rise to power had begun when he was called in to make a hand at whist with the prince and princess, the parents of the future George III; and rumor darkly whispered that he kept his influence after the untimely death of the prince in 1751 by becoming the princess's lover. Tutor of the young prince, he became the favorite upon the accession of George III; and after the fall of Pitt, the King called upon Bute to form a ministry. Bute accepted and immediately began the purge of the Whigs — for which he incurred their undying hatred.

The Whigs struck back at Bute — the "Northern Thane" — by making political capital of the King's fondness for Scotchmen. They swore that this "accursed Scotch Administration" would be the ruin of England: Scotch politicians were descending upon England

---

[28] *London Chronicle*, September 1, November 30, 1763.
[29] *Ibid.*, June 18, 1763. *The Political Controversy*, London, 1762, I, 30, 158.

in Bute's train by "thousands" — in many respects an invasion more terrible than that of the Picts. It was said that "the Northern roads groan under broad-wheel waggons all swarming with penurious scorbutic wretches" drawn to the English Exchequer like flies to honey.[30] The young King who had declared upon his accession that he rejoiced in the name of Briton seemed to have forgotten that Englishmen were the greatest of the Britons and ought to have first choice when offices and emoluments were handed out. Under this heavy load of Scotchmen even George III's popularity began to decline. Both Bute and the King saw in 1762, while the Seven Years' War was still raging, that they must ingratiate themselves with the people by some bold stroke of policy before the Whigs' propaganda had done its work.

Having all but knocked Spain out of the war, they therefore determined to make peace with France and Spain despite the fact that England's ally, Frederick of Prussia, was in danger of being overwhelmed by the Russian, Austrian, and French armies. Pitt, now in the opposition benches of the House of Commons, demanded that such crushing terms be meted out to France and Spain that they would never again be able to menace the British Empire. Above all, he wished to prevent France from reassuming her position as a maritime and commercial power. Therefore he insisted that the North American fisheries become a British monopoly and France be shorn of her West Indian islands. England, Pitt believed, had an unexampled opportunity to destroy for all time the fighting power of her "eternal" enemy, France, if she but dealt firmly with the beaten Bourbons.

But Bute and the King, in their eagerness to present the English people with a victorious peace, did not take full advantage of their strong position at the peace table. Although shattered and exhausted, France was not permanently crippled by the British government. The monopoly of the fisheries, upon which Pitt had set his heart, slipped through the fingers of the English negotiators when the islands of Miquelon and St. Pierre off the coast of Newfoundland were restored to France. Moreover, she was allowed to retain the most important of her West Indian islands. Despite Pitt's insistence that Great Britain make a clean sweep of French possessions in North America, Bute and George III accepted the demand of the French government that they content themselves with choosing

[30] *Ibid.*, I, 30, 158.

between the acquisition of Canada and the island of Guadeloupe. Guadeloupe was one of the French West Indian islands captured by the British during the war. It was rich in sugar — and the British Empire was sorely deficient in sugar colonies. Its acquisition, therefore, was in accord with doctrines of mercantilism which emphasized the necessity of a self-sufficient empire and it promised to be a boon to the British consumer, gouged by the monopolistic British West Indian planters who held the price of sugar in Great Britain high above that of the world market. Canada, on the other hand, was regarded by many Englishmen as a barren waste, producing only furs and timber and affording a small market for the sale of British merchandise. Despite these shortcomings, Canada was chosen over Guadeloupe, largely for reasons of strategy. With Canada in British hands, an end might be brought to the long series of destructive wars waged by France and England for the mastery of North America. Control of the Indian tribes which, under French instigation, had long harried the frontiers of the British colonies would mean peace and prosperity for British America.[31] The security of the empire thus played a vital part in the decision of the British government to take Canada rather than Guadeloupe, although some Englishmen remarked that security for the empire had begun to bear a disqueting resemblance to "universal Empire" — an ambition usually ascribed only to France.[32]

The acquisition of Canada was based upon a long-range view of British interests in North America, but here the long view proved costly. Canada increased the financial problems of Great Britain and thereby further obliged the British government to look to its colonies for added revenue. The sugar of Guadeloupe, on the other hand, would have brought much-needed revenue to the home government and would have immediately stimulated British trade and shipping to a far greater degree than did Canada. In taking Canada, the British government placed another financial millstone around its neck; nor could the other North American acquisitions of the Seven Years' War be expected to ease the mother country's burden.

[31] W. L. Grant, "Canada versus Guadeloupe," *American Historical Review*, July 1912, XVII. F. W. Pitman, *The Development of the British West Indies*, 334–360, emphasizes the part played by the British sugar planters in determining the government's decision to take Canada rather than Guadeloupe.

[32] *An Examination of the Commercial Principles of the late Negotiation*, London, 1762, 94.

The Floridas, taken from Spain in 1763, were regarded as a waste of swamp and sand which, groaned an Englishman, would be "the dwelling of desperate villains" and the chief products of the country seemed likely to be "disease and lamentation." [33] Great Britain, in the eyes of some Englishmen, had done little more in 1763 than take white elephants in North America off the hands of France and Spain. With the exception of the West Indian islands taken from France not a single colony acquired by the Peace of Paris could pay its own way, much less contribute to the financial needs of the mother country. Yet throughout the Seven Years' War, while Englishmen were tightening their belts and waging the most costly war in their history, they had been told that British conquests in North America would amply repay the costs. New colonies would be formed and from them Englishmen could expect a steady stream of riches, besides the wealth that would be drawn from the older provinces. "From hence," it was said, "every loss was to be repaired, every burden to be alleviated, and all past calamities softened into oblivion." The realization that Great Britain had acquired, from the immediate financial point of view, only new liabilities came therefore as a rude awakening to British taxpayers.[34] "Alas great Pitt," exclaimed one of the Great Commoner's admirers, "are all thy conquests, trophies, spoils, shrunk to this little measure." [35]

This conviction that England had won the war but lost the peace was not shared by the American colonists. From their point of view, the Peace of Paris was the best that could have been made: it eliminated the menace of France in Canada and paved the way for the westward expansion of the British colonies. In drawing up the terms of peace, the British government seemed to have had the interests of the British-American colonies close at heart and had finally recognized that "the *foundations of the future grandeur and stability of the British empire lie in America.*" For this reason, probably at no time during the entire colonial period was there more good will toward Great Britain in America than at the conclusion of the Seven Years' War.[36]

[33] *The Political Register*, London, 1769, V, 164–165.
[34] *The Works of Edmund Burke*, Boston, 1826, I, 245–246.
[35] *The Political Register*, London, 1769, V, 164. *The Correspondence of William Pitt, Earl of Chatham*, London, 1838, II, 197.
[36] *The Writings of Benjamin Franklin*, IV, 4. Jonathan Mayhew, *Two Discourses Delivered October 9th, 1760*, Boston, 1760, 47.

After the outbreak of the revolutionary movement in the American colonies, many Englishmen concluded that Great Britain had made a serious error in taking Canada from France. The French, it was recognized, had kept the Americans loyal — never had the colonists loved the mother country more than when the French and Indians were burning up the frontiers. Those who were fond of giving advice after the event pointed out that the colonists needed a strong hostile power on their borders to remind them of their dependence upon Great Britain and to keep them from developing illusions of grandeur. The fact that Americans had "no enemy but a few Savages to contend with," it was remarked in 1775, was "now the true cause of their assuming the important airs of a self-sufficient and powerful state." [37] The best cure for American pride and presumption, some Englishmen suggested, was to restore Canada to France, dismantle the frontier forts, and "let in upon them their old Friends the French Indians." [38] Indeed, public opinion in Great Britain became so critical of the acquisition of Canada that the administration was obliged in 1775 and 1776 to defend it as a measure dictated by the need of security and the larger interests of the empire.

It may well be doubted whether the revolutionary spirit would have so easily taken possession of Americans had the French held Canada after 1763. In an ever-increasing degree after the conquest of New France, Americans were coming to regard themselves as the masters of the continent and the idea of "a great Empire" was beginning to act like heady wine upon them. With the "turbulent Gallics" still in Canada, however, this sense of self-importance might have been moderated by the realization that British military aid was vital to the defense of the colonies. Perhaps Americans would then have been willing to pay a heavier price for British protection; at least one of the arguments that Americans used against the Stamp Act — that they were being taxed to maintain an army which they did not need — would not have held true. But it is also true that the acquisition of Canada gave Britain an opportunity to deal with her colonies without fear of driving them into the arms of the French. Americans exclaimed in 1765 that if the French

[37] *Gazetteer and New Daily Advertiser,* January 16, 1775.
[38] *Parliamentary Register* (House of Lords), V, 95. *St. James's Chronicle,* January 25, 1766.

were still in Quebec, "the British parlem't would as soon be D[amne]d as to offer to do what they do now."[39]

The peace of 1763 was the first important achievement of George III's personal rule in foreign affairs. When the preliminaries of the peace had been approved by Parliament, the Princess Dowager exclaimed, "Now my son is King of England." After surveying the peace terms of 1763, many Englishmen concluded that if the young King enjoyed a long reign, he would be obliged to take his country again into war with France. The Gallic peril still hung heavy over England because, said Pitt, the restoration of the West Indian islands and Miquelon and St. Pierre gave France "the means of recovering her prodigious losses and of becoming once more formidable to us at sea." At best, Pitt believed that the Peace of Paris would last ten years. Choiseul, the French minister, certain that he had outwitted the British in the peace settlement, declared that within five years France would be ready to launch a war of revenge.[40]

Even upon the peacemakers it dawned that in their haste they had given too much quarter to France. Dismayed by their own handiwork, they began to fear that France, still possessing great powers of rejuvenation and burning for revenge, might force war upon Great Britain when Britain wanted nothing more than to settle down comfortably and enjoy the fruits of victory. The Family Compact was not broken — France had given Spain Louisiana in compensation for Spain's losses in the unsuccessful war against Great Britain; but Great Britain had sacrificed its friendship with Prussia in order to make a separate peace. Great Britain's isolation might spell France's opportunity to regain its lost territories and prestige. Alarming reports came out of France of preparations for another war. As early as September, 1763, it was reported that the French navy was being rebuilt; and Lord Egmont, the First Lord of the Admiralty, predicted that the new fleet would be ready for action in 1764 and that an attack might be made upon Newfoundland.[41] The British Empire seemed indeed menaced on every

[39] *The American Historical Review*, July 1921, XXVI, 747. Thomas Lyttelton, *A Letter to the Earl of Chatham on the Quebec Bill*, London, 1774, 35. Lord Fitzmaurice, *Life of William Earl of Shelburne*, London, 1912, I, 137.
[40] Richard Pares, *War and Trade in the West Indies*, New York, 1936, 611.
[41] *London Chronicle*, September 8, 1763. *The Grenville Papers*, edited by William James Smith, London, 1852–1853, 173.

side. It was for this reason that the men who had made the Peace of 1763 became the first to raise their voices for more armaments and troops with which to defend the empire against the dangers that loomed unexpectedly on the horizon. Immediate measures must be taken to protect British America, they declared, or "else all the labour of the last war may be lost in a moment; the colonies may be conquered by our enemies in one campaign." [42]

Fears for the safety of the British colonies were magnified by Pontiac's Rebellion. The ease with which the Indians overran the frontier was final proof to British statesmen that the mother country could not view with indifference the defenseless state of the colonies. The Indians, it was clear, were potential allies of the French and Spaniards, and, by flanking the exposed frontiers of the British colonies, constituted a major threat to their security. This peril was met in two ways: by the issuance of the Proclamation of 1763 and by the effort to station an army of ten thousand men in British America.

One of the chief reasons why Americans had rejoiced in the peace terms of 1763 was that the West seemed to have been thrown open to their expansion. The removal of the French menace had, it was believed, made possible at long last the settlement of the American West by British subjects. "What fair Hopes," exclaimed the Reverend Dr. Samuel Cooper of Boston in 1759, "have we of being compleatly delivered from that Enemy, that has so often interrupted our Tranquillity, and checked our Growth! What scenes of Happiness are we ready to figure to ourselves, from the Hope of enjoying, in this good Land, all the Blessings of an undisturbed and lasting Peace! From the Hope of seeing our Towns enlarged; our Commerce increased; and our Settlements extending themselves with Security of every Side, and changing a Wilderness into a fruitful Field." [43] The victory over France was a triumph of Protestantism over Catholicism — and now the faithful were to be rewarded with the substantial goods of this world. But Americans, in their exultation, forgot the Indians until they were rudely reminded by Pontiac's uprising that the redskins still barred the

---

[42] *The Justice and Necessity of Taxing the American Colonies Demonstrated together with a Vindication of the Authority of Parliament*, London, 1766, 10–11.

[43] The Reverend Samuel Cooper, *A Sermon Preached Before His Excellency Thomas Pownall*, Boston, 1759, 46.

way to the riches of the West. Since the Indians had taken to the warpath in 1763 partly because they feared they were about to be deprived of their lands by the advancing line of white settlement, the British government issued a proclamation which established a line of demarcation – roughly the summit of the Alleghenies – westward of which no British subject could purchase land or settle. Hastily drawn and designed only to meet a temporary emergency, the Proclamation of 1763 became the foundation of a permanent British policy toward the American West. Instead of being quickly withdrawn, as had perhaps been intended, the Proclamation was maintained without modification; and it was not until Americans had become an independent people that they resumed the westward advance and thereby fulfilled the promise of the destruction of New France in 1763.

The Proclamation of 1763 was retained by the British government long after Pontiac and his warriors had laid down their arms because it was a solution – or at least the best the British government was capable of making – of the Indian problem. By enabling the Crown to keep white settlers out of the Indians' hunting grounds it eliminated one of the chief causes of border warfare. The Proclamation came to be regarded, moreover, as an answer to the question – insistently raised after 1765 – how the American colonists were to be kept loyal to the mother country and prevented from defrauding their English creditors. By confining Americans to the seaboard, there seemed little likelihood that they could escape the long arm of Britain. But once Americans put the Appalachians between themselves and the mother country, it was pointed out, they could throw off British sovereignty and invite all subjects of the British Crown who believed themselves oppressed to join them in this "American Paradise." British merchants were warned that the withdrawal of the Proclamation would lead to a retreat of debtors "bag and baggage over the almost inaccessible Alleghany Mountains"; "was a man in debt," it was said, "he might sell off his stock, and clamber over the American Alps with the money in his pocket and there he would be nearly as safe from his creditors in England as if he was beyond the verge of nature." [44] And to

---

[44] *An Appeal to the Public*, London, 1774, 52. *The Regulations Lately Made Concerning the Colonies and the Taxes Imposed upon Them, Considered*, London, 1765, 19–22. *Virginia Gazette* (Purdie and Dixon), December 17, 1772. Mein, 14.

crown these evils, Americans would begin to manufacture for themselves after they had established themselves beyond the mountains and British manufacturers and merchants would find their former customers vanished into thin air.

For several years after the issuance of the Proclamation of 1763 Americans refused to believe that it represented a permanent British policy. George Washington thought that it would remain in force only until the Indians had been persuaded to sell their lands. He advised his friends to continue to seek and mark lands west of the line so that when the Proclamation was withdrawn they would be in a position to take possession of the choicest acreage. The chief fear of Americans was not that the West would remain permanently closed but that English promoters and capitalists would persuade the British government to grant them the most desirable lands in the region. Virginians were alarmed lest the Ohio and Kentucky country be granted to Englishmen with influential connections at court. But a powerful group of English officials were beginning to speak of the "finality" of the Proclamation line. Although Lord Shelburne urged the establishment of new settlements, Barrington and Hillsborough opposed any attempts to open the West to settlement. Hillsborough, Secretary of State for the Colonies, fell from power in 1772 partly over the issue of Western lands, but his successor, Lord Dartmouth, declared in 1774 that all efforts to promote Western settlements were "a gross Indignity and Dishonour to the Crown and an act of equal Inhumanity and Injustice to the Indians." [45] In 1774, when some Virginians laid claims to lands west of the line of 1763, Governor Dunmore permitted the lands to be surveyed. He was sharply reprimanded by Lord Dartmouth and ordered to permit no more surveys west of the mountains — to the chagrin of Patrick Henry and a large number of speculators and ex-soldiers who held bounty claims on these lands. [46]

Had not the Revolution intervened, the British government would have withdrawn or modified the Proclamation of 1763, but Americans were never informed of this intention. Instead, in 1773, the British government instructed the colonial governors to make no further grants of Crown lands anywhere in the colonies — bringing

[45] Lord Dartmouth to Lord Dunmore, September 8, 1774, P.R.O., C.O. 5, 1352, Library of Congress Transcript.
[46] *William and Mary College Quarterly*, Second Series, April 1925, V, 160–161.

colonial expansion to a complete halt.[47] Thus, as long as its rule endured, the British government sought to thwart one of the strongest forces in American life. The Americans, said a royal governor, "for ever imagine the Lands further off are still better than those upon which they are already settled"; if they attained Paradise, they would move on if they heard of a better place farther west.[48] Life in the American wilderness did not lead men to believe that any government had the right to forbid them to possess themselves of unused lands if they were strong enough to take them. By prohibiting Western settlement, as by its forest-conservation policy, the mother country put itself in opposition to the American practice of exploiting natural resources wherever it could be done with profit. Moreover, in the Proclamation of 1763, the British government was showing, in the eyes of American backwoodsmen, an insufferable tenderness for the Indians. In its panic, the Crown seemed to have handed over to the Indians the richest lands of the continent. Safe behind the mountains, the tribes could now recruit their strength until they were able to take the warpath thousands strong against the white settlements. A question that meant life and death along the border had been settled in the snug comfort of their ministerial offices by men who had never seen a redskin rampant with blood lust. No Indian hunting ground, whether established by the British or American government, long resisted the inroads of American frontiersmen; and the government which sought to protect and cherish the Indians was certain to earn the hatred of Westerners.

As for establishing an army of ten thousand men in the colonies, Americans found the plan no better than the Proclamation of 1763. British alarm for the security of the colonies left Americans cold. They pointed out that no standing army had been maintained in British America while France was in possession of Canada and Louisiana; why then, they asked, was an army required after the French had been almost completely driven from the hemisphere and the New England colonies were menaced by no more redoubtable an enemy than the "formidable power of the Scatacook Indians, a warlike tribe of near thirty fighting men, situated on the western borders of the Connecticut"? The British fleet could prevent in-

[47] *Colonial Records of North Carolina,* IX, 668–669.
[48] Lord Dunmore to Lord Dartmouth, December 24, 1774, P.R.O., C.O. 5, 1533, Library of Congress Transcript.

vasion of the colonies and as long as bluejackets commanded the seas there was no necessity of burdening the colonies with redcoats. It was true that British armies were good for business: they brought specie into the country; they consumed the farmers' surplus, and they were excellent customers of grogshops. Besides, British officers promised to enliven social life in the colonial towns: "Philadelphia is charming, and really very sociable people," wrote a young British officer in 1756; "the women there are extreamly and most passionately fond of red coats, which is for us a most fortunate piece of absurdity." [49] But puritanical patriots feared that Americans would pick up fashionable vices from the rakes and wastrels that were supposed to flourish in the British army: from this association, American men promised to become less frugal and women less chaste.

[49] Collections of the New York Historical Society, *The Lee Papers*, New York, 1872, I, 3.

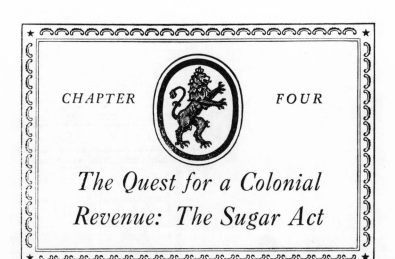

CHAPTER FOUR

The Quest for a Colonial Revenue: The Sugar Act

AMERICANS objected to the presence of a large British force in North America chiefly because they dreaded a standing army and because they expected to be compelled to pay for the troops' support. Some colonists believed that the British government intended to use the army to cram unpopular acts of Parliament down their throats, not to defend them against their enemies. Daniel Dulany of Maryland predicted that the redcoats would be "employed in the national Service of Cropping the Ears, and Slitting the Nostrils of the Civil Magistrates, as Marks of Distinction." [1] To add to these misgivings, reports were heard in the colonies in 1762 and 1763 that the mother country was determined to tax Americans to maintain a huge army among them. George Washington, for instance, learned "on good authority" that the home government contemplated raising £300,000 a year in America; and the colonial agents wrote despairingly from London that they could do nothing to avert the blow.[2]

As Americans soon learned, these reports were well-founded. Great Britain had incurred such a heavy debt during the war that the government was obliged to seek new sources of revenue if a British army were to be maintained in the colonies. Pitt had effected great conquests, but the bill came high. He believed that Great Britain, locked in a life-and-death struggle with France, could not afford to haggle over pounds and shillings: every resource must be thrown without stint into the winning of the war. But after Pitt had conquered an empire for his countrymen, many complained of his prodigality and his ignorance of finance. After his fall from power, the finances of Great Britain passed into even more inexpert hands. It was said of Sir Francis Dashwood, Chancellor of

[1] Dulany, 59.
[2] *Pennsylvania Magazine of History and Biography*, Philadelphia, 1879, III, 148. *Boston Gazette*, November 5, 1764. *The New London Gazette*, April 6, 1764. Richard Jackson to Benjamin Franklin, November 12, 1763, Franklin MSS., American Philosophical Society.

the Exchequer under Lord Bute, that "his knowledge of accounts was confined to the reckoning of tavern bills" and that to him "a sum of five figures was an impenetrable secret." [3] With the national debt swollen to £140,000,000, it was evident that retrenchment was the need of the hour and that the crisis was so acute that a man of business rather than a borough-monger or fashionable rake was required to head the British Exchequer.

Meanwhile, in 1763, Lord Bute, laboring under the double stigma of being a Scotchman and the author of the peace treaty of 1763, retired from English politics, declaring as he surrendered the seals that "fifty pounds a year and bread and water were luxury compared with what I suffer." For Bute's successor, the King turned to George Grenville, a Whig leader who, instead of following the Whigs into opposition after the fall of Pitt, had attached himself to the King and had served as speaker of the House of Commons under Bute. Like his chief, Grenville owed his elevation not to Parliament but to the King, and he depended for support in the House of Commons not upon the Whig magnates or upon his personal following, but upon the King. Once again, the Whigs were given bitter proof that it was the King of England who made and unmade ministries at pleasure. [4]

George Grenville was a rare figure in eighteenth-century English political life. A man of business, stiff, opinionated, and dour, he enjoyed repute as a financier: as Dr. Samuel Johnson remarked, could Great Britain have obliged the Spaniards to pay for the return of Manila in the peace treaty of 1763, Grenville, in contrast to his predecessor at the Exchequer, could have counted the money. He was horrified by the cost of the Seven Years' War and had consistently attempted to bridle Pitt's prodigality. So powerful was his zeal for thrift and economy that he thought more in 1762 of stopping the war than of squeezing concessions from France and Spain; it was said of him that he considered "a National saving of two Inches of Candle" as a triumph greater than all Pitt's victories. [5] He seems, indeed, to have regarded himself as the only man who could save England after William Pitt had run through the treasury.

[3] *Memoirs of the Marquis of Rockingham*, I, 117–118. *Grenville Papers*, London, 1858, II, 219.

[4] *Memoirs of the Marquis of Rockingham*, I, 109.

[5] *Grenville Papers*, II, 109, 290–292, 293–295. *The Political Controversy*, London, 1762, I, 154. D. A. Winstanley, *Lord Chatham and the Whig Opposition*, Cambridge, 1912, 10, note. *Public Advertiser*, December 30, 1765.

Although Grenville's critics said that he acted upon the principle that the people of England are never so happy as when they are told they are ruined, his alarm for Britain's financial stability was genuine and it became the foundation of his domestic and colonial policy.

Grenville's chief concern was revenue and economy; they were his passion, which he pursued relentlessly until he was brought to the quicksands in which the British Empire foundered. He could not endure the sight of red ink, an unbalanced budget, or waste and extravagance – these invariably inspired him with a fatal determination to set matters right. He sought to lead the empire into a heaven of black ink and sound bookkeeping; but "the Gentle Shepherd" – as Pitt called Grenville – took the wrong turning and never attained the promised land.

The condition of the colonial customs might well have agitated A British financier less penny-wise than George Grenville was. To collect two thousand pounds in customs duties in the colonies cost the British government eight thousand pounds. Smuggling was rampant and openly connived at by British officials. The chief posts in the colonial customs had been made sinecures and were filled by placemen who lived in England; their poorly paid agents were found by the colonial merchants to be "needy Wretches who found it easier, and more profitable, not only to wink but to sleep in their Beds; the Merchants' Pay being more generous than the King's." [6] James Otis said that "a very small office in the customs in America has raised a man a fortune sooner than a government" because customs officers found it possible to do what the King himself could not do: dispense with acts of Parliament. While the custom-house officers thus feathered their nests, British officials estimated that £700,000 worth of merchandise was smuggled annually into the colonies – a serious loss to British merchants and manufacturers as well as to the government itself. "The Americans take nothing from us which they cannot do without," lamented an Englishman, "and . . . they smuggle as fast as they can upon their extensive coasts." [7] In New York, the Indian trade was carried on to an alarming extent with goods smuggled from Holland; and the royal

---

[6] *Virginia Gazette* (Purdie), May 27, 1773. *The Regulations Lately Made Concerning the Colonies . . . Considered*, 60. *Grenville Papers*, II, 114. *Public Advertiser*, January 13, 1766.

[7] Josiah Tucker, *Four Tracts*, Gloucester, 1774, 134.

governor warned that if this were tolerated, "the greatest part of the commerce of the American Colonies will be withdrawn from the Mother Country, and be carryed to Holland." [8] These violations of the Acts of Trade, it was held in England, made the colonies worse than independent "for so much of their Trade as is thereby diverted from its proper channel, they are no longer British Colonies, but Colonies of the Countries with which they trade." [9]

In Virginia and Maryland, tobacco was smuggled out of the country by New Englanders, some of them perhaps loyal Harvard men, who thus deprived William and Mary College of the proceeds it received by law from tobacco duties. The smuggling of New Englanders became proverbial in Great Britain where it was believed that the Saints, far from regarding contraband running as a crime, found "religious Merit" in it because it defrauded the mother country. A New Englander, it was said, derived "his right of cheating the Revenue, and of purjuring himself, from the example of his fathers and the rights of nature"; and he would continue to "complain and smuggle, and smuggle and complain, 'till all Restraints are removed, and 'till he can both buy and sell, whenever, and wheresoever, he pleases. Any thing short of this, is still a Grievance, a Badge of Slavery." [10] Yet, in fairness to New Englanders, it ought to be said that most of this illicit trade was in violation of the Molasses Act of 1733 and was essential to the survival of New England commerce, rather than in violation of the Laws of Trade and Navigation which, in some respects, conferred positive advantages upon Northern merchants.

Grenville attempted to suppress smuggling by multiplying certificates, affidavits, cockets, warrants, and bonds, thus enmeshing the colonial merchants in a web of red tape. For example, shipmasters were now compelled to give bond before instead of after loading, as had been the previous rule; and they were required to post bond even for a cargo of non-enumerated goods, which had formerly been exported without bond. The customhouse officers were directed to take up their posts in the colonies and officers of

[8] *Documents relative to the Colonial History of the State of New York*, VII, 271–272.
[9] *The Regulations Lately Made Concerning the Colonies . . . Considered*, 92.
[10] Tucker, 134. *Public Advertiser*, April 6, 1775. Mein, 2.

the Royal Navy were ordered to aid in the enforcement of the Acts of Trade, much to their disgust at being degraded to the position of customhouse officers, and to the anger of the colonists, who protested, as did Burke, that Grenville had given "to the collection of the revenue the air of hostile combination." [11] Red tape had no terrors for American smugglers; but the British navy was not so easily brushed aside. "Men of war, cutters, marines, with their bayonets fixed, judges of admiralty, collectors, comptrollers, searchers, tide waiters, land waiters, with a whole catalogue of pimps, are sent hither," groaned the merchants, "not to protect our trade, but to distress it." [12]

To increase the efficiency of the customs, the powers of the Admiralty Courts were enlarged. Established in the colonies since 1696, the Admiralty Courts were one of the most effective – and most hated – instruments for enforcing the Acts of Trade. Here suspected violators of British commercial laws were tried by a judge without benefit of jury, as indeed was true in Great Britain itself. This deprivation of the jealously guarded right to trial by jury was justified, Englishmen pointed out, by the likelihood that a smuggler, if tried by his peers, would find himself at the tender mercies of a jury of smugglers. But the Admiralty judges to whom was entrusted this great power were by no means disinterested: they received a commission of 5 per cent upon the amount of the fine and condemnation. As a result, the hapless merchant who fell into the jaws of these "dreadful courts" was apt to be plucked clean. Prior to 1764, however, the merchants were protected against the worst abuses of this system by the provision that if seizures were made upon false information or contrary to law, the informer was liable to suit under the common law. George Grenville deprived the merchants of even this small guarantee of justice. Under the new procedure instituted in 1764, a customhouse officer might make a seizure in any of the colonies and carry the trial to Halifax, whither the owner must follow to defend his property. If the Admiralty judge decided that there was probable cause for seizure, the owner had no redress. Thus American merchants were faced with the prospect of seeing their property, "after being seized by a numerous swarm of horse-leeches, who never cease crying Give! Give! to be thrown into a prerogative court, a court of admiralty,

[11] *Works of Edmund Burke*, Boston, 1826, I, 313.
[12] *Boston Gazette*, September 16, 1765. *Public Advertiser*, December 16, 1765.

and there to be judged, forfeited, and condemned without a jury." [13]

Besides seeking to suppress smuggling, Grenville attempted to strengthen the monopolistic position of British merchants in the colonies. In 1764, higher duties were imposed on imported merchandise; French lawns and cambrics in particular were heavily taxed. At the same time, the English merchants and manufacturers were favored by the enumeration of lumber, raw silk, pot-ashes, and whale fins. By thus obliging the colonists to export these articles only to the mother country, the price was lowered in Great Britain at the expense of the colonial producers. In the same manner, the profit was taken out of the logwood trade. Early in the eighteenth century, the Northern colonies opened up with Europe a large trade in logwood which they procured from the British settlements in Honduras. This commodity served in some measure as a staple with which the Northern colonies were able to redress their adverse balance of trade with Great Britain. Some merchants, however, took Honduras logwood to Holland and smuggled back Dutch goods; therefore the English merchants demanded the cessation of the logwood trade between the colonies and the European continent. Grenville obliged by placing logwood upon the enumerated list. Coffee and pimento imported into the colonies were also taxed and Americans were forbidden to import wine directly from the Madeiras and Canary Islands lest they smuggle in European goods with their wine cargoes. This inflicted no little hardship upon colonial merchants because wine made up a large part of the return cargo of the food and fish ships that trafficked in the Mediterranean. The American merchants were now obliged to bring their wine to England before it could be carried to the colonies — to the distress of well-to-do colonists who exclaimed that wine was "more necessary than ever, to keep up our spirits" during the postwar depression.[14] But the British government seemed to have adopted the policy that "the best regimen for recruiting an emaciated body was to leave it no juices at all." [15]

[13] *Boston Gazette*, July 15, 1765. *New York Mercury*, January 28, 1765. *Virginia Gazette* (Dixon and Purdie), May 28, 1767. Stephen Hopkins, *The Rights of the Colonies Examined*, Providence, 1765, 15. William B. Reed, *The Life and Correspondence of Joseph Reed*, Philadelphia, 1847, I, 57. *Rhode Island Colonial Records*, Providence, 1861, VI, 458.

[14] *South Carolina Gazette*, October 22, 1764. Robert Macfarlane, *History of the Reign of George III*, London, 1770, 220.

[15] Thomas Whately, *Considerations on the Trade and Finances of this Kingdom, A Collection of Tracts*, London, 1767, II, 23.

The suppression of colonial smuggling and the tightening of the mercantilist system, however, did little to ease the financial burdens of the mother country. Grenville's immediate problem was to find the means of maintaining ten thousand men in the colonies. All of his economies and careful prunings of expenses were insufficient to meet the financial problems raised by the necessity of defending the empire which was rapidly rising upon the ruins of the French and Dutch colonial empires.

Before turning to the American colonies for revenue, however, the British government loaded British taxpayers with new stamp duties, window taxes, and excise taxes upon malt and cider. During the Seven Years' War, Pitt risked his popularity by laying an additional duty upon beer when it was calculated that "every poor hardworking man" in London drank four quarts of beer a day. But Britons were in no mood for taxes, and the government quickly learned that although the tinkers, tailors, and cobblers of England were the first to roar for war, they were also "the first to roar against the additional Halfpenny on their Pot of Porter, when that war had made the levying of it necessary." [16] The squires not only roared against taxes; the cider tax was violently resisted in the country districts and the excise officers who had been appointed to collect the tax were denounced as "boisterous ruffians, swelling with insolence of office," empowered to "invade and ransack, at pleasure, the asylum of domestic peace and security; nay, even to rifle the private retreats, or *penetralia* of female modesty." The excise officers were roughly handled by mobs of countrymen who believed themselves to be defending the rights of Englishmen; and in consequence, the British government was obliged to repeal the cider tax in 1765. Thus Englishmen gave Americans an example of how unpopular taxes might be nullified — an example which was not lost upon the colonists when they were confronted with the Stamp Tax.[17]

English squires protested with good cause against higher taxes. Because of the prevailing inequitable system of taxation, the greater part of the tax load fell upon the shoulders of the landowners, whereas the merchants escaped with comparatively light imposts. Long after the end of the Seven Years' War, the squires were

[16] *New Hampshire Gazette*, January 25, 1765.
[17] *A Letter to a Member of Parliament*, London, 1765, 2. *London Chronicle*, June 30, April 28, May 10 and 31, 1763.

obliged to pay the wartime land tax of four shillings in the pound; and it seemed inevitable that unless new sources of revenue were found the rate would be increased to the ruinous level of six shillings in the pound. The squires therefore complained that they were paying the bills for a war which had chiefly benefited the English merchants and the American colonists. While the merchants pocketed the wealth of the empire, the country gentlemen found their pockets emptied by tax collectors. The squires sourly observed that it was "the *trading* and not the *landed* interest which sets up most new carriages" and flaunted its wealth at court. Commerce, they believed, had "grown into a hydra, whose heads, unless lopped off, would devour the great landed property of the kingdom," and "citizens, merchants, planters, nabobs, Americans buy up their estates from them, turn them out of their patrimonial boroughs, live more luxuriously than they do." [18] In the opinion of the country gentlemen, relief from taxation could alone save them from falling completely under the domination of the mercantile class.

It is the plight of the landowners rather than bribery and corruption that explains the administration's huge majorities in Parliament. The scheme of drawing a revenue from the American colonies required no vote buying; on the contrary, the squires pricked up their ears whenever the ministers mentioned the "sweet welcome sound" of revenue. They joyfully looked forward to "rolling in American revenue" and were entranced by "the dazzling name of Sovereigns of America." [19] To the squires, a colonial revenue meant paring the land tax to the peacetime rate of two shillings in the pound and paying off the national debt with the help of the colonists. It would, they declared, "set us free, break asunder the galling shackles of our national debt . . . make the poor man easy, the rich man easier, and give content and abundance to all." [20] John Wilkes observed that the squires were not "burthened or perplexed with many ideas" and with none of a liberal character, but they clung obstinately to the conviction that a colonial revenue was essential to their welfare.[21] A British government that sought to

[18] *A Letter to the Reverend Josiah Tucker, D.D., by Samuel Estwick,* London, 1776, 110.
[19] *Ibid.*
[20] *Gazetteer and New Daily Advertiser,* February 10, 1775.
[21] *Parliamentary History,* XIX, 811. *The Political Controversy,* London, 1762, I, 365.

surrender the right of taxing the colonies could not have survived
the onslaught of the exasperated squires in the House of Commons.
After 1765, it may be questioned indeed whether it was the ministers
of George III or the country gentlemen who were most insistent
that the colonies be taxed.

It is significant that after the fall of the Whigs in 1762 the merchants began to lose their influence in British politics, although
it was briefly revived during the Stamp Act crisis. In general, however, the country squires and politicians came into their own under
George III and the merchants were obliged to make way for the
new masters of the empire. Crowded out of the Commons by
nabobs and placemen, the merchants were either ignored or "insulted and treated with contempt by Officers of the Treasury, the
Customs, and others that ought to be servants of the public, and
not Lords over the people." [22] This shift in political power was to
have far-reaching consequences upon British colonial policy.

After the Ministry had perceived that the English orange had
been squeezed dry of revenue, it turned almost inevitably to the
American colonies. Americans had won security as a result of the
Seven Years' War; they were now in a position to monopolize the
Indian trade; the fishery was safe from molestation by hostile fleets,
and new bounties had been given colonial producers. Moreover,
because of Pitt's generosity, the colonies had not incurred a crushing burden of debt during the war; whereas the interest on Great
Britain's national debt was almost £5,000,000 a year, the total debt
of the American colonies was only £2,600,000. At the end of the
war it was calculated that the public debt in the colonies was eighteen shillings per person; that of Great Britain stood at eighteen
pounds per person. In 1775, Lord North declared that Englishmen
paid on an average twenty-five shillings annually in taxes whereas
Americans paid only sixpence.

At the same time, the Seven Years' War so enriched the colonists
that it was believed in England that they had it within their power
to save the mother country from bankruptcy. Free spending by
British soldiers had spread prosperity and American contractors had
profiteered at the expense of the British armed forces. Americans
could now reap the fruits of victory: "We have opened to them new
funds of wealth," said an Englishman; "and if we apply'd a part
of it to the national service, the deduction was only from our

[22] *Gazetteer and New Daily Advertiser*, February 1, 1766.

boon not from their property." [23] Many Americans had become wealthy through privateering and smuggling. The Dutch island of St. Eustatius was the starting point of a large number of colonial fortunes and contraband French molasses brought wealth to numerous men later distinguished in the Revolution. The origins of the Hancock family fortune, in particular, would not have borne scrutiny by customhouse officers. Evidences of this abounding wealth had already reached the mother country. During the war, wealthy American merchants and planters spread themselves to entertain British officers. Their rich plate, sumptuous furniture, and fine wines dazzled these gentry, who returned to the mother country with tales of rich colonists who were making immense fortunes and paying virtually no taxes.[24] It began to be said in England: "The colonies are in a flourishing condition, increasing every day in riches, people and territory. Britain is exhausted; she is manifestly sinking under oppressive and insupportable burdens." [25]

Certainly the American colonies seemed in 1763 to be riding the crest of a wave of prosperity and easily capable of paying taxes to the mother country. In the South, travelers observed that "you may really go from house to house living upon Delicatesses, and drinking Claret you would not despise at the first tavern in London." It was a common sight to see a Virginia gentleman burning up the road with his chariot and four, flanked by Negro outriders. Horse racing, jockey clubs, and theaters flourished — where they were not forbidden by puritanical laws. It was observed that in the once puritanical city of Boston, the maids "exceed their mistresses in dress . . . they must have their hyson and green, and a black to attend at their pleasure." The Boston mall, modeled upon St. James's Park, was crowded with resplendently dressed ladies and gentlemen who, it was reported, were more gorgeous than courtiers on a coronation day and who curtsied and simpered in the latest London fashion.[26] Philip Fithian, a perspicacious young gentleman from New Jersey, noted that the Virginia belles were got up in the latest London stays: "I imputed the Flush which was visible in her

[23] Whately, II, 152. Ramsay, *The History of the American Revolution*, I, 74–75.
[24] John Fothergill, *Considerations Relative to the North American Colonies*, London, 1765, 41–42.
[25] *London Chronicle*, November 24, 1774. *Gazetteer and New Daily Advertiser*, December 23, 1765. *Public Advertiser*, February 17, 1766.
[26] *New Hampshire Gazette*, February 1, 1765.

Face," he remarked of one of these ladies, "to her being swathed up *Body & Soul & limbs together*." One day he confided to his diary a rare and wonderful sight: "This day," he wrote, "I saw a Phenomenon, Mrs. Carter without Stays." [27] English travelers complained that the colonial upper class overdressed in its anxiety to be in the height of the mode; the governor of South Carolina felt obliged to rebuke the Carolina gentry for their extravagance by preaching the necessity of "Diligence, Industry, and Frugality, telling them, that by pursuing these Maxims, the Dutch from low beginnings climbed up to be high and mighty States; and that by following the contrary methods, the Commonwealth of Rome fell from being the mistress of the World." [28] The lessons of history were quite lost upon the colonists: they continued to adorn themselves with fine Flanders lace, Dutch linens, French cambrics, silks, and gold and silver lace.

The latest London fashions were often seen in the American colonies before they reached the provincial towns of England itself. The colonial upper class aspired to be as English as possible; in its eyes, "Americanism" meant boorishness and rusticity. The ideal of wealthy colonists was the English country gentleman or merchant; accordingly, they had their clothes made to order by English tailors; their balls and assemblies compared favorably with those of English provincial society; and their towns boasted imitations of Ranelagh Gardens and Vauxhall.[29] The most sought-after guest by New York hostesses was the traveler recently returned from London who "can move a Minuet after the newest fashions in England; can quiver like a butterfly; is a perfect connoisseur in dress; and has been author to all the new cock't hats and scatches in town; has learnt the art of address from the gentility of Covent Garden, which, by Jove, he swears has ruined his constitution. Amongst the accomplished beaux, he has learned those elegant expressions, Split me, Madam; By Gad, Dam me; and fails not to use them on

[27] *Philip Vickers Fithian, Journal and Letters*, edited by John Rogers Williams, Princeton, 1924, 193, 270, 286. William Eddis, *Letters from America*, 107, 112.
[28] *Historical Collections of South Carolina*, edited by B. R. Carroll, New York, 1836, II, 228.
[29] *Quarterly Journal of the New York State Historical Association*, October 1932, XIII, 373–379. *Some Cursory Remarks made by James Birket in his Voyage to North America, 1750–1751*, New Haven, 1916, 21. *Reflections on the American Contest*, London, 1776, 16.

all occasions. So entirely is he taken up with England, that he always mentions guineas when he speaks of money." [30]

But it is plain that this prosperity was not confined to the wealthy; life was becoming less hard for the common people as comforts and luxuries came increasingly within their reach. "You cannot well imagine," wrote James Murray of Massachusetts in 1760, "what a Land of health, plenty and contentment this is among all ranks, vastly improved within these last ten years. The war on this Continent has been equally a blessing to the English Subjects and a Calamity to the French, especially in the Northern Colonies." [31] The common people lived better and drank better; one of the proofs commonly cited of American prosperity was the vast increase in the amount of liquor consumed and the growing prevalence of gambling and tavern lounging. Governor Pownall of Massachusetts declared that every other house in Boston was a tavern: it was here, exclaimed John Adams, that "disease, vicious habits, bastards & legislators are frequently begotten." In Williamsburg, Virginia, while the assembly was in session, the town was crowded with people "hurrying back and forwards from the Capitoll to the taverns, and at night Carousing and Drinking in one Chamber and box and Dice in another, which Continues till morning Commonly." "There is not a public house in virginia," said a traveler, "but have their tables all baterd with the boxes, which shows the Extravagant Disposition of the planters." [32] So widespread had become this affluence that an Englishman sourly remarked some years later that he saw no purpose to the Seven Years' War other perhaps than "to enable the grateful Colonies to rebel against the Mother Country, perhaps a generation or two sooner, than otherwise they would have done." [33]

Americans urged the mother country to look at the opposite side of the medal: the heavy debts contracted during the war which required all their energies to liquidate; the superficial nature of the prosperity of the colonies — it was, said Americans, owing solely to the credit advanced by British merchants, who, if they demanded repayment of their debts, "wou'd entirely change the appearance,

[30] Esther Singleton, *Social New York Under the Georges*, New York, 1902, 374.
[31] *Letters of James Murray, Loyalist*, Boston, 1911, 111.
[32] *American Historical Review*, July 1921, XXVI, 742.
[33] Josiah Tucker, *An Humble Address*, Gloucester, 1775, 14.

and our poverty wou'd appear," and the plight of the planters, who, by depending upon their future crop to pay their debts, were obliged to buy clothing and other necessities at the merchants' own price. "Come and see how well we are able to bear additional taxes," they invited. "See our poor starving! our liberties expiring! our trade declining." Were they to find that they had "been lavish of their blood and treasure in the late war, only to bind the shackles of slavery on themselves and their children," Americans asked, while by their sacrifices they raised the mother country "to an height of glory and wealth, which no European nation hath ever reached, since the decline of the Roman Empire?" [34]

But by British standards the colonists were lightly taxed; and no allegations to the contrary met with any credence in Great Britain. Although, to ward off British taxes, Americans declared their debts to be an insupportable burden, many of the provinces had succeeded by 1767 in freeing themselves entirely from debt. In this matter, it must be confessed that Americans adopted a most disingenuous policy: by complaining loudly of their taxes and debts, they tried to conceal from the mother country the true state of affairs. In 1767, for example, William Samuel Johnson, the Connecticut agent in London, learning that the province was almost out of debt, urged the local authorities to keep the fact secret from the British government lest it lead to a demand for further taxation by Parliament.[35]

Despite these precautions their high living proved a source of embarrassment to the American patriots when they came to plead poverty as an excuse for not paying taxes to the British government. Englishmen had heard too many reports of "the prodigious Increase of *American* Luxury" to believe the colonists' protests that they were poor and debt-ridden. When Americans sought to take shelter from taxation under the claim of destitution, Englishmen asked: What about "your Gold and Silver Laces; — your rich Brocades, Silks, and Velvets; — your Plate and China, and Jewels; — your Coaches and Equipages; — your sumptuous Furniture, Prints, and Pictures?" Moreover, their concerts, assemblies, and the "Va-

[34] *Rhode Island Colonial Records*, Providence, 1861, VI, 381. *Essex Gazette*, February 14, 1769. *Newport Mercury*, October 21, December 9, 1765. Oxenbridge Thacher, *The Sentiments of a British American*, Boston, 1764, 3.

[35] *Correspondence of General Thomas Gage*, I, 118. *Collections of the Massachusetts Historical Society*, Fifth Series, Boston, 1885, IX, 333.

riety and Profusion of Wines and Liquors" did not well accord with Americans' talk in 1765 of depression, bankruptcy, and hard times.[36]

Nor did it avail Americans to raise the cry, when they were asked to contribute to the expenses of the British Empire, that the Seven Years' War was an imperialistic war, waged by England for her own aggrandizement and by which she had been enriched with the spoils of two hemispheres. When Parliament attempted to tax the colonies, Americans declared that if Great Britain was heavily burdened with debt, it was owing entirely to her own extravagance and ambition — for which the colonies bore no responsibility whatever. To British demands for revenue, they answered that they were no more bound to "pay one farthing in discharge of the national debt, than we are to contribute towards lessening the national debt of Japan." Englishmen replied that they had been dragged into war by their self-seeking colonists and that the terms of peace had redounded solely to the benefit of Americans.[37] "The English," remarked a shrewd observer, "speak of the Blood and Treasure they have expended. The Americans that they have encountered an inhospitable Climate, for the purposes of Great Britain. . . . There is no Weight in any of these Declamations. Whatever was done by either of them, was done for their own Advantage." [38] However the facts may have been distorted in 1765, it is clear today that although the spark that plunged Europe into the Seven Years' War was the rattle of musketry and the yell of savages upon an obscure Ohio meadow, the struggle there begun was merely a chapter in the history of the second hundred years' war waged by England and France for world domination and in which the future of both the colonies and the mother country was equally at stake.

Nevertheless, Englishmen persisted in their conviction that the war had been fought for the colonies and that the greater part of the cost of the struggle had been laid by the taxpayers of the mother country "at the altar of American prosperity." [39] Britons had been taxed even in their beer to save the colonies from "merciless Papists"; and after such sacrifices Englishmen believed that

[36] Tucker, 123–124.

[37] *Newport Mercury*, September 2, 1765.

[38] Fred J. Hinkhouse, *The Preliminaries of the American Revolution as seen in the English Press*, New York, 1926, 111.

[39] *The Supremacy of the British Legislature over the Colonies candidly discussed*, London, 1775, 32

they might reasonably expect some show of gratitude by the colonists, who, as a result of their war boom, drank the finest port and Madeira. One of the strongest arguments for the taxation of the colonies was their flourishing, almost tax-free state. English propagandists soon found that this never failed to set Britons clamoring for a colonial revenue — nothing was sweeter to their ears than to be told "what *we* have done for them; what money *we* have spent; what blood *we* have lavished; and what trouble *we* have had in establishing and protecting them to this day." [40]

In seeking ways and means of raising a colonial revenue — certain to bring joy to British taxpayers — George Grenville hit upon rum and thereby made that intoxicant one of the essential ingredients of the American Revolution. For by taxing molasses — the raw material from which rum is manufactured — Grenville threatened New England with ruin, struck a blow at the economic foundations of the Middle colonies, and at the same time opened the way for the British West Indians — whom the continental colonists regarded as their worst enemies — to wax rich at the expense of their fellow subjects on the mainland.

Perhaps the bitterest rivalry within the empire lay between the British West India planters and the New England merchants and rum distillers. New England floated in a sea of rum; and without a free flow of molasses from the French West Indies the Saints would be left high and dry. New England and the Middle colonies exported large quantities of fish, flour, horses, and lumber to the French, Dutch, and Spanish West Indies and received in return specie or molasses. This was the Northern colonists' chief source of specie and it enabled them to continue to buy British manufactures despite their adverse balance of trade with the mother country. The molasses procured from the foreign islands was carried to the New England distilleries where it was manufactured into rum to be sold to thirsty Americans, Indians, and fishermen on the Newfoundland banks. Rum was also extensively used in the so-called triangular trade. New England ships, heavily laden with this potent liquid which bore the nickname of "Kill-Devil," crossed the Atlantic to the coast of Africa, where the rum was exchanged for slaves. The slaves were carried to the West Indies and exchanged for specie or for more molasses with which to manufacture more rum to be used in the purchase of more Negroes.

[40] *St. James's Chronicle*, January 28, 1766.

Trade between the French, Dutch, and Spanish West Indian islands and the New England and Middle colonies was firmly established by 1730 and had become essential to the well-being of the Northern merchants and farmers. The British West Indies alone could neither supply the Northern colonies with sufficient quantities of molasses to meet their needs nor absorb the lumber, fish, and provisions produced by the continental provinces. Only Jamaica, of the British West Indies, could offer a considerable supply of molasses, but it was far more expensive than the molasses sold by the French West Indies.[41] The French government forbade its subjects overseas to manufacture rum lest it compete with French brandy — consequently the French sugar producers were obliged to dump their molasses unless the American traders took it off their hands. This the Americans did gladly, but they virtually set their own price. The British planters, on the other hand, placed a relatively high value upon their molasses, which they were free to manufacture into rum. As a result, the bulk of the business went to the foreign islands: of the 14,000 hogsheads of molasses annually imported in Rhode Island, only 2500 came from the British plantations. Likewise, as a market, the British West Indies were utterly inadequate to consume the surpluses of the continental colonies. It was estimated that in 1760 they produced 100,000 barrels of flour, besides vast stores of beef, pork, fish, and lumber which had no market except in the Caribbean possessions of France, Spain, and Holland. Moreover, the colonists' most profitable trade lay here: their fish, lumber, and provisions sold at double the price they brought in the British islands, netting the colonial merchants a fat profit of 30 per cent.[42] Inevitably, therefore, trade tended to gravitate toward the foreign islands and the Northern colonists regarded the Dutch, French, and Spaniards as their best customers.[43]

But the British West Indians were far from content to see virtual free trade prevailing between the British continental colonies and the foreign West Indies. During the seventeenth century, the British islands had largely supplied the European continent as well as

[41] An Essay on the Trade of the Northern Colonies of Great Britain in North America, London, 1764, 15.

[42] New York Mercury, January 23, 1764.

[43] The Scots Magazine, Edinburgh, 1764, XXVI, 568. Providence Gazette and Country Journal, October 20, 1764. Correspondence of William Pitt, edited by G. S. Kimball, New York, 1906, II, 377. An Essay on the Trade of the Northern Colonies of Great Britain, London, 1764, 15-16.

England itself with sugar; but this trade had been lost largely because of the enumeration of sugar and the rapid growth of the British market which absorbed most of the sugar produced in the British islands. Nevertheless, the British sugar planters still hoped to regain the European market from the French into whose hands it had passed when the output of the British plantations failed to keep pace with the demand. It will be recalled that in 1739 the British planters had won the privilege of exporting sugar direct to Europe, although they were not in a position to take full advantage of this boon. Because the French possessed more fertile sugar lands and enjoyed the advantage of smaller capitalization charges, the competitive position of the British planters in the European market seemed hopeless. They recognized, indeed, that unless they crippled French sugar production at the source of supply, they could not hope to drive the French from the continental market. The British planters believed that with the aid of the home government this could be quickly accomplished. Clearly, the French planters were most vulnerable to attack in their trade with the continental British colonies, which, while not prohibited by express law, was nonetheless a violation of mercantilist principles. This trade was essential to the prosperity of the French islands: without it, they would be unable to buy their necessities at low prices and dispose of their molasses. And so the British sugar producers reasoned that by excluding Northern merchants from the foreign islands they would ruin their competitors and at the same time compel Americans to send to the British islands all their fish, lumber, and provisions — with the result that prices would be driven down to rock bottom. The West India sugar barons would then be in a position to reap the fruits of their monopoly; and they could comfortably set about exploiting the European consumer as well as the British and the continental Americans.[44]

The British planters therefore demanded the prohibition of all commerce between the foreign sugar islands and the continental British colonies. New England's commercial existence and the prosperity of the farmers of the Middle colonies depended upon keeping the sea lanes open. In the outcome of this struggle within the Imperial household, the British government possessed a decisive voice. It was soon apparent that the West Indians enjoyed a considerable

[44] *Proceedings and Debates of the British Parliaments Respecting North America*, edited by L. F. Stock, Washington, 1937, IV, 96.

advantage over the Northern merchants in reaching the ear of the mother country. The mercantilists regarded the British West Indies as the cornerstone of the empire. The islands were almost completely dependent upon the mother country for their manufactured goods; they gave employment to large numbers of English ships and seamen; and as producers of sugar, indigo, and cotton they enabled the empire to achieve in a large measure the mercantilists' goal of self-sufficiency. Moreover, the planters and their merchant allies constituted a powerful pressure group in English politics. Altogether, while New Englanders were tolerated in the household, the West Indians were the spoiled darlings of the family.

During the eighteenth century, it is true, Englishmen began to look with greater favor upon New Englanders than during the previous century when they had been regarded as poachers upon a preserve which rightly belonged to British merchants alone. When Sir Josiah Child remarked that New England was "the most prejudicial plantation to the kingdom of England," he added that New England was also a large importer of British merchandise and thereby benefited English merchants and manufacturers. New England's shipbuilding also began to be recognized as vital to British maritime supremacy. "Tho we esteem New England and the Northern Colonies of small Advantage of us," observed Joshua Gee, "yet if Things were truly stated, they are as profitable as most other of our Plantations. . . . If ever a Stop should be put to the Building of Ships in New England, &c and carrying our Timber from thence," he continued, "we should soon sink in our Navigation, and that of the Dutch flourish in its former Height and Grandeur." The small injury done English merchants by New Englanders ought not to obscure the great good they wrought, it began to be said; yet if the British government were compelled to choose between the Northern merchants and the West India planters, there could be little doubt where its sympathies would lie.

The British government refused, however, to yield to the West Indians' demands for an outright prohibition of the trade between the foreign West Indian islands and the continental British colonies. Instead, the Molasses Act of 1733 imposed a duty of sixpence per gallon upon foreign molasses imported into British America. Superficially, the Molasses Act was a revenue measure; and it provoked an outburst in the New England colonies against taxation without representation. The Rhode Island Assembly's protest against the act clearly foreshadows the constitutional arguments of the revolutionary period. Richard Partridge, the Rhode Island agent in England, declared that the Molasses Act was worse than the prohibitory bill introduced by the West Indian interest "because of the levying a Subsidy upon a Free People without their Knowledg agst their consent, who have the libertys and immunitys granted them [of] Natural born Subjects," and because it established a precedent by which endless taxes might be imposed upon Americans by the British Parliament.[45] For its temerity in insisting that the Molasses Act was a violation of its charter liberties and the principle of no taxation without representation, the Rhode Island Assembly was rebuked in Parliament and members of the House of Commons voiced their alarm over the progress of republicanism in that benighted province.[46]

Nevertheless, the Molasses Act seemed far less likely to raise a colonial revenue than to stop completely the trade between the Northern colonies and the foreign West Indies. The tax of sixpence per gallon was prohibitively high. Whatever hopes Parliament may have had of a colonial revenue in 1733 were blasted by the effect of the Molasses Act. In substance, the West Indians had triumphed in 1733; and while the principles of mercantilism had been sacrificed, the mercantilist structure of the British Empire had not been impaired. The Northern merchants might draw what consolation they could from the fact that they were threatened with ruin by a prohibitive duty rather than by an outright prohibition.

Against the Molasses Act, Americans had only their smugglers to depend upon — but these redoubtable gentry proved more than a match for the British. After a brief effort to enforce the act in Massachusetts in the 1740's, the English government tacitly accepted defeat and foreign molasses was smuggled into the Northern colonies in an ever-increasing quantity. Thus the New England merchants survived — but only by nullifying an act of Parliament.[47]

In 1763, the Molasses Act was about to expire — if it can be said that such a dead letter could expire. The question was thus placed squarely before George Grenville whether Great Britain should

[45] The Correspondence of the Colonial Governors of Rhode Island, edited by Gertrude S. Kimball, Boston, 1903, I, 34.

[46] Proceedings and Debates of the British Parliament Respecting North America, IV, 189–191.

[47] The Correspondence of the Colonial Governors of Rhode Island, II, 133–134, 137, 146.

renew a law which had been observed chiefly in the breach or whether an effort should be made to raise revenue by taxing the importation of foreign molasses into the British colonies. Grenville, in his quest for revenue, found many signposts pointing in the direction of molasses. Had the Molasses Act of 1733 been enforced, it would have yielded a considerable revenue to the British government. Henry McCulloh, an Englishman whose views had marked influence upon Grenville, had urged in 1761 that the duties on foreign molasses and rum be lowered in the interests of revenue.[48] Of even greater significance was the report of the Commissioners of the Customs in 1763, urging the reduction of the molasses duty and the strict enforcement of British commercial laws in the colonies as a means of increasing the customs revenue of the British government. The Commissioners pointed out that a duty on foreign molasses was particularly timely after the conclusion of the Seven Years' War because the Northern colonies, now joined by Canada, would require much larger supplies of molasses than before, and, because they could buy cheaply from the foreign sugar islands, the trade could easily bear taxation.[49] It was pointed out that New Englanders were underselling British rum on the African coast and that, even if they were obliged to increase prices, they enjoyed a great advantage inasmuch as the New England product was more fiery and therefore held in greater esteem. The tax, it was observed, might easily be passed on to the consumers: it could not be supposed that the Negroes and Indians who constituted the best customers for New England rum were such financiers "as to be very sensible to a Difference of Three Half-pence on a gallon of Rum." [50] Moreover, there was the device of watering, with which, it was well known, the New Englanders were not unacquainted. In other words, if the British government taxed New England distillers, they might in turn make the public pay.

These considerations led Grenville to propose to Parliament the measure known as the Sugar Act of 1764. By this law, the duty on foreign molasses imported into the British colonies was

[48] Henry McCulloh, *Miscellaneous Representations Relative to Our Concerns in America*, London, 1761, 12.

[49] *Report of the Commissioners of the Customs*, September 16, 1763, Additional MSS., 8133, Library of Congress Transcript.

[50] *The Regulations Lately Made Concerning the* **Colonies** . . . *Considered*, 82–83.

reduced from six- to threepence a gallon. There could be no question, however, that, unlike the Molasses Act of 1733, the Sugar Act was designed to raise a revenue. The preamble declares that "it is expedient that new provisions and regulations should be established for improving the revenue of this Kingdom . . . and . . . it is just and necessary that a revenue should be raised . . . for defraying the expenses of defending, protecting, and securing the same."

The Sugar Act struck Americans, however, not so much as a revenue measure as a virtual prohibition of trade between the Northern colonies and the foreign West Indies.[51] The threepence duty in itself had no terrors for the colonists — they had long borne a sixpence duty — but the evident determination of the British government to collect the duty dismayed them. With British men-of-war enforcing the commercial laws and a rejuvenated British customs service at work, the happy days of smuggling seemed forever ended. A duty of threepence, the merchants insisted, could not be borne — indeed, the margin of profit in rum was so small that molasses could bear no duty whatever. The colonial merchants demanded in effect free trade with the foreign West Indies or easy smuggling — but from George Grenville they received neither. The Chancellor of the Exchequer gave Americans a double dosage of bitter medicine: an insupportably high duty plus strict enforcement.

This legislation was declared to have caused greater alarm in New England than the forays of the French and Indians during the darkest days of the Seven Years' War. Certainly the menace of the Sugar Act led Americans to unite, which fear of the French and Indians had never done. When it was learned in Boston that the British government intended to collect duties on foreign molasses, the merchants appointed a corresponding committee to consolidate the opposition of the Northern merchants to the Sugar Act and to "promote a union and coalition of their councils." The Massachusetts House of Representatives likewise appointed a committee to correspond with the other colonial assemblies. Thus, said the governor of Massachusetts, was laid a "foundation for connecting the demagogues of the several governments in America to

[51] Collections of the New Haven Colony Historical Society, *The Ingersoll Papers*, New Haven, 1918, 296.

join together in opposition to all orders from Great Britain which don't square with their notions of the rights of the people." [52] While the Sugar Act delivered a devastating blow at the welfare of the Northern colonies, it brought prosperity to the British West India planters. After the passage of the act, the British islands were so flooded with provisions, horses, lumber, and fish from the Northern colonies that these commodities fell precipitately in price. The British planters were now in a position to buy cheap and sell dear; and they proceeded to take full advantage of their good fortune. Rum became so expensive in the Northern colonies that an alarmed American declared it would soon be out of the reach of the "poorer sort" except as a medicine. But the Sugar Act threatened to do more than make Americans thirsty. While molasses and sugar rose in price, lumber and other staples of the Northern colonies fell. Farmers lost an important market for their foodstuffs; lumber rotted on the wharves; and colonial merchants began to wind up their affairs.[53] Moreover, shut off from their principal source of specie — the foreign West Indies — colonists saw their reserves rapidly dwindle and the value of their paper money jeopardized. The stagnation of trade produced by the Sugar Act was an important factor in intensifying the postwar depression which had already begun to grip the colonies; and it helped materially to produce the conditions out of which opposition to the Stamp Act sprang.

It is not surprising therefore that Americans overlooked the fact that the Sugar Act was primarily a revenue measure. Because they were still thinking in terms of their long-standing quarrel with the West Indians they leaped to the conclusion that the Sugar Act was the work of their traditional enemies, the sugar planters. The British House of Commons, it was believed, had fallen under the control of these "Creolians" who had determined to reduce the continental Americans to the plight of those "sooty sons of Africa" who labored on the West India plantations. How else, Americans asked themselves, could Parliament have been brought to pass a law whose only purpose was the "aggrandizing a number of prodigal all-grasping West Indians, at the expense of whole Colonies of loyal and valuable subjects"? Parliament had in effect handed the con-

[52] Collections of the Connecticut Historical Society, XVIII, *Fitch Papers*, Hartford, 1920, II, 261. *Boston Gazette*, November 28, 1763.
[53] *Fitch Papers*, II, 296, 297. *New Hampshire Gazette*, January 25, 1765.

tinental colonies over to their worst enemies: they were now crushed between the red Indians on the frontier and the no less sinister West Indians overseas.[54] The triumph of the West Indians in Parliament had sealed the fate of the continental colonists: they were to be made "the Dupes, Hewers of Wood, and Drawers of Water to a few West India Planters." [55] In New England, the blow was rendered even more severe by the fact that the Sugar Act was regarded as a triumph of immoral, loose-living members of the Church of England over pious, sober Congregationalists. "As for the West Indies," said Ezra Stiles of Connecticut, "they will die in their iniquities. . . . Assuredly I account the West Indies, both priests and people, most amazingly debauched." [56] The Sugar Act had consummated an unnatural marriage of the energetic, vigorous continental colonies to the old, static West Indies. A great empire had been delivered over to "a few dirty Specks, the Sugar Islands"; the continent must henceforth move in the wake of the sugar planters of the British Empire.[57] The Sugar Act had, it seemed evident, called a halt to the economic development of the Northern continental colonies as truly as the Proclamation of 1763 had established metes and bounds for the expansion of the Middle and Southern colonies. "Must the quantity of fish, flour, lumber, horses &c produced in the northern colonies, be lessened much more than half," asked the merchants in anguish, "until they be made to dwindle down to the diminutive size of these markets" to which the British government had restricted them?

Nevertheless, the British government was not acting in 1764 at the behest of the West India interest. The West India bloc in Parliament, although formidable, was not sufficiently powerful to make the British government a mere tool. It was the government, rather than the sugar planters and their friends, which controlled Parliament; Benjamin Franklin observed that even before 1760, "if the Ministry make a Point of carrying *any thing* in Parliament, they can carry it." [58] In 1765, this was borne out when the

[54] Collections of the New York Historical Society, *Letter Book of John Watts*, New York, 1928, LXI, 212, 261–262. *John Penn to Thomas Penn*, June 16, 1764, Penn MSS., Historical Society of Pennsylvania.

[55] *Providence Gazette and Country Journal*, September 8, 1764.

[56] L. B. Namier, *England in the Age of the American Revolution*, London, 1930, 279.

[57] *Providence Gazette and Country Journal*, October 27, 1764.

[58] *Proceedings of the American Antiquarian Society*, Worcester, 1934, New Series, XXXIV, 248.

Stamp Act was carried in Parliament over the opposition of the West India interest; and again in 1766 when a tax of one penny per gallon was imposed upon British as well as foreign molasses imported into the British continental colonies. The West India interest in Parliament, it is true, voted for the Sugar Act, but not because it had drawn up the measure. In fact, the West Indians proposed a heavier duty but finally accepted the administration's figure because they hoped that the threepence duty would prove prohibitory. There was virtually no opposition in Parliament to the Sugar Act; only one member — John Huske, who had been born in Boston — voted against it. The explanation for such overwhelming support was not that the West Indians demanded the measure but that the Ministry and Parliament were eager to taste the sweets of a colonial revenue and to punish the Northern merchants for their unpatriotic conduct during the Seven Years' War.[59]

At least three New Englanders recognized immediately that the Sugar Act was not the work of West India planters still playing their old game of barring the Northern merchants from the foreign sugar islands but the first step taken by the British government toward its goal of a colonial revenue. Sam Adams, Oxenbridge Thacher, and Thomas Hutchinson saw in Grenville's preamble a challenge to the doctrine of no taxation without representation.[60] The Sugar Act, Adams and Thacher declared, was no mere regulation of trade in the interests of mercantilism; it was a tax, levied for revenue, and designed as an entering wedge for parliamentary taxation of the colonies. It was owing to their influence that the Massachusetts General Court, in a private letter to its agent in London, declared that the Sugar Act violated the right of levying taxes conferred by charter solely upon the Massachusetts Legislature. Sam Adams went so far as to warn the British government in the newspapers that New Englanders would forcibly resist the act: the doctrine of passive obedience, he ominously remarked, had no followers in America.

This radical stand found little support elsewhere in the colonies. Indeed, George Grenville was encouraged by the moderation of American opposition to the Sugar Act to proceed with his schemes

[59] *Fitch Papers*, II, 278. Namier, 277, 279.
[60] Thomas Hutchinson to Robert Jackson, August ?, 1763, *Hutchinson Correspondence*, Bancroft Collection, New York Public Library. Thacher, 5. *Boston Gazette*, July 23, 1764.

of colonial taxation. Constitutional arguments against the act were sparingly put forth — in contrast to the emphasis laid upon law and right after 1765. For the most part, Americans relied upon the contention that the act injured Great Britain as well as the Northern colonies. It was, they pointed out, to England's interest to have prosperous subjects overseas because they spent their money upon British manufactures. The colonists declared that they could not buy from Great Britain if their trade with the foreign sugar islands was destroyed; instead of selling to the colonists, Englishmen would be obliged to make charitable donations for their support and to write off the immense debt owing them by Americans. The British Empire, they insisted, could not exist half "boom" and half "broke"; the West Indies and the mother country itself could not escape the consequences of the ruin of the Northern colonies. Americans regarded the British Empire as a great commercial entity in which all found opportunity for profit; although the mother country enjoyed special privileges, no part ought to be favored at the expense of the whole or at the expense of other parts. "We are all link'd in a Chain of Dependance on each other," said a New York merchant, "and when properly regulated, by the most prudential Laws, form a beautiful Whole, having within ourselves the rich Sources of an active Commerce and diffusive Happiness." [61] It was therefore as a measure inimical to the prosperity of Great Britain and the Northern colonies and as a departure from the fundamental principles of the empire that the Sugar Act was attacked by Americans.

There was good reason why the wisdom rather than the constitutionality of the act should have been called in question in 1764. Americans were not yet convinced that the British Parliament was lost to reason and fair words. The Sugar Act did not bear with equal weight upon all the colonies: the Southern were relatively unaffected while the blow fell heaviest upon New England. Political radicalism did not flourish in the colonies as a whole until Americans began to feel that they were a powerful and united people; and this conviction had hardly begun to make its influence felt in 1764. There were other circumstances which prevented Americans from perceiving that the Sugar Act was a departure from the time-honored British policy of regulating colonial trade. The

[61] *New York Mercury*, January 24, 1764.

language of the act was similar to that of other regulatory acts except for a brief clause in the preamble which branded it as a revenue measure. The tax was concealed as a duty upon trade, and thereby escaped the attention of many. The Sugar Act was, remarked John Dickinson, "the first comet of this kind, that glared over these Colonies since their existence"; it was not remarkable, therefore, that Americans at first failed to read its portents. By holding the West Indians to blame, Americans further beclouded the issue. Lastly, the act dealt such a shattering blow at colonial prosperity that the merchants were not primarily concerned whether or not the money raised by it was pre-empted by the British Treasury; their chief purpose was not to engage in polemics with the British government over the disposition of the money raised by the molasses duty, but to save their businesses from ruin.

CHAPTER   FIVE

The Quest for a Colonial
Revenue: The Stamp Act

George Grenville

I

W HEN GRENVILLE laid the Sugar Bill before Parliament, he announced that it might be necessary to impose further taxes upon the colonies in the form of stamp duties. To make sure of his ground, he demanded that if any member questioned Parliament's right to tax the colonies, he should speak out or forever hold his peace. No one rose to challenge this right; and Grenville congratulated himself upon having spiked the guns of the Whig opposition. Having made certain of his rear, he set about conciliating the colonial opposition. He laid his plans carefully; already he had seen honest Englishmen rioting against tax collectors and he did not intend to stir up a hornet's nest in the colonies if the honey could be quietly removed. Grenville declared that he wished to give "universal satisfaction" in levying new taxes; and although he was nettled by reports that Americans were denying the right of Parliament to tax them, he yielded to the request of the colonial agents that the stamp duty be postponed for a year in order to give the colonists an opportunity to suggest a better method of raising revenue.

As Grenville later pointed out, in consenting to a year's delay before imposing taxes he was displaying extraordinary benevolence. But the magnanimity of the First Lord of the Treasury did not spring from the fact that he was overflowing with the milk of human kindness; he merely adopted his best bedside manner in order to extract a revenue from the colonies painlessly. By breaking the bad news gently, he hoped to reconcile Americans to paying taxes imposed by Parliament. A year's postponement also gave them an opportunity to consent to the Stamp Act and thereby keep intact the principle of no taxation without consent. It demonstrated — or so Grenville believed — that the mother country was not acting precipitately and that there was no intention to subvert colonial liberties but merely to raise a revenue in the most expeditious and least burdensome manner possible.

As might have been foreseen, the colonists did not succeed during this year of grace in warding off the Stamp Act. The best plan the colonial agents could put forward as an alternative to Grenville's scheme was a return to the requisition system. This proposal left Grenville cold. He was on firm ground in his conviction that requisitions had been tried and found wanting; and he suspected that Americans loved the requisition system chiefly because they had learned how to evade it. Grenville likewise rejected suggestions of taxation by means of a colonial congress such as that projected in the Albany Plan of 1754 because he believed that the colonies would quarrel between themselves over their share of taxes and that Parliament would be compelled to intervene to keep Americans from cutting each other's throats. As for a tax upon Negroes, Grenville objected with reason that it would fall almost exclusively upon the Southern colonies and the West Indies and was therefore unacceptable.[1]

As the shortcomings of all other taxes were thus revealed, Grenville's fondness for a stamp tax grew apace. He came to regard it, indeed, as the best tax that could be devised for the American colonies. It had proved its worth in England where stamp duties yielded over a hundred thousand pounds to the Exchequer, with comparatively small collection costs. The chief merit of the English Stamp Act was that it was almost self-executing; it did not require enforcement officers with powers of entering houses and prying into citizens' private affairs. If documents did not bear a stamp they were void: therefore it was the duty of the citizen himself to procure stamps. To extend this system into the colonies would require little cost — only one additional officer added to the staff at Lincoln's Inn to act as warehouseman.[2] Moreover, conditions in the American colonies seemed to make stamp duties an ideal form of taxation from the viewpoint of the British government. The people were extremely litigious — indeed, they haled each other into court upon the slightest pretext — and since all legal papers required a stamp, this weakness for going to law promised to redound to the profit of the British Exchequer. Some Englishmen even claimed that in destroying "that nest of small petty-fogging attorneys whose

---

[1] *Collections of the New Haven Colony Historical Society*, New Haven, 1918, IX, 294, 313. *The Claim of the Colonies to Exemption*, London, 1765, 34.

[2] *A Copy of a Letter from John Huske, Esq. to the Committee of Merchants in Boston*, August 14, 1764. Additional MS. 33030, folio 334.

business it was to create disturbances and law suits, and live by the plunder," the Stamp Act was conferring a positive benefit upon Americans.[3] Moreover, colonists were avid readers of newspapers — and all newspapers were required to bear a stamp. The tax fell upon those best able to pay, and yet was not "soak the rich" taxation likely to turn the colonial upper class against the British government. Grenville prided himself upon asking nothing unreasonable. If it was not worth the price of a stamp to clear a ship from a colonial harbor it was surely not worth while to make the voyage; if a wife was not worth the price of the stamp required on marriage licenses, it would be better to remain a bachelor.[4]

Despite Grenville's devotion to the Stamp Act, he never claimed to have originated the scheme of raising a colonial revenue by means of stamp duties, although it is true that after the Stamp Act came to a bad end, he had little reason to boast of any part he might have had in its paternity. Had he, on the other hand, been eager to cast off the luckless brat, he could have found several other Englishmen upon whom to put the blame. William Keith, governor of Pennsylvania, and a "Club of American Merchants" had urged as early as 1739 that stamp duties be imposed by Parliament upon the colonies in order to maintain an army sufficient to stop the French and Indians' forays upon the frontiers. Pointing out that the "loose, disorderly and insignificant Militia" of the colonies was utterly unreliable, they declared that the revenue realized from stamp duties would relieve colonial governors of the necessity of wrangling with their assemblies for funds; it would put the united strength of the colonies into the hands of the Crown; and it would create among Americans "a more just and favourable Opinion of their Dependency on a *British* Parliament, than what they have at present."[5] Walpole, however, refused to heed this siren song of an American revenue partly because he strongly suspected that there were rocks ahead and partly because he had his hands full at home collecting taxes.[6] Nevertheless, the idea cropped up repeatedly.

[3] *Parliamentary History*, XVII, 1213.
[4] *The Regulations Lately Made*, London, 1765, 101. *The Claim of the Colonies to Exemption*, London, 1765, 32. *Two Papers, on the Subject of Taxing the British Colonies in America*, London, 1767, 20. *London Chronicle*, February 18, 1766.
[5] *Two Papers, on the Subject of Taxing the British Colonies in America*, London, 1767, 9–22.
[6] Reginald Lucas, *Lord North*, London, 1913, I, 216.

In 1754 and 1757 the Treasury Board discussed the question of a colonial stamp act but action was postponed until after the Seven Years' War. Meanwhile, New York and Massachusetts had imposed stamp duties of their own, but they were quickly dropped, thereby serving warning upon the British government that even when levied by the colonists' own legislatures, stamp duties were not a popular tax. Yet in 1761 the issue was again raised by Henry McCulloh, on whose ideas Grenville placed great store. McCulloh pointed out that the colonies were ripe for taxation and that stamp duties were the best means of opening the melon.

The Stamp Act was one of the most popular taxes ever passed by Parliament — partly because the members were not taxing themselves or their constituents. The measure slipped through the House of Commons with less heated debate than many turnpike bills aroused.[7] Grenville declared in the House that he "hop'd in God's name . . . none would dare dispute their Sovereignty" over the colonies; and during the short debate not a single member questioned the right of Parliament to tax them.[8] Those who spoke against the bill confined their arguments to the inexpediency of taxing the colonies, exhausted and debt-burdened after a long and expensive war. The opposition came chiefly from the absentee West India planters, a handful of members who were connected with the colonies, and "a few of the heads of the minority who are sure to athwart and oppose ye Ministry in Every Measure of what Nature or kind soever." [9] In the absence of Pitt, who was ill, three spokesmen for the colonies emerged from the debate: Alderman Beckford, a West India planter; General Conway, whose recent dismissal was believed to have embittered him against everything proposed by the Ministry; and Colonel Barré, a towering, one-eyed veteran of the wars. Conway urged that the House depart from its usual practice by admitting petitions from the colonial assemblies against the bill, but he was "elegantly refuted" by Solicitor General Yorke in what was regarded as one of the best speeches ever made in the House.[10] The climax of the debate came

---

[7] *Newport Mercury*, June 3, 1765. *Writings of Benjamin Franklin*, IV, 390.
[8] *Papers of the New Haven Colony Historical Society*, New Haven, 1918, IX, 289, 291.
[9] *Ibid.*, IV, 317, 336.
[10] *Newport Mercury*, June 3, 1765.

in a passage of arms between Charles Townshend and Colonel Barré in which Barré, "with Eyes darting Fire, and an outstretched Arm," apostrophized the Americans as "Sons of Liberty." But even Colonel Barré hastened to add that no member of Parliament ought to deny its right to tax the colonies, "and he was pleased to add, that he did not think the more sensible people in America would deny it." [11] Had Pitt been able to speak against the bill, the opposition might have been more formidable; but Pitt could not have prevented the passage of the Stamp Act. Indeed, the majority was so great that the bill was read in its final form "without a syllable being said" and was passed without a division. The only indication of the voting strength of the supporters and opponents of the measure came when Alderman Beckford, contending that the Stamp Act would "not go down" in the colonies, moved that the House adjourn. The House voted him down 245 to 49. [12]

The Stamp Act was a modest beginning in direct taxation of the colonies by Parliament; in later years, Grenville pointed out that he had proposed to collect from Americans only a fraction of the expenses of protecting the colonies. The British government did not in the Stamp Act, or at any later time, propose that the colonists be saddled with part of the British national debt. It asked merely that they contribute a part of the total expense — estimated at £350,000 a year — of maintaining the British army in North America. Towards this end, the Stamp Act was expected to raise about £60,000 annually. [13] This amounted to only one shilling per head in the colonies, or about one third the value of a day's labor each year. The moderation of the tax was later used against Grenville by his critics in England who called him "a wretched Financier" who sought to "bring into the Treasury a Pepper-Corn, at the Risque of Millions to the Nation." [14] In 1765, however, the insignificance of the sum to be raised by the stamp duty convinced many Englishmen that it would, for that reason, meet with no opposition in the colonies: "They must be the veriest beggars in the world," remarked an Englishman, "if such inconsiderable duties

[11] *Maryland Gazette*, June 6, 1765. *Papers of the New Haven Colony Historical Society*, IV, 336.

[12] *New Hampshire Gazette*, June 7, 1765. *Parliamentary History*, XVI, 98.

[13] *The Present State of the Nation*, London, 1768, 37. *Gazetteer and New Daily Advertiser*, November 21, 1765.

[14] *Public Advertiser*, January 15, 1770.

appear to be intollerable burthens in their eyes." [15] It seemed far more likely that after the tumult and shouting had subsided, Americans would pay the tax without argument. George Grenville later remarked that he would have staked his life that the Stamp Act would succeed in the colonies. It seemed impossible that "twelve lubberly young fellows, who have always enjoyed the benefit of their father's house," would fail to come to the old gentleman's aid when he found himself unable to carry the burden alone. However peevish and reluctant Americans might be at first, they would soon perceive that Great Britain was asking no more than its due.[16]

Certainly, Grenville spared no pains to make the act palatable to Americans. He directed that only colonists were to be appointed stamp masters in the hope that Americans would find it easier to pay the tax if it were collected by their fellow colonists. His judgment seemed to be confirmed by the flood of applications for the post that poured in from prominent colonists. A stamp master received a salary of three hundred pounds a year; the office was regarded as "genteel"; and it offered the prospect of valuable patronage. Colonel Mercer, the Virginia stamp master, for example, expected to employ twenty-five assistants. To colonists such as Richard Henry Lee of Virginia, struggling to keep a large family afloat, the office was indeed a boon. But the prizes went not to the most deserving or the most needy but to those who knew the right people in England. An acquaintance with Benjamin Franklin was particularly valuable because Franklin, having determined after his futile opposition to make the best of the Stamp Act, stood close to the Ministry and was in a position to reward his friends. If Grenville was blind in failing to foresee the explosion in America against the act, Benjamin Franklin was equally so. He helped place some of his closest friends in a position from which they were fortunate to escape with their lives. He made his friend John Hughes stamp master of Pennsylvania, and Jared Ingersoll became stamp master of Connecticut at Franklin's urging. "Upon my Honor," Ingersoll later remarked, "I thought I should be blamed if I did not accept the Appointment."

While Grenville was thus engaged in making the Stamp Act itself as agreeable as possible to Americans, he had neglected, it will

[15] Gazetteer and New Daily Advertiser, November 13, 1765. The Conduct of the Late Administration Examined, London, 1767, 63.
[16] The Regulations Lately Made, London, 1765, 3.

be remembered, to smooth its way by removing colonial grievances. On the contrary, he had added to those grievances until Americans had become so "sower'd & imbitter'd" toward the British government that "even the most constitutional tax would have been thought a hardship." [17] The Stamp Act was merely the culmination of a number of oppressive acts which had convinced many Americans that the British government was seeking to destroy colonial prosperity. After dealing hard blows at colonial business by means of commercial restrictions, the British government had crowned its oppression by demanding that Americans pay taxes directly to the British Exchequer. The Sugar Act, the prohibition of paper money, and the mercantilist legislation of 1764 had put Americans in no mood to appreciate the excellences of even the best of all possible taxes.

Grenville gave these storm warnings no heed; instead of watching the barometer, he kept his eyes glued upon a colonial revenue. It has been said that Grenville lost the colonies because he read the American dispatches; but it is clear that if he read the letters of the colonial governors, he acted contrary to their advice. They pointed out that it was fatal to attempt to tax the colonies immediately after their trade had been put in a strait jacket; a breathing spell rather than a tightening of the laces seemed to be in order. Moreover, British authority in America needed to be strengthened before clashing with the colonists; "the patch-work government of America," it was observed, could not stand attack. Without taking any precautions or preparing to meet resistance, one colonial governor complained, the British government had bluntly told Americans, "Obey the act and be damned!" It was not remarkable therefore that Americans, finding a weak government attempting to play the tyrant, shouted, "We'll be damned if we do!" [18]

Grenville likewise ignored the warnings of colonial officials that the economic state of the colonies made taxation inadvisable. The bubble of war prosperity was pricked in 1764 largely as a result of the withdrawal of British armies and the return to France and Spain of their rich West Indian islands which had been in British hands during the last years of the war. The hard times following upon

---

[17] *The Crisis, or a Full Defence of the Colonies*, London, 1766, 27.

[18] Lawrence Shaw Mayo, *John Wentworth*, Cambridge, 1921, 121. Governor Bernard to Richard Jackson, October 22, 1765, Bernard MSS., Harvard University Library.

the Seven Years' War that caused Englishmen to look to the colonies for revenue struck the colonies themselves at almost the same time. In 1765, when the Stamp Act was about to go into effect, colonial trade seemed "burthened beyond all Possible Bearing, bleeding, dying"; and "private debts were never so pressing in the memory of man. Never was a time of more general distress and calamity since the first beginnings of the country." [19] Americans grumbled about the high cost of living, the price of English-manufactured goods, and the precipitous decline in real-estate values. Within two years of the Peace of Paris, Rhode Island real estate was selling for half its former value; hard money had disappeared from the colony; laborers were unemployed; and merchants groaned over their ledgers. In New York lands were being sold at ruinous prices at forced sales, and bankruptcies and "the most pitiable Scenes of Distress" resulted as creditors squeezed their debtors. Some of the most important commercial houses in Boston failed; others were obliged to sell their ships; and unemployed artisans began to leave the towns and high taxes for the country.[20] "It seems as if all our American World must inevitably break, & the Lord have Mercy on the London Merchants," wrote William Livingston of New York.[21]

Meanwhile, in England, George Grenville was congratulating himself upon having preserved the empire from financial collapse. Through new imposts he had succeeded in raising the revenue of the mother country by £234,000 a year – provided the new taxes could be collected; and by his economies he had saved the government £130,000 during his tenure as First Lord of the Treasury.[22] Happily for his own piece of mind, George Grenville was not obliged to face the crisis which his measures had raised in the colonies. In July 1765, the King, long suffering under Grenville's lectures, his insistence that the King break connections with Lord

[19] The Burd Papers, edited by Lewis Burd Walker, Philadelphia, 1897, 65–67. Extract of a Letter from Mr. William Donaldson of New York, 1766, Lee MSS., Harvard University Library. Boston Gazette, July 29, September 16, 1765. South Carolina Gazette, October 22, 1764.

[20] Additional MSS., British Museum, 33030, information of Barlow Trecothick. Diary of John Rowe, edited by Anne Rowe Cunningham, Boston, 1903, 75. John Dickinson, The Regulations respecting the British Colonies on the Continent of America Considered, London, 1765, 30–31.

[21] William Livingston to Messrs. Champion and Haley, December 10, 1765, Livingston MSS., New York Public Library.

[22] A Collection of Scarce and Interesting Tracts, London, 1767, II, 68–69.

Bute, and his petty economies — he even attempted to reduce expenses at Buckingham Palace — found his patience giving way. "Every day I meet with some insult from these people" (Grenville and the other members of the cabinet), cried George; "I have been for near a week as it were in a feaver my very sleep is not free from thinking of the men I daily see." His mind, he declared, was "ulcer'd, by the treatment it meets with from all around." [23] In his exasperation and despair, he exclaimed that he would as soon see the devil in his closet as Mr. Grenville. It was in this spirit that the King sought Grenville's successor; for in July 1765, he called upon the Marquis of Rockingham, the leader of a small band of Whigs whom George had proscribed in 1762, to form a Ministry. Rockingham consented, but he soon discovered that he had accepted a poisoned chalice from the hands of George Grenville.

II

WHILE the Stamp Act was still pending in Parliament, the colonial assemblies displayed a certain reluctance to affront the mother country by unequivocally denying parliamentary authority. The Virginia burgesses, for example, remarked that they wished to avoid "the least Disposition to any Sort of Rudeness" towards Parliament; at worst they could call the Stamp Act "a long & hasty Stride." The Massachusetts petition was a model of propriety because Thomas Hutchinson, as a member of the council, carefully blue-penciled all "indecencies" in the draft of the House of Representatives.[24] New Yorkers declared that their petition contained "nothing but Assertions of our undoubted Rights, in the most soft and dutiful Terms we could devise," and was distinguished by "British, Roman and Grecian Sense" — but none of these recommendations carried weight in Great Britain where New Yorkers

[23] *Letters from George III to Lord Bute,* edited by Romney Sedgwick, London, 1939, 240–241.
[24] *Boston Gazette,* January 20, 1766. *The Virginia Magazine of History and Biography,* XII, 9.

were regarded as neither Greeks, nor Romans, nor even as true-born Britons.[25]

In general, the assemblies preferred to keep the question of Parliament's constitutional right to tax the colonies discreetly in the background while they sought to ward off the blow by demonstrating their inability to pay the stamp duties. They appealed to the self-interest of the mother country by pointing out that the Stamp Act defeated its purpose of raising a colonial revenue. Because Americans had been cut off from their chief source of specie – the foreign West Indies – by the Sugar Act, they could not pay for stamps in hard money as required by the British government. The colonists declared that they could no more pay the mother country sixty thousand pounds a year in specie than "a tax in pagodas of the East Indies, or in diamonds of the first water"; and it was predicted that if the Stamp Act went into effect, it would soon be as difficult to raise the dead as to raise one hundred pounds in specie from an American.[26] And after the colonists' gold and silver had been scooped across the Atlantic it would be the British merchants and manufacturers that would be the first to suffer from the bankruptcy of their best customers.[27]

The colonists soon found, however, that their arguments were wasted upon Parliament. Not one of their petitions was read in the House of Commons. It had become a rule of the House that no petitions on money bills were acceptable and this rule was invoked against the colonial assemblies in 1765.

Smarting under this rebuff and with the postwar depression beginning to make itself felt, the colonists cast off the moderation that had hitherto marked their opposition to the Stamp Act. Instead of spending their year of grace in resigning themselves to taxation by Parliament and decently interring their liberties, the colonists' anger began to swell ominously. As Grenville soon learned, by postponing the stamp duties for a year he had helped produce the

[25] *Newport Mercury*, January 7, 1765. *An Apparition of the late Maryland Gazette* (no date), 1765.

[26] *The Examination of Doctor Benjamin Franklin Relative to the Repeal of the American Stamp Act*, London, 1767, 4. *Public Advertiser*, May 29, 1767. *New Hampshire Gazette*, October 4, 1765.

[27] Had the specie raised by the Stamp Act been expended by the British government in the colonies, this situation would not have existed. The Commissioners of the Treasury recommended that this be done, but the Ministry did not follow their advice. *The Conduct of the Late Administration Examined*, London, 1767, 38.

storm that later descended upon him. The more Americans examined the Stamp Act, the more vexatious and oppressive it appeared. "EveryThing that can be thought of among a Trading active People," it was found, "is subject to this Duty." [28] Under the provisions of the act, Americans could not engage in commerce, exchange property with each other, recover debts, buy a newspaper, institute lawsuits or make wills, without paying for a stamp. Every diploma awarded by a college or academy required a stamp of two pounds and — what was more important to the common man — every tavern owner who retailed spirituous liquor was obliged to pay twenty shillings for his license. To crown these hardships, infractions of the Stamp Act were to be tried without a jury in the hated Admiralty Courts.

To damn the act further in Americans' eyes, it struck directly at the interests of some of the most influential groups in the colonies. Grenville incautiously forfeited the support of those elements of colonial society whose approval was essential to the success of his undertaking. The colonial tavern owners, printers, lawyers, and merchants were alike injured by the Stamp Act. The tavern owners — who were often the leading politicians of their neighborhood — were outraged by the heavy tax upon licenses. The printers feared a ruinous drop in circulation as a result of the tax upon newspapers; to express their resentment, they sent each other wooden shoes "as a proper Badge of the Slavery the Stamp Act must reduce all Printers in America to." [29] As a result, colonial newspapers quickly took up the hue and cry. Occasionally, the printers themselves turned mob leaders: in Philadelphia, the printers Hall and Bradford raised "a Rabble of Boys, Sailors and Negroes" to riot against the Stamp Act. [30] The lawyers believed that their practice would be wrecked by the duties upon legal documents. And the colonial merchants, usually one of the most conservative groups in the colonies, found their welfare threatened by the duties upon cockets and clearances which promised to add materially to the hardships of carrying on legal as well as illegal trade.

There could be little doubt that taxation by Parliament was cer-

[28] *New Hampshire Gazette*, September 6 and 27, 1765.

[29] James Parker to Benjamin Franklin, April 25, 1765, Franklin MSS., American Philosophical Society.

[30] John Hughes to the Stamp Act Commissioners, January 13, 1766, P.R.O., Treasury, I, 452.

tain to be far more burdensome to Americans than was the requisition system. Whereas royal requisitions could be easily evaded, there were no loopholes in taxes imposed by Parliament: they were collected by a corps of tax gatherers backed by the power of the Admiralty Courts. Moreover, the financial necessities of the Crown seemed small indeed when compared with the ravenous appetite of Parliament for a colonial revenue. British taxpayers staggered under a huge national debt and it could not be doubted that they would seek to ease themselves by thrusting part of the load upon the colonists. They seemed likely to demand that Parliament tax Americans to the limit of their endurance because every shilling drawn from America would represent a shilling saved to taxpayers in the mother country.[31] Thus in taxing the colonists members of Parliament would in effect be untaxing themselves and their constituents. For this reason, Americans denounced the Stamp Act as the work of "some demon" who, "in an evil hour, suggested to a short-sighted financier, the hateful project of transferring the whole property of the King's subjects in America, to his subjects in Britain." It is not remarkable that the colonists now fondly looked back upon the requisition system which they had consistently attempted to subvert during the eighteenth century. "I would much more willingly see my Property arbitrarily dispos'd of by a privy Seal," exclaimed a colonist, "than extorted from me by the unwarrantable Power of a Parliament, whose Members would naturally endeavour to lessen their own Burthens." [32] From Parliament, it was believed, Americans could expect only "the malevolent Influence of that Jealousy, which would sacrifice a Rival even in the Person of a Brother"; the King, on the other hand, however stern and uncharitable, was a parent who wished to see the colonies prosperous and contented.[33]

What made Americans confident that the British Parliament would load them with "new, endless, and insupportable taxes" as soon as it had made good its claim to a colonial revenue was the fact that the British national debt had attained the unprecedented total of £140,000,000. Most Americans were agreed that this debt — equal to ten days' expenditure by the British government in the

---

[31] Stephen Hopkins, *The Grievances of the American Colonies Candidly Examined*, London, 1766, 33. William Pulteney, *Thoughts on the Present State of Affairs with America*, London, 1778, 24.

[32] *Considerations upon the Rights of the Colonists*, New York, 1766, 21-22.

[33] *Ibid.*

present war — could never be repaid. Englishmen were believed to be too extravagant and too prone to wage new and more costly wars to balance their budget and liquidate their debts. They had therefore determined to foist this burden upon the "honest and industrious of these colonies, whom Satan envies as he did Adam and Eve in Paradise." [34] But it was doubtful if even sober, hard-working Americans could rescue Great Britain from debt. "The unbounded luxury and profusion of that nation will make money more and more necessary to them," it was said, "and we may as well think of filling a bottomless pit, as of satisfying their wants, when £7 or £800 sterling is paid for a coach — thousands given in pensions — £10,000 lavished on a ball." [35] Here, surely, seemed to be "a pit that will soon swallow up all the wealth of *America*, and, like *Pharaoh's* lean kine, will n'er be the fatter for it all." [36] After all their labor, Americans might well find that they and their children as well as their land and property would "be sold to the best bidders, to reduce a small part of that enormous sum." [37]

But heavy taxes were neither the sole nor perhaps the greatest evil to be feared: the Stamp Act threatened to divest them of their political liberties at the same time that it fleeced them of their money. It came to be widely believed in the colonies that the British government planned to stamp out liberty in the empire and that the Stamp Act was the first step toward reducing Americans to slavery. Certainly, if the principle of parliamentary taxation were once established, it was apparent that the colonial assemblies would be stripped of the power of the purse and that Parliament would be in a position to make the governors and judges totally independent of popular control. Overnight, the work of the patriots who had defended the rights and privileges of the assemblies against the prerogative during the eighteenth century would be undone; where the Crown had repeatedly failed, Parliament would succeed at a single blow. If Parliament could tax the colonies, there was no limit to what it could do; John Adams believed that it could even establish the Church of England in America if it saw fit. Certainly, it could impose taxes without end because "by the same power, by which the people of England can compel them to pay *one penny,*

[34] *Essex Gazette,* July 21, 1772.
[35] *Pennsylvania Chronicle,* October 10, 1768, Postscript.
[36] *Ibid.*
[37] *South Carolina Gazette,* October 3, 1768.

they may compel them to pay the *last penny* they have" — with the result that property in the colonies would not be worth holding.[38]

Despite the menace to colonial liberty and property rights raised by parliamentary taxation, few colonists doubted until May 1765 that the Stamp Act would be enforced: there was panic and despair but little hope that the act could be successfully resisted. No leader arose to urge Americans to defy the British government. James Otis of Massachusetts declared that "let the parliament lay what burthens they please on us, we must, it is our duty to patiently bear them, till they will be pleased to relieve us." [39] Daniel Dulany of Maryland, although denying the constitutional right of Parliament to tax the colonies, made clear his opinion that Americans must submit to the Stamp Act.[40] Benjamin Franklin likewise advised his countrymen not to attempt forcible resistance to British authority. Thus the act seemed likely to encounter little more than sullen resentment until the Virginia House of Burgesses blew a blast upon the "trumpet of sedition" that awakened Americans from their lethargy and aroused a spirit of resistance against which the authority of the mother country could not stand.

In Virginia, a group of young men in the House of Burgesses had grown restive under the rule of the tidewater aristocrats. They were eager to make their mark in politics and to enjoy the sweets of office, yet they found themselves thwarted by the planter oligarchy which monopolized political office. Patrick Henry, the leader of these young malcontents, had by no means satisfied that itch for popularity which he had confessed to the Reverend Mr. Maury, the unfortunate parson of the "Parson's Cause." Richard Henry Lee, perennial office seeker, still yearned to overthrow the tidewater oligarchs, although he himself was an aristocrat. Having dispatched a petition to the King and a Memorial to the House of Commons against the Stamp Act, the leaders of the House of Burgesses were content to let matters rest: in May 1765, they contemplated no further action and the session was about to come to a close. But the younger men did not share this complacency:

[38] *Newport Mercury*, October 7, 1765; *Providence Gazette*, March 12, 1766. Jonathan Trumbull, *The Life of Jonathan Trumbull*, Boston, 1919, 114. Joseph Priestly, *The Present State of Liberty in Great Britain and her Colonies*, London, 1769, 24.

[39] James Otis, *Rights of the Colonists*, Boston, 1765, 57, 59–60. *Boston Gazette*, August 20, 1764. *New York Gazette or Weekly Post Boy*, February 20, 1766.

[40] Dulany, 4.

they were determined to speak their minds in such ringing terms that all America and Britain would hear them. Before playing their hand, however, they waited until many members had gone home and the assembly had become one of the "thinnest ever known." [41] Patrick Henry, "moderate and mild and in religious matters a Saint, but ye very Devil in Politicks," [42] shattered the calm of the assembly by unexpectedly rising to "blaze out" at the British government in a speech which singed even the sacred person of George III. Henry declared that "in former times Tarquin and Julius had their Brutus, Charles had his Cromwell, and he Did not Doubt but some good american would stand up, in favour of his Country." At this point, the speaker stopped him and declared that he was uttering treason. The speaker then rebuked the members of the House for not having interrupted Henry when he made his treasonable declarations; but after Henry had apologized and declared his loyalty to the King he was permitted to go on.[43]

Having carried off these introductory remarks in his best style, Henry whipped out of his pocket a sheaf containing seven resolves which he urged the House to adopt. The substance of the first five resolves was that Americans possessed all the rights of Englishmen; that the principle of no taxation without representation was an essential part of the British Constitution; and that Virginia alone enjoyed the right to tax Virginians. The sixth and seventh resolves went beyond anything that had been heard in the House: they declared that Virginians were "not bound to yield obedience to any law or ordinance whatever, designed to impose any taxation whatsoever upon them, other than the laws or ordinances of the General Assembly"; and that "any person who shall, by speaking or writing, assert or maintain that any person or persons other than the General Assembly of this Colony, have any right or power to impose or lay any taxation on the people here, shall be deemed an enemy to His Majesty's Colony." The sixth resolve clearly implied the right to resist taxation by Parliament; the seventh would have suppressed freedom of speech in the name of American liberty. Ultimately, Americans were to accept both of Henry's principles, but in May 1765 they seemed little less than treasonable. Henry had two more resolutions in his pocket, but sensing that they were

[41] New Hampshire Gazette, July 26, 1765.
[42] Virginia Magazine of History and Biography, XV, 356.
[43] American Historical Review, July 1921, XXVI, 745.

certain to be defeated he wisely refrained from reading them to the already dumbfounded burgesses.

The struggle over Henry's resolutions became a test of strength between the old conservative leadership and the new, more aggressive representatives, most of whom, like Patrick Henry, came from the western counties. The most distinguished names in Virginia were to be found among those who voted against Henry's resolutions. John Randolph, Attorney General of Virginia and a judge of admiralty; Peyton Randolph, formerly speaker of the House; and George Wythe, one of the leading lawyers of the colony, led the fight against the resolutions. They were aided by Colonel Richard Bland, the author of *An Enquiry into the Rights of the British Colonies*, whose erudition made him a dangerous opponent. He was, remarked one of his friends, "a very old experienced veteran at ye Senate or ye Bar — staunch and tough as whiteleather — has something of ye look of musty old Parchme'ts w'ch he handleth and studieth much." [44] These conservatives insisted that the petition and memorial of the Virginia Assembly took essentially the same ground as did Henry; and since the petition and memorial had only recently been sent to England, it was improper for the assembly to hurl defiance at the British government before a reply had been received. But neither these arguments nor the prestige of his opponents daunted Henry: as in the Parson's Cause, he was not arguing a case but delivering an oration — and in that he had no peer in the House.

The vote was a victory for Patrick Henry and the "Young, hot and Giddy Members" over the old, cool, and conservative tidewater gentry.[45] Henry had been a member of the House of Burgesses for less than a month, yet he scored a triumph over men who had dominated the assembly for years. It is significant, however, that this victory was won when only 39 of the 116 members were present. And despite the fact that Henry enjoyed the advantage of a rump House, his sixth and seventh resolutions were defeated and the first five resolutions were passed by narrow majorities. The greatest majority for any one of Henry's resolutions was 22 to 17;

[44] *Virginia Magazine of History and Biography*, XV, 356. *William and Mary College Quarterly*, July 1912, XXI, 243. Lord Dunmore to Lord Dartmouth, June 25, 1775, P.R.O., C.O. 5, 1533.

[45] Governor Fauquier to the Lords of Trade, June 5, 1765, P.R.O., C.O. 5, 1331.

the smallest was 20 to 19 for the fifth resolution. After Henry's departure from Williamsburg, even the fifth resolution was expunged by the burgesses. The royal governor hoped that all the resolves would be rescinded by a full House, but he was quickly disillusioned. "The Leaven of the North," he lamented ". . . fermented the Minds of the Virginians" and they rallied round Henry as a "Noble Patriot." The people declared that "if the least Injury was ofered to him [Henry] they'd stand by him to the last Drop of their blood. some of them muter betwixt their teeth, let worst Come to the worst we'l Call the french to our sucour." Consequently, Governor Fauquier decided not to call the assembly lest it be led into worse mischief than passing Henry's resolves.[46]

The adoption of Henry's resolutions signalized a fundamental shift of political power in Virginia from the tidewater to the west. But it is probable that the lowland gentry soon would have been restored to power with the aid of the royal governor had not Richard Henry Lee and Patrick Henry turned muckrakers and exposed the scandalous shortages in the books of Speaker Robinson, formerly treasurer of the province. Robinson, a tidewater aristocrat, had fallen into the habit, during his tenure of office, of loaning public money to his highly placed friends. These gentlemen had found it impossible — as friends sometimes do — to repay the loans. The result was that Robinson's badly unbalanced books gave Henry and Lee an opportunity to discredit the planters' regime and to turn the wrath of the people against men some of whom bore the proudest names in the province. Robinson's friends insisted that he was the victim of "the Sensibility of his too benevolent Heart"; but he left at his death in 1766 an estate worth £300,000.[47] For many years, the tidewater aristocrats had reason to regret that Speaker Robinson had been so liberal with the public money and had not died a poorer man.

Although four of Henry's seven resolves were rejected by the House of Burgesses, they were printed in full in the colonial newspapers, thus giving the impression that all seven had been adopted by the Virginia legislators. This is why the first reaction of many patriots to the Virginia Resolves was one of shocked alarm and

[46] Governor Fauquier to Secretary Conway, December 11, 1765, P.R.O., C.O. 5, 1345. *American Historical Review*, July 1921, XXVI, 747.

[47] Governor Fauquier to the Earl of Shelburne, December 18, 1766, P.R.O., C.O. 5, 1345. *Virginia Gazette*, August 8, 1766.

why they hastened to disclaim any complicity in them. James Otis of Massachusetts pronounced them treasonable as did Alexander McDougall and John Morin Scott of New York. Scott, later to become one of the most radical of the Sons of Liberty, fully demonstrated their subversive nature as "a numerous Turtle Party, at Crown Point." Benjamin Franklin, who was rapidly becoming resigned to the Stamp Act, deplored the rashness of the Virginia burgesses and urged Pennsylvanians to shun their example.[48]

Yet many Americans found themselves warmly in accord with the first five Virginia Resolves. Henry had in fact expressed what thousands of colonists were thinking but dared not speak. His resolves dispelled the indecision and doubt which had prevented effective resistance to the Stamp Act; where the Old Dominion trod, the other colonies did not fear to follow. The resolves gave "the Signal for a general outcry over the Continent" and made certain that resistance would be based upon a denial of Parliament's right to tax the colonies. In this sense, they mark the beginning of the revolutionary movement in the American colonies. As the other colonies took their stand beside Virginia in the defense of American liberty, the issue which ultimately divided the British Empire was for the first time clearly joined.[49]

[48] William Gordon, *History of the Rise*, I, 119. *Writings of Benjamin Franklin*, IV, 392. *New York Journal or General Advertiser*, January 12, 1769; April 12, May 31, 1770.

[49] *The Correspondence of General Thomas Gage*, edited by C. E. Carter, I, 67. Ramsay, *The History of the American Revolution*, I, 84-85.

CHAPTER SIX

The Stamp Act Crisis

Old New York
Broad Street

IN IMPOSING the Stamp Act, Grenville departed from the time-honored British policy of ruling the colonies by taking advantage of their sectional and social divisions. Instead, he gave them a fundamental and well-nigh universal grievance which swept aside their petty jealousies in a mounting wave of anger against Great Britain. Despite his efforts to gild the pill, Grenville did not succeed in making taxation more palatable to Americans: rather, it appeared that the British government, in its efforts to lay hands upon their property, had bluntly ordered them to stand and deliver. From Grenville's time to the present day, this method has revealed certain shortcomings when employed against Americans.

The Stamp Act was no more calculated to divide Americans along class lines than it was designed to play upon sectional and provincial differences. "Even the meanest peasant," it was said, felt the tax, but it is evident that the blow fell heaviest upon the wealthy, propertied class and particularly upon the merchants and lawyers — the chief prop of British rule in North America. Almost over-night, the conservative class which during most of the colonial period had stood as a bulwark of British dominion became openly mutinous and began to mobilize colonial society against the British government. With his eyes upon replenishing the British Exchequer, Grenville had in fact hit upon a recipe for producing a union of the colonies which, in its results, was to exceed the brightest hopes of American patriots.

In August 1765, the colonial pot, which had been simmering ominously since the adoption of the Virginia Resolves, boiled over and spread terror among the Crown Officers and stamp masters. Boston took the lead in rioting — which surprised no one who knew the Boston mob — and the other colonial seaports quickly followed its example. Mobs chased some of the bluest-blooded patricians in America through back alleys, wrecked their houses and guzzled their liquor; and although the patriots did not shed any of their victims' blood, this was largely owing to the agility of the gentry in getting out of harm's way and to their alacrity in yielding to the demands of the mobs. Of even greater significance was the organization of the Sons of Liberty — clubs of patriots which took their name from Colonel Barré's apostrophe in the House of Commons to Americans. The colonies were soon covered with a network of these clubs which served as headquarters for the patriot leaders who set the mobs to work terrorizing stamp masters, burning the stamps, and mobbing all supporters of British "tyranny." The organization of these radical societies in British America marked the first effective intercolonial union and paved the way for the later Continental Congresses. It is ironical that the patriots in the various provinces found it possible to maintain close touch with each other and to co-ordinate resistance to the mother country by utilizing the colonial post office which had been created by the British government itself. In giving Americans a common grievance and making possible the rapid transmission of news and correspondence in British America, the mother country unwittingly laid the foundations for united action between the provinces and for the Declaration of Independence.

Crown Officers and stamp masters alike believed that the Sons of Liberty had begun a reign of terror in which every supporter of British sovereignty would be crushed by the patriot mob. Yet mobs and riots were nothing new in colonial seaports: rival gangs frequently battled in the streets and sailors on shore leave brawled lustily in brothels, taverns, and waterfront dives. Efforts by British officers to impress seamen in American ports usually produced a riot; and at one time the mob had held sway in Boston for three days. But these outbreaks of proletarian violence differed greatly from the Stamp Act riots. Whereas the upper class had taken no part in earlier disorders, they now organized, encouraged, and directed the mobs that rose against the Stamp Act. Men of wealth and repute either actively supported the mobs or condoned them as a means of preserving American liberty. John Morin Scott of New York, the son of a wealthy merchant, a graduate of Yale, a popular lawyer, and the owner of an "elegant seat" on Manhattan Island as well as extensive holdings in the Schoharie Valley, was deeply implicated in the mob uprisings in New York City. John Hancock of Boston, one of the richest men in America and the financial "angel" of the Massachusetts patriots, was much more intimate with the Boston mobsters than the Tories deemed any gentleman ought to be. William Livingston, one of the principal lawyers and landowners of New York, worked hand in hand with the mob leaders of the colony. At the head of the Philadelphia mob marched William Allen, son of the Chief Justice of the province, "animating and encouraging the lower class." It is probable that the Charleston, South Carolina, riots were directed by Christopher Gadsden, one of the wealthiest merchants in the province. When the Charleston mob swarmed into the house of Henry Laurens, he recognized many of them as gentlemen of his acquaintance despite their disguise of soot, slouch hats, and sailors' clothing. Indeed, in 1765 some of the "best people" in America might have been found either in the mob or encouraging it to rise up against British "tyranny."

To the Crown Officers, the support given the mob by "Persons of Consequence" was the most alarming aspect of the resistance. Had they been obliged to deal merely with an outbreak of "plebeian frenzy" they did not doubt that it could have been easily overcome; but they recognized that the weight of the gentry threatened to turn the scales against British authority. It seemed likely, indeed, that had it not been for the instigation of the upper classes, the lower class would have remained quiet, content to see the British government impose taxes which would have fallen most heavily upon the wealthier colonists.

By appointing Americans stamp masters, George Grenville did not save them from the wrath of the Sons of Liberty; instead their position was made even more precarious. They were said to have been appointed by the British government just as West India planters used Negro overseers for their slaves: they drove men of their own color harder and whipped them more severely than did white overseers.[1] "A Foreigner we could more cheerfully endure," exclaimed a Son of Liberty, "because he might be supposed not to feel our Distresses; but for one of our Fellow Slaves, who equally shares in our Pains, to rise up and beg the favor of inflicting them — is not that intolerable?"[2] The stamp masters found themselves the most hated men in America; their best friends refused to speak to them "except to upbraid them with their baseness." Upon their heads descended the full weight of guilt for the Stamp Act: if the patriots could not lay hands on Grenville and Lord Bute, they could

---

[1] *New Hampshire Gazette*, June 7, 1765.
[2] *Boston Gazette*, August 19, 1765.

at least terrify the stamp masters out of their wits, wreck their houses, drink their liquor, and finally chase them across the border into a neighboring province to make sport for the Sons of Liberty. Most stamp masters probably did not suspect when they received their appointment that it was to be a traveling job — usually with a mob at their heels. In their headlong dash across country, they may well have outridden Revere himself. Had you seen a disheveled figure with a hunted look in his eye thundering down a colonial highway in 1765, you might well have concluded that here was an American stamp master, on his way to the nearest British fort or man-of-war.

As for selling stamps, few of the stamp masters ever enjoyed the satisfaction. Most of them took a good look at the mob, resigned their commissions, and let the stamps take care of themselves. Oliver, the Massachusetts stamp master, resigned after the mob had run amuck in one of the worst riots ever seen in the Bay Colony; and William Coxe, in New Jersey, abandoned his office without making an effort to execute it, despite Governor Franklin's promises of protection. On the other hand, Zachariah Hood of Maryland refused to yield to the mob and as a result became one of the best-traveled stamp masters in America. His store was pulled down, he himself was burned in effigy, and threats were made against his life — whereupon Hood fled for New York, riding so hard that he killed his horse on the road. But the fugitive found no more security in New York than in Maryland; although British soldiers were in the fort, they themselves were threatened with attack by the mob. Only the country seemed to afford refuge and so Hood went into hiding at Flushing, Long Island. Even this seclusion he was not permitted long to enjoy: the New York Sons of Liberty took up the scent, ferreted the unhappy stamp master out of his hideaway, and forced him to resign on pain of being handed back to the Maryland Liberty Boys.

Colonel Mercer, the Virginia stamp master, journeyed from London to the Old Dominion to find himself hanging in effigy and even his own father engaged in writing newspaper articles against the Stamp Act. He quickly perceived that he had unsuspectingly walked into a hornets' nest. Williamsburg was filled with jurors and witnesses from the back country who had come to attend the trials at the General Court. These rough-and-ready customers from the backwoods seemed disposed to take vengeance upon the stamp master despite the fact that he possessed some of the bluest blood in Virginia. To prevent an outbreak by the westerners, the merchants and planters of the colony took matters into their own hands by parading through the streets of Williamsburg to demand Mercer's resignation. Mercer begged for time; he consulted the governor, who refused to permit him to resign; he took a look at the mob which clamored for his resignation and ended by promising not to act as stamp master. Instantly he became a hero: he was raised upon the shoulders of the people and carried around town to the music of French horns. That night the bells were set ringing, the town was illuminated, and a "splendid ball" was held to celebrate the event. But despite these amenities, the humor of the mob was unpredictable and Colonel Mercer left on the first boat for England, in order, as he declared, to take care of pressing business in the mother country.

George Meserve, the New Hampshire stamp master, returned to America in 1765 to find that if he landed at Boston it was unlikely that he would ever take leave of the Saints with a whole skin. By resigning his commission, he got safe passage through Boston, but this was unsatisfactory to the New Hampshire patriots. They insisted upon burning his commission to make sure that he could not fulfill his office. Meserve surrendered it with alacrity: "I did not know whether I should have escaped from this Mob with my life," he wrote, "as some were for Cutting off my head, others for Cutting off my Ears and sending them home with my Commission." [3] It is not remarkable that property owners did not regard stamp masters as desirable tenants and insisted that they take out full insurance on the houses they occupied.

Taking warning from all this, the Crown Officers juggled the stamps from one to another like hot potatoes. The stamp masters appealed to the governors to take custody of the stamps: the governors appealed to the commanders of the armed forces; and the commanders appealed to Parliament. In few colonies was there a stronghold in which the stamps could be safely stored. The governor of Maryland, rather than entrust the stamps to the care of the militia — which, he observed, was nothing more nor less than turning them over to the mob — ordered the shipmaster who brought the stamps to Maryland to keep them aboard and head for deep water. In Virginia and New Jersey as well, the stamps were

[3] George Meserve to Secretary Conway, July 31, 1766, P.R.O., C.O. 5, 934.

stowed below decks to keep them out of the patriots' bonfires. Because of the weakness of the British armed forces, the mere act of bringing the stamps ashore was an invitation to riot and mob uprising. In South Carolina, the stamps were placed in Fort Johnson for safekeeping. The garrison consisted of fourteen men; the commanding officer spent most of his time in Charleston, leaving the gunner in command. This stronghold fell without resistance to a hundred and fifty Sons of Liberty who found the stamps stored in the barracks. Nevertheless, rumors persisted that not all the stamps had been destroyed; a large quantity, it was said, had been stored in the houses of Henry Laurens and Chief Justice Shinner. The mob gathered fast and marched against the suspected Tories. At Laurens's house they made "a direct attack upon his cellar," where, though no stamps were found, they lighted on some of the choicest liquor in Charleston. After this highly satisfactory assault, the mob paraded to the house of Chief Justice Shinner, who, having been forewarned of what the patriots were seeking, received them hospitably at the door and ushered them into the living room where brimming bowls of punch had been placed. The judge joined the patriots in drinking their favorite toast, "Damnation to the Stamp Act"; whereupon the Whigs staggered homeward, no doubt convinced that they had done a good night's work in combating British tyranny.[4]

The patriot leaders were not content that American wrath should be vented wholly against the British government; they had not forgotten that there were tyrants at home as well as abroad. They dreaded the oppression of the colonial office-holding class scarcely less than the British government; and they were well aware that taxation by Parliament promised to permit the oligarchs to live in luxury upon the labor of their tax-ridden fellow colonists. It was wise policy, therefore, to smear the office-holding aristocracy with the Stamp Act. These oligarchs — who began to be known as Tories — were declared to be responsible for this hated tax. James Otis swore that he could point out the very room in Boston where the "foul cockatrice" was hatched. Thomas Hutchinson and the Olivers, the foremost oligarchs of New England, were accused of having taken the chief part in its procreation. These "detestable Villians who want to be exalted — and richly deserve it" were denounced

---

[4] John Drayton, *Memoirs of the American Revolution*, Charleston, 1821, 44-45, 47-48. *South Carolina Gazette*, I, October 31, 1765.

as "lowering dastards, haughty tyrants, and merciless parricides," "first born sons of Hell," and "infernal, corrupted, detested incendiaries . . . who have invited despotism to cross the ocean." [5] They were charged with having sold their country's liberty in order that they might lord it over their fellow citizens and rob them of their hard-won money. For this crime, said John Hancock, there were about a dozen Bostonians who ought "to be beheaded." [6]

Although Andrew Oliver, Hutchinson's brother-in-law, had been appointed stamp master for Massachusetts Bay, Hutchinson himself, far from being the author of the Stamp Act, had opposed its passage on the ground that internal taxation ought to be left in the hands of the colonial assemblies.[7] Innocence availed him little, however: the mob was convinced that he was responsible for the taxation of the colonies. In the great riot of August, 1765, Hutchinson's house was wrecked by the mob and the manuscript of his *History of the Province of Massachusetts Bay* scattered in the mud outside his door. The patriots had done their work well; for the rest of his life, Hutchinson vainly attempted to clear his name of the stigma which Otis and Adams had attached to it in 1765.

Franklin's equivocal conduct in connection with the Stamp Act gave his enemies in Pennsylvania the opportunity they had long awaited. Having failed to prevent the passage of the act, Franklin determined to make the best of it. A blackout of liberty in the colonies seemed to him inevitable; therefore he advised his countrymen to "make as good a night of it as we can." [8] While urging them to light the candles of frugality and industry, he had procured the office of stamp master for Pennsylvania for his good friend and political ally, John Hughes, a Philadelphia baker. Franklin admonished Hughes to execute his office faithfully "whatever may be the Madness of the Populace or their blind Leaders"; if he were obliged to choose between the favor of the colonists and that of the British government he ought, said Franklin, to sacrifice his popularity with the people in order to uphold British authority — the best guarantee of "the Safety as well as Honour of the Colonies." [9] In general,

[5] *Boston Gazette*, October 8, 1764; September 16, 1765; March 31, 1766. John Adams, *History of the Dispute with America*, London, 1784, 9, 13.

[6] *The Works of John Adams*, Boston, 1850, II, 169.

[7] Massachusetts Archives, *Hutchinson Correspondence*, II; Thomas Hutchinson to Ebenezer Silliman, November 9, 1764.

[8] *The Writings of Benjamin Franklin*, IV, 390.

[9] *Ibid.*, 392.

Franklin's henchmen took his advice — to their acute discomfort and Franklin's own embarrassment. John Hughes stubbornly refused to resign despite the menaces of the Philadelphia mob; and Joseph Galloway wrote in favor of the Stamp Act in the newspapers.

The proprietary party in Pennsylvania seized upon these circumstances to turn the mob against Franklin and his followers. Samuel Smith, a native of New England and the moving spirit of the mob, declared that it was Franklin himself who had first broached the Stamp Act in order to ingratiate himself with the Ministry. With one eye on the German vote, Smith accused Franklin of having proposed a double stamp duty upon German newspapers; and with the other on the Presbyterians he cried that Franklin was attempting to have the Test Act extended to the colonies. Indeed, Franklin was blamed for every oppressive act of the British government and it was made to appear that all the time he had been in England he had engaged in plots against the liberties of his fellow Americans.[10]

The Philadelphia mob was soon straining at the leash and Dr. Franklin might well be thankful that the Atlantic was between him and the City of Brotherly Love. Mrs. Franklin was urged to leave town, but she stoutly insisted upon standing her ground. She rounded up all available arms and ammunition and prepared with her friends to withstand a siege. Her precautions seemed well-advised. When the mob summoned John Hughes to resign, the governor, mayor, recorder, and all the magistrates hurriedly left town. Philadelphia was spared a riot like the Boston outbreaks largely because Joseph Galloway, Franklin's right-hand man, called out the White Oaks and Hearts of Oak — clubs of Philadelphia tradesmen — who posted themselves throughout the town and broke up the demonstrations before they became dangerous. As a result, the mob had to content itself with burning the effigy of the stamp master instead of chasing him through the streets like a hunted animal.[11]

---

[10] Mrs. Deborah Franklin to Benjamin Franklin, September 22, 1765, Bache MSS., American Philosophical Society. Samuel Wharton to Benjamin Franklin, October 13, 1765; Edmund Quincy to Benjamin Franklin, November 5, 1764; Franklin MSS., American Philosophical Society. William Allen to Thomas Penn, December 13, 1764, Penn MSS., Historical Society of Pennsylvania.

[11] *Pennsylvania Journal and Weekly Advertiser*, September 4 and 11, 1766. *A Collection of Interesting Authentic Papers . . . from 1764 to 1775*, edited by John Almon, London, 1777, 57. Joseph Galloway to Benjamin Franklin, June 7, 1766, Franklin MSS., American Philosophical Society. Richard Penn

It is significant that resistance in Pennsylvania came principally from the proprietarians rather than from Franklin's partisans, although Joseph Galloway confessed himself unable to keep party lines intact: "Too many of our friends," he lamented, "were inclined to unite with those wretches [the proprietarians] against the Stamp Act." [12] John Hughes followed Franklin's advice and upheld British authority to the last despite great personal danger and the unkind cuts of his friends. He even found himself expelled from the Heart and Hand Fire Company with whose brother members he had fought some of the best fires in Philadelphia and drunk some of the deepest bumpers.[13] Franklin was able to remove the stain from his own reputation by his remarks before the House of Commons when the repeal of the Stamp Act was under discussion; but Galloway and many other of Franklin's followers continued to move in the direction of Toryism until they were driven into exile in 1775.

II

AT ALMOST the very time that Henry laid his resolves before the Virginia burgesses, James Otis proposed in the Massachusetts House of Representatives that an intercolonial congress be summoned in order that the provinces might act in concert against the Stamp Act. Despite "the sneers of the Tories," Otis's plan was adopted and the colonies were invited to send delegates to a congress to be held in New York in October, 1765. The composition of this Stamp Act Congress ought to have been convincing proof to the British government that resistance to parliamentary taxation was by no means confined to the riffraff of colonial seaports. The members were some of the most distinguished men in the colonies. Tories might take what encouragement they could from the failure

---

to Thomas Penn, December 15, 1765, Penn MSS., Historical Society of Pennsylvania.

[12] Joseph Galloway to Benjamin Franklin, November 14, 1765, Franklin MSS., American Philosophical Society.

[13] *Pennsylvania Journal and Weekly Advertiser,* December 19, 1765.

of all the colonies to respond to the call. New Hampshire, North Carolina, Georgia, Nova Scotia, and Virginia were not represented; and the delegates from South Carolina, Connecticut, and New York were not given authority to sign for their colonies. The Pennsylvania Assembly appointed delegates only after a bitter struggle in which the members voted fifteen to fourteen to join the colonies at New York. In the congress itself, moreover, lines were quickly drawn between the radicals and conservatives. The majority was determined to assert the rights and privileges of the colonies without infringing upon the prerogative of the Crown and the constitutional powers of Parliament; but a radical minority was disposed to treat Parliament with scant courtesy. Lynch and Gadsden of South Carolina, leaders of this latter group, favored petitioning only the King and ignoring Parliament on the ground that Americans did not hold their rights from Parliament and had been insulted by the refusal of the House of Commons to accept the petitions of the colonial assemblies against the Stamp Act. The South Carolinians were overruled, however, and the congress drew up an address to the King, a memorial to the Lords, and a petition to the House of Commons, thus demonstrating the dependence of the colonies upon Parliament as well as upon the King.[14]

While acknowledging that Americans owed "all due subordination" to Parliament, the Stamp Act Congress put forward the doctrine of no taxation without representation. This stand for American freedom almost broke up the congress. Timothy Ruggles of Massachusetts, the president, refused to sign the petition on the ground that it was inexpedient for the colonies to claim the sole right of taxation at the same time that they pleaded for repeal of the Stamp Act.[15] The speaker of the New Jersey Assembly, Ogden, left the Congress without signing its petitions, declaring that the colonies could do more towards repealing the act by acting separately than by making a united protest.[16] Ruggles almost lost his seat in the Massachusetts House of Representatives for walking out of the congress and Ogden was burned in effigy in almost every

[14] *Letters to and from Caesar Rodney*, edited by George H. Ryden, Philadelphia, 1933, 26. R. W. Gibbes, *Documentary History of the American Revolution*, New York, 1885, 9.

[15] *Boston Gazette*, May 5, 1766, Supplement; May 12, 1766.

[16] *New York Mercury*, December 16, 1765. William Franklin to the Lords Commissioners of Trade and Plantations, December 18, 1765, House of Lords MSS.

town in the Jerseys and was obliged to resign his seat in the assembly; but the action of the conservatives had revealed differences between Americans at a time when union was essential. Much of the damage was repaired, however, by the prompt approval of the congress's work by every colony except Virginia, whose legislature remained prorogued by the royal governor. But Virginia had already made clear her position by the adoption of Patrick Henry's resolutions.

Had Great Britain attempted to enforce the Stamp Act, there can be little doubt that British troops and embattled Americans would have shed each other's blood ten years before Lexington. As Benjamin Franklin remarked, a British army would not have found a rebellion in the American colonies in 1765 but it would have made one. The Sons of Liberty attempted to create a military alliance of the Northern colonies to prevent the landing of British regulars; and Colonel Putnam declared that ten thousand men would spring to arms in Connecticut alone. "Many of us have vindicated our country's wrongs in the bloody field, have despised the yells of savages, and trod down the armies of France," said the Sons of Liberty. "Shall we then crouch to tyranny obtruding itself under the sanction of a law, when we have defied foreign legions to force it upon us? Have native Americans stood undaunted before the roaring cannon, and shall they be affrighted at the threats of haughty ministers, and their vile instruments?"[17] Rather than permit the act to be enforced, the patriots swore that they would "fight up to their knees in blood"; although the colonies were turned into "a most doleful scene of outrage, violence, desolation, slaughter," they would continue the fight from the western country until the British invaders had been driven into the sea.[18] "Daughters of Liberty" declared that they would accept no suitors who were not willing to resist the Stamp Act "to the last Extremity." Even in Philadelphia, the Quaker stronghold, war and bloodshed were regarded as inevitable if the British government called upon the army to break American resistance; and the hard-drinking Maryland planters, perhaps emboldened by copious draughts of punch, became flaming patriots before they slipped under the table, "Daming their souls if they would pay (the Stamp duties) and Damn them but

[17] *Providence Gazette*, March 12, 1766.
[18] Charles Chauncy, *A Discourse on "The Good News from a Far Country,"* Boston, 1766, 21.

they would fight to the last Drop of their blood before they would Consent to any such slavery." [19]

The Sons of Liberty, whether in or out of their cups, had little doubt of victory over the British army if it came to a showdown of military force. They believed that the "true old British Lyon" had strayed away from the mother country and, having swum the Atlantic, was now heard "to roar most terribly" in Virginia, New York, Rhode Island, and Boston. The fierce females of America had welcomed him to these shores and had borne him offspring that would make the poor, moth-eaten old fraud the British were attempting to palm off as the original turn tail at the first encounter. [20]

Englishmen roundly cursed "the damned Blunder that was made in sending over the Stamp-Duty" without men-of-war and British troops to enforce it. Certainly, British weakness in the colonies was an invitation to Americans to rise up against unpopular taxes. The British army of ten thousand men which Grenville proposed to station in North America was still on paper in 1765; and the fifteen battalions of British regulars then serving in the colonies were widely dispersed through Canada, Florida, and the western posts, rather than centered in the colonial seaports where they were urgently needed. British officers found it impossible to assemble immediately five hundred men in the seaports "on any emergency foreign or domestick."

The Stamp Act did not miscarry everywhere in the British Empire: it was only where British authority was weak and colonial traditions of self-government strong that it was successfully resisted. It is significant that the line drawn in 1776 between rebellious and loyal colonies was foreshadowed in 1765. Opposition was most effective in the older, more settled continental colonies; in the newer colonies and in most of the West Indian Islands, the act was executed without difficulty. Barbados and Jamaica submitted quietly; in Jamaica, indeed, the people were so unconcerned that two Negro slaves carted the stamps overland for more than ten miles without interference. Of the British West Indies, only St. Kitts and Nevis rose up against the stamps, but in St. Kitts, resistance came chiefly

---

[19] John Penn to Thomas Penn, December 15, 1765, Penn MSS., Historical Society of Pennsylvania. *American Historical Review*, October 1921, XXVII, 72.

[20] *Newport Mercury*, September 30, 1765.

from the sailors on the American ships in the harbor who, it was said, behaved like "Young Lions." [21] In Halifax, the citizens did not mark their disapproval with even a riot — which caused many royal governors who found the more southerly colonies too hot for comfort to look to that port, hitherto regarded as a frigid place of banishment, as a haven in a storm. Likewise, Quebec offered no resistance, largely because the French-speaking inhabitants had no traditions of home rule and because the English-speaking settlers were too few to organize opposition.

In the newly acquired colony of East Florida and in Georgia, where frontier conditions largely prevailed, British authority was particularly strong. In East Florida, the Stamp Act made smooth progress until the stamp master was obliged to flee St. Augustine to escape not the mob but his creditors. [22] The Georgia patriots were overcome by the close co-operation between the royal governor, the merchants of Savannah, and the Georgia rangers — a redoubtable body of fighting men for whose support many royal governors would have been willing to pay dear. When the Sons of Liberty staged an uprising in Savannah, Governor Wright, gun in hand and flanked by the merchants and rangers, told the patriots that "if they had anything to ask, this was not a manner to wait upon the governor of a province." This unexpected firmness, rare in a royal governor, nonplused the Whigs and they quickly dispersed, leaving the field to the governor and his friends. To crown the patriots' discomfiture, when a Son of Liberty who had been spending the day in the "Wars of Bacchus" tried to break in upon the governor and his supporters in their tavern, he was badly beaten up and "immediately kicked out." [23]

The continental patriots, disgusted by the submission of the "base, servile Barbadians" and other West Indians, proposed to starve them into repentance. All commercial intercourse with "Creole Slaves" was stopped: "Let them want the comfortable Enjoyment of every delicious Dainty from us," exclaimed a patriot, "till they are brought to a State of Despondency, without any

---

[21] *Pennsylvania Journal and Weekly Advertiser*, December 26, 1765.

[22] James Grant to Grey Cooper, September 8, 1766; James Grant to Charles Lowndes, April 26, 1766, P.R., Treasury K, Bundle 452.

[23] *Pennsylvania Journal and Weekly Advertiser*, February 13, 1766. Governor Wright to the Lords of Trade, February 1 and 7, 1766, P.R.O., C.O. 5, 649.

Thing but stinking Fish and false Doctrine."[24] Fortunately for the West Indians, the repeal of the Stamp Act spared them from this fate — although not from stinking fish, which the New Englanders continued to unload upon them.

Americans had challenged the authority of Parliament to tax the colonies; they had rioted against the Stamp Act and driven the stamp masters to cover; yet the crisis had not yet been passed. November first, the day the Stamp Act was to go into effect, was ushered in with funerals of Liberty, "aged 145" (which placed its birth in 1620 — the year the Pilgrims landed), the ringing of muffled church bells, flags hanging at half mast, and heavy drinking in the taverns. Many Americans wore crape; and even the dice and backgammon boxes at the Merchants' Coffee House in New York were covered with crape. In Boston, to the surprise of the Crown Officers, there was no riot; but in New York a violent outbreak took place which almost led to bloodshed between American patriots and British troops.

New York City was the powder keg of the colonies. As the headquarters of the British army in North America, and the central link in the colonial chain, it afforded a strong base from which to divide the colonies and beat down opposition to the Stamp Act with military force. But the British government had made no preparations to utilize the strategic position of the city. The guns of the fort were in disrepair, the carriages rotten; powder was scarce; the fort itself was commanded by neighboring buildings with little cover available for its defenders; and the garrison consisted of only 151 men and officers. Instead of presenting a threat to the Sons of Liberty, the British troops in New York seemed to be at the mercy of the patriots.

In 1765, under the direction of Colonel James, the British began to repair the fort and prepare for defense. Colonel James was one of those British officers who wore their hats at the "damn my eyes cock" and who yearned to see the army — which contained some of the best foxhunters in the empire — take up the sport of hunting down American "rebels." Despite the weakness of the British military forces in New York, Colonel James infuriated the patriots by declaring that he would "cram the Stamps down their Throats"

[24] *Boston Gazette*, January 6, 1766. *Newport Mercury*, March 10, 1766. *The Works of John Adams*, II, 173, 174. *Pennsylvania Journal and Weekly Advertiser*, April 15, 1766.

with his sword; if they resisted, he swore he would "drive them all out of the Town for a Pack of Rascals, with four and twenty men." On the night of November 1, 1765, the New York mob gave him its answer. Thousands of townspeople drew up menacingly before the gate of the fort as if to make a frontal assault. The British troops who manned the guns might easily have killed hundreds by opening fire upon the crowd but, as a British officer later pointed out, twenty thousand men would have gathered within two days to storm the fort and take vengeance upon the garrison.[25]

Despite the fact that the patriots commanded a formidable mob of almost three thousand men recruited largely from the waterfront laborers, artisans, sailors on shore leave, and Negro slaves, they had no stomach for assaulting British cannon and fortifications with small arms; after making a futile effort to burn the fort, they contented themselves with hurling abuse and curses at the garrison, beating at the gate with sticks, daring the troops to fire, and giving "three Whozaus in defyance." After tiring of this sport, the mob prepared to burn Lieutenant Governor Colden's coach; when they found it impossible to cram an oversized effigy of the Lieutenant Governor into the coach they "placed a *drunken Indian* in his Honour's Seat." [26] Nor was Colonel James forgotten by the mob; although he was safe behind the ramparts of the fort, the patriots had the satisfaction of wrecking his furniture, burning his library, and drinking up his cellar. In fact, the only article saved from the ruin was a red curtain which the mob hoisted as a flag.[27]

Outside of the fort, after the riot of November first, British authority in New York existed only by sufferance. When Governor Moore arrived on November 18 to assume the governorship of the colony, he found Lieutenant Governor Colden quaking behind the locked doors of the fort, through which no townspeople were allowed to pass lest the garrison be overcome by surprise. The new governor succeeded in restoring order and winning the good will of the people — but only by refusing to take measures to enforce the Stamp Act.

[25] *The Correspondence of General Thomas Gage*, edited by C. E. Carter, I, 73.

[26] *New York City During the American Revolution*, New York, 1861, 47.

[27] Narrative of Ebenezer Hazard, Diary of Events in America, 1765-1770, MSS., Library of Congress. *Pennsylvania Journal and Weekly Advertiser*, November 14, 1765.

Having cleared the colonies of stamps and stamp masters, the Sons of Liberty clamored for business as usual without stamps. "What signify all our arguements against the Stamp Act," they asked, "if we by it, in any instance, are turned out of, or stopped in our ordinary way of transacting our affairs?" [28] By doing business without stamps, the Sons of Liberty would complete their triumph over the British government and demonstrate its utter helplessness in the face of American opposition; to suspend business because of the lack of stamps might, on the other hand, be construed as acquiescence in the act.

The demand that the courts and ports be opened without benefit of stamps precipitated a struggle between conservative and radical patriots upon the issue that later divided Americans into Whigs and Tories. It was observed that it was the "men of little note" who were most insistent upon business as usual; men of wealth and position whose property would be the first to suffer from British retaliation urged that no outright defiance be made until Parliament had been given a fair opportunity to repeal the act. These conservatives feared that the people were becoming too aware of their strength and importance and that if they were permitted to dictate to the courts of law one of the strongest bulwarks against majority rule would be destroyed. The mob seemed to be making itself sovereign in the colonies and its next victims were likely to be the Whig gentry. "It is the opinion of many of the better sort of people," said General Gage, "that if the provinces were left much longer in the situation they are now in, the Inhabitants wou'd rise and attack each other." [29] The Maryland stamp master, Zachariah Hood, observed during his enforced tour of the colonies that in New York the upper class was deeply alarmed by the "plebeian phrenzy"; in the "Grait Confushion," he noted, "every one begunn to dread the Consequence." [30] In the eyes of the gentry, the principal work of the Sons of Liberty seemed to be "committing riots, breaking city lamps, violently assaulting the peace officers, and cutting off their noses, rescuing criminals; or marching away to fall upon a parcel of his Majesty's subjects, at the request of any whose interest it is to distress them." [31] Gangs

[28] *New York Gazette or Weekly Post Boy*, January 9, 1766.
[29] *The Correspondence of General Thomas Gage*, I, 91.
[30] Archives of Maryland, *Sharpe Papers*, III, 237.
[31] *Boston Gazette*, August 18, 1766.

borrowing the popular name of Sons of Liberty began to rob and pillage private houses, and although the patriots denied any hand in these outrages, the name "Son of Liberty" came to have a distinctly bad odor.[32] Open intimidation of even the popularly elected assemblies was practised by the "true" Sons of Liberty, however: in Connecticut, five hundred Liberty Boys with cudgels aloft marched three times around the Courthouse where the Connecticut Assembly was sitting. Grieved by these events, James Otis begged Americans to stop rioting and to send "dutiful and loyal Addresses to his Majesty and his Parliament, who alone under God can extricate the Colonies from the painful Scenes of Tumult, Confusion and Distress." [33]

But that "over-ruling gentry, the mob," had become too powerful to be deterred by such importunities. Conservative patriots who resisted the popular demand that business be resumed without stamps found themselves denounced as Tories. Printers who wished to stop the publication of their newspapers because stamps could not be had were told that unless they continued to bring out their papers as usual they would have the mob at their doors. Most of them prudently continued publication. The New York lawyers were accused by the radicals of "snoring over the Liberties and Properties of their Fellow Subjects in the most supine Indolence"; and the New Jersey lawyers were visited by delegations of Sons of Liberty who insisted that the courts be opened without delay.[34]

Because of the opposition of upper-class conservatives and the colonial judges, the radicals, although successful in opening the ports, were thwarted in many provinces in their efforts to compel the higher courts to transact business. In South Carolina, in particular, the judges waged a vigorous struggle to keep the courts closed. Robert Pinckney, Provost Marshal of the province, declared that if an unstamped writ were brought before him "he would pay no more regard to such a Writ than he would to a Cabbage

[32] New York Mercury, September 7, 1765. Boston Evening Post, April 14, 1766.
[33] James Otis to the Honorable Henry Sherburne, November 26, 1765, MS. Library of Congress.
[34] New York Gazette, November 20, 1765. Charles Steuart, Surveyor General of the Eastern Middle District of America, to the Commissioners of the Customs, December 8, 1765, House of Lords MSS. Unpublished Letters of Charles Carroll of Carrollton, I, 112–113. Pennsylvania Journal and Weekly Advertiser, February 13, 1766. A Collection of Interesting, Authentic Papers . . . from 1764 to 1775, edited by John Almon, London, 1777, 48.

Leaf or a Piece of Blank Paper." Chief Justice Shinner likewise braved the wrath of the people by refusing to consent to the opening of the courts. For this defiance, the South Carolina Assembly demanded his suspension, the mob became so threatening that he was obliged to sleep with firearms beside his bed, and he was reduced to such destitution that before the repeal of the Stamp Act he had "a French half Crown, and eighteen pence English Silver Coin, left to send to Market for the Support of his Family; as almost every debt he owed were running upon him." [35] The patriots had almost succeeded in ruining the Chief Justice; but the higher courts in the province remained closed.

[35] Lieutenant Governor Bull to the Lords of Trade, May 8, 1766, P.R.O., C.O. 5, 378.

CHAPTER · · · SEVEN

The Repeal of the Stamp Act

REPEAL

OF THE STAMP ACT

I

F EW Americans expected the riots and bravado of the Sons of Liberty to compel England to repeal the Stamp Act. They believed, nevertheless, that they held a trump card which, if well played, would eventually force the mother country to yield. By threatening Great Britain with ruin, they hoped to induce the British merchants and manufacturers to force the government into repealing the act. In the eyes of many Americans, John Bull was no longer a hearty beef-eater but a lean, miserly fellow whose deepest anguish was the loss of a shilling. Lost to all finer sensibilities, their horizon bounded by loaves and fishes, the English had to be hit hard in their pocketbooks before Americans could expect justice.

The first attempt to bring economic pressure upon Great Britain by means of boycotting British merchandise had been made by New Englanders in 1764. In retaliation for the Sugar Act, they adopted Poor Richard as their guide and proceeded to seek the simple life — thus saving their money while they injured British trade. Many Whigs philosophically regarded the Sugar Act as a wholesale chastisement compelling Americans to give up enervating British luxuries and return to the austerity of the Founding Fathers. The growing importation from Great Britain of plate, fine clothing, carriages, and "Gewgaws" had long alarmed puritanical colonists who believed that the moral fiber of Americans was being undermined by soft living. In New England, even funerals had become the occasions for a display of finery — particularly of black gloves. The patriots inveighed against this unseemly ostentation to such purpose that in 1764 a funeral was held in which "a long Train of Relations followed the Corpse (which was deposited in a plain Coffin) without any Sort of Mourning at all." [1] At the same time, the merchants of Boston forswore the wearing of lace and ruffles;

[1] *The Scots Magazine*, Edinburgh, 1764, XXVI, 568. *Boston Gazette*, September 24, 1764.

and gay Boston began once more to assume the drabness of a puritan metropolis.

The Stamp Act inspired a more thoroughgoing boycott of British merchandise. Believing themselves confronted with ruin, the colonial merchants countermanded their orders for British goods and gave their creditors to understand that dark days were in store unless the Stamp Act was repealed immediately. In their own fall, American merchants seemed likely to carry down with them the pillars of English business and finance. The colonial boycott became in 1765 a formidable threat to British trade and commerce; and the British merchants and manufacturers, already suffering from the postwar depression, bitterly repented their shortsightedness in giving Grenville a free hand in the colonies. Unlike the squires, businessmen had from the beginning regarded the Stamp Act with misgivings. Although they were eager to see smuggling suppressed, they saw no benefits to themselves from parliamentary taxation of the colonies. Taxation, they believed, would injure trade by draining the colonies of the specie with which they bought British manufactures and creating ill feeling between Englishmen and their customers overseas. "They will never consent to enrich us," lamented the merchants, "while they think we oppress them."[2] But above all they did not wish Parliament to thrust its hand into the pockets of the colonists because their own hands were already there, busily engaged in removing whatever small change Americans might happen to accumulate. "We at present have their all," they said of the colonists, "can we have more?"[3] The British government had jeopardized their trade and their debts for the sake of a "peppercorn" of sixty thousand pounds.

The colonial boycott, riots, and denials of Parliament's right to tax Americans persuaded many Englishmen that a full-scale rebellion had broken out. In particular, the Duke of Bedford and his followers clamored for reprisals against the rebellious "peasantry" overseas. The Duke was one of the Whig lords who, like George Grenville, had made peace with Lord Bute and served under him in the Ministry of 1761–1763. Falling out with Bute and the King,

[2] *The Necessity of Repealing the American Stamp Act Demonstrated*, London, 1766.

[3] *The True Interest of Great Britain with respect to her American Colonies Stated and Impartially Considered*, by a Merchant of London, London, 1765, 40, 43.

Bedford in 1765 became the head of a party known as the "Bedford Party" or "Bloomsbury Gang," the members of which were distinguished even in eighteenth-century English politics by their rapacity. They were also marked by the extreme rancor which they displayed toward Americans: throughout the struggle with the colonies they were among the first to urge the spilling of American blood. In 1765 they were prepared to act upon the approved principles, if not of statecraft, at least of medical science. In the overheated condition of the colonists, a little bloodletting might bring them to their senses, they suggested. Tear up colonial charters, abolish the assemblies, and dispatch a fleet and army to cram the stamps down the colonists' throats, read their prescription for curing American distemper and putting an end to all "clamorous bawlings." The Bedfords screamed for dragoons and cannon so furiously that it was said they were ready to "butcher all America" rather than give up the Stamp Act.[4] Certainly, they believed that if the colonists were forced to obey the Stamp Act, they would soon fall into the wholesome habit of obeying all acts of Parliament, including revenue acts — and when that happy day arrived the Duke and his followers promised themselves a good share of the spoils. The Bedfords proposed to settle the colonial problem by giving the colonists no rights or privileges to dispute about and little money or property to complicate their lives. But above all they advocated strong-arm methods: it was fatal to British prestige abroad, they exclaimed, "to talk big at the Courts of Madrid & Paris and be Timid and Pusillanimous at Boston & Rhode Island."[5] The New Yorkers had besieged the fort and hung the governor in effigy; was Great Britain to stay its hand, they asked, until the mob had stormed the fort and hung the governor in earnest? Was Parliament, "the most august Assembly on Earth, which so lately made every Quarter of the Globe tremble," to be dictated to by mobs in England and America — and were mob leaders to become more powerful than cabinet ministers?[6] "The weavers were at your doors last year because you would not Pass a Law to please them," they told members of Parliament; "the

---

[4] *Public Advertiser*, December 27, 1765. *Gazetteer and New Daily Advertiser*, March 12, April 4, 1766.

[5] Archives of Maryland, XIV, *Correspondence of Governor Horatio Sharpe*, Baltimore, 1895, III, 247.

[6] *Public Advertiser*, January 14, 1766.

Americans are this year up in Arms because they do not like what you have Passed." [7] It was high time for Parliament to show that it was master; and there could be no more effective demonstration of its authority than stamping out sedition in America. To the Bedfords, the issue was simply whether "American insolence shall rule British councils, or, Whether Britain shall rule an American rabble?" [8]

The crucial nature of the decision England was called upon to make was perhaps best expressed by John Hughes, the Pennsylvania stamp master who found time from his bouts with the mob to write letters to the British government. "The Issue of this Act," said Hughes, "will absolutely determine Britain's Sovereignty in America, for if by these rebellious actions we can get this act repealed, I have no doubt but some of my children may live to see a duty laid by Americans on some things imported from Britain, for I do not know an instance of a Mob's sitting down contented with one thing, unless they have a force able to quell them." [9]

The Bedfords and even many honest Englishmen believed that the Stamp Act was merely the ostensible cause of the upheaval in the colonies. The colonists seemed ready to clutch at any straw which gave them a pretext of quarreling with the mother country and enabled them to move closer to their goal of complete independence of all British authority. It was difficult to believe that Americans were deeply agitated by the Stamp Act alone: it was, in the first place, such a moderate tax that only "the veriest beggars in the world" would rise up against it, unless, indeed, they were seeking to prevent the British Parliament from taxing them "were they never so rich." Had Parliament taxed American small beer half a penny a quart, few Englishmen would have been surprised to see the colonists rising in mobs — that was to be expected of Englishmen. But to riot about a stamp tax seemed convincing evidence that either Americans were hair-triggered gentry who took up their cudgels upon the slightest provocation or the Stamp Act was merely the ostensible cause of the trouble. Many Englishmen concluded that the fundamental grievance of the colonists was the restrictions imposed upon their commerce; that the real British

[7] *Correspondence of Governor Horatio Sharpe*, III, 246–247.
[8] *Gazetteer and New Daily Advertiser*, March 17, 1766.
[9] *Pennsylvania Journal and Weekly Advertiser*, September 4, 1766, Supplement.

tyranny, in their eyes, was the mercantilist system. If this was true, they could be appeased only by granting them free trade — then, having thrown off every irksome restraint of British sovereignty, Americans might be content to pay Great Britain the empty honor of calling her the mother country. But in the meantime Americans rioted against the Stamp Act and defied the British government because they regarded Great Britain as "a Millstone that is tied about their Necks to sink them; a very Leech, or Bloodsucker, that drains them of their Wealth." They yearned for complete independence from Great Britain; indeed, they imbibed "notions of Independence and Liberty with their very Milk." [10] They were republicans from the cradle; and they blamed the British government for every evil that befell them after they cut their teeth. Any attempt to appease these inveterate enemies of British authority was certain to fail: every concession would be regarded as a sign of weakness and new demands would be made upon the British government until not a shred of sovereignty remained to the mother country. Parliament, it was feared, would soon be unable to pass any legislation whatever that did not inspire the cry of "tyranny" in America; a "red-hot Provincialist" like James Otis had merely to blow his whistle to bring "their High Mightinesses, the Mob," tumbling out of garrets and taverns to nullify another act of Parliament.[11]

Despite these gloomy forebodings, the Rockingham Ministry which had assumed office in July 1765, after the fall of George Grenville, was resolved to try appeasement. Representing the mercantile interests of Britain, the ministers, though themselves chiefly landed gentry, were appalled by the prospect of losing the colonial market. Of all the Whig factions, the Rockinghams were most benevolent toward the colonies. While they were as determined as were the Bedfords or the King's Friends to maintain the sovereignty of Great Britain, they insisted that Americans must be treated as customers rather than as rebellious rogues who merited a sound whipping. They were not willing to agree that the customer was always right, but they did believe he ought to be kept in good

[10] London Chronicle, February 13, 1766. Public Advertiser, February 12, 1766.
[11] Ibid., January 22, February 3, March 31, 1766. Gazetteer and New Daily Advertiser, February 14, 1766. A Plain and Seasonable Address to the Freeholders of Great Britain on the Present Posture of Affairs in America, London, 1766, 16. Considerations on the American Stamp Act, London, 1766, 33.

humor and they did not advocate the modern totalitarian method of merchandising at the point of a bayonet. Instead of proclaiming the colonies in rebellion, the Ministry termed the riots "Important Occurrences" in the speech from the throne. In their eyes, Americans were merely copying the example of true-born Englishmen. If the outbreaks of mob violence in the colonies were to be regarded as rebellion, they pointed out that England, with its mobs of coal heavers, was in a chronic state of rebellion. They regarded riots as merely an "effervescence of liberty" and "a favorable crisis, by which nature throws off the peccant humours in the body politic." [12]

Rockingham and his followers were willing to take Americans at their word and treat the Stamp Act as the real cause of conflict between the mother country and colonies. They believed that if the act were repealed, tranquillity would be restored in the empire and Great Britain would not be obliged to make further concessions to purchase the good will of the colonists. The Rockingham Whigs thus staked their political future — and, indeed, the future of the British Empire — upon Americans' dutiful behavior after the repeal of the Stamp Act had been brought about. If the colonists continued refractory and insisted upon relaxation of the Laws of Trade, the Rockingham Whigs declared that they would be ready to join the Bedfords in employing force to subdue them.

The strength of the Rockingham party in Parliament hardly warranted hope that it could carry the repeal of the Stamp Act over the opposition of the now thoroughly aroused members. Consisting of a mere handful of the devoted followers of the Marquis of Rockingham, the Whig Ministry was dependent for its majorities upon the King and the so-called "King's Friends" under the leadership of Lord Bute. Moreover, the weak character and ordinary abilities of the Marquis of Rockingham were no good augury for the friends of the colonies. A dyspeptic and somewhat querulous young man, like the Duke of Newcastle in the purge of 1762 he had suffered the loss of his Lord Lieutenancy, but had refused to restore himself to favor by truckling to Bute and

[12] *American Historical Review*, April 1912, XVII, 586. *Public Advertiser*, March 6, 1766. *Considerations on the American Stamp Act, and on the Conduct of the Minister Who Planned It*, London, 1766, 31. *A Letter to a Member of Parliament wherein the Power of the British Legislature and the Case of the Colonists are briefly and impartially considered*, London, 1765, 2.

Grenville. Rockingham was an ardent lover of the turf and like the other Whig lords was seldom absent from Newmarket when the horses were running. But he showed excellent judgment in secretaries as well as horses: his secretary was Edmund Burke, who gave the Whigs a philosophy and held the party together during the dark days of the Revolutionary War.

The Rockingham Ministry recognized that in the distress of the British merchants it possessed a trump card to win repeal of the Stamp Act. It was clear that repeal could not be carried solely by appeals to Englishmen's sense of justice; it must be demonstrated that the Stamp Act, instead of benefiting Great Britain, was actually doing injury. The argument for repeal could be clinched only by reference to the pounds and shillings at stake. Here the plight of the merchants was of great propaganda value to the Ministry and was utilized with remarkable astuteness. Working hand in hand with the Rockinghams, the London merchants appointed a committee to organize opposition to the Stamp Act. The committee wrote circular letters to thirty trading and manufacturing towns, urging the merchants and manufacturers to flood Parliament with petitions demanding repeal.[13] The businessmen of Great Britain needed little prompting: most of them were thoroughly alarmed by the turn of events in the colonies and disposed to regard the repeal of the Stamp Act as their only salvation. As a result, petitions began to pour into Parliament from the manufacturing towns and seaports of Great Britain; and reports of impending riots and rebellions began to appear in the newspapers. It was reported that manufacturers were laying off men in such numbers that there would shortly be an army of one hundred thousand unemployed in Manchester, Liverpool, and Bristol, ready to march on London and force repeal by breaking the heads of obstinate members of Parliament.[14] Alarming stories of destitution were spread abroad: "No such Thing as a Loom going in Spitalfields, nor a Pair of Shoes making in Yorkshire . . . and as for the Tanners, they

[13] Thomas Penn to ?, December 15, 1765, Penn MSS., Historical Society of Pennsylvania. Additional MSS. 33030, British Museum, Information of Barlow Trecothick. L. Stuart Sutherland, "Edmund Burke and the First Rockingham Ministry," *English Historical Review*, XLVII, 62–64.

[14] Historical Manuscripts Commission, *Report on the MSS. of Reginald Randon Hastings*, London, 1934, III, 146. Horace Walpole, *Memoirs of the Reign of King George the Third*, London, 1845, II, 296–297. *Considerations Relative to the North American Colonies*, London, 1765, 14.

were ready to throw themselves into their own Lime Vats at seeing all their Hides upon their Hands." [15]

In repeal of the Stamp Act, the Rockingham Ministry found itself supported by William Pitt, who hitherto had not deigned to aid the hard-pressed Whigs. But Pitt had not won a great empire for England to see it destroyed by a "short-sighted financier"; and he now declared publicly that he rejoiced that America had resisted and had frustrated Grenville's scheme of a colonial revenue. Pitt went far beyond the Rockingham Whigs and the great majority of Englishmen in his view of colonial rights. He denied that Parliament could impose internal taxes such as the Stamp Act upon the colonists because they were not represented in Parliament; like Lord Camden, he believed that God and Nature had joined representation and taxation and that it was beyond the power of Parliament to tear them asunder. On the other hand, Pitt acknowledged that Parliament could pass laws restricting colonial trade, navigation, and manufactures — it could do everything, in fact, except take Americans' money by internal taxation "out of their pockets without their consent." By Pitt's theory of the British Constitution, the colonial assemblies had the sole power of laying internal taxes upon the colonists, yet Parliament remained "sovereign and supreme, in every circumstance of government and legislation whatever." Thus, although Americans possessed certain political rights, they had no economic liberties whatever except those granted them by Parliament. The British House of Commons held despotic powers over American trade, commerce, and manufactures; and from its authority there was no appeal. Indeed, in this respect Pitt, the champion of the colonies, was less liberal than even George Grenville. Pitt declared that if the colonists began manufacturing for themselves contrary to an act of Parliament, he would favor sending men-of-war to bombard their cities; in his eyes, the right of controlling the economic life of the colonies was so vital to the mother country that if it were ever lost he advised Englishmen to sell their lands and board ship for America.

Meanwhile, Benjamin Franklin was assiduously buttonholing members of Parliament and urging the repeal of the Stamp Act in the newspapers. But even with the aid of the merchants, Pitt, and Benjamin Franklin, it was not certain that the Rockingham Ministry could carry repeal through Parliament. The Stamp Act

[15] *Public Advertiser*, November 30, 1769.

had passed by a large majority; the Rockingham Ministry enjoyed only an inconsiderable personal following in Parliament; and the defiant attitude of the Americans made repeal doubly difficult. From the beginning of the debate, it was plain that the House of Commons was in no mood to yield to American rioters. Although the House refused to adopt the proposal of George Grenville, the author of the Stamp Act and "fond of it beyond the love of a politician," that the British army be called upon to enforce the act, it declined at the same time to accept Rockingham's whitewashing of the American riots as "important occurrences." They were, the House declared, "Tumults and Insurrections of the most dangerous Nature." [16]

In this crisis, the decision of the King was vital in determining British policy. George III, the most powerful political manager in the kingdom, held the balance of power in the House of Commons; and therefore both foes and friends of repeal looked to the King for support. Although George III had called the Rockingham Whigs to power, he was reluctant to aid their efforts to repeal the Stamp Act. The King was profoundly disturbed by the "abandoned licentiousness" of his subjects both at home and overseas: "If a due obedience to Law . . . does not once more become the Characteristic of this Nation," he said, "we shall soon be no better than the Savages in America." When he was urged to step forward as the champion of repeal and vie with Pitt for popular applause, he declared that "they would ruin him, themselves, and the nation, by trying for popularity." [17] The King favored modifying the Stamp Act; it was only when he was told that modification was impossible and that he must choose between repeal and enforcement that he decided upon repeal. He did not, however, put pressure upon his followers in Parliament to vote in accordance with his decision: as a result, Lord Bute and his henchmen voted against repeal.[18]

While the great debate proceeded, the lobbies were so crowded with merchants that it seemed "the whole trading interest" of the empire had gathered to learn the decision of Parliament.[19] Their

[16] *Public Advertiser*, December 27, 1765; January 14, 1766. *St. James's Chronicle*, February 6, 1766. *Parliamentary History*, XVI, 96. *Good Humour, or, a Way with the Colonies*, London, 1766, 15. Walpole, II, 220-221.

[17] *Grenville Papers*, III, 370. *The Correspondence of King George the Third*, I, 161, 394.

[18] *The Correspondence of King George the Third*, I, 267, 269.

[19] Walpole, II, 289, 299.

presence undoubtedly smoothed the way for repeal. It was essential that Parliament did not seem to give way to the riotous colonists; the pleas of the merchants made it possible to regard repeal as a concession to English businessmen in the interest of trade and commerce. A way was opened for government to retreat with honor. It was the merchants, rather than the colonists, who seemed to have won the victory. When the King went to Parliament to pass the repeal, "to shew respect to the Merchants" they were received in the Princes' chamber by His Majesty; but it is significant that no effort was made to call in the colonial agents to show respect to the Americans.[20]

Despite the fact that the merchants thus saved the mother country from humiliation at the hands of her unruly children overseas, it was impossible to repeal the Stamp Act without at the same time asserting the right of Parliament to tax the colonies. If permitted to stand alone, repeal could certainly be construed by the colonists as a virtual renunciation by Parliament of its authority over the empire. It must therefore be made clear that while Parliament acted out of tenderness towards them and the English merchants, it did not surrender one jot of its authority. To drive this point home, before the repeal of the Stamp Act took place, Parliament passed the Declaratory Act by which it claimed authority over the colonies in "all cases whatsoever" and declared that they always had been and "are and ought to be" subject to the British Crown and Parliament. In England, the Declaratory Act and the repeal of the Stamp Act were known as the "Twin Brothers" and Americans were warned that one could not be considered apart from the other.

The Declaratory Act was far more popular in England than the repeal of the Stamp Act; Englishmen caressed one of the Twin Brothers and cuffed the other. Whereas over a hundred votes had been cast in the House of Commons against the repeal, the Declaratory Act passed unanimously in the Commons and fell short of unanimity by only five votes in the House of Lords. It was supported by all parties except Pitt's followers, but they could do nothing to impede its passage. The Great Commoner declared that "if he was an American he would not thank Parliament for the repeal of the Act if it was not done on the principle of our having no

[20] Thomas Penn to ?, March 18, 1766, Penn MSS., Historical Society of Pennsylvania.

right to lay an internal tax upon that country," and he warned the House that Americans would not accept the repeal upon any other grounds.[21] But Colonel Barré's motion to strike out "in all cases whatsoever" — an unpleasant reminder to Americans of the Act of 1719 by which Parliament had declared sweeping authority over Ireland — was supported by only ten members, including Pitt. The Rockingham Whigs approved of the Declaratory Act and it was observed that Edmund Burke and many other Whigs "particularly distinguish'd themselves" in advocating it in Parliament. Upon the issue of parliamentary authority over the colonies, factions in England displayed a unanimity which promised to bring the mother country squarely into collision with the colonies, where an equally strong conviction prevailed that Parliament's authority was strictly limited by God, Nature, and the British Constitution.

For the great majority of Englishmen and Americans, the repeal of the Stamp Act and the passage of the Declaratory Act brought to an end the dispute between the mother country and her colonies. It meant peace for the empire; the threat of civil war was dispelled. "Let the past, like the Falling out of Lovers," exclaimed an Englishman, "Prove only the renewal of Love." [22] For the moment at least, the course of love ran smooth; and Englishmen and Americans, like a married couple, were willing to stop wrecking the furniture and let bygones be bygones.

When the good news arrived in Boston, the Whigs called out the Sons of Liberty, not for a riot but for a frolic. John Hancock, whose wealth had made him the "angel" of the patriot party and of needy Whigs like Sam Adams, gave "a grand and elegant entertainment to the genteel part of the town," and rolled out a pipe of Madeira for the common people; while Otis and other patriots who lived near the Common kept open house. Fireworks in the form of pyramids and obelisks showered sparks upon the merrymakers, and the evening was concluded by the stupendous spectacle of "sixteen dozen of serpents" set off simultaneously.[23] The Virginians celebrated characteristically with "a ball and elegant entertainment at the Capitol"; the New York Sons of Liberty crowded into their taverns and spent the evening drinking toasts and ex-

[21] Historical Manuscripts Commission, *Report on the MSS. of Mrs. Stopford-Sackville*, London, 1894, I, 105.
[22] *Correspondence of Governor Horatio Sharpe*, III, 284.
[23] *The Scots Magazine*, Edinburgh, 1766, XXVIII, 380.

changing compliments with the "friendly Brothers of St. Patrick" who had also gotten together for some serious drinking.[24] Fired by rum and patriotism, the patriots rushed into the streets, where they passed the evening in the "throwing of Squibbs, Crackers, firing of muskets and pistols, breaking some windows and forcing off the Knockers off the Doors." [25] In Connecticut, however, the celebrations were marred by the fact that a large number of patriots blew themselves up with gunpowder or were killed by the bursting of cannon. In Hartford alone, six men lost their lives when a schoolhouse in which they were preparing fireworks blew up — which proved, the Tories observed, that rum and gunpowder do not mix.[26] In a more sober vein, the New England clergy made a field day of the event — in all, over five hundred sermons were preached in thanksgiving for the repeal. "We may now be easie in our minds, contented with our condition," declared the Reverend Charles Chauncy of Boston in 1766.[27] Reconciliation with the mother country now became the ideal of many of those who had been foremost in opposition to the Stamp Act. They rejoiced again in the prospect of the "growing greatness of the British Empire" and hailed the Lords and Commons as the "Guardians of the English Nation." [28] Many of the stamp masters were permitted to resume their professions of lawyers, innkeepers, or storekeepers. It became a patriotic duty to buy British merchandise: the Philadelphia merchants voted to give their suits of homespun to the poor "and on the King's Birthday appear in new Suits of Broad Cloth made in England." [29]

Americans were at first too busy celebrating the repeal to pay much heed to the Declaratory Act. To conservatives, repeal meant that property was safe from the mob as well as from the British Parliament; the need of order and subordination was uppermost in their minds and they had little desire to stir up a new conflict with

[24] Virginia Gazette (Purdie), March 14, 1766.

[25] Wilbur C. Abbott, New York in the American Revolution, New York, 1929, 73.

[26] Providence Gazette and Country Journal, September 13, 1766. The Reverend Samuel Peters, The General History of Connecticut, New York, 1877, 239.

[27] Chauncy, 23.

[28] New Hampshire Gazette, May 22, 1766. The Reverend Nathaniel Appleton, A Thanksgiving Sermon on the Total Repeal of the Stamp Act, Boston, 1766, 18.

[29] Thomas Wharton to Benjamin Franklin, May 22, 1766, Franklin MSS., American Philosophical Society.

the British government. And yet the repeal of the Stamp Act and passage of the Declaratory Act afforded no basis for a permanent settlement of the dispute between mother country and colonies. The immediate menace to the internal peace of the empire had been removed; but beneath the surface there remained all the old sources of conflict. It needed only another English minister of the caliber of George Grenville to ignore the danger signals and plunge Great Britain into a quarrel with the colonies from which she could not retreat with honor.

The Declaratory Act failed to weaken in the slightest the colonists' conviction that their assemblies were local parliaments. In he Virginia House of Burgesses, for example, it was suggested that the Declaratory Act be laid upon the table for the inspection of members who would then "without mentioning anything of the Proceedings of Parliament . . . enter upon their Journals, as strong Declarations of their own Rights as Words can express. Thus one Declaration of Rights will stand against another, and Matters will remain in *Status quo*." [30]

The repeal of the Stamp Act left British taxpayers no better off than when George Grenville took up the quest for a colonial revenue in 1764. The squires still staggered under a land tax of four shillings in the pound; the British Exchequer still awaited replenishment from the colonies; and Americans still paid light local taxes and glorified their refusal to contribute to the needs of the mother country as "English liberty." Instead of helping to lighten Great Britain's financial burden, the Stamp Act left a fresh deficit in the Exchequer of 631 pounds, 9 shillings — representing administration costs and the expense of printing the unused stamps.[31] The British government had clearly met with a stunning reverse and the full impact of the blow threatened to fall upon the hapless British taxpayer — and particularly upon the already overtaxed squires. The repeal of the Stamp Act meant that the country gentlemen must once again shoulder the financial burden of defending the colonies. Their visions of colonial revenue went glimmering for it seemed improbable that Great Britain, after backing down in the case of the Stamp Act, could ever "command a single shilling" from her colonies.[32]

[30] *New York Gazette and Weekly Post Boy*, July 3, 1766.
[31] Kate Hotblack, *Chatham's Colonial Policy*, London, 1917, 177.
[32] Samuel Estwick, *A Letter to the Reverend Josiah Tucker, D.D.*, London, 1776, 121.

The repeal brought no truce in the struggle between the colonial assemblies and royal governors and it established no constitutional equilibrium in the colonies. The royal governors were now more hated than before: most of them, it was said, would have enforced the Stamp Act with as much satisfaction as Grenville himself had they had a British army at their backs. Within a month of the repeal, the governor and assembly of Massachusetts were engaged in heated controversy. The fermentation of the Stamp Act had, wrote the governor, "stirred up all the ill humours." The Whigs purged the Council, baited the royal governor, styling him "an infamous pimp" who had "called up that Fiend Discord, from the Pit," drew up a black list of thirty-two supporters of the Stamp Act in the House of Representatives and drove most of them from office in the elections of 1766.[33] Moreover, the leadership of the radicals was strengthened by the repeal of the act. "The great witless Vulgar," lamented the Tories, were still "following, huzzaing, and adoring" the Whig chiefs who continued their practice of "indefatigably stabbing the most distinguish'd, virtuous characters, — poisoning the minds of the people — sapping and assaulting the whole structure of our government." [34]

The Stamp Act had led many Americans to examine closely the position of the colonies in the British Empire; and the deeper they delved, the more evidences of tyranny they brought to light. Those who had believed themselves to be fellow subjects of Englishmen and entitled to all the rights of free men now found that they were in fact treated as infants "whose every motion was to be directed by the arbitrary will of their jealous parent." In political affairs they were kept tightly in leading strings by the British government; in economic matters they were "the faithful drudges" of British merchants and manufacturers.[35] The repeal, it was now seen, left much to be done before American liberty was placed upon a firm foundation. George Grenville had planted suspicion of the designs of the British government so deeply in the minds of Americans that even the most trivial exercise of British sovereignty began to be regarded askance. Certainly, after 1765, Americans were remarkably thin-skinned on the subject of British oppression; they cried "tyranny" upon small provocation and detected black plots

[33] *Boston Gazette*, June 2, 1766, Supplement.
[34] *Boston Evening Post*, December 21, 1767.
[35] *The Political Register*, London, 1768, III, 289–290.

against colonial liberty in every act of the British Ministry. Immediately after the repeal of the Stamp Act, this temper was evident. The Massachusetts House of Representatives declared that the printing of acts of Parliament in Massachusetts against the wishes of the legislature was "an unconstitutional expense on this people, and a grievance." [36] The governor of North Carolina found in 1766 that the people were "as jealous of any restraint put on their consciences as they have of late shewn for that on their property"; indeed, the dissenters of Mecklenburg County insisted that provincial laws designed for the benefit of the Church of England were as oppressive as the Stamp Act. In New York, the customhouse and post office were denounced as unconstitutional creations of the British Parliament which ought to go the way of the Stamp Act. [37] But of even greater significance was the change that had taken place in the minds of Americans since the passage of the Stamp Act. It was a change which held out no prospect of calm sailing for British imperialists who still kept their eyes fixed upon a colonial revenue. "People are so habituated to wild extravagant language & actions," said Thomas Hutchinson in 1766, "that they appear in a different light from what they did, & nothing more than the noble sallies of a true patriotic Spirit." [38]

The truth is that the patriots now knew the real weakness of British authority in the colonies. In the eyes of the Sons of Liberty, the Stamp Act had demonstrated that the mother country was helpless in the face of determined American resistance. The work of the British merchants in procuring the Stamp Act was disregarded; the Sons of Liberty took upon themselves full credit for having forced the British government to yield. "Every dirty fellow, just risen from his kennel," sourly remarked a Tory, "congratulated his neighbour on their glorious *victory over England*." [39] The Sons of Liberty declared that had they not rushed into the breach, "George Grenville would have this day rode triumphant, in the full execution of his grand and deep laid plot of subverting the British constitution." [40]

[36] *Massachusetts State Papers*, edited by Alden Bradford, Boston, 1815, 64.
[37] James Parker to Benjamin Franklin, June 11, 1766, Franklin MSS., American Philosophical Society.
[38] Thomas Hutchinson to Thomas Bollan, November 22, 1766, MSS. Hutchinson Correspondence, New York Public Library.
[39] Mein, 38.
[40] *Providence Gazette and Country Journal*, March 12, 1766.

The repeal of the Stamp Act came to be widely regarded in Great Britain as the cause of the later troubles in the colonies. It was supposed to have weakened British authority by encouraging Americans to believe that they had forced the mother country to concede their demands. The bill by which the Stamp Act was repealed ought to have been titled, exclaimed an Englishman in 1774, "*a formal renunciation of the legislative authority of* BRITAIN *over her* COLONIES." [41] It had begun the series of humiliating retreats that ultimately destroyed the loyalty and subordination of the American colonists and made the British government an object of contempt rather than veneration. It had invited the aggression of colonial radicals upon British authority; New Englanders, it was said, had "not only verified, but improved upon the old Adage, 'Give the Devil an Inch and he will take an Ell.'" George III declared during the American Revolutionary War that the only thing he regretted was the repeal of the Stamp Act. The Rockinghams became the scapegoats of this disastrous beginning in appeasement: "If the pusillanimous gang, of infamous memory, who repealed the Stamp Act," it was said in 1774, "had been gibbetted long since, the Americans had been at this time our very liege and dutiful subjects." [42]

Yet the coercion of the colonists in 1765 would have been no more a solution of the problems of the British Empire than was the use of force in 1775. Even a British victory would have failed to place British rule upon a firm foundation. To conquer America, the minds as well as the bodies of the colonists had to be subjugated — but the British government throughout the revolutionary period failed to perceive this truth. It thought only of compelling Americans to yield, not of winning them to its views or of adjusting its policies to their ideas. The way to reason with an American, in the eyes of most British officials of the period, was to cow him with a whip. The very fact that George III and his ministers lamented in later years that the colonists had not been *forced* to obey the Stamp Act reveals how little they understood the basic causes of the dispute that ultimately disrupted the empire.

[41] *Gazetteer and New Daily Advertiser*, March 11, 1774.
[42] *Essex Gazette*, May 10, 1774.

CHAPTER EIGHT

The Ideological Conflict:
I. The American Mind

John Locke

THE struggle over the Stamp Act disclosed that two irreconcilable conceptions of the nature of the British Empire and the rights of Americans had sprung up on opposite sides of the Atlantic. George Grenville had brought into open conflict two opposing ideologies and thereafter the empire knew no peace. "It seems," wrote the royal governor of Massachusetts in 1765, "that Great Britain and America are got so widely different in their Notions of their relation to one another, that their Connection must be destroyed, if this Question is not determined soon." [1] In England, liberty had ceased to be an ideal to be fought for: leadership in the struggle for popular rights had fallen to the level of John Wilkes and the prevailing ideal was not freedom but the maintenance of the established order. In the American colonies, as in the England of Pym and Hampden, liberty was regarded as the highest goal of human effort and the energies of the ablest men were enlisted in its behalf. Two spiritual worlds existed within the British Empire; from their collision sprang the American Revolution and the triumph of the forces that ultimately created American democracy.

From 1765 to 1775, the American revolutionary movement remained largely a struggle to impress American conceptions of law and justice upon the British government. The dispute was waged over the nature of the British Constitution and the rights of subjects; the goal of the colonists was to reform the British Empire, not to withdraw from it. Ideas were the weapons with which Englishmen and Americans fought for a decade before they resorted to arms; the War of American Independence did not begin until both sides had become convinced that force alone could decide the issues that divided the empire. The source of the American Revolution may be found in these conflicting ideologies and in the actions which they inspired on different sides of the Atlantic. As long as Americans

[1] Governor Bernard to Richard Jackson, October 22, 1765, Bernard MSS., Harvard University Library.

and Englishmen held irreconcilable views as to the nature of the empire and the rights of subjects, it is clear that a collision resulting in the break-up of the empire could scarcely be avoided.

The great strength of the revolutionary movement up to 1775 was the conviction of Americans that they were engaged in a struggle to attain the rights of Englishmen. "We claim nothing but the liberty and privileges of Englishmen," said George Mason of Virginia, "in the same degree, as if we had still continued among our brethren in Great Britain." [2] Americans thought of themselves as Englishmen — better Englishmen, indeed, than those who had remained at home. They conceived themselves to be Englishmen of the truest breed — the descendants of Pym and Hampden — who carried on the work of these "heroes of liberty." They grounded their cause upon English precedents and declared repeatedly that they were merely following "the good people of Britain who have set them the example." As long as the rights of Englishmen remained the goal, most Americans warmly supported the patriot leaders; when the rights of Americans and independence of Great Britain were put forward, the colonists began to divide into hostile camps.

It is significant that the most English part of British America was New England — the spearhead of the revolt against Great Britain. Here English travelers found the speech, the manners and appearance, of the people similar to those of the mother country; New England, it was frequently observed, was appropriately named. New England was among the first to raise the standard of rebellion, partly because New Englanders were so English. "The liberties so long enjoyed" by them, said a foreign observer in 1768, had "only swelled the pride and presumption" so characteristic of Englishmen, until they had become more English than the English themselves.[3] At the same time, the homogeneity of New Englanders served to make them conscious of their strength. A Virginian explained New England's leadership of the revolutionary movement on the ground that the Puritan colonies "approached more nearly, than a single colony, to that period of power when independence would have become a natural event, and dependence a political absurdity." [4]

---

[2] Kate M. Rowland, *The Life and Correspondence of George Mason*, New York, 1892, I, 387.

[3] Friedrich Kapp, *The Life of John Kalb*, New York, 1884, 64.

[4] *Virginia Gazette* (Purdie), April 12, 1776.

The first impulse of Americans upon learning of the Stamp Act was to reach for their pens. Even while the mobs rose to prevent its execution, colonial writers were engaged in drawing up a constitutional justification for resisting British authority. Within the space of a few months, the groundwork of American political theory had been laid and constitutional defenses had been erected against the oppressions of the mother country.

The explanation for this rapid formulation of principles is that Americans possessed a ready-made political philosophy with which to combat British tyranny. During their long struggle against the prerogative, the colonists had employed arguments which served as well against parliamentary taxation as "government by instruction." Despite colonial separatism, this political philosophy was essentially the same in all the colonies. Before 1765, each colony went its own way, unheedful of the similar struggle waged by its neighbors against the authority of the Crown. The Stamp Act swept all the rivulets into one central stream of resistance and revealed that Americans already possessed the prerequisite to united action against the mother country: a common ideology. In their efforts to achieve home rule, all the colonial assemblies had based their claims upon natural law and the rights of Englishmen. The traditions of the English struggle for liberty were the common property of Americans and thus formed another bond of union. And it is clear that Americans were inspired by the example of the "heroes of liberty" of classical antiquity: an American patriot recommended that his countrymen read thoroughly the history of Greece and Rome, "from whence they will imbue a just hatred of tyranny and zeal for freedom." The colonists became so steeped in the letters and history of ancient civilization that they began to conceive of themselves as "Old Romans": one patriot, for example, urged his fellow Rhode Islanders to awaken "all that is Roman in Providence"; an orator was said to defend liberty "with Attic Eloquence and Roman Spirit"; and George Mason said of Patrick Henry that "had he lived in Rome about the time of the first Punic War, when the Roman people had arrived at their meridian glory, and their virtue not tarnished, Mr. Henry's talents must have put him at the head of that glorious commonwealth." [5]

[5] *Virginia Gazette* (Rind's), March 3, 1768. *New York Gazette and Weekly Mercury*, May 23, 1768. Rowland, I, 169.

But above all, the political writings of John Locke furnished Americans, whether Carolinians or New Englanders, with an arsenal of arguments against the arbitrary rule of both King and Parliament. If any one man can be said to have dominated the political philosophy of the American Revolution, it is John Locke. American political thinking was largely an exegesis upon Locke: and patriots quoted him with as much reverence as Communists quote Marx today. Indeed, it is not too much to say that during the era of the American Revolution, the "party line" was John Locke.

In writing his *Two Treatises of Government* in 1690, John Locke did not dream that he was producing a textbook for American revolutionists. He was seeking, rather, to justify the English Revolution of 1688 and to glorify the supremacy won by Parliament over the Crown. He was not thinking of a future revolution, like Marx and Engels; he was attempting to give a philosophical vindication of a revolution that had already largely attained its ends. It is ironical, therefore, that the man who sought to justify the events of 1688–1689 should have given to the world a book from which Americans drew the "principles of 1776" and that his arguments in favor of parliamentary supremacy should have been used by Americans to destroy that very authority in the British Empire.

It was Locke's doctrine that there was a state of nature in which men enjoyed complete liberty; that they had created by means of compact an authority superior to their individual wills; that the government thus established was endowed with only certain specific powers – above all, with the protection of property; and that tyranny began when government invaded the natural rights of man. All these principles which led to the concept of government by consent and limited by law, while not original with Locke, were transmitted to Americans chiefly through his writings. But Americans were not interested in Locke as a vindicator of the "glorious revolution"; they believed his principles to be universal in scope and insisted upon bringing him down to date by applying his doctrines to the dispute between the mother country and the colonies.

Locke's doctrine of the supremacy of the legislature – by which he meant supremacy of the British Parliament over the Crown – was seized upon by the colonists to justify their contention that

the colonial legislatures were superior to the prerogative. His insistence that taxes could not be levied without the people's consent
— by which he meant that the King could not levy taxes without
Parliament's consent — was turned by Americans against Parliament's attempt to tax the colonies without their consent. His conviction that subjects might rebel if their government ceased to
respect the law — which clearly referred to the tyranny of James
II — was used by Americans to sanction rebellion against the King
and Parliament. At every turn, Locke's principles stood Americans
in good stead and confounded British imperialists. It is not remarkable that Americans enthusiastically adopted Locke as their guide
and prophet.

What Americans particularly relished in John Locke was his
emphasis upon natural law. He contended that the laws of nature
were still an enduring force in human affairs despite the fact that
mankind had established organized society. Indeed, he maintained
men had created government merely in order to make their natural
liberties more secure; therefore government at all times must respect
the laws of nature or forfeit its right to exist. These laws of nature
were believed to be moral laws which every man knew intuitively
— a sort of ready-made knowledge of right and wrong which was
"interwoven in the constitution of the human mind." It was soon
made clear that there was no agreement on opposite sides of the
Atlantic as to what the laws of nature were; but their ambiguity,
far from weakening their authority in the eyes of American patriots, made them the more highly esteemed. Tom Paine remarked
that a man who had recourse to the laws of nature would seldom
find himself worsted in arguments; and it was remembered that
Aristotle advised lawyers to resort to them when they found themselves in a tight spot. Americans continued to insist that the British
Constitution was founded upon natural laws and that God and
Nature had ordained that there were certain things — clear to
every man — which King and Parliament could not do. Natural
law thus became the chief bulwark of American liberty because it
strictly limited the authority of the mother country over the
colonies.

The law of nature which most immediately concerned Americans was the principle that no government could take its subjects'
property without their consent. "If any one shall claim a power

to lay and levy taxes on the people by his own authority," said
John Locke, "and without such consent of the people, he thereby
invades the fundamental law of property, and subverts the end of
government." Here Americans found a direct reference to their
dispute with Parliament: they were being taxed without their consent — therefore was not the end of government being subverted?
If the law of nature had forever joined taxation and representation
as Locke contended, the British Parliament was acting contrary to
the will of God in seeking to draw a revenue from the colonies.

Locke's readiness to sanction rebellion against an oppressive government seemed to conservatives to open the floodgates to endless
revolutions which, they feared, would not be "glorious" from their
point of view. If the right of revolution was one of the natural rights
of man which he carried with him into society, it seemed likely that
he would find no lack of occasions to put it to use. To American
patriots, however, the right of revolution appeared to be their trump
card against British tyranny. As early as 1773, Sam Adams was proclaiming in Boston that Americans had no need of constitutional
arguments for "they are upon better ground. All men have a natural
right to change a bad constitution for a better whenever they have
it in their power." [6]

Because Englishmen and Americans failed to agree upon the interpretation of the laws of nature — or, indeed, upon their existence
— the colonists were driven to the position that their liberties would
not be secure until the British Constitution had been put in writing
and approved by both Englishmen and Americans. The colonists
would not have been content — as were Canadians, Australians, New
Zealanders, and South Africans until 1931 — with a theoretical but
unexercised supremacy of the British Parliament. "Who," asked
John Dickinson, "are a free people? Not those over whom government is reasonably and equitably exercised but those who live under a government so constitutionally checked and controlled that
proper provision is made against its being otherwise exercised."
There must be written guarantees against tyranny; and there could
be no peace until Parliament had solemnly renounced its right to
tax the colonies: "Their dread of being taxed by Parliament is the
grand sinew of the League," wrote Governor Tryon of New York,
"no arguments or address can persuade them that the British Nation

[6] Thomas Hutchinson to William Williams, April 7, 1773, Israel Williams
MSS., Massachusetts Historical Society.

does not mean to exercise that principle and deeply impressed with that consideration they look upon themselves as mere tenants at Will of all they possess." Parliament's abstention from the exercise of its right of taxation was not enough: the danger remained that the rule of law might be overthrown by the "will and pleasure" of Parliament — which would put even Turkey in "a better situation than Great Britain or America; as the passions and lustful rapacity of one, is more easily satisfied than that of *seven* or *eight* hundred" (members of Parliament).[7] But with a "Magna Charta Americana" which permanently limited the rights of Parliament and guaranteed the liberties of Americans, the government as well as the governed would know clearly what they could and what they could not do. The British Empire might then move forward as an empire of free men, unvexed by disputes between Englishmen and Americans over their rights and privileges.[8]

Natural law was the first line of defense of colonial liberty. There was also a secondary line upon which much skirmishing took place and which some Americans regarded as the main field of battle. The colonial charters seemed to offer an impregnable defense against abuses of parliamentary power because they were supposed to be compacts between the King and people of the colonies which, while confirming royal authority in America, denied by implication the right of Parliament to intervene in colonial affairs. Charters were grants of the King and made no mention of Parliament. They were even thought to hold good against the King, for it was believed that the King derived all the power he enjoyed in the colonies from the compacts he had made with the settlers. Some colonists went so far as to claim that they were granted by "the King of Kings" — and therefore "no earthly Potentate can take them away." [9] John Adams said that when the grantees of the Massachusetts Bay Charter carried it to America they "got out of the English realm, dominions, state, empire, call it by what name you will, and out of the legal jurisdiction of Parliament. The king might, by his writ or proclamation, have commanded them to return; but he did not." By this interpretation, the charters accorded Americans "all the rights and privileges of natural free-born subjects of Great Britain" and gave colonial assemblies the sole right of imposing

[7] *Pennsylvania Journal*, September 20, 1770.
[8] *Virginia Gazette* (Rind's), March 24, 1768.
[9] *The Other Side of the Question*, by a Citizen, New York, 1774, 16.

taxes.[10] Accordingly, when Americans were told that they had no constitutional basis for their claim of exemption from parliamentary authority, they answered, "Our Charters have done it absolutely." "And if one protests," remarked a Tory, "the answer is, 'You are an Enemy to America, and ought to have your brains beat out.' "[11]

But, in fact, these "glorious charters, granted to the virtuous resolution of our brave forefathers," were hardly the faultless armor of a righteous cause that many Americans supposed them to be.[12] Although they were regarded as constitutions in the colonies, in law they were simply medieval grants. The growth of colonial institutions stretched charter powers far beyond what was originally intended and raised grave doubts of their legality. Charters were open to attack from the prerogative, the courts, and Parliament. As grants from the King, they made colonial liberty appear to be derived from royal authority. In the opinion of English lawyers, they were no more sacred than the charters of the East India Company and municipal bodies in England. Moreover, all charters were now under the control of Parliament and the King could no longer grant the exemptions from parliamentary authority which Americans claimed under their instruments; many English lawyers, for example, argued that the charters were "given in high Times by the King without consent of Parliament, and so are void in themselves." The ambiguity of the charters made possible contradictory interpretations which further weakened them as safeguards of colonial liberty. They declared that the emigrants should enjoy the same privileges in the New World "as if they had remained, or had been born within the realm." This provision could be construed in contradictory ways. Americans maintained that they were thereby relieved from the obligation to pay taxes levied by Parliament in which they were not represented, no taxation without representation being one of the rights of Englishmen who remained at home. Englishmen, on the other hand, insisted that if the colonists had remained in England, they would have been compelled to pay taxes imposed by Parliament — therefore they must pay taxes although they were in America.[13]

---

[10] *Principles and Acts of the Revolution*, edited by H. Niles, 16.

[11] *Pennsylvania Journal and Weekly Advertiser*, September 4, 1766, Supplement.

[12] *Ibid.*, January 28, 1768.

[13] William Knox, *The Controversy Reviewed*, London, 1769, 71. *Parliamentary History*, XVI, 175.

The Pennsylvania Charter expressly recognized taxation by Parliament — and this, Englishmen contended, ought to be regarded as explanatory of the purpose of all colonial charters. The charter of Maryland, on the other hand, denied the right of Parliament to tax Marylanders directly — and Americans insisted that this provision ought to be read between the lines of every charter. Thus neither side could win a clear-cut victory on the strength of charters alone; but the colonists would have been ill-advised had they placed all their eggs in the charter-rights basket.[14]

Indeed, the charter-rights argument threatened to do serious injury to the colonial cause; Christopher Gadsden of South Carolina, deploring the strong attachment of New Englanders to their charters, exclaimed that charters might be "the bane of us at last."[15] The disadvantage of resting the American case upon charters was that most of the colonies did not have them: therefore they failed to lay down those broad "inherent and indefeasible" rights in whose defense Americans as a whole could be united. The danger to American union in colonial charters was recognized by some Massachusetts patriots who complained that the people paid more attention to upholding their charter rights than to the cause of America. "We have got a Charter, they say, and let the Virginians, New Yorkers and New Hampshire People come away from England as they did, our Ancestors came away by compact between the King and them, and the Parliament has nothing to do with us."[16] This argument, it was observed, "cuts up at once the principal Ground for an Union of the Colonies." Fortunately for the patriot cause, this pitfall was avoided. Charter rights were steadily pushed into the background by the laws of nature; and the patriot leaders followed Patrick Henry, who had no faith in charters but, as Jefferson said, "drew all natural rights from a purer source — the feelings of his own heart."[17]

From 1765 to 1775, Americans sought to reconcile British authority with colonial liberty: a constitutional subordination to the

---

[14] *The Claim of the Colonies to an Exemption from Internal Taxes Imposed by Authority of Parliament, Examined. In a Letter from a Gentleman in London to his Friend in America*, London, 1765. *Public Advertiser*, January 3 and 22, 1775.

[15] Gibbes, 9. Hopkins, *The Grievances of the American Colonies Candidly Examined*, 17.

[16] *Massachusetts Gazette*, February 16, 1772.

[17] *The Works of Thomas Jefferson*, XII, 33.

mother country rather than independence was their goal. "Nothing is more earnestly our wish," they declared, "than that the most perfect happy union may be preserved betwixt Great Britain & her Colonies"; even the Sons of Liberty pledged themselves "to prevent as much as in us lies, the Dissollution of so inestimable an Union. . . . May the English Empire continue in the highest earthly Prosperity and Glory, so long as Time may be enumerated." As James Otis said, Americans were "firmly persuaded that their interest and happiness is closely and inseparably connected with that of Great Britain." [18] They were not seeking so much to make a revolution as to preserve the old empire from the heavy hand of Parliament.

The American contention that the authority of Parliament over the colonies was limited was not as utterly without historical foundation as British imperialists believed it to be. Although it was true that Parliament had exercised such authority before the passage of the Stamp Act — the Navigation Acts, the restrictions upon colonial manufactures, the destruction of the Massachusetts Land Bank, the suppression of paper money in the colonies, and the establishment of the colonial post office were all cases in point — yet the question remained whether Parliament's sovereignty was not founded in usurpation. In 1649, the English Parliament had declared, in the act establishing the Commonwealth, that "the people of England and of all the dominions and territories thereunto belonging are . . . a Commonwealth," and therefore under the control of Parliament. The legality of this measure was open to question: could Parliament assume sovereignty over colonies which, according to the colonists' view, had been solely under the jurisdiction of the King? The Revolution of 1688 had established parliamentary supremacy in England; but after 1765 Americans denied that they had consented to this revolution and insisted that the accessions of authority won by Parliament were null and void as regards the colonies. Viewed in this light, the colonists were the victims of repeated usurpations by Parliament, and the constitution of the empire had been overturned.

[18] Boston Sons of Liberty, *Circular Letter*, February 3, 1766. Portsmouth Sons of Liberty to the Boston Sons of Liberty, April 10, 1766, Belknap MSS., Massachusetts Historical Society. *Boston Gazette*, December 9, 1765.

II

AMERICANS were too practical a people to rely wholly on theoretical arguments based on interpretations of charters or the broader and vaguer authority of the Rights of Man. With great vigor they put forward the contention that they were already so heavily taxed by the Acts of Trade that further burdens could not be borne. They countered Parliament's demands for revenue by asserting that the effect of the Navigation Acts was to enrich British merchants and manufacturers and enable them to pay their taxes and was therefore "very nearly the same thing as being taxed ourselves, and equally beneficial to the crown." [19] John Adams concluded that the Navigation Acts taxed Americans more severely than any other subjects of George III. Compelling Americans to buy and sell at Great Britain's price, he observed, meant that they were obliged to sell in the cheapest market and buy in the dearest — a burden for which they ought to receive full credit as their share of the cost of defending the British Empire.[20] Staggering under this weight of taxes, Americans declared that if direct taxation by Parliament were superimposed upon the Acts of Trade, they would be reduced to both ruin and slavery.

Early in the revolutionary period, opposition to the Acts of Trade assumed proportions highly disquieting to the British merchants and Ministry. Americans began to reason that any tax or restraint which prevented them from making a shilling was almost as iniquitous as a law which took money out of their pockets. In 1769, for example, it was pointed out that "this *restraining Power*, will have as pernicious an Effect, both upon our Liberty and our Property, as any other with which our Enemies could wish to curb us," because "under a Pretence of regulating our Trade we may be strip'd of our Property; and with an Appearing of limiting our Manufactures, we may insensibly be rob'd of our Liberty." [21] With

[19] *The Writings of Alexander Hamilton*, I, 117. *The Writings of Benjamin Franklin*, III, 236.

[20] Adams, 44. Edward Bancroft, *Remarks on the Review of the Controversy between Great Britain and her Colonies*, London, 1769, 75.

[21] *New York Gazette and Weekly Mercury*, February 29, 1768. Richard Bland, "An Enquiry into the Rights of the British Colonies," *The Political Register*, London, 1769, IV, 23.

increasing insistence, the question was raised during the period from 1765 to 1775: "Why is the trade of the colonies more circumscribed than the trade of Britain? And why are impositions laid upon the one, which are not laid upon the other?" "Can any one tell me why trade, commerce, arts, science, and manufactures, should not be as free for an American as for an European?" a colonist inquired. "Is there any thing in the nature of our allegiance, that forbids a colonist to push the manufacture of Iron much beyond the making a horse shoe or a hob-nail?" [22] The more closely Americans examined British mercantilism after 1765, the more certain they became that the purpose of the mother country's commercial laws was to make them "the slaves of Britain." [23] Free trade with the world was put forward as one of the objectives of American independence; and after the Declaration of Independence, the Laws of Trade were declared to be "a glaring monument of the all-grasping nature of unlimited power" which sacrificed American commerce and industry "to the interest of a selfish European island." [24]

This mounting opposition to the Laws of Trade was an expression of the growing tendency among Americans after 1765 to call in question the authority of Parliament. The more the British government insisted that no line could be drawn between the supreme authority of Parliament and the total independence of the colonies, the more Americans were disposed to deny all parliamentary authority and acclaim the King as the sole "Head of the Empire." As the revolutionary movement progressed, the demand for complete equality with Great Britain began increasingly to take the form of attacks upon the Declaratory Act. "To suppose any Subordination" (to Parliament), it was often said, "would be destroying the very spirit of the English Government." [25]

It is significant that none of these claims to complete freedom from parliamentary control are to be found in the state papers drawn up by colonial leaders from 1765 to 1775. Instead, the right of Parliament to regulate colonial trade is at all times specifically acknowledged; there is no suggestion in these petitions and memorials that resistance to British mercantilism is contemplated. This

[22] *Boston Gazette*, August 12, 1765.
[23] *Virginia Gazette* (Purdie), March 29, 1776.
[24] *Principles and Acts of the American Revolution*, edited by H. Niles, 63 Ramsay, *The History of the American Revolution*, I, 117.
[25] *The American Alarm*, by a British Bostonian, Boston, 1773, 2–3.

conspicuous absence was owing to the fact that the purpose of the American patriots was to strike a bargain with the British government whereby in exchange for submission to British regulation of colonial trade and manufactures, the right of direct taxation was to be invested solely in the assemblies. Far from seeking to destroy parliamentary authority altogether, they insisted upon giving Parliament the right of overseeing "everything that concerns the proper interest and fit government of the common-wealth, of keeping the peace, and subordination of all the parts towards the whole, and one among another." Daniel Dulany, for example, saw no inconsistency in acknowledging the sovereignty of Parliament at the same time that he demanded for the colonial assemblies the sole right of taxation.[26] James Otis declared that the conception of independent legislatures united only by the Crown was treason to the British Constitution: the colonial assemblies, he insisted, were subordinate to the British Parliament. Down to the eve of the Declaration of Independence, the petitions and declarations emanating from the Continental Congress and the colonial assemblies agreed in giving Parliament control of colonial trade and general supervision over the empire. And until 1775 the colonists' offer to sacrifice their economic liberty in exchange for the right of "internal taxation" stood open. This proposal offered the best basis of compromise between the conflicting views of Americans and Englishmen that was put forward during the revolutionary period. It was rejected because the English government refused to retreat from its position that sovereignty was indivisible and that taxation was its most vital element.

It is true, however, that Americans, despite their willingness to grant Parliament the privileges of controlling colonial trade and manufactures, were almost united in their opposition to giving it the right to establish any effective machinery to enforce its laws in the colonies. Furthermore, although Americans spoke of Great Britain as "home" or "the mother country," they never acknowledged that the right to obedience was one of the prerogatives of motherhood; and they never permitted sentimental veneration for the parent country to stand in the way of their efforts to usurp its authority. By the colonists' theory, Parliament's power over the colonies seemed to be "somewhat like that allowed by the deists to

[26] Dulany, 17, 46–47. Hopkins, 10.

the Almighty over his creatures: he may regard them with eternal happiness if he pleases, but he must not punish them on any account." [27] They clamored against the Courts of Admiralty and customhouse officers but at the same time gladly acknowledged the right of Parliament to give bounties and pay the expenses of the empire. "A strange kind of allegiance this," exclaimed an outraged Briton, "and the first that has ever appeared in the history of mankind!" Englishmen therefore concluded — and not without reason — that Parliament's right to regulate trade would prove an empty honor and that Americans would smuggle to their hearts' content while they laughed up their sleeve at the mother country. Nor would it have resolved the dispute with the mother country or permanently prevented the rupture of the empire had Great Britain acknowledged the validity of the principle of no taxation without representation, in exchange for the subordination of colonial commerce and manufacturing to its control. Fundamentally, the colonies were seeking equality with the mother country and the Navigation Acts and the restraints upon colonial manufacturing were evidences of the superiority of the mother country and the inferiority of the colonies in an empire which Americans were coming to regard as a union of equals.[28]

In 1765 and 1766, Americans, in their eagerness to effect a compromise between parliamentary sovereignty and colonial liberty, followed William Pitt in making an untenable distinction between internal and external taxation. Parliament, they conceded, had the right to lay external taxes — port duties — but could not levy internal taxes such as stamp duties. Thus, at least at the beginning of the revolutionary period, Americans were not demanding a strict application of the principle of no taxation without representation. The right of Parliament to tax colonial trade was admitted — despite the fact that Americans, by their own statements, were not represented in Parliament. The colonists' position was therefore that certain kinds of taxes were illegal without representation, not that all such taxation was forbidden. They believed, however, that by drawing a distinction between internal and external taxation they had rendered Parliament harmless to attack their liberties or their pocketbooks. Prior to 1764, Parliament had imposed port duties — external taxes — upon certain commodities imported into the colonies in order to regulate colonial trade and to enforce British mercantile law; and it was of this practice that Americans were thinking when they acknowledged the right of Parliament to impose external taxes. Certainly, they did not intend to give it the right to raise a colonial revenue.

Yet in the Sugar Act of 1764, the British government had already given an indication of how the right of regulating trade could be turned against Americans' political liberties and a revenue extracted from the colonies. Taking warning from this act, a few American political writers declared that Americans were leaving the back door open for British tyranny; there was no essential difference between internal and external taxation, and if the British government had a right to impose taxes upon trade, it also had a right to tax lands, houses, and everything the colonists possessed. But this logic cut too deep: instead of taking the ground that Parliament had no authority whatever to tax them, the colonists continued to distinguish between internal and external taxation.

It was ominous for the peace of the British Empire that few Englishmen except William Pitt admitted a difference between external and internal taxation and that fewer still agreed that Parliament could impose the one but not the other. The great majority of Englishmen took their stand upon the principles of the Declaratory Act and insisted that Parliament must have power to bind the colonies in all cases whatsoever. George Grenville declared in 1766 that external and internal taxes were "the same in effect, and only differ in name"; and that the colonies were "as much represented in one kind of taxation as the other." Within a year of the repeal of the Stamp Act, Charles Townshend opened Americans' eyes to the folly of attempting to reconcile parliamentary authority with American freedom by any such artificial distinction as that between external and internal taxation.

At the same time that the colonists tried to restrict the power of Parliament they exalted the person, although not the authority, of the King. They insisted that the American provinces were the "King's colonies" over which Parliament was unconstitutionally seeking to make itself master. The Stamp Act, for example, was denounced as an encroachment by Parliament upon the royal prerogative. "Did the Ministers of our Sovereign fully comprehend the Nature and Extent of their Master's Prerogative in America," said a Pennsylvanian, "they would impeach that Man for high Treason who first broached the Right of the British Parliament to tax the Colonies." [29] Even the Sons of Liberty, the leading radicals in the provinces, declared that in opposing the Stamp Act they were representing the King's interests and deserved His Majesty's thanks for their exertions in behalf of constitutional government. George III, they exclaimed, was "the Rightful Lord" and "Sovereign King" of America; and he was, besides, "one of the best of earthly kings," "a prince of heaven-born virtues and ever tender to the cries of injur'd innocence." In their enthusiasm for George, they pronounced the House of Hanover to be "amongst the choicest of God's providential gifts to Great-Britain and the British colonies." [30] If George III should ever find himself obliged to leave England to escape mobbish Londoners, he was promised a refuge in America where it was expected that he would find greater happiness in ruling loyal Americans than unruly Britons. Americans, it was proudly said, had never revolted against the House of Hanover (which could not be said of the Scotch) and there was not a single Jacobite in all America. "Whoever insinuates that Americans can be disloyal to the Brunswick line, or disaffected to the English Constitution," exclaimed a patriot, " — may such a damn'd rebellious villain be banish'd from our peaceful land." [31]

The eagerness of Americans to exalt the King and weaken the authority of Parliament alarmed the English Whigs, who were attempting to do precisely the opposite. Alexander Hamilton's doctrine that George III was King of America independent of any act of Parliament struck consternation among these Whigs, who began to fear that Americans were so enamored of George III that they would aid him in despoiling Parliament of its authority and ruling by prerogative. [32] Lord North attempted to widen this breach between the American and English Whigs by declaring that the Americans were Tories because they wished to enhance the prerogative — in contrast to the Ministry which sought only to main-

[29] *Virginia Gazette* (Purdie and Dixon), November 11, 1773.
[30] *Newport Mercury*, February 3, 1766. *New Hampshire Gazette*, June 20, 1766. *Some Important Observations*, Newport, 1766, 28.
[31] *New York Journal or General Advertiser*, March 8, 1770. *Pennsylvania Packet or General Advertiser*, August 29, 1774. *South Carolina Gazette*, August 3, 1769.
[32] *The Writings of Alexander Hamilton*, edited by Henry Cabot Lodge, I, 67.

tain the rights of Parliament.[33] Even Jonathan Mayhew, the Boston divine, urged Americans not to exalt the King into the sole sovereign of the colonies lest they enable him to strike down English and American liberty.

The English Whigs might have set their fears at rest: Americans did not propose to make George III a tyrant but a strictly constitutional King — in fact, little more than a figurehead. His chief function, they believed, was to protect liberty throughout the empire; if he sought to destroy liberty, he ceased to be King. "Virginians," an American exclaimed in 1773, "you have nothing to fear, for Centuries to come, while you continue under the Protection of the Crown. You are defended against its Encroachments by the Power you have derived from the People. Should the King of Britain ever invade your Rights, he ceases, according to the Principles of the British Constitution, to be King of the Dominion of Virginia." [34] The prerogative, in American opinion, ought only to be exercised to "maintain an Equilibrium" among British subjects.[35] Thomas Jefferson considered the King to be "no more than the chief officer of the people, appointed by the laws, and circumscribed with definite powers, to assist in working the great machine of government, erected for their use, and consequently subject to their superintendence."

George III vastly increased his popularity in England because, as was said, when "the Americans had offered to lay kingdoms at the feet of the Crown" and to nullify Parliament's control of the purse, he spurned the offer and insisted upon being a constitutional King.[36] The King, it was claimed by his admirers, recognized that the dispute was "not between the King and the Ministry on the one part, and the Colonies on the other; but between the British nation and the Colonies." [37] It is evident, however, that George III could not have squared his ideas of kingship with those held by the colonists, and if he had attempted to rule the empire with the revenues he received from America, he would have had to go on

[33] *Parliamentary History*, XVIII, 771. Jonathan Mayhew, *The Snare Broken*, Boston, 1766, 34.

[34] *Virginia Gazette* (Purdie and Dixon), November 11, 1773.

[35] *New York Gazette or Weekly Post Boy*, January 9, 1766. *The Writings of Thomas Jefferson*, II, 59–60.

[36] Earl of Abingdon, *Thoughts on the Letter of Edmund Burke*, London, 1776, 57.

[37] *Gazetteer and New Daily Advertiser*, March 15, 1774.

short rations indeed. To follow Jefferson's metaphor, George III would not have been content to be a handyman around "the great machine of government"; he believed that he ought to be in the driver's seat. Therefore, he abetted Parliament's attempt to establish its supremacy over the empire. Having brought Parliament under his control, he found it more expedient to rule through Parliament than to try to rule by means of the prerogative — a step certain to bring down upon him the wrath of Britons.

Americans made the King the chief bond of union in the empire largely because they had succeeded in shearing away much of his authority. The prerogative had ceased to have any terrors for them; they had learned how to cope with royal governors and instructions and had steadily enlarged their liberties at the expense of the Crown. They had made the old empire, as it existed prior to 1763, compatible with colonial liberty and a large measure of government by consent. And so Americans professed devotion to George III not so much because they loved kings as because the King's authority was weak in comparison with that of Parliament. By supporting the King and opposing Parliament, they believed that they were perpetuating the constitutional order that had proved so advantageous to the maintenance of colonial liberty.

Americans' fulsome and, as they later learned, totally unwarranted praise of George III was designed to build up the King for the role of "sole sovereign of the empire" in which the patriots had cast him. Despite their concessions to the principle of parliamentary sovereignty, many colonists made no attempt to conceal their conviction that the best of all possible solutions of the empire's problems was a federation of self-governing commonwealths owing allegiance to the King alone. This view was clearly held by Benjamin Franklin in 1773 when he declared that the King, with the respective colonial parliaments, was the only legislator of the empire; Parliament, he believed, had no right to make any law whatever binding upon the colonies. Alexander Hamilton gave this conception wider currency when he wrote in 1774 that the King was "the great connecting principle. The several parts of the empire, though otherwise independent on each other, will all be dependent on him." [38]

If George III were to occupy this exalted position in the empire, it was clear that he must bear a good character: it would be

[38] *The Writings of Benjamin Franklin*, VI, 144. *Works of Alexander Hamilton*, I, 80.

fatal to Americans' purposes if he proved the tyrant the English Whigs pictured. Since the ideal king did not exist, the American patriots were obliged to create him. Accordingly they fabricated the myth of George III as a benevolent, pure-souled monarch who, could he but be rescued from the clutches of his advisers, would certainly save the empire. To keep the King's skirts clear of British tyranny, Americans adopted the doctrine of ministerial responsibility. They closed their eyes to the realities of English politics — that it was the King who appointed the Ministry and who controlled Parliament — and charged that all the oppressions of the mother country emanated from the Ministry. As a result, the luckless ministers bore the brunt of American wrath, and vituperation was hurled at Bute, North, and Grenville — "enemies to the freedom of the human race, like so many Master devils in the infernal regions" — while the King went unscathed. Americans also found this distinction between the King and Ministry helpful in nullifying the royal prerogative. The Crown's orders must be obeyed, they acknowledged, but "the neer arbitrary commands of a minister . . . are no more obligatory, than the bulls of Pope Joan." It was found convenient to ascribe to the Ministry every exercise of the prerogative that Americans regarded as objectionable.

There were no stauncher imperialists in Britain itself than in the American colonies. But Americans conceived the British Empire to be based upon liberty and its purpose to extend liberty throughout the world. In the British Empire, as it was idealized by Americans, there was no place for arbitrary government. Sovereignty was limited and divided between King, Parliament, and the colonial assemblies. It was an empire of laws, not of men; its constitution was fixed because it was founded upon the immutable laws of nature; and government was carried on with the consent of the governed. In practice, this theory reduced the empire to a federation of commonwealths — which, to Englishmen of the eighteenth century, was equivalent to its annihilation. To Americans, however, it was the surest means of perpetuating the empire: they believed that "harmony will reign through the whole empire . . . and it may be extended farther and farther to the utmost ends of the earth, and yet continue firmly compacted until all the kingdoms of the world shall be dissolved." [39]

[39] *Essex Gazette*, January 14, 1772. *Virginia Gazette* (Purdie and Dixon), April 29, 1773.

III

IT HAS been seen that in their political and economic views Englishmen and Americans were at odds; it now remains to discuss the third source of conflict — religion. From the beginning of the dispute, the colonial clergy took up "the Cudgels, and beat the Drum ecclesiastic." [40] The politicians found no difficulty in winning the support of the "black regiment"; indeed, the New England clergy had been preaching for generations the doctrines which after 1765 became the tenets of colonial patriotism. There was no definite partition between preaching and politics; the clergy were old hands at sowing subversive political doctrines from their pulpits and following "the Pharisaical practice of their forefathers the Cromwellians, of praying while they are plotting mischief." After 1765, however, the clergy entered the fray in full canonicals. The Tories groaned that these men of God were "unceasingly sounding the Yell of Rebellion in the Ears of an ignorant & deluded People"; "Boys who had just thrown away their satchels and who scarcely read English," it was said, "mounted the pulpit and ventured to decide on matters which had puzzled the sages of the law." [41] Ministers who "belched from the pulpit" the most furious attacks upon the mother country were revered as Christian philosophers and applauded by their congregations. "Popish Priests have not a more powerful Influence over their deluded and credulous Hearers," remarked an Englishman. "Neither Swords nor Pistols, neither Fleets nor Armies, will be of any Avail towards reducing them to Obedience, if Religion shall be called in to enforce, to encourage, to sanctify Opposition. If the Americans shall be taught to believe Resistance to be lawful and consistent with their Duty to God, it will not be long before they sound the Trumpet of War, and publicly appear in Arms." [42]

The Congregational and Presbyterian clergy drew a close parallel in their sermons between resistance to the tyranny of Archbishop

---

[40] *Gazetteer and New Daily Advertiser*, May 18, 1770.

[41] *Massachusetts Gazette*, January 11, 1776. *Rivington's New York Gazetteer*, March 9, 1775. *Extracts of private letters from Boston*, Mr. H. to Mr. M., December 5, 1774, Hardwicke MSS. 35912, Library of Congress Transcript.

[42] *St. James's Chronicle*, September 29, 1774.

Laud and Charles I and the struggle against the tyranny of the Parliament and ministers of George III. "No people," they declared, "are under a *religious obligation* to be slaves, if they are able to set themselves at liberty"; on the contrary, there was a religious duty to oppose a tyrannical king.[43] They taught that rulers must obey the commands of God as expressed in the law of nature: "all commands running counter to the declared will of the Supreme Legislator of heaven and earth are null and void, and therefore disobedience to them is a duty, not a crime." Parliament likewise, they declared, was bound by the same laws which fettered kings — "the eternal laws of truth, wisdom, and equity, and the everlasting tables of right reason." They told their congregations that the only form of government to which true Christians could submit was a government by consent in which the people, ceaselessly vigilant against oppression, retained the right to overthrow unjust rulers. "The people know for what end they set up and maintain their governors," said Jonathan Mayhew, "and they are the proper judges when they execute their trust as they ought to do it." [44] The purpose of government was the common good of society; and revolution was the proper answer to rulers who forgot this primary principle. It is apparent that the colonial clergy served their parishioners John Locke and Holy Writ in equal measure.

Preachers were politicians and politicians preachers during the revolutionary period partly because the religious as well as the political liberties of Americans seemed threatened by the mother country. For many years, the Society for Propagating the Gospel in Foreign Parts had urged the creation of an Anglican bishop for the colonies. The society's missionaries in the Northern colonies clamored for an American bishop to strengthen the hand of the Church in America, although even without the aid of a bishop they were making alarming inroads upon New England Congregationalism. On the other hand, in the Southern colonies where the Church of England was established, few laymen supported the demand of the society or its missionaries. Southern vestries had gained prescriptive rights in the nomination and induction of

[43] Jonathan Mayhew to Thomas Hollis, August 8, 1765, Hollis MSS., Massachusetts Historical Society.
[44] John W. Thornton, *The Pulpit of the American Revolution*, Boston, 1860, 16, note, 86, note, 87, 95, 98.

clergymen which were certain to be lost if a bishop were placed over the provinces.[45] Nevertheless, after 1763, when the British Empire seemed about to undergo a thorough reorganization, pressure for an American bishop was greatly increased. The Bishop of London labored among English cabinet members, urging them to forward the cause of religion by permitting the Church to send a bishop across the Atlantic to the shepherdless flock in the colonies. He pointed out that the Church of England was placed at a great disadvantage by being deprived of its ecclesiastical government in America while dissenting sects enjoyed full privileges. The necessity of going to England for ordination hampered the growth of the Church to such an extent that even in Virginia it was being swamped by the rising tide of sectarianism. The western country was filling up with Baptists, Presbyterians, and New Lights, all bitterly opposed to the Established Church of England. The Anglicans were being besieged, it was said, by "a Banditti of furious Dissenters" — and their position became steadily more precarious as new recruits for the dissenters poured in from Pennsylvania. This colony threatened eventually to overwhelm the Churchmen by sheer force of the numbers it spewed into the Southern colonies: "Africk never more abounded with new Monsters," declared an Episcopalian, "than Pennsylvania with new Sects who are continually sending out their Emissaries around." [46]

The work of the Bishop of London and the Society for the Propagating of the Gospel gave Whig propagandists an opportunity to dust off the specter of ecclesiastical tyranny — "the most cruel, intolerable, and impious of any" — and to throw Americans into alarm for their religious liberties. Let the bishops but get their foot in the stirrup, exclaimed the Reverend Jonathan Mayhew, and "their 'beasts, the laity,' may prance and flounce about to no purpose; and they will at length be so jaded and hacked by these reverend jockeys, that they will not have even spirits enough to complain that their backs are galled." [47] "America," exclaimed an overwrought Whig, "is a Virgin as yet, undebauch'd by proud tyrannical Ecclesiastics," but these gentry were clearly up to their

[45] Boucher, xlix, preface. *The Francis Letters*, edited by Beata Francis and Eliza Keary, London, 1901, 98.

[46] *Colonial Records of North Carolina*, VIII, 286. *Maryland Historical Magazine*, Baltimore, 1913, VIII, 177. Arthur Lyon Cross, *The Anglican Episcopate and the American Colonies*, New York, 1902, 126.

[47] Thornton, *The Pulpit of the American Revolution*, 50.

old tricks and a fate worse than death seemed in store for the colonies. They conjured up visions of "episcopal palaces, or pontifical revenues, of spiritual courts, and all the pomp, grandeur, luxury and regalia of an American Lambeth." [48] Americans would be compelled to fall upon their knees in the streets and adore the miter as the "Apostolic Tyrant" rode by in his "gilded equipage." Moreover, it was believed that an American bishop would be "a political animal . . . and in this lies his Sting." [49] He would dominate the colonial governors and councils, strengthen the position of the colonial oligarchy, and drive dissenters from political life by means of a Test Act. Having brought the colonial governments under his control, he would establish the Church of England in all the colonies and impose taxes for the support of the hierarchy. Indeed, the propagandists did their work so well that it was said by Americans that "the sight of lawn sleeves in this country would be more terrible to us than 10,000 Mohawks." [50] The Presbyterians and Congregationalists saw the dread shadow of "that monster of wickedness, Archbishop Laud," again cast upon America. The Puritans had preferred the company of Indians and rattlesnakes to that of bishops; it now seemed that their descendants were to be driven from America or, as Jonathan Mayhew said, obliged to submit to "that yoke of episcopal bondage, which so miserably galled the necks of our Forefathers." Instead of converting "the poor, perishing heathens and papists in Canada," it was feared that an American bishop would seek to "disturb and destroy honest Presbyterians or Congregationalists." [51] Had a bishop and his court set out to the colonies they might have found American dissenters as prepared to resist their landing as though they were "a formidable army of *dons* and *monsieurs*"; and probably the bishop would have met with the same treatment that was given the East India Company's tea at Boston. [52]

Churchmen protested that colonial dissenters raised such a hue and cry against an American bishop that it might be supposed that a "Cargo of Inquisitors" armed with all the instruments of torture

---

[48] *New York Gazette or Weekly Post Boy*, March 14, 1768.

[49] Francis Alison to Ezra Stiles, March 29, 1768, Stiles MSS., Yale University Library. *New York Journal or General Advertiser*, March 3, 1768.

[50] *The Scots Magazine*, Edinburgh, 1768, XXX, 373.

[51] *New York Gazette and Weekly Mercury*, April 4, 1768; March 27, April 10 and 17, 1769.

[52] *Ibid.*

known to the Holy Office was on its way to the colonies.[53] They insisted that an American bishop would be merely a "Primitive Bishop," without spiritual courts, and his work would be confined to ordaining, confirming, and superintending the colonial clergy and saving the Indians from the "stupid Bigots" and "independent fire-brands" that Eleazar Wheelock, the founder of Dartmouth College, was sending among them. Moreover, an American bishop would have no political powers: "We desire not Bishops to punish the Iniquity of Whigs (God will do that in his own Time and Manner)," said the Churchmen, "but to govern and take Care of our Churches." [54] But even if an American bishop became tyrannical, Americans could drive him out: it would be "as easy to ship him," it was pointed out, "with a coop of poultry, and four or five dozen of Madeira, and shew him the way out of *Sandy* Hook, as it is now to obstruct his coming in." [55]

The partition between the Church of Rome and the Church of England had always seemed dangerously thin to dissenting Americans; now, with Roman Catholicism no longer actively persecuted in England, many Americans concluded that the mother country was about to return to Rome and that an American bishop of the Church of England might prove to be the Trojan horse by which Popery would subjugate North America. Thus the whole British Empire would be carried into the camp of antichrist and, between the Pope and the British Ministry, tyranny would be riveted upon the colonies as well as the mother country. There seemed, certainly, an abundance of straws in the wind to prove that Catholicism was making rapid strides in England. Englishmen were displaying, from the point of view of many Americans, an alarming disposition to tolerate it. The Church of Rome was coming to be regarded as a religion instead of a "horrid system of tyranny over the bodies and souls of men," and it was even rumored that Mass was being publicly said in London; idolatry and worse went on in the chapel of the Sardinian minister; the town swarmed with "popish priests,"

[53] *New York Gazette and Weekly Mercury*, March 27, 1769. Samuel Johnson, *A Short Vindication of the Society for the Propagation of the Gospel*, Boston, 1763, 90.

[54] *New York Gazette and Weekly Mercury*, April 10, 1769.

[55] *New York Gazette or Weekly Post Boy*, April 18, 1768. Convention of Clergy at King's College to Sir William Johnson, November 29, 1766; Samuel Auchmuty to Sir William Johnson, November 14, 1768, Sir William Johnson MSS., Library of Congress.

"Infidels and Sceptics, if not right down Atheists." [56] Such goings-on were abomination to Protestant provincials. Thomas Hollis, the benefactor of Harvard, struck consternation among his New England friends with hair-raising accounts of the rapid progress of Popery in Great Britain.[57] English politicians and prelates fawned upon powerful Roman Catholics, declared Hollis: when the lower clergy attempted to slay "that foulest Hydra Popery," they were rebuked by their superiors — which pointed to a deep-laid plot to restore the sovereignty of Rome over England.[58] The Reverend Jonathan Mayhew, who combined the talents of a divine with those of a first-rate propagandist, mourned the sad state of England in which Pope-baiting had gone out of fashion: "Is the infernal gunpowder plot? are other treasonable and execrable conspiracies of English papists, forgotten?" he asked. ". . . Are all their diabolical treacheries and cruelties buried in oblivion?" [59] This grist, grinding steadily in the mills of colonial propagandists, prepared the American mind for the outburst against the Quebec Act and against Great Britain itself as virtually a Roman Catholic power.

In a world apparently slipping beneath the yoke of Popery, the American patriots were resolved to keep North America a refuge for Protestantism. One of the peculiar charms of New England, remarked Mayhew, was that a Roman Catholic was rarely seen and thereby the Saints were preserved from all contamination. The New England clergy, in particular, refused to yield to the tolerating temper of the times: the Church of Rome, they insisted, was "so far from being the only true church, and chaste spouse of Christ, that she is a most corrupt one, a filthy prostitute, who hath forsaken her first love, and is become indeed, the 'mother of harlots.' " [60]

The bugbear of an American bishop who would serve as an entering wedge for Popery terrified colonists throughout the revolutionary period. To some Americans, "No Bishop" was hardly less

[56] Mayhew, *Popish Idolatry*, Boston, 1765, 50.

[57] Thomas Hollis to Jonathan Mayhew, October 10, December 18, 1764, Hollis MSS., Massachusetts Historical Society.

[58] *Ibid.*, December 6, 1763. Mayhew, *Observations on the Character and Conduct of the Society for the Propagation of the Gospel in Foreign Parts*, Boston, 1763, 45.

[59] Mayhew, *Remarks on an Anonymous Tract*, Boston, 1764, 72–73.

[60] Mayhew, *Popish Idolatry*, 43.

important than "no taxation without representation." These fears were whetted by English Whigs who warned the patriots that the government was determined to create an American bishop the moment the colonists relaxed their vigilance, because it was obliged "to gratify the lawn-sleeves by way of compense for so often voting against their consciences for the court." [61] But the fact was that the British government did not entertain the slightest intention of burning its fingers with an American bishop. The government was interested in matters of revenue, not in matters of faith; and the pleas of the ecclesiastics failed to change the official opinion that there was "no manner of Occasion for any Bishop." Indeed, it was quite clear to the English Ministry that an American episcopate entailed the surrender of the goal toward which British policy was wholly directed: the centralization of authority over the empire in the British capital. By obliging candidates for Holy Orders to come to the mother country for ordination, the colonies were kept in a dependent status and the religious centralization of the empire was preserved. The creation of an American bishop would be a step toward the attainment of Americans' goal: equality in all things with the mother country. It was therefore a foregone conclusion that no bishop would ever be sent to the colonies. Although Americans believed that they alone had warded off the peril of jeweled, tyrannical ecclesiastics, tithes, spiritual courts, and perhaps the Pope himself, the decision was actually made in London and for reasons other than those held by Americans.

The struggle over an American episcopate was much more than a religious quarrel: it was a phase of the conflict between privileged aristocracy and popular leaders that was being waged in the colonies. During the eighteenth century, people of wealth and fashion in the Northern colonies began to display a decided preference for the Church of England. The royal governors were usually Churchmen; and, as social arbiters and the colonists' chief link with the fashionable world, they probably were more influential in making converts to the Church of England than were the far more pious and harder-working missionaries of the Society for the Propagating of the Gospel. The colonial aristocracy began to look upon the Church of England as the most genteel pathway to Heaven; Presby-

[61] Theodore Sedgwick, Jr., *A Memoir of the Life of William Livingston,* New York, 1844, 137. Samuel Johnson to Sir William Johnson, July 7, 1767, Sir William Johnson MSS., Library of Congress.

terianism and Congregationalism were regarded, on the other hand, as low and vulgar religions.

In New York, in particular, Churchmen seemed in their own eyes to be a small island of respectability in a vast sea of uncouth dissenters. Despite their numerical inferiority, they possessed a great deal of the wealth and political power of the province. The Church of England was established in the four lower counties of New York, although its communicants were even here in a minority; the governor and council were usually Episcopalians; and members of the Established Church received the cream of the patronage, together with huge land grants from the royal governor. In New York, only the assembly remained in the hands of dissenters; but even here the Churchmen were making inroads upon the Presbyterians and members of the Dutch Reformed Church. Wealthy old Dutch families tended to gravitate toward the Church of England aristocracy. Because the Dutch held the balance of power between Anglicans and Presbyterians, their support materially assisted the Churchmen to win control of the province.

In Pennsylvania, the Episcopalians worked hand in glove with the Quaker oligarchy. Although a small minority of the population, they exerted an influence out of all proportion to their numbers, largely because of their wealth and social prominence. Through "that designing subtile Mortal Dr. Smith," president of the College of Philadelphia and a member of the Church of England, they molded the ideas of impressionable young colonists. The Presbyterians complained that at college students acquired such "a taste for high life" that they became Episcopalians — a religion which permitted them to sin with impunity; and others became such bigoted Churchmen that they set off for England to take Holy Orders.[62] On the other hand, the dissenters controlled Harvard, Yale, and Princeton — a fearsome triumvirate in the eyes of the Episcopalians. Yale in particular they regarded as "a college remarkable for its persecuting spirit, its republican principles, its intolerance in religion and its utter aversion to Bishops and all Earthly Kings." [63]

The privileged position of the Churchmen aroused the jealousy

[62] *The Literary Diary of Ezra Stiles,* edited by F. B. Dexter, New York, 1901, I, 554. Francis Alison to Ezra Stiles, October 30, 1766, Stiles MSS., Yale University Library. William Allen to Thomas Penn, November 12, 1766, Penn MSS., *Official Correspondence,* X, Historical Society of Pennsylvania.
[63] Thomas Jones, *History of New York During the Revolutionary War,* New York, 1879, 5.

and resentment of the dissenters, particularly the Presbyterians, numerically the strongest sect in New York and Pennsylvania. To overthow the Episcopalians a union of the "antiprelatical churches" was urged early in the revolutionary period; and the menace of a bishop, certain to rivet the oligarchic Churchmen in power, brought the Presbyterians and Congregationalists together shortly after the passage of the Stamp Act. Permanent Committees of Correspondence were appointed and an intercolonial organization of the two churches was created. Shortly thereafter, a "Society of Dissenters" was formed in New York to oppose the Church of England by entering into correspondence with all dissenters in America, Great Britain, and Ireland.[64]

The union of all dissenters was never fully realized, however. The Baptists ran foul of New England religious laws which, they declared, "savoured more of tyranny than any law of Great Britain respecting the Colonies." Eighteen Baptists were imprisoned in the town of Warwick, Massachusetts, when they refused to pay taxes for the support of a Congregational minister; in reprisal, they appointed an agent to go to England and procure the revocation of the Massachusetts Charter.[65] In Virginia and North Carolina, the Baptists were persecuted by the Anglicans — they were, indeed, a downtrodden sect against which every man's hand was raised. In consequence, they saw little to be gained from joining their oppressors in the struggle against British tyranny. "Tho some few Baptists and Quakers are hearty with us," declared Ezra Stiles, "yet too many are so much otherwise, that was all America of their Temper or Coolness in the Cause the Parliament would easily carry their Points & triumph over American Liberty." [66]

The dissenters in the Northern colonies deliberately stirred up religious hatred against the "DOMINEERING *Episcopalians*" in order to hasten the overthrow of the Anglican governing class. All Episcopalians were declared to be Tories — "The political tenets

[64] Lewis R. Harley, *The Life of Charles Thomson*, Philadelphia, 1906, 61–62. Francis Alison to Ezra Stiles, August 20, 1766; March 29, 1768, Stiles MSS., Yale University Library. *New York Gazette or Weekly Post Boy*, June 13, 1768. *New York Gazette and Weekly Mercury*, July 24, 1769. Rev. Charles Inglis, *The State of the Anglo-American Church in 1776, Documentary History of the State of New York*, edited by E. B. O'Callaghan, Albany, 1850, III, 1050.

[65] *Boston Evening Post*, March 12, 1770; September 9, 1771; March 1, 1773; April 18, 1774. *Massachusetts Gazette*, March 3, 1771.

[66] *The Literary Diary of Ezra Stiles*, New York, 1901, I, 490.

of high episcopacy," it was said, "is branded on the forehead of every tory" — and their efforts to establish a bishop in America were denounced as a plot to strip Americans of all their liberties, civil as well as religious.[67] In this way, colonial propagandists turned against the Anglican aristocracy the hatred felt by Americans for British tyranny and its abettors. It was good propaganda, but poor history, to assert that there was a close connection between the Stamp Act and the English bishops and that an American bishop was to be paid with the money taken from the colonists by parliamentary taxation — thus making the proposed episcopate an "ecclesiastical stamp act, which, if submitted to, will at length grind us to powder."[68] The controversy gave colonial patriots an almost inexhaustible fund of propaganda to employ against oligarchs at home and tyrants abroad; as Jonathan Boucher said, it "served to keep the public mind in a state of ferment and effervescence; to make them (the people) jealous and suspicious of all measures not brought forward by demagogues; and above all, to train and habituate the people to opposition."[69]

But the fight was far from one-sided. The Episcopalians struck back at the Presbyterians by denouncing them as rebels and republicans; they hated kings as well as bishops, it was said — "as soon look for *Chastity* in Brothels as for Loyalty among Independents."[70] They accused the Presbyterians and Congregationalists of seeking to establish a "DEMOCRATICAL DESPOTISM" in America; their professions of loyalty to the King were intended merely to mask their purpose of destroying monarchy. "Your old Game," they told the dissenters, "is to spit in the King's Face, and when he is angry, swear that it was a *Tory Churchman* who stood behind you, and spat over your Shoulder."[71] To the end, the Churchmen believed that the Revolution was a Presbyterian-Congregationalist plot; these bigoted Calvinists, said John Hughes of Pennsylvania, were "ripe for open Rebellion, when they poisoned the Minds of the people enough" and had gathered together "Forty Thousand Cut-throats" to fall upon the Episcopalians. Hughes reported that they were

[67] *New York Journal*, July 20, 1775.
[68] Sedgwick, 136.
[69] Boucher, 149.
[70] *New York Gazette and Weekly Mercury*, May 15, 1769.
[71] *Ibid.*, August 7, 1769. Views on Doctor Mayhew's Book of Observations on the Character and Conduct of the Society for the Propagation of the Gospel in Foreign Parts, by a Gentleman of Rhode Island, Providence, 1763, 3.

"as averse to Kings, as they were in the Days of Cromwell," and that as early as 1766 some had begun to cry out, "No King but King Jesus." But their true purpose, he believed, was to form "a Republican Empire, in America, being *Lords* and *Masters* themselves." [72]

While imputing these black designs to the Presbyterians, the Churchmen proclaimed themselves to be the upholders of monarchy and British authority in the colonies. They pictured the Church of England as the front line in the defense of the British Empire; if it were overthrown, they predicted that the colonies would quickly throw off their allegiance to the mother country. Both the Whigs and the Tories later pointed out that the British government had erred in not throwing its full support behind the Church in America. Thomas Bradbury Chandler declared that had the Church been established in all the colonies, the Revolution might have been averted; and James Madison said that the Church was a powerful weapon in the hands of the government with which to keep Americans loyal and contented.[73] Yet it is true that the members of the Church of England in the Southern colonies — where the Church enjoyed the advantages of establishment — seldom permitted their religion to stand in the way of taking up arms against the mother country; it was chiefly the Northern Churchmen — the "oligarchs" — who took the hard and thorny road that led to Tory exile.

The most significant religious union achieved during the revolutionary period was the joining together of Northern dissenters and Southern Anglicans against British misrule. After 1774, New Englanders began to distinguish sharply between Northern and Southern members of the Church of England and they ceased to inveigh against the Established Church as a lady of soiled virtue who kept company with the "Whore of Babylon." On the contrary, they took pains to point out that "the Gentlemen of the Established Church of England are men of the most just and liberal Sentiments, and are high in the Esteem of the most sensible and resolute Defenders of the Rights of the People of this Continent." [74] In Philadelphia, attending the first Continental Congress, Sam Adams passed on word to

[72] John Hughes to the Stamp Act Commissioners, January 13, 1766, P.R.O., Treasury I, 452, Library of Congress Transcript. Joseph Galloway to Benjamin Franklin, November 14, 1765, Franklin MSS., American Philosophical Society.

[73] E. Alfred Jones, *The Loyalists of New Jersey*, Newark, 1927, 42.

[74] *Boston Gazette*, September 26, 1774.

his friends at home that "many of our warmest Friends are Members of the Church of England"; and it was Adams — one of the most rancorous enemies of the Northern Episcopalians — who proposed that the Reverend Mr. Duché, an Anglican clergyman, be invited to preach a sermon to the assembled delegates.[75]

[75] *Ibid.*

CHAPTER NINE

The Ideological Conflict:
II. The English Mind

Edmund Burke

THE marked conservatism in political matters that distinguished the eighteenth-century English mind was owing largely to the fact that as a result of the revolutionary settlement of 1689 and the preoccupation of the first two Kings of the House of Hanover with their German territories and mistresses, the long-sought goal of parliamentary supremacy had been achieved. With this end attained, English liberalism withered at the roots and the Whig Party split into factions. In the opinion of the English governing class, the fruits of the Revolution of 1688–1689 had been gathered and were, so to speak, "in the bag"; any further shaking of the tree promised only to bring down the sour fruit of democracy and levelism. The aristocracy had succeeded in shearing away a large part of the King's authority and bringing Parliament under its control; the revolution had stopped with the aristocracy on top and there, the Whig Lords maintained, it ought to remain. Even when, in 1761, the King cast the Whigs out of the green pastures of offices and sinecures, they made no immediate attempt to overthrow the system which George III had borrowed from them; nor did they appeal to the people by holding aloft the standard of reform. Instead, they sought to get back into power by attempting to manipulate once more the system of rotten boroughs and parliamentary corruption through which they had once ruled England.

Although it must be recognized at the outset that some factions of the Whigs — particularly the followers of the Marquis of Rockingham — and English Radicals such as John Wilkes, John Horne Tooke, Joseph Priestley, Richard Price, and Catherine Macaulay, adopted a liberal, conciliatory position in the dispute between Great Britain and the colonies, it cannot be claimed — as has so often been done — that they represented English public opinion. At the same time it is pointed out that there were liberals in England during the period of the American Revolution it ought to be observed that they were out of power. For the most part, they were also out of public favor. As they themselves acknowledged, they were voices crying in the wilderness of English Toryism. What is of vital importance in studying the origins of the American Revolution is not that Charles James Fox and Edmund Burke disapproved of the policy of George III, but that George III and his ministers had a policy, ruled England and the colonies in conformity to it, and, until disaster overtook them, stood high in the graces of the English people. Here will be emphasized the ideology of the group of men who ruled the British Empire in one of the most critical periods of its history.

During the eighteenth century, many Englishmen came to hold a very different view of John Locke from that of the colonists. In their eyes, Locke was well enough as an expounder of the principles of the "glorious revolution"; but the age of revolutions was happily passed and the *Treatises of Government* was a museum piece, not a manifesto calling the oppressed to arms. They deplored that, in Americans' hands, Locke had become a menace to the established order and bitterly regretted that the works of this "exploded author" had not been burned after they had fulfilled their usefulness in the "glorious revolution." "Are the Closet Reveries of an Author," they exclaimed, "to direct the Operations of Government, to over-rule the Parliament, and to destroy the Constitution?" [1]

The gulf that divided the ways of thought of Englishmen and Americans was further revealed by the different way in which William Pitt was regarded in the mother country and in the colonies. At the very time that Pitt was hailed in America as the savior of the empire, in England he was denounced as its betrayer. When Pitt in the House of Commons praised American resistance, an indignant member declared that the Great Commoner ought to be sent to the Tower, whereupon the House, in the words of an eyewitness, "immediately joined in the idea and gave such shouts of applause as I never heard, so much that Mr. Pitt seemed greatly disconcerted and got off awkwardly enough when he was permitted to speak in his justification." [2] Pitt was declared to have sacrificed the rights of the mother country "to the pitiful ambition of obtaining *an huzza from American rioters*"; by approving rioting and rebellion he had encouraged Americans in their unruly ways and had made more difficult the task of those who upheld the rights of Great

---

[1] *St. James's Chronicle*, December 22, 1774.
[2] *Report on the MSS. of Mrs. Stopford-Sackville*, London, 1904, I, 105.

Britain over the colonies. Instead of giving aid and comfort to the American rebels, it was remarked that Pitt ought to have been "solacing his distempered joints with flannel, and cooling his overheated body by a milk and water gruel diet." [3]

The colonies, it was argued, must pay taxes imposed by the mother country because they received its protection. An Englishman observed that "the duty of paying taxes to the protective power is so strongly connected with christianity, that the colonists must practically give up the scriptures, or submit to the reasonable demands of the British legislature." [4] Without British aid, they would be overrun by every covetous European power. It was therefore regarded as no more unjust "to demand a penny for a penny-loaf" than to impose taxes upon the colonists in exchange for the protection of the British fleet and army.[5] As Englishmen saw it, during the colonies' infancy they had "wanted great parliamentary aids" and had received them without stint from the mother country. Wars had been undertaken in their defense; bounties had been lavished upon many of their products; and their growth and prosperity had been encouraged by wise and benevolent laws. Now the mother country called upon them to help pay the expense of their own protection; but it received as answer the claim that because they had not paid direct taxes in the past, they enjoyed a right of exemption from taxes levied by Parliament. This argument at least had the virtue of reducing the dispute to simple terms that every Englishman could understand: "The payment of their just portion to defray the charges of their own defence, is all the oppression under which they [the colonists] groan." [6]

One of the convictions most firmly planted in the minds of eighteenth-century Englishmen was the superiority of true-born Britons to the American colonists. Too often, Americans were regarded as degenerate Englishmen or as "the scum or off scouring of all nations" — "a hotchpotch medley of foreign, enthusiastic madmen" — a mongrel breed of Irish, Scotch, and Germans, leavened with convicts and outcasts.[7] "Mr. Hancock may be a very good English-

[3] *Gazetteer and New Daily Advertiser*, January 28, February 11 and 15, 1766. *Public Advertiser*, February 1, March 8, 1766.

[4] J. Fletcher, *American Patriotism further confronted with Reason, Scripture, and the Constitution*, London, 1777, iii (preface).

[5] *Gazetteer and New Daily Advertiser*, April 1, 1767.

[6] *Ibid.*, March 23, 1774.

[7] *Morning Post and Daily Advertiser*, January 7, February 17, 1775.

man amongst Bostonians," it was said, "but he is no more an Englishman amongst Englishmen, than General Gage is a King amongst Sovereigns." [8] These "insignificant dependents" were not recognized as fellow subjects; on the contrary, they were held no more the equals of Englishmen than were the King's subjects in Hanover. Americans, in the eyes of many Englishmen, were not "heroes of liberty" who had sought freedom in the wilderness rather than submit to tyranny in the Old World: they were merely "runaways," who, had they possessed the least spark of courage, would have remained at home to assist "their fellow subjects in the glorious struggle against arbitrary power in Church and State, instead of basely deserting them in distress, and running away like cowards to another world, to make their fortune." [9] British propagandists found that one of the most effective ways of silencing the advocates of conciliation was to remind Englishmen of the low birth and general inferiority of the colonists; and, in consequence, every effort at compromise broke upon this inflexible conviction that it would be an insufferable humiliation to treat the colonists as equals.

This doctrine of innate British superiority exercised great influence upon the mother country's colonial policy. Just as mercantilism emphasized the economic subordination of colonies, so English political philosophy took as an accepted fact their political subordination. "The very word COLONY," it was said, "implies DEPENDENCY." [10] When Englishmen spoke of "our colonies" they meant that they were masters and the colonists subjects; and so they must remain forever. There was no room in this philosophy for the gradual growth of the colonies into commonwealths equal in all respects with the mother country: Charles Townshend declared that "sooner than make our Collonies our Allies he wod wish to see them returned to their Primitive Desarts." [11] The status of colonies was fixed for all time; regardless of their strength and population they must remain inferior to the mother country: indeed, as they became wealthy and populous they attained no new liberties or rights — instead they were to be taxed directly by the British Parliament. As Dr. Johnson said, "We do not put a calf into the

[8] *Public Advertiser*, August 25, 1775.
[9] *Ibid.*, January 25, 1775. *Gazetteer and New Daily Advertiser*, July 29, 1768.
[10] *Public Ledger*, January 7, 1775.
[11] *Correspondence of Governor Horatio Sharpe*, III, 248.

plow, we wait till he is an ox." The metaphor was appropriate: the colonies were to be treated — at least in their own eyes — as a beast of burden.

To an ever-increasing degree, British imperialists were calling upon the practices followed in French and Spanish colonial administration to furnish precedents for British policy toward the American colonies. Since the French and Spanish governments enjoyed the right of imposing taxes upon their colonies, ought not the British government to exercise the same privilege? Moreover, the vast extent of the British Empire had captured the imagination of many Englishmen. Here was a new Roman Empire arising; ought not the example of ancient Rome toward her colonies to be copied even to the extent of taxing them? [12] This was, of course, overlooking the fact that the American colonists, for the most part, were neither Frenchmen, Spaniards, nor Romans, but Englishmen with all the Englishman's high notions of liberty strengthened by contact with the American wilderness. Americans were ill-prepared by a century and a half of British neglect to become overnight servile subjects of the type envisaged by British imperialists. There was much truth in Burke's warning that "the British colonist must see something which will distinguish him from the colonists of other nations." [13]

Every demand made by Americans for liberty was declared to be an effort by the "upstart Colonies" and "mushroom plantations" to dictate to true-born Britons. If Great Britain yielded an inch, they would seek to rule the mother country. "Is not every thing English maddened in our bosoms at the remotest tho't of crouching to the creatures of our formation?" exclaimed an Englishman. "Have we erected Colonies to be our masters?" [14] Britain's true policy was to exact obedience, if necessary, with the rod; for colonists, like children, must obey the mother country in all things. Englishmen habitually thought of the relationship of Great Britain and America in terms of parent and child; George Mason of Virginia complained that Great Britain's bearing toward the colonies was seldom "free from the authoritative style of a master to a schoolboy." [15] The official British mind was well expressed by Lord Hillsborough when

---

[12] *A Letter to the Gentlemen of the Committee of London Merchants Trading to North America*, London, 1766, 14.
[13] *The Works of Edmund Burke*, Boston, 1826, I, 322.
[14] *Essex Gazette*, May 10, 1774. *Parliamentary History*, XVI, 1015.
[15] Rowland, I, 382.

he declared that "the colonies are our subjects; as such they are bound by our laws; and I trust we shall never use the language of supplication, to beg that our subjects will condescendingly yield obedience to our inherent pre-eminence." It was this belief in British superiority and American inferiority which led Benjamin Franklin reluctantly to surrender his hopes of reconciliation. The British, he said, despised Americans too much. Even American Tories who fled to England from patriot mobs could not endure the pretensions of Englishmen: "It picques my pride, I confess," wrote Samuel Curwen, late of Philadelphia, "to hear us called *our colonies, our plantations,*' in such terms and with such airs as if our property and persons were absolutely theirs, like the 'villains' and their cottages in the old feudal system." [16]

For Englishmen to be taxed even in their necessities "for the Defence of a Country which will not contribute a Farthing" seemed to true-born Britons to be a monstrous inversion of nature. It made Englishmen "hewers of wood and drawers of water" for the colonists, when, in a rightly ordered empire, the colonists ought to be the servants of the mother country. "The colonies were acquired with no other view than to be a convenience to us," remarked an Englishman; "and therefore it can never be imagined that we are to consult their interests preferably to our own. . . . We have in a manner created the colonies, and have a right therefore to give them laws." [17] "I have always considered the Colonies as the great *farms* of the public, and the Colonists as our tenants," said another; and many regarded "the American colonists as little more than a Set of Slaves, at work for us, in distant Plantations one Degree only above the Negroes that we carry to them." [18] The Marquis of Carmarthen spoke the mind of the majority of Englishmen of all classes when he declared that "we sent them to those Colonies to labour for us. . . . For what purpose were they suffered to go to that country, unless the profit of their labour should return to their masters here?" [19] Richard Price, the English radical, complained that "the meanest person among us is disposed to look upon himself as having a body of subjects in *America;* and to be

[16] Samuel Curwen, *Journals and Letters of the late Samuel Curwen,* New York, 1842, 90.

[17] *The Constitutional Right of the Legislature of Great Britain to Tax the British Colonies in America, Impartially Stated,* London, 1768, 58.

[18] Hinkhouse, 102.

[19] *Newport Mercury,* December 9, 1774. *Parliamentary History.* XVII, 1208.

offended at the denial of his right to make laws for them, though perhaps he does not know what colour they are, or what language they talk. . . . We have been so used to speak of the Colonies as *our* Colonies and to think of them as in a state of subordination to us, and as holding their existence in *America* only for our use." [20]

The great danger in permitting Americans to remain untaxed while they "rioted in ease and luxury" was that they might take advantage of their favored position to make themselves masters of the empire. Englishmen would quickly see the profit to be gained by leaving the mother country for the untaxed felicity of the colonies: "and consequently we must dwindle and decline every Day in our Trade, whilst they [the colonies] thrive and prosper exceedingly. The Consequence of this will certainly be, that the Inhabitants will run away as fast as they can from this Country to that, and Old England will become a poor, deserted, deplorable Kingdom." [21] By coddling Americans and grinding the faces of Englishmen, America was certain to pay "a Sum that she likes, and no more; in a few Years she would not pay Six pence." Thus the colonies would make themselves supreme over the mother country: "They will open the Budget," exclaimed an agitated Englishman; "Mr. Otis or Mr. Hancock will be Lord of the Treasury and Chancellor of the Exchequer; they will cast up our Land Tax, Malt Tax, &c. and then determine how much Money we want." Bleak days indeed were in store for the mother country if Englishmen found themselves in the power of their colonists: we shall be obliged to "cringe to America for our Food and Raiment," it was predicted, "they will turn us out of Doors to starve, unless, indeed, we are to become as much Slaves as their own Negroes." [22] For this reason, many Englishmen feared that "Britain, by promoting the grandeur of that country [British America], diminishes her own importance, and rears up a rival to her commerce . . . America hangs like a wasting disease on the strength of Britain." [23]

Most Englishmen did not share Burke's view that Great Britain's neglect of the colonies had been salutary. It seemed more likely that the troubles of the mother country came from sparing the

[20] Richard Price, *Observations on the Nature of Civil Liberty, etc.*, London, 1776, 31–32.

[21] *Gazetteer and New Daily Advertiser*, June 1, 1767.

[22] *Public Advertiser*, July 27, 1775.

[23] *The Importance of the British Dominion in India compared with that in America*, London, 1770, 58.

rod and spoiling the child. It was not surprising that men who had been "bred up almost in Independency" rioted against the Stamp Act and sought to sweep away all British authority in America.[24] "Our forefathers," lamented an Englishman in 1770, "listened more to the dictates of humanity, than those of true policy, when they permitted the counter-part of the constitution of England to be established on every navigable river in America. Instead of strengthening the empire with provinces, they weakened it by raising rivals, where there only ought to be subjects." [25] Now "these saucy Americans" needed to be taught humility and obedience; and it was better to take them in hand while they were yet in their infancy than to postpone the reckoning until they had become great lubberly fellows who might knock their old mother down when she attempted to apply the birch.[26] Time seemed to be on the side of the Americans: one Englishman pointed out in 1769 that by 1944, Americans — the most powerful people in the world — would visit the ruins of London.[27] Clearly, Americans must be taught who was master in the household, exclaimed an Englishman, before they felt strong enough to "wrestle with us for Pre-eminence."

To many Englishmen, the rapid growth of the American colonies was a source of greater alarm than gratification. Their philosophy of empire made no provision for colonies that threatened to outstrip the mother country in population and rival her in trade and commerce. They feared that "opulence and security have begot a desire of independence"; and because Americans were too prosperous to be good subjects, it was well to give them a taste of salutary poverty.[28] It was common to hear London coffeehouse politicians declare that the colonies "are now extremely populous, and extremely rich; they are every day rising in Numbers, and in wealth, and must, in the nature of things, aspire at a total independence, unless we are beforehand with them, and wisely take the power out of their hands." [29] Englishmen inveighed against "our

[24] Fothergill, 26.

[25] *General Evening Post*, London, May 5, 1770.

[26] *Morning Chronicle and London Advertiser*, January 21, 1775. *Public Advertiser*, January 10, 1775.

[27] *Gazetteer and New Daily Advertiser*, February 28, 1769.

[28] *Ibid.*, March 13, 1766; January 21, 1775. *The Parliamentary Register*, II, 54.

[29] *The Crisis, or, a Full Defence of the Colonies*, London, 1766, 19. Collections of the New York Historical Society, *The Colden Papers*, New York, 1923, VII, 232–233.

too large and too powerful Colonies" which they gloomily contrasted with the declining, exhausted, and tax-ridden mother country. Just as Americans apprehended future evils at the hands of Parliament, so Englishmen feared for the future when the colonies, swollen in population and power, would be beyond the control of the mother country. "It may be even more dangerous and ruinous for Britain," an Englishman observed in 1776, "to suffer the colonies to become too rich, than too poor; by the latter, we should undoubtedly injure ourselves; but by the former, we should certainly be undone." [30] Therefore, it was argued, "Good policy persuades us to stop those provinces in their career to opulence and importance." [31]

It was widely feared in England that the natural prolificness of Americans was redressing the balance of power between the colonies and Great Britain to the latter's disadvantage. So rapidly was the population of the colonies increasing that it seemed not improbable to some Englishmen that within a century "the Seat of Royal Residence may be transferred from St. James's to Faneuil Hall and this devoted Island made a pitiful Province to its Provinces!" [32] New York might prove to be "to London what Byzantium was to Rome." [33] A few Englishmen believed that it was impossible to prevent the course of empire from moving westward and that the mother country, instead of attempting to halt its inevitable progress, ought to get aboard the bandwagon and ride to undreamed-of glory with the Americans. By treating Americans as allies, it was prophetically pointed out in 1766, they might some day prove Great Britain's salvation in war: they had "already often aided us in our *American* Wars, and they will soon be able to do so in *Europe*." [34] Lord Camden, one of the most liberal of the Whig peers, held it to be self-evident that Great Britain must one day lose the American colonies and that the best that could be done was to win their friendship by good treatment for the trying days that lay ahead. "It is impossible that this petty island can continue in dependence that mighty continent, increasing daily in numbers and in strength," he said. "To protract the time of separation to a distant

---

[30] *Gazetteer and New Daily Advertiser*, February 18, 1766.
[31] *Ibid.*, February 11, 1766.
[32] *Public Advertiser*, December 31, 1770; January 7, 1775.
[33] Hinkhouse, 107, 109.
[34] Nicholas Ray, *The Importance of the Colonies of North America*, London, 1766, 6.

day is all that can be hoped." [35] One Englishman urged in 1765 that the parting be delayed by awarding American scholarships to be used in British universities and that choice posts in the colonies be given to Americans who had studied in Great Britain. "The Americans," he reasoned, "by mixing with our own Youth at the University, will diffuse a Spirit of Enquiry after America, and its Affairs; they will cement Friendships on both Sides" of the Atlantic.[36] Shades of Cecil Rhodes!

But these voices were little heeded; the curbing of America's growth was to most Englishmen the goal of British policy and even the Stamp Act was prized by some because it threatened to hamper colonial development. It was at least partly for this reason that the Proclamation of 1763 was retained. "I [think it would] be for our interest to keep the Settlers within reach of the Sea-Coast as long as we can," remarked General Gage; "and to cramp their Trade as far as it can be done prudentially." [37] Large cities, also, ought to be discouraged in the colonies because they attracted skilled workers who would set up industries and thus injure British commerce and manufactures. Englishmen were becoming increasingly aware after 1765 that England's problem was no longer to build up the American colonies but to keep them down.

This was all the more urgent because when upper-class Englishmen snuffed the breeze from America, they found it tainted with "the Gangrene of *American* Republicanism." [38] The dread that "American principles" of liberty and political equality might overthrow the established order in Great Britain itself was never absent from their minds; in their eyes, the frontier of the aristocratic way of life was the Atlantic Ocean. Above all, Americans must not be permitted to instill "the Leaven of Republican Principles into the *Canaille*" of England who, it was observed, were already ominously near to bursting with discontent and ill humor.[39] It was for this reason that the repeal of the Stamp Act was opposed — it would reveal to unprivileged Englishmen as well as Americans that they were "intitled to return to that savage freedom on which every restrictive law is an usurpation." [40] Overnight, millions of sub-

[35] *Parliamentary Register*, II, 85.
[36] Fothergill, 48.
[37] *The Correspondence of General Thomas Gage*, II, 616.
[38] Tucker, *An Humble Address*, Gloucester, 1775, 75.
[39] *Public Advertiser*, January 22, 1766.
[40] J. Fletcher, *American Patriotism further confronted with Reason, Scripture, and the Constitution*, London, 1777, 10, 53. Tucker, *An Humble Appeal,*

jects would be released from their allegiance; all acts of Parliament would be null and void; subordination would be at an end and the social order of Great Britain would be turned into "a Ruin and Heap of Rubbish." [41] Revolution would break out when the honest British workman, "groaning under the late beer tax" and maddened by thirst, learned that the pampered Americans had been relieved of their taxes. Englishmen were at least as high-spirited as Americans; the British government would quickly learn that "a Mob of oppressed and wretched Englishmen" was as formidable as a mob of Americans and in a vastly better position to take vengeance upon unpopular ministers. Moreover, if Parliament knuckled under to the American colonists, it would probably be confronted with a hundred thousand seasoned Irish rioters, determined to batter their way to freedom with their shillelaghs. Repeal the Stamp Act, said these prophets of doom, and the whole British Empire would come crashing down upon the heads of the English aristocracy. Republicanism and levelism would triumph everywhere and greasy English mechanics, Irish bog-trotters, and American "peasants" would rule the new order.

Englishmen regarded New England in general and Boston in particular as the hotbed of American republicanism. The inhabitants of this peculiarly benighted region seemed to be "full of a levelling, republican spirit, which would never be rooted out" except by force. Here was the breeding ground of the subversive ideas that produced turmoil and the class struggle throughout the British Empire, setting the common people against their betters by spreading the doctrine that there was no "pre-eminence in persons." Boston, to conservatives everywhere in the empire, was a horrible example of the rule of numbers; the dire results of giving the common people an equal voice with gentlemen of property and breeding in the management of public affairs seemed exemplified in this mobbish metropolis. "Persons of the best characters and best estates," it was lamented, had little voice in Boston: they remained away from town meetings because they were certain to be outvoted by the mechanics, laborers, and small tradesmen who came to cheer and vote for Adams and Otis. Some Englishmen lived in dread that Boston would spawn an agitator, who, travers-

---

88. *Protests against the Bill to Repeal the American Stamp Act*, Paris, 1766, 10–11. *Parliamentary History*, XVI, 167–168, 186.
    [41] *Public Advertiser*, February 3, 1766. *Gazetteer and New Daily Advertiser*, January 23, 1766.

ing the Atlantic, would seek to establish another Commonwealth in Great Britain. In 1774, it was widely believed that Josiah Quincy of Boston — a most "pestilent Fellow" — had determined to essay this role when he "came over from Boston with the lighted Torch of Rebellion in his Hand, and went Brandishing it up and down the Country, in hopes of kindling the Flame of Civil Discord and Fury."

The doctrine that English conservatives feared above all was that of no taxation without representation. Certainly nothing was more likely to overthrow the privileged class than the application of this "rare levelling principle" in Great Britain. The inequities of English representation had become a glaring abuse which enabled the Whig oligarchy, and later the King, to rule England without benefit of the English people. Twenty-nine out of thirty Englishmen did not enjoy the suffrage; and a majority of the House of Commons was elected by a few thousand voters who, it was said, were willing to "sell their birth-right to the best bidder, be his extraction from the dunghill, his manners from the beargarden, his morals from the brothel, and his understanding of the meanest cast." In most of the towns, the corporation members were the only voters; in some boroughs, there were no voters at all. Cornwall and Devon sent seventy representatives to Parliament; Manchester, Birmingham, and Sheffield had none. London, Westminster, and Southwark elected only six members; Old Sarum and a few other rotten boroughs in its vicinity sent as many.

Instead of acknowledging that this system was a negation of the principle of no taxation without representation, Englishmen sought to gloss over its injustices with the doctrine of virtual representation. By this theory, a member of the House of Commons, regardless of the nature of his constituency, represented the interests of all Englishmen. Even though he were elected by "Pot-wollopers or Chimney-sweepers" he became, by virtue of his translation to the House, the spokesman of the great interests of the nation: financial, mercantile, and agricultural. In other words, a member of Parliament represented the property and interests of England rather than individuals and was expected to promote the welfare of the whole empire rather than that of his own constituents. The unfranchised and the franchised stood upon the common ground inasmuch as their good was consulted by Parliament impartially.[42]

[42] Fletcher, 21, 23.

It was therefore not unconstitutional that twenty-nine out of thirty Englishmen should not have the privilege of voting for members of Parliament. "It is," said an Englishman, "the very constitution itself." [43] By extending this doctrine to the colonies, it became one of the most useful legal fictions ever invented in England. It justified the taxation of millions of unfranchised Americans and gave legal sanction to Parliament's claims to absolutism in the empire. Since all its members represented Americans as well as Englishmen, Parliament could tax them without violating the principle of no taxation without representation. [44]

Although the English masses accepted virtual representation with little protest, the doctrine made no converts in America. The colonists insisted that they had no representatives, virtual or actual, in Parliament, and challenged any member of the House of Commons to prove that he was their representative. By what right, they asked, did "a Lordly, though *unlettered, British elector*, possessed of a turnip garden . . . appoint a legislature, to assess the ample domains of the most sensible, opulent American planter?" [45] It was "the absurdity of absurdities," exclaimed an American, that the "paltry fellows" who jockeyed, bought, and pandered their way into the House of Commons should regard themselves as the representatives of Virginians or Pennsylvanians whom they had never seen. [46] In the colonists' opinion, a representative ought to know the needs and wishes of his constituents — which disqualified the English parliamentarians who, although they frequently crossed the Alps, were well acquainted with the monuments of antiquity, and "had much pleasure in conversing with the Ciceroni of Rome," knew nothing about the colonial lumber trade, molasses, or the problems of a tobacco planter. [47]

Americans pointed out that virtual representation worked far

[43] *An Englishman's Answer to the Address from the Delegates*, New York, 1775, 8–9. Tucker, *An Humble Appeal*, 91.

[44] M. de Pinto, *Letters on the American Troubles*, London, 1776, 14. The Earl of Abingdon, *Thoughts on the Letter of Edmund Burke, Esq.*, Oxford, 1779, lxxiv, note.

[45] *Principles and Acts of the Revolution*, edited by H. Niles, 11.

[46] *Pennsylvania Evening Post*, April 18, 1775. *Pennsylvania Journal and Weekly Advertiser*, July 11, 1765. *Considerations upon the Rights of the Colonists*, New York, 1766, 20–21. *New London Gazette*, September 29, 1765.

[47] *Pennsylvania Chronicle*, April 10, 1769. *Virginia Gazette* (Rind's), March 10, 1768. *The Later Occurrences in North America, and the Policy of Great Britain Considered*, London, 1766, 6.

greater injustice in the colonies than in England. Even the richest man in America would be debarred from voting for the members of Parliament who would represent him. Pitt once said that every Englishman had at least the right of huzzaing at an election — but Americans could not claim even this small privilege. It seemed probable, therefore, that once Americans admitted that they were virtually represented in Parliament they would find their sufferings were actual and their privileges theoretical. Daniel Dulany declared that it was "a mere Cob-web, spread to catch the wary, and intangle the weak"; to expect Americans to be caught was "only adding to ye oppression ye cruel mockery of our understandings." [48]

The defects and abuses of English parliamentary government could not, Americans held, be employed to justify tyranny in the British Empire. James Otis declared that no prescription in England ran against American liberties: "If for the sake of imagin'd superior advantages," exclaimed Otis, "any of the people of Britain have sold their birthright, or if thro' corruption it has been wrested or wheedled from them, pray what is that to America?" [49] Nor could the defects of colonial representation be used to swindle Americans out of their liberties. When Englishmen attempted to justify virtual representation by pointing out that many Americans were taxed without representation by their colonial assemblies, Sam Adams answered that this was no precedent "for the parliament to tax a whole continent without allowing them the privilege or right of being represented." [50]

Daniel Dulany acknowledged that the doctrine of virtual representation might justly be applied to Great Britain, but most Americans agreed with James Otis when he exclaimed that if Birmingham and Manchester were not represented they ought to be. "Right reason and the spirit of a free constitution," said Otis, "require that the representation of the whole people should be as equal as pos-

---

[48] *Virginia Gazette* (Rind's), March 24, 1768. *Unpublished Letters of Charles Carroll of Carrollton,* 89.

[49] *Boston Gazette,* July 15, 1765.

[50] *Massachusetts Gazette,* February 7, 1765. *Boston Gazette,* July 15, 1765. Soame Jenyns, *The Objections to the Taxation of our American Colonies, by the Legislature of Great Britain Briefly Consider'd,* London, 1765, 7–8. Dulany, 3, 4. Francis Alison to Ezra Stiles, June 13, 1765, Ezra Stiles MSS., Yale University Library.

sible." If perfect equality of representation was impossible, continued Otis, "no good reason however can be given in any country why every man of a sound mind should not have his vote in the election of a representative. If a man has but little property to protect and defend, yet his life and liberty are things of some importance." [51] With James Otis proclaiming the rightness of universal suffrage in Great Britain itself, the English governing class might well conclude that the American colonies, and Boston in particular, threatened the mother country with a "futurity of Whiggism."

Despite Americans' refusal to accept the doctrine of virtual representation, Englishmen continued to assert that it was one of the basic principles of the empire. Americans, it was said, "are too dull to understand any arguments drawn from *virtual representation*"; as a prominent New Dealer once remarked of American businessmen, they were "too damn dumb." This peremptory demand that Americans swallow virtual representation struck one American as having very much "the same force as Lord Peter's, when he undertook to convince his two brothers that a slice of brown loaf was good mutton; says he, to convince you what a couple of blind puppies you are, I will use but this plain argument, *by God it is good natural mutton*." [52]

Although most Englishmen paid lip service to the doctrine of no taxation without representation, they held up to scorn Americans' appeals to natural law. Did the New England Saints suppose themselves to be in an "original state of true Indian innocence," asked an Englishman, that they quoted laws of nature so glibly? The law of nature, said Jeremy Bentham, was "nothing but a phrase" which worked anarchy in the state; "the natural tendency of such doctrine," he declared, "is to compel a man by the force of conscience, to rise up in arms against any law whatever that he happens not to like." [53] The Puritans had attempted to destroy the Church of England by subjecting it to a literal interpretation of the Bible; now their descendants promised to do the same to the British Empire with the laws of God and nature. It was clear that God and nature were invariably upon the side of the Americans; an English-

---

[51] *Boston Gazette*, July 22, 1765.
[52] *Newport Mercury*, September 2, 1765.
[53] *Gazetteer and New Daily Advertiser*, January 11, 1775. *The Works of Jeremy Bentham*, edited by John Bowring, Edinburgh, 1843, I, 287.

man had no credit in Heaven. "An American rioter and rebel," remarked an Englishman, "thinks he has a right to defraud the customs, to perjure himself at the Custom-house, to tar and feather Custom-house Officers. . . . But the laws of nature, that give such surprizing rights to the American traitors, give no rights of retaliation to the King's Officers." [54] Englishmen complained that in a fair argument it was not difficult to drive Americans from the field, "but when we have got fast hold of what we suppose the main argument, and are ready to squeeze it to death, it immediately slips like an eel through our fingers," and they found themselves clutching at thin air.[55] In conservatives' eyes, the laws of nature were simply the last refuge of scoundrels who, finding themselves worsted in fair argument, resorted to a jargon about a state of nature which they were never in and "natural and inalienable rights" which never existed.[56]

It is true that not all English thinkers denied the existence of natural law: Blackstone, for example, contended that the laws of Parliament were an exposition of natural law. But this doctrine did not bring Americans and Englishmen into harmony for the question remained: What were the laws of nature? Here there was sharp and violent disagreement: "Were my countrymen now in England dipped once in the River Delaware," remarked an Englishman, "I dare say, that it would make an almost miraculous change in their opinions." [57] Americans stoutly insisted upon the right of interpreting natural law, which, Britons remarked, was submitting the laws of the empire not to God or Nature, but to a "Jury of Bostonians." [58]

In rejecting natural law, Englishmen also denied the colonists' contention that there were metes and bounds to the authority of Parliament. The authority of Parliament was, in their opinion, unlimited: the supremacy of Parliament had come to mean to Englishmen an uncontrolled and uncontrollable authority. Indeed, the divine right of kings had been succeeded by the divine right of Parliament and Parliament was displaying "a kingly fondness for

[54] *Gazetteer and New Daily Advertiser*, February 21, 1775.
[55] Allan Ramsay, *Thoughts on the Origin and Nature of Government*, London, 1766, 27–28.
[56] *A Letter from an Officer Retired to his Son in Parliament*, London, 1776, 10.
[57] Robinson, 163.
[58] *Public Advertiser*, January 25, 1775.

prerogative." [59] It was the refusal of Americans to bow before this new divinity that precipitated the American Revolution.

The absolutism of Parliament admitted of no divisions of authority within the empire: Parliament must have all power or it had none. In Englishmen's eyes, sovereignty was indivisible: it could not be parceled out between the colonies and mother country. "The supremacy of the British legislature must be compleat, entire, and unconditional," said Lord Mansfield; "or on the other hand, the colonies must be free and independent." [60] By this theory, Parliament enjoyed the right of taxing the colonies, for the right of taxation was regarded as the most important part of sovereignty. "America must forever hereafter be considered as a separate kingdom," it was said, "if our parliament cannot tax that country. A country which we cannot tax is a country not subject to us." [61] Americans were told by way of answer to their objections to parliamentary taxation that "to suppose that America is not to be bound by the statutes of the British legislature . . . in all respects, must confound every idea of its being part and parcel of the British empire . . . and totally destroy your title to the protection of the British fleets and armies; . . . to be a part of the empire, lying out of the jurisdiction of the imperial legislature, would be a most palpable absurdity, fairly affronting to common sense." [62]

Viewed in this light, the colonial assemblies were not local parliaments as Americans supposed, but merely corporations subject to the will of Parliament. Indeed, Dr. Samuel Johnson compared them to "the vestry of a larger parish, which may lay a cess on the inhabitants and enforce payment," and which had no more right "to plead an Exemption from . . . parliamentary Authority, than any other Corporation in England." [63] To recognize these provincial assemblies as local parliaments was "to suppose that a body of Adventurers could carry the Legislative Powers of Great Britain along

[59] Macpherson, 15. Cavendish, *Debates*, I, 496. *Gazetteer and New Daily Advertiser*, January 3, 1775. *American Archives*, edited by Peter Force, Washington, 1837, II, 1641.
[60] *Parliamentary Register*, II, 37–38. Cavendish, II, 84. *A Plain and Seasonable Address to the Freeholders of Great Britain on the Present Posture of Affairs in America*, London, 1766, 10. *Public Advertiser*, March 10, 1774.
[61] Macpherson, 77. *Gazetteer and New Daily Advertiser*, November 25, 1765.
[62] *An Englishman's Answer, to the Address from the Delegates*, New York, 1775, 5, 7. Fletcher, 5–6. John Wesley, *A Calm Address to our American Colonies*, London, 1775, 3–5.
[63] Samuel Johnson, *Taxation No Tyranny*, London, 1775, 44. Jenyns, 10.

with them" in their journey across the Atlantic – which struck most Englishmen as an absurdity. Sovereignty resided in Great Britain regardless of how many Englishmen chose to go to the New World; and the King and Parliament remained the legislature of the colonies for all time.[64]

This doctrine ruled out the American conception of the British Empire as a federation of self-governing commonwealths. The shortest way to ruin a great empire, in the opinion of most Englishmen, was to federalize it. "As despotic monarchies have, for the most part fallen into pieces, by a delegation of too much power to the viceroys of different provinces," it was argued, "so our popular government runs the risque of ruin, by transferring too much of its own freedom to its remote colonies." At best, the empire would become a "confederacy of petty states," leaving England with only a precarious hegemony where once she had exercised absolute authority.[65] But worse, it was apprehended that once the colonies had been erected into commonwealths, every county and town in England would demand its independence until the authority of Parliament would be divided among "one diminutive Assembly of States at *Edinburgh*, another at *York*, a third at *London, Bath, Exeter*, etc." [66] Thus "endless Anarchy and Confusion" would spring up on every side and while Englishmen were cutting each other's throats to attain their natural liberties, the French and Spaniards would be quietly preparing to invade England and divide the British Empire.

Despite the menace to the peace of the empire raised by the conflicting ideologies of Englishmen and Americans, many of the upper-class Englishmen who constituted the ruling clique were slow to bestir themselves. Instead of acting vigorously against their disaffected subjects overseas, they were disposed to trust to England's genius for "muddling through." Until 1774, as a result, the home government tended to assess too lightly the opposition in British America to its authority. It regarded the ferment overseas as a reflection of the mobs and riots in the mother country; mobs were too frequent in London to be alarming when they appeared in New York and Boston. The colonial disturbances could be plausibly explained as evidence that "the spirit of riot, which has so long disturbed the repose of this island, has at length infected our colo-

[64] *New York Mercury*, May 27, 1765. Pulteney, 16–17.
[65] *The Repository . . . of Politics and Literature*, London, 1771, I, 467.
[66] *Public Advertiser*, March 24, 1766. MacFarlane, 245, 246, 252.

nies." [67] Thus the American struggle for liberty appeared to be of no greater consequence than the huzzaing of a few drunken yokels and mechanics at the English hustings. It was not that the times were out of joint: it was merely that a few office-hungry politicians in Great Britain and America had taught the lower classes "in the jollity of their drunkenness, to cry out that they were undone," and in this state they "signed papers that they have never read, and determined questions that they do not know; roared against oppression and tyranny . . . and staggered home with impunity, swearing they were in danger of slavery, while every one they met, who did not join in their cry, was in danger of a broken head." [68] Many of the English ministers were too cynical to believe that the colonial patriots were sincere: it seemed more probable that, as Dr. Johnson said, they were "incendiaries, that hope to rob in the tumults of a conflagration, and toss brands among a rabble passively combustible." [69] This led inescapably to the conclusion that the revolutionary movement was the work of a few self-seeking "factious demagogues, whom if you could catch and hang, all would be quiet." [70] A dozen Americans swinging on Tyburn would set matters right in the British Empire; there was no necessity to examine into the grievances of the colonists, only to weed out the irreconcilables. As late as April, 1775, on the eve of the battle of Lexington, the British government was still deluding itself that if Hancock and Adams could be brought to trial in England and punished in a manner to strike terror among the other colonial rabble-rousers, the rebellion would collapse. [71]

After Englishmen had become convinced in 1775–1776 that the Americans were seeking to make themselves independent of the mother country, there can be little wonder that they chose to attempt to keep the "erring children" forcibly within the empire rather than permit them to go in peace. It was not only a matter of preserving "the beauty, excellence and perfection of the British constitution" from defilement at the hands of the provincials; the existence of Great Britain as a great power seemed to depend upon

[67] *Pennsylvania Journal,* January 30, 1766. *Public Advertiser,* December 9, 1769.
[68] *Parliamentary History,* XVI, 759.
[69] Johnson, *Taxation No Tyranny,* 68.
[70] *The Writings of Benjamin Franklin,* VI, 135.
[71] *Public Ledger,* April 7, 1774. *Gazetteer and New Daily Advertiser,* February 3, 1775.

maintaining its sovereignty over the American colonies. English-men had never played for higher stakes: if they lost, Great Britain appeared certain to "revert to her primitive insignificancy in the map of the world," and perhaps fall prey to France and Spain.[72] The commercial prosperity of England was believed to depend upon the colonial market; the British fleet drew vital masts and naval stores from New England and the Southern colonies; and the trade with British America was a great "nursery" of British seamen. With the fate of their country in the balance, many Englishmen found the sovereignty of Great Britain "a cause to fight for, to bleed and die for."

II

CONFRONTED with the fact that the British Empire was a house divided against itself, a handful of Englishmen began to seek means of reconciling the jarring views of Englishmen and Americans. They recognized that the colonists would not yield their conviction that the principle of no taxation without representation was an integral part of the laws of nature and the British Constitution; yet it was equally clear that Englishmen would never surrender the supremacy of Parliament over the empire. This deadlock threatened to disrupt the empire unless men of good will on both sides of the Atlantic succeeded in composing their differences. The English advocates of compromise found a way out of the blind alley into which George Grenville had led the mother country, in the proposal that colonial representatives be admitted to Parliament. It was far wiser, they pointed out, to throw open the door to Americans than to keep them outside until they had battered the house down.

This scheme of imperial federation would, it was hoped, bring peace to the empire by removing the colonists' grievances and, at the same time, strengthen Parliament's claim to supremacy over the empire. Thus, dissension would be silenced; the colonists would look upon the mother country with new trust and affection; and Amer-

[72] *Parliamentary History*, XVIII, 356–357.

icans and Englishmen might once again lie down "in Peace and Concord and mutual Felicity." The granting of such representation would ensure the colonists' obedience and settle for all time the constitutional dispute that racked the empire. It was, besides, no more than just. Certainly, it was as fitting that a North American colony should be represented in Parliament as "a little Cornish borough of ten barns and ale-houses." [73] In taxing Americans without representation, Great Britain was treating them worse than Irishmen, for despite the Declaratory Act of 1719 Ireland was not taxed by the British Parliament. Furthermore, there was ample precedent for permitting citizens who raised the cry of no taxation without representation to elect representatives to Parliament. The statute of Henry VIII, for example, which gave the city of Chester the right to choose representatives to Parliament, declared that in their unrepresented state "the inhabitants thereof have been oftentimes touched and grieved with acts and statutes made within the said court of parliament, as well derogatory unto the most ancient jurisdiction, liberties and privileges thereof, as prejudicial unto the *common weal, quietness, and peace,* of his Majesty's subjects." [74]

The most active exponent of colonial representation was Thomas Crowley, a Quaker merchant who had traveled in the colonies and had gained some idea of the tenacity with which Americans clung to their political liberties. From 1765 to 1776, Crowley unremittingly urged imperial federation by means of an Act of Union. In 1766 he suggested that the Stamp Act be suspended until the next general election, when all qualified electors throughout the British Empire would be empowered to elect representatives to Parliament. No final decision ought to be made upon the rights of Parliament over the colonies, he said, until the subject had been thoroughly debated "in the first parliament of the British empire." No American, Crowley believed, could object to taxation by this truly imperial Parliament; but to prepare for all contingencies, he proposed to establish guarantees in the Act of Union which would prevent Americans from paying higher taxes than Englishmen.

The most thoroughgoing scheme of imperial federation, how-

---

[73] *Newport Mercury,* February 17, 1766. *Reflexions upon Representation in Parliament,* London, 1766, 26, 31. Thomas Crowley, *Letters and Disquisitions on various Subjects,* London, 1776, 9.

[74] *Ibid.,* 8–9.

ever, was that suggested by Francis Maseres in 1770. Maseres was a liberal-minded lawyer of the Inner Temple who had served as attorney general of Quebec from 1766 to 1769. In a pamphlet entitled *Considerations on the Expediency of Admitting Representatives from the American Colonies into the British House of Commons*, he declared that the idea of colonies independent of parliamentary control could not be accepted by any true friend of the British Empire. On the other hand, taxation by Parliament worked undoubted hardship upon the colonists and therefore it was "equitable and expedient" to grant them representation. He proposed to admit eighty representatives from the continental colonies and the British West Indies. No property qualifications were to be required of American representatives and they were to be elected yearly by the colonial assemblies in order to make them less open to bribery by the Crown and more active in their constituents' behalf. Maseres believed that the colonies ought to petition for this privilege — yet since it was evident that they would not, he advised Englishmen to swallow their pride and "comply . . . with the froward humour of the Americans" by making the first move. If the colonists rejected this offer, it would be clear to Englishmen that they were dealing with men who were bent upon attaining complete independence. The result of this unmasking of the colonists, Maseres believed, would be that all parties in Great Britain would unite against them and that they would speedily be brought under parliamentary control without the boon of representation.

Maseres advocated that the colonial assemblies be left in control of the internal affairs of the colonies; the authority of Parliament, although "supreme and incontestable," was to be exercised only in matters of general concern, such as taxation for the prosecution of war, regulations of trade, and issuance of money. There was to be no effort to create a civil list — royal government in America would continue to be dependent upon taxes levied and paid by the people. When it was thus stripped of all menace to colonial liberty, Maseres prophesied that the authority of Parliament would become "a blessed bond of union to all the various dominions." He argued that Americans need not fear to be outvoted in Parliament — Scotland sent only forty-five representatives yet Scotland could not complain that its interests were sacrificed to those of England. Moreover, the influence wielded by the West Indians revealed how powerful the American bloc might be in the House of Commons.[75]

In the *Wealth of Nations*, Adam Smith pleaded for Irish and colonial representation in Parliament to save the empire from impending dissolution. He believed that federation would bring many blessings, not the least of which was delivering the colonies from "those rancorous and virulent factions which are inseparable from small democracies." The only way to preserve Americans from destructive intestine feuds, he contended, was to transfer the scene of political struggle across the Atlantic. He admitted that Americans and Irishmen would be obliged to pay higher taxes after they had accepted imperial federation, but he urged them not to be blinded by the British national debt to the benefits of a closer connection with the mother country. As late as 1778, Adam Smith was still calling for federation although he was compelled to admit that the scheme had scarcely a single supporter outside of a few solitary philosophers like himself. Yet rather than plunge the colonies back into the old colonial system, Adam Smith wished to lay the foundations of the empire anew upon the principle of federalism. No other plan, in his opinion, tended more "to the prosperity, to the splendor, and to the duration of the empire." [76]

It is significant that none of the great English Whigs — Pitt, Camden, Burke, or Shelburne — approved imperial federation. Pitt, Shelburne, and Camden, it is true, upheld the American view that Parliament could not tax but could legislate for the colonies; but Burke and the vast majority of Whigs believed that Parliament enjoyed absolute sovereignty without admitting colonial representatives. Burke condemned the scheme as a "visionary union" which endangered the stability of the mother country's institutions. England, he feared, would be inundated with newfangled notions of representation; and the power of the Crown would be strengthened by the presence of colonial members who, because they received no salaries as members of Parliament, would be cheaply bought by the King. Besides, there was the "infinite difficulty" of apportioning representation "on a fair balance of wealth and numbers" throughout the British colonies. Burke, indeed, saw no end of objections to

[75] Francis Maseres, *Considerations on the Expediency of Admitting Representatives from the American Colonies into the British House of Commons*, London, 1770, 9, 21–22, 39–40.

[76] Adam Smith, *The Wealth of Nations*, 587–590. *American Historical Review*, July 1933, 714–720.

the scheme: petitions, contested elections, and double returns from
the colonies would involve the transportation of the petitioners and
members "with all their train of attorneys, solicitors, mayors, select
men, provost-marshals, and above five hundred or a thousand witnesses." No doubt the sight of this army trooping into the House
would be diverting to the members, but there was danger of losing
in time of war a goodly portion of the House and perhaps a considerable part of the inhabitants of the colonies. If this "constitutional fleet, loaded with members of parliament, returning officers,
petitions, and witnesses, the electors and elected," fell a prize to
the French or Spaniards, they would make a rich haul of American
politicians and throw the governmental machinery of the empire
into confusion.[77]

Imperial federation savored too strongly of equality between
mother country and colonies to be acceptable to many Englishmen.
It went against the grain of true-born Britons and outraged their
conviction that because the mother country was "the source and
origin of the colonies," it enjoyed a "natural right to dominion and
authority." Joshua Steele, an English pamphleteer, declared in
1766 that the proposal of admitting colonial representatives to Parliament "would go so much against the stomachs of some of our
countrymen, that it could never be got down; nay, would disgust
them to that degree, that I think they would not suffer any plan
to be brought before them that savoured of such a doctrine." [78]
Certainly, this was the view of the British government; and the
colonies were never invited to send representatives to Parliament
until Lord Carlisle, at the head of a Peace Commission, undertook to
wean them from the French Alliance late in 1778.

Most Englishmen took the ground that Parliament was sovereign
over the colonies without benefit of colonial representatives. The
colonists — except, of course, transported convicts — had gone to
the New World of their free will; and they ought to have known
that they thereby surrendered their right of voting for members of
Parliament. Assuredly, they had no right to complain because Englishmen could not work the miracle of bridging the Atlantic and
thus making colonial representation feasible. "Must British Subjects
remain *ungoverned,*" it was asked, "because they choose from in-

[77] *Works of Edmund Burke,* Boston, 1826, I, 305-307. *Correspondence of
Edmund Burke,* II, 311.
[78] Joshua Steele, *An Account of a Late Conference on the Occurrences in
America,* London, 1766, 23. *The Political Register,* London, 1768, II, 42-43.

terested Motives to continue where they themselves declare they *cannot be represented?* They may as well complain that we do not make them immortal." [79]

Some of the ablest Americans saw in imperial federation the best hope for the preservation of the empire. James Otis and Benjamin Franklin, both of whom were ardent imperialists at heart and revolutionists only by necessity, believed that it would strengthen the empire and leave colonial liberty intact. Otis pointed out that if American representatives sat in Parliament, English administrators would no longer be "as ignorant of the state of this country, as of the regions in Jupiter and Saturn"; instead, they would be able to turn to capable, informed colonists for advice and information.[80] Franklin would have made the admission of colonists to Parliament the occasion of a thorough reorganization of the British Empire. He proposed that the first truly imperial Parliament in history should wipe the slate clean and begin fresh: the Acts of Trade and all acts restraining colonial manufactures ought, he said, to be repealed in order that all legislation for the empire be the joint work of Englishmen and Americans. Franklin's scheme of federation was far more sweeping than those projected by his contemporaries; most of them assumed a priori the right of Parliament to legislate for the colonies without colonial representation and none proposed to tamper with the Acts of Trade. In 1766, Franklin drew up for his friend Thomas Pownall, likewise an advocate of imperial federation, a resolve to present to the House of Commons requesting colonial representation. The resolve was never presented; and although Franklin continued to toy with the idea, he never again attempted to bring it before Parliament, partly because his education in English politics cooled his romantic enthusiasm for British imperialism. "When I consider," wrote Franklin in 1774, "the extream Corruption prevalent among all Orders of Men in this old rotten State, and the glorious publick Virtue so predominant in our rising Country, I cannot but apprehend more Mischief than Benefit from a closer Union." [81]

Joseph Galloway of Pennsylvania, author of the plan of union rejected by the Continental Congress in 1774, was a firm believer

[79] *Public Advertiser,* January 21, 1775.
[80] James Otis, *Considerations on Behalf of the Colonies,* London, 1765, 9, 49, 73.
[81] William Franklin to Benjamin Franklin, August 22, 1767, Franklin MSS., American Philosophical Society. *Writings of Benjamin Franklin,* III, 239–240; IV, 400, 456.

in imperial federation. As early as 1765 he declared that the admission of the colonies to full participation "in the supreme councils of the State" must be granted or "that profound and excellent fabrick of civil polity will, ere long, crumble to pieces." [82] His plan of 1774 which called for the creation of an American Congress was in his own eyes second-best to giving the colonies representation in Parliament and was proposed only because he recognized, as did Otis and Franklin, that imperial federation was a lost cause.

The high-water mark of the movement for federation was reached in British America between George Grenville's announcement of the government's intention to tax the colonies and the outbreak of resistance to the Stamp Act in 1765. During this period, the idea of representation seemed to many colonists to offer the best security against oppressive taxation. Since Parliament had resolved to raise a revenue in the colonies, it was believed to be to Americans' interests to be represented there. When Richard Stockton of New Jersey learned of Grenville's plans, he declared that the colonies "must each of them send one or two of their most ingenious fellows, and enable them to get into the House of Commons, and maintain them there till they can maintain themselves, or else we shall be fleeced to some purpose." [83]

Little was heard in the colonies in favor of imperial federation, however, after the Stamp Act riots. James Otis recanted his opinion: and Americans hastened to place themselves on record as opposed to colonial representation. The Stamp Act Congress declared that the colonies could not be represented in Parliament; and the Massachusetts Circular Letter of 1768 said that taxation without any representation whatever was to be preferred to any schemes of imperial federation. The colonists discovered that it was a law of nature that they could not be represented in Parliament. The "vast and hazardous ocean" which separated them from the mother country was satisfactory evidence to most Americans that God ordained that separate legislatures must exist in the colonies. The scheme of imperial federation was condemned as the work of visionaries to whom "the vast Atlantic is no more . . . than a mere ferry." [84]

[82] Joseph Galloway to Benjamin Franklin, 1765, Franklin MSS., American Philosophical Society.

[83] Reed, I, 30.

[84] *New York Gazette or Weekly Post Boy*, January 9, 1766. *Public Advertiser*, April 22, 1774. John Cartwright, *American Independence, The Interest and Glory of Great Britain*, Philadelphia, 1776, 50. Bancroft, 118.

American representatives would be unable to communicate with their constituents; they would lose touch with the colonies; and if they sought to consult with Americans, they would spend most of their lives tossing about the Atlantic.[85]

The colonists' opposition to imperial federation revealed that they were seeking something more than the rights of Englishmen: they were striving for home rule. Colonial representation might have given Americans equal rights with Englishmen, but because it meant centralization of power in Great Britain, it was rejected. The roots of their opposition to imperial federation go back to the earliest period of colonial history. In 1641, the English Puritans urged the New Englanders to send a delegation to the English Parliament. "But consulting about it," wrote John Winthrop, "we declined the motion for this consideration, that if we should put ourselves under the protection of the parliament, we must then be subject to such laws as they should make, or at least such as they might impose upon us in which course though they should intend our good, yet it might prove very prejudicial to us."[86] When John Hughes, the Pennsylvania stamp master, urged Americans to petition for the privilege of sending members to Parliament, he was met with much the same answer: "O, no, we will not agree to that, because we have representatives of our own, and have always given money when we have been called on by the king or his ministers, and if that will not do, let us have a house of Commons in America, to settle what shall be the quota of each colony when money is wanted."[87] They insisted, in other words, upon being taxed by their own representatives in *America*. Dr. Samuel Johnson was quite right when he remarked that Americans would not "exchange solid money for such airy honour" as representation in Parliament.[88] As William Knox said, while the colonists exclaimed "against parliament for taxing them when they are not represented, they candidly declare they will not have representatives, lest they should be taxed

[85] It was pointed out, however, that "a voyage from America hath been very often performed in twenty days, and less expence than a journey from Scotland by land in a coach would cost." *London Chronicle*, April 9, 1774.

[86] *John Winthrop's Journal*, edited by J. K. Hosmer, Boston, 1908, II, 24.

[87] *A Collection of Interesting, Authentic Papers, relative to the Dispute between Great Britain and America*, edited by John Almon, London, 1777, 52–53.

[88] Johnson, *Taxation No Tyranny*, 54. Thomas Wharton to Benjamin Franklin, April 27, 1765, Franklin MSS., American Philosophical Society.

. . . the truth however is, that they are determined to get rid of the jurisdiction of parliament *in all cases whatsoever.*" [89]

Americans were seeking to escape from the jurisdiction of Parliament: imperial federation would mean that they had placed themselves irrevocably under its authority. Nevertheless, extremists on both sides of the Atlantic feared that the idea of imperial federation might furnish a basis for compromise between mother country and colonies. They therefore sought to discredit it beyond hope of redemption by directing against it a steady stream of propaganda. Colonial propagandists predicted that the American representatives would not remain virtuous after they had established themselves in London. They would quickly sink to the level of English politicians: places and pensions would be dangled before them, and they would forget their constituents completely in the round of feasts, balls, and debaucheries believed to be practised in fashionable London circles. One New Englander cynically remarked that he knew a merchant who would carry American representatives to England "for half what they would sell for when they arrived there." Thus it might be expected that a cargo of exemplary, righteous Whigs sent over by the colonies would return broken-down rakes and unprincipled timeservers. It was said that the only colonists in favor of the plan were those who imagined that they would be elected to Parliament and thereby given an opportunity to "riot seven years in the pleasures of England" safe from the scrutiny of their constituents. With such representation, the colonists would find that the greater part of the British national debt was being foisted upon them.[90]

In the hands of British propagandists, the admitting of colonial representatives to Parliament was made to the certain ruin of the mother country. Social and political upheaval would follow fast upon the heels of the newly elected American members, who might be expected to be little better than fifth columnists of democracy. Under their inspiration, every town and district would demand the right to elect representatives, with the result that boroughs would become valueless and property rights and the constitution would be overwhelmed together. The high American birth rate would soon en-

[89] Knox, 91.

[90] Martin Howard, *A Letter from a Gentleman at Halifax to his Friend in Rhode Island*, Newport, 1765, 12. *Newport Mercury*, January 23, 1775. *New York Journal or General Advertiser*, November 26, 1767.

able American representatives to dominate the House of Commons and to "remove the seat of empire to the inhospitable banks of the Oronoque or the Ohio, from the delightful borders of the Thames." These "plantation Senators" would seek to aggrandize the colonies at the expense of the mother country; the representation of the British West Indies in Parliament would mean, it was predicted, the triumph of sugar cane over hops and "barbacued hog over the roast-beef of the English." [91] The House of Commons, some Englishmen feared, would suffer severely in tone and respectability if uncouth colonials were permitted to take their seats in Westminster. Americans were deficient in the fine manners expected of members of Parliament: they could not even take snuff properly, much less play a creditable part in debate. New Englanders were pronounced to be "a crabbed race not very unlike their half-brothers, the Indians, for unsocial principles, and an unrelenting cruelty"; and who would think of inviting a Mohawk to sit beside an English gentleman in Parliament? [92] Colonial rabble rousers would disgust members of Parliament who were unaccustomed to the antics of such low fellows. The scheme seemed, indeed, in many Englishmen's eyes, to be nothing less than inviting "the spawn of our transports" to "occupy the highest seats in our commonwealth." Having unloaded their convicts upon the colonies, Englishmen were understandably reluctant to receive them back as members of Parliament.[93]

Above all, Englishmen held dear their religion and their wives, yet even they seemed threatened by an "American invasion" of the British Parliament. "Would our morals be safe under Virginia legislators, or would our church be in no danger from pumpkin senators?" Englishmen anxiously asked; would not New England set about erecting "scaffolds for witches and quakers" and prisons for bishops and would not lecherous Virginians "attempt to corrupt our already too much corrupted morals?" [94] Although Americans answered that Virginians would bring about a much-needed reform in English morals and that New Englanders would save English

[91] *The Political Controversy*, London, 1762, I, 33. Tucker, *Four Tracts*, 177, 179. *Newport Mercury*, October 29, 1764; January 6, 1766. *The Constitutional Right of the Legislature of Great Britain to Tax the British Colonies in America, Impartially Stated*, London, 1768, 51.
[92] *Gazetteer and New Daily Advertiser*, November 7, 13, 1765.
[93] *The Political Register*, London, 1768, II, 43.
[94] *Gazetteer and New Daily Advertiser*, November 13, 19, 1765.

Protestantism from the rising tide of Popery, the apprehensions of Englishmen were by no means set at rest.[95]

Many English politicians opposed imperial federation because of the unhappy consequences, from their point of view, of the Union with Scotland. A horde of office-seekers from the north seemed to have descended upon England and in the person of Lord Bute, "the northern Thane," had attained the highest office in the land. The Scotch Menace became one of the best vote-getting issues in England: on the hustings and in the newspapers it was declared that Scotch members of Parliament sold themselves to the King rather than to the Whigs — a high political crime — and devoted themselves to pillaging England for the benefit of their famished constituents. The Scotch had feared that with the Act of Union, Scotland would be swallowed by England as Jonah was swallowed by the whale; but it now appeared that Jonah had swallowed the whale. While English office-seekers were striving to keep their heads above this "foul northern inundation," it would be folly to invite another flood from across the Atlantic.[96]

In the opinion of many Englishmen, Americans already enjoyed in the persons of the English Whigs as partisan representatives as they would have had if flaming patriots from Boston itself were admitted into the Commons. To reinforce these supporters of the American cause with actual representatives from the colonies would be to endanger British sovereignty and to import the dark abominations of Boston into the heart of the realm. Moreover, it was pointed out that the colonial agents in England already served to represent the interests of Americans at court and in Parliament. Elected by the colonial legislatures, such distinguished men as Benjamin Franklin and Edmund Burke served the colonies in capacity of agent, pleading their cause before the court, Privy Council, and, upon occasion, before Parliament. But the colonial agents could not be regarded as representatives of Americans in the British Parliament. Unless they were already members, they had no right to speak in the Commons or Lords and they had no power to bind the colonies. Their failure to prevent the passage of coercive legislation served, however, to prejudice Americans against imperial federation.[97]

[95] *Providence Gazette*, March 12, 1765, Supplement.
[96] *The Political Register*, London, 1767, I, 308–309. *The Works of Thomas Jefferson*, XII, 109.
[97] Edwin P. Tanner, "Colonial Agents in England during the Eighteenth

Hope for its success grew dim indeed after the colonial Nonimportation Agreement of 1768–1770. The hatred of Boston — the prime mover of the boycott — which swept England was turned against the idea of colonial representation. Should Englishmen, it was now asked, be obliged to take their seats with Boston "rebels" in the House of Commons — men who seemed to be as rancorous enemies of Great Britain as ever Carthaginians were of Rome? When Trecothick, a Boston-born member of the House of Commons, canvassed for re-election in 1768, he was told that since no Carthaginian would have been permitted to sit in the Roman Senate, so no Bostonian ought to be allowed to sit in the British Parliament. "I think we might now, with equal propriety, seek a representative from among the French or Spaniards, as from Boston," said an Englishman in 1768; "for neither of these countries have, as yet, outdone the Bostonians in malicious combinations against our existence." [98]

Century," *Political Science Quarterly*, 1901, XVI, 901. Beverly W. Bond, Jr., "The Colonial Agent as a Popular Representative," *Ibid.*, 1920, XXXV. *The Correspondence of Edmund Burke*, II, 312.

[98] *Gazetteer and New Daily Advertiser*, January 5, 1768. *The Political Register*, London, 1768, II, 123-125. *Pennsylvania Chronicle*, December 12, 1768.

CHAPTER   TEN

The Townshend Duties

Hon. Charles Townshend

I

AFTER the repeal of the Stamp Act, the Rockingham administration continued to seek to appease the colonists. The duty on molasses was reduced from threepence to one penny per gallon — although British as well as foreign molasses was now taxed; free ports were opened in the West Indies to permit the colonists to trade with the foreign islands; and bounties upon colonial products were increased. But for these as well as for the other measures by which they sought to bind up the wounds left by the Stamp Act, they won little popularity in England. The squires bitterly complained that the Whigs had "sacrificed the landed gentlemen to the interests of traders and colonists." [1] By the repeal of the Stamp and Cider Acts, the Whigs had cut over £130,000 from the government's revenue — which the squires feared would be made good by a land tax of six shillings in the pound. The King, for his part, was weary of the Whigs and wished heartily to be rid of them, although he feared to make a change lest he again fall into the hands of George Grenville, for whom his loathing was unabated. But William Pitt, who had refused to join the Rockingham Ministry and publicly declared himself in agreement with the King's views upon the necessity of extirpating partisan politics in England, now stood ready to make his peace with George III. Indeed, Pitt seemed to be the King's best hope of saving himself from the dictatorial George Grenville and "to extricate this Country out of faction" by uniting all Englishmen in a single party founded upon the principle of loyalty to the Crown. Therefore, in August 1766 — a little more than a year after the Rockingham Whigs had taken office — the King dismissed them and summoned William Pitt, soon to assume the title of Lord Chatham, to form a ministry. [2]

---

[1] *A Collection of Scarce and Interesting Tracts*, London, 1767, 68–69.
[2] *Letters from George III to Lord Bute*, edited by Romney Sedgwick, London, 1939, 250–254. *A Collection of Scarce and Interesting Tracts*, London, 1767, 68–69. *Gazetteer and New Daily Advertiser*, March 17, 1766. L. Stuart

No appointment could have been more welcome to Americans. In their eyes, Chatham was the hero of the Stamp Act repeal. It was he who had thundered against the tyranny of the act; he had opposed the Declaratory Act; and it was he who had declared that Americans had a God-given right to tax themselves. He was regarded, indeed, as the man who had saved the British Empire from Grenville and Bute, just as he had preserved it from the French during the Seven Years' War. Statues of Chatham were erected in several cities: in New York, a white marble statue of Pitt in a Roman toga was raised in Wall Street. The colonists emptied their deepest bumpers toasting "the illustrious MR. PITT, under GOD, and the KING, the Saviour of Britain, and the Redeemer of America." [3] Some of the panegyrics lavished upon Chatham would seem to have been written after the bowls had been emptied and Americans were in a high state of mellowness. Chatham, said Ezra Stiles, was "the most penetrating political Genius, the most upright & Sagacious Legislator, that ever appeared on earth. I am sure Lycurgus, Plato, Cicero, Selden, or the venetian Paul," he continued, "had not the amazing Compass & force of Genius, which shines in Lord Chatham." He was hailed as the American "Moses," "Guardian angel of British Liberty," "that stupendous COMET," "the glory of Britain, the wonder of the world, who twice rescued these infant colonies from ruin." [4]

Chatham's popularity in the colonies had been chilled, however, by his acceptance of a peerage. His admirers hoped to the last that he would refuse the "bribe" and remain the Great Commoner; but it was soon apparent that "no girl could shew more impatience for a new toy" than did Pitt for a peerage. The spectacle of the Great Commoner "sinking into a peerage" dismayed the patriots. "The corrupt and profligate," they groaned, rejoiced in Pitt's translation to the Lords and sang "Te Deum, as the Devil probably did for the fall of man." [5]

But there was no reason to suppose that in accepting a title

Sutherland, "Edmund Burke and the First Rockingham Ministry," *English Historical Review*, XLVII, 66–67.

[3] Chauncy, 31.

[4] Ezra Stiles to Benjamin Gale, July 31, 1767, Stiles MSS., Yale University Library. *The South Carolina Historical and Genealogical Magazine*, Charleston, 1927, XXVIII, 79. *New Hampshire Gazette*, June 20, 1766. *Boston Gazette*, February 1, 1768. Mayhew, *The Snare Broken*, iv, viii.

[5] *The Lee Papers*, I, 57–58.

Chatham had surrendered his conviction that Parliament could not tax the colonies. So long as he remained in power, colonial political liberties seemed secure and Americans need have no fears of the Declaratory Act. Nevertheless, despite Chatham's good will towards the colonists and his "American principles," his administration marked the reopening of the dispute with the colonies and the second great effort by the British government to raise a revenue from America.

Chatham quickly found that the chalice handed him by Rockingham still contained dregs of the poison left by George Grenville. By no means all the grievances dating from Grenville's administration had been removed by the repeal of the Stamp Act: the slate was not yet sufficiently clean to satisfy the American patriots. The Mutiny Act of 1765, in particular, continued to embitter relations between mother country and colonies. When first drawn up, the Mutiny Act had given British officers in the colonies the right to quarter troops in private houses. Contrary to the belief widely held in America, this provision was not the work of George Grenville but of the army officers themselves; and it intended not to destroy colonial liberty, as Americans supposed, but to remedy the shortage of barracks and public houses which made it impossible to quarter large bodies of troops in the colonial seaports.[6] This provision of the Mutiny Act was struck out when it became apparent that it would meet with resistance in the colonies; but the damage had already been done and Americans were convinced that the British government harbored designs to turn their houses into barracks and expose "the Chastity of our Wives and Daughters . . . to the insulting Arrogance of a rude and unpolished Soldiery." Even after the Mutiny Act had been altered to give British officers the right to quarter troops only in empty houses and barns where barracks were lacking, it was still under suspicion. But no British army was sent to dragoon the colonists and the Americans were soon too busy terrorizing stamp masters and hanging prominent British statesmen in effigy to pay it much heed.

It was not until after the repeal of the Stamp Act that the Mutiny Act came to be regarded as an intolerable grievance. By its provisions, the American assemblies were required to provide barracks,

<hr/>

[6] *New Hampshire Gazette*, July 26, 1765. *Pennsylvania Chronicle*, April 25, 1768. *Grenville Papers*, London, 1853, III, 12–13. *Correspondence of William Pitt, Earl of Chatham*, London, 1839, III, 208.

fuel, candles, vinegar, salt, and beer or cider for British troops. The Stamp Act had sought to raise money in the colonies for the needs of the British army; yet it was clear that if Parliament could compel Americans to supply British troops with necessities, the mother country had lost nothing by repealing the Stamp Act and might still oblige Americans to pay the bills for "defending, protecting, and securing" the colonies. Thus, under the Mutiny Act, Parliament could violate the principle of no taxation without representation as effectively as though the Stamp Act remained upon the statute books. What difference was there, asked the colonial patriots, between Parliament's taxing the colonists directly and requiring colonial assemblies to lay taxes upon their constituents to serve the ends of Parliament? If colonial assemblies were to be compelled to obey the "Dictatorial Mandates" of Parliament, they pointed out, the "very Essence of the Idea of a free Representation is totally extinguish'd and destroy'd." Indeed, if the colonial legislatures were to take orders from Parliament in matters of taxation, they might as well close their doors and save American taxpayers money. Blackstone, the famous constitutional lawyer, declared that the Mutiny Act was a tax; and as such it established a precedent for what was expected to be the next step of the British government: to oblige the colonies to pay for the support of the troops quartered in America and thus to achieve by stealth and stratagem what the Stamp Act had failed to accomplish by forthright methods.[7]

The Massachusetts Whigs first set the colonies the example of nullifying the Mutiny Act. In 1766, a ship with two companies of artillery aboard was driven by storms into Boston Harbor. The commanding officer applied to the governor, as the Mutiny Act directed, for barracks, fuel, and candles; and Governor Bernard sent this request to the Council. The councilors acted in obedience to the law and ordered the supplies to be sent to Castle William, where the storm-bound soldiers had taken refuge. Immediately, Boston was in an uproar. James Otis declared that he "would as soon vote for the Devil as he would for such Councellors as were betraying the liberties of their Country by inserting Acts of parliament into the provincial law books." The Massachusetts Council, he observed, needed a purging: it had, said Otis, "got the disease of Mary Mag-

[7] *Pennsylvania Chronicle*, April 25, May 23, 1768. *New York Journal or General Advertiser*, December 1, 1768. *Virginia Gazette* (Rind's), July 21, 1768. *American Historical Review*, 1911, XVII, 569.

dalen, had 7 devils in it, which must be cast out before it could recover." [8] As a result of Otis's tirade, the House of Representatives refused to vote supplies for the troops. Since this contumacy was not punished by the British government, it was not remarkable that other colonies sought to save both their principles and their money by following the New Englanders' example. Henceforth British officers found themselves engaged in a bitter struggle with the colonial assemblies to enforce the Mutiny Act. The action of Massachusetts had, wrote General Gage, "near annihilated all the Authority of the British Legislature over the Colonies." [9]

The storm center of this dispute was New York. Because New York was the headquarters of the British army in North America, furnishing the troops with supplies as required by the Mutiny Act promised to be a relatively heavy burden to New York taxpayers. The New York legislators, fired by the conviction that the Mutiny Act imposed an unconstitutional tax, refused outright to obey it, but at the same time they offered to obey royal requisitions for supplies for the troops — thus exalting the prerogative at the same time that they refused to obey acts of Parliament. To cap the province's iniquity in English eyes the New York merchants chose this moment to dispatch a petition to Parliament requesting to be freed from some of the restraints imposed upon colonial commerce by the Acts of Trade.

Most of the colonies declined to follow New York in brazenly defying the British government; in their opinion, circumlocution was the better part of valor. They preferred to accompany their grants of supplies to British troops with qualifications designed to preserve their constitutional principles and liberty of action. They provided for the soldiers either by acts of their own assemblies which took no notice of the Mutiny Act or, as in South Carolina, by refusing to include certain articles such as salt and beer as required by Parliament, in order to make their grant appear voluntary. New Jersey evaded the act by appointing commissioners who were instructed to act according to the custom of the province. Only Pennsylvania executed the Mutiny Act to the letter and thereby acknowledged it to be a binding law.

Opposition to the Mutiny Act became so widespread in the

[8] Governor Bernard to John Pownall, December 16, 1766, Bernard MSS., Harvard University Library.
[9] *The Correspondence of General Thomas Gage,* II, 546, 592.

colonies that Chatham concluded that the Stamp Act had "frightened those irritable and umbrageous people quite out of their senses"; and William Beckford, another stanch friend of the colonists, believed that "the devil has possessed the minds of the North Americans." [10] All over England there were heard demands for strong action against the colonies; appeasement had failed, was the cry, England must now act to preserve its sovereignty. If the colonies were permitted to nullify the Mutiny Act, they might nullify all acts of Parliament. In England, therefore, enforcement of the Mutiny Act was regarded as essential to the maintenance of British sovereignty just as in the colonies its defeat was believed to be essential to the preservation of colonial liberty.

Whatever its initial benevolence toward the colonies, the hand of the Chatham Ministry was forced by Americans' resistance to the Mutiny Act. Failure to act vigorously in this crisis might well have cost the ministers their seats. It was observed that George Grenville, champion of forceful methods in the colonies, began quickly to regain his popularity in the House of Commons and his prophecies of the dire consequences of repealing the Stamp Act were widely quoted. It was vital that the Ministry steal some of George Grenville's thunder. Benjamin Franklin once remarked that whenever Englishmen heard of discontent in the colonies, they cried: "Send over an army or a fleet, and reduce the dogs to *reason*." [11] In 1767, the Duke of Bedford and his followers screamed, as always, for bloody reprisals upon the colonies: send eight or nine regiments to New York, they urged, and let the Sons of Liberty fight if they dared. Charles Townshend, the Chancellor of the Exchequer, one of the surest weathercocks in England, quickly sensed from which direction the wind was blowing. In a speech before the Commons, Townshend declared that the colonies must be forced to yield to British authority because, as he said, "if we once lose the superintendency of the colonys this nation is undone"; and the thunderous applause which greeted his declamation left no doubt as to the eagerness of the House to come to grips with the colonists. In the House of Lords, Lord Camden, one of the few Englishmen who favored repealing the Declaratory Act, "held very stout language" against the colonies and was congratulated upon having at

---

[10] *Pitt Correspondence*, III, 193, 203, note, 206. *Collections of the Massachusetts Historical Society*, Fifth Series, Boston, 1885, IX, 216, 489.
[11] *Writings of Benjamin Franklin*, V, 128.

last seen Americans in their true light as rebels and seditious rogues.[12]

Chatham had inherited the Mutiny Act from George Grenville and the dispute with the colonies was not of his making. He bore a greater share of responsibility, however, for the measures undertaken during his administration which brought the quarrel between mother country and colonies to as white a heat as when George Grenville himself had applied the bellows. Like George III, Chatham was eager to slay "the hydra faction" and drive party politics out of England; and the composition of his Ministry reflected his aversion to party. He attempted to create a Ministry of all the talents which embraced men of every political hue and complexion. He insisted upon no uniformity of attitude toward the central issues of British politics nor did he seek to assemble about him men who seemed likely to work together in harmony. As a result, his Ministry was composed of "patriots and courtiers, king's friends and republicans; whigs and tories; treacherous friends and open enemies." It was observed that there was a more fundamental difference between the members of the government under Chatham than between the ins and the outs.

The most glittering ornament in Chatham's "Mosaic Ministry" was the Chancellor of the Exchequer, Charles Townshend. "Champagne Charley" Townshend was one of the flashiest politicians in England — the man who, in Burke's eulogy, was the fair-haired boy of the House of Commons, whose wit rocked the Whig taverns and whose charm made him the most sought-after man in society. But the qualities which endeared Townshend to fashionable hostesses and politicians were not useful in conducting the affairs of a great empire. Townshend changed his ideas almost as easily as he changed waistcoats; he had been known to harangue "most inimitably on both sides of the question" in the House of Commons and to be cheered in turn "by every party in the House." Even Townshend's ability to make a brilliant speech when drunk, while vastly increasing his prestige in the House, hardly fitted him to steer a course through the dangerous shoals that beset the path of British statesmen after 1763.

At the time of his appointment to the Chancellorship, Charles Townshend was not regarded as an enemy of the colonies. Although he had voted for the Stamp Act, he had also been active in its re-

---

[12] *Report on the MSS. of Mrs. Stopford-Sackville*, I, 120. *The Address of the People of Great Britain to the Inhabitants of America*, London, 1775, 34.

peal. In 1766, James Otis and Sam Adams had been instructed by the Massachusetts House of Representatives to thank him for his efforts in behalf of American liberty. Townshend was unwilling to enter Chatham's Ministry in 1766 because his salary in the pay office was twice the sum he would receive as Chancellor of the Exchequer. He declared that he would accept office under Chatham only if the King commanded him to do so. Not the least of George III's mistakes was his insistence that Townshend, the play-boy of British politics, become Chancellor of the Exchequer.[13]

Unhappily for the British Empire, Chatham's chronic gout laid him low in 1766 and he was obliged to retire to Bath. But the Earl's gout was beyond cure of physic and the Bath waters; his mind and body became increasingly impaired, and he began to reveal un-mistakable signs of insanity. With Chatham, the ostensible head of the Ministry, languishing at Bath, Townshend began to assume more and more "Ministerial airs" and to regard himself as Chatham's successor. Townshend's claims to head the Ministry were indeed well founded: he was the ablest speaker in the government, and almost alone of the cabinet members he had the facility of im-provising a policy to meet the successive crises which the Ministry of Lord Chatham encountered. He was well aware of his qualifica-tions and pointedly neglected to ask Chatham's advice. When the opposition denounced the administration on the ground that it was dominated by an "invisible influence," Townshend heatedly de-clared that he acted on his own and took orders from no great man behind the scenes.[14]

The restiveness of the squires under the wartime land tax of four shillings in the pound could no longer be ignored by an English Ministry. The disgruntlement of the squires had increased apace since the repeal of the Stamp Act and they were now in a rebel-lious mood. On the other hand, the expense of defending and ad-ministering the American colonies continued to mount alarmingly. The colonies cost the British government nearly four hundred thousand pounds a year; and Englishmen were becoming increas-ingly "alarmed and astonished at the growing charges and the heavy accounts and draughts brought in from America." A certain Major Farmer for example, sent to take possession of the Illinois country, drew £30,000 from the Exchequer. These expenses had to be borne

[13] *Pitt Correspondence*, III, 26, note. *New York Gazette*, May 6, 1766.
[14] *Report on the MSS. of Mrs. Stopford-Sackville*, I, 119.

by British taxpayers; the British government, as Englishmen were never weary of pointing out, could not *"command a single shilling"* from the rich and overbearing Americans.[15]

Here, clearly, was Townshend's opportunity of making a bid for popularity that would carry him to the premiership. In January 1767, therefore, he startled the House by declaring that he knew of a way to draw a revenue from the colonies without giving offense to Americans. He "laughed most unmercifully" at the distinction made by Americans — and by Chatham himself — between internal and external taxation, declaring that it was ridiculous to everyone except the Americans — and, he might have added, Lord Chatham. It was, he said, "perfect nonsense"; Parliament had the right to impose both external and internal taxes upon the colonies as it saw fit; and, he intimated, the rights of Parliament ought never to grow rusty from disuse. The spectacle of a member of Chatham's Ministry decrying the ideas of the head of the government did not apparently surprise the members: they were accustomed to hearing the ministers berate each other publicly and they were far too intent upon following Townshend's speech to be aware of the inconsistencies of his conduct. At the mention of the word "revenue" — "O blessed Word" — the squires pricked up their ears. The friends of the colonies observed with dismay that Townshend's "flippant boasting was received with strong marks of a blind and greedy approbation from the body of the House." George Grenville, believing that his colonial policy was at last to have its vindication, was immediately upon his feet pressing the Chancellor to pledge himself to raise a colonial revenue. Townshend could not have withdrawn had he wished; and under Grenville's prodding, he promised the House an American revenue which would reduce taxes in the mother country.[16]

Townshend had committed the Ministry to an American revenue — but he had acted without consulting his colleagues and contrary to their principles. Above all, Townshend had openly defied Chatham, the head of the Ministry: although Chatham was ready to "act with vigour to support the superiority of Great Britain over her

---

[15] *A New and Impartial Collection of Interesting Letters,* London, 1767, II, 138. *Virginia Gazette* (Purdie and Dixon), May 28, 1767. Lord Fitzmaurice, *Life of William Earl of Shelburne,* I, 304.

[16] Cavendish, II, 16. D. A. Winstanley, *Lord Chatham and the Whig Opposition,* 141. *Autobiography and Political Correspondence of Augustus Henry, Third Duke of Grafton,* edited by Sir William Anson, London, 1898, 137.

colonies," he was firmly opposed to taxing them. Yet the errant Chancellor was not dismissed. Chatham was nursing his gout at Bath and could not discuss business; and there was no one else in the cabinet with sufficient authority to remove Townshend. Moreover, the majority of the cabinet was thoroughly out of patience with the colonies and eager to vindicate British authority. Townshend had a plan and he was sufficiently strong-willed to impose it upon his reluctant colleagues. The ministers wished to be popular and to enjoy a long lease of power; and the House of Commons had given unmistakable signs that the shortest road to popularity was to impose taxes upon the colonies.

The demand for a revenue from the American colonies might have been less vehement had the British government been able to tap the resources of India. The nabobs returned to England laden with the spoils of the East; but the British government itself derived comparatively little direct financial benefit from India. By 1767, the corruption, mismanagement, and oppression of the East India Company had brought its affairs to the attention of Parliament. The East India Company exercised many of the rights of sovereignty in India and drew immense wealth from the country in the form of trade profits and territorial revenues. Its plight was owing primarily to the dishonesty and rapacity of its agents who lined their pockets with the company's money. Yet despite its dwindling revenue, the company paid lavish dividends to its stockholders; in 1766, the Court of Directors raised the dividend from 6 to 10 per cent in the face of an adverse financial report. The difficulties of the company seemed the British government's opportunity to strengthen its financial position. The London merchants were willing to pay a large sum to the government if the monopoly of the East India Company were abolished; and the government stood to profit from this arrangement by an increase in revenue from customs duties. Chatham and Shelburne would have gone farther: they proposed to divest the East India Company of its territorial revenues and transfer them to the British government. Chatham denounced "the lofty Asiatic plunderers of Leadenhall-street" — the headquarters of the company — who were pouring the wealth of the East into the laps of nabobs instead of into the coffers of the British Exchequer.[17] But Chatham found himself opposed in the cabinet by Charles Townshend, who proclaimed himself the

[17] *Pitt Correspondence*, IV, 16. *Political Register*, London, 1768, II, 137.

champion of charter rights and insisted that the charter of the East India Company be held sacred by the British government. He declared that the territorial revenues as well as the trade profits rightfully belonged to the company. As a result, he became the darling of the nabobs; and when he spoke in the Commons, the price of East India Company stock soared. With good reason, the directors and stockholders of the East India Company blessed Townshend; it was largely owing to his opposition that the cabinet was divided and Chatham's plan defeated in the House.[18]

The settlement ultimately arrived at in Parliament left the East India Company in possession of its territorial revenues as well as its trade profits, but it was obliged to pay the government £400,000 a year and submit to restrictions upon its dividends. Townshend even voted against giving the government the power to limit dividends, thus resisting to the bitter end any extension of governmental authority over vested interests. Burke and the Rockingham Whigs likewise insisted upon the inviolability of the East India Company's charter. In their eyes, Chatham's plan was merely "a design of fleecing the Company" to enrich the Crown and enable it to rule without Parliament. Burke declared that government regulation was "an infringement upon charter-rights as the spirit of Englishmen ought not to brook; and such a violation of the constitution, as might indeed be paralleled, but could not be exceeded in the annals of any country, how despotic soever." [19] But Townshend's and Burke's efforts in behalf of the East India Company, though not wholly successful, proved costly for the British government. The territorial revenues derived from India were permitted to remain in the hands of the East India Company — revenue which might have relieved the pressing financial needs of the British government. Not all the wealth of India, however, would have weakened the conviction held by many Englishmen that the colonies must be taxed. Townshend's successful opposition to the appropriation by the government of the East India Company's territorial revenue merely gave added point to the necessity of taxing the colonies to relieve British taxpayers.

The squires impatiently waited for Charles Townshend to pro-

[18] *Report on the MSS. of Mrs. Stopford-Sackville*, I, 124. *Parliamentary History*, XVII, 124. Fitzmaurice, I, 295, 298, 299. *Pitt Correspondence*, III, 196, note, 199, 200.
[19] *Parliamentary History*, XVII, 819.

duce the plan which, he had assured the House, would work the miracle of raising a colonial revenue and decreasing taxes at home without offending the colonists. But Townshend made no move and his silence began to arouse the suspicion that he was merely throwing a sop to the country gentlemen to keep them quiet while they were being bled white by taxation. Several ministers put the squires into a panic by declaring that the four-shilling tax must be continued until the national debt had been paid. Townshend himself told the House that it would be necessary to maintain the wartime rate on the land tax for at least another year in order "to give room for the most brilliant operation of finance, which this country ever saw." The country gentlemen demanded deeds not words; and despite Townshend's promises of speedy relief from taxation, the members began to show an alarming disposition to take matters into their own hands. The landed gentry, it was said, was "not again to be told that it is still *virtually* war." [20]

The opposition recognized that the discontent of the squires gave them a golden opportunity to overthrow the Ministry. All factions of the opposition set about encouraging the country gentlemen to throw off the traces. Rockingham instructed his followers that "a little *pathos* about the middling *small* landed gentry and country clergy is not amiss." So effective was this attack that in the House of Lords the Ministry soon had a majority of only three, including the votes of the King's brothers "and some lords brought down from their very beds." George III observed with dismay this coalition of factions; "the Bedfords, and the Rockinghams," he exclaimed, "are joined with intention to storm my closet." [21] Yet not all the King's men in the House could stamp out the revolt. In defiance of the Ministry, the Commons voted to reduce the land tax from four to three shillings in the pound, thus depriving the British government of almost half a million pounds a year in revenue and presenting Charles Townshend with the necessity of making good the loss by finding other sources of supply. [22]

The bad news from London threw Chatham into a "sort of constant hectick fever." He immediately came up to town so "full of

[20] *Memoirs of the Marquis of Rockingham*, II, 36, 40. *The Parliamentary Register*, II, 41. *Parliamentary History*, London, 1816, XVI, 362.
[21] *Pitt Correspondence*, III, 258, 261.
[22] *Ibid.*, III, 224, 232. Augustus Henry, Duke of Grafton, *Autobiography*, 122–124. *Virginia Gazette* (Purdie and Dixon), June 18, 1767.

gout" that he could not move hand or foot; only his determination to get rid of Townshend, to whose bungling he ascribed the defeat on the land tax, sustained him. In London, he opened negotiations with Lord North, the head of the "Bute faction" in the House, to take Townshend's place at the Exchequer, but North declined to risk sailing with an invalid skipper and a mutinous crew. In the midst of Chatham's efforts to save his administration, his ailments returned with redoubled fury — it was whispered that "a bungling physician has checked his gout, and thrown it upon his nerves" — and he was obliged to return to the seclusion of his estate. Only "a good natural fit," his doctors said, could dispel his gout and purge his mind of its dark humors. It is clear that Charles Townshend as well as the gout had got on Chatham's nerves and was playing havoc with his already shattered constitution. Indeed, Charles Townshend was uncommonly poor company for a nervous man. In any event, Chatham was seen no more in London; he withdrew to his closet, and bare mention of business caused him to writhe in agony. Even his colleagues in the Ministry who supported his policies were denied an opportunity to see him: his "knocker is tied up, and he is inaccessible," sorrowfully remarked Lord Camden.[23]

In Chatham's absence, Charles Townshend, still the strong man of the Ministry despite his defeat on the land tax, assumed command of the badly disorganized administration forces. He believed that the Ministry could yet be saved if a vigorous colonial policy were adopted. He had promised the House of Commons a colonial revenue and now, with half a million pounds sliced from the government's revenue, it was clear that he must make good his word. What had been originally perhaps merely "flippant boasting" to put the squires in good humor became now vital to the existence of the Ministry. Townshend declared that "England was undone" if the colonies were not taxed: certainly the Ministry was undone if an American revenue was not forthcoming. To meet this crisis, he adopted Grenville's policy of economy and taxation. Townshend demanded that colonial expenses be reduced by withdrawing the greater part of the British troops in North America from the frontier and holding the West with a mere skeleton force. The British army was not to be withdrawn entirely from the colonies —

[23] *Grenville Papers*, IV, 250. Grafton, 161. *Virginia Gazette* (Purdie and Dixon), June 18, 1767.

Townshend declared that he would resign his office rather than leave America open to a French invasion — but it was to be posted in the settled regions where its maintenance was less costly to the British government. "An American army, and consequently an American revenue, are essentially necessary," he exclaimed; "but I am willing to have both in the manner most easy to the people, and will pursue the most moderate measures consistent with the attainment of these important objects." He declared in the cabinet that unless his demand for taxation and economy were adopted he would resign as Chancellor. Townshend's resignation would, in all probability, mean the end of the Ministry; and so, finding the wolves dangerously near, the ministers determined to save their seats by throwing the colonies to the pack.[24]

After his triumph in the cabinet, Townshend laid before Parliament his long-awaited proposals for enforcing the Mutiny Act and drawing a revenue from the colonies. Contrary to the Bedfords' wish that all the colonies concerned in resisting the Mutiny Act be punished, Townshend decided to single out New York. Moreover, the Chancellor declared that he "could bear to hear of nothing military." Such squeamishness in a British minister was no doubt shocking to the Bedfords, but Townshend brilliantly defended his refusal to use military force and to punish the colonies indiscriminately. The Bedfords' policy, he declared, was certain to produce another union of the colonies against the mother country: only by attacking each colony singly and with the civil rather than with the military power could Great Britain keep Americans apart.

He proposed, therefore, to suspend the New York Assembly until it signified its willingness to comply with the Mutiny Act. Townshend prided himself upon the moderation and forbearance he displayed toward New York; and, unlike his other measures relating to the colonies, he had the approval of most of his colleagues in the cabinet. Although Conway disapproved, Grafton expressed the view of the majority when he pronounced it to be a "temperate, but dignified proceeding, and purposely avoided all harsh and positive penalties." Shelburne, Camden, and Chatham himself commended the measure; New York's disobedience had been so flagrant that liberalism toward the colonies was rapidly evaporating. Chatham and his followers, it will be observed, were now in office: they were no longer critics and obstructionists but the upholders

[24] Fitzmaurice, I, 308–309. Winstanley, 141–142. Grafton, 127.

of British sovereignty. This change of circumstances obliged them to do the very thing they had bitterly condemned when out of power.[25]

Having laid down excellent precepts for the guidance of the House of Commons to prevent colonial union, Townshend, with all the inconsistency for which he was famed, proceeded to violate them by imposing taxes upon the colonies – the most certain method of uniting Americans. He advised that Parliament levy duties upon glass, lead, paint, paper, and tea, the proceeds of which were to be appropriated by the British Exchequer and used to defray "the charge of the administration of justice, and the support of civil government, in such provinces where it shall be found necessary," and the cost of defending the colonies. At the same time, Townshend urged that an American Board of Commissioners of the Customs be established to enforce navigation acts and revenue laws. It was noted that in laying these proposals before the House, Townshend completely discarded his air of levity: he indulged in none of the "wanton sallies of a man of parts and pleasure," speaking instead in a businesslike manner "but too well calculated," remarked an observer, "to inflame the passions of a legislature whose authority was called in question."

The first reaction to the duties was disappointment at the smallness of the sum to be raised by them. Townshend did not expect them to produce more than £40,000 a year – which was small change, many members observed, in comparison with the loss of revenue suffered by the government in the reduction of the land tax. After much labor, Townshend seemed to have brought forth a mouse – to the chagrin of the squires who had looked forward to a mountain of gold from the colonies. Their only consolation was the reflection that from this small beginning, great things might grow, and, in Townshend's own words, once the precedent had been established, colonial revenue "might in time ease this country of a considerable burden." But it was evident that the country gentlemen and the Bedfords would be obliged to wait for this blessing: the Townshend duties alone would not in themselves relieve British taxpayers or contribute to the happiness of political jobholders.

Opposition to the Townshend duties created strange bedfellows

[25] Winstanley, 130, 140. Horace Walpole, *Memoirs of the Reign of King George the Third*, London, 1845, III, 21–24. Grafton, 126.

in British politics: Burke and Grenville both cast their votes against the act. Burke was in opposition because he believed that the Townshend duties did not differ essentially from the Stamp Act; he predicted that Americans would likewise see the similarity and England would not receive a shilling from America in the form of taxes whether external or internal. Grenville declared that the Townshend duties would do greater injury to British merchants and manufacturers than good to the British Exchequer: as taxes upon British commodities they were impolitic and "uncommercial." Grenville, too, warned Townshend that the Americans would trump up arguments against external taxes as easily as they had against internal taxes: "They will laugh at you," he said, "for your distinctions about regulations of trade." Grenville was a sadder but hardly a wiser man after he had burned his fingers with the Stamp Act: he still insisted upon the necessity of drawing a revenue from the colonies. He proposed, as an alternative to the Townshend duties, to raise £400,000 a year by requisitions upon the colonies. But Pitt's description of Grenville as "a miserable financier" who had succeeded in fetching "a pepper-corn into the exchequer, to the loss of millions to the nation," still stuck to him. Certainly, most members of Parliament preferred to attach themselves to "that high-flying kite," Charles Townshend, in his quest of a colonial revenue, rather than try another leap in the dark with George Grenville.[26]

The Townshend duties, like the Stamp Act, "stole through the House; no man knew how it passed." [27] The vote in the House of Commons was 180 to 98; but the opposition based its arguments upon the impolitic nature of the duties rather than upon the danger that they would revive the constitutional dispute between mother country and colonies. The British Empire was lost as well as acquired in a state of absence of mind. After the Townshend duties had produced an explosion in the colonies that rocked the empire, many members of Parliament wondered how it happened that they had unwittingly lighted this train of gunpowder. Lord Rockingham, who made no effort to defeat the duties, later declared that they "originated from no plan of policy whatever, but were merely the result of picque and passion" on the part of Charles

[26] Cavendish, I, 39, 217. *Parliamentary History*, XVI, 106. Grafton, 176, 180. *Pitt Correspondence*, III, 178.
[27] Cavendish, I, 215.

Townshend. The great majority of the House, it is evident, voted for Townshend's duties because they wished to raise a colonial revenue, punish the colonies for their ill-behavior after the repeal of the Stamp Act, and exercise the rights to which Parliament laid claim in the Declaratory Act. Great Britain must exercise its right of taxing the colonies, it was urged, otherwise Americans would give free reign to their "high and imperious ambition of being themselves, a nation of independent states." [28]

In his own opinion, Townshend had hit upon an infallible method of raising a colonial revenue; simply by taking Americans at their word, the British government could get everything it wanted from the colonies. Townshend and his supporters made much of the fact that the taxes levied by Parliament in 1767 were port duties which, by the colonists' own definition, were external taxes and therefore within the power of Parliament to impose. These duties were, it was said, "perfectly consistent with Doctor Franklin's own arguments, while he was soliciting the repeal of the stamp-act." [29] Americans could keep their principles — it was enough for Townshend if the British government secured a revenue; and he was content to let them spin out theories and draw distinctions — which did not exist — between internal and external taxation as long as they paid taxes in hard cash to the British government. If Americans could swallow the absurdity that there was a real difference between internal and external taxes, this proved, at least to Townshend's satisfaction, that they were a singularly doltish people who might easily be duped into paying taxes provided they were not called taxes. Townshend's attitude toward the colonists was not altogether dissimilar to that of a shell-game operator toward bumpkins at a country fair. Of course, they would fight if they were held up — the Stamp Act proved that — but Townshend, like a good bunco artist, preferred to trick them out of their money.

It is singular that Townshend, to whom consistency was the least prized of virtues, should have believed that Americans would surrender their liberties in order to be consistent. They had, it is true, acknowledged the legality of external taxation; but did that mean that they would cling to the principle even after it had become

[28] Walpole, III, 28. *Parliamentary History*, XVII, 1350. *Parliamentary Register*, II, 39. Grafton, 127.
[29] *An Englishman's Answer to the Address from the Delegates*, New York, 1775, 16.

apparent that it would cost them their freedom? Townshend's fundamental mistake lay in underestimating the intelligence as well as the strength of the American colonists.

Charles Townshend made an important contribution toward precipitating the American Revolution; and he belongs in that group of British statesmen who unwittingly helped to establish the United States of America. The central constitutional problem of the British Empire during the period from 1763 to 1776 was to find a compromise between the unlimited sovereignty of Parliament and the complete independence of the colonies. American political theorists and William Pitt put forward such a compromise by drawing a distinction between internal and external taxation. The British government refused to accept this distinction and insisted in the Declaratory Act of 1766 that the colonies must be subject to Parliament "in all cases whatsoever." For the most part Americans had overlooked the Declaratory Act and remained firmly attached to the doctrine of the limited sovereignty of Parliament. It was Townshend's work to demonstrate to Americans the futility of the distinction they had made between internal and external taxation and, in a larger sense, to reveal to them the folly of seeking any middle ground between the absolute sovereignty of Parliament and the rights of the colonies. He made it clear to Americans that Parliament's claims of jurisdiction over the colonies were not an empty assertion made to salve the pride of the mother country but a real threat against colonial liberty. Viewed in this light, the Declaratory Act was seen to be "a clear, concise, and comprehensive *definition* and sentence of *slavery*" — "the death-warrant" of colonial liberty which needed only "a Czarish king to put it into execution." [30] One way of reducing a great empire is to remove all bases for compromise between conflicting views. Charles Townshend carried the dispute between the colonies and the mother country a long stride toward the impasse in which Americans were to find no alternative but to submit to the despotic control of Parliament or deny its jurisdiction altogether. One fact he overlooked. Americans would throw off the jurisdiction of Parliament — and with it all British sovereignty — rather than submit to what they regarded as slavery.

[30] *Principles and Acts of the Revolution in America*, edited by H. Niles, Baltimore, 1822, 19, 176.

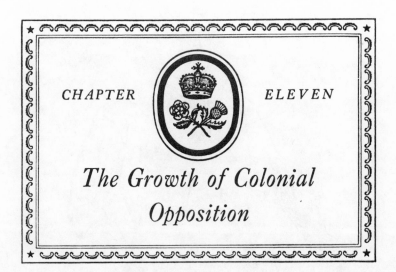

CHAPTER   ELEVEN

The Growth of Colonial
Opposition

Lord North

I

IN THE preamble to the Townshend duties, as Edmund Burke remarked, the colonial assemblies "thought they read their own annihilation." Even more seriously than the Stamp Act, the Townshend duties threatened to deprive the assemblies of the power of the purse.[1] The preamble of his law provided that the money raised by the duties upon tea, colors, glass, and paper should be used "for defraying the charge of the administration of justice, and the support of civil government" in the colonies. This meant that the civil list which the Crown had unsuccessfully attempted to establish in British America was now to be created by Parliament. Townshend ingeniously sought to take money from Americans by means of parliamentary taxation and to employ it against their liberties by making colonial governors and judges independent of the assemblies. No measure could have been more certain to encounter opposition in the colonies. James Otis declared that he preferred that the money raised by the Townshend duties should be sent to England "or to the German Gulph, or to the bottom of the sea," than to enable Hutchinson and his fellow oligarchs to "share in the spoils of their country."[2] But Charles Townshend had the satisfaction of dying in the belief that he had discovered the secret of painlessly stripping Americans of their money and their liberty. In the autumn of 1767, before opposition had manifested itself in the colonies, Townshend was unexpectedly plucked from this world, mourned by his friend Burke as the "delight and ornament of this House, and the charm of every private society which he honoured with his presence."

The suspension of the New York Legislature by Parliament for its refusal to obey the Mutiny Act evoked the first outcry in the colonies against the Townshend Acts. In the eyes of men who re-

[1] Cavendish, II, 18.
[2] *Collections of the Massachusetts Historical Society*, Fifth Series, Boston, 1885, IX, 239.

garded the provincial assemblies as local parliaments this measure was peculiarly sinister inasmuch as it reduced those assemblies to "poor contemptible air castles" which might be punctured at any moment by an act of Parliament. And, although the New York Assembly alone was punished, if the right of Parliament were admitted, every assembly on the continent that refused to obey parliamentary edicts might be annihilated. In its treatment of the New York Legislature, the Ministry had seemingly given warning of its intention to deprive Americans in general of their rights and privileges unless they handed over their money at its command. "Nothing," it was said, "could be more grating to the sons of liberty in every province. It was the club of power which, while it knocked down the New York assembly, threatened every other with the like." [3] The patriots inveighed against this "imperious mandate" and "high handed encroachment" as a "more despotic stride" than any taken by "the most arbitrary monarch of Europe" and they compared it to "the annihilation of the parliaments of France by Lewis the fifteenth." [4] Throughout the colonies, there were "horrid apprehensions of being reduced to a state of slavish dependence." [5] Rather than surrender their liberties without a struggle, the Boston Sons of Liberty began to talk, as they did during the Stamp Act crisis, of "wading thro' seas of blood, though stunn'd with the awful roar of cannon." [6]

This spirit was reflected by the New York fire-eaters who were eager to defy Parliament and call upon the other colonies for aid. By refusing to grant money to "those mercenaries" — that is, the British troops — the radicals told New Yorkers that they were certain of joining "the glorious company of martyrs to the British constitution." [7] On the other hand, the conservative, propertied members of society clearly perceived the risk of engaging in a quarrel with the mother country without assurances that their fellow Americans would spring to New York's defense; the colony, they pointed out, might "stand single in the Quarrel, and fall a helpless Sacrifice to the Indignation of the Commons of Great Britain." [8]

---

[3] Gordon, I, 216.
[4] *Massachusetts Spy*, March 17, 1775.
[5] *Pennsylvania Journal and Weekly Advertiser*, January 28, 1768.
[6] *Boston Gazette*, August 31, 1767.
[7] *Pennsylvania Journal and Weekly Advertiser*, May 28, 1770.
[8] *New York Gazette or Weekly Post Boy*, February 26, 1770. *Pennsylvania Journal and Weekly Advertiser*, February 22, 1770.

Englishmen were united upon the policy of coercing New York —
even Chatham approved punishing the colony — and therefore New
Yorkers must expect the full weight of British resentment. The
uncertainty of outside support and the certainty of British retaliation weakened the position of the radicals. The act suspending
the New York Legislature was to go into effect in October 1767,
but shortly before the deadline the assembly voted, by a majority of
a single vote, to supply the troops.

Yet if New Yorkers feared to hurl outright defiance at the British government, they did not hesitate to disobey by stealth. The
assembly made no mention of the Mutiny or Suspending Acts
by which it was required to appropriate money for the troops; instead, it voted £1500 for the troops in an act without preamble. By
this means, the assembly made its grant appear to be a free gift.
The Ministry, eager to wash its hands of this unprofitable dispute,
accepted the action of the New York Legislature as compliance
with the Mutiny Act, although George Grenville bitingly observed
that if Americans were permitted to ignore parliamentary laws
by such subterfuge, Parliament would shortly find itself without
real authority upon the North American continent.

Resistance to the other measures introduced by Townshend was
less rapid in getting under way. It might be supposed that after
Charles Townshend had revealed the determination of the British
government to seek out the weaknesses of the colonists' defenses
against parliamentary taxation and perhaps strike a fatal blow at
their freedom, Americans would have promptly taken the ground
that Parliament had no authority whatever over them. But the colonists were not yet prepared to regard the problem as a choice between slavery and complete independence of Parliament; instead,
they continued to think in terms of reconciling parliamentary authority with colonial freedom. Rather than deny altogether the
rights of Parliament over the colonies, they sought to find a basis
of compromise which, while preserving the principle of no taxation without representation, would admit a limited exercise of sovereignty by the Lords and Commons. The Massachusetts Circular
Letter of 1768 was the clearest statement made by Americans during
the revolutionary period of how colonial liberty could be preserved within the empire.

The purpose of the Massachusetts patriots in drawing up the
Circular Letter was to unite the continent against the Townshend

Acts upon the most advanced ground possible. The immediate necessity was to persuade Americans to take a firm stand against "external" taxation by Parliament in order to procure the repeal of the acts. The failure of Americans to adopt a strong position against all forms of parliamentary taxation in 1765 had enabled Charles Townshend to tax them in 1767 without violating "American principles." The Circular Letter was designed to throw up impregnable defenses against taxation by Parliament from every quarter and to make certain that colonial liberties were not destroyed by the Trojan horse of trade duties.

In spite of radical outbursts, conservatism still characterized the American mind, and since the Massachusetts patriots were seeking to unite Americans upon certain principles, they conformed to it in the Circular Letter of 1768. The Circular Letter cannot be said to express the real views of Sam Adams, who drafted it; but it does reveal that Adams was willing to sacrifice his radicalism in order to unite Americans. Even the word "joining" was omitted from the Letter lest it be construed as a call for a Continental Congress. Although the Letter called in question the right of the British government to pay the salaries of colonial governors and judges, it did not seek to throw off parliamentary sovereignty; on the contrary, Parliament was acknowledged to be "the supreme legislative Power over the whole Empire." Nevertheless, the Letter made it clear that the power of both Crown and Parliament over the colonies was limited and that the British Empire was governed by a fixed constitution based upon the immutable laws of nature. These laws, it was held, vested the power of the purse exclusively in the colonial assemblies; no taxes, internal or external, could be imposed by Parliament upon Americans because the principle of no taxation without representation was one of those fixed laws which neither King nor Parliament could override. Brushing aside the doctrine of virtual representation as unworthy of serious consideration, the Circular Letter declared that Americans were not represented in Parliament and never could be — and therefore could not accept the idea of imperial federation.

At the same time that the Massachusetts House of Representatives was debating the Circular Letter, colonial newspapers were bringing to their readers the *Letters of a Pennsylvania Farmer* by John Dickinson of Philadelphia. Dickinson, a lawyer educated in the Middle Temple, was a conservative patriot who throughout the revolutionary period was enamored of the legal aspects of the controversy between Great Britain and the colonies. He regarded the struggle as a fascinating law case and would have had it conducted with the same dignity and gentlemanly restraint that distinguished a court of law. In 1768, his moderation was fully in accord with the far from revolutionary temper of the American people. In his Farmer's Letters he popularized the fundamental doctrines which were later to be expressed in the Circular Letter: that Parliament was sovereign but that external taxation was illegal. Dickinson recognized, however, that an "incidental revenue" might accrue from duties designed to regulate trade. He argued that no exception could be taken to this addition to British revenues provided the intention of the government was to regulate trade rather than to raise revenue. In other words, the intent governed. In effect, as English writers were quick to point out, this meant that Great Britain could raise a small revenue in the colonies but not a large one. It represented, as well, another attempt to water down the doctrine of no taxation without representation in order to make it more acceptable to Parliament. Later, American patriots had no reason to thank John Dickinson for his fine-spun theories and hair-splitting distinctions. Thomas Jefferson, indeed, blamed him for having set back the revolutionary movement and pronounced Richard Bland, who had written in 1765, to be a more liberal thinker than John Dickinson. But the Farmer's Letters, at the time of their publication, were an immediate sensation and Dickinson came to be regarded as the spokesman of the American colonies.[9]

Most Americans saw no impropriety in the Massachusetts Circular Letter; its purpose seemed merely to win a redress of grievances by showing the British government how widespread was opposition in the colonies to the Townshend Acts. Moreover, it was distinctly mild in tone compared with what Americans were reading in their newspapers. It was far from a call to arms against British oppression; even many conservative supporters of colonial rights found little fault with it. It seemed to be merely a respectful, loyal, and temperate statement of the colonies' case against the Townshend Acts. Judging it in this light, the Virginia patriots in April 1768 approved the Massachusetts Circular Letter and sent a circular

[9] John Devotion to Ezra Stiles, February 8, 1768, Stiles MSS., Yale University Library.

letter of their own to the colonial assemblies reinforcing the Massachusetts plea for union against British taxation.[10]

The Circular Letter encountered strong opposition in Pennsylvania, where James Galloway and the Quaker political machine still held a tight rein. Although it was notorious that Galloway had advocated submission to the Stamp Act, his Toryism did not cost him any loss in prestige or influence in the Pennsylvania Assembly and in 1766 he was elected speaker. Galloway sought to keep Pennsylvania from taking part in other colonies' quarrels with the British government; and as long as he remained at the helm, the Pennsylvania Assembly seemed more likely to pass laws against "the trespassing spirit of encroaching hogs" than to engage in the defense of American liberties.[11]

Galloway deplored that the Farmer's Letters had been written by a Pennsylvanian — they were, he remarked, fit only for the "selectmen of Boston, and the mob meetings of Rhode Island." [12] His views were reflected by those Pennsylvania conservatives who protested against Bostonian laudation of Dickinson as a "BENEFACTOR OF MANKIND" who had saved America from tyranny. When an image of Dickinson was placed in the Boston Waxworks alongside George Whitefield and the Prodigal Son returning to his father, they swore that Bostonians were turning Dickinson's head and would soon make him a mob leader. They were even more deeply alarmed when John Hancock paid a visit to Philadelphia in order to sit at the feet of the Farmer. The next step, Philadelphia Tories sourly observed, would be the importation of town meetings into the Quaker City in imitation of the "*orderly republicans of Boston*" whose purpose, it was believed, was to create "an *American* bedlam, for mad *Whigs*." [13]

The Massachusetts Circular Letter, therefore, was under suspicion in Philadelphia merely because it came from Boston. After it had been read to the legislature it was ordered to be laid upon the table — where the conservatives hoped it would be buried for-

[10] William Allen to Thomas Penn, September 23, 1768, Penn MSS., Historical Society of Pennsylvania. *Pennsylvania Chronicle*, August 8, 1768; May 15, 1769.

[11] R. H. Lee, *Memoirs of the Life of R. H. Lee*, Philadelphia, 1825, 77.

[12] *Memoirs of the Historical Society of Pennsylvania*, Philadelphia, 1895, XIV, 281.

[13] *Pennsylvania Chronicle*, August 15 and 22, 1768. *Essex Gazette*, September 10, 1771.

ever. This action made the Pennsylvania Assembly a byword among patriots throughout the colonies: It was responsible, they declared, for "all the Bloodshed and Calamities" that might follow this refusal to preserve colonial unity against the British government.[14]

In this crisis, it was the English government itself which made certain that the Massachusetts Circular Letter should not be consigned to the wastebasket by the Pennsylvania Tories. In England, the Circular Letter was regarded as "little better than an incentive to Rebellion" and as laying the foundation for "a powerful *confederacy* and *combination*"; and George Grenville pronounced the Farmer's Letters to be an "impudent, seditious, infamous libel." [15] If strong action were not immediately taken, ran the cry, Americans would soon *deny* the authority of Parliament in "all cases whatsoever." The Ministry, disorganized by the death of Townshend and the continued ill-health of Chatham, was obliged by the popular clamor to leave off quarreling at least long enough to reprove the colonists. At a cabinet meeting in 1768, it was decided to send a circular letter to the colonies containing "kind and lenient" expressions which, it was hoped, would avert the danger of another union of the colonies. But Chatham's Ministry, although no longer vexed by Charles Townshend, had not seen the last of its evil geniuses. In 1768, Lord Hillsborough, an Irish peer, was appointed to the new office of Secretary of State for the Colonies in which control of American affairs was henceforth centralized. He was a man of so little tact and wisdom that George III later remarked that he did not know "a man of less judgment than Lord Hillsborough" and refused to approve his appointment as Lord Lieutenant of Ireland. In 1768, however, high hopes were placed in Hillsborough, particularly by those who knew him least. Enjoying greater authority over the colonies than any British administrator before him, he was expected to deliver the empire from its troubles. Hillsborough had hardly warmed the seat of his office before he blasted these expectations. He was entrusted with the task of writing the Ministry's circular letter; but in his hands the kindness and leniency were omitted and threats and sternness substituted. Camden and Grafton denounced Hillsborough for acting

[14] *The American Querist*, London, 1768–1769, 162–164.

[15] *Transactions of the Colonial Society of Massachusetts*, 1910–1911, Boston, 1912, XIII, 336. *Gazetteer and New Daily Advertiser*, September 30, 1768.

contrary to the will of the cabinet but the damage had been done — the circular letter was already on its way across the Atlantic.[16]

Had British policy been to unite the American colonies, the statesmen of the reign of George III would be regarded as the greatest in English history. When a British Minister took up his pen to address himself to the colonies, he was almost certain to produce a state paper which gave hope, comfort, and propaganda to the enemies of British authority. Lord Hillsborough's Circular Letter deserved to rank not far below the Stamp Act and Townshend duties among the contributions of British ministers to the formation of the American Union.

In this ill-starred dispatch, Hillsborough declared that because the Massachusetts Circular Letter was calculated "to promote an unwarrantable combination, and to excite open opposition to the authority of Parliament" the colonial governors were instructed to order the colonial assemblies to take no notice of it whatever — "which," he observed, "will be treating it with the contempt it deserves." Assemblies which insisted upon approving the Massachusetts Letter were to be prorogued or dissolved immediately. As for the Massachusetts General Court, it was to be required to rescind the Circular Letter on penalty of being dissolved by the royal governor. No Massachusetts Assembly, declared Hillsborough, would ever sit down to business in the colony until it had declared its "disapprobation of that rash and hasty proceeding." This clearly implied that the British government was prepared to compel submission even if it were necessary to deprive the colonists of their representative institutions.

Hillsborough's Circular Letter was denounced as a "Ministerial Mandate," fit perhaps for Turks and Frenchmen but not for Englishmen who possessed a spark of love of liberty. It was called "the most daring insult that ever was offered to any free legislature"; if Americans were to be prevented from making a united protest against British oppression they were in "a worse Situation than their Negroes (who have the privilege of Petitioning their masters whenever they please)."[17] After reading this high-handed ultimatum, many Americans began to consider whether it were not "nigh time to think of the Preservation of their Liberty in the best man-

[16] Grafton, 230–233.
[17] John Penn to Thomas Penn, July 31, 1768, Penn MSS., Historical Society of Pennsylvania. *Pennsylvania Chronicle*, December 19, 1768.

ner they can." George Washington, loyal to England as he was, declared his readiness to take up arms in defense of American freedom.[18]

Indeed, Lord Hillsborough had incautiously dropped a bombshell on the colonies which, instead of striking panic among Americans, made them fighting mad. Colonial assemblies that had been lukewarm toward the Massachusetts Circular Letter now enthusiastically adopted it — and were promptly prorogued for their pains. Even the Pennsylvania Legislature was roused by Hillsborough's "mandate"; "those persons who were the most moderate are now set in a flame and have joined in the General Cry of Liberty," reported the governor. It was Lord Hillsborough's Circular Letter that was treated with contempt by Americans — not the Massachusetts Letter. Instead of destroying the union of the colonies, Hillsborough had played into the hands of Sam Adams and the Massachusetts Whigs. Not even the most optimistic of the Massachusetts patriots had anticipated such good fortune as they now encountered. "*One spirit* animates all America," they exclaimed after the full consequences of Hillsborough's policy had been seen; "and both the *justice* and *importance* of the cause is so plain, that to *quench* the spirit, *all the colonies* must be absolutely *destroyed.*" Here was a lesson for British ministers: "the *tighter* the cord on unconstitutional power is drawn round this bundle of arrows, the *firmer* it will be." [19] Unfortunately for the British Empire, the lesson went over the heads of the statesmen at Westminster.

Nor did Hillsborough succeed in frightening the Massachusetts General Court into disavowing the Circular Letter. When they learned that they were ordered to rescind the Circular Letter the patriots exclaimed: "Good God! shall we be forever thus abus'd without Redress! Shall we be incessantly defamed as Rebels and Traytors?" [20] By a vote of 92 to 17, the House of Representatives refused to rescind, despite the royal instructions contained in Hillsborough's letter to Governor Bernard. Throughout America, the "glorious 92" were acclaimed heroes while the 17 rescinders were damned as traitors and British tools. Paul Revere pictured in a widely circulated cartoon the rescinders marching into hell.

[18] *The Revolutionary Diplomatic Correspondence of the United States,* edited by Francis Wharton, Washington, 1889, II, 342.
[19] *Boston Evening Post,* April 10, May 15, 1769.
[20] *Boston Gazette,* July 11, 1768.

"SEVENTEEN such Miscreants sure will startle Hell," it was re-marked ". . . and the outdone DEVIL will resign his sway." Most of the rescinders were purged at the next election when Sam Adams associated them with Popery, which, to most New Eng-landers, was synonymous with tyranny, oppression, and every other abomination.

The Townshend duties struck at the roots of colonial liberty; but unlike the Stamp Act they did not greatly injure business. The merchants could easily pass the tax on to the consumer; and of all the commodities taxed by Townshend only tea was an important article of colonial trade and Townshend had actually made it cheaper in the colonies. All duties imposed upon the exportation of tea were removed in 1767 — the East India Company promised to reimburse the government for its loss of revenue — and the only remaining duty was that paid upon entry into the colonies. In consequence, Americans now paid a tax of threepence a pound instead of a shilling as heretofore and they could look forward to drinking tea at a cheaper price than ever before — if they could swallow the tax which was now expressly designed to raise revenue.[21]

Nevertheless, the merchants still nursed grievances which soured them against the Townshend duties, however innocuous those duties may have been in themselves. Although the Rockingham Ministry had attempted to pacify the merchants by reducing the duty on foreign molasses to one penny, it had also extended the tax to include molasses imported from the British West Indies to the continental British colonies. This expedient had by no means silenced the complaints of the New England merchants and dis-tillers: one penny was a tenth of the value of a gallon of molasses and a 10 per cent tax was not easily borne.[22] Moreover, this duty was an important source of revenue: it produced on an average £12,194 a year during the period from 1767 to 1775. Nothing had been done to remove the other grievances of colonial merchants against the economic policy of the mother country. The Northern colonies still labored under the disadvantage of a "prodigious Bal-ance" of trade in favor of Great Britain. Colonial commerce was severely restricted by the Acts of Trade; specie was scarce and

[21] *Collections of the Massachusetts Historical Society*, Fifth Series, Boston, 1885, IX, 236.

[22] *Newport Mercury*, December 21, 1767. *Journal of John Leeds of Quebec*, 1768, Additional MSS. 28605.

paper money could no longer be used as legal tender. "There is such a scarcity of money," lamented a New York merchant, "that even when our work is done, our customers, tho' they may be able and honest, yet often know not where to find cash to pay for it." A long list of articles was still enumerated; and wine, oil, and fruit could not be imported directly into the colonies from Spain, Portugal, or the Madeiras.

But worst of all from the merchants' point of view were the measures taken by Townshend to enforce British commercial laws in the colonies. To remove all doubts concerning the legality of writs of assistance, Townshend expressly provided for their issuance by colonial courts — which spelled disaster for merchants whose warehouses were crammed with contraband. Moreover, four Vice Admiralty Courts were established, at Halifax, Philadelphia, Boston, and Charleston, to enforce the trade laws more expeditiously and to render unnecessary appeals to England. Of even greater significance in explaining the hostility of the colonial merchants to the Townshend duties was the establishment of a Board of American Commissioners of the Customs.

In creating an American Board of Commissioners of the Customs Townshend believed, as when he imposed duties upon articles of colonial trade, that he was taking Americans at their word. Prior to 1767, there were four Surveyor Generals in the British continental colonies who acted under the authority of the Board of Commissioners in London. Because they did not possess the power of making final decisions, it was necessary to refer all important matters to the Board at London and to await its ruling. This delay caused much complaint among American merchants, many of whom urged the creation of an American Board of Commissioners clothed with the same powers as the English Board.[23] Charles Townshend obliged; but here, as in the duties he levied upon trade, he gave the colonists more than they had bargained for. An American Board consisting of five Commissioners of the Customs was established in the colonies independent of the English Board and acting directly under the authority of the Lords of the Treasury in England. The American Board, in other words, was co-ordinate with rather than subordinate to the English commissioners: and all the royal customs officials in the colonies were made responsible to the American Board of Com-

[23] *Proceedings of the Massachusetts Historical Society*, 1910, XLIII, 484. *Virginia Gazette* (Purdie and Dixon), December 17, 1767.

missioners. The Chancellor of the Exchequer was willing to satisfy Americans' demands for equality with Englishmen at least to the extent of putting them under the same disabilities as Englishmen.[24]

Townshend's chief purpose in creating these commissioners was to plug the leaks in the customs which remained after Grenville's imperfect calking. Only six seizures of contraband were made in New England during 1765 and 1767; and only one of the cases prosecuted was won by the Crown. In 1766, the Boston customhouse officers were resisted in broad daylight when they attempted to inspect the house of a notorious smuggler; and in Rhode Island the officers did not dare to take action against the powerful clique of illicit traders.[25] Townshend saw that no amount of taxation by Parliament would ever produce a colonial revenue until the tax-collecting agencies in the colonies had been placed upon a sound footing; for this purpose the American Board of Commissioners of the Customs was created. The commissioners were given authority to appoint searchers, tide waiters, collectors, surveyors, clerks, land waiters, and comptrollers to assist them in executing their duties. Acting in close co-operation with the Courts of Admiralty, these officials, together with the informers who followed in their train, added greatly to the hazards of smuggling. The commissioners and their underlings furnished another example of how jobs in the royal service in British America tended to be monopolized by a small group of men in whom the people had no confidence. Charles Paxton, one of the commissioners, was an intimate friend of Thomas Hutchinson. One of the officials of the Philadelphia customhouse was "that execrable Villain; the condemned Vagabound; the rank, bloody, and as yet unhanged EBENEZER RICHARDSON" who had killed a young Boston Whig in a riot. To crown the chagrin of the merchants, the commissioners insisted upon dismissing the old customhouse employees — many of whom the merchants had safely purchased — and putting in their places "petty Scotch Laddys" who seemed to be able to live on their salaries alone.[26]

Not one of Townshend's measures brought British "tyranny" home to the colonial merchants as did the Commissioners of the

[24] *American Historical Review*, July 1940, XLV, 780.

[25] Memorial of the Commissioners of the Customs, February 12, 1768, House of Lords MSS. *Hutchinson Correspondence*, II, Thomas Hutchinson to ?, July 18, 1767.

[26] *Pennsylvania Journal and Weekly Advertiser*, July 26, 1770. *Boston Gazette*, May 24, 1773.

Customs. They were, swore the merchants, "so many BLOOD SUCKERS upon our TRADE"; the King had no more right to impose such "a set of Miscreants" upon free Americans than he had to establish a court of inquisition. The commissioners, "by their dissolute Lives and Evil Practices," exclaimed a Whig, threatened America "with a curse more deplorable than Egyptian Darkness." [27] They drew such vast sums from the colonies that their money chests were declared to be the "common receptacle of the earnings of the industrious yeomen, merchants and tradesmen of North-America." [28] The lineage of the commissioners was traced back to Charles II's efforts to enforce the Laws of Trade in the colonies in order to support the "whores and other flimsy creatures" with whom he surrounded himself. "When things are ripe for it," promised the Whigs, "they will be prosecuted in Law for Robbery" and the whole iniquitous system of customhouses and commissioners wiped out because they were no more known to the Constitution than "a troop of Cossacks." [29]

The Commissioners of the Customs considerably increased the British government's revenue from the colonial customs but they did not succeed in suppressing smuggling except perhaps in Boston. Elsewhere, Americans still experienced no great difficulty in turning a dishonest penny. Little tea was imported into Philadelphia from England after 1769 yet thanks to the activities of the smuggling fraternity there was no scarcity. Since Pennsylvania consumed over two thousand chests of tea a year, it is apparent that the commissioners came off second best in their encounters with the illicit traders of the Middle colonies. In New York, much the same conditions prevailed. Besides tea, large quantities of calicoes, spices, and other Indian commodities were brought into the province illegally. Despite the best efforts of the commissioners, the East India Company lost the greater part of its colonial market to the Dutch smugglers who swarmed everywhere except at Boston. Had the commissioners succeeded in wiping out smuggling as Townshend hoped, there would have been no necessity for the Tea Act of 1773 which led to the Boston Tea Party.[30]

[27] *Essex Gazette*, January 4, 1774. *Pennsylvania Chronicle*, March 21, 1768. *New York Gazette or Weekly Post Boy*, May 8, 1769.
[28] *Boston Gazette*, August 31, 1772.
[29] *Massachusetts Spy*, May 23, 1771.
[30] Reed, I, 52, 56. *Proceedings of the Massachusetts Historical Society*, XLIII, 484–490.

When confronted by British tyranny, it was inevitable that Americans should again resort to a boycott of British goods. Manifestly, by buying British merchandise, particularly that taxed by Townshend, Americans were helping the mother country destroy colonial liberty — buying a rod, in fact, for their own breech.[31] The repeal of the Stamp Act had convinced them colonial trade was so vital to Great Britain that it was within their power to bankrupt the mother country. Hitherto in history, it was pointed out, it had been "the unfortunate lot of mankind, to wade through human blood, for a permanent security of their rights"; but Americans, more fortunate than other peoples of the earth, seemed to be able to bring their oppressors to terms simply by refusing to buy their goods.[32]

The Boston merchants were the first American businessmen to clamor for economic reprisals against Great Britain, partly, no doubt, because they not only shared the grievances of the other colonial merchants against British policy, but labored under unique disadvantages as well. Boston had been made the headquarters of the Commissioners of the Customs and its trade was kept under closer scrutiny than that of any other colonial seaport. Furthermore, Boston was rapidly losing its pre-eminence as the leading American port; shipbuilding was stagnant; and the citizens lamented that "many an honest and industrious tradesman" had "fallen into decay."[33] These discontented, impoverished citizens were tinder for the propaganda dispensed by Sam Adams and the Sons of Liberty; and even many of the wealthier merchants were ready to join the radicals against the mother country in the hope that prosperity could be restored by forcing the British government to relax the restrictions upon colonial trade.

But even in Boston the demand for a boycott came chiefly from the patriot leaders and the people; the merchants were at first reluctant to sacrifice their property at the feet of "that Celestial Goddess Liberty." The merchants of the other ports were even less disposed to act; and in 1767 James Otis warned the Boston Town Meeting against picking a quarrel with the mother country over the Townshend duties "when every other Town in the Province and every other Province in America seemed to acquiesce in them and

[31] *South Carolina Gazette*, June 1, 1769.
[32] *Pennsylvania Journal and Weekly Advertiser*, September 20, 1770.
[33] *Boston Evening Post*, November 9, 1768.

be contented." [34] After the Boston merchants had become convinced of the necessity of a boycott, the Philadelphians and New Yorkers refused to join. It was not until almost a year after the duties had gone into effect that the Nonimportation Agreement was finally consummated. The anger generated in the colonies by Lord Hillsborough's Circular Letter played an important part in turning the scale — for most of the colonial merchants were patriots as well as businessmen; but of equal significance was the decision made by the Commissioners of the Customs in the summer of 1768 to demand specie in payment for duties. Immediately the New York merchants informed the Bostonians that they were ready to enter into a nonimportation agreement to compel the government to repeal the Townshend duties and the Philadelphians soon followed.[35] The Townshend duties now seemed likely to destroy colonial purchasing power by draining off the inadequate supply of hard money to England. In Philadelphia, there was soon "scarce a dollar to be seen" and the citizens were forced to hammer up their plate to settle their bills with the customhouse. Bostonians calculated late in 1768 that "if the Silver already drawn from us by the new Duties [Townshend's] was to be beat into thin Plates . . . it would entirely cover the main Road from this Town to the Borders of York Government." [36] There could be little question after the commissioners had announced their intention of requiring payment in specie that the prosperity of the colonial merchants was directly threatened.

The agreement made less rapid progress in the Southern colonies. Virginia did not join until 1769 and then only with reservations which permitted the importation of a large amount of British merchandise. The principal opposition to the agreement came from the extremely wealthy planters who, living "genteely and hospitably, on clear Estates" thought it "hard to be curtail'd in their living and enjoyments," and from the merchants who were for the most part factors of the great Scottish and English firms. But the small planters welcomed the Nonimportation Agreement as a means of de-

[34] Governor Bernard to Lord Shelburne, November 21, 1767, Bernard MSS., Harvard University Library.

[35] *Memoirs of the Historical Society of Pennsylvania*, Philadelphia, 1895, XIV, 441–442. *History of the State of New York*, New York, 1933, III, 203.

[36] *New York Gazette and Weekly Post Boy*, February 1, 1768. *Boston Weekly News Letter*, July 7, 1768. *Massachusetts Gazette*, November 19, 1767. William Allen to Thomas Penn, September 23, October 8, 1767, Penn MSS., Historical Society of Pennsylvania.

fending the rights of the colonial assemblies and of getting out of debt to their English creditors. Washington reported in 1769 that many hitherto prosperous men were so deeply in debt that the market was being flooded with their estates. The Nonimportation Agreement, by placing British luxuries outside their reach, gave them a much needed "breathing spell" in which to practise economy and retrenchment.

In July 1769, Charleston, South Carolina, joined the agreement largely through the efforts of a small group of Whig merchants led by Thomas Lynch, Christopher Gadsden, and John MacKenzie. These men — "mere Tribunes of the people," as the royal governor termed them — went beyond most of the other colonies by making the objective of the boycott not merely the repeal of the Townshend duties but the abolition of the Board of Commissioners of the Customs and the curtailment of the powers of the Admiralty Courts.[37] And, in contrast to the Virginians' ill success, the Charleston merchants effectively boycotted slaves on the ground that they were British merchandise of a particularly objectionable character.

American women were from the beginning thrust into the thick of this struggle with the mother country. As the chief consumers of British luxuries, their action promised to be decisive: the home front lay in the boudoir. "One prudent matron," it was said, "by a strict economy at the head of her family, will do more for the good of her country than five hundred noisy sons of liberty, with all their mobs and riots."[38] The leaders urged these "female patriots" to renounce "Tinsel Gewgaws and exuberant Fineries"; to cease to increase "the Revenues of *Anti-Christ*, by fluttering in Italian silks"; to spin instead of drinking tea and gossiping; and to avoid "like an infectious disease . . . the unmannerly delicacy of splendid furniture, sumptuous sideboards, and . . . every mode of foreign Cookery."[39] Women with marriageable daughters were reminded that by teaching their daughters to be thrifty housewives they would be married the sooner — cautious bachelors would no longer avoid marriage because of the fear of bankruptcy. The ladies were told that they would be more alluring in "decent plain

---

[37] Lieutenant Governor Bull to Lord Hillsborough, December 5, 1770, P.R.O., C.O. 5, 394. *Colonial Records of North Carolina*, VIII, 197–198. *Virginia Gazette* (Rind's), June 1, 1769; July 26, 1770.

[38] *Virginia Gazette* (Rind's), June 1, 1769.

[39] *New Hampshire Gazette*, January 25, February 1, 1765.

Dresses made in their own Country than in the gaudy, butterfly, vain, fantastic, and expensive Dresses brought from Europe"; the "delicate Madams" who made the experiment reported gratifying results: "their Husbands like them full as well or better in a Cotton Smock, as in a Holland one." To reward the Sons of Liberty and punish the Tories, it was suggested that ladies permit themselves to be courted only by patriots: then, exclaimed the Whigs, "how soon might we expect to see industry flourish, and raise its languid head." [40] The ladies of Newport, Rhode Island, declared that they were willing to make all the sacrifices asked of them, provided their husbands and lovers gave up "their dearer and more beloved Punch, renounce going so often to Taverns, and become more kind and loving Sweethearts and Husbands." Said the women: —

> "Most gladly we aside our Tea wo'd lay,
> Could we more Pleasure gain some other Way." [41]

Whether or not the Nonimportation Agreement kept the Sons of Liberty at home o' nights, it is evident that the Daughters of Liberty did much to make it a success: "That disagreeable noise made by the rattling of the foot wheel was accounted fine music," it was said, "and preferred to the music of a violin that was imported from England since the non-importation agreement." [42] In a rapture of patriotism, the women of New York declared that they would "cheerfully sacrifice the most darling Appurtenances of the Toilet on the Altar of public Emolument"; "Off with our fine Feathers in a Moment," they cried, "if the public Interest so requireth." [43]

The effort to purge the colonies of British luxuries was accompanied by a "Buy American" campaign. Pennsylvanians were urged not to drink English punch or toddy which, American physicians attested, was a baneful concoction which caused agues, fevers, and rheumatic pains; they ought, instead, to heal their ravaged constitutions with healthful Pennsylvania-made beer and cider. Benjamin Franklin advised Americans to turn from rum — which was manufactured from West Indian molasses — to whiskey, which could be made from home-grown ingredients. This, likewise, promised to be a highly salubrious change: it was predicted that Americans

[40] *New York Gazette and Weekly Post Boy*, April 10, 1769.
[41] *Newport Mercury*, December 14, 1767. *New Hampshire Gazette*, February 15, 1765.
[42] *Essex Gazette*, May 19, 1772.
[43] *Ibid.*

would be "a more hardy and manly Race of People when our Constitutions are no longer jaundiced, nor our Juices vitiated by abominable West India Distillations." [44] Rhode Island ladies were asked to demonstrate their patriotism by "taking the Snuff of Rhode Island" and only drinking home-grown New England balm, which, it was claimed, "far surpasses the Teas of India, whether in Fragrance, Colour or Virtue." Colonial physicians sought remedies and cures in American plants and herbs; a Dr. Chalmers of Charleston, South Carolina, declared, for example, that he had found a sovereign cure in his own province for "the Dry Belly-Ach or Nervous Colick" and for "Catarrhal Peripneumony." [45]

The wearing of homespun became *de rigueur* for colonial patriots. The graduating classes at Harvard and Princeton took their degrees in homespun; at "elegant entertainments," the gentlemen all appeared in homespun; and the South Carolina assemblymen renounced the wearing of wigs and stockings, with the result, noted an observer, that should a new governor arrive in Charleston, "he would probably from their dress, take them for so many unhappy persons ready for execution, who had come to petition for a pardon." [46] A gentleman set out on a journey from New York to Philadelphia clad in homespun and "his whole Apparel and Horse Furniture were of American Manufacture." The *Boston Gazette* was printed on home-manufactured paper; college undergraduates enthusiastically boycotted British merchandise; and Dr. Frelinghuysen of Princeton delivered an oration on "The Utility of American Manufactures." At the London coffeehouses pieces of broadcloth manufactured in the colonies were exhibited; and John Hancock was reported to have offered free passage to Boston to English artisans. "All the country seems possessed with a madness of manufacture and economy," wrote Governor Wentworth of New Hampshire; in the seaports, soldiers were offered high wages if they would desert and practise trades. [47]

Self-sufficiency — the goal of the mercantilists — now became the

---

[44] *Providence Gazette and Country Journal*, September 8, 1764. *Virginia Gazette*, February 25, 1773. *Newport Mercury*, November 12, 1764.

[45] *Pennsylvania Chronicle*, November 28, 1773. *Newport Mercury*, August 20, 1764.

[46] *Pennsylvania Journal and Weekly Advertiser*, October 18, 1770. *Boston Gazette*, March 27, 1769; July 30, 1770. *Boston Evening Post*, January 4, 1768. *New York Journal and General Advertiser*, December 28, 1769.

[47] L. M. Mayo, *John Wentworth*, 126. *Pennsylvania Journal and Weekly Advertiser*, October 25, 1770.

ideal of the colonists; but they conceived of it as self-sufficiency not for the British Empire but for the British continental colonies alone. The purpose of the patriots was to make the colonies economically independent of Great Britain; and to achieve this end they attempted to press into service the vast agricultural and mineral resources of the continent. The American Society for Promoting Useful Knowledge was established in Philadelphia — a similar organization existed in New York — to devise means of improving agriculture, opening up new fields for enterprise, and experimenting with exotic plants and herbs. Vineyards were laid out in Virginia in the hope that the wine of Virginia would soon vie with that of Madeira; tea was planted in New England; and silkworms and mulberry trees were cultivated in the Southern colonies. The more optimistic patriots believed that the colonies would one day become large exporters of silk and tea. A Philadelphian pointed out that China and the American colonies lay in the same latitude and that Philadelphia therefore might be expected to compete with Peking. "Could we be so fortunate as to introduce the Industry of the *Chinese*," he remarked, "their Arts of Living and Improvements in Husbandry, as well as their Native Plants, America might, in Time, become as populous as *China*." [48]

Many Americans recognized that if the colonies were to wage successful economic war with the mother country, it was necessary that they manufacture for themselves the necessities they had formerly imported from Great Britain. As the Tories unkindly pointed out, Americans had the alternative in 1768 of buying from Great Britain or going naked. For this reason, colonial manufacturing came to be widely regarded as "the only way to unrivet the chains, and burst asunder the bands of Iron that are fastened on us." [49] Moreover, some Northern merchants, fearing that British restrictions upon commerce would ultimately drive them from trade, began to look to manufacturing for salvation. A group of merchants in Boston and New York pooled their capital, formed an association to establish spinning factories, and sent to England for men skilled in making woolen and linen cloth. [50] In Virginia, likewise, the declining profitableness of agriculture led many planters — George Washington and Richard Henry Lee among

[48] *Pennsylvania Chronicle*, March 7, 1768. *Boston Gazette*, January 25, 1768.
[49] *South Carolina Gazette*, October 22, 1764. *Boston Evening Post*, June 5, 1769.
[50] *The Ingersoll Papers*, New Haven, 1918, 297–298.

them — to look to manufacturing to recoup their fortunes. These men pointed to the great natural resources which God had placed before Americans as proof that He intended them to be an industrial as well as an agricultural people. God had created an "American Canaan" and had ordained that Americans were to be the greatest people on earth: "Let us be ashamed to be dependent on other Countries for our Manufactures," exclaimed a New Yorker. ". . . Let it be our glory to make use only of such Articles as are manufactured in this Country." [51]

Thus some colonists had already caught a vision of an America bristling with factories and workshops. They believed that only by manufacturing for herself could America become rich and powerful since workshops and factories were essential to "the happiness and glory of a state." It was argued that manufacturing had made Great Britain powerful: it had "made her merchants nobles, and her nobles princes" and it would do as much for America.[52] Furthermore, the industrialization of the colonies would strengthen them against British tyranny by peopling them with thousands of workers from Europe and the mother country. America would become the asylum of the oppressed factory employees of the world: "By establishing manufactories," exclaimed a colonist, "we stretch forth a hand from the ark to invite the timid manufacturers to come in." Within a century, it seemed certain that manufacturing would make America powerful enough to "bid defiance to the whole world." [53]

Nevertheless, there were serious obstacles in the way of attaining this felicity. Lack of capital, high wages, and the general predilection of the people for agriculture conspired against the plans of the patriots. On every side, it was acknowledged that the colonists would not turn to manufacturing except under compulsion; they were farmers, and farmers they wished to remain. Likewise, Americans' fondness for fashionable clothing imported from Great Britain was not easily overcome. They delighted in "a laced coat, or brocaded gown" and it was said that they would prefer to be seen "strutting about the streets, clad in foreign fripperies, than to be nobly independent in the russet grey" of homespun.[54]

[51] *New York Journal or Weekly Advertiser*, April 7, 1768.
[52] *Pennsylvania Evening Post*, April 13, 1775.
[53] *Ibid.*
[54] *Pennsylvania Chronicle*, July 25, 1768. *Newport Mercury*, November 23, 1767.

The patriots proposed to overcome the handicap of high wages and scarcity of labor by putting the "idle and indolent" and women and children to work. Alexander Hamilton, in particular, impatiently awaited the day when thousands of American children would be happily trooping off to the factories. The high birth rate of the colonies offered hope that some day America would be able to compete with Great Britain if children were properly utilized. One colonist deemed it proper that they be employed "from the time they are able to move their hands or feet." [55] High wages were denounced as the bane of the colonies: "It is certain," remarked an American, "that high wages more frequently make labouring people miserable; they too commonly employ their spare time and cash, in debauching their morals and ruining their health." [56] Clearly, to save the American workingman from himself, it was necessary to beat down wages to a salutary level; and many of the advocates of manufacturing were ready to do this service for American labor.

Most of the projects to make the colonies the commercial rivals of the mother country never got beyond the paper stage, however, and colonial manufacturing proved a disappointment to its supporters. Americans seemed to believe that it was only necessary to frighten the mother country with the bogey of colonial manufacturing to bring about a repeal of the Townshend duties; and the newspapers did their part by printing stories of nonexistent workshops and by puffing backhouse workbenches into extensive factories. Even so, the spirit and determination evinced by the colonists was highly disquieting to British businessmen. Most disturbing of all, in Philadelphia local industry had clearly attained proportions which menaced British monopoly of the colonial market. "I assure your Lordship," wrote General Gage to Lord Barrington, "that Foundations are laid in Philadelphia, that must create Jealousy in an Englishman." [57] The East India Company encountered such sharp competition from the Philadelphia china factory that it was obliged to cut the price of its china in the province to keep abreast of this troublesome rival.

In 1763, there had been little fear in England of colonial manufacturing. It was believed that the scarcity of labor and the abun-

[55] *Virginia Gazette* (Rind's), April 14, 1768.
[56] *Pennsylvania Chronicle*, March 27, 1769.
[57] *The Correspondence of General Thomas Gage*, I, 161.

dance of land had solved the British government's problem of how to keep Americans down on the farm and out of the factories. Benjamin Franklin had fostered this complacency by assuring Englishmen that the colonists were certain to remain an agricultural people for centuries to come. But Charles Townshend had aroused a new spirit in the colonies; the mercantilist foundations of the empire were threatened and the English merchants feared that their highly profitable monopoly would dissolve before their eyes. "Every hour that increases the number of their [the colonists'] Artificers," they exclaimed, "is a dagger in the vitals of Great Britain"; "every man, deserting from our army, is better and of more value to America than his weight in gold." [58]

The colonists' efforts to coerce the mother country by means of boycotts and manufacturing cost them virtually all their friends in England. They were flying in the face of Chatham himself, who had repeatedly said that if they attempted to manufacture for themselves against the will of Parliament, he would be the first to demand that the British navy and army blast them out of their workshops. Their conduct seemed to be little short of rebellion against Great Britain's authority: "They have beat the Drum and openly declared themselves their own Masters," it was said.[59] It seemed likely that the Bostonians would next resolve not to import acts of Parliament. Already they had begun to appear in Englishmen's eyes as worse enemies of Great Britain than even the French: the "generous rivals" of John Bull across the Channel did not try to turn Great Britain into a desert as did the colonists. The Boston Saints in particular appeared to "brandish the sword of Boston against our legislature, and threaten our starving manufacturers with clean teeth and empty bellies"; and by seeking to starve Englishmen, they proved that they would also cut Englishmen's throats "if they could effect that carnage." [60] Although they proclaimed themselves the champions of liberty, Americans seemed in English eyes no more willing to permit freedom of speech than were New England Puritans disposed to grant religious toleration. In Boston it appeared to be "as meritorious to find out an importer, as it was some

[58] Pennsylvania Chronicle, March 14, 1768; June 26, 1769. Writings of Benjamin Franklin, V, 244.
[59] Public Advertiser, November 2, 1768. Gazetteer and New Daily Advertiser, May 18, 1770.
[60] Gazetteer and New Daily Advertiser, January 5, February 3, 1768.

time ago to find out a witch"; and property was "perpetually at the mercy of every ruffian who bellows the cause of liberty." [61]

The Grafton Ministry which succeeded the administration of Lord Chatham found no reason to bless Townshend's memory. Townshend had stirred up the hornets' nest, leaving to his successors the problem of pacifying the hive. "God knows there is little pleasure in being a minister," exclaimed Lord North.[62] As early as 1768, the Ministry seriously considered repealing the duties imposed by the late-lamented Chancellor of the Exchequer. Lord Grafton, the head of the Ministry, regarded them as unprofitable and mischievous; Lord Hillsborough, the new Secretary of State for the Colonies, declared the Townshend Act was "so anti-commercial that he wished it had never existed"; and Lord North, who had succeeded Townshend as Chancellor of the Exchequer, remarked that the duties were so "preposterous" that he was amazed they had been passed by the British Parliament. The members of Grafton's cabinet were agreed that the duties injured British merchants and manufacturers, that they served as "premiums to encourage American manufacturers" and that the small revenue they yielded could never compensate for the losses they occasioned to British trade as a result of the colonial boycott.[63]

The Grafton Ministry would have rejoiced at the opportunity to retreat with honor from the dilemma. But retreat, after Americans had attempted to coerce the mother country by riots and boycotts and had denied the right of Parliament to tax them, was not easy for the British government. The taxation of the colonies could no longer be treated as a mere matter of revenue; the sovereignty of Parliament over the colonies had become inextricably bound up with the right of taxing Americans. Because Americans had chosen to wage the struggle against parliamentary taxation upon the broad principles of natural law, the rights of Englishmen, and the British Constitution, the Ministry was obliged to maintain at all costs the right of taxation in defense of British sovereignty over the colonies. The right of taxing the colonies came to be regarded as the very citadel of parliamentary authority; if it fell, few

[61] *The Repository*, London, 1771, II, 249, 324.

[62] Cavendish, II, 33.

[63] *Collections of the Massachusetts Historical Society*, Fifth Series, Boston, 1885, IX, 292, 296, 305, 338. *South Carolina Historical and Genealogical Magazine*, 1929, XXX, 234. *Parliamentary History*, London, 1813, XVI, 853.

Englishmen doubted that the colonies would be independent of the mother country in fact if not in name. In 1764–1765, the British government had sought a colonial revenue primarily in the interests of relieving the strain upon British taxpayers; but by 1769, the right of taxation had become more important as an assertion of British sovereignty than as a means of producing revenue for the British Exchequer. "A peppercorn, in acknowledgment of the right," exclaimed Lord Clare, "was of more value than millions without it." [64]

Yet Grafton and three other members of the Ministry regarded the Townshend duties as so "uncommercial" that they were prepared to throw them all overboard and rely upon the Declaratory Act, the Acts of Trade, and the molasses tax to uphold parliamentary sovereignty. But Lord North, the Chancellor of the Exchequer, refused to approve the entire repeal of the Townshend duties. North declared that Parliament ought to exercise its rights under the Declaratory Act and to tax Americans if only to remind them that Parliament was still sovereign over the empire.

A repeal of the Townshend duties in the face of American resistance struck Lord North as a disastrous defeat which the colonists would quickly impute to weakness. It would, he prophesied, mark the end of parliamentary authority in the empire; the right of Parliament to regulate colonial trade would go the way of its right to tax; and the Acts of Trade and Navigation would be overthrown, leaving England only the empty title of sovereign. "Upon my word," he exclaimed, "if we are to run after America in search of reconciliation, in this way, I do not know a single act of parliament that will remain." [65]

In this deadlock in the cabinet, the action of the British merchants was decisive. It probably was within the power of the men who had repealed the Stamp Act to have procured, by unremitting petitioning and agitation, the total repeal of the Townshend duties. But the merchants failed to rise as they had in 1766; and as a result the cabinet voted by a margin of five to four to retain the tax on tea while repealing the duties upon all other commodities taxed by Townshend. And so, by a majority of one vote, the British government committed itself to continuing the policy of taxing the colonies. Grafton believed that had Chatham still been at the head

[64] Cavendish, II, 20, note.
[65] *Ibid.*, I, 487.

of the government, his vote and influence would have carried the total repeal of the duties. But after all, there was a limit to the number of times that Chatham could save the British Empire.[66]

From this debate, Lord North emerged as the strong man of the cabinet. He had prevailed over Grafton, the head of the Ministry; henceforth it was North and Hillsborough who controlled the government's colonial policy. Although North was a "great, heavy, booby-looking" man who embarrassed his colleagues by taking cat naps in the House of Commons, he was not one of those "first-rate geniuses in incapacity" who seem created by Providence to reduce great empires.[67] Even his enemies admitted his ability in managing the House; and his skill in finance was sounder, if less flashy, than that of Charles Townshend. It was his boast, however, that he had never voted for a popular measure.

Lord North was under no illusions that he was appeasing Americans by partially repealing the Townshend duties. The dispute between mother country and colonies, he said, would continue as long as Parliament asserted its right to tax the colonies and Americans denied it. He believed, however, that if Great Britain made a strategic withdrawal in 1769, the Nonimportation Agreement would be destroyed and colonial union brought to an end. In effect, Lord North proposed to drive a wedge between the American colonists by well-timed concession without in any way impairing the sovereignty of the mother country. Thus, although American malcontents would not be satisfied, it was hoped that "ye *Well disposed* may gain ye Lead, in a divided People, against ye *Seditious.*" [68] Moreover, the partial repeal of the duties would quiet English merchants, ruin colonial manufacturing built up behind the boycott, and silence the opposition in Parliament.

Although Lord North regarded the Townshend duties as "uncommercial" and therefore subject to repeal, he excepted the tea tax on the ground that it did no injury to the commercial interests of the mother country. But, in fact, none of the duties imposed by Townshend was more clearly uncommercial than the tea duty.

[66] *Pennsylvania Magazine of History and Biography*, 1936, IX, 477. *Collections of the Massachusetts Historical Society*, Fifth Series, Boston, 1885, IX, 298.

[67] *Memoirs of the Marquis of Rockingham*, I, 344. *Pitt Correspondence*, IV, 119.

[68] Thomas Pownall to the Reverend Mr. Cooper, May 25, 1769, British Museum, Kings MSS. 205, Library of Congress Transcript. *Collections of the Massachusetts Historical Society*, Fifth Series, Boston, 1885, IX, 349–350, 358.

The East India Company suffered exceedingly from Townshend's measures because of the vast amount of Dutch tea that was smuggled into the colonies after British tea had been taxed to raise revenue for the British Exchequer. The tea duty cost the East India Company thousands of pounds yearly. The true reason why the tax on tea was retained by North was that it alone of the Townshend duties furnished a sizable revenue to the mother country. The other duties levied proved to be mere irritants: they yielded a trifling revenue and led the colonists to attempt to manufacture for themselves. Tea brought between eleven and twelve thousand pounds a year into the King's Chest; yet it could not be produced in the colonies and would not stimulate colonial manufacturing.[69]

In accord with the cabinet's decision, Lord Hillsborough in 1769 addressed a letter to the colonial assemblies announcing the Ministry's intention to propose in the next session of Parliament the repeal of the duties upon glass, paper, and paint. At the same time, the colonists were assured that the Ministry "at no time entertained a design, to propose to parliament, to lay any further taxes on America, for the purpose of raising a revenue." This action was taken, Lord North later made plain, purely because the taxes imposed by Townshend wrought serious injury to British commerce and trade: the American boycott had not affected in any way the government's decision. Thus the Ministry pictured the repeal of the Townshend duties, like that of the Stamp Act, as a concession to British merchants and manufacturers rather than a yielding to American mobs and economic reprisals.

When Parliament in 1770 debated this decision of the Ministry, Lord North, now First Lord of the Treasury in place of Lord Grafton, steadfastly refused to consider any proposals for repeal of the tea duty. He declared that leniency merely led Americans to heap new indignities upon the mother country. Only when he saw America at the feet of Great Britain, he said, would he make another attempt to appease the colonists. Although North later explained that he had meant merely that the colonies must seek redress of grievances by means of petitions and that he had never intended to establish arbitrary government over the empire, his excuses fell upon deaf ears in the colonies. North was henceforth regarded as "an enemy of mankind" and he never succeeded in living down

---

[69] *South Carolina Historical and Genealogical Magazine*, XXX, 231. Cavendish, I, 486.

the unfortunate remark. When an American learned that Lord North had been attacked by a mob in London, he was overjoyed, although he confessed that his gratification would have been complete had the mob left North "a lifeless Corpse in his chariot." [70]

The answer of the colonists to Hillsborough's offer of the partial repeal of the Townshend duties was to screw their demands higher and to raise the cry that the British government was attempting by guile to divide Americans. Certain that the mother country was in disorderly retreat and would soon be compelled to accept any terms dictated by the colonies, the radicals urged Americans to demand the abolition of the Commissioners of the Customs, the Admiralty Courts, and all the obnoxious measures passed by Parliament since 1763. The people were told that all this was within their grasp; they had only to continue the boycott a few months more and every grievance of which they complained would be removed by the panic-stricken Ministry. But many merchants were heartily weary of the struggle; they wished to meet the government halfway by calling off the Nonimportation Agreement and trusting that good behavior would induce the mother country to repeal the remaining taxes. Lord North had wrought better than he knew: a dangerous rift was becoming apparent between the merchants on the one hand and the patriot leaders and their followers on the other over the question of protracting the boycott.[71]

[70] Edward Warren, *The Life of John Warren*, Boston, 1874, 30.
[71] *Boston Gazette*, May 7, 1770. *Pennsylvania Journal*, May 10, 1770. *New York Gazette or Weekly Post Boy*, July 2, 1770. *South Carolina Gazette*, June 1, 1769.

CHAPTER TWELVE

The Collapse of Colonial Opposition

Faneuil Hall

BOSTON, MASS.

I

THE uncompromising temper of the patriots was owing largely to the lack of military force behind British rule in the colonies: they saw no reason to yield as long as they held a whip over the British lion. It is important to recognize that from the beginning of the dispute with Great Britain, Americans found themselves confronted by a government which, while making sweeping claims of authority over the colonies, had little force with which to back up its pretensions to imperial power. In the opinion of many American Tories, the great fault of the mother country was not that it was tyrannical but that it was not strong enough to hold the colonists in check: the Ministry, said Jonathan Boucher, was guilty of "having done both too much and too little; too much in the way of hostility for reconciliation, and too little for compulsion." [1] A policy of alternate coercion and appeasement convinced Americans that they had little to fear from the Ministry, however it might bluster and threaten. The mother country began to appear an impotent old shrew with an uncommonly evil temper but quite unable to bring her unruly children overseas to book. This discouraged the Tories from actively supporting the home government at the same time that it had "a direct tendency to heighten the unjust claims of the colonists, confirm them in their stubborn and refractory behavior, and rivet in their minds the stupid thirst for an absolute independency." [2]

It should also be borne in mind that during the revolutionary period Great Britain was attempting to rule colonies which lay beyond three thousand miles of ocean usually requiring from two to three months to traverse. Obviously, the difficulties of the British government in formulating and executing its policies were vastly increased by the problems created by space and time – prob-

[1] Boucher, 371.
[2] Robert Auchmuty to Joseph Harrison, March 15, 1770, Chalmers MSS., Harvard University Library.

lems which present-day governments are no longer obliged to face.
The Stamp Act riots had demonstrated that it was impossible for
a royal governor to exercise "one single Act in the Administration
of Government, if it appears repugnant to the Sentiments of the
People."[3] For example, the governor of Connecticut took an oath
to enforce the Stamp Act; when the Sons of Liberty buried the
Stamp Act in a coffin with the King's colors flying over it, "they
not only buryd the Stamp Act but the Gov[ernor] (in effigy)[4] also."
"For any Man to set himself up as an Advocate for the S[tam]p
Act in the Colonies," said William Franklin, the royal governor of
New Jersey, "is a meer Piece of Quixotism, & can answer no good
Purpose whatever. And if he is an Officer of Govt. he not only
becomes obnoxious, but is sure to lose all the Authority belonging
to his Office."[5] The colonial magistrates gave the Crown Officers
little aid against the mobs; like the militia, they were often to be
found in the mobs themselves. A Tory of Norfolk, Virginia, paraded
through the streets bound to a cart, saw the mayor of Norfolk in
the crowd; but instead of stopping the riot, complained the Tory,
he "threw stones at me himself."[6] Usually when the mob was
abroad the magistrates kept out of sight lest some law-abiding
citizen call upon them to disperse the rioters. At the most, they
consented to plead with the Sons of Liberty to keep the peace; but
entreaties were of little avail with men who had drunk so deep
of power. The magistrates held the patriots in such terror that in
New York when some children — sons of the Sons of Liberty —
marched through the streets "with some lanthorns upon Poles and
hallowing," the town officers made no attempt to break up the
demonstration. They "either approve of it," remarked a British
officer, "or do not dare to suppress . . . the children."[7]
Had the magistrates taken their lives in their hands by arresting
riotous Whigs, they would have procured few convictions before

[3] Governor Benning Wentworth to the Lords Commissioners for Trade and
Plantations, December 16, 1765, House of Lords MSS. *The Barrington-
Bernard Correspondence*, edited by Ed. Channing and A. C. Coolidge, Harvard
Hist. Studies, XVII, 115, 121.
[4] *The Literary Diary of Ezra Stiles*, 512.
[5] William Franklin to Benjamin Franklin, November 13, 1765, Franklin
MSS., American Philosophical Society.
[6] *William and Mary College Quarterly*, January 1913, XXI, 167.
[7] Collections of the New York Historical Society, *The Montresor Journals*,
New York, 1882, 346. *A Collection of Interesting, Authentic Papers . . . from
1764 to 1775*, edited by John Almon, London, 1777, 48.

colonial juries. Jurymen were notoriously prejudiced in favor of smugglers and patriotic mob leaders; they could be depended upon coolly to set aside the weight of evidence and bring in the verdicts that the patriots expected of them. In Boston, grand juries were nominated by the town meetings; and not infrequently it happened that a mob leader was chosen to sit upon the grand jury appointed to investigate the riot in which he had played a distinguished part. When the Attorney General of Massachusetts attempted to bring to trial the patriots suspected of having been involved in the riot of June 10, 1768, he found that no one would testify against them although over three hundred people had participated in the disturbance. Their reluctance was not remarkable, observed the royal governor, because "the Head of the Mob sat upon the Grand Jury ready to mark those who would testify against his Mob." [8]

The Nonimportation Agreement revealed, as strikingly as had the Stamp Act, the woeful weakness of the British government in the provinces. Americans who stood out loyally in support of the mother country were obliged to face the mobs without protection. Violators of the agreement were tarred and feathered, hounded from colony to colony, and forced to take refuge, when they could, on board British men-of-war. The civil government did not raise its hand: "Officers of the Crown," reported General Gage in 1769, "grow more timid, and more fearful of doing their Duty every Day." [9] As Edmund Burke said, Americans were finding that they had "a great resource" in the incapacity of the mother country.

Well aware of their own strength and the powerlessness of the British government, the colonial mobs were with difficulty held in check by the patriot leaders. Having once tasted the exhilaration of driving Tories and stamp masters to cover, they wished to return to the sport and seek out bigger game. The Commissioners of the Customs, finding that the Boston mob had a weakness for beating up customhouse officers, fully realized that they, as the heads of the customs, were its most eagerly sought-after victims. The failure of the Sons of Liberty to attack them when they first landed in Boston was, they perceived, merely a reprieve. The commissioners weathered an outbreak in March 1768, but it was becoming increasingly clear that the mob could not be long held in leash. The

[8] *Hutchinson-Oliver Letters*, Boston, 1774, 31. Governor Bernard to Lord Hillsborough, September 9, 1768, Bernard MSS., Harvard University Library.
[9] *The Correspondence of General Thomas Gage*, II, 518.

crisis occurred when the customhouse officers attempted to seize a cargo of wine which John Hancock was trying to smuggle into Boston. It was said that Hancock had sworn not "to sell or to drink wine polluted by the payments of unconstitutional duties." But rather than become a teetotaler, John Hancock took the easier course and became a smuggler. In June 1768, the customhouse got wind of his activities, boarded his ship *Liberty* and demanded to see its cargo. Hancock and his men showed scant respect for these officials of His Royal Majesty. They locked them up in the cabin, landed the cargo, and when the work was done heaved the customhouse officers overboard. Meanwhile the mob had learned what was going on at Hancock's wharf; and to punish the customhouse officers for their presumption seized the Collector and the Controller, drove them through the streets, and dragged the Collector's son along by the hair of his head. The Commissioners of the Customs did not wait for their turns to come: they fled to Castle William and thus put three miles of blue water between themselves and the Boston Sons of Liberty.[10] When one of the commissioners was reported to have taken refuge in Newport, the Sons of Liberty searched "Out-houses, Bales, Barrels, Meal Tubs, Trunks, Boxes, Packs, and Packages . . . in short every Hole and Corner sufficient to conceal a *Ram Cat*, or a *Commissioner*," but they found neither.[11]

Of even greater significance than their ability to turn mobs upon defenseless Tories and Crown Officers was the patriots' control of the press. From the beginning of the revolutionary movement, the newspapers rang the changes "so often upon tyranny, oppression and slavery" that a Tory declared that "whether sleeping or waking, they are continually vibrating in our ears." Virtually all the newspapers were Whiggish, and the Tories lamented that the people heard nothing but what "their ringleaders chuse they should hear" — which, conservatives insisted, was not the unvarnished truth. The American Revolution was one of the first great popular movements in which the newspapers played a vital part: "The PRESS hath never done greater Service since its first Invention," exclaimed an American patriot, as he surveyed the wonders wrought by propaganda.[12] The newspapers kept the people in alarm for their liberties and made the controversy between mother country and

---

[10] *Gazetteer and New Daily Advertiser*, May 18, 1770.
[11] *New York Gazette and Weekly Mercury*, September 12, 1770.
[12] *Maryland Gazette*, April 17, 1766.

colonies a great popular crusade in which every American could take part. The Tories groaned that by dint of reading newspapers, even "the peasants and their housewives in every part of the land were able to dispute on politics and positively to determine upon our liberties." [13] What was worse, in Tory opinion, was that Americans believed everything they read in the Whig newspapers. "Tell them thro' the channel of a seditious news-paper the most improbable tale about grievances," exclaimed Jonathan Sewall of Massachusetts, "and they believe it more firmly than they will those many parts of Holy Writ which enjoin submission to rulers, as a Christian duty." When George Grenville rose in the House of Commons and, waving a copy of the *Boston Gazette* above his head, told the members that the Americans were being prepared for rebellion by means of subversive newspapers, he displayed a discernment which was little evidenced by the acts of his administration.[14]

The fact that the colonial press was in the hands of the patriots from the outset placed the Tories at a serious disadvantage. As early as 1766, Joseph Galloway of Pennsylvania complained that he could find no printer to publish his article on the Stamp Act because they had "combined together, to print every thing inflammatory and nothing that is rational and cool." [15] Americans always contended that they were too well educated to be swayed by demagogues and that the revolutionary movement sprang spontaneously from an enlightened, freedom-loving people. But the very fact that most colonists possessed at least a rudimentary education made them susceptible to written propaganda — if they were beyond the reach of old-fashioned demagogues, they were vulnerable to modern methods of working upon the masses.

The patriots fully appreciated the vital role played by newspapers in forwarding the revolutionary movement. After the passage of the Virginia Resolves in 1765, the governor dissolved the

[13] *Boston Evening Post*, May 22, 1769.
[14] *Pennsylvania Chronicle*, February 29, 1768. *Gazetteer and New Daily Advertiser*, January 19, 1775. Robert Auchmuty to Thomas Hutchinson, March 3, 1775, Egerton MSS. 2695, British Museum. Daniel Leonard, *The Origins of the American Contest with Great Britain*, New York, 1775, 4. Jonathan Sewall, "A Cure for the Spleen," *Magazine of History*, 1922, 38. *Letters of Captain W. G. Evelyn*, edited by G. D. Scull, Oxford, 1879, 46.
[15] Joseph Galloway to Benjamin Franklin, January 13, 1766, Franklin MSS., American Philosophical Society.

assembly and threatened the printer of the *Virginia Gazette* with the loss of his salary as official printer unless he kept his paper clear of radicalism. In consequence, the Whigs found that the only newspaper in the Old Dominion was "totally engrossed for the vile Purpose of *ministerial Craft.*" [16] Moreover, it suspended publication for four months in 1765–1766 on the ground that no stamps could be procured. The Virginia press was thus silenced during one of the most critical periods of the revolutionary era. The Sons of Liberty in the Middle colonies quickly came to the rescue, however, by sending a printer to Virginia to establish a Whig newspaper in the province. The royal governor soon found himself unable to maintain his control over the press: the old *Virginia Gazette* threw off the traces and became a Whig sheet and thus all the governor got for his pains was the establishment of two radical newspapers in place of one. [17]

The most significant work of the papers lay in uniting the colonies behind the leadership of the seaports. After the repeal of the Stamp Act, British taxation fell almost wholly upon the trading towns: the country people did not see the commissioners, customhouse officers, and admiralty judges who to the seagoing patriots were the embodiment of British tyranny. It was vital to the success of the revolutionary movement that the farmers — who composed the great bulk of the population — be persuaded to come to the aid of the townsmen; yet they revealed an alarming disposition to regard the quarrel as being exclusively between the seaports and the British government. To convince the farmers of their stake in the struggle, the town patriots were obliged to aim their propaganda at the weakest place in the people's armor: their fear of taxation by the British government. As a result, it was the farmers who, during the revolutionary period, snuffed tyranny in every tainted breeze and who lived in fear of future evils at the hands of the mother country. It would be more exact to say, however, that they did not snuff tyranny — they read about it in their weekly newspapers.

When serving up their propaganda, the Whigs believed that

---

[16] *Maryland Gazette*, October 17, 1765. *New York Journal or General Advertiser*, November 27, 1765.

[17] James Parker to Benjamin Franklin, May 6, 1766, Franklin MSS., American Philosophical Society. *New York Journal or General Advertiser*, November 27, 1766.

seasoning and spice ought to be used liberally. "People who have weak appetites must be warmed," said they.[18] This recipe succeeded admirably in making the farmers quake for their liberty and property. A colonial farmer could scarcely pick up his newspaper without encountering dire warnings of his fate if the British Parliament succeeded in establishing its right to tax the colonies. Then, predicted the Whig journalists, Americans would be buried beneath an avalanche of imposts: hearth taxes, window taxes, taxes upon imports, taxes upon exports, land taxes — nothing, it seemed, would escape the gimlet eye of the tax gatherer. As Americans studied this dismal catalogue, they might well conclude that they would shortly "be brought to a morsel of bread, or but one meal of meat in a week" in order that Englishmen might consume double rations.[19] "Perhaps before long," remarked Alexander Hamilton, "your tables, chairs, and platters, and dishes, and knives, and forks, and every thing else, would be taxed. Nay, I don't know but they would find means to tax you for every child you got, and for every kiss your daughters received from their sweethearts; and, God knows, that would soon ruin you."[20] If farmers permitted Parliament to tax merchandise imported into the colonies, the fatal precedent would be established whereby they would be reduced to poverty and slavery. For them to contend that they had "a Right to hold the Lands which they have honestly purchased," the Whigs pointed out, "will be as great a piece of *Folly*, as it was for the Merchants *vainly* to pretend that *they* had a *Right* to keep *their own* Money, which they had *fairly gained* after *many a Risque* in their Trade."[21] With these warnings dinned in their ears, it was not remarkable that country people began to ask each other: "What would you say, if a Fellow should come to take a list of your Cattle that Parliament might tax you for them at so much a head? . . . If Parliament can take away Mr. Hancock's wharf and Mr. Row's wharf they can take away your Barn and my house."[22]

To prove that this alarm was not baseless, Americans had merely to point to Ireland as a dreadful example of what might happen

[18] *Proceedings of the Massachusetts Historical Society*, Boston, 1860, Second Series, IV, 382.

[19] *Essex Gazette*, January 18, 1774.

[20] *Works of Alexander Hamilton*, I, 36–37.

[21] *Boston Gazette*, December 23, 1771; August 1, 1774.

[22] *Old Family Letters*, edited by Alexander Biddle, Philadelphia, 1892, 140.

here. American grievances were slight indeed when contrasted with those of Ireland; there could be little doubt that the real tyranny in the British Empire was felt in Ireland rather than in the colonies. The sufferings of Ireland were of great propaganda value to the American agitators. Once a rich and prosperous country, Ireland had been crushed by heavy taxes, rack rents, and commercial restrictions until the Irish had nothing they could call their own: all their wealth had been placed at the disposal of "worn out Panders and Whores" from England. As a consequence, the island seemed to be "sinking beneath the infamous Load; and must, ere long, die a Martyr to the *absolute Controul of the Parliament of Great-Britain*." With Ireland drained dry, there was danger that America would become the "Milch cow" for English courtiers and officeholders. In this way, the fear that British America would be turned into another Ireland was employed to strengthen the determination of Americans to resist parliamentary taxation in its very beginning.

Although the royal governors lamented that the Whig newspapers were "crammed with Treason," and dreaded the publication day of the *Boston Gazette* — known among the Tories as the "Weekly Dung Barge" — they were unable to put a stop to these effusions. The legal machinery was in many provinces utterly inadequate: in Massachusetts, for example, all prosecutions were entrusted to the King's Attorney, who was paid not by the King but by the people — and the King's Attorney usually knew who buttered his bread.[23] The patriots possessed in the Zenger decision of 1735 legal guarantee of the freedom of the press. Moreover, radical printers enjoyed the protection of powerful politicians and sometimes the authors of the most inflammable articles were themselves politicians. Thus when the *Boston Gazette* printed what Governor Bernard termed "a blasphemous Abuse of Kingly Government itself," the authors, leading members of the House of Representatives, prevented the House from taking action. When the Massachusetts Council ordered the printer of the *Massachusetts Spy* to answer charges of printing a seditious article, the printer, relying upon his friendship with Sam Adams and other prominent Whigs, sent answer that he was "*too busy in his office* and should

[23] Governor Bernard to Lord Hillsborough, December 2, 1768, Bernard MSS., Harvard University Library.

not attend." [24] It was thus made abundantly clear to the royal governors that a colonial printer could not be convinced of sedition and libel by a colonial jury even if he were brought to trial. And always the threat of mob violence hung above the head of every enemy of American liberty and discouraged action by servants of the Crown. When it was learned that radical newspapers were being distributed by the post riders throughout America, the New York Council decided that it was "prudent at this time to delay making more particular inquiry lest it should be the occasion of raising the Mob." [25]

Against the overwhelming power of the colonial radicals, the British government held what it fondly believed was a trump card — military coercion. It was not until 1768, however, that the British army was called upon to restore order in the colonies and then only in such a halfhearted, bungling manner that the experiment ended in a disgrace for British arms and a resounding victory for the patriot leaders.

After the Boston mob had succeeded in driving the Commissioners of the Customs to Castle William in terror for their lives the cry was raised in England that measures be taken to show "those Braggarts their Insignificancy in the Scale of Empire" and that Boston be reduced to "a poor smuggling Village." [26] The pressure of public opinion finally stirred the sluggard Ministry of Lord Grafton into action and four regiments of British troops were dispatched to Boston to preserve order. Learning of this decision, the Massachusetts patriots, led by Sam Adams, called a convention of delegates from the towns to sit in place of the General Court, now dissolved because of its refusal to rescind the Circular Letter. In summoning this extralegal convention, the Boston patriots were usurping powers which belonged constitutionally only to the Crown, but this, perhaps, was the least of their offenses. Many of them were determined to fight off the British troops if they should attempt to land in Boston; and the Massachusetts Convention of 1768 was intended to lay the foundation for armed resistance to British authority. But the country people had no stomach for fight-

---

[24] *Essex Gazette*, November 19, 1771. *Journals of the Massachusetts House of Representatives*, Boston, 1768, 206–207.

[25] *Documents relative to the Colonial History of the State of New York*, VIII, 760, 767–768.

[26] *Public Advertiser*, October 1, November 2, 1768.

ing British troops; and the town radicals were forced to yield to the conservatism of the rural members of the convention. The result was that despite the threats of the Sons of Liberty that British soldiers would never invade Massachusetts soil, the troops were permitted to land and take up their positions in the Puritan metropolis in September 1768, without a shot being fired.

As a punishment for engaging in the treasonable designs imputed to the Massachusetts Convention, the British government proposed to apply an obsolete act of Henry VIII to the colonies which would have permitted the removal of American patriots to England for trial. This threat solidified the union of the colonies. In 1769 the Virginia House. of Burgesses dispatched a circular letter to the colonial legislatures denouncing this invasion of Americans' rights; and to lend emphasis to their word the burgesses drew up and adopted a nonimportation agreement to which they urged all Virginians to subscribe. It was characteristic of British policy that having threatened to punish the colonial ringleaders, the government backed down; the act of Henry VIII was dropped and the patriots went unscathed. It was likewise characteristic that the Massachusetts Assembly, dissolved in 1768 for refusing to obey the royal command to revoke the Circular Letter, was permitted to sit in 1769 without mention being made of the original cause of dissolution and with the resolutions denying the right of the British Parliament to tax the colonies still upon the journals. Thus, by a policy of "doing and undoing, menacing and submitting, straining and relaxing," the British government itself undermined its authority in American colonies.[27]

The presence of British troops in Boston was a standing menace to the Nonimportation Agreement: it was feared that at any moment the British government might attempt to break the boycott with the aid of the redcoats. This danger was greatly diminished, however, when in 1769 the home government withdrew to Halifax two of the four regiments that composed the garrison at Boston. This action left the weakened British force exposed to the wrath of the patriots who smarted under the charge of cowardice for having permitted the redcoats to land on New England shores. The troops that remained in Boston were too few to preserve order yet sufficiently numerous to goad the patriots and constantly to remind them of the menace of military despotism.

[27] Ramsay, *The History of the American Revolution*, Trenton, 1811, I, 118.

The weakening of the garrison at Boston in fact set the stage for the Boston Massacre. After two regiments had sailed away to Halifax a patriot remarked ominously that "the Soldiers must now take care of themselves, *nor trust too much to their Arms*, for they are but a handful, in comparison with the Sons of Liberty who could destroy them in a Moment, if they pleased." [28]

Both soldiers and civilians in Boston suspected each other of planning to strike. The townspeople's apprehensions were played upon by Sam Adams and William Cooper who, drawing liberally upon their imaginations, published in the *Journal of Events* lurid accounts of rapes, beatings, and other atrocities perpetrated by the redcoats. The soldiers' nerves were frayed to a ragged edge by being waylaid in dark streets by Whig cudgel boys; haled into court upon every conceivable pretext; and by frequent scuffles with the ropewalkers of Boston. "I don't suppose my Men are without fault," said Colonel Dalrymple, "but twenty of them have been knocked down in the Streets and got up and scratched their heads and run to their Barracks and no more has been heard of it whereas if one of the Inhabitants meets with no more than just a Kick for an Insult to a Soldier the Town is immediately in an Alarm and not one word the Soldier says in his justification can gain any credence." In October 1769, a mob attacked a British detachment on its way to barracks and filled the air with sticks and stones to such good effect that the troops were obliged to break ranks. The troops did not fire upon the townspeople although one soldier discharged his gun into the air which brought them to a momentary halt. "This," remarked Colonel Dalrymple, "is but a prelude to some motion more consequential, at least never was the popular Insolence at such a pitch." [29]

The rougher elements of the population were led to believe that they could heap indignities upon the troops with impunity. They were told that the soldiers would not fire even in self-defense without the order of a civil magistrate; and it was well known that no magistrate in Boston would dare to issue such an order. The royal officers themselves took this view: Lieutenant Governor Hutchinson could not persuade the town officers to intervene in the quar-

[28] The Case of Captain Thomas Preston of the 29th Regiment, House of Lords MSS.

[29] Colonel Dalrymple to General Gage, October 28, 1769, House of Lords MSS., Egerton MSS. 2666, British Museum, 55.

rels of the soldiers and citizens; and the Tories declined to invite a disaster by championing the troops against the citizens. "I consider myself to be without support," exclaimed Colonel Dalrymple, commander of the troops in Boston. "Government here is in the hands of the Multitude." [30]

Throughout the winter of 1769–1770, the townspeople and soldiers awaited the almost inevitable incident that would ignite the powder keg. It came early in 1770 when a party of soldiers, falling in with the ropewalkers, engaged in a free-for-all in which one soldier was seriously injured by a blow from a piece of iron. Shortly thereafter one of the ropewalkers asked a soldier if he wanted a job. When the soldier replied that he did, the ropewalker told him "to go empty his ——house." There was another brawl and word spread through Boston that the feud was to be settled by an outright battle between the townspeople and soldiers.[31]

On the night of March 5, 1770, when a mob of citizens began to attack the sentry at the customhouse, Captain Preston concluded that the Whigs intended to loot the King's Chest in which the customs revenue was stored. Quickly gathering reinforcements, he drew his men up before the customhouse and attempted to parley with the mob. He found, however, that the townspeople were in no mood to reason: they were "striking their Clubs of Bludgeons one against another and calling out, come on you Rascals, you bloody-backs, you Lobster Scoundrels; fire if you dare, G——d damn you, fire and be damned, we know you dare not." Preston stood between the mob and the soldiers, attempting to make his voice heard above the din, when the mob "advanced to the points of the Bayonets, struck some of them, and even the Muzzles of the Pieces, and seemed to be endeavouring to close with the Soldiers." At this moment, after one of the soldiers had been knocked down, the command "fire" was heard and the soldiers emptied their guns into the mob. Preston was later accused of having ordered his men to fire; he denied the charge and it is improbable that he gave such a command. At the time of the volley, Preston was directly in the line of fire and came perilously near being struck himself.[32]

[30] *Ibid.*
[31] *Ibid.*, 56, 69. *Gazetteer and New Daily Advertiser*, April 30, 1770.
[32] *The London Magazine*, 1770, XXXIX, 222. The Case of Captain Thomas Preston of the 29th Regiment, House of Lords MSS. *Gazetteer and New Daily Advertiser*, December 18, 1770. *A Narrative of What Happened at Boston*, March 5, 1770, P.R.O. War Office, Class I, IX.

When the smoke cleared, five Bostonians lay dead or dying in the street. The townspeople immediately fell back; but after a few moments of hesitation they came forward again, apparently to take away the dead and wounded. The soldiers, however, believed that they were to be attacked again and they began to make ready to fire until Preston struck up their firelocks with his own hand. After the street had been cleared, there could be little doubt that the mob was preparing a second attack. The streets echoed to the beat of drums and the cry of "To Arms! To Arms! To Arms! Turn out with your Guns!" Preston was told that four or five hundred people were assembling and had sworn to take the life of every British soldier that had fired upon the citizens. Rather than face this overwhelming force, Preston and his men retreated until they were joined by the 29th Regiment, which had gotten under arms. Although several officers were knocked down by missiles before they finally reached the guardhouse, no casualties were suffered and the danger of a counter massacre was averted at least for the night.[33]

Supported by a large number of townspeople, Sam Adams demanded the removal of the troops from Boston and Lieutenant Governor Hutchinson was obliged to comply. The Boston selectmen immediately began to take *ex parte* testimony from the townspeople regarding the affray; and the Whigs rushed through the press an account of the events of March 5 which made the Massacre appear to be the result of a deliberate plot by the British soldiers to murder innocent Whigs.[34] But the jury found the soldiers guilty only of manslaughter and they were permitted to plead their clergy — in other words, to prove their ability to read (which made them "clerks") and so gain exemption from the jurisdiction of the secular courts. Accordingly, their punishment was reduced to a mere burning upon the hand. (By English criminal law, laymen who were accorded the benefit of clergy were burned with a hot iron on the left thumb in order that, being thus marked, they could not again claim their clergy.) Sam Adams tried the soldiers over again in the newspapers under the name "Vindex" but nothing could be done to upset the jury's verdict or to mete out more severe punishment upon the soldiers. Instead, the Boston Whigs found themselves arrayed as the fomenters of the Massacre; and "mobbish

[33] *Ibid.*
[34] John Lathrop, *Innocent Blood Crying to God from the Streets of Boston*, Boston, 1771, 18.

Boston" became even more unsavory than before to conservatives throughout the colonies.

The Boston Massacre probably hastened the inevitable reaction against the inordinate power which the people had gained in the Northern colonies. The bloodshed in Boston served warning upon the mercantile aristocracy of the seaports that unless the mobs were curbed the colonies might find themselves at war with the mother country. "It's high time a stop was put to mobbing," they vowed, "without which property will soon be very precarious, as God knows where it will end." [35] The merchants recoiled from this prospect: they had no heart to fight Great Britain and they had even less desire to see a social revolution in the American colonies.

Yet it was becoming visibly evident that the Nonimportation Agreement was passing out of the control of the merchants into that of the politicians and the mob. Radicals were becoming increasingly intolerant of those "timid or trimming Whigs" who sought safety in the middle of the road. "When a Country is divided," they declared, "*Neutrality* is little better than *Treason.*" [36] The Whig businessmen were themselves beginning to feel the sharp pricks of "Democratick Tyranny" from a "lawless banditti." [37] Overriding the wishes of the merchants, the patriot leaders insisted upon publicly burning or sending imported goods back to England. When they decided that the merchants had been too lenient with importers, the mechanics appointed committees from among themselves to punish the culprits. The merchants exclaimed that it was insufferable that "men of liberal Education," wealth, and position should be "dictated to by illiterate Mechanicks" and by "every insignificant *whiffler* that can scarce spell his name" and they began to seek means of freeing themselves from these upstarts.[38]

The New York merchants were the first to succeed in casting off the control of the people and re-establishing their authority. It is significant that in New York the class struggle had attained a greater height than in any other colony and that the provincial aristocracy had more to lose by a popular upheaval. New York, even

[35] *New York Gazette and Weekly Mercury*, July 23, 1770.

[36] *Boston Gazette*, August 7, 1769. *Boston Weekly News Letter*, September 1, 1768.

[37] *Hutchinson Correspondence*, II, Thomas Hutchinson to ?, June 26, 1770.

[38] *Boston Chronicle*, January 15, 1770. *New York Journal or General Advertiser*, January 18, 1770. *New York Gazette and Weekly Mercury*, August 13, 1770.

more than Massachusetts, was ruled by an oligarchy which owed its predominance to disparities and abuses which were certain to be swept away if the people should ever come into their own.

New York, although an appendage of the British Crown, was even more truly an appendage of the two great opposing factions of the provincial aristocracy — the Delanceys and the Livingstons. James Delancey, head of the so-called "Ottoman Family," controlled the New York Assembly and Council and even eclipsed the royal governor himself. Governor Clinton became, in fact, a mere figurehead largely because he "continued at his bottle after dinner, and committed the important affairs of government to the Ottoman Chiefs." While the governor guzzled, James Delancey gathered up the threads of power; and until his death in 1760 he dominated the colony and "settled elections at a beer-house with his companions by sending out his minions." [39] A staunch Churchman, Delancey helped establish King's College and endeared himself to the Episcopalians of New York. His son, Captain Oliver Delancey, inherited this political machine together with a fortune of one hundred thousand pounds. Young Delancey was educated at Eton and Cambridge, and had become a captain in the British army during the Seven Years' War. An ardent turfman, he imported one of the first racing stables in America and divided his affection between "cock-fighting, horse-racing, and women." In Philadelphia he was regarded as a rake and wastrel and when he descended upon that temple of sobriety in 1770 with a retinue of twenty-three young blades "a Cocking," an alarmed citizen urged that the town be shut against Delancey and his party lest they bring "a Reproach on our Place, and perhaps debase our Manners." [40]

The chief rivals of the Delanceys were William Livingston and his followers who cultivated the Presbyterian vote in New York. The Livingston family, like the Delanceys, was extremely wealthy; in fact, the Livingstons were one of the largest landowning families in the province. After the death of James Delancey in 1760, the Livingston party dominated the assembly; and it was not until 1768 that young Oliver Delancey came into his full patrimony and assumed control of the legislature of New York as his father had done before him.

[39] *Pennsylvania Journal and Weekly Advertiser*, March 29, May 3, 1770.
[40] *New York Gazette or Weekly Post Boy*, March 26, 1770. *New York Journal or General Advertiser*, April 19, 1779.

Both the Delanceys and the Livingstons strove to make the New York Assembly a provincial Parliament. If Whiggery meant the exaltation of the legislature at the expense of the Crown's authority, virtually all New York politicians were Whigs. The Delanceys and the Livingstons were agreed upon the necessity of home rule but neither proposed to admit the people to a share in power. In their eyes, the sole question at issue was what faction of the aristocracy should reap the benefits of a successful assertion of colonial rights; the dispute with the British government was being carried on by gentlemen and for gentlemen. Thus New York politics consisted, for the most part, of the sound and fury of two aristocratic families, both of which aspired to dominate the province. The choice open to the people in this struggle seemed to be whether they were to be ruled by Great Britain or by a provincial oligarchy.

At the beginning of the revolutionary movement, a large proportion of the upper class of New York was to be found openly or secretly aiding the Sons of Liberty. The patriot party in New York was far more aristocratic in character than that in New England. But most of these gentry wished only to strengthen their own position in the colony and to secure a larger share of authority for the New York Assembly which they confidently expected to dominate. When it became clear that if the revolutionary movement were not stopped it would escape from their control and lead to the rule of the common people, they attempted to halt the tide. They became Tories; but it always remained one of the peculiarities of New York Tories that many of them had formerly been hand in glove with the mob leaders and had helped open the bag of the winds that whisked them to "Hell, Hull, and Halifax."

During the Stamp Act period, the Livingstons and the Delanceys were engaged in a heated contest for the privilege of leading the struggle against British tyranny. Both factions claimed to be the true upholders of freedom and the defenders of local liberties, particularly the rights of the legislature. " 'Tis upon our Assemblies that Breakers will first fall," they declared, "and if they are outwitted or overpowered, America is undone." [41] New Yorkers were treated to the spectacle of two sets of aristocrats descanting eloquently upon liberty, striking Ciceronic postures and courting the favor of the common people. James Delancey openly hobnobbed with such

[41] *New York Journal or General Advertiser*, March 3, 1768. *Pennsylvania Journal and Weekly Advertiser*, May 3, 1770.

proletarian leaders as Isaac Sears and Alexander McDougall. Delancey was the only representative of the "first people" of New
York City who openly attended the meetings of the Sons of Liberty;
and he spoke so eloquently of his patriotism that the common
people "thought they had discovered a *Cato* that would die in his
country's cause." [42] But Delancey soon shattered these hopes;
shocked by what he heard in the cabals of the Sons of Liberty, and
offended by the low company he was compelled to keep, he withdrew from the society and organized a group of Sons of Liberty of
his own. Henceforth, there were two factions of this patriot organization in New York — but it was observed that a gentleman
could belong only to the genteel organization sponsored by Delancey.[43]

Unlike the New England Tories, the New York aristocrats sought
to win the support of the common people. As rivals for the people's
favor, they could scarcely treat them with disdain; for this reason,
the New York aristocracy was able to hold its ground with greater
success than was the upper class elsewhere in the Northern colonies.
Delancey won great popularity by permitting hunting on his estate
near New York City, thus supporting the claim of New Yorkers
that they had the right of fishing and hunting on the entire island
of Manhattan. During elections, Captain Delancey "posted himself
in the broad way, and stopped every elector that passed within his
call, that he had the least hopes of turning." Here was no repulsive,
snobbish aristocrat but a neighborly, affable fellow, ready to meet
the common people on equal terms, at least during elections.[44]

Delancey's tactics against the Livingstons soon proved their worth.
In the election of 1768, he called for a purge of all lawyers from
the New York Assembly; and since most of the lawyers were
Livingston men, this move threatened to destroy their control of
the assembly. The popular hostility to lawyers gave Delancey a
burning campaign issue: these "pettifogging Attorneys" were denounced as "the bane of Society" who aspired to get all the property in the province into their hands. "Does not *this* Country as
much swarm with *them*," asked the Delanceys, "as *Norway* does
with Rats, or our Salt-Meadows, in a calm Summer's Evening with

---

[42] *Pennsylvania Journal and Weekly Advertiser*, March 29, 1770. *New York Journal or General Advertiser*, May 10, 1770; December 28, 1775.
[43] *Pennsylvania Journal and Weekly Advertiser*, May 3, 1770.
[44] *Ibid.*, March 29, 1770.

Musquetoes? And do not both kinds of Vermin sustain themselves by drawing the Blood from our very Bodies?"[45] The Delanceys proposed to replace the lawyers with merchants who would devote themselves to the commercial interests of New York and thereby redress the balance against the heavy representation from the country districts. The mob was on the side of the Livingstons — "If there is not fair play shown [in the election]," said Peter Livingston, "there will be bloodshed, as we have by far the best part of the Bruisers on our side, who are determined to use force, if they [the Delanceys] use any foul play." The close connection between the mob and the Livingstons served to discredit them in the eyes of the New York merchants, most of whom were eager to be free of mob rule; in their opinion, the Livingstons were "*a restless set of republicans*" who stopped at nothing to win the support of the lower classes. The election went decisively against the Livingston faction and control of the New York Assembly passed into the hands of Delancey and his partisans. William Livingston acknowledged the overwhelming rout of his forces by retiring to New Jersey, leaving only the radicals to contest the rule of the Delanceys.[46]

The struggle for office carried on by the two "ancient families of the province" had long been a stench in radical nostrils. The aristocrats — whether they called themselves Delanceys or Livingstons, Tories or Whigs — seemed to "bellow for liberty to get into power"; the very men who paid lip service to liberty secretly yearned for the power of "Turkish Bashaws, French Grandees, and the Romish Clergy." The radicals insisted that neither the Delanceys nor the Livingstons had the right to call themselves Sons of Liberty — that title could be borne only by the true Sons of Liberty who met at Hampden Hall. These patriots were not members of the old aristocratic families of the province — most of them were new men who had come up from the bottom by the hard way. John Lamb was a liquor dealer; Isaac Sears — "King Sears" — was the son of a Yankee fish peddler and had himself been a sailor, privateersman, and small merchant; and Alexander McDougall — the "John Wilkes of New York" — had risen from equally humble circumstances.[47]

[45] *New York Journal or General Advertiser*, February 25, 1768; March 4, 1768, Supplement.

[46] *Ibid.*, April 19, 1770.

[47] C. H. Levermore, "The Whigs of Colonial New York," *American Historical Review*, 1896, I, 247. *New York Journal or General Advertiser*, April 5, 19, 1770. *New York Gazette or Weekly Post Boy*, January 29, 1770.

These men were the true tribunes of the people of the American Revolution and expressed the hopes and ideals of the people far more fully than did the well-born leaders of the province. Inflexible in their stand against British tyranny, they were also resolved to wage war upon tyranny at home. They believed that the revolutionary movement was a mighty force which, by sweeping old institutions before it, was making way for a new democratic society. To them, the Delanceys and the Livingstons were not leaders but obstacles in the way of this revolution.

The radicals found in 1770, however, that the revolution was far from complete and that the old order could still strike back vigorously when attacked. Outraged by the open corruption and intimidation practised in New York, the radicals attempted to introduce voting by ballot there. Although the ballot was used in Massachusetts, Pennsylvania, and Connecticut, voting by viva voce still prevailed in New York and other colonies. As a consequence, elections were not free; in New York "the intollerable tyranny of the great and opulent who . . . have openly threatened them [the poorer citizens] with the loss of their Employment, and to arrest them for debt, unless they gave their Voices as they were directed," made possible the domination of the province by the aristocracy. The radicals believed with good cause that as long as voters stood in terror of their landlords and employers, the rule of the "Knights of the most noble Order of Perriwiggs" could not be overthrown.[48] But, as could be foreseen, the conservatives rallied to the defense of viva voce voting and denounced the ballot as "a dangerous Innovation, directly contrary to the old Laws and Customs of the Realm, and unknown in any royal British Government on the Continent."[49] The assembly heeded the objections of the conservatives by voting down the ballot; and although John Lamb summoned the patriots to assemble at Liberty Tree — a tree consecrated by the Sons of Liberty to the cause of freedom — and marched from there to the assembly, and though Lamb himself appeared before the bar of the House, the legislators could not be brought to reverse their position.

[48] George W. Edwards, *New York as an Eighteenth Century Municipality,* New York, 1917, II, 50. *New York Gazette or Weekly Post Boy,* January 8, 1770.
[49] *New York Journal or General Advertiser,* January 4, 1770. *New York Gazette or Weekly Post Boy,* January 1, 1770. *Boston Gazette,* January 15, 1770.

Early in 1770, when the efforts of the people and their leaders to seize control of the Nonimportation Agreement threatened the foundations of aristocratic domination in New York, the privileged class struck in retaliation at Alexander McDougall, one of the most radical of the Sons of Liberty. McDougall was born in Scotland and brought early in life to New York by his father, a milkman, who set his son to work peddling milk in the city. But young McDougall was drawn to the sea; he became a mate, and in 1758 the captain of a privateer, preying chiefly upon Dutchmen in the West Indies. He found the Dutch good game, married a rich lady in the West Indies, and returned to New York where he set up a "Slop-Shop." He did not immediately distinguish himself among the New York Whigs; indeed, Isaac Sears at one time called him "a rotten-hearted fellow," which, in the opinion of the Tories, eminently qualified him to be a New York Liberty Boy.[50] It was not until the controversy over the Mutiny Act that McDougall emerged as a first-rate agitator. After the New York Assembly had saved itself from dissolution by providing the British troops with supplies as required by the Mutiny Act, McDougall published anonymously a pamphlet addressed "To the Betrayed Inhabitants of the City and Colony of New York" in which he asserted that the assembly had violated its trust by voting supplies to the British troops. He declared that the only honorable course open to the assembly was to follow the example of the Massachusetts and South Carolina Legislatures and refuse to appropriate money for the soldiers. "Will you suffer your liberties to be torn from you by your own representatives?" demanded McDougall. "Tell it not in Boston; publish it not in the streets of Charlestown." [51] To protest against this tyranny created by the people's own representatives, McDougall sounded the tocsin for a mass meeting of the citizens in the fields.

The New York Whigs, although always ready to lead an attack upon British authority, were outraged by this assault upon their own stronghold, the New York Assembly. They denounced the author as a Cataline and a Wilkes who sought to "trample down all legal authority, and shake the government to the foundation"; and led by James Delancey and his aristocratic partisans they attempted to bring the seditious pamphleteer to justice.[52] Confession by a printer's

[50] *New York Journal or General Advertiser*, May 3, 1770.
[51] *Boston Gazette*, January 8, 1770.
[52] *New York Gazette and Weekly Mercury*, April 9, 1770. *New York Gazette or Weekly Post Boy*, May 7, 1770.

devil and the frightened proprietor of the newspaper put the finger of guilt upon Alexander McDougall. He was immediately arraigned at the bar of the assembly; his defense was voted to be "a high contempt of the House" and he was ordered imprisoned. This action gave McDougall an opportunity of becoming an "American Wilkes" and none could deny that he made the most of it. Determined to make a *cause célèbre* of his case, McDougall refused to give bail, insisting instead upon going to jail. "I rejoice," he exclaimed, "I am the first sufferer of Liberty since the commencement of our glorious struggle. . . . The cause for which I suffer is capable of converting Chains into Laurels, and transforming a Gaol into a Paradise." [53]

The persecution of McDougall by the New York Assembly turned the unfranchised masses against a legislature in which they had no more actual representation than in the British Parliament and which now seemed determined to ape the tyranny of the House of Commons. Never before had it been clearer that the liberty of the New York Assembly did not mean the liberty of the people and that their exertions in behalf of freedom were merely increasing the power of the local aristocracy. While the plain people concentrated their attention upon the menace of British tyranny, the "Ottoman Family" of the Delanceys established themselves in power and persecuted tribunes of the people like McDougall who sought to defend liberty on the home front. Was this the liberty for which New Yorkers had fought? "What have we been contending for ever since the noble Virginians first set the glorious example!" exclaimed a disillusioned patriot. "A libel! curse on the Star Chamber law." The aristocratic leadership of New York was for the moment thoroughly discredited: "Trust not in the rich," the people were advised, "they trust in their wealth, and will sneak in an hour of distress. If the middle class sleep, perdition is just before us." [54]

McDougall spent almost three months in prison, receiving delegations of patriots, feasting upon choice viands contributed by his sympathizers, and striking the pose of an American John Wilkes. Because Wilkes had been imprisoned for the libel contained in the forty-fifth number of the *North Briton*, his admirers regarded this number with peculiar veneration. The followers of Alexander

[53] *Pennsylvania Journal and Weekly Advertiser*, February 22, 1770.
[54] *Virginia Gazette* (Purdie and Dixon), March 22, 1770. *Pennsylvania Journal and Weekly Advertiser*, March 22, 1770.

McDougall adopted this practice from the English Wilkites. On February fourteenth, for instance, "the Forty-fifth Day of the Year, forty-five Gentlemen, real Enemies to internal Taxation, by, or in Obedience to external Authority, and cordial Friends of American Liberty, went in decent Procession to the New Gaol; and dined with him [McDougall], on Forty-five Pounds of Beef Stakes, cut from a Bullock of Forty-five Months old." [55] McDougall aroused great enthusiasm among the "female lovers of liberty"; and hardly a day passed but some patriotic ladies managed to get up a procession to visit the handsome prisoner. On one momentous day, he received forty-five virgins who sang forty-five songs, which prompted a Tory to remark that "he that is courted in a gloomy Prison by Forty-Five (virgins) in one Day, cannot fail of being a MAN INDEED." McDougall, it seemed, was in the "paradise of Mahomet, graced with forty-five black-eyed virgins, who are continually caressing him; while those angels of light, the TRUE sons of liberty, are offering incense at his shrine." One Tory, however, threw cold water on this bliss by declaring that all the virgins were forty-five years old.[56]

The New York aristocracy began to suspect that in Alexander McDougall it had got "a bear by the tail." [57] This irrepressible orator, reveling in his martyrdom and fomenting hatred of the aristocracy, promised to make the trial room a forum from which to denounce "the tools of arbitrary power." Moreover, a horde of Whigs from New England and Pennsylvania seemed likely to descend upon New York to ensure that McDougall received a fair trial. Therefore, although he was indicted on charges of libel by the New York grand jury and his trial was set for October 1770, the trial never took place. Having at last persuaded him to give bail and move out of jail, the conservatives were happy to be rid of the affair.[58]

The New York merchants found themselves endangered by Alexander McDougall and the mob on one side and by double-dealing merchants in the neighboring colonies on the other. Although the boycott was striking evidence of the unity of the colonies, the complete unity essential to the success of the scheme had

[55] *Boston Gazette*, February 26, 1770.
[56] *New York Journal or Weekly Advertiser*, April 12, 1770. *New York Gazette and Weekly Mercury*, April 9, 30, 1770.
[57] *Pennsylvania Journal and Weekly Advertiser*, March 22, May 3, 1770.
[58] *Ibid. New York Gazette or Weekly Post Boy*, April 2, 1770.

not yet been attained. The colonies had closed their doors in varying degrees to British merchandise: in some, the agreement had been stultified by permitting the importation of almost all articles of trade except those taxed by Townshend; in others, even necessities had been excluded in order to bring speedy retribution upon the mother country. There were, moreover, gaping holes in the boycott: Rhode Island merchants imported British merchandise freely and to make matters worse sold it to former customers of Boston. Portsmouth, New Hampshire, merchants took similar advantage of the Bostonians' self-sacrifice. Further, it was manifestly more difficult to enforce the boycott in Virginia and Maryland where most of the planters were themselves importers of British merchandise; so many wares were brought into these colonies contrary to the agreement that George Mason began to fear that Virginia would become "the receptacle of all the goods refused by the other colonies." [59] New York merchants believed that Albany was secretly trading with England through Quebec while South Carolinians denounced Georgia merchants who continued to import British goods and sell them at high prices in South Carolina itself. The Charleston merchants voted to have no commercial dealings with Georgia and urged that the people of that recusant colony be "amputated from the rest of the brethren as a *rotten part* that might spread a dangerous infection." [60] Philadelphia merchants for their part regarded themselves as victims of Baltimore's trickery; and everywhere merchants who obeyed the agreement saw themselves "beguiled out of their Trade Either by their Neighbouring Governments or by Men of no Principle among themselves." [61]

All these suspicions and recriminations were nourished by Tory propaganda which from the beginning had pictured the Nonimportation Agreement as a scheme of Whig merchants to unload their goods on the public at fancy prices. The Tories spread tales of vast secret importations; accused prominent Whigs like John Hancock of making a fortune out of New Englanders' gullibility; and planted seeds of doubt among the colonies. To quiet these rumors, the

[59] Rowland, I, 144–147.
[60] *Pennsylvania Journal and Weekly Advertiser*, July 19, 1770. *South Carolina Gazette*, May 17, 1770, Supplement. *New York Gazette and Weekly Mercury*, July 19, 1770.
[61] Thomas Clifford to Lancelot Cooper, June 21, September 15, 1770, Clifford MSS., Historical Society of Pennsylvania. *Massachusetts Gazette*, January 11, 1776. *Public Advertiser*, October 20, 1770.

Boston politicians determined to send back to England a shipload of British merchandise that had been landed at the port. The ship was loaded and set sail but this gesture was largely nullified by the rumor that the cargo consisted of boxes filled not with British luxuries but with "billets of wood, shavings and brick bats."

It is clear that of all the colonial ports New York most rigorously enforced the Nonimportation Agreement. While Boston was reducing its imports from Great Britain by half during 1769, New York cut its imports from £482,000 in 1768 to £74,000 in 1769.[62] Where the agreement was carried out in good faith, the pinch of scarcity soon began to be felt: prices skyrocketed; nails could not be obtained; and building came to a standstill. Unemployment spread rapidly among the town artisans; but the farmers remained comparatively prosperous because of the high price of food. Tea became a luxury: priced at four shillings per pound before 1768, it reached eleven shillings in the winter of 1769. The wearing of homespun put many Americans' patriotism to a severe test: "My Homespun Clothers were so ill dyed," exclaimed a Philadelphian, "that that Dye Stuff came off on my Shirts and painted them of the same Colour which occasioned so much Rubbing by the Washerwoman to get them clear that she wore out my Shirts for me." [63] Despite the fact that the hardships of the Nonimportation Agreement fell most heavily upon the town artisans, they remained its most steadfast supporters. On the other hand, the merchants, finding their supplies exhausted and further importations barred, began to clamor for a relaxation of the boycott before they were completely ruined.

In May 1770, the merchants revealed the first signs of cracking under the triple strain of suspicion, empty warehouses, and mob rule. The Philadelphia importers proposed to open the port to all British merchandise except tea; and fifty Boston merchants took up the cry for an end of the boycott. But their attempt to come to terms with the British government was thwarted by the town mechanics and the patriot leaders who demanded that the boycott be maintained until all taxes had been repealed. The position of the

[62] *Collections of the Massachusetts Historical Society*, Boston, 1885, IX, 424, 432.

[63] *The Burd Papers*, edited by Lewis Burd Walker, Pottsville, 1899, 53. *Publications of the Colonial Society of Massachusetts, Transactions*, 1916–1917, Boston, 1918, XIX, 248–249. *New York Journal or General Advertiser*, July 12, 1770.

merchants grew steadily worse and in June 1770 the New Yorkers proposed a meeting at Norwalk, Connecticut, of delegates to be appointed by the merchants of the Northern seaports "to adopt one general solid System, for the Benefit of the Whole, that no one Colony may be liable to the Censures or Reproaches of another but all share the same Fate." The refusal of the other seaports to attend this meeting convinced the New Yorkers that they were "starving on the slender Meals of Patriotism" while "Rogues laugh'd and thriv'd." [64]

Despite the insistence of the mob that the boycott be protracted to the bitter end, the New York merchants resolved to break the agreement. In the very teeth of "their High Mightinesses, the Mohawks," the merchants openly flouted the rule of the patriots.[65] They drew up a petition demanding the ending of the boycott and procured twelve hundred signatures from among the wealthier citizens. The patriots attempted to stop the petition by parading the streets with flags on which was inscribed "Liberty and no Importation" but the merchants drove them off with their walking sticks. The New York gentry rejoiced that the mob had been "muzzl'd at last" and triumphantly prepared to throw open the port to British merchandise.[66]

The defection of New York marked the end of the Nonimportation Agreement, although efforts were made to keep it alive in the other colonies. From England, Benjamin Franklin attempted "by an electrical stroke, to reinvigorate the exhausted Brethren of Pennsylvania"; and the Bostonians tried to induce the New York mob to rise against the merchants, but these appeals were without result.[67] Most Americans continued to boycott British tea but the Nonimportation Agreement had been struck a fatal blow by the New Yorkers.

The patriots always contended that the British government had been about to yield when New York surrendered: "LIBERTY, like ripened fruit, was again falling into our lap," exclaimed the Charleston patriots. In other words, the trumps were all in the

[64] New York Gazette and Weekly Post Boy, July 2, 1770.
[65] New York Gazette and Weekly Mercury, November 19, 1770. Boston Evening Post, September 10, 1770. Pennsylvania Journal and Weekly Advertiser, October 25, 1770. Boston Evening Post, July 16, 1770. New York Gazette and Weekly Mercury, July 23, 1770.
[66] Documents relative to the Colonial History of the State of New York, VIII, 217, 219. Letters of General Thomas Gage, II, 546–547.
[67] Public Advertiser, November 13, 1770.

colonists' hand when those "parracidial, treacherous *Dons*," the New York merchants, threw in their chips.[68] It was believed that the next session of Parliament would have seen the complete repeal of all taxes: the manufacturers were "absolutely *out at elbows*"; the workers were starving; and the government would not long withstand the popular demand for conciliation with the colonies. The patriots could only conclude that "a secret Exertion of Ministerial Influence" such as that which had brought the House of Commons under the King had been employed against American liberties: "Corruption with gigantic strides, has crossed the Atlantic, and *New York* feels it in *her Heart*." [69] George III might have been touched by this testimonial to his talents but it is clear that the colonists overrated their sovereign's skill in corrupting his subjects.

For some time after 1770, New York merchants found it decidedly unhealthy to travel about the colonies. Connecticut innkeepers posted the names of those who stopped at their hostelries in order that the mob might suffer no delay in disposing of them. New Jersey towns put in supplies of tar and feathers with which to welcome visiting New Yorkers. One importer was stopped at Woodbridge, New Jersey, and was "genteely ducked to cool his courage." [70] Indeed, the merchants in all the colonies suffered by the action of the New Yorkers. They were now under suspicion as turncoats; and many Americans resolved in 1770 that never again would they trust themselves to their leadership. The lesson learned from the failure of the Nonimportation Agreement was that the common people must be entrusted with control over the boycott and that merchants must be watched carefully lest they sell out the cause.[71]

The New York radicals, concluding that the conduct of New York would be "a stench in the nostrils of every true-born American, till time is no more," proposed to move en masse to Perth Amboy where they believed they would find "easy navigation, de-

[68] *Pennsylvania Journal and Weekly Advertiser*, June 21, September 20, 1770. *New York Gazette and Weekly Mercury*, July 30, 1770. *New York Journal or General Advertiser*, May 24, 1770.

[69] *South Carolina Gazette*, August 20, 1770, Supplement. Thomas Cooper to Thomas Pownall, October 12 and November 5, 1770. British Museum, Kings MSS., 203, Library of Congress Transcript.

[70] *Pennsylvania Journal and Weekly Advertiser*, August 9, 1770.

[71] William Pepperell to Arthur Lee, November 21, 1770, MS. Massachusetts Historical Society. Lee, II, 302.

lightful prospect, and healthful situation," and no Tory merchants.[72] In this refuge, they promised themselves, they would be free from the domination of that "abandoned crew of the most perfidious tyrannical traytors, who have ever been striving to enslave their fellow-citizens that happen to have less money and low cunning than themselves." [73] Once established in Perth Amboy, the patriots expected to pay New Yorkers back in their own coin by ruining New York as a port. The scheme fell through, however, when the patriots found that the Boston Whigs were not disposed to carry their hostility to New York to the point of setting up Sears, Lamb, McDougall & Company in business at Perth Amboy.

After the good news from New York, Englishmen breathed easier. There was no longer danger that "the Kingdom of the Saints will shine forth, and Boston become the Seat of Empire" and give law to England.[74] New Yorkers were applauded for having freed themselves from the tyranny of Boston and for having displayed the best qualities of Englishmen when confronted with oppression. Even if New Yorkers were slaves, it was observed that it was "surely more honourable to have this kingdom for a sovereign, than to have the rabble of Boston or Philadelphia." [75] The failure of this "great and last Effort of American Patriotism" was regarded as final proof that the colonies could not prevail against a firmly united England: the mother country had stood her ground and "down they tumbled one after another like Nine-pins." [76] Great Britain now seemed invulnerable even in what had been supposed was her weakest spot: her dependence upon the colonial market. Lord North's stock as a statesman rose rapidly: his handling of the colonial dispute was hailed as a masterly exhibition of tact and firmness. But in the long run this easy triumph proved disastrous for England: after 1770, Englishmen made the fatal mistake of taking colonial opposition lightly — and of this error Lord North himself was signally guilty when in 1773 he acted upon the assumption that Americans preferred cheap tea to liberty.

[72] *Pennsylvania Chronicle*, July 30, 1770.
[73] *Ibid.*
[74] *Public Advertiser*, November 23, 1770.
[75] *The Repository*, London, 1771, II, 314-315.
[76] *Public Advertiser*, November 13, 1770.

CHAPTER   THIRTEEN

The Decline of the
Revolutionary Movement

Thomas Hutchinson

IN BREAKING the Nonimportation Agreement, the New York merchants administered a severe setback to the revolutionary movement. For three years after the collapse of the boycott, the patriot leaders were compelled to struggle against widespread indifference and "political Lethargy" among the people. They lamented that "the Spirit of Patriotism seems expiring in America in general," and many of them gave up the fight as lost and began to make their peace with the Tory oligarchs. Christopher Gadsden of South Carolina urged Sam Adams to send him "a receipt effectually to cure supineness" but Adams had no sovereign cure for the slump in idealism even in Massachusetts. In New York, the patriots found only "backwardness, frivolous delays, and . . . total dearth of spirit." [1] But what most alarmed the patriots was the weakening of the bonds of colonial union. Correspondence between the leaders in various colonies almost ceased and Massachusetts seemed to have been "left in the lurch" by the other colonies. When Sam Adams urged John Dickinson to take up his pen and again awaken the American people to their peril, Adams met with polite evasion. John Dickinson had married a rich Quakeress and settled down in a splendid country house outside Philadelphia. The patriots suspected that good living had weakened his principles; certainly, he was unwilling to bestir himself in the cause of colonial liberty until he saw better prospects of success. [2]

American manufactures were forgotten as a flood of British merchandise poured into the colonies after 1770. Ladies deserted their spinning wheels and idled over their tea tables and talked fashions instead of politics. The roads were crowded with "Coaches, Chariots and Chaises"; and many of the staunchest patriots renounced frugality and "puritanism." The colonies had never seemed so prosperous as during the period of the decline of the patriot

[1] Reed, I, 47. *Newport Mercury*, August 3, 1773, Supplement.
[2] John Dickinson to Samuel Adams, April 10, 1773; Christopher Gadsden to Samuel Adams, June 5, 1774, Adams MSS., New York Public Library.

party: lands were increasing in value, roads were being improved, and the people were in general contented and happy. "In short," said a Philadelphian, "everything of a domestic kind is as we would wish and nothing but some unhappy misunderstanding with the Mother Country can hurt us." Americans were eager to start making money again; too much politics, it had been learned, was bad for business.[3]

Virginians began to display what New England patriots thought shocking affection for their new governor, Lord Botetourt. Botetourt was an affable, bumbling peer, a lord of the bedchamber and an accomplished courtier. Some members of Parliament, at the time of his appointment to the governorship, questioned his ability to read and write; later, in the House of Commons, Barré and Burke "made everybody laugh ready to die for near an hour with their comments on Lord Botetourt's two speeches" to the Virginia Assembly. Barré "challenged the whole ministry, and defied them to make common sense of it." But if Botetourt was not a scholar or a wit, he was eminently a gentleman; and Virginia aristocrats, who dearly loved a lord, fell under the charms of this amiable but somewhat torpid peer. "Fulsome panegyrics" began to pour in upon the governor and Virginia ladies brought out their most expensive fineries for the governor's "court." Even Lord Hillsborough – to whom Botetourt owed his elevation – began to rise in the estimation of some Virginians for having favored the colony with a gentleman of such impeccable lineage and manners. American patriots were dismayed: they began to fear that Virginians were allowing themselves to be wheedled out of their liberties by fine manners and a coat of arms; "titles, Burgundy and a gilt coach" seemed stronger in Virginia than love of liberty. It is notable, however, that even Lord Botetourt was unable to prevent the passage of the Virginia Resolutions in 1769; and his untimely death shortly thereafter set at rest all apprehension that Virginians were about to be undone by a lord of the bedchamber.[4]

[3] Thomas Clifford to Thomas Frank, November 16, 1771, Clifford MSS., Historical Society of Pennsylvania. Thomas Barton to Thomas Penn, April 28, 1773, Penn MSS., *Official Correspondence*, XI, Historical Society of Pennsylvania. *Essex Gazette*, May 19, 1772. *Massachusetts Gazette and Weekly News Letter*, January 2, 1772.

[4] Cavendish, II, 26. Rowland, I, 136, 152. *New York Gazette or Weekly Post Boy*, June 19, 1769. *Virginia Gazette* (Rind's), February 2, 1769; January 2, 1772.

After spending six years in outer darkness, the Tories now came into the light of day. No longer were they obliged to speak their opinions with frequent glances over their shoulders; freed from the terror of the mob, they openly drank to the health of Lord North and emptied their bumpers to the toast: "Confusion to S. Adams and party." [5] But the Tories were slow to take advantage of this swing of fortune — instead of actively taking the field against the Whigs, they preferred to tend their estates and businesses and let time work in their favor. Governor Hutchinson was compelled to remind them that they did not live "in the Commonwealth of Plato but in the dregs of Romulus" and that full advantage must be taken of this opportunity to complete the rout of the patriots.

Although the dispute with Great Britain was very nearly forgotten by Americans, this brief era of good feelings was disturbed by acrimonious bickerings between the assemblies and the royal governors. The assemblies still sought to transform themselves into local parliaments while the Crown continued its efforts to bring them under control by means of the prerogative. In South Carolina, for example, the struggle took the form of a passage of arms between the assembly and governor over moneys voted by the assembly to assist John Wilkes; in Massachusetts, the bone of contention was the removal of the assembly by means of a royal instruction from Boston to Cambridge. In Maryland, the assembly accused the governor and council of imposing taxes without its consent. From this controversy sprang an interchange of public letters between Daniel Dulany and Charles Carroll in which Dulany, formerly a Whiggish champion, took the Tory side. [6]

For the most part, the patriots' grievances were stale, flat, and unprofitable and the British government made no move to oblige them by giving them a fresh supply. By 1772, the Whigs were scraping the bottom of the propaganda barrel when there occurred a great fire at the naval base in Portsmouth, England. Sabotage was suspected and Parliament passed an act inflicting the death penalty upon anyone found guilty of setting fire to the King's ships or dockyards in Great Britain or the colonies. American propagandists seized upon this act as another example of British tyranny over the

[5] *Massachusetts Spy*, July 23, 1773. Reverend Jacob Duché, *Observations on a Variety of Subjects*, Philadelphia, 1774, 35.
[6] *Correspondence of "First Citizen," Charles Carroll of Carrollton and "Antilon," Daniel Dulany, Junior*, 54.

colonists. But this straw, so eagerly clutched by the patriots, could not sustain them; it proved impossible to twist the Dockyard Act into British oppression. Despite the outcries of the Whigs, the act seemed to be nothing more than a wise precaution to safeguard the British fleet.

Not only was the quarrel between the British government and the colonists becoming a matter of desultory sparring but the solidarity of Americans themselves showed signs of cracking. The boundary disputes which flared up between the colonies during this period were one of the most alarming evidences of American disunion. Connecticut laid claim to the Wyoming Valley in western Pennsylvania and fighting soon broke out in the disputed area between the New Englanders and Pennsylvanians. Flaunting white cockades, the Connecticut settlers harried the frontier with such ruthlessness that the governor of Pennsylvania swore they were worse than the Indians.[7] Serious trouble occurred likewise in the New Hampshire Grants where New York speculators attempted to dispossess the settlers who held their lands from grants by New Hampshire. The stake held by Massachusetts citizens in the New Hampshire Grants threatened to embroil that province in the quarrel; a demand was soon raised in New England for an expeditionary force to take the field against the "Yorkers"[8] and "drive them all back over the Atlantic to Holland again." A body of volunteers set out from Massachusetts to aid the frontiersmen but it was soon evident that these hardy mountaineers needed no aid. The agents sent out by the New York speculators to take possession of the lands were so roughly handled by the Green Mountain Boys that they were glad to escape with a whole skin, for, by way of example, one "high-spirited valiant man took a small ox goad, and coldly belaboured one of the officers who had gloried much in being the instrument of the New York oppression."[9] But even while applauding the spirit displayed by the Green Mountain Boys, the patriots could not forget that Americans were quarreling between themselves at a time when they ought to be concentrating their energies against British "tyrants" and colonial oligarchs.

[7] John Penn to Thomas Penn, April 24, 1770, Penn MSS., Historical Society of Pennsylvania.
[8] *Essex Gazette*, May 26, 1772. *Publications of the Colonial Society of Massachusetts, Transactions, 1922–1924*, Boston, 1924, XXV, 35.
[9] *Essex Gazette*, May 26, 1772.

Likewise, the outbreak of class and sectional struggles within the colonies revealed that the impact of revolutionary ideals upon Americans might produce a civil war instead of a united stand against the mother country. The Southern and Middle provinces were dominated by wealthy landowners and merchants who, feeling the pricks of British tyranny more acutely than any other group, sought to persuade the farmers of the interior to join them in their attacks upon British authority. But this Eastern ruling class was at no time disposed to sacrifice any of its privileges in order to bring the Western farmers wholeheartedly into the revolutionary movement. Instead, the aristocracy urged Americans to center their attention wholly upon British tyranny and not seek to apply revolutionary principles to conditions at home. No grievance, they held, could be so great as to justify Americans in breaking their ranks and engaging in quarrels between themselves while the threat of British oppression hung over the colonies.

Despite this appeal for unity, Americans were by no means persuaded to forgo the struggle for social justice at home in order to present a united front to Great Britain. The roots of discontent struck too deep to be easily removed. In New York, for example, the owners of the great estates had for years been engaged in harassing the small farmers with ruinous lawsuits; whenever a tenant attempted to free himself from the control of his landlord by taking up new lands he found that the great landowners — who laid claim to the best lands in the province — brought ejectment proceedings against him. But in 1766, the tenants refused to pay rent to the landlords and prepared to march upon New York City in the expectation that the urban Sons of Liberty would come to their aid. But the Sons of Liberty remained unconcerned while British regulars dispersed the embattled farmers.[10] These men were fighting for liberty as certainly as were their compatriots at Lexington and Concord, ten years later, but Americans did not rally to their side. The natural rights of Americans did not yet include the right of unprivileged groups to free themselves from the exploitation of their wealthy fellow countrymen.

The Carolina backwoodsmen found their grievances against the tidewater aristocracy far more insupportable than those against the British government and in 1770 they too rose in revolt. An in-

[10] Irving Mark, *Agrarian Conflicts in Colonial New York*, New York, 1940, 131–163.

equitable system of representation kept the interior counties under the control of the numerically inferior seaboard districts. This open discrimination against Westerners in the colonial assemblies gave rise to most of the abuses against which the frontiersmen protested. They were heavily taxed; they were at the mercy of dishonest sheriffs; they were victimized by clerks and law officers who charged extortionate fees and they were oppressed by the lawyers — "There should be no Lawyers in the Province," they exclaimed, "they damned themselves if there should." [11]

During the Stamp Act period, the Charleston patriots warned the frontiersmen that if the stamp duties were collected they would be obliged to surrender their cattle, horses, and crops as tribute to the British government. This propaganda worked too well for the entire satisfaction of the Charleston Whigs. The frontiersmen drew together to resist British tyranny; but they soon began to use their new-found unity for other purposes.[12] The back country was infested with horse thieves who took advantage of the absence of courts to terrorize the inhabitants. The frontiersmen now constituted their own courts, which, like the later vigilantes of the West, meted out punishment to evildoers. "They are every day, excepting Sundays, employed in the Regulation Work, as they term it," wrote an observer. "They have brought many under the lash, and are scourging and banishing the baser sort of people . . . with unwearied diligence. Such as they think reclaimable, they are a little tender of; and those they task, giving them so many acres to extend in so many days, on pain of flagitation, that they may not be reduced to poverty, and by that be led to steal from their industrious neighbours." [13]

These Regulators, as they were called, lost no time in turning their strength against their "Crafty and cruel Oppressors" in the seaboard counties. They denied the jurisdiction of the Charleston courts; and sheriffs and marshals who attempted to serve writs or warrants among the Regulators found the country exceedingly unhealthy. Until circuit courts were established in accordance with their demands, they took the law entirely into their own hands. They refused to pay taxes until they were convinced that the

---

[11] Colonial Records of North Carolina, VIII, 70.
[12] Peter Timothy to Benjamin Franklin, September 3, 1768, Franklin MSS., American Philosophical Society.
[13] Pennsylvania Chronicle, October 3, 1768.

money was being used constitutionally by the provincial government and raised the cry of no taxation without representation against the colonial assembly. They declared that they were deprived of "the rights of British subjects" by wealthy Easterners as truly as were the colonial merchants by the British government. The wind in which the Regulators snuffed tyranny came not from the British Isles but from the lowland counties of the American seaboard; and against the oppression of the aristocracy, the Regulators looked to the Crown for protection.[14]

Harmon Husbands, leader of the Regulators and a member of the North Carolina Assembly, was expelled from that body for his activities in behalf of the frontiersmen. To make sure that he would not inflame the back-country people he was arrested and put in the jail at New Bern, North Carolina, for safe-keeping. The Regulators were enraged at this treatment of their leader; quickly mobilizing their forces they swore that they would burn the town. The Eastern gentry rallied to the support of Governor Tryon, the royal governor of the province, who found himself in possession of such a large force that he undertook to invade the Regulators' country and fight them on their own ground. The governor and his followers encountered an army of frontiersmen at the Alamance where about six thousand men met in battle. Fifteen of this host lost their lives but it was observed that trees were almost whittled through by the "incredible number of balls" that struck them.[15] The Regulators were routed; some of the prisoners captured by Tryon were executed but the greater number were permitted to march disconsolately home to nurse their grievances until the outbreak of the War of Independence gave them an opportunity to strike back at the Eastern Whigs.

While the American patriots were tasting these draughts of adversity, the English radicals were being obliged to drink of the same bitter brew. John Horne Tooke and John Wilkes, the two great pillars of English radicalism, fell out and brought the house down by their quarrels — to the joy of the conservatives in both mother country and colonies. To see two such firebrands as John Wilkes and Sam Adams quenched at the same time was indeed an auspicious beginning for Lord North's Ministry.

The American patriots had long regarded John Wilkes as an ally

[14] *Ibid. Colonial Records of North Carolina*, VIII, 700, 702.
[15] *Colonial Records of North Carolina*, VIII, 655.

who would keep the Ministry so busy at home that it would have no time to deal with the colonies, however intransigent they might become. Every riot in England they regarded as a boon for the colonies inasmuch as it would "deter the most adventurous desperado from risquing further experiments on a people who need but a spark to set them all in flames." [16] In their eyes, the American struggle for liberty was merely a part of the struggle against oppression waged upon many fronts in the empire; and John Wilkes was one of the stoutest champions of the cause. Efforts were made to merge more closely the radical movements in Great Britain and the colonies: the American patriots struck up a correspondence with Wilkes and sent him cheering letters when his fortunes were darkest. The chief link between the Wilkites and the American Whigs was Arthur Lee of Virginia, who had taken up his residence in London; it was Lee who inserted in the Middlesex petition a resolution denouncing the oppression of the colonies by the British government. Wilkes-Barre, Pennsylvania, was named in honor of the British radical; and one Bostonian gave his two children the names John Wilkes and Oliver Cromwell. Sam Adams was spoken of as "a sort of Wilkes in New England." On his part, Wilkes made the oppression of the colonies part of his catalogue of grievances against the British government — a catalogue which already included persecution for seditious libel, expulsion from the House of Commons, and exclusion from the House after he had been duly elected by the voters of Middlesex.

American patriots found the program of the English radicals vastly more to their liking than that of the English Whigs. Wilkes, Horne Tooke, Glynn, Sawbridge, and Oliver — the moving spirits of English radicalism — demanded triennial Parliaments, the ballot, and the purification of English political life, in contrast to the mild palliatives proposed by the Whigs. Unlike the Whigs, the radicals had no love for the Declaratory Act and would have given the colonists a large measure of economic as well as political liberty. John Horne Tooke held firm to his conviction that "when the people of America are enslaved, we cannot be free; and they can never be enslaved whilst we continue free. We are stones of one arch, and must stand or fall together." [17] The radicals welcomed

[16] *Proceedings of the Massachusetts Historical Society*, Boston, 1914, XLVII, 202.

[17] M. C. Yarborough, *John Horne Tooke*, New York, 1912, 78. Arthur Lee to Samuel Adams, June 14, 1771, Adams MSS.

American independence and rejoiced that the separation had come before English vices and corruption had penetrated to the New World. "Is it generous," they asked, "because we are in a sink, to endeavour to draw them [the colonies] into it? Ought we not rather to wish earnestly, that there may at least be ONE FREE COUNTRY left upon earth, to which we may flee, when venality, luxury, and vice have completed the ruin of liberty here?"[18]

This staunch stand for colonial liberty endeared the English radicals to the American patriots. They became Wilkites — which John Wilkes once remarked he never was. They warmly invited Wilkes and his friends to seek shelter in "the peaceful desarts of America" if arbitrary power drove them from England; and they were enraptured when they learned that Mrs. Macaulay, "the celebrated female historian," talked of "ending her days on the banks of the Ohio," and that John Wilkes, if he failed to win a seat in Parliament, spoke of retiring to Boston, where, it was said, he would be sure of finding kindred spirits in plenty.[19] It is not probable, however, that Wilkes's morals would have been acceptable to the Bostonians, who could no more bear a rake than a bishop. In the colonies, furthermore, Wilkes would have lost much of the nuisance value upon which he relied to procure office; and he would have been only one mob leader among many. There was more to be gained by terrorizing George and his ministers than by striking panic among royal governors and customhouse officers: a riot before the royal palace was worth ten before the Boston Town House. But Wilkes never seriously entertained the idea of fleeing to America; although the secret was unknown to the colonial patriots, he aspired to come to the colonies as nothing less than the governor of Canada.

The refusal of the House of Commons to permit Wilkes to take his seat after the Middlesex election led the radicals to form the Society for Supporting the Bill of Rights of which prominent American patriots became members. This organization enabled Americans to contribute financially toward winning the struggle for freedom in England and they were not remiss in backing Wilkes with their money as well as good wishes. In 1770, the Virginia patriots shipped Wilkes forty-five hogsheads of tobacco as a "small acknowledgment for his sufferings in the cause of liberty." The South Carolina

---

[18] Price, 41–42.
[19] *Virginia Gazette* (Purdie and Dixon), April 27, 1769. *Pennsylvania Chronicle*, May 30, 1768.

Assembly, not to be outdone, voted to send the Society £1500 sterling to frustrate "the unjust and unconstitutional measures of an arbitrary and oppressive ministry." The governor and council refused to accede to this grant; and the Crown issued peremptory instructions to the governor to consent to no money bills until the assembly had withdrawn its grant to Wilkes. The assembly, instead of yielding, launched a vigorous attack upon the system of "government by instruction" which kept the colony in a turmoil for the next four years.[20]

The gift of the South Carolina Assembly caused no less dissension in England among the members of the Society for Supporting the Bill of Rights than in South Carolina itself between the Crown and the assembly. During a long career spent in gaming, debauchery, and keeping fancy mistresses, Wilkes's debts had reached an appalling total. What was worse, his creditors' patience was wearing dangerously thin by 1770. The Society for Supporting the Bill of Rights deemed it wise, therefore, to take Horne Tooke's advice and use these windfalls from Virginia and South Carolina to keep Wilkes out of a debtors' prison. Wilkes, however, wanted "*ready money*, not money to pay his debts," and he was angry with the South Carolinians for having made their grant to the Society rather than directly to himself. He railed at the Carolina legislators and swore that he had been deliberately affronted by those boorish colonists who had no understanding of a gentleman's sensibilities. Although Wilkes was able to lay his hands on the tobacco sent him by his Virginia admirers, Horne Tooke steadfastly refused to turn over the money sent the Society by the Carolina Assembly.[21]

In the heat of this fracas, Tooke swore that Wilkes was seeking to convert the Society for Supporting the Bill of Rights into "a sponge which should suck up the generosity of the public to be squeezed into his pocket." Wilkes, said Tooke, "had always hated the Americans, was always the declared foe of their liberties" and valued them only for what he could wheedle from them by playing upon their love of liberty.[22] In reply, Wilkes published a letter written him by Tooke in which that clergyman apologized for having

[20] Lord Charles Montague to Lord Dartmouth, September 26 and October 21, 1771; July 25 and November 4, 1772. Lieutenant Governor Bull to Lord Dartmouth, July 24, 1773; March 10, 1774, P.R.O., C.O. 5, 394. *South Carolina Gazette*, November 4, 1772.

[21] Leigh, 30. Yarborough, 80–81.

[22] *Essex Gazette*, September 10, 1771. Yarborough, 82–84.

had "the infectious hand of a bishop waved over him." Tooke resigned his benefice, which he found thoroughly uncomfortable, and withdrew from the Society for Supporting the Bill of Rights to form a rival organization known as the Society for Constitutional Information. Thus the power of the Wilkites was broken and they no longer menaced the established order. They thereby lost much of their value to American patriots, who, after 1771, found it increasingly difficult to feel that they were closely united with a group of English radicals in a struggle to defend common liberties. Rather, they seemed to stand alone against British tyranny and only by relying upon their own strength did they seem likely to achieve victory.

Conservatives in both England and America rejoiced in the calm that followed the downfall of the Wilkites and the colonial patriots: "at length . . . after a violent and tedious Hurricane" in which the empire had tossed and pitched until its seams had almost split, a safe haven had been reached. The British government was little disposed to renew the quarrel with the colonies. Lord North was quite content to let sleeping dogs lie; his only regret was that they did not sleep more soundly. North was himself eager to catch up on his sleep in the House; after six years of uproar and confusion, it was observed that the noble lord now spent many happy hours dozing in his seat. One agitated member declared that he wished Lord North had "some one at his elbow, to pull him every now and then by the ear . . . to keep him awake to the affairs of America." But North refused to bestir himself — if, indeed, he heard; his recipe for a quiet administration was to keep American affairs out of the House of Commons and give Americans no fresh grievances. So well did North succeed that, for over two years, the colonies were not so much as mentioned in parliamentary debates.

Thus in both England and America the radicals' craft lay becalmed, their crews mutinous, and their rigging rotting from disuse. The colonial patriots waited impatiently for a breeze; but it was not until March 1772 that the lull was broken. In that month, the armed schooner *Gaspee*, Lieutenant William Dudingston in command, appeared off the Rhode Island coast and began to seize the ships and cargoes belonging to the powerful smugglers' rings of Newport and Providence. The Rhode Island merchants had hitherto smuggled with little interference from the British government; in

1770 the collector was mobbed at Newport and the superior court of the colony refused to grant general writs of assistance to the customhouse officers. Lieutenant Dudingston was something new in Rhode Islanders' experience; a fire-eating sea dog, he was determined to stamp out smuggling without regard for Americans' sensibilities. He was even reported to have said that he would be delighted to see Newport burn about the heads of its citizens; "he would be damn'd," he swore, if he or his crew would lift a finger to put out the fire.[23]

Dudingston cruised about Narragansett Bay, boarding and examining every vessel that he came upon, and threatening to blow recalcitrant skippers out of the water. The smuggling fraternity was outraged by these tactics and Dudingston soon found himself pictured as an enemy to the rights of man. It was charged that he was "haughty, insolent, and intolerant, personally ill treating every Master and Merchant of the Vessels he boarded, stealing Sheep, Hogs, Poultry &c. from the Farmers round the Bay, and cutting down their Fruit and other Trees for Fire-Wood; in a Word, his Behaviour was so *piratical* and provoking that Englishmen could not patiently bear it." Indeed, he seemed to Rhode Islanders to be "more imperious and haughty than the Grand Turk himself."[24] His activities became so distressing that Newport soon buzzed with rumors that an armed ship would be fitted out by the merchants to rescue any vessel taken by the *Gaspee* for violating the Laws of Trade. But Admiral Montague cooled Rhode Islanders' ardor for this enterprise by declaring that he would hang all concerned as pirates.[25]

Tension had reached the breaking point in Rhode Island when the *Gaspee* ran aground while chasing a smuggler. The ship was certain to remain stranded until midnight at high tide. High and dry, unable to run or fight, she lay at the mercy of Rhode Islanders; and it was soon evident that the smugglers were prepared to make the most of their opportunity. Shortly after nightfall, a drummer went through the streets of Providence crying that the *Gaspee* was aground and urging the citizens to hasten to the house of Mr. James Sabin, where an expedition was gathering to dispose of the schooner once and for all.

[23] *Newport Mercury*, November 9, 1772.
[24] *Virginia Gazette* (Purdie and Dixon), February 18, 1773. *Newport Mercury*, November 9, 1772.
[25] *Records of the Colony of Rhode Island*, Providence, 1862, III, 63.

The patriot crew set out from Providence in small boats to destroy the hated revenue cutter before she could be floated. When they reached the ship she was still fast aground. Captain Dudingston, hearing the approaching boats, "mounted the starboard gunwhale in his shirt" and hailed "Who comes there?" Captain Whipple, commander of the privateer *Game Cock* during the Seven Years' War, answered: "I am the sheriff of the county of Kent, G——d——n you, I have got a warrant to apprehend you, G——d d——n you; so surrender, G——d d——n you." Upon Dudingston's refusal, one Bucklin fired and Dudingston fell, whereupon Bucklin exclaimed, "I have killed the rascal." Dudingston cried out, "Good God, I am done for," and collapsed with bullets in his arm and groin. After ransacking the ship, which yielded at least several silver spoons, they put Dudingston and his servant in a small boat, but not before Captain Whipple had had his sport with the wounded officer. Holding a handspike over Dudingston's head, he exclaimed, "Stand aside, let me dispatch the piratical dog"; and after Dudingston had begged for his life abjectly, he was turned loose in an open boat, while Whipple and his men burned the *Gaspee* to the water's edge.[26]

Despite its desire to wash its hands of the American dispute, the English government could not tamely suffer this outrage upon its authority. In the destruction of the *Gaspee*, American "licentiousness" seemed at last to have grown into treason: if the British government passed over this "attrocious offence," it would lose all title to respect in British America. It was well known that the Sons of Liberty regarded the *Gaspee* affair as a test case: "If the Nation shows no resentment against that Colony for so high an affront to the Mother Country," it was said, "they say they are safe & they may venture upon any further Measures which are necessary to obtain & secure their Independence without any danger of ever being called to acct for it." The effect upon the Tories would be equally disastrous; "if the *Gaspee* rioters were not punished," declared Thomas Hutchinson, "the Friends to Government will despond and give up all hopes of being able to withstand the Faction."[27]

In this critical hour, the home government, apparently recognizing the vital importance of decisive action, struck back at the Rhode

---

[26] *Records of the Colony of Rhode Island*, III, 70, 71, 72, 82–86.

[27] *Hutchinson Correspondence*, III, Thomas Hutchinson to ?, August 27, 29, 1772. *Documents relative to the Colonial History of the State of New Jersey*, X, 395, 397.

Island "rebels" by appointing a Commission of Inquiry to examine into the *Gaspee* affair and to hold suspects for trial in England. The Crown Officers and Tories hailed this move as evidence that the British lion was at last roused and that sedition would meet with its just reward. But the patriots screamed that the commission was a Court of Inquisition which combined the iniquities of the holy office and the Court of Star Chamber. It made the position of Americans "infinitely worse than that of a subject of France, Spain, Portugal or any other the most despotic power on earth." [28] The commissioners were pronounced to be "a pack of Egyptian tyrants" whose very presence in Rhode Island was "the most insulting violation of the rights of Americans that could be devised." [29] It was with these epithets ringing in their ears that the commissioners began their investigation in Rhode Island.

They were handicapped from the beginning by the singularly short memories displayed by the citizens of Providence under questioning; the events of the night the *Gaspee* was destroyed were to most of them a complete blank. No one recognized any of the rioters; no one admitted any part in stirring up the mob. The commissioners were nonplused by this behavior; but they could do nothing in the face of the Rhode Islanders' refusal to talk. They concluded that the ringleaders were "Men of Estate and Property" who enjoyed the protection of the entire community; therefore no informer dared risk his life by giving evidence. As a result, the commissioners ferreted out no culprits to send to England for trial and Tyburn remained undecorated by an American Whig. The commissioners indeed discovered that Rhode Island was a "downright Democracy" but this was hardly news to the English government. Yet the government made no effort to pursue the *Gaspee* affair after the commissioners had confessed their failure. Instead of finding and punishing the guilty colonists, it contented itself with making Dudingston a captain for his sufferings at the hands of Captain Whipple and his men.

The spectacle of American rioters again slipping through the fingers of the British government struck dismay among the Crown Officers. The failure of the commission, wrote the Collector of the Customs in Rhode Island, marked the end "to security to government servants . . . an end to collecting a revenue and enforcing

[28] *Pennsylvania Journal and Weekly Advertiser*, January 20, 1773.
[29] Lee, I, 91.

the acts of trade." Britain, despite its bluster, lamented a Tory, "sat down silently under the Affront, laughed at by the *Rhode Islanders*, and held in Derision by Foreigners." [30] On the other hand, this triumph over the British government was heady wine to colonial radicals: the indecision, rapid veering from appeasement to severity, and the inability of the government to punish the colonists effectively, encouraged Americans to regard the Atlantic as a barrier beyond which the long arm of Great Britain could not reach. Colonists seemingly need have little fear of punishment from the doddering old lady overseas. Certainly, the failure of the British government to punish the scuttlers of the *Gaspee* was a direct encouragement to Bostonians to stage the Tea Party. After the Rhode Island Commission had revealed the weakness of the British government, Admiral Montague concluded that the Bostonians were "almost ripe for independence, and nothing but the ships (in Boston harbor) prevents their going greater lengths, as they see no notice taken from home of their behaviour." [31]

From the point of view of the mother country, the destruction of the *Gaspee* had another untoward result: it gave a strong impetus to colonial union. The presence of the Commission of Inquiry in Rhode Island was widely pictured as an attack upon liberty in all the colonies and Americans were told that in this crisis they must unite and stand their ground "with a truly Roman spirit of liberty." [32] The Court of Inquiry in Rhode Island and the payment of judges' salaries from the English Exchequer led the Virginia burgesses to propose in 1773 that Committees of Correspondence be appointed by all the assemblies in America to resist British oppression.

The burning of the *Gaspee* thus reopened the dispute between England and America. The era of good feelings proved to be merely a breathing spell in the contest. The short-lived harmony was further shattered by the government when, late in 1772, it declared its intention of erecting a civil list in Massachusetts by paying the salaries of the royal governor and judges from the revenues collected by the American Commissioners of the Customs. Sam Adams met the crisis by organizing the Boston Committee of Correspond-

[30] Robert Nicholas, *Considerations on the Present State of Virginia*, 1774, 12. Publications of the Navy Records Society, LXIX, *The Sandwich Papers*, London, 1932, I, 53.

[31] *Ibid.*, I, 50.

[32] *Pennsylvania Journal and Weekly Advertiser*, January 20, 1773.

ence and, with the aid of rural patriots, covering New England with a network of similar committees. Charging that the effort to subvert the constitution by establishing a civil list was made at the behest of Hutchinson and his fellow oligarchs, Adams thoroughly aroused New Englanders and put Boston at the head of what soon became the most formidable revolutionary machine created in the American colonies.

It was a windfall from Benjamin Franklin that enabled Adams and the Boston patriots to turn the full force of the Committees of Correspondence against Thomas Hutchinson, since 1771 governor of Massachusetts Bay. By means which he never divulged, Franklin acquired in 1773 the letters written by Hutchinson when he was lieutenant governor of the province to Thomas Whately, then a member of Parliament, and the letters of Andrew Oliver, one of the leading "oligarchs" of Massachusetts and since 1770 its lieutenant governor, to his English correspondents. Franklin was well aware that private letters had been used before by the patriots with highly gratifying results: Governor Bernard had been ruined in New England by the publication of his correspondence with British statesmen. In 1770, letters written by Thomas Hutchinson and Colonel Dalrymple, the commander of the troops in Boston, had been published in the *Boston Gazette*. Knowing that he was suspected of Toryism by some of the leading patriots in Boston and that his position as agent for Massachusetts in London was none too secure, Franklin determined to set at rest all doubt of his patriotism by sending the Boston radicals the private correspondence of Thomas Hutchinson and Andrew Oliver that had come into his possession.

It has been said that Franklin took this step because he wished to preserve the British Empire by proving to the New England radicals that the real enemies of colonial liberty were renegade provincials like Thomas Hutchinson and not the British ministers whom they misinformed of conditions in the colonies. This is to suppose that Franklin was singularly unacquainted with the views of the Massachusetts patriots. They had long since made up their minds concerning Thomas Hutchinson and they had already accused him of most of the iniquities under heaven. They had also made up their minds concerning the source of British tyranny; when it suited their purpose, they were ready to ascribe it to Hutchinson and his fellow "oligarchs" but they were well aware that Hutchinson and his friends were sustained in office by British imperialists. What they wanted above all were documents which would prove Hutchinson's guilt to the world. Did Franklin send these documents across the Atlantic hoping that they would bring sweetness and light into imperial relations? A man who had played with lightning surely ought to have known better.[33]

Whatever his motives, Franklin hoped to conceal his part in the affair. His position in England was delicate and he was reluctant to reveal himself as a fomenter of discord in the empire. And so, while loosing the bag of the winds, he sought to stir up no more than a moderate gale and, above all, to stay out of the draft himself. He therefore sent the letters to a half-dozen prominent Massachusetts patriots with the stipulation that no copies were to be made; they were to be shown only to confidential friends and then were to be returned to England.

Franklin was setting a dinner before hungry men and forbidding them to eat. As might have been foreseen, they fell upon the feast even though it was necessary to brush aside all of Franklin's instructions. The patriots wrote Franklin that "nothing could have been more Seasonable than the arrival of these letters"; with good reason, they exulted that Hutchinson had been delivered into their hands and they proceeded to make the most of this windfall. The letters were read to the Massachusetts House of Representatives; the House voted that they tended to "subvert the Constitution and to introduce arbitrary power"; and they were ordered to be printed in order that the black designs of the Massachusetts oligarchs might be exposed to the world.[34]

Hutchinson's letters by no means convicted him of all the crimes against liberty of which he was accused. They consisted, for the most part, of expressions of disapproval of the work of the radicals not much stronger than were to be found in his official messages to the Massachusetts General Court. But, these being confidential letters to a friend, Hutchinson occasionally let down his guard. He remarked, for instance, that "there must be a diminution of what are called English liberties" in Massachusetts if the empire was to be preserved. This statement, coupled with interpolations by Sam

[33] Carl Van Doren (*Benjamin Franklin*, New York, 1939, 445) takes the opposite view.
[34] Samuel Cooper to Benjamin Franklin, June 14, 1773, Franklin MSS., American Philosophical Society.

Adams and William Cooper, who acted as "editors" of Hutchinson's letters, sufficed to damn him in the eyes of liberty-loving Americans as one of those "homebred, pestilential fiends" who had encouraged British tyranny. His enemies did not add that he favored these restrictions largely because he wished to prevent the revocation of the Massachusetts Charter — a step he believed inevitable if tumult continued in the colony. In his opinion, liberty could be saved from complete overthrow only by restoring order. "I tremble for my Country [Massachusetts]," he wrote in 1769. "I wished to leave its Constitution at my death in the same state it was in at my birth." [35]

Having rushed Hutchinson's letters through the press, the Boston Committee of Correspondence sent copies to all the important towns in the province. In a circular letter accompanying them, the committee declared that the fact that it was able to make the governor's letters public was proof that God, who had benignantly watched over New England from its first settlement, again "wonderfully interposed to bring to Light the Plot that had been laid for us by our malicious and invidious Enemies." Hutchinson thus became one of that long list of hell-inspired wretches who "remain on Record as Monuments of Divine Vengeance" for seeking to thwart God's plans for New England. It was clear that the struggle between God and the Devil for New England had entered its crucial phase: the patriots were on the side of the angels and there seemed no question from what quarter Thomas Hutchinson was receiving aid. [36]

As a result of the publication of these letters, Franklin, despite his precautions, was smoked into the open by the fire he had lighted. Although the Massachusetts Whigs declared that he might console himself with the reflection that he had labored for "the Security and Happiness of Millions," Poor Richard would have preferred to forgo this particular immortality. Because of his part in the affair, Franklin, the dreamer of a great British Empire founded upon justice and freedom, found himself pilloried in 1774 by Attorney General Wedderburn in "a most severe Phillipic on the celebrated American philosopher, in which he loaded him with all the licensed scurrility

[35] *Hutchinson Correspondence*, II, Thomas Hutchinson to ?, September 1, 1769.

[36] Circular Letter, June 22, 1773, Committee of Correspondence Papers, MSS. New York Public Library. *Boston Gazette*, April 11, 1774.

of the bar, and decked his harangue with the choicest flowers of Billingsgate." "Men will watch him with a jealous eye," exclaimed Wedderburn, "they will hide their papers from him, and lock up their escritoires. Having hitherto aspired after fame by his writings, he will henceforth esteem it a libel to be called a *man of letters.*" The fact that Franklin was a Bostonian by birth was held to be sufficient explanation for his iniquities. "I ask, my Lords," said Wedderburn, "whether the revengeful temper, attributed by poetic fiction only to the bloodyminded African, is not surpassed by the coolness and apathy of the wily New Englander?" It is said that Franklin never again donned the suit he wore on this black day when he smarted under Wedderburn's "more than hellish rancour" until the signing of the Treaty of Paris in 1783.[37]

After this ordeal, London coffeehouses buzzed with the question: "Was not Mr. W.'s Phillipick against the Doctor a capital performance?" The wits were entranced and the propagandists were soon in full cry after Franklin. He was called "a viper . . . festering in the bosom of Government"; the Wilkes of America who "with a brand lighted from the clouds set fire" to the empire. He was reviled as a scheming provincial who sought to remove the seat of empire from London and to make himself dictator of Boston: indeed, it was said, "the old Dotard thought he saw himself the Founder of Empires and the Father of Kings." Franklin was called "a Skunk, or American Pole Cat" and when he set sail for America in 1775 he was said to be planning to put himself at the head of rebels "and to try whether he cannot do more Mischief with the Sword, than with the Pen."[38] Franklin winced under this notoriety hardly less than did John Adams, who later protested against the practice of ascribing the American Revolution to Benjamin Franklin. "The History of our Revolution will be one continued Lye from one end to the other," John Adams said. "The essence of the whole will be that *Dr. Franklin's electrical Rod smote the Earth and out sprang General Washington.*"[39]

The publication of the Hutchinson-Oliver letters destroyed the last shreds of reputation the two men possessed in New England.

[37] John Lord Campbell, *The Lives of the Lord Chancellors*, London, 1850, VI, 103–104. *Hutchinson-Oliver Letters*, 106, 110. Hinkhouse, 158. *Pennsylvania Packet and General Advertiser*, April 18, 1774.
[38] Tucker, *An Humble Appeal*, 40. Robinson, 166, 169. *Public Ledger*, February 26, 1774.
[39] *Old Family Letters*, edited by Alexander Biddle, Philadelphia, 1892, 55.

Their position had become clearly untenable. The General Court voted their impeachment and petitions were sent to England asking their removal. When Andrew Oliver died in March 1774, Peter Oliver and Hutchinson feared to attend the funeral because of the "rude & brutal behaviour of the rabble." [40] Hutchinson swore that there "never was greater tyranny in Constantinople"; and he reluctantly acknowledged that Massachusetts must be subdued before British authority could be restored. Although the demand of the Massachusetts Assembly for Hutchinson's removal was refused, the patriots succeeding in ridding themselves of him forever: in 1774 he was replaced by General Gage, who took office after the passage of the Boston Port Act.

The fate of Thomas Hutchinson and the organization of Committees of Correspondence by the Virginia burgesses and the Boston radicals ought to have been fair warning to the British government that American patriotism was beginning to revive and that a new colonial union was in the making. More clearly than ever before, the mother country was served notice to tread warily in its colonial policy. Lord North ought to have remained quietly dozing in the House of Commons; at no time would neglect of the colonies have been more salutary. It was unfortunate for the British Empire that Lord North did not nap more soundly.

[40] Peggy Hutchinson to Mrs. Mary Hutchinson, March 9, 1774, Egerton MSS., British Museum.

CHAPTER FOURTEEN

Tea Revives the Dispute

The Boston Tea Party

I

IT WAS not the colonists but the East India Company which disturbed Lord North's slumbers and impelled him to take action. The East India Company had again fallen on evil days and the British government was obliged to come to its rescue. And, to the Prime Minister's consternation, in his efforts to save the East India Company he blundered into a dispute with the colonies from which the British government found it impossible to retreat with honor.

The settlement of 1767 had not brought order into the tangled affairs of the East India Company. The corporation continued to be plundered by its officials and the natives remained at the mercy of ruthless and irresponsible Englishmen who were bent upon getting rich in the shortest possible order. By 1773, the plight of the company had become critical; it had no cash; it could not pay bills drawn upon it; and its credit was almost exhausted. The value of its stock fell from 280 to 160 while millions of pounds of unsold tea and India goods rotted in its warehouses. The distress of the company jeopardized the £400,000 which the British government since 1767 had received annually from it and threatened the loss of England's foothold in India. Accustomed as Lord North was to blink at trouble, he could not close his eyes to the predicament into which the East India Company had fallen.[1]

The directors of the company feared that the government would seize this opportunity to strip it of its territorial revenues and put its affairs under the direct control of the Crown. They appealed to the Whigs for aid; and the Whigs rallied to the company's support as they had in 1767. They warned that interference by the government would establish the supremacy of the Crown over Parliament; Edmund Burke declared that Lord North was seeking to decorate the Crown "with the collected spoils of the East" in order

[1] *Correspondence of Edmund Burke*, I, 343. *Pennsylvania Journal and Weekly Advertiser*, March 31, 1773. *Public Advertiser*, January 4, February 25, 1773.

to enable the King to rule without Parliament.² The City of London protested against any infringement of the company's rights on the ground that it would be "a direct and dangerous attack upon the liberties of the people." The American colonists likewise expressed their sympathy with the East India Company in its efforts to stave off governmental control. Because it was a chartered corporation, the fate of the East India Company was believed to be bound up with that of the chartered colonies and hence with the defense of American liberty.³

But Lord North had little interest in extending the authority of the Crown: his chief concern was to preserve the East India Company from bankruptcy and to save the government's equity. It was this consideration, rather than any deep-laid plot of depriving Parliament of control of the purse or enslaving the colonies, which influenced North when he set out in 1773 to make the American colonies safe for the East India Company's tea.

It was well known that the company's distress was partly owing to the refusal of the American colonists to buy British tea after it had been taxed by Charles Townshend. They drank instead smuggled Dutch tea in such quantities that the salvation of the East India Company seemed to require that the colonial tea market be regained by driving out the smugglers.⁴ But the directors were not eager to be thrust again into the thick of the dispute over taxation which troubled relations between Great Britain and the colonies. They believed that their business was to sell tea, not to uphold the rights of Parliament over the colonies; and they had little confidence that their tea could be sold to Americans until the issue of taxation without representation had been set at rest. The directors therefore urged the government to repeal the threepence duty paid into the customs on every pound of tea imported into the colonies. Only by this means, they reasoned, could the government be certain of driving the smugglers from the field and recovering the colonial market.⁵

North refused to heed this advice: it was enough, he believed, to give Americans cheap tea — they would drink it regardless of the

² *Pitt Correspondence*, IV, 276, 285. *Correspondence of Edmund Burke*, I, 388-389.
³ *Boston Evening Post*, October 25, 1773. *Parliamentary History*, XVII, 889.
⁴ Historical MSS. Commission, 11th Report, London, 1887, V.
⁵ *Manuscripts of the Earl of Dartmouth*, I, 346. *Parliamentary History*, XVII, 841. Grafton, 266.

tax. As in 1769, he insisted that the tea duty stand lest the right of Parliament to tax the colonists fall into disuse. North at no time lost sight of the importance of maintaining parliamentary sovereignty over the colonies; and he considered taxation to be the most vital element of sovereignty. He scoffed at warnings that Americans prized principle more than cheap tea and would spurn the East India Company's tea because it was taxed. He confidently expected Americans to set about contentedly brewing their tea, forgetting in its cheapness that they were helping the British government to raise a revenue which might be used against their liberties.

By the Tea Act of 1773, the threepence tax on tea imported into the colonies was retained; the British government made the East India Company a loan of £1,400,000 and renounced the £400,000 it had compelled the company to pay annually since 1767. Moreover, the company was no longer required to reimburse the government for any losses in revenue it might suffer as a result of its remission of duties paid upon importation into Great Britain. This, coupled with permission to export tea directly to America without putting it up for public sale in England, put the company in an excellent competitive position. By eliminating the middleman — the English merchants who bought tea at the company's auctions in London and then resold it to American merchants — the company was able to sell tea in the colonies cheaper than in England itself. More significantly, its tea now undersold that of the Dutch smugglers. Instead of twenty shillings a pound, tea now sold for ten shillings — a price which even the smugglers could not meet. There seemed excellent prospect, therefore, that this cheap tea would "overcome all the Patriotism of an American" and that the colonists would hail Lord North as one of the great benefactors of thirsty humanity.[6]

Not without some misgivings on the part of the directors, the East India Company set about unloading its surplus tea upon the colonies. Two hundred and ninety-eight chests of tea — valued at £10,994 — were dispatched to Boston; 257 chests to Charleston, South Carolina; and 698 chests to New York and Philadelphia. For the safe delivery of this tea, the British merchants trading to North America stood security.[7]

---

[6] *American Historical Review*, January 1898, III, 266–269. *The Address of the People of Great Britain to the Inhabitants of America*, London, 1775, 45.
[7] P.R.O., C.O. 5, 133. *An Account of Tea, Exported by the East India*

At first, many Americans rejoiced in the prospect of slaking their thirst by drinking up the tea that filled to bursting the warehouses of the East India Company. There were some killjoys, however, who pointed out that tea, unlike wine, did not grow better "by sweating several years, in a warehouse"; and it even began to be whispered that the tea was rotten and the East India Company was trying to dispose of it in the colonies because it could find no market elsewhere.[8] And sober second thought brought home to Americans the menace of this taxed tea: even if their constitutions were unimpaired, their political liberties and their economic well-being seemed certain to suffer.

The smugglers appeared destined to be the first victims of the Tea Act. Undersold by the East India Company, they could look forward only to ruin at its hands. Because their interests were more immediately threatened by the Tea Act than those of any other group, it was the smugglers — and not the slave drivers, as Dr. Johnson supposed — who raised the "loudest yelps" for liberty and took the lead in fomenting opposition to the East India Company.

The most active tea smugglers in the colonies in 1773 were the merchants of Rhode Island, New York, and Philadelphia. Although Englishmen supposed that Boston was a nest of smugglers, its citizens had long since lost their pre-eminence as runners of contraband. This reformation was owing not to any awakening of conscience to the sinfulness of smuggling but simply to the fact that there was stricter enforcement of the laws in Boston than in other colonial seaports. As the headquarters of the Commissioners of the Customs and with a British fleet stationed in its harbor, Boston felt the full force of the British government's war upon illicit trade. New York, on the other hand, was almost a wide-open town for smugglers: in 1774 there was not a boat of any kind belonging to the New York customhouse; the customs officers were still bribed by the merchants; and large quantities of contraband were brought into the port without interference. Much the same state of affairs prevailed in Philadelphia where the merchants salved their consciences with the argument that "every man has a natural right

---

Company to his Majesty's Colonies in North America, with the Quantities, to whom Consigned, &c.

[8] Rivington's New York Gazetteer, November 18, 1773.

to exchange his property with whom he pleases and where he can make the most advantage of it." [9]

It is significant that the first outcry against the Tea Act came from Philadelphia and New York, the smugglers' strongholds, while Boston remained relatively quiet — an unaccustomed role for the "metropolis of sedition." The merchants of Philadelphia and New York held meetings to protest against the importation of East India tea and to demand the resignation of the tea consignees several weeks before the Boston merchants took action. Indeed, in October 1773 it seemed far more probable that the tea would be destroyed in New York or Philadelphia than in Boston. The Philadelphia patriots had prepared a reception for Captain Ayres of the tea ship which might well have persuaded that sea dog to give the City of Brotherly Love a wide berth. The Whigs declared that they would "heave him keel cut, and see that his bottom be well fired, scrubbed and paid — His upper works too will have an overhauling." They had calculated, they said, "to a gill and a feather, how much it will require to fit him for an American exhibition." [10]

Although the smugglers led the attack upon the Tea Act, the law-abiding merchants followed closely upon their heels. The menace of monopoly united virtually all businessmen — whether smugglers or honest traders — in opposition to the East India Company. The company had chosen to send its tea to a picked group of merchants — called "consignees" — who were directed to sell it to tea dealers in the colonies. The colonial importers saw in this measure a threat to free enterprise: once the East India Company had established itself firmly in the colonies, it would presumably eliminate the middlemen altogether and sell tea directly to the people through its agents. A monopoly of the tea market would be followed by a monopoly of wines, spices, silks, and other commodities, until the American merchants had been squeezed completely out of business.

Viewed in this light, the Tea Act was more inimical to the interests of American merchants than were the Townshend duties: in place of a tax that could be passed on to the consumer, there was now danger that all business would be swallowed up by the East India Company and its Tory favorites. John Hancock declared

[9] *Documents relative to the Colonial History of the State of New York*, VIII, 511. *Pennsylvania Gazette*, November 10, 1773. *Rivington's New York Gazetteer*, August 25, 1774.
[10] *Newport Mercury*, December 7, 1773.

that if the Tea Act had gone into effect, "we soon should have found our trade in the hands of foreigners [i.e., Englishmen] . . . nor would it have been strange, if, in a few years, a company in London should have purchased an exclusive right of trading to America." [11] It was supposed that one of the first acts of the East India Company, once its position was secure in the colonies, would be to ruin the Philadelphia china factory which competed with its wares; the promoters of the china factory warned that its destruction would "clip twenty Years from the Growth of *American Improvements*." [12] No longer regarded as a helpless corporation in the grip of the British government, the East India Company now appeared to the colonists as the merciless exploiter of India seeking new worlds to conquer. "It is shocking to Humanity," said a New Yorker, "to relate the relentless Barbarity, practised by the Servants of that Body, on the helpless Asiatics; a Barbarity scarce equalled even by the most brutal Savages, or *Cortez*, the *Mexican* Conqueror." It was recalled that in India the company had "monopolized the absolute Necessaries of Life," with the result that "thousands perished by this black, sordid and cruel Avarice." And because the nabobs' rapacity knew no bounds, they were believed to have leagued themselves with the British government in order to pillage the colonies. "Thank GOD," exclaimed John Dickinson, "we are not Sea Poys, nor Marattas, but *British Subjects*," yet he urged watchmen as they made their rounds to call out, "*Beware of the East-India Company*." [13]

But the peril uppermost in the minds of patriot leaders in 1773 was that the Tea Act threatened the foundations of American political liberty. The triumph of the East India Company over American merchants would in fact be a victory for the British government over colonial rights: "What the Parliament could not Fleece from us by Taxes," exclaimed the New York merchants, "the Crown will by Monopoly." [14] The tea duty imposed by Townshend and retained by Lord North in 1773 was designed to raise a revenue for the purpose of maintaining armies and a civil list in the colonies — thereby nullifying the privileges of the colonial as-

[11] *Principles and Acts of the Revolution*, edited by H. Niles, 16.
[12] *Pennsylvania Gazette*, August 1, 1771.
[13] *Memoirs of the Historical Society of Pennsylvania*, Philadelphia, 1895, XIV, 460, 463. *The Alarm* (Broadside), New York, 1773.
[14] *Pennsylvania Gazette*, February 8, 1773.

semblies. The preamble to the Townshend duties still remained upon the statute books; and never before had the danger been greater that its ends would be achieved. The colonists were well aware that the tea duty had been retained because the British government wished to keep alive the right of taxation and that the successful collection of this tax would place them at the mercy of Parliament. Crediting Lord North with more duplicity than he was guilty of, they assumed that he was now striving to take by ruse what he could not capture by storm. Once the American defenses had been breached by the tea duty, it was expected that North and the King's Friends would "enter the Bulwarks of our sacred Liberties, and will never desist, till they have made a Conquest of the whole." [15]

It was fortunate for the colonial merchants that the British government had not repealed the tea duty. If the East India Company's tea had not been taxed — if it had not been mixed with the question of Americans' political rights — the colonists would have been under strong temptation to make the most of their opportunity to buy cheap tea even though it meant the ruin of the American merchants. Under such circumstances they might have drunk the East India Company back to solvency; and the Boston Tea Party might have been an entirely decorous affair in which the Bostonians regaled themselves instead of the fishes with the East India tea.

The besetting fear of the patriots was that Americans, if they would not sell their liberties for a mess of pottage, would gladly do so for a dish of tea. The colonists' fondness for tea seemed to both the imperialists at Westminster and the patriots overseas to be the Achilles' heel of American patriotism. Per Kalm, the Swedish traveler, found that there was "hardly a farmer's wife or a poor woman, who does not drink tea in the morning," and he ascribed to excessive tea drinking the fact that American girls often lost their teeth before they were twenty years old.[16] It was estimated that at least one million Americans drank tea twice daily; in Philadelphia, it was remarked that "the women are such slaves to it, that they would rather go without their dinners than without a *dish of tea*." The Whigs groaned that tea was the "Idol of America" and

[15] New York Committee of Correspondence to the Boston Committee of Correspondence, February 20, 1774, *Committee of Correspondence Papers*.

[16] Per Kalm, *Travels in North America*, Warrington, 1780, I, 361. Abbé Claude C. Robin, *New Travels Through North America*, Boston, 1784, 23.

that its devotees were lost to reason. Since 1767, when tea was first taxed by Townshend, tea drinking had been under fire as an injurious unpatriotic habit. American physicians testified that tea caused spleen, and weakened "the tone of the stomach, and therefore of the whole system, inducing tremors and spasmodic affections." [17] Tea drinkers were warned that they were in danger of becoming "weak, effeminate and valetudinarian for life." But it not only shortened Americans' lives: it destroyed their civil liberties because every dish of British tea brewed in the colonies paid tribute to the British government. "Do not suffer yourself to sip the accursed, dutied STUFF," exclaimed a colonist. "For if you do, the devil will immediately enter into you, and you will instantly become a traitor to your country." [18]

As the chief tea drinkers in the colonies, women were certain to play a crucial part in the struggle. No matter how strictly the Sons of Liberty abstained from tea, if their wives and daughters continued to sip the "baneful weed" the enemies of colonial liberty would surely triumph. Patriots who had no fear of redcoats and men-of-war dreaded this attack upon Americans at their breakfast tables; in this war of the teacups, everything depended upon the hardihood of American women. An indignant patriot swore that Lord North was attempting "to damn half mankind by tempting *female weakness* with *empoisoned* TEA." [19] Englishmen congratulated themselves upon their astuteness in attacking the patriots in their weakest spot. It was believed that even the stiff-backed Saints of New England would be overborne by their wives "for the New-England husbands however they may intimidate British merchants and the British administration, are, in their own houses, too much on the hen-pecked establishment, to be able to carry such a measure against the Sovereign and absolute authority of their fair helpmates." The Whigs, however, were far from giving up the fight for lost: "With the Ladies on our Side," they exclaimed, "we can make every Tory tremble." [20]

But Lord North, less fortunate than the devil, his supposed boon

[17] Singleton, 378. *Essex Gazette*, January 4, 1774. *Pennsylvania Chronicle*, May 2, November 28, 1768.

[18] *Newport Mercury*, January 24, February 28, 1774. *Pennsylvania Packet*, October 11, 1773.

[19] *Boston Evening Post*, June 24, 1775.

[20] *Gazetteer and New Daily Advertiser*, June 14, 1770. *New Hampshire Gazette*, July 22, 1774.

companion, failed to tempt frail woman. On the contrary, the women of America spurned the taxed tea and drank home-grown "Labradore" in its stead, pronouncing it "vastly more agreeable" than anything out of China. When tea was found in the possession of a tea addict in Bedford, Massachusetts, he was given the alternative by the patriots of either surrendering his tea or being turned over to the ladies for punishment. The offender wisely chose to give up his tea, whereupon he received "three cheers from the sons and a glass of American wine from the daughters of liberty." [21]

Deprived of these invaluable allies, the British government had little else upon which to depend for the enforcement of the Tea Act. Lord North anticipated no trouble in the colonies and, like George Grenville before him, made no preparations for overcoming resistance. Indeed, he was so certain there would be no mishap that instructions regarding the disposition of the tea were not even sent British officials in the colonies: the East India Company alone was expected to see to it that its tea was sold to Americans. As a result, most of the royal governors refused to touch the tea when it became apparent that, instead of tea, Americans were brewing trouble; almost without exception they pleaded want of instructions as an excuse for remaining safely on the side lines. [22]

The tea consignees sorely needed the protection of the British government, for like the stamp masters they found themselves exposed to the full fury of the Sons of Liberty. In the opinion of their fellow colonists, they had been appointed to do the dirty work of the British Ministry; and, as in the case of the stamp officers, the patriots declared that it was "as great a grievance to be under the hands of monopolizers and extortioners among ourselves, as under foreign task-masters and tax-gatherers." When they were presented with the choice of resigning their posts or withstanding "the insults of many rascally Mobbs Convened in the Dark high charged with Liquor to do every act of Violence their mad Brain could invent," the consignees looked in vain to the British officials for aid. The only place of safety in the colonies was aboard a British man-of-war; but the chances of fighting one's way through mobs to this haven were not encouraging. The tea consignees, in short, had an excellent opportunity of making themselves martyrs to the

[21] *Newport Mercury*, February 7, 1774.
[22] John Penn to the Right Honourable Lady Juliana Penn, May 13, 1774, Penn MSS., Private Correspondence, Historical Society of Pennsylvania.

cause of British authority in America; yet this prospect had little charm for them. As merchants, they wished to carry on their business in the colonies, not to ruin themselves for the sake of the East India Company or the British Parliament. Therefore they resigned their posts with little ado and thrust the problem of protecting the tea upon the reluctant Crown Officers.

The situation in Boston set that town apart from the other colonial seaports. There existed among the Saints a powerful, organized party prepared to go any length to strike a "Home Blow" at British tyranny. The heavy importations of taxed British tea into Boston from 1768 to 1773 while the other colonists were patronizing the Dutch smugglers made necessary, in the opinion of the patriots, a bold stroke which would wipe out the stain of Toryism. And lastly, Governor Thomas Hutchinson, smarting under the publication of his confidential letters, had resolved to make a decisive stand upon the Tea Act against the radicals; another retreat, he believed, would be fatal to British sovereignty over the colonies. Therefore, the tea consignees — among whom were Hutchinson's sons — were supported by the royal government in Massachusetts, whereas in most of the other colonies they were compelled to stand alone against the patriot mobs. Largely because of this aid, the Boston consignees refused to follow the example of their fellow consignees by resigning their posts. Instead, they took refuge at Castle William, where, surrounded by cannon and redcoats, they lived very cozily with the Commissioners of the Customs who had likewise found Boston too hot for comfort. Safe behind the ramparts, these much-harassed gentry passed their time drinking bumpers to Peggy Hutchinson and "the other Toasts of the Town" and hobnobbing with the army officers.[23] The baffled patriots, finding the birds flown, were obliged to take drastic action to redeem Boston's reputation as a patriot stronghold.

Hutchinson's resolute stand gave the Boston Whigs little choice between submission and the destruction of the tea. Convinced that Adams and his "crew" would yield at the last moment and determined not to give an inch of ground to the patriots, Hutchinson refused to permit the tea ships in Boston Harbor to leave port with their cargoes. His obduracy convinced the patriots that they must dispose of the tea before December 17, 1773 — last day of

[23] Thomas Hutchinson, Junior, to Elisha Hutchinson, December 14, 1773, Egerton MSS., British Museum 2659.

grace before it was liable to seizure by the customhouse authorities for nonpayment of duty. The patriots feared that once the tea was in the possession of the customs officers it would be sold secretly to the people in order to raise money to pay the salaries of the governor and judges. Therefore, on the night of December 16, after the citizens assembled at Faneuil Hall had made an eleventh-hour attempt to persuade Hutchinson to release the tea ships, the "Mohawks" struck. Three companies of fifty men, each led by a captain, had been appointed to board the three tea ships which lay under the guns of the British men-of-war in the harbor. Although the men masqueraded as Indians, their disguise would not have deceived a redskin — or, more important, a British Crown Officer. For example, George Hewes, one of the "Indians," had time only to darken his complexion with soot from a blacksmith's shop on Boylston's wharf and run to a friend's house to borrow a blanket before he joined his fellow Mohawks. More effective protection was afforded by the hundreds of spectators who covered the waterfront, making it impossible for any royal officer to see closely the men aboard the tea ships. No resistance was offered the Indians; on the contrary, the sailors aboard the ships helped hoist the tea chests from the hold, break them open, and heave them overboard. Neither the ships nor any other items of their cargo were damaged; the Whigs boasted that all that was found missing the next morning was the tea and one padlock.[24]

The identity of the Indians was a well-kept secret; although the Attorney General of Massachusetts pronounced the destruction of the tea to be treason, he was unable to ferret out any culprits. Only one citizen of the hundreds who witnessed the destruction of the tea was willing to testify — and then only on condition that the trial take place in England, three thousand miles away from the Boston mob. A trial in Boston would serve no good purpose: as Hutchinson pointed out, the jury would certainly be composed of the Indians or their sympathizers. It was rumored, however, that the tea was destroyed by "King Hancock, and the damn'd sons of liberty" in blackface and feathers. Hancock and Sam Adams

[24] Deposition of Hezekiah Coffin, Jethro Coffin and William Hewley, January 11, 1775; Deposition of James Bruce, James Bruce, Junior, and John Tinney, January 11, 1775, P.R.O., C.O. 5, 133, Library of Congress Transcript. *Hutchinson Correspondence*, III, 589. William Smith MSS., Entry for December 20, 1773, New York Public Library. *Massachusetts Spy*, February 2, 1775.

were alleged to have led the braves aboard the tea ships and to have assisted in throwing the tea into Boston Harbor. Franklin ridiculed the story, pointing out "the Improbability that, when the lower Actors tho't it prudent to disguise themselves, any of the principal Inhabitants should appear in the Affair." [25] Nevertheless, George Hewes declared many years later that Sam Adams and John Hancock were among those that poured at the Boston Tea Party, claiming that he helped Hancock heave a chest overboard. He recognized Hancock, he said, "by his ruffles" and exchanged with him the countersign: "an Indian grunt, and the expression *me know you.*" [26] Certainly, the presence of Hancock and Adams would have bolstered patriot morale by demonstrating that the leaders were as deeply involved in the enterprise as were the rank and file.

Not all the East India Company's tea was dumped into Boston Harbor on the night of December 16, 1773. One of the ships carrying tea to Boston was wrecked on Cape Cod. Much of the tea aboard was washed ashore and burned by the patriots but part of it was saved and stored in Castle William by the British, to the great chagrin of Sam Adams, who declared that had he known that the "Indians" of Cape Cod were so "sick at the knees," the Boston braves would have "marched on snowshoes to do the business for them." [27]

The Tories railed against "ye wicked Bostonians, who have given it to the fishes"; and Thomas Hutchinson declared that a full-fledged tyranny had been established in Boston. Hutchinson believed that the Sons of Liberty in disguising themselves as Mohawks did the Indians a grave injustice, for "such barbarity none of the Aboriginals were guilty of" — although the redskins had slain his great-grand-mother, Anne Hutchinson.[28] Daniel Leonard, the Massachusetts Tory, declared that the Tea Party was "a more unaccountable phrenzy, and more disgraceful to the annals of America, than that of the witchcraft." As always, however, the Whigs were prepared to justify their assault upon British authority. They contended that the villainy of that "damn'd arch traitor," Thomas Hutchinson, made the destruction of the tea imperative. Had the

[25] *The Writings of Benjamin Franklin,* IV, 223.
[26] George R. T. Hewes, *Traits of the Tea Party,* New York, 1835, 180, 193.
[27] Sam Adams to James Warren, January 10, 1774, Adams MSS., New York Public Library.
[28] Thomas Hutchinson to Israel Williams, December 23, 1773, Williams MSS., Massachusetts Historical Society.

royal governor not encouraged the tea consignees to resist the people and had he permitted the tea ships to return to England, they argued that there would have been no necessity for the Tea Party. The Whigs pictured it as an act of self-defense; and since "the great Law of Nature and Reason has possessed every Society with a Right to defend itself from Ruin, without having Recourse to Books or Statutes, or recorded Customs," the destruction of the tea was legitimate resistance to tyranny within the definition laid down by John Locke. It was accordingly pronounced to be a "glorious illegality" perpetrated by "a band of virtuous patriots" — "an act of absolute moral and political necessity, and therefore exempt from even good laws." [29]

Nevertheless, signs were not wanting that the Boston patriots had outrun public opinion even in New England. Many towns rebuked the Bostonians for their rashness and dissolved their Committees of Correspondence on the ground that they were "calculated to introduce anarchy, confusion and blood-shed among the people." Some committees, in their eagerness to clear their skirts of complicity in the acts of the mobbish metropolis, instructed their representatives in the General Court to bring the "Indians" to justice. Much of this alarm among the country people was owing, however, less to moral indignation than to the fear that they would be obliged to pay for the tea; and the punishment meted out to Boston by the British government for the Tea Party, together with the refusal of the Bostonians to reimburse the East India Company, put an end to these recriminations. [30]

In Charleston, South Carolina, there occurred what the Boston patriots had most feared might be awaiting them: the tea was seized by the customhouse officers for nonpayment of duty and stored. Although threats had been made to destroy the tea aboard ship in Charleston Harbor, the Whigs were restrained by the fear that violence against the East India Company would cost them their bounty upon indigo and the privilege of exporting rice to southern Europe. They therefore permitted the tea to be landed and to be taken into the custody of the customhouse. The subsequent events at Charleston refuted, at least to the Tories' satisfaction, the Bos-

[29] *Rivington's New York Gazetteer*, January 27, 1774. *Virginia Gazette* (Purdie and Dixon), March 3, 1774. Cartwright, 106.

[30] *Essex Gazette*, February 8, 1774. *Massachusetts Spy*, February 3 and 24, 1774. *Massachusetts Gazette*, May 26, 1774.

tonians' contention that if the tea were seized by the customhouse, the duty would be paid and it would be sold to unsuspecting citizens. No duty was ever paid upon the tea stored in Charleston nor was it sold until July 1776, when the South Carolina delegates to the Continental Congress petitioned Congress for permission to dispose of it.[31] By the same token, said the Tories, had the tea at Boston fallen into the hands of the customhouse officers it "might have lain till doomsday, and would never have hurt you or your posterity."[32] But the Whigs answered, with no small justification, that there was no powerful faction in Charleston, as in Boston, headed by the royal governor, which was determined to make the Tea Act a test case of British sovereignty.

The Boston Tea Party was merely the first of a series of tea parties given by Americans at the expense of the East India Company and colonial tea importers. In March 1774 over a score of chests of tea arrived in Boston. This tea did not belong to the East India Company: it was the property of a New England merchant but it bore the hated tax and hence was fair game for the patriots. The Committees of Correspondence from the towns in the neighborhood of Boston were called into consultation by the Boston patriots. To the consternation of the radicals, a majority of the committeemen favored returning the tea to England unharmed; no violent solution was countenanced. But while the committeemen proposed, the "Indians" disposed: "His Majesty OKNOOKO-TUNKOGOG King of the Narraganset Tribe of Indians, on receiving Information of the arrival of another Cargo of that Cursed Weed TEA immediately Summoned his Council at the Great Swamp by the River Jordan, who did Advise and Consent to the immediate Destruction thereof."[33]

In other colonies as well, Americans sang "Tea Deum." At Greenwich, New Jersey, the tea cargo of the ship *Greyhound* was burned by the local tribe of Indians; in November 1774, seven chests of tea were thrown into the Cooper River at Charleston,

[31] *Letters of Members of the Continental Congress*, edited by E. C. Burnett, I, 24.

[32] *Boston Evening Post*, May 23, 1774. Lieutenant Governor Bull to Lord Dartmouth, December 24, 1774, P.R.O., C.O. 5. Thomas Wharton to Samuel Wharton, January 4, 1774, Wharton MSS., Historical Society of Pennsylvania. Samuel Seabury, *The Congress Canvassed*, New York, 1774, 22.

[33] *Boston Gazette*, March 14, 1774. *Newport Mercury*, April 11, 1774. *Committees of Correspondence Papers*, Entries of March 7 and March 8, 1774.

South Carolina, while crowds cheered from the wharves; and in Annapolis, Maryland, the ship and cargo of a tea importer were burned. The New York patriots could not be prevented from joining in this sport, despite the fact that the governor of New York was Tryon, the conqueror of the North Carolina Regulators. Tryon came to the colony with a formidable reputation as a fighting man and the Tories confidently expected him to cram the tea down the throats of the Sons of Liberty.[34] He attempted to land the tea and store it pending instructions from the British government, but the citizens refused to permit it to be brought ashore. When Tryon ordered the tea ship convoyed by His Majesty's sloop *Susan* to the wharf at New York, two thousand citizens met in the New York City Hall to express their determination that the tea should never be landed. Committees were appointed to prevent the tea being removed from the ship. On December 16, the day the tea was destroyed at Boston, an outbreak of violence seemed inevitable at New York. Had the governor made a move to bring the tea ashore, thousands of patriots would have rushed to the waterfront with equally fatal results to the tea and any Crown Officers who stood in their way. A tea party was averted in New York at this time only because Governor Tryon decided not to run the risk of a mob uprising. But in March 1774, the New York Mohawks fell upon tea consigned to merchants in the city and — in the manner of the redskins at Boston — brewed it with salt water.[35]

After 1773, the patriots insisted upon the complete proscription of tea throughout the colonies. They reasoned that only by abstaining altogether from tea could Americans be certain that they were not drinking dutied British tea. Even the smugglers were warned not to import tea lest they unwittingly aid the British government in its efforts to raise a colonial revenue. A close scrutiny was maintained by the patriots over the business affairs of the merchants; and for the first time in their careers, the Sons of Liberty found themselves suppressing smuggling. They did the job so thoroughly that they boasted that there was no longer need for the

[34] *Pennsylvania Gazette*, November 17, 1773.
[35] William Smith MSS., Entries of December 13 and 15, 1773, New York Public Library. *Rivington's New York Gazetteer*, May 12, 1774. Henry White, Abraham Lott, Pigou and Booth to the Court of Directors of the East India Company, December 1, 1773, P.R.O., C.O. 5, 133, Library of Congress Transcript.

"tide-Waiters, Pimps, or Informers" of the customhouse. It is significant that it was the radicals who demanded the complete prohibition of tea — the merchants, whether Whig or Tory, were obliged to take orders from men whom they considered on a social level with their employees. Nevertheless, under patriotic pressure tea disappeared from the colonies: "You may ride days, nay weeks," a traveler observed, "and never get a drop." The women of Boston, "to their immortal honor," took a solemn oath never to drink another cup; and whole chests were burned upon village commons, thus sacrificing "the obnoxious Drug at the Shrine of American Liberty." [36] Coffee drinking became patriotic in the colonies and Americans were weaned from the teacup to the coffee cup, where, for the most part, their devotion still rests.

[36] *Letters on the American Revolution*, edited by Margaret Wheeler Willard, Boston, 1925, 4. *Newport Mercury*, January 27, February 14, 1774. *Essex Gazette*, December 28, 1773, January 4, 1774. *Boston Evening Post*, January 23, 1774. *Virginia Gazette* (Purdie), April 7, 1775.

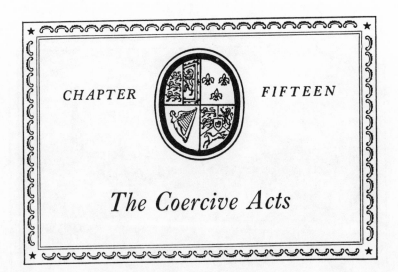

CHAPTER FIFTEEN

The Coercive Acts

The Port of Boston

MASSACHUSETTS

THE Tea Party generated an "electrical Shock" of such voltage that all England was agitated. Few doubted that the Saints had risen in rebellion and were about to declare themselves independent of the mother country. Many Englishmen compared the Tea Party with the rebellion of 1745: instead of Charles Stuart at the head of Highland clans, Sam Adams now led "a banditti of hypocrites" against Great Britain.[1] After having long abused the mother country and planted thorns in her bed, the Bostonians had at last given her "a Blow in full Face of the World" — "the most wanton and unprovoked insult offered to the civil power that is recorded in history." Lord North was dumbfounded by the news from Boston; he declared that it was impossible for any man to have foreseen that these perverse colonists would rise up against a tax which made tea cheaper than it had ever been before. He insisted that he had given the colonists "a relief instead of an oppression" and that of all mankind, only "New England Fanatics" would have rebelled against it.[2] The turn of events dismayed North: the colonial pot was again at full boil and there seemed little rest in store for British ministers until those seething waters had been quieted.

The Tea Party silenced almost the last appeaser in England. Even the Whigs were aghast at the rashness of the Bostonians. Chatham declared that the Tea Party was "certainly criminal" and that Boston ought to make restitution. Few Englishmen believed that the mother country could retain its sovereignty if it retreated in the face of such outrage: it was now said upon every side that the colonists must be chastised into submission. If Americans were to enjoy the privilege of rejecting acts of Parliament as they chose, there could be little doubt that "they will without ceremony reject the

---

[1] *Gazetteer and New Daily Advertiser*, April 2, 1775.
[2] *Parliamentary History*, XVIII, 177, 604, 763. *Public Advertiser*, May 17, 1774. *Independency of the Object of the Congress in America*, London, 1776, 2–3.

whole statute books, and so save Parliament any further trouble," and that "in process of time, if this kingdom is tame enough, they may proceed to control and tax it, instead of Parliament regulating and taxing them." [3] As Lord North said, the dispute was no longer over taxation but whether Great Britain possessed any authority whatever over the "haughty American Republicans." "We must master them or totally leave them to themselves and treat them as Aliens," said George III; unless the mother country acted firmly, its laws would have no more currency in America than Papal Bulls.[4] "It is, no doubt, very easy for our Parliament to repeal all their late Acts," an Englishman observed; "but nothing less than the Almighty Power . . . would be able to repeal from the perverted Minds of those Americans the Impression which such a Conduct would leave behind it. Every Act which had been passed against them would be produced as so many Proofs of our Folly and Injustice; every Repeal of those Acts, as equal Proofs of our Weakness, Disunion and Timidity." [5] Englishmen believed that they had erred upon the side of patience and kindness: "Men accustomed to think themselves masters," said Dr. Johnson, "do not love to be threatened," yet they had taken insults and abuse from Americans that no true-born Briton ought to be expected to endure. But the mistress of the seas, the conqueror of France and Spain and the terror of the evildoers of the world, could no longer sit still while a knot of agitators and firebrands in her own colonies sought to destroy the empire. If England were to continue to hold up her head in Europe as a great power, she could not permit "a petty little province, the creature of our own hands, the bubble of our own breath," to hurl defiance across the Atlantic with impunity.[6]

The demand for a final reckoning with the colonies was strengthened by the fact that the dispute was chiefly with the Bostonians, the most hateful, to Britons, of all the colonists. Had the tea not been destroyed at Boston, the advocates of compromise might have made their voices heard; but to surrender to Boston in 1774 was a humiliation which few Englishmen could bear. "I would rather," exclaimed an Englishman, "all the Hamilcars, and all the Hanni-

[3] *Gazetteer and New Daily Advertiser*, January 10, 1775. *Parliamentary History*, XVII, 1166. *The Sandwich Papers*, LXIX, 63.
[4] *The Correspondence of King George the Third*, III, 154.
[5] *Public Advertiser*, May 17, 1774, and January 26, 1775. *Gazetteer and New Daily Advertiser*, March 19, 1774.
[6] *Rivington's New York Gazetteer*, May 12, 1774.

bals that Boston ever bred; all the Hancocks, and all the Sad-Cocks, and sad dogs of Massachusetts Bay; all the heroes of tar and feathers, and the champions, maimers of unpatriotic horses, mares, and mules, were led up to the Altar, or to Liberty Tree, there to be exalted and rewarded according to their merit or demerit, than that Britain should disgrace herself by receding from her just authority."[7] From its settlement, Boston had seemingly been "a nest of rebels and hypocrites"; "obstinate, undutiful, and ungovernable from the very beginning." All the colonial troubles, it was said, could be traced to Boston; it had spread seditious doctrines over America and had committed "more atrocious Acts of Outrage than any other Part of the Colonies."[8] As the "first movers, and the main spring of all this contention," Bostonians gloried in their misbehavior and dignified sedition by calling it patriotism and love of liberty.[9] They had proved themselves to be "a canker worm in the heart of America" and a "rotten limb which (if suffered to remain) will inevitably destroy the whole body of that extensive country."[10] The Saints had made such inroads upon British authority that the question now seemed to be whether Boston, "the center of American politics, and source of all the controversy, shall be, to all intents and purposes, the capital of the British empire, the seat and center of government," or whether London should retain its pre-eminence. It was observed that every year "the American capital gains very large and dangerous strides upon the British capital"; but by rushing into premature rebellion, the Saints had given Great Britain an opportunity to smash this wasps' nest before the authority of the mother country had been totally destroyed.[11]

In the opinion of many Englishmen, the Boston Saints deserved nothing less than "canonizing" for the Tea Party. They declared that "it would be best to blow the town of *Boston* about the ears of its inhabitants, and to destroy that nest of *locusts*"; and, for good measure, they urged that "about one hundred of these puritanical rebels" be hung.[12] "I wish the Bostonians were at the d——l," exclaimed a member of Parliament, "for they are likely to be a

[7] *Gazetteer and New Daily Advertiser*, February 3, 1775.
[8] *Parliamentary Register*, V, 194. *Public Advertiser*, April 8, 1774.
[9] *Gazetteer and New Daily Advertiser*, May 6, 1774.
[10] *Morning Chronicle and London Advertiser*, March 12 and 14, 1774.
[11] *Gazetteer and New Daily Advertiser*, January 31, 1775.
[12] *Ibid.*, April 8, 1774.

continual plague to us." [13] Those who raised the cry of *Delenda est Bostoniensis* urged Englishmen to cast off their scruples over using force against their subjects overseas; having treated Great Britain "like a foreign enemy," Bostonians merited the same harsh treatment that France and Spain would have meted out to their colonists had they risen in rebellion.[14]

Lord North refused to yield to this clamor for bloody reprisals. Instead of battering Boston about the heads of the Sons of Liberty, he favored the more refined method of starving them into submission. This was the purpose of the Boston Port Bill which was introduced into Parliament in March 1774. It provided that the Puritan metropolis be closed to all shipping — in effect removing it thirty miles from the sea — until the citizens had paid the East India Company for the tea destroyed at the Tea Party, compensated the revenue officers for the losses they had incurred at the hands of the mob, and otherwise given the Crown evidence of their good intentions. North believed that by singling out Boston for punishment he had provided against a new colonial union; but to make certain that Americans did not permit their sympathy for Boston to draw them into the quarrel, he proposed to keep them busy scrambling for Boston's trade. He anticipated great popularity for himself among the New York and New Hampshire merchants, who, it was expected, would leap at the opportunity of growing rich on Boston's ruin.

Lord North's Port Bill was also recommended by its economy. Four or five frigates stationed in Boston Harbor and a few regiments of British regulars in Boston itself to keep order would, he told the House, "do the business." The events of 1768 gave good grounds for believing that the Bostonians would submit without a struggle and that the other colonies would not come to their aid. When the British fleet hove-to off Boston, it was predicted, "the Boston voters will scamper behind their counters . . . assume an affecting hypocritical air, clap their hands, cast up their eyes to heaven, wonder if the King knows their oppressive situation," and declare that Parliament was misled by the wicked Ministry or it "would not have so grievously vexed the hearts of the Lord's people." [15] That Boston

[13] Historical Manuscripts Commission, *Report on the MSS. in various Collections*, Dublin, 1909, VI, 112.
[14] *St. James's Chronicle*, November 8, 1774. Fletcher, 42.
[15] *Massachusetts Spy*, May 5, 1774.

would stand alone seemed certain to North and his colleagues. "Will the Colonies, who have been repeatedly persecuted, deluded and betrayed by the Bostonians, engage in a REBELLION to support them?" asked an Englishman.[16]

The Boston Port Bill was passed by the House of Commons on March 25, 1774, without a division "but after a pretty long debate." An overwhelming majority was determined to deal firmly with the "Boston mutineers"; certainly no member had to be bribed to vote for the bill. George III rejoiced that at last England was united: "The feebleness and futility of the Opposition to the Boston Port Bill," he declared, "shows the rectitude of the measure." [17] What little opposition there was came chiefly from those who contended not that Boston was punished with undue severity but that the bill gave too great power to the Crown. Charles James Fox and Lord Shelburne, for example, declared that Boston should not be compelled to apply to the Crown for relief: the townspeople's quarrel was with Parliament and therefore Parliament ought to have the power of relaxing the restrictions it imposed.[18] A few objected that by the Port Bill, the innocent as well as the guilty suffered; but Dr. Samuel Johnson thundered that the Bostonians were like rebels who had seized and fortified a town — thus putting "the harmless burghers and the criminal garrison" in equal danger of destruction.

The patriots were well aware that the British government would not pass over the Tea Party lightly. The day after the dumping of the tea, Admiral Montague remarked to the townsmen: "Well, boys, you have had a fine pleasant evening for your Indian caper, haven't you. But mind, you have got to pay the fiddler yet!" But the Port Act was more than they had bargained for. Even Thomas Hutchinson was shocked by its severity. For a riot no worse than many witnessed in the mother country and perpetrated — so the Bostonians claimed — not by the citizens but by "strangers," Boston seemed condemned to be "inhumanly murder'd in cold blood . . . and by such an act of despotism as an eastern divan would blush at." But both Whigs and Tories rejoiced that the quarrel had been brought to a head; the long period of indecision was over, the issue was fairly joined between Great Britain and the colonies. "The per-

[16] *Ibid.*
[17] *The Correspondence of King George III*, III, 83–84.
[18] *Parliamentary History*, XVII, 1182–1184, 1302.

fect Crisis of American politics" seemed to have arrived; there could no longer be doubt that the die had been cast and that either America or Great Britain must triumph.[19]

The news of the Port Act reached Boston on May 11, 1774. Immediately the Committee of Correspondence dispatched a circular letter to the committees of the neighboring towns urging them to meet at Faneuil Hall. The Boston Town Meeting was summoned and the Committees of Correspondence were quickly put in action. Terrified conservatives could think only of paying for the tea and begging the British government for mercy. But the radicals wanted no reconciliation with Great Britain upon such terms: paying for the tea would be a backward step, and Sam Adams and his followers intended to go forward — even if independence were at the end of the road. They refused to recross the Rubicon. Rather than pay a farthing in damages to the East India Company they declared they would "abandon their city to flames." If the East India Company had been injured, they pointed out, it was no more than it deserved for having sold itself to the British government to destroy American liberties. Certainly, Americans owed it nothing because it had chosen to risk its property to further the government's schemes of tyranny.

Paul Revere, the patriot "express," was dispatched to New York and Philadelphia with appeals for aid. The Boston patriots were well aware that they could not stand alone against the British government; if the other colonies deserted them, they recognized that they must beg forgiveness and "acknowledge the right of parliament to da——n us whenever they please."[20] They sought, therefore, to persuade Americans that Boston was the first line of defense of American freedom and that if it were destroyed, British tyranny would sweep almost unchecked over the continent. The best that the colonies could hope for after the fall of Boston "was to be the last that would be devoured; because the British government was making war upon liberty wherever it existed in the empire, and there could be no refuge in neutrality." The frontier of American liberty was on the Charles, said the Whigs, and this frontier must be held against the British government at all costs. They swore that the true reason why Boston had been punished was that it had been

[19] *Proceedings of the Massachusetts Historical Society*, Boston, 1860, IV, Second Series, 30.
[20] *Ibid.*, VIII, 328.

foremost in the struggle for American rights: it was the Puritan metropolis that "when this Brat of Despotism was in Embryo . . . discovered it." The blow was aimed at Boston because "*there* lie the VITALS of *American freedom*" and the British government hoped to annihilate colonial liberty at one blow.[21]

These warnings carried conviction to many Americans who recognized that provincial isolationism afforded little security. Although Boston alone had destroyed the tea in 1773, New York, Philadelphia, and Charleston had all brewed a bitter dish for the British government and the East India Company. "Where is the mighty difference," asked the Charleston patriots, "between destroying the tea, and resolving to do it, with such firmness as intimidated the Captains to a return? Besides, did not every province applaud the Bostonians?" If Boston had given the British government the most flagrant provocation, it was equally clear that all the colonies were tarred with the same brush. After the government had dealt with Boston it seemed likely that the turn of the other offending seaports would come next and that Americans would be made "the most abject slaves of the earth." As George Washington saw it, the question was whether Americans should "supinely sit and see one province after another fall a prey to despotism?" A South Carolinian declared that if Boston submitted, he expected to see "our courts of justice removed — our harbour blockaded — navigation stopt — our streets crowded with soldiers . . . and, after a little time, the now flourishing Charles-Town reduced to a neglected plain." Charleston certainly could not regard itself as being in the good graces of the British government: although its behavior was not "equal in Criminality to the Proceedings in other Colonies," wrote the lieutenant governor of South Carolina, it could be considered "in no other light than that of a most unwarrantable Insult to the Authority of this Kingdom." [22] It was for this reason South Carolinians urged that even if Boston were in the wrong, she ought to be supported because her punishment established a precedent that might be used against every other seaport in America.

June 1, 1774, the day the Port Act went into effect, was marked by demonstrations throughout the colonies similar to those that had greeted the Stamp Act. In Philadelphia, the shops were closed,

[21] *Essex Gazette*, March 24, 1774. *Massachusetts Spy*, July 28, 1774.
[22] *Newport Mercury*, May 16, June 27, July 25, 1774. *Essex Gazette*, May 24, June 14, 1774.

flags hung at half mast, churches were filled with wrathful Whigs, and the muffled bells of Christ Church "rung a solemn peal at intervals, from morning till night." In New York, effigies of Hutchinson, Wedderburn, Lord North — "that blood-thirsty wretch" — and the devil were carried through the streets and burned. In Connecticut, the Port Act was burned publicly and "executed by the common hangman . . . in honour to the immortal goddess of liberty."

Lord North's calculation that Americans' suspicion of "mobbish Boston" and their eagerness to share in its trade would permit the British government a free hand with the Saints proved ill-founded. After the Port Act, Bostonians underwent a metamorphosis in the eyes of many colonists: from riot lovers and levelers, they became "an innocent, a virtuous, a religious and loyal people, ever remarkable for their love of order, peace and good government." Despite his pains, Lord North had succeeded only in making Bostonians martyrs to American liberty. Newport, Rhode Island, pledged its assistance to its "virtuous brethren in that capital, who have so nobly stood as a barrier against slavery"; "Let America think herself happy," exclaimed a South Carolina patriot, "that she has such a number of staunch friends to liberty as the *New-England* colonies abound with." [23] "The blow struck at that truly magnanimous Community, the respectable Town of Boston," said a Salem patriot, "is a Blow at all the colonies"; and the citizens of Marblehead declared that in supporting Boston they propped "the tottering Liberties of America." [24] So the Port Act, instead of isolating Boston, seemed to be "the very means to perfect *that union* in America, which it was intended to destroy, and finally restore the excellent constitution even of the mother country itself." [25]

It was thus disclosed that the question was not whether Americans would support Boston in this crisis but how far they would go in giving aid. Sam Adams and the Boston Committee of Correspondence believed that Boston could be saved from ruin by an immediate suspension of trade between Great Britain and the colonies. They therefore drew up a "Solemn League and Covenant" in which Americans were asked to pledge themselves not to purchase British merchandise or to export commodities to the mother country until the Port Act had been repealed. By this means, Adams

[23] *Newport Mercury*, June 27, 1774. *Massachusetts Spy*, July 28, 1774.
[24] *Essex Gazette*, May 24, June 14, 1774.
[25] *Massachusetts Spy*, June 30, 1774.

hoped to resume the economic war with the mother country, but — it is significant — under the leadership of the radicals and common people instead of that of the merchants. The adoption of the Solemn League and Covenant would have meant that the struggle for colonial liberty would have been directed not merely against the mother country, but against the wealthy, conservative mercantile class that had hitherto succeeded in controlling the revolutionary movement.

The New York merchants immediately recognized that this scheme hatched by Adams and the Boston committee was a bird of ill omen. In 1770, they had won a hard-earned victory over the mob; yet now they were being asked to place their property and welfare in the hands of men whom they regarded as their bitterest enemies. They dreaded the Solemn League and Covenant like the plague; and when Sears and McDougall began to clamor for its adoption in New York, they exerted all their influence to thwart the radicals. McDougall was flattered and cajoled by the merchants, who urged him to "shoot no Bolt, because it would expose our Weakness." "Time will do every Thing for us," he was told, "if we maintain our Firmness without Violence." [26] At the same time, they undertook to purge the New York Committee of Correspondence which, because of the "Languor of the Chief Citizens," had been permitted to fall under the control of the radicals. In May 1774, the "people of weight" appeared in such numbers at the public meeting called to consider the adoption of the Solemn League and Covenant that they succeeded in dissolving the Committee of Correspondence and creating a Committee of Fifty-one which was dominated by the "most prudent and considerate People of the Place." Thus Sears and McDougall were rudely jostled out of the saddle and New York was put under the tight rein of the moderates.

To head off the Solemn League and Covenant and frustrate the radicals' aspirations to leadership, the New York Committee of Fifty-one proposed that a Continental Congress be called. Forced to choose between a Continental Congress and the Solemn League and Covenant, conservatives found a Congress much the lesser evil. Many, indeed, welcomed a Congress as the only means of keeping the extremists within bounds. It was possible that moderation might

[26] William Smith MSS., May 18, 1774, IV, New York Public Library. *Document relative to the Colonial History of the State of New York*, VIII, 433.

prevail in a Continental Congress; but if the colonies accepted the leadership of Boston, there seemed little doubt that the door would be slammed upon compromise and Americans would shortly find themselves at war with Great Britain.[27]

The fate of the Boston-made Solemn League and Covenant and New York's counterproposal of a Continental Congress was decided at Philadelphia. The Quaker City offered small hope of success to the radicals; indeed, isolationist sentiment was stronger there than in New York. Many Philadelphians believed, as did Benjamin Franklin (who was still in London), that Boston ought to pay for the tea and they advised Bostonians to lose no time in getting into sackcloth and ashes. Few citizens wished to lash themselves to the mast and go down with Boston; they bore little love for "mobbish Boston" and distrusted everything, including the Solemn League and Covenant, that came out of the Boston Committee of Correspondence.[28]

A handful of Philadelphia radicals led by Charles Thomson — the "Sam Adams" of Philadelphia — Joseph Reed, and Thomas Mifflin favored the adoption of the Solemn League and Covenant, but without the help of John Dickinson they could not hope to carry even moderate proposals of support for the Puritan metropolis. The erstwhile "Pennsylvania Farmer" was the most influential man in the province and his decision would sway thousands of Pennsylvanians. But Dickinson, unlike Sam Adams, had not become progressively more radical; on the contrary, he had not altered the views he had expressed in 1767–1768 and had not overcome his suspicion of Boston. Many of his supporters feared that his aversion to disorder had triumphed over his love of liberty. His insistence upon decorum and moderation in opposing British tyranny seemed to have refined the revolutionary movement into a tea-table dispute. Although he still expressed concern for the fate of colonial liberty, he ruled out the only means by which liberty could be successfully defended. Dickinson, in short, pinned his faith on reason and moderation; he was convinced of the rectitude of Great Britain and genuinely loved the mother country and the British Empire. He

---

[27] John Drayton, *Memoirs of the American Revolution*, Charleston, 1821, I, 131.

[28] Thomas Wharton to Thomas Walpole, May 2, 1774; Thomas Wharton to Samuel Wharton, May 17, 1774, Wharton MSS., Historical Society of Pennsylvania.

carried, it is clear, far too heavy intellectual baggage to be a swift-moving revolutionist. The faster Sam Adams and other radicals pressed forward, the more Dickinson sought to apply the brakes. For such a timid soul, the radicals had only contempt; "His nerves were weak," they remarked.

But Dickinson was far too much of a public idol to permit the radicals publicly to express such views. Instead, they had to flatter him, remove his doubts about supporting "mobbish Boston," and induce him to come forward as an advocate of aid to the Saints. Charles Thomson well knew that if Dickinson opposed assistance, the weight of his name would certainly sink the cause of Boston in Pennsylvania. Therefore, the Philadelphia radicals laid a trap, baited, for Dickinson's special benefit, with an opportunity to appear as the advocate of "moderation." They agreed that Thomson, the fieriest patriot in Philadelphia, should make a speech at the meeting called to discuss the plight of Boston in which he would urge the adoption of the Solemn League and Covenant. After this proposal had been supported by the other extremists, Dickinson would step forward as the champion of moderation and suggest that while Philadelphians proclaimed their solidarity with Bostonians they should at the same time decline to enter into the Solemn League and Covenant. There was only one serious obstacle to this scheme: Dickinson's reluctance to attend the meeting and play the part assigned him. It was only on the very day of the meeting that, plied with wine and arguments by the patriots, he agreed to be present upon the understanding that "matters were so conducted that he might be allowed to propose and carry moderate measures."

The radicals recognized that they and Boston were getting only half a loaf, but they regarded half a loaf as better than none at all — which would certainly be their portion if Dickinson did not speak.[29]

The meeting called in Philadelphia to discuss the Boston Port Act closely followed this prearranged plan. Charles Thomson made a violent speech demanding full support of Boston even to the point of adopting the covenant. He was drowned by the clamor of the conservatives who had turned out in large numbers to forestall any attempts to align Philadelphia with Boston. In the midst of the tumult, Thomson found it convenient to faint. While he was being carried out, Dickinson took the floor and spoke gravely of the need of moderation in all things — including patriotism. Although recommending that Philadelphia make common cause with Boston, he cautioned against rushing headlong into rebellion alongside the hotheads of that city. Instead of approving the Solemn League and Covenant, Dickinson advised Philadelphians to appoint a Committee of Correspondence and draft an answer to the letter of the Boston committee. This basis of compromise was adopted and the "company broke up in tolerable good humour, both thinking they had in part carried their point." The radicals had good cause for rejoicing: it marked another triumph for their policy of leading the people "step by step till they had advanced too far to retreat." [30]

The reply of the Philadelphia Committee of Correspondence written by John Dickinson, while not a total rejection of their appeal, administered the final blow to Bostonian hopes that the Solemn League and Covenant would be adopted throughout the colonies. Dickinson rejected the covenant, advised the Boston patriots to practise "Firmness, Prudence and Moderation," and gave his approval to the New Yorkers' plan of a Continental Congress. Letters from the Philadelphia radicals left no doubt that the Bostonians would be obliged to resort to "moderate prudent Measures prior to a *Non* Importation" if they hoped for support from the Middle colonies. "A Non Importation to be urged immediately, without some previous Step taken to obtain Redress," wrote Thomas Mifflin to Sam Adams, "may disunite us and ruin the Cause of America." [31]

The summoning of an American Congress had long been part of the patriots' program for uniting the colonies against Great Britain.[32] The Stamp Act Congress and the New England Confederation were harked back to in every crisis as precedents for colonial union; but in 1774 the Boston radicals had little heart for the plan. They wanted a boycott without tarrying, and a Continental Congress seemed likely to delay, if not altogether prevent, retaliation against the mother country. Their program called for immediate cessation of trade with Great Britain to be followed by a Continental Congress.

[30] *Letters of William Lee*, edited by W. C. Ford, I, 90–91. Thomas Wharton to Thomas Walpole, May 31, 1774, Wharton MSS., Historical Society of Pennsylvania.

[31] Thomas Mifflin to Samuel Adams, July 30, 1774, Adams MSS.

[32] *Newport Mercury*, March 22, 1773. *Essex Gazette*, February 25, 1772. Samuel H. Parsons to Samuel Adams, March 3, 1773, Adams MSS., New York Public Library. *American Historical Review*, VIII, 312.

They justified their insistence upon haste in resorting to economic reprisals largely because Boston was facing starvation and could be spared the horrors of a siege only by the quick repeal of the Port Act. The assembling of a Continental Congress might, they warned, be too late to save Boston.[33]

As the Tories observed, the Port Act was the first act of Parliament that Bostonians could not evade. Business in Boston came to a standstill; real estate fell precipitately in value; and "nine tenths of the Inhabitants [were] render'd wretchedly miserable." For the first time, an American city was obliged to deal with the problem of large-scale public relief. As they tightened their belts and prepared to endure siege, the Boston Whigs began to fear they would become martyrs indeed to the cause of American liberty.[34]

But in this emergency the colonists rallied to the support of the beleaguered city and by means of donations of sheep, rice, and wheat enabled the Bostonians to hold out against Lord North's blockade. The New York patriots promised Boston a supply of food sufficient to withstand a ten years' siege; the citizens of Brooklyn sent one hundred and twenty-five sheep to Boston and declared that if these were not enough to frustrate the British tyrants they were "ready to march in the van, and sprinkle the American altars with our heart's blood." Thus, when the English Tories expected to be entertained with news of famine in Boston, they found the patriots "bullying and insulting us with the Plenty they enjoyed, boasting that their Sheep and their Flour, their Fish and their Rice came faster than they could use them." The Boston Saints seemed indeed to have attained their beatification: they were living upon the fat of the land and were heroes into the bargain. "The malcontents" in Boston, it was reported, "are as sleek and as round as robins, especially our Demogogues, saving Hancock," whose vices were believed to have undermined his constitution. So much food poured into Boston that some Tories began to believe that the Saints were about to receive "a *literal* completion of the promise, that the *Saints shall inherit the earth.*"[35] "In God's name," exclaimed Samuel Seabury, "are not the people of Boston able to relieve their own poor?

[33] Josiah Quincy, Jr., *Memoir of Josiah Quincy*, 150. Thomas Mifflin to Samuel Adams, July 30, 1774, Adams MSS.

[34] *Massachusetts Spy*, August 25, 1774.

[35] Thomas B. Chandler, *A Friendly Address*, New York, 1774, 40. *Boston Gazette*, September 26, 1774. *Gazetteer and New Daily Advertiser*, February 11, 1775. *Rivington's New York Gazetteer*, February 23, 1775.

Must they go begging . . . from Nova-Scotia to Georgia, to support a few poor people whom their perverseness and ill conduct have thrown into distress? If they are really under such violent concern for their poor, why don't they pay for the tea?" [36]

The Tories' chagrin at the willingness of Americans to "pamper the Boston fanatics" was matched by their vexation over the course of events in Virginia. When the Port Act went into effect, some of the members of the Virginia Assembly signified their sympathy by fasting — but, as the Tories unkindly pointed out, simply by changing the hour of dining from afternoon to evening so "nothing was gained by the Fast but full Bellies at Night instead of the Day." But the burgesses did not, as the Tories hoped, "fob them [the Bostonians] off with nothing but Fasting and Prayer." The governor dissolved the assembly, whereupon the burgesses moved to the Raleigh Tavern and voted that the attack upon Massachusetts was an assault upon all the colonies and that a Continental Congress must be convened. Meeting in convention on August 1, 1774, the Virginia delegates showed that they intended to support the principles of the Solemn League and Covenant at the forthcoming Continental Congress. They resolved, if American grievances were not redressed, not to import British merchandise, including tea, after November 1, 1774, and to stop the exportation of tobacco after August 10, 1775.

There could be little doubt that the Continental Congress was to be a battleground between conservatives and radicals. The conservatives who had issued the call for a Congress expected that its first act would be to advise Boston to pay for the tea and make its peace with the British government. Then, it was hoped, the Congress would draw up a plan of "Constitutional Union" between Great Britain and the colonies which, by the inclusion of an American Bill of Rights, would ensure American liberty within the British Empire. Because its chief task was supposed to be to effect a reconciliation between Great Britain and the colonies, "a Message of Peace unmixt with Threats or threatening Behaviour" ought to be dispatched to the mother country; above all, there ought to be no attempt at economic coercion of the mother country until petitions and remonstrances had clearly failed to accomplish a redress of grievances. "Would it not be a ridiculous and unconstitutional Conduct," asked a Philadelphia merchant, "to implore the favor and

[36] Seabury, 17.

protection of a great State and at the same time using every Method to distress and starve her Inhabitants?" [37] In the conservatives' opinion, the duty of Congress was to extend the olive branch, not to throw down the gauntlet.

The outcome of this impending struggle in Philadelphia was determined in a large degree by the measures adopted by the British government during the summer of 1774. The passage of the "Coercive" or "Intolerable" Acts by the British Parliament immeasurably strengthened the position of the radicals in the Continental Congress and set the stage for their eventual triumph.

Having put Boston under siege, Lord North — without waiting the outcome of his efforts to reduce the Puritan stronghold — undertook to reform the Massachusetts Constitution. Many Englishmen had long since concluded that New Englanders were past saving but Lord North believed that they could be redeemed if British authority were strengthened and the loyal majority freed from the tyranny of the "Boston faction." The necessity of changing the Massachusetts government had been apparent to British statesmen from the period of the Puritan settlement; but although the province was shorn of many of its rights and privileges, eighteenth-century British imperialists learned from their defeats at the hands of the Massachusetts General Court that the Saints were far from chastened. Yet nothing was done until Lord North, confronted with what he regarded as the insufferable unruliness of the Bostonians, determined in 1774 to purge the Massachusetts Constitution of its "crudities" — by which he meant its democracy — and, by giving it a large dose of aristocratic and monarchical principles, to restore the authority of the mother country and put the "respectable characters" of the province in power.

Accordingly, in three acts of Parliament — known together with the Boston Port Act and the Quebec Act as the Coercive Acts or Intolerable Acts — the government of Massachusetts Bay was transformed. The Massachusetts Government Act of May 1774 provided that councilors should no longer be elected by the House of Representatives but should be chosen by the Crown and hold office "for and during the pleasure of his Majesty." At the same time,

---

[37] Harrison Gray, *A Few Remarks Upon Some of the Votes and Resolutions of the Continental Congress*, Boston, 1775, 6. Joseph Galloway, *Historical and Political Reflections*, London, 1780, 64. Edward Burd to ?, July 4, 1774, Shippen MSS., Historical Society of Pennsylvania.

the royal governor was given authority to appoint and remove, without consent of the council, all judges of the lower courts; and restrictions were imposed upon holding the town meetings which effectively prevented the patriots from making them instruments of democratic control. The Administration of Justice Act protected soldiers, magistrates, and customhouse officers who took part in suppressing riots or other disturbances from trial by juries of Sons of Liberty by providing that when, in the opinion of the governor, a fair trial could not be had in the province, it might be transferred to England or to another colony. The Quartering Act directed the local authorities to find quarters for troops, if barracks were not available, at the scene of trouble and not, as had been done in 1768, several miles away in Castle William.

The effect of the Coercive Acts was to produce an outburst in Massachusetts which swept away almost all British authority outside Boston where British troops held sway. The Committees of Correspondence in New England quickly went into action against the "mandamus councillors," as the royal appointees were called. They were pronounced to be "monsters more hideous than Hydra," and "traitorous villains" who had consented to be made the tools of "foreign usurpation." [38] The Whigs contended that no obedience was due them, because the Massachusetts Government Act was unconstitutional: "No power on earth," said the Boston Committee of Correspondence, "hath a Right without the consent of this Province to alter the minutest title of its Charter or abrogate any Act whatever made in pursuance of it, and confirmed by the Royal assent. . . . We are entitled to life liberty and the means of Sustenance by the grace of Heaven and without the King's leave." [39]

The Boston committee's call to arms against the mandamus councilors quickly roused the country. Although Lord North was "curs'd from morn to noon, and from noon to morn by every denomination of people," he was well out of the Yankees' reach; but the mandamus councilors were conveniently near their tar barrels and fowl roosts. Spurred by the Boston Whigs, New Englanders set grimly about the business of nullifying the Coercive Acts. Daniel Leonard of Taunton, a mandamus councilor, found bullets whistling uncomfortably close to his ears; Colonel Watson, after

[38] Thomas Young to Samuel Adams, August 19, 1774, Adams MSS.
[39] Committee of Correspondence Papers, MSS. New York Public Library, Letter of Boston Committee, August 26 and 27, 1774.

taking the oath as councilor, discovered that people shunned him on the streets and young patriot "Puppies" abused him to his face. Bidding "farewell to all Peace & Comfort in this World," the colonel made for Boston and the protection of British troops. Back-country Whigs declared that not even the Boston Sons of Liberty could have fallen upon the mandamus councilors with greater spirit; and one countryman boasted that "it is more dangerous being a tory here than at Boston, even if no troops were there." Peter Oliver — one of the Massachusetts oligarchs — who had seen Boston mobs at their worst, remarked after he had witnessed the countrymen in action, "I never knew what mobbing was before. I am sick enough of Confusion & Uproar. I long for an Asylum, some blessed Place of Refuge." [40] Rather than face these mobs of farmers, the councilors streaked for Boston, which soon gained the reputation of an "Asylum for Magistrates." The judges and sheriffs appointed by General Gage were hot on their heels. At Great Barrington, a mob of farmers surrounded the courthouse and stopped legal proceedings. Courts of justice were forcibly closed; the judges were compelled to resign their offices and a judge was pulled bodily from the bench in Berkshire County. Colonel Gilbert of Freetown, a staunch Tory, was treated to a crowning indignity: the patriots put glass under his saddle, whereupon his horse threw him and the colonel "lighted on his head, and remained senseless for some time, to the infinite joy and amusement of the rebels." [41]

At the same time that the patriots were nullifying the Coercive Acts, they were putting them to good purpose as propaganda. The Act for the Impartial Administration of Justice was ready-made for the purposes of colonial propagandists. Known as the "Murder Act" in Massachusetts, it was pointed out that under its provisions "every inhabitant in Massachusetts Bay" was "exposed to the lawless violence of a Soldiery to be destroyed as wild & savage beasts of the forests," and that every villain "who ravishes our wives, deflowers our daughters, can evade punishment by being tried in Britain, where no evidence can pursue him." [42]

The New England patriots rested their case against the Coercive Acts on the ground that the British government had treated the

[40] Peter Oliver to ?, August 19, 1774, Egerton MSS. 2659, British Museum.
[41] *Gazetteer and New Daily Advertiser*, February 11, 1775.
[42] Lee, I, 207. Mentor (William Lee) to Samuel Adams, May 14, 1774, Adams MSS.

Massachusetts Charter as a scrap of paper. If charter rights had no sanctity in the eyes of British ministers, how, the patriots asked, could the law of nature be expected to protect American liberties? "The same power that can take away our right of electing councillors by our representatives," said Joseph Warren, "can take away from the other colonies the right of choosing even representatives" and load them with taxes.[43] Americans were told that poll taxes, land taxes, and cattle taxes would follow their acquiescence in the Coercive Acts; if they could not pay, the Whigs predicted that the British government would "take your land for the rates, and make you and your children slaves." With the tax gatherers would come "a voluptuous crew of harpies . . . a parcel of scoundrels, the offscouring of the earth," who would seize "your pleasant habitations, your orchards and gardens, your wives and daughters" while Americans were forced "to dig Tobacco, Iron, and whatever our good and virtuous Masters" in England required.[44] These warnings struck deep alarm into American hearts. Here was barefaced tyranny, no longer in the breeze, but actually seen and felt in Massachusetts Bay. The blow struck at Massachusetts seemed merely the prelude to a general "Massacre of American Liberty" and its outcome would determine whether Great Britain had "a constitutional Right to exercise *Despotism* over America!" "If the Parliament is to have the absolute Government of us, we have here [in the Coercive Acts] a Specimen of what we are to expect," declared a South Carolinian. "If a few ill-minded Persons take upon them to make Water against the Door of a Custom-house Officer, or of the Cellar where the Tea is lodged, upon the same Principle all in Charles-Town ought to be laid in Ashes." [45]

Nevertheless, it could still be argued that the Coercive Acts did not endanger the liberties of Americans as a whole. Conservatives pointed out that the mandamus councilors of Massachusetts were similar to the councilors of every royal province. Indeed, Pennsylvania had recently petitioned for the very form of government which the Massachusetts patriots now found intolerable. Under a royal governor and council, New Yorkers had been "as happy

[43] Richard Frothingham, *Life of Joseph Warren,* 340.

[44] James Burd to Edward Shippen, August 8, 1774, Shippen MSS., Historical Society of Pennsylvania. *Newport Mercury,* December 5, 1774.

[45] *South Carolina Gazette,* June 20, 1774. William Henry Drayton, *A Letter from the Freemen of South Carolina to the Deputies of America,* Charleston, 1774, 7.

as any people in *America*." New Englanders objected to the Coercive Acts because they were republicans and levelers, declared the Tories; and therefore Boston's quarrel with the British government was their own and not Americans': "God grant," they prayed, "that it never may be." The Tories compared the Bostonians to the fox in the fable who, having lost his tail, denounced the use of tails and tried to persuade the other foxes to cut off theirs. It would be disastrous, they pointed out, for Americans to embark upon a conflict with the mother country by abetting Boston in its wrong-doing. They would be placing themselves in a false position by countenancing the work of a mob that no Virginia or Carolina gentleman would tolerate in his own country.[46]

But it was the British government itself rather than the Whigs which gave the most crushing answer to the Tories. In the Quebec Act of June 1774, the mother country sealed its infamy in the eyes of many Americans and gave colonial propagandists their juiciest plum since the Stamp Act. In essentials, the Quebec Act continued the undemocratic government over the province of an appointed governor and council; extended the boundaries of Quebec southward to the Ohio River and westward to the Mississippi; restored French civil law; and pledged the British government to tolerate the Roman Catholic religion in Quebec. Every provision of the act — however just or liberal — was turned against the British government with devastating effect by the American patriots.

In American nostrils the breeze from England, already heavily laden with tyranny, now smelled "strong of Popery." The colonists leaped to the conclusion that the British government had proclaimed its toleration of Roman Catholicism in Quebec in order to throw against the disaffected Protestant colonies a "horde of Popish slaves" who would help the Ministry establish a "universal despotism in the British Empire." "We may live to see our churches converted in mass houses, and lands plundered of tythes for the support of a Popish clergy," exclaimed the patriots; "the Inquisition may erect her standard in Pennsylvania and the city of Philadelphia may yet experience the carnage of a St. Bartholomew's day." [47] Alexander Hamilton declared that the act would bring millions of Papists from Europe until the Protestant colonies found themselves encircled by "a Nation of Papists and Slaves." He urged

[46] *South Carolina Gazette*, July 4, 1774. Nicholas, 14. Chandler, 19, 24.
[47] *Pennsylvania Packet or General Advertiser*, October 31, 1774.

his countrymen whose ears were "stunned with the dismal sounds of New England's republicanism, bigotry, and intolerance" to remember that a Papist was more to be feared than a Calvinist despite the fact that "a superstitious, bigotted Canadian Papist, though ever so profligate, is now esteemed a better subject to our Gracious Sovereign George the Third, than a liberal, enlightened New England Dissenter, though ever so virtuous." [48]

American propagandists enjoyed a field day in conjuring up bugbears from the Quebec Act. They pictured it as a deep-laid plot to turn the empire over to the Pope. By associating those twin malefactors, the Pope and the Devil, with the British Ministry, the patriots succeeded in establishing a close connection between the infernal regions, Rome, and Whitehall. The Pope was said to have invited Lord North to come to Rome, "his Holiness having a mind to reward his good services done the Catholic faith, by conferring on him some dignified office in the Romish Church." [49] The next step seemed for Lord North to establish Roman Catholicism throughout the British Empire by kissing "his Holiness's great toe, and humbly acknowledge his supremacy throughout Christendom." [50] Members of Parliament who voted for the Quebec Act must, it was argued, be converts to Roman Catholicism — else how could they have helped establish "the Roman Idolatry over two Thirds of Territories of the British Empire, and there Exciting a Jubilee in Hell & Thanksgiving throughout the Pontificate?" [51]

The Quebec Act, by extending the southern boundaries of Quebec to the Ohio River, ruined the prospects of many Western land speculators. Schemes such as the Vandalia colony in which Washington, Patrick Henry, and a group of Philadelphia merchants had invested were crippled and the stock rendered worthless. Moreover, by establishing metes and bounds to the westward progress of the colonists the act indicated that the British government was resolved to stand upon the policy of the Proclamation of 1763, at least as regards the region north of the Ohio. It was Great Britain itself which now was seen to be preventing the spread of Englishmen and English liberties over the American continent, thus denying

[48] *The Works of Alexander Hamilton*, edited by H. C. Lodge, I, 181, 196. *New York Journal or General Advertiser*, March 30, 1775.
[49] *Newport Mercury*, November 14, 1774.
[50] *Ibid.*
[51] Ezra Stiles to the Reverend Dr. Dwyer, April 10, 1775, Stiles MSS., Yale University Library.

the "manifest destiny" of Americans to expand the frontiers of freedom. "The finger of God," the colonists were told, "points out a mighty Empire to your sons: the Savages of the wilderness were never expelled to make room in this, the best part of the Continent, for idolators and slaves." [52]

Englishmen always contended that in the Quebec Act they had pleased God, if not the Continental Congress. It was, they insisted, a signal act of justice to the Canadians who smarted under the persecution of those who took advantage of their ignorance of English civil law; it was a milestone in the history of religious toleration; and, if the grant of a popular assembly was withheld, it was only because the people of Quebec were not sufficiently mature politically to enjoy representative institutions. Viewed in this light, the Quebec Act acknowledged Canadians' natural right to enjoy their own laws and religion — and Americans, of all people, could not cavil because the British government saw fit to do justice to their French-speaking fellow subjects. [53]

Yet it is true that the British government made no effort to apply its new-found liberalism to Ireland, where there was as great need for justice and toleration as in Canada. Although the Quebec Act had been under consideration for several years before its enactment, it seems evident that its passage at a time when serious trouble was brewing in the colonies was not wholly coincidental. It was widely recognized that the act, while demonstrating Great Britain's beneficence toward its French-speaking subjects, also served as an effective "political *check* to the growing independence of our American children." [54] It was pointed out during the debate in Parliament that the Canadians, if guaranteed their religious liberties, might be used to curb "those fierce fanatic spirits in the Protestant colonies" who, it was believed, inherited the Roundheads' hatred of monarchy. The Canadians, it comforted some Englishmen to know, stood ready after the Quebec Act "to butcher these Puritan Dogs." And, less than a year after its passage, Lord North acknowledged that the Canadians — now reconciled to British rule by the Quebec Act — might be armed to assist in crushing the American revolt. [55]

[52] *New York Journal or General Advertiser*, July 20, 1775.
[53] John Wesley, *Some Observations on Liberty*, London, 1776, 30.
[54] *An Appeal to the Public*, London, 1774, 54. *Parliamentary History*, XVII, 1406.
[55] *Ibid.*, XVIII, 681. *Public Advertiser*, December 21, 1774.

Certainly the English Whigs were not willing to accept the Quebec Act as unadulterated magnanimity. Barré called it a "monstrous production of tyranny, injustice, and arbitrary power." Camden, Chatham, Fox, and Shelburne declared that the government's intention was to subvert the liberties of the Protestant colonies by means of a "Popish army"; and Shelburne said darkly that liberty was endangered in England itself by the "Popish hordes" of Ireland which awaited the signal of the Ministry to hurl themselves across St. George's Channel.[56]

News of the Quebec Act reached the colonies when the Continental Congress was preparing to meet in Philadelphia. Perhaps more than any other act of the British government, it made possible the victory of the radicals and made the people "generally ripe for any plan the Congress [might] advise, should it be war itself." [57]

Prior to the Quebec Act, the British government had struck only at Massachusetts; but now it appeared to menace the religion, property, and civil liberties of all Americans. Had the British government confined itself to punishing Massachusetts alone, American union would have been much more difficult of achievement by the radicals: "Had he [Lord North] even stopped short of the Quebec Bill," said a colonist, "there might have been some distant prospect of less general confederacy; but that open, and avowed design of subjugating America, has alarmed the most inattentive, and given us but one mind." In New England, it destroyed General Gage's last hope of keeping town and country apart: the farmers were now convinced that their religious liberties were endangered and, observed Gage, "they cannot be made to believe the contrary." In consequence, "the Flame blazed out in all Parts at once beyond the conception of every Body"; and the mother country began to appear in American eyes as a foreign, despotic and "Papist" power.[58]

[56] *Parliamentary History*, XVIII, 656, 657, 681, 734, 742.
[57] Reed, I, 78.
[58] *The Correspondence of General Thomas Gage*, I, 374.

CHAPTER   SIXTEEN

The Continental Congress

John Dickinson

I

THE Continental Congress met in one of the most conservative of the seaport towns from which the revolutionary movement stemmed. Philadelphia patriots complained that there was more Toryism in Pennsylvania than in all the colonies combined; certainly the Quakers who dominated the province were more concerned in putting down radicalism at home than resisting tyranny from abroad.[1] The character of the delegates who assembled in Philadelphia in September 1774 was likewise a good augury to the conservatives. The Continental Congress was composed of "the ablest and wealthiest men in America"; Chatham pronounced it to be "the most honourable Assembly of Statesmen since those of the ancient Greeks and Romans, in the most virtuous Times."[2] In the opinion of the radicals, however, there were far too few "Old Romans" among the delegates. John Adams calculated that they were "one third Tories, another Whigs, and the rest mongrels"; and he found "Trimmers & Timeservers" upon every side. Fifth columnism was at work, as the patriots soon learned; despite the best efforts of Congress to preserve secrecy, the British government was informed of all its proceedings.[3]

Nevertheless, the aristocratic complexion of Congress was no guarantee against its radicalism. Its delegates included both the well-heeled and the down-at-heel but the line which divided the extremists from the conservatives was not one of wealth or social position: some of the bluest-blooded members were among the most radical in combating British tyranny. The work of the Continental Congress soon demonstrated that the American aristocracy

[1] *Pennsylvania Gazette*, May 15, June 26, 1776. *Principles and Acts of the Revolution*, edited by H. Niles, 11.

[2] John Penn to Lady Juliana Penn, September 6, 1774, Penn MSS., *Official Correspondence*, XI, Historical Society of Pennsylvania. *Writings of Benjamin Franklin*, VI, 350.

[3] Stephen Sayre to Samuel Adams, April 4, 1775; William Lee to Samuel Adams, April 10, 1775, Adams MSS., New York Public Library.

was divided against itself and that this division worked in favor of the triumph of radicalism.

It is significant that from the beginning the Continental Congress associated itself with the democratic elements in Philadelphia. Instead of meeting in the State House as Joseph Galloway desired, the members chose Carpenter's Hall, the meeting place of the Philadelphia Carpenters' Guild — a move which conservatives deplored as an unseemly attempt to curry favor with the working class of Philadelphia. They soon received another disquieting indication of the temper of Congress: Charles Thomson, the leading radical of Philadelphia, was chosen secretary although his radicalism had prevented him from being elected to that body by the voters of Philadelphia.

The conservatives stood ready to meet violent counsel from the New England delegates. They had raised their defenses against Northern radicalism by putting Americans on their guard against New England firebrands. But they had not reckoned with Yankee shrewdness. The New England delegates, who had been expected to roar like lions, proved meek as lambs. At the meetings they were so quiet and unobtrusive that they seemed to have come to Philadelphia solely to enjoy the peace and restful surroundings of the City of Brotherly Love. This surprising behavior nonplused the conservatives: their denunciations of New Englanders died upon their lips and they were obliged to face the attack of the enemy from an unexpected quarter.

While the New Englanders discreetly remained in the background the Virginians and Carolinians stepped forward as champions of the patriot cause. These patricians were protected by their birth and breeding from the conservatives' sharpest shafts. A New Englander was peculiarly vulnerable to attack because of the strong prejudice that existed in the colonies against the "pumpkin gentry" and their democratic ways; but Virginia and Carolina planters could hardly be pilloried as "upstarts" and "levelers." They gave the revolutionary movement a respectability and "tone" which New Englanders alone could not have bestowed upon it. "There are some fine fellows come from Virginia, but they are very high," remarked a Pennsylvanian. "The Bostonians are mere milksops to them." [4] The true fire-eating Whigs seemed to come from south of the Potomac: Christopher Gadsden of South Carolina urged that Gage

[4] Reed, I, 75.

and the British troops in Boston should be attacked before reinforcements could arrive; Richard Henry Lee of Virginia proposed the Nonimportation and Nonexportation Agreement; and Patrick Henry argued that the empire already was dissolved and that the colonies were in a "state of nature." [5]

Nevertheless, it was Virginia that prevented the Continental Congress, in drawing up its list of colonial grievances, from delving further back into history than 1763. The Virginia delegates were bound by instructions to confine their attention to measures dating from 1763, in order, as they put it, that greater odium might be cast upon the reign of George III. This meant that no mention could be made of the Navigation Acts or restraints upon colonial manufacturing and that "the many aggressions which had been committed by Great Britain upon her infant Colonies" could not be cited. Virginia thus kept the lid on a Pandora's box of complaints which some of the radicals were eager to open. Those who wished to lay bare all the oppressions of the mother country since the settlement of the colonies would also have insisted upon a full redress of grievances. In their opinion, it would be disastrous for American liberty if the colonies gained nothing more than the repeal of the oppressive measures passed since 1763. Yet when an attempt was made to enumerate the full catalogue of wrongs, the Virginia delegates found allies in the members from North Carolina and Maryland who rallied to the side of the Old Dominion and obliged the radicals to yield to Virginia's wishes. [6]

In stating its grievances, the Continental Congress therefore confined its attention to the period beginning with George Grenville's administration. It conceded that Parliament had the right to regulate colonial trade and declared that a full settlement of the controversy might be made on the basis of a repeal of all oppressive measures enacted since 1763 and a return to the principles of the "Old Empire." Thus the members of the Congress "stated the lowest terms they thought possible to be accepted, in order to convince the world that they were not unreasonable." Moreover, in their petition to the King they addressed him as their "Most Gracious Sovereign" and assured him that if he would but turn his "royal indignation" upon those "designing and dangerous men" in the Ministry who were "prosecuting the most desperate and irritating projects of oppres-

[5] Drayton, *Memoirs of the American Revolution*, I, 165.
[6] *Ibid.*, 167-168. *The Correspondence of Ralph Izard*, New York, 1844, 22-23.

sion," all would be well in the empire — an oversimplification of the dispute between mother country and colonies which some of the radicals soon regretted they had consented to.

The consequence of the collaboration of Southern gentlemen and New England "republicans" was, as the Tories declared, that "Adams, with his crew, and the haughty Sultans of the south, juggled the whole conclave of the Delegates." [7] Few conservatives believed that because the New England delegates appeared in public as angels of patience and good will they were not working underground digging pits for the feet of the conservatives; and the party found convincing proof of such sapping and mining in the fate of Joseph Galloway's plan of union which was presented to Congress in September 1774.

Despite repeated rebuffs by Congress, Joseph Galloway still hoped to thwart the plans of the radicals. He believed that if he could persuade Congress to open negotiations with Great Britain the crust of prejudice and misunderstanding would be broken and reconciliation be assured. He saw that the conservatives must lose no time in assuming the leadership; if Sam Adams and the radicals took the helm, he knew that there would be no port short of independence. Though he personally believed that colonial representation in Parliament offered the best prospects of reconciling British sovereignty with colonial liberty, he recognized the futility of making such a proposal in 1774. Therefore, as a second-best plan he suggested that an American legislature or Grand Council be created, the members of which were to be elected by the colonial assemblies. The colonies would continue to exercise authority over internal affairs; the Grand Council was to have jurisdiction over the general concerns of the colonies and to enjoy "all the like rights, liberties and privileges, as are held and exercised by and in the House of Commons of Great Britain." The Grand Council was in fact to be an inferior branch of the British Parliament. Acts might be introduced in Parliament relative to colonial affairs which, if passed, were to be sent to the Grand Council for its approbation; the assent of both the Grand Council and the Parliament was necessary to give validity to laws. The Crown was to be represented by a Resident General who held office during the King's pleasure, exercised executive authority, and held a veto power upon all acts of the Grand Council.[8]

[7] *Rivington's New York Gazetteer*, February 9, 1775.
[8] *Journals of the Continental Congress*, Washington, 1905, I, 49-50.

With this plan of union, Galloway expected to take the wind out of the sails of the radicals. He was well aware that the majority of Americans wished to remain united to the mother country and that if they could be convinced that British sovereignty was compatible with colonial freedom, they would cease to follow the radicals toward revolution. The chief recommendation of his plan, he believed, was that *"the strength of the whole empire may be drawn together on any emergency, the interest of both countries advanced, and the rights and liberties of America secured."* To those conservatives who objected that his scheme was too democratic inasmuch as it did not provide for a privy council consisting of the "principal Gentlemen of Fortune in each Colony," Galloway answered that he could not afford to offend the "Democratic Spirits" in Congress however necessary he considered a privy council to be. He took into account the prejudices of Americans and made his plan as broadly popular as possible.[9] How well he had wrought was seen by the narrow margin by which the radicals defeated his proposal in Congress.

At the outset, they won a precarious triumph by securing the postponement of debate upon Galloway's plan, but it remained for the radicals to prevent its reconsideration and keep it from getting abroad among the people. Galloway claimed that he was terrorized into dropping his plan by Sam Adams, who had already begun to make the Philadelphia mob as effective in intimidating conservative Congressmen as the Boston mob was in frightening Tory members of the General Court. Rather than face these formidable dispensers of tar and feathers, Galloway allowed his scheme of union to lie buried on the table of Congress. But, in all probability, Galloway's failure to press his plan was less owing to fear of the mob than to his perception, a few days after it had been presented, that the Congress had gone over to the camp of the radicals. The adoption of the Suffolk Resolves dashed Galloway's hopes and enabled the radicals to expunge all mention of his plan from the journals of Congress.

The delegates had hardly more than settled themselves comfortably in their lodgings and learned the way to the best taverns before a rumor spread like wildfire over the colonies that General

---

[9] *Documents relative to the Colonial History of the State of New Jersey,* X, New Series, 578, 585. *The Examination of Joseph Galloway Before the House of Commons,* London, 1779, 48.

Gage had begun a "horrid butchery" in Massachusetts. Boston was reported laid in ashes by the cannon of the British ships in the harbor. Immediately, General Israel Putnam roused the country and the roads to Boston were soon full of armed men "cursing the King and Lord North, general Gage, the bishops and their cursed curates, and the church of England." [10] When the news reached Philadelphia, thousands of men prepared to take the road to Boston and the patriots were enthralled to see how "the awful genius of America rouses from his slumber." Although the report soon proved false, the "Powder Alarm," as it was called, proved that the British government was now obliged to deal not merely with a handful of Boston Liberty Boys but with a continent, and that, as the Whigs remarked, "if our liberties are extorted from us, they will be by the hardest blows and not without some bloody noses." [11]

The Powder Alarm had called the attention of the Congress to the danger that fighting between British troops and New Englanders would involve the Middle and Southern colonies in war with the mother country. This question would not down; and in September 1774 it was again placed squarely before Congress. The Suffolk County Convention, called in lieu of the proscribed town meetings in Massachusetts, adopted on September 9, 1774, the resolutions introduced by Joseph Warren known as the Suffolk Resolves. These resolutions declared that no obedience ought to be paid the Coercive Acts; that taxes ought to be collected by the Provincial Congress and withheld from the royal government until the government of Massachusetts had been "placed upon a constitutional foundation"; that military preparations ought to be made against the danger of attack by the British troops in Boston; and that, if a patriot leader was seized by the British, the citizens were justified in imprisoning "every servant of the present tyrannical and unconstitutional government." Paul Revere was sent to Philadelphia with a copy of the Suffolk Resolves and incendiary accounts of Gage's seizure of cannon and his preparations to fortify Boston Neck. On October 8, to the joy of the radicals, Congress approved the Suffolk Resolves, although the people of Massachusetts were advised to behave peaceably towards Gage and the British soldiers "as far as can possibly be consistent with their immediate safety, and the security of the town." As long, therefore, as New Englanders maintained

---

[10] *Boston Gazette*, October 24, 1774. *Newport Mercury*, September 12, 1774.
[11] *Boston Gazette*, October 10, 1774. *Newport Mercury*, September 12, 1774.

a "firm and temperate conduct," they could be sure of the support of the rest of the colonies. In this way, Congress stamped its approval upon a defensive war.[12]

More bitter proof was soon presented to conservatives that they had miscalculated in supposing that the Continental Congress would uphold the cause of reconciliation. Those who had expected that by joining in the cry for a Continental Congress they were averting a boycott were given a rude jolt when, on September 27, 1774, Congress voted for nonintercourse with the mother country. In October 1774, nonimportation, nonexportation, and nonconsumption were agreed upon under the name of the "Continental Association" and Americans were called upon to gird themselves for another struggle with the mother country.

Congress found little difficulty in drawing up a Nonimportation Agreement although some of the delegates balked at forgoing wine. "I drank Madeira at a great rate and found no inconvenience in it," wrote John Adams from Philadelphia; and many members of Congress were prepared to go so far as to say that they found it delightful. Although wine was banned by the Association, in 1776 John Hancock proposed in Congress that Madeira be permitted free entry, in order, it was said, to curry favor with Southern Congressmen and to slake his own well-known thirst. But in 1774 the members of Congress were in a self-sacrificing mood. The Association prohibited "every species of extravagance and dissipation, especially all horse-racing, and all kinds of gaming, cock-fighting, exhibitions of shews, plays, and other expensive diversions and entertainments." For the duration at least, Americans seemed committed to Spartan simplicity.

Because the merchants were under suspicion as profiteers and traitors as a result of the failure of the boycott in 1770, Congress took the control of the Association out of their hands. In the first place, the people were asked to pledge themselves not to buy British merchandise — the Nonconsumption Agreement — thus leaving ill-disposed merchants no market for their proscribed wares. Secondly, the enforcement of the Association was entrusted to local committees usually dominated by the radicals. It was believed that these safeguards made it impossible for "the whole mercantile interest of America, joined together in devotion to the ministerial system of tyranny, to beguile the country yeomanry." The merchants had

[12] *Journals of the Continental Congress*, I, 33-35, 55, 61.

clearly been demoted from command to a humble position in the ranks: the committees frequently demanded that their ledgers and invoices be opened for inspection and maintained a far more effective watch upon shipping than had the customhouse officers from whose "tyranny" the unhappy businessmen had recently freed themselves.[13]

It was agreed that the Nonimportation and Nonconsumption Agreements were to go into effect on December 1, 1774, and to apply against Great Britain, Ireland, and the British West Indies. But here the smooth passage of the Association ended. A dispute so violent that it almost broke up Congress arose over the question of whether the Nonexportation Agreement was to be absolute or merely partial. Many delegates believed that complete nonexportation would ruin Southern agriculture as surely as the Port Act was ruining Boston. John Rutledge, one of the members from South Carolina, declared that whereas nonexportation would not seriously injure the Northern colonies, it would lay waste the staples of the South. He saw in the proposal an attempt by the Northerners to profit by the misfortunes of the Southern provinces. "Upon the whole," he declared, "the affair seemed rather like a commercial scheme, among the flour Colonies, to find a better vent for their flour through the British Channel, by preventing, if possible, any rice from being sent to those markets: and, for his part, he could never consent to our becoming dupes to the people of the north."[14] To forestall this evil, Virginia pleaded for a postponement of the agreement until the autumn of 1776; and a compromise was ultimately arrived at between Northern and Southern members by which it was deferred until September 1775. But the South Carolina delegation was not yet satisfied. The majority declared that they would not sign the Association unless rice and indigo were excepted; and to lend force to their threat they walked out of Congress. To bring them back to the fold, it was necessary to make another compromise whereby rice but not indigo was given free outlet to European markets. Although the colonial union was saved by this device, the Association was gravely weakened. Discontent started up among the Northerners, who asked why, if South Carolinians were privileged to export their rice, should not the other

[13] Reed, I, 70. Quincy, 180. Lord Dunmore to Lord Dartmouth, December 14, 1774, P.R.O., C.O. 5, 1553, Library of Congress Transcript.
[14] Drayton, *Memoirs of the American Revolution*, I, 170.

colonies be allowed to send their wheat, flour, and lumber to Europe and the West Indies?

In their zeal to defend American liberty by distressing the mother country, some Americans went so far as to refuse to pay their debts to their British creditors. The citizens of Annapolis, Maryland, resolved on May 22, 1774, that no suits could be brought in Maryland for recovery of debts owing Englishmen until the Boston Port Act had been repealed. Some thirty townspeople indignantly protested that this action was "founded in treachery and rashness" and would ruin American reputation for honesty and fair dealing. Washington and many other Virginians, although deeply in debt to British merchants, likewise disapproved of this measure on the ground that since Americans were struggling for justice, they ought not to commit injustice themselves. In Washington's opinion, only the "last extremity" could justify such drastic action.[15]

The men behind the Continental Association recognized that even if payments on their debts were not withheld, the British merchants and the common people of Ireland and England whom Americans had been taught to regard as their best friends overseas would be gravely injured. But tyranny had made such vast strides, they contended, that all parts of the empire must make sacrifices to prevent its triumph; Americans were jeopardizing their own well-being by engaging in economic war with the mother country, and the people of England and Ireland must not expect to go unscathed. If Americans failed to arrest its progress, despotism would be established everywhere and "Britain and Ireland may shudder at the consequences": "Soldiers who have sheathed their Swords in the Bowels of their *American* Brethren," the patriots told the people of England, "will not draw them with more reluctance against you." Irishmen were assured that the Association was designed to combat "the iniquitous scheme of extirpating liberty from the British Empire"—and was therefore a work in which every Irishman could heartily join. And if the Association pinched Irishmen too hard, they could emigrate to America where they would receive a warm welcome, as befitted refugees from implacable tyranny.[16]

---

[15] *Letters to George Washington*, edited by S. M. Hamilton, Boston, 1901, III, 355. *Correspondence of Ralph Izard*, I, 23. *Pennsylvania Packet or General Advertiser*, June 13, July 18, 1774. *Letters of Members of the Continental Congress*, I, 369. *The Writings of George Washington*, III, 229.

[16] *Journals of the Continental Congress*, II, 169–170, 214–215, 216. 218.

In drawing up the Association, Congress took its first steps toward curbing the liberties of the individual in the name of American liberty. The Whig committees were directed "attentively to observe the conduct of all persons touching the association" and the names of violators were ordered published in the newspapers. These mild measures did not always succeed in silencing opposition; but the patriots were prepared in such emergencies to resort to the tar barrel and the poultry yard. Obstinate Tories were decorated with feathers and paraded through the towns in order to warn their fellows of what lay in store if they continued to resist the popular will. As a result, the very name of these committees became so terrifying to the "nonsubscribers" of the Association that one Charleston, South Carolina, Tory was observed to turn "as pale as his shirt" when he received a letter from the Charleston committee.[17]

The Tories swore that the despotism of the Continental Congress was more intolerable than British tyranny at its worst. An American could no longer drink a dish of tea, take a glass of Madeira, or buy an English pin by the edict of this revolutionary body which had usurped authority over British America. Americans need no longer snuff the breeze for tyranny: it hung rankly over the colonies though it came not from Westminster but from Philadelphia. In particular, Tories found the Continental Association "big with rank Tyranny" beyond anything yet produced by the Holy Office:—

"Could the Inquisition, Venice, Rome, or Japan,
Have devised so horrid, so wicked a Plan?"

they asked. The very Americans who had "blustered and bellowed and swaggered and bragged" that they would not submit to oppression by Parliament now tamely permitted themselves to be "bullied by a congress and cowed by a committee" who had enlisted the aid of "their *High Mightinesses* the MOB" to complete "the utter subversion of all *Law*, and the total destruction of all LIBERTY."[18] The Tories predicted that the committeemen who compelled merchants to open their ledgers for their inspection would next insist upon examining "your tea-cannisters, and molasses-jugs, and your

[17] Gibbes, 138.
[18] Isaac Wilkins, *Short Advice to the Counties of New York*, New York, 1774, 11, 12. *The American Querist, by a North American* (Myles Cooper), New York, 1774, 25.

wives and daughters' petty-coats"; nothing less than a "good hiccory cudgel" could preserve the virtue of American womanhood from these prying Whigs. The only liberty that the patriots wanted, said the Tories, was the liberty "of knocking out any Man's Brains that dares presume to speak his Mind freely about the present Contest." [19] They had already almost attained the "state of nature": they "swear and drink, and lie and whore and cheat, and rob, and pull down houses, and tar and feather, and play the devil in every shape, just as the devil and their own inclination lead them," exclaimed a Tory; "and yet they cry out for liberty; what the deuce would they have, or what would they be at?" [20]

As they surveyed the work of the first Continental Congress, the Tories cried out in dismay that it was no better than a Boston town meeting. In its proceedings, they saw "not a word of peace and reconciliation — not even a soothing expression"; instead, they encountered only abuse of Parliament as "a Pack of Banditti" and insolent defiance of Great Britain which made the "breach with the parent state a thousand times more irreparable than it was before." [21] Far from seeking to remove the burdens upon the colonies, Congress had busied itself in inventing new grievances. At best, the members had been more intent upon showing the world that they were scholars and masters of polished English than statesmen whose mission was to bring peace to a great empire. Congress, it seemed clear, had fallen under the control of the "sly favourers of an American Republic" and these gentry had succeeded in hatching "a venomous brood of scorpions, to sting us to death." What particularly stung the Tories was the adoption of the Suffolk Resolves. They could explain this measure only upon the supposition that the members "came into this vote immediately after drinking thirty two bumpers of the *best* madeira." Congress sober was horrified by what Congress drunk had done; but the deed could not be undone because Paul Revere was already on his way back to Boston with the certificate of approval of the Suffolk Resolves in his pocket. The repentant Congressmen, so the story ran, "prudently determined to do

[19] *Rivington's New York Gazetteer*, December 22, 1774. *Newport Mercury*, January 2, 1775. *New York Gazette and Weekly Mercury*, June 25, 1770.
[20] Jonathan Sewall, "A Cure for the Spleen," *Magazine of History*, 1922, 33.
[21] Seabury, 5. Crean Brush, *The Speech of a Member of the General Assembly of New York*, New York, 1775, 10. *A Dialogue, Between a Southern Delegate and His Spouse, on his Return from the Grand Continental Congress*, New York, 1774, 10–12.

no business after dinner" thenceforth.[22] But the Whigs scotched this libel by pointing out that the Suffolk Resolves were adopted in the morning, when it might be presumed that even the heaviest tipplers were sober.[23]

Recognizing that the Continental Congress had fallen into the hands of the radicals, the Tories retreated to the last refuge of minority parties in America: local rights. They declared that Congress had "erected itself into *the supreme legislature of North America*" by usurping powers which rightfully belonged to the colonial assemblies as well as to the British government. "Virginia and Massachusetts madmen," exclaimed Samuel Seabury, the New York Tory, "met at Philadelphia, have made laws for the province of *New York*, and have rendered our Assembly *useless*." [24] The Tories contended that the provincial assemblies were the only true guardians of American liberties: "If any laws of the British Parliament are thought oppressive . . . *they* are the proper persons to seek for redress. And they are the most likely to succeed. . . . They are the *real* not the *pretended* representatives of the people." The assemblies, together with the British government, were Americans' best hope of saving themselves from the formidable tyranny which the Tories believed was rising in Philadelphia. Had the Tories been able to identify liberty with provincialism, they would have wielded a powerful weapon against the patriots and perhaps have averted independence. But in 1774 provincialism was on the wane: in the first flush of patriotic fervor, union and liberty had become the popular watchwords. Therefore, the Continental Congress continued to be regarded as a great bulwark against British oppression and not, as the loyalists pictured it, the enemy of local liberty.[25]

The Continental Association was generally regarded as an infallible means of bringing Great Britain to its knees. Americans whipped out of their pockets statistics which proved beyond doubt the dependence of Great Britain upon the colonies and its utter inability to survive the loss of the colonial market. It seemed certain that the colonies could produce "national bankruptcy" in Great

[22] Gray, 9.
[23] *Boston Gazette*, January 30, 1775.
[24] Samuel Seabury, *A View of the Controversy Between Great Britain and her Colonies*, New York, 1774, 17. Brush, 9.
[25] Seabury, *A View of the Controversy Between Great Britain and her Colonies*, 7-8; *Free Thoughts on the Proceedings of the Congress*, 19, 24; *The Congress Canvassed*, 16-17. Wilkins, 12.

Britain within a year: "Before nine months," the South Carolinians warned Lord North, "millions of people, who depend on America for their daily bread, will curse you with their dying groans." [26] The British government was expected to suffer the loss of almost a million pounds in revenue a year; the British West Indies would be ruined in six months, thereby bankrupting the West India merchants and planters; and by stopping the export of flaxseed to Ireland, the Irish linen industry would be prostrated and three hundred thousand people would be thrown out of work. Riots and revolution would sweep England; the outcry of millions of starving citizens would "shake the throne of Majesty itself"; Lord North would be rushed off to the Tower; and the English would recognize the futility of contending with a people who could ruin them merely by sitting down. Thus, without firing a shot, Americans would "cut up the whole System of Tyranny by the Roots." [27]

Americans were not yet ready to make war upon the mother country but they found highly comforting this assurance that pacific measures alone would restore their liberties. "We shall afford a new phaenomenon in the history of mankind," said an American in 1775, "and furnish posterity with an example to teach them that peace with all the rights of humanity and justice, may be maintained by the exertion of economical as well as military virtues." "We have no need or arms to defend ourselves," exclaimed another patriot. "We want nothing but self-denial, to triumph." [28] The prevailing ideology of the times, it is clear, was that measures short of war would be sufficient to win for the colonies everything they demanded from the mother country; and American opinion was far more united upon the necessity of defending colonial liberty by economic reprisals against Great Britain than ever it was upon declaring independence.

Tories, of course, were convinced that nothing good could come of the Association. They believed that the privations it caused in the colonies would produce twenty mobs here before one had been raised in Britain. Farmers would find no outlet for their surplus — although, as Tories said, the Whigs were greedy, it was too much to expect them to eat all the wheat, rye, beef, pork, and butter that

[26] *Boston Gazette*, June 27, 1774. *Essex Gazette*, June 7, 1774.
[27] *Pennsylvania Packet or General Advertiser*, November 28, 1774. *Writings of Benjamin Franklin*, VI, 305, 309; V, 222, 224.
[28] *Pennsylvania Evening Post*, April 11, 1775. *Massachusetts Spy*, July 28, 1774.

had formerly been exported to Europe and the West Indies. "The devil is in it if their bellies are not filled," said Samuel Seabury.[29] Town artisans and laborers would be thrown out of employment by the stoppage of trade; the merchants would be ruined; and thousands of starving Americans would take to the highways, robbing and pillaging their fellow men. Those that did not starve or rob seemed certain to freeze to death.

Many radicals agreed with the Tories that the boycott was certain to fail in its purpose of coercing Great Britain. The Adamses, for example, believed war inevitable; in their opinion, the colonies were inviting destruction by delaying their preparations for a struggle to the death with the mother country. "I expect no redress, but, on the contrary, increased resentment and double vengeance," said John Adams to Patrick Henry. "We must fight." "By God," exclaimed Henry, "I am of your opinion." [30]

A question which hardly entered into the calculations of those who predicted a bloodless conquest of Great Britain by means of the Continental Association was the danger that armed conflict between New Englanders and the British troops in Boston would precipitate war. Massachusetts had been guaranteed the support of Congress if war was forced upon the colony; but only a handful of Americans seemed to have foreseen in the winter of 1774–1775 that fighting was imminent. Few believed as did Patrick Henry that "the next gale from the north will bring to our ears the clash of resounding arms" and fewer still shared his joy in the prospect of conflict.

[29] Seabury, *Free Thoughts on the Proceedings of Congress*, 9–11; *A View of the Controversy Between Great Britain and her Colonies*, 25.
[30] Quincy, 162.

CHAPTER   SEVENTEEN

Lexington and Its Aftermath

The Battle of Lexington

I

IN 1774, the memory of the Boston Massacre was still fresh in New England and the pent-up hatred of British military rule might well have given the Southern Whigs pause before they joined forces with the New Englanders. Bostonians had never been permitted to forget those "corpses wallowing in gore, upon our Exchange." On March 5 of every year, a Massacre Oration was delivered in which the horrors of that night became progressively more horrible. Benjamin Church, one of the orators of the day, described the British troops as a "brutal banditti," and "grinning furies gloating o'er their carnage." The spot in King's Street where the patriots had fallen was sacred ground on which the children of New England were enjoined not to tread without remembering that "your feet slide on the stones bespattered with your father's brains." [1] The Whigs lamented that they had permitted the soldiers to leave Boston alive after March 5, 1770; they richly deserved, it was said, "to have had their Bones piled up in the Common as a Monument of Massachusetts Bravery." [2] One of the survivors of the Massacre, Christopher Monk, who never completely recovered from his wounds, was paraded on Massacre Day for the edification of the patriots. John Hancock, the orator of 1774, pointed to the "miserable Monk" and urged the audience to "observe his tottering knees, which scarce sustain his wasted body; look on his haggard eyes; mark well the death-like paleness on his fallen cheeks." These Massacre Orations kept alive the hatred of British redcoats and caused New Englanders to burn with warlike ardor: a Tory observed "the greasy rebellious Rogues swelling themselves up" as they listened to Hancock's speech.[3]

Although the patriot leaders had repeatedly declared that British troops should never again enter Boston, they offered no resistance

---

[1] Lathrop, 5.
[2] *Principles and Acts of the Revolution*, edited by H. Niles, 12, 20.
[3] *Ibid.*, 14. Mein, 104.

when several British regiments took possession of the town in 1774. Instead they fell back upon the strategy of making the redcoats as uncomfortable as possible. The city refused to provide barracks, with the result that the troops were obliged to remain encamped on the Common until November, to the great unhappiness of Boston cows, who were thus deprived of their favorite pasture. The Committee of Correspondence ordered Boston carpenters not to help the troops construct barracks; no lumber was permitted to be brought into the city; and the merchants refused to sell the soldiers blankets, tools, or material of any kind. General Gage was forced to bring carpenters and bricklayers from Nova Scotia in order to make the climate of Boston endurable for the British army.

With the Massacre vividly impressed upon their memories, New Englanders expected the worst from the redcoats: they would begin to seduce, attack, and rape American womanhood afresh, just as they had done before they were driven out of Boston in 1770. These fears were seemingly borne out by the conduct of the troops. Their sex crimes were so luridly described in the newspapers that it began to appear to the Whigs that "neither our Wives, Daughters, nor even Grandmothers would be safe." As before the Massacre, the newspapers were filled with a dismal catalogue of "robberies, rapes and murders" perpetrated by these fiends. The Daughters of Liberty were, as usual, the worst sufferers and the Whigs lived in constant dread of seeing "a ruffian's blade reaking from a daughter's heart, for nobly preserving her virtue." But this concerted assault upon the virtue of American womanhood was only part of the heavy indictment made by Whig propagandists against the British army. They screamed that the British government was up to its old tricks of undermining New Englanders' morals by sending a licentious soldiery among them: its purpose was to make Americans forget their patriotism and "look jolly, frolick and revel, frequent bawdy houses, race horses and fight cocks on Sundays, drink profane and obscene toasts, damn the sons of liberty." [4] It was said that grave citizens could not go abroad without hearing barrack-room profanity and congregations were disturbed by the playing of "Yankee Doodle" outside the meetinghouses. Moreover, the troops rioted in waterfront bawdy houses and their "savage barbarity" made the streets unsafe. One trooper was reported to have broken into a shop and to have fallen with drawn sword upon the help-

[4] *St. James's Chronicle*, November 17, 1774.

less proprietor and his servant, "damning His Eyes but He would kill Every Inhabitant He mett." A coach from Providence was attacked, the windows broken and the passengers mistreated; and a group of officers "heated with liquor . . . with drawn swords, ran through the streets like what they really were, madmen, cutting every one they met." The troops were declared to have tarred and feathered patriots and ridden them round the town on rails; "and now," exclaimed an unhappy Whig, "the pretty boys are playing Congress, and the feathering Colonel is Chairman of the Farce." [5] And it was darkly whispered that Mass was being said for dead British soldiers and that the crucifix would soon be publicly raised in Boston.

The patriots might rail against British troops, but their presence helped to relieve the distress wrought by the Port Act. The soldiers brought with them cash which enabled at least the proprietors of grogshops to endure the closing of the port. Some Englishmen opposed the sending of an army to Boston on the ground that it would benefit the rebels: the British government, they declared, ought to have used the navy, which would help starve the Saints instead of alleviating their miseries. The British troops, it was remarked, were "too numerous indeed for Ambassadors, and too few for soldiers" — and instead of humbling the Bostonians, it was feared that they were enriching them and thereby defeating the purpose of the Port Act.[6]

However atrocious the conduct of the "bloody soldiery," General Gage, the commander of the British troops and new governor of Massachusetts, was not, the patriots were obliged to admit, the "Turkish Bashaw" they had expected. He attempted to win over the Whigs by fair dealing: he took care to keep the military subordinated to the civil power; and he listened at all times to the complaints of the townspeople and kept the Tories waiting in his anteroom. Indeed, in the opinion of many Tories and Englishmen, Gage was an "old woman" who coddled the Bostonians when

[5] *Massachusetts Spy*, September 1, 1774. *Newport Mercury*, March 27, April 3, 1775. *Letters on the American Revolution*, edited by Margaret Wheeler Willard, Boston, 1925, 81. Elbridge Gerry to Samuel Adams, December 19, 1774, Adams MSS., New York Public Library. Jane Mecom to Benjamin Franklin, November 3, 1774, Franklin MSS., American Philosophical Society.

[6] E. Lechemere to Messrs. Lane Son and Fraser, May 30, 1774, MS. Massachusetts Historical Society. *London Chronicle*, November 26, 1774.

they merited a whipping. He seemed to lack the polished manners and air of a man of the world that were necessary, in the opinion of others, to tame the Saints. Had the British government been wise, wrote a British officer in Boston, it "would have sent out as Governor a Man of Fashion and Politeness, who would have complimented, entertained, flattered, and danced us all into good Humour." Instead, Gage was awkward and dull — "Even at his own Table," it was said, "he is at a Loss amongst his own Officers, for common Chit-Chat." [7]

During the winter of 1774-1775, the "menaces of blood and slaughter" which reverberated through the New England countryside became increasingly ominous. New Englanders were clearly preparing to take full advantage of the approval placed upon a defensive war by the Continental Congress; and if the British troops ventured far from Boston they might well expect a warm reception from the Yankees. Companies of minutemen were being formed; military stores collected; committees of observation appointed to watch the movement of the British troops in Boston; and everywhere "sedition flowed copiously from the pulpits." Some clergymen even handed out pikes and muskets to the men after preaching a sermon on the iniquities of antichrist and his boon companion Lord North. When General Israel Putnam came down to Boston he could scarcely get out of town because he was "so much carressed, both by the officers and citizens." [8] Early in March, 1775, the guard on Boston Neck seized over thirteen thousand cartridges which the patriots were attempting to smuggle into the country. The outbreak of fighting in New England waited only upon a move by the British troops which would fulfill the conditions of defensive war laid down by the Continental Congress.

General Gage was well aware of these warlike preparations. A traitor in the Massachusetts Provincial Congress kept Gage informed of developments — perhaps Benjamin Church, whose expensive mistress had already involved him in the financial difficulties from which he attempted to extricate himself by selling Whig secrets to the British. Gage learned, for instance, that the Provincial Congress was thrown into "great Consternation" by the news which reached Massachusetts on April 2, 1775, that Parliament had firmly

[7] St. James's Chronicle, November 17, 1774. Proceedings of the Massachusetts Historical Society, VIII, 385-386.
[8] New York Gazette and Weekly Mercury, October 3, 1774.

supported the Ministry and that reinforcements were on their way to Boston. Some hotheads were in favor of immediately raising an army and attacking the British troops before aid could arrive; but cooler councils prevailed, and the Congress resumed its policy of watchful waiting for Gage to take the offensive. But preparations continued to be made for war: delegates were sent by the Massachusetts Provincial Congress to the other New England colonies to persuade them to join Massachusetts in raising an army of eighteen thousand men. The patriots had little doubt that the British would soon move to enforce the Coercive Acts and stamp out rebellion in the country. Gage's grapevine gave him ample warning that the New Englanders would meet force with force.[9]

On the other hand, British officers were eager to take the field because they keenly felt the humiliation of their position in Boston. Here was a British army cooped up in the Puritan metropolis while rebellion was spreading through the country and the Yankees were preparing for war. Edmund Burke taunted the army by pointing out in Parliament that the British troops served only to protect the Tory councilors and magistrates who came streaming into Boston for protection: "he had often heard," he remarked, "of such places for thieves, rogues, and female orphans; but it was the first time he ever heard of an asylum for magistrates." The British army, most military men agreed, ought to crush the rebellion instead of protecting refugees from the patriot reign of terror. Moreover, the British soldiers longed to settle old scores with the patriots. Not only had the Whigs succeeded in keeping the troops out of barracks until winter: they plied the men with cheap rum to induce them to desert. Desertion was bad enough, but the frequency with which "Kill Devil" — New England rum — lived up to its reputation by sending British soldiers to their graves was highly alarming. British officers, viewing the toll taken among their men, concluded that this devil's broth was more to be dreaded than the New England army: "It will destroy more of us than the Yankies will," exclaimed a British officer, little dreaming that the Yankees would prove at least as potent as their rum.[10]

In general, British officers held a very low opinion of the Yankees as fighting men. However loudly they might rant and bluster, in the hour of danger they would run for cover, it was believed, thus

[9] Allen French, *General Gage's Informers*, Ann Arbor, 1932, 21. 22, 23, 27.
[10] *The Sandwich Papers*, I, 57.

making the conquest of New England by the British army simply
a matter of marching; the New England soldiers would offer no
problem that could not be met by an experienced sheep herder.[11]
"I am satisfied," declared Major Pitcairn in March 1775, "that one
active campaign, a smart action, and burning two or three of their
towns, will set everything to rights." The expedition to Salem undertaken by a British detachment in that same month strengthened
this conviction. The British were told to expect trouble but when
they arrived in town not a sign of hostility was evident. Yet the
moment the British officer and his men had left Salem, Major
Pitcairn noted with contempt, "the people got arms and paraded
about, and swore if he had stayed half an hour longer they would
have cut him to pieces." [12] When Gage began to build fortifications
on Boston Neck in 1774, Thomas Young, one of the leading patriots of the town, hurriedly decamped, swearing that "HE
WOULD BE DAMNED IF HE (GAGE) SHOULD NAB HIM."
Nor was the appearance of New England militia calculated to
arouse the apprehension of British officers. "It is a curious Mas-
querade Scene," observed an Englishman, "to see grave sober
Citizens, Barbers and Tailors, who never looked fierce before in
their Lives, but at their Wives, Children, or Apprentices, strutting
about in their Sunday Wigs in stiff Buckles with their Muskets on
their Shoulders, struggling to put on a Martial Countenance. If
ever you saw a Goose assume an Air of Consequence, you may
catch some faint Idea of the foolish, aukward, puffed-up Stare of
our Tradesmen: the Wig, indeed, is the most frightful Thing about
them, for its very Hairs seem to bristle up in Defiance of the
Soldiers." [13] A "Lady of Quality" observed a similar spectacle at
Wilmington, North Carolina, where two thousand militiamen
marched in review in such heat that "they had certainly fainted
under it had not the constant draughts of grog supported them."
"They made indeed a most unmartial appearance," she remarked —
but she noted a significant fact that escaped the attention of most
British officers. "The worst figure there," she said, "can shoot from
behind a bush and kill even a General Wolfe." [14]

[11] *Letters of Captain W. G. Evelyn*, 28–29, 39, 40. *Proceedings of the Massachusetts Historical Society*, XLIX, 370.
[12] *The Sandwich Papers*, I, 60–61.
[13] *St. James's Chronicle*, November 17, 1774. *The Sandwich Papers*, I, 58.
[14] *Journal of a Lady of Quality*, edited by E. W. Andrews, New Haven,
1927, 190.

General Gage partly shared the views of his officers. He remarked that the Yankees "will be Lyons, whilst we are Lambs but if we take the resolute part they will undoubtedly prove very meek." Gage believed that the New Englanders could be awed into submission by a display of force, but he reported to the British government that his army was too weak to strike terror among even such poor-spirited creatures as the New England Saints. "If you think ten Thousand Men sufficient," he wrote the British government, "send Twenty, if one Million is thought enough, give two; you will save both Blood and Treasure in the End." [15] In the absence of an overwhelming military force, Gage relied upon threats to induce New Englanders to give up the struggle against the mother country. Gage told some of the "Great Wigs" of Boston that "he swore to it by the living God, that if there was a single man of the King's troops killed in any of their towns he would burn it to the ground. What fools you are, said he, to pretend to resist the power of Great Britain: she maintained last war three hundred thousand men, and will do the same now rather than suffer the ungrateful people of this country to continue in their rebellion." [16] The fact that New Englanders were not easily bluffed ought to have warned Gage that they were not the errant cowards he and his staff believed them to be.

With over seven thousand people on relief and a prey to the manipulations of expert propagandists, there seemingly was danger that Bostonians would attack the British troops despite the injunction by the Continental Congress against offensive war. An outbreak did occur in March 1775, when Dr. Joseph Warren delivered the annual Massacre Oration; but the Whigs bridled their tempers and, in spite of provocation by the redcoats, refused to be drawn into beginning hostilities. In the meanwhile, the country districts were seething ominously and the western part of the colony, long regarded as the most conservative section, became a hotbed of radicalism. It was well for the patriot cause that the first scene of bloodshed was not in Boston: the metropolis was already under suspicion throughout America and its citizens were believed to be eager to precipitate war. The New England yeomen, on the other hand, while not altogether immune from suspicion, were not "mobbish Bostonians." By refraining from attacking the British troops

---

[15] *The Correspondence of General Thomas Gage*, II, 659.
[16] *The Sandwich Papers*, I, 60–61.

in Boston, the townspeople left embattled farmers to fire the first shots against Great Britain. Thenceforth, it was "the Freeholders and Farmers of the Country . . . worked up to a Fury" who bore the brunt of the struggle. If the revolutionary movement, in its immediate origins, began in the colonial seaports and was chiefly a protest of merchants and townsmen against British oppression, it drew its strength from the men who tilled the soil. Without their aid, Great Britain would have remained sovereign in America.

While the lines of battle were being drawn in Massachusetts, Pennsylvania, Georgia, and New York were on the verge of breaking the unity of the colonies and Lord North was dangling the bait of appeasement before their eyes. Although the Pennsylvania patriots insisted that "all the wealth, virtue, and understanding in the province" were "on the side of Liberty," and that there were only a handful of Tories in Philadelphia, most of whom were "young lads . . . just emerged from behind the counter," it was clear that Pennsylvania was in the grip of rock-ribbed conservatism whether it be called Whiggery or Toryism. "That damn'd slow heavy quakering Nag your Province is mounted upon," said Charles Lee to a Pennsylvanian, "ought to be flogg'd and spurr'd though she kicks and plunges." [17] Tories in the Philadelphia coffeehouses spoke out boldly and refused to be cowed by the Whigs. Joseph Galloway made a speech in the Pennsylvania Assembly in which he denounced the Continental Congress, "proved the Necessity of Parliamentary Jurisdiction over the Colonies in all Cases whatsoever," and came dangerously near carrying a motion to send a separate petition to the King. The Georgia Assembly actually did dispatch a separate petition, although it was recognized that this "tended to annihilate the Weight of the Grand Congress." [18]

Everywhere in the colonies conservatives took heart from the Tory reaction which occurred in New York during the winter of 1774–1775. The formation of the Committee of Fifty-one had effectively broken the power of the radicals in New York. This committee nominated New York's delegates to the Continental Congress, and thereby made certain that only hand-picked conservatives represented the colony at Philadelphia. Jay and Alsop — both "safe" men — were nominated in place of the far more

[17] *The Lee Papers*, I, 168.
[18] *Documents relative to the Colonial History of the State of New Jersey*, First Series, X, 573–574.

popular and more radical John Morin Scott and Alexander Mc-
Dougall. The members of the Committee of Fifty-one — most of
whom subsequently became Tories — were determined to prevent
"a few rash Men" from gaining the upper hand in New York as
they had in Massachusetts; and they even enabled the New York
merchants to sell supplies to the British troops in Boston, despite the
efforts of New York patriots to stop the traffic. After this rebuff,
the Whigs were so intimidated that they did not dare talk politics
in public; Isaac Sears became "the butt of every puny jester, and
the laughing stock of the whole town." He seemed, indeed, to be
an "exploded cracker"; early in 1775 he was arrested and imprisoned,
only to be rescued by "a rascally Whig Mob" to the disgust of
the Tories, who complained that the New York magistrates who
surrendered Sears to his friends had "not the spirit of a louse." [19]

Delancey and his followers repudiated their connection with the
patriots and became the nucleus of the Tory Party in New York.
These aristocratic officeholders, merchants, and churchmen now
constituted a serious menace to the disorganized Whigs. The majority of New Yorkers, so reported the Crown Officers to the
British government, considered that "the Dispute with Great Britain
is carried far enough, and abhor the thought of pushing it to desperate Lengths." New Yorkers began to show alarming scruples —
in the eyes of the Whigs — about burning prominent British statesmen in effigy. More Tory newspapers and tracts were published
in New York than in all the other colonies combined; *Rivington's
New York Gazetteer*, which the patriots declared was printed by
"a little junto of hireling prostitutes placed under the command
of an unsavory high flying jacobite priest," particularly distinguished itself in propagating Toryism. The Tories rejoiced that
at last the press was free in New York but, as events were to show,
they reckoned without the Whig mob.[20]

A stunning blow was delivered by New York against the pa-

---

[19] *Documents relative to the Colonial History of the State of New York*,
VIII, 433, 486, 493. *Pennsylvania Evening Post*, May 27, 1775. Thomas Jones,
History of New York during the Revolutionary War, New York, 1879, 38.
Rivington's New York Gazetteer, August 18, September 29, 1774. *New York
Journal and Weekly Advertiser*, December 28, 1775. Thomas Wharton to
Thomas Walpole, May 31, 1774, Wharton MSS., Historical Society of Penn-
sylvania. Thomas Young to John Lamb, November 19, 1774, Lamb MSS.,
New York Historical Society.

[20] *Documents relative to the Colonial History of the State of New York*,
VIII, 493. *Boston Gazette*, January 16, 1775.

triot cause through the refusal of the New York Assembly to adopt the Continental Association. Although the Association was enforced in New York by local committees which looked to the Continental Congress rather than to the local government for authority, the action of the assembly showed that the conservatives who ruled the colony were determined to keep their skirts clear of the "treason" and "rebellion" which they suspected was being hatched in Philadelphia. Early in 1775, the assembly moved to separate itself entirely from the Continental Congress by sending a separate petition to the King and refusing to send delegates to the second Continental Congress. The New York Tories declared that the provincial delegates to the first Congress had been honest men when they left New York but had been corrupted by the bad company they had fallen in with at Philadelphia. "Let no honest man hereafter trust himself at a Philadelphia Congress," they exclaimed; even the purest New Yorker could not escape contamination in that sink of Virginia and New England republicanism. Although the patriots clamored for a Provincial Congress and popular election of delegates to the Continental Congress, the power of the Tories was so great that it seemed unlikely that New York would again be represented at Philadelphia.

New York was thus clearly revealed to be the weakest link in the chain of colonies laboriously fashioned since 1765. From the beginning of the dispute with Great Britain, there had been grave doubt whether the New Yorkers would stand firm; now the worst of these fears seemed realized. Some outraged patriots urged that the colonies break off all commercial relations with the "assassins" of American liberty and that New York be included in the boycott of Great Britain, Ireland, and the West Indies until the Tories had been overthrown. Others demanded that the New England militia hurl itself upon New York. "Take care of yourselves," they told the New Yorkers, "we have more than Men enough to block up the Enemy at Boston; and if we are like to fall by Treachery, by Heaven, we will not fall unrevenged on the Traitors." [21]

New York's loyalty made the province the white hope of the British Ministry. George III at his levee expressed his pleasure at New York's faithfulness; but the satisfaction of the British government was diminished by the fact that at no time did the province

[21] *Virginia Gazette* (Purdie), March 17, 1775. *Pennsylvania Packet or General Advertiser*, May 15, June 13, 1775.

show the slightest disposition to acknowledge the principles of the Declaratory Act. Indeed, the petition of the New York Assembly was not read in Parliament because it called in question parliamentary rights. It is evident that in "the only province that was moderate, and in which England had some friends," there were few supporters of parliamentary taxation. By insisting upon this right, Parliament made it difficult even for conservative Americans to uphold British sovereignty.[22]

Meanwhile, the English Whigs, like the colonial moderates, were seeking some common ground upon which the empire could be reconstituted. Lord Chatham proposed in 1775 that the British troops in America be withdrawn and the colonies given an opportunity to defray their share of imperial expenses by means of a free gift. Burke urged the repeal of the Coercive Acts, modification of the Admiralty Courts to meet Americans' objections, and a return to the requisition system. Although neither Burke nor Chatham went so far as to favor the surrender of parliamentary sovereignty over the colonies, their plans were rejected by large majorities in Parliament. They were proof, however, that Englishmen were not united upon the policy of coercing the colonies without one last effort at peaceful settlement of the dispute. To unite the country behind the Ministry, to divide the colonists, and to make an eleventh-hour attempt to avert civil war in the empire, Lord North determined to present a conciliatory plan of his own.

The Prime Minister heartily wished himself out of the scrape and was prepared to make considerable concessions to pacify the Americans. He virtually repudiated the idea of direct taxation of the colonies by Parliament by disclaiming early in 1775 any intention of drawing a "considerable revenue" from them and by declaring that he had always known that "American taxation could never produce a beneficial revenue." He attempted to wipe his hands of all responsibility for such taxation: he insisted that he had merely retained measures already upon the statute books; and so far from making an effort to collect a revenue in America, he had not even considered "any particular means for enforcing" the tea tax. Instead of direct parliamentary taxation he proposed the adoption of a requisition system in which Parliament, instead of the Crown,

[22] *Parliamentary History*, XVIII, 644, 648, 649. *Colden Papers*, VII, 268. *The Correspondence of General Thomas Gage*, I, 383. *The Sandwich Papers*, I, 57.

would lay its demands before the colonial legislatures. As long as the colonists taxed themselves to the satisfaction of Parliament, Parliament would refrain from taxing them. North made it clear that he intended no infringement of the principles of the Declaratory Act; Parliament, he declared, would merely forbear to exercise its rights.[23] By this means, he hoped to extricate himself from a situation which was rapidly becoming more and more untenable to a man of his peace-loving temperament.

Lord North believed that the great merit of his plan was that it would prove to the satisfaction of every honest Englishman whether or not the colonists were sincere in their professions of willingness to settle amicably their dispute with Great Britain. If Americans refused to accept the terms of these Conciliatory Propositions, "the temper and moderation of Parliament, and the obstinacy and disaffection of the Americans" would be beyond dispute. At the same time that he united Englishmen, North hoped to spread disunion among the colonists. New York was the rainbow in the Tory heaven and North had his eye upon this errant colony when he proposed his Conciliatory Propositions. If New York could be persuaded to agree to the government's proposals, the union of the colonies would be broken and the Continental Congress would collapse as had the Nonimportation Agreement in 1770. A wedge would be driven between New England and the Southern colonies, thus isolating the Saints while the British fleet and army reduced them to reason.[24]

Instead of uniting Englishmen, the immediate effect of Lord North's propositions was to jeopardize the position of the Ministry in the House of Commons. The majority in Parliament clearly wished to coerce the colonies into submission rather than to hold out the olive branch. It was observed that "uncertainty, surprize, distraction were seated on every countenance" when Lord North broached his plan, and even his staunchest followers "turned pale with shame and disappointment." The Bedfords began to consider ditching him and it was only after an impassioned plea by Sir Gilbert Eliot for unity against the colonists that the Conciliatory Propositions were accepted by the Commons. Many Englishmen,

[23] *Parliamentary History*, XIX, 762–763.
[24] *Pennsylvania Evening Post*, April 27, 1775. *Parliamentary History*, XVIII, 625, 740, 781. *South Carolina Genealogical and Historical Magazine*, Charleston, 1903, IV, 4.

nevertheless, would have been dismayed had Lord North's plan been assented to by Americans: they believed that Great Britain would derive no benefit from this arrangement because "an assembly of mulish republicans" would "grant nothing toward the support of majesty and the *whore of Babylon*" unless forced to by the government.[25]

Lord North's Conciliatory Propositions were not a plan of "Constitutional Union" such as Americans could accept without surrendering their principles. They did not penetrate to the roots of American discontent. Lord North would have made the colonial assemblies the agents of Parliament in levying and collecting taxes — but, as Americans said, "it is not merely the mode of raising, but the freedom of granting our money, for which we have contended."[26] At best, North's plan seemed to be a desperate effort "*to coop up*, the crazy Bottom of Old England with temporary Expedients"; or a "dirty, humiliating contrivance" to break up the Continental Congress in order to carry "the diabolical ministerial designs of despotism into execution with the greater ease." Under the best of circumstances, it would have found few friends in the colonies, but before it could be submitted to the people its fate was sealed by the outbreak of fighting between the British troops and New England farmers. North's Conciliatory Propositions reached New York the day after news of Lexington and Concord.[27]

In sallying out of Boston on the night of April 18, 1775, the British troops were in search of the powder which Gage's informants told him the patriots had stored at Concord. Gage had received orders to arrest Hancock and Adams, who were known to be near Lexington, and the Tories hoped fervently that the British troops would bag the patriot leaders and send them "home to England hand-cuffed, as well as hand-cocked . . . to pay a debt outstanding of old arrears due to Tyburn tree." But it was the Whigs' powder magazine rather than the capture of the patriot leaders which brought the British to Lexington and Concord.

[25] *Parliamentary History*, XVIII, 340. *Pitt Correspondence*, IV, 404. *Writings of Benjamin Franklin*, VI, 388. *A letter to the People of America*, London, 1778, 47.

[26] *American Archives*, edited by Peter Force, Fourth Series, II, 1201.

[27] *Massachusetts Spy*, December 29, 1775. *Public Advertiser*, February 23, 1775. *Letters of William Lee*, I, 142. Alexander Innes to Lord Dartmouth, May 1, 1775, P.R.O., C.O. 5, 396. *Parliamentary History*, XVIII, 443. *Journals of the Continental Congress*, II, 226, 230.

Secrecy was vital to the success of their plan, but the country was roused before their arrival by Dawes and Revere, and when the British force marched into the town, the militia was drawn up on Lexington Common. According to the patriots' account, the British made the first hostile move. Colonel Smyth of the 10th Regiment ordered his men to rush "the peasants" with bayonets fixed; but the charge was stopped short by the fire of the militia, who quickly took shelter behind walls and trees. Pushing on to Concord, the British were fired upon before they could destroy all the powder; and their retreat to Boston was made under the grueling fire of enemies who fought like Indians from behind houses, trees, and walls.

The shot heard round the world set the wild echoes of propaganda flying. If the events of April 19, 1775, seem today chiefly remarkable in showing the courage of British troops under fire and the determination of Americans to defend their rights by force of arms, in 1775 these factors were obscured by the work of propagandists on both sides of the Atlantic. Throughout the dreadful day, Americans declared, the British troops had shown "the ferocity of a mad wild beast," killing "geese, hogs, cattle, and every living creature they came across," and taking particular relish in murdering women and children.[28] When they did not find Hancock and Adams where they were believed to be hiding, these British "barbarians killed the women of the house and all the children in cold blood, and then set the house on fire." Houses were wantonly burned by the score: "women in child-bed were driven by the soldiery naked into the street; old men, peaceably in their house, were shot dead" and innocent children were brained by blows from muskets. In the wake of the retreating British, Joseph Warren declared, there were "depredations, ruins and butcheries hardly to be matched by the armies of any civilized nation on the globe"; it was said that even the Iroquois would "blush at such horrid murder, and worse than brutal rage." [29] Amidst this carnage, the redcoats moved like furies, devastating the countryside, disregarding "the cries of the wounded, killing them without mercy, and mangling their bodies in the most shocking manner." [30] The

---

[28] *American Archives*, Fourth Series, II, 428.
[29] *Ibid. Collections of the Massachusetts Historical Society*, Fifth Series, Boston, 1888, X, 285. *New York Journal or Weekly Advertiser*, May 4, 1775.
[30] *Boston Evening Post*, May 11, 1775.

fight at Lexington and Concord, although not one of the decisive battles of the world, was certainly one of the decisive stories of atrocity.

The American Revolution now had its martyrs. The blood shed at Lexington was used by propagandists to cast an ineradicable stain upon the mother country. "This pretended mother," exclaimed a patriot, "is a vile imposter — an old abandoned prostitute — a robber, a murderer — crimson'd o'er with every abominable crime, shocking to humanity." Innocent Whigs were slaughtered, it was declared, because they had striven to defend the British Constitution; their only offense was that they were freemen seeking to maintain their liberties. The British had begun, said John Dickinson, an "impious war of tyranny against innocence" which aimed at destroying liberty everywhere in the empire.[31] The patriots had no doubt that Lexington was only the beginning of British attempts to liquidate the American Whigs by means of wholesale massacres. Fortunately for the cause of liberty, exclaimed the patriots, the British government had tipped its hand before its preparations were complete; and there yet remained time to defeat its purpose by vigorous counteraction.

It is significant that the Whigs' version of the battle, replete with British atrocities in all their gruesome detail, was the first to reach the people of England and America. A large batch was rushed to Franklin in London with instructions that printed copies be sent to every town in England and to the Lord Mayor, Aldermen, and members of the Common Council of London. General Gage accused the patriots of stopping the posts, breaking open the mails, and removing letters in order to prevent the British account of the battle from getting abroad. How well they succeeded is shown by the fact that the Whigs' story arrived in North Carolina two months before General Gage's letter describing the action. The delay had been fatal to the loyalist cause, lamented the royal governor of North Carolina; Whig propaganda had done its work of "confirming the seditious in their evil purposes, and bringing over vast numbers of the fickle, wavering and unsteady multitude to their party."[32]

In England, though it came late, the propagandists likewise en-

[31] *New York Journal or Weekly Advertiser*, May 25, 1775, Supplement. *Life of Arthur Lee*, II, 307. *American Archives*, Fourth Series, II, 429, 433.
[32] *Colonial Records of North Carolina*, X, Letter of Governor Martin, June 30, 1775.

joyed a field day. It was charged that Americans had scalped dead and dying British soldiers. One British officer testified that the Yankees were "full as bad as the Indians for scalping and cutting the dead Men's Ears and Noses off, and those they get alive, that are wounded and can't get off the Ground." [33] If a wounded English soldier who fell into the hands of the American rebels did not have his scalp lifted, he was almost certain to have his eyes "googed" out by his captors. As for the atrocities of which they were accused, the British insisted that they had only burned houses from which the Whigs were firing; that the militia at Lexington had fired first; and that the Americans "ran to the Woods like Devils" and poured a murderous fire upon the retreating British. Americans did not fight fair, the troops declared; they skulked from tree to tree, taking pot shots at the troops and loading "on their bellies" instead of remaining upright while they recharged and thus presenting the British with a fair target in the approved European fashion. [34]

The results of the first encounter of British troops and American militia struck consternation among the Ministry. Here American "peasants" had not run, as Lord George Germain and other Tories had predicted; and Germain observed with alarm "the many jovial faces upon this event" as the opposition looked forward to the speedy overthrow of the ministers. [35] It was difficult to portray Lexington as a British victory. "A most vigorous retreat," Burke called it — "twenty miles in three hours — scarce to be paralleled in history; the feeble Americans, who pelted them all the way, could scarce keep up with them." [36] The Tories felt obliged to assure the English people that Great Britain still had its navy to use against the colonists — and great things could be expected of the mistress of the seas despite reverses on land.

The British were unable to extract much consolation from the events which followed the retreat of the redcoats to Boston. After Lexington, the British army remained in Boston, hemmed in by an increasing force of provincials. In June 1775, the New England troops stole a march upon the British by occupying Breed's Hill

---

[33] *Newport Mercury*, May 29, 1775.
[34] *Ibid.* Macpherson, 67.
[35] *Report on the MSS. of Mrs. Stopford-Sackville*, I, 134.
[36] *Correspondence of Edmund Burke*, London, 1844, II, 27–28. *Newport Mercury*, May 8, 1775.

in Charlestown which commanded the harbor and city of Boston. To prevent the militia from entrenching themselves in this strong position, the British launched a frontal attack upon the American lines before the provincials had had an opportunity to construct strong defenses. The battle of Bunker or more properly Breed's Hill ended with the British in possession of the field but with a staggering casualty list as the price of victory. Another such victory, it was said in England, and there would be no one left alive to carry the good news home.

At the battle of Bunker Hill, an "irregular peasantry, commanded by a physician" (Dr. Joseph Warren), had again proved that Americans were a match for British regulars. "We expected to find them a cowardly rabble who would lie quietly at our feet, and they have disappointed us," observed an English radical.[37] Even some British officers began to see the light: General Gage warned the Ministry that the colonists were "not the despicable Rabble too many have supposed them to be"; "These People," he declared, "Shew a Spirit and Conduct against us, they never shewed against the French, and every body has Judged of them from their former Appearance, and behaviour, when joyned with the Kings Forces in the last War, which has led many into great mistakes. . . . They are now Spirited Up by a Rage and Enthousiasm, as great as ever People were possessed of."[38]

Lexington and Bunker Hill engaged British honor more deeply than ever before in the American dispute: it was now essential that British prestige be restored by a decisive victory over the colonists. A compromise settlement in 1775 would have left the colonists claiming victory over British arms; the mother country could not retreat with honor after British soldiers had shown their heels to American farmers. "The Arms of this Country," it was said in England, "*must* not be permitted to succumb to *Rebels*."[39] It was necessary, therefore, to win a clear-cut victory; only by shedding Americans' blood could their pride be humbled and a proper sense of the might and majesty of Great Britain be instilled. There could no longer be any thought of magnanimity; conciliation must wait upon victory and the complete submission of the colonies.

[37] Richard Price, *Observations on Civil Liberty and the Justice and Policy of the War with America*, London, 1776, 56.
[38] *Correspondence of General Thomas Gage*, I, 407; II, 686.
[39] *Public Advertiser*, June 20, 1775.

CHAPTER EIGHTEEN

The Empire in the Balance

Benjamin Franklin

THE WORK of the British "barbarians" at Lexington fired the blood of the New Yorkers and destroyed the moderation which had been the best hope of the British government. Instead of clamoring for reconciliation with Great Britain on the basis of Lord North's Conciliatory Propositions, now, like true-born Whigs, they hung Lord North in effigy. The wheel seemed to have spun full round. "Not one month ago," remarked Gouverneur Morris in May 1775, "and Whiggism was branded with Infamy. Now each person strives to shew the Excess of his zeal by the madness of his actions." [1] The Tories were disheartened to find "the most violent Proposals meeting with universal Approbation" and the city in the hands of "high flying demagogues." The royal governor declared that British authority was "entirely prostrated" by the people; arms belonging to the city were seized and distributed among the citizens; committees were appointed to enforce the Association; supplies destined for the British troops at Boston were confiscated; and Isaac Sears, at the head of three hundred men, demanded the keys of the customhouse. They were surrendered without a struggle and the port was closed by the patriots. Because of the danger of attack, the small British garrison in New York was withdrawn to a man-of-war in the harbor. As the soldiers marched out of their barracks to embark, the patriots seized the soldiers' baggage, arms, and ammunition and the troops made no effort to recover them. By June 1775, New York had fully redeemed itself. Dr. Thomas Cooper, President of King's College, and a prominent Tory pamphleteer, was attacked by a mob which broke down the college gate. Rivington, the Tory printer, was obliged to take refuge on a man-of-war in New York Harbor. Freedom of the press, as far as the Tories

[1] *The Lee Papers*, I, 178. *Public Advertiser*, June 15, 1775. Letter to "Dear Vardell" from "A Real Churchman," May 2, 1775, Egerton MSS. 2135, Library of Congress Transcript.

were concerned, was at an end in New York until the British army returned in 1776.[2]

Throughout the colonies, the news of Lexington brought demands from the radicals for vengeance upon the "British butchers" and an end to all thought of compromise with the mother country. Some declared that the union between Great Britain and the colonies was now dissolved and that Americans were in a "state of nature"; the first volley at Lexington, they said, had proclaimed American independence. It now seemed certain that Americans would be forced to fight to protect their liberties and, as the Boston Committee of Correspondence put it, in order "to defend our wives and children from the butchering hands of an inhuman soldiery." As a result, the continent began to prepare for war: "Travel through whatever part of this country you will," wrote a colonist in July 1775, "you see the inhabitants training, making firelocks, casting mortars, shells and shot, and making saltpetre."[3] In Maryland, citizens wore cockades in their hats and, remarked a Tory, "the churlish drum and fife are the only music of the times." In Virginia, the people were said to be "even madder than in New England"; the burgesses attired themselves in the frontiersman's hunting shirt and it was fashionable to carry a tomahawk. The King's arms were seized in Charleston, South Carolina, militia officers resigned their commissions under the royal government, and a new army was created under the authority of the Provincial Congress. Even Philadelphia began to assume a warlike appearance; evidences of the spirit of "Ancient Sparta," declared a Whig, were now seen on every hand. The city was decorated with flags inscribed: "Liberty or Death." "Even our Women and Children," it was said, "now talk of nothing but of the Glory of Fighting, suffering and dying for our Country."[4] When the delegates to the second Continental Congress reached Philadelphia in May 1775, they were escorted into the city by companies of riflemen and infantry. Americans were stripping for action even though they continued to think in terms of reconciling colonial liberty with British sovereignty.

Lexington turned men's eyes to Philadelphia and the Continental

[2] *Documents relative to the Colonial History of the State of New York,* VIII, 571–572, 581–583.

[3] *The Remembrancer,* 2nd Edition, London, 1775, I, 149. *American Archives,* Fourth Series, II, 433.

[4] Lord Dunmore to Lord Dartmouth, June 25, 1775, P.R.O., C.O. 5, 1533, Library of Congress Transcript. *American Archives,* Fourth Series, II, 433.

Congress for leadership. Promises of support for *"whatever meas-ures"* Congress might recommend poured in; New York sent a full delegation to Philadelphia and, at least for the moment, all thoughts of separate petitions by colonial congresses or assemblies were laid aside. Americans were caught up in a wave of nascent nationalism. At no time during the last decade had there appeared greater unanimity in the colonies. From the battle of Lexington until early in 1776 when the issues of independence and republican-ism sharply divided Americans, the "United Colonies" were firmly joined. "America is grown so irritable, by oppression," declared the Whigs, "that the least shock in any part is, by the most powerful and sympathetic affection, instantaneously felt through the whole continent."[5]

It is not too much to affirm that the possibility of keeping the dispute between mother country and colonies upon the plane of constitutional argument ended with the fighting at Lexington and Bunker Hill. What conservatives in both England and America most dreaded — a civil war — had begun and the issue could only be de-cided by a victory of arms. To many Americans, however, this truth was not evident. They still clung to the hope that their liberty could be preserved within the British Empire without war. For a decade, Americans had sought to defend their rights by methods short of war. They had been led to believe that fighting would not be necessary: the British government would, at the last hour, grant their demands, the empire would be reconstituted upon a new basis and emerge stronger and more majestic than ever before. Even after war had begun, the majority of Americans re-fused to admit that this hope was dead: they still sought ways and means of reconciliation rather than victory over the mother coun-try. Their military preparations were made not to destroy British sovereignty but to protect American liberty. Even Lexington and Bunker Hill did not convince Americans that they were engaged in a war to the death with the mother country; in the eyes of many, it merely made the necessity of reconciliation more urgent. But had they known the determination of the British government not to yield one jot of its sovereignty over the colonies and to retrieve British honor by winning a military decision over the rebellious "peasants," they would have been less optimistic over the chances of a peaceful settlement. They would have seen what is so evident

[5] *Pennsylvania Evening Post*, May 18, 1775.

today: that Lexington brought the first phase of the revolutionary movement to an end; the dispute between the mother country and colonies could no longer be confined to nonimportation agreements, remonstrances, and petitions. The war was on; the American Revolution had moved from a constitutional to a military sphere. "They have now dipt their hands in Blood," exclaimed a royal governor. "God Almighty knows where it will end." [6]

It is indicative of the strength of the colonists' veneration for the mother country that not even the bloodcurdling description of British atrocities by Whig propagandists could bring many Americans to forget that they were in arms against a country they had only recently called "home." "We are contending," wrote James Duane of New York, "with the State from whence we spring, with those who were once our fathers, our guardians, our brethren, with those fleets and armies which were lately our protection, and contributed to rescue us from Gallic tyranny and oppression. . . . Cemented by the ties of blood, religion and interest, victory itself however decided must be fatal; and whichever side prevails must weep over its conquests." [7]

But even the staunchest advocates of reconciliation were obliged to confess that their task had become vastly more difficult after Lexington. In the spring of 1775, conservative members of the Continental Congress were planning to stand out boldly for a peaceful adjustment of differences with Great Britain. John Dickinson, in particular, looked forward confidently to effecting lasting good will between mother country and colonies. The King, men thought, could yet save all; he stood apart from the dispute; and he had only to dismiss his wicked ministers to set all to rights in the empire. But the outbreak of fighting clouded this prospect. "What topics of reconciliation," Dickinson asked in anguish after the news of Lexington had reached him, "are now left for men who think as I do, to address our countrymen? To recommend reverence for the monarch, or affection for the mother country? Will the distinctions between the prince and his ministers, between the people and their representatives, wipe out the stain of blood?" [8] But he was

---

[6] Lord William Campbell to Lord Dartmouth, August 19, 1775, Historical Manuscripts Commission, *Report on the MSS. of the Earl of Dartmouth*, 14th Report, London, 1895, II, Part X, 354.

[7] *Letters of Members of the Continental Congress*, edited by E. C. Burnett, Washington, I, 98.

[8] Lee, II. 311.

soon hard at work to erase the memory of bloodshed and to preserve the union of colonies and mother country by safeguarding American liberty within the empire.

The impact of Lexington upon the Continental Congress gave no encouragement to conservative hopes that a plan of "Constitutional Union" would yet come out of Philadelphia. In May 1775, Congress resolved that "these colonies be immediately put into a state of defence"; the Massachusetts militia was taken over by Congress; an army of twenty thousand men was ordered to be raised; and George Washington was appointed to command. The "Declaration on Taking Arms" which was read when Washington took command of the troops struck a new and militant note: "Our cause is just," it declared. "Our union is perfect. Our internal resources are great, and, if necessary, foreign assistance is undoubtedly attainable." Congress directed that paper money be printed and in July 1775 Benjamin Franklin drew up "Articles of Confederation and Perpetual Union," which, although too bold to be entered upon the journals of Congress, were openly discussed by the members.

Despite these setbacks, the conservatives sought desperately to find some basis upon which the British Empire could be reconstructed. They urged Congress to revert to the position taken by the first Continental Congress and petition Parliament to return to the colonial system in force before 1763. This meant the renunciation by the mother country of a colonial revenue and its efforts to enforce the Acts of Trade by means of the Board of Commissioners of the Customs. Turning the clock back to 1763 implied, in brief, a defeat for the British imperialists and a victory for American Whigs — but it was not a sufficiently sweeping victory to content the radicals. The liberties enjoyed by the colonists prior to 1763, which before Lexington seemed fully ample for American prosperity and happiness, now appeared to many Americans little better than slavery. "Good God," exclaimed a Virginian, "were we not abject slaves (in 1763)? We wanted but the name. . . . It was not till 1763 that we were openly insulted, and treated as slaves." [9] By returning to 1763 fundamental grievances would be untouched: American trade and manufactures would be cramped by British restrictions; colonial laws would have to be approved by the British government; and Americans would "always be peeled and

[9] *Virginia Gazette* (Purdie), March 29, 1776.

pillaged" for the benefit of English pensioners and courtiers. Moreover, the sacrifices already made for American liberty would have
been in vain if such a poor palliative were accepted as the terms of
peace.[10] The "blood and treasure" already expended by Americans,
exclaimed the radicals, made reconciliation impossible except upon
the colonists' own terms. Thus the blood of the "precious Sons of
Liberty" spilled in the cause of liberty was used to silence the advocates of reconciliation. Now that men were being asked to die,
a richer reward than a return to 1763 had to be offered for their
sacrifice.[11]

The radicals in the Continental Congress rejoiced that Great
Britain's "unexampled cruelties" now barred the path of compromise. They proposed to gird for war before another blow could
be struck. Their program was to open American ports to foreign
powers; construct a navy; set up state governments; break off
negotiations with Great Britain; seize the Tories and hold them
as hostages for the Bostonians. But Congress was still far from being
under the control of the radicals. John Dickinson of Pennsylvania
— whom John Adams referred to as a "piddling genius" in a letter
which fell into the hands of the British and was published in the
Tory newspapers — insisted upon sending another petition to the
mother country.

Despite the fact that neither the King, Lords, nor Commons had
ever deigned to answer the petitions of the first Continental Congress, John Dickinson had not yet been convinced of the futility
of petitioning. Oppression had not diminished his love of the mother
country; in the dispute with Great Britain he saw no irrepressible
conflict generated by political and economic forces but merely
the handiwork of misguided men in Great Britain. "I grieve for
the Fate of a brave and generous Nation," he said, "plung'd by a
few profligate men, into such Scenes of unmerited and inglorious
Distress": "why should Nations meet with hostile Eyes, because
Villains and Ideots have acted like Villains and Ideots?" So strong
was his affection for Great Britain that he even wished the Continental Association to be carried out "with tenderness, so as to

---

[10] *Pennsylvania Gazette*, March 6, 1776. *Principles and Acts of the Revolution*, edited by H. Niles, 157. Jacob Green, *Observations on the Reconciliation
of Great Britain and the Colonies*, Philadelphia, 1776, 20, 23, 26. *New York
Journal or General Advertiser*, February 22, 1776.
[11] *American Archives*, Fourth Series, V, 129, 856, 973.

convince our brethren in *Great Britain* of the importance of a connection and harmony between them and us, and of the danger of driving us to despair." He believed that the interests of mother country and colonies were irrevocably united; the prosperity and happiness of each were dependent upon the other. War he regarded as the worst of evils: America could perhaps gain "a dear bought and at best a frequently convulsed and precarious independence," but Great Britain, weakened by the loss of her colonies, might fall a victim to France and Spain. For these reasons, he refused to admit that the road the colonies had been traveling since 1764 led to rebellion; nor would he agree that the day of petitions and remonstrances was over. Closing his eyes to the bloodshed and preparations for war on both sides of the Atlantic, he wished to carry on the dispute from his desk, certain that ultimately the British people would respond to Americans' appeals to their reason and cast out the handful of miscreants who had brought the empire to the brink of civil war.[12]

Dickinson declared that no petition from the colonies had ever been rejected unless it offended the dignity of King or Parliament. He proposed in 1775 to dispatch a petition to the King that would be free from this fault; soft words and a humble demeanor, he believed, would work wonders upon even the most prejudiced members of Parliament.

The radicals regarded petitioning not only as a futile but as a calamitous measure. They argued that no petition would be acceptable to Parliament unless it acknowledged the principles of the Declaratory Act; Lord North, it was remembered, had said that America must be at the feet of Great Britain — and petitioning seemed to be the shortest road to this final abasement. The debates in the House of Commons which had reached America had made it clear that a large majority of the members believed that the colonies must be taxed to ensure the sovereignty of the mother country — and no amount of petitioning could change this conviction. They had no hope that another exhibition of American literary ability would have the slightest effect in softening the hearts of British imperialists. Moreover, the radicals were of the opinion that with fighting already begun, Americans ought to be busy with their muskets rather than their pens.

[12] John Dickinson, *A New Essay on the Constitutional Power of Great Britain over the Colonies in America*, Philadelphia, 1774, 28–29.

Dickinson was supported by a clear majority in Congress, and the radicals were therefore obliged to rest upon their oars while he made another of the interminable soundings that marked the progress of the Congress toward independence. But, as in previous attempts, he could find no bottom. Despite the moderation that distinguished the "olive branch" petition, it was rudely rejected by the British government. Dickinson's careful use of words, his polishing and refining, went for naught. The petition was denounced in England as "an insult and mockery"; "Was General Washington himself, with 50,000 Americans, encamped on Blackheath," exclaimed an Englishman, "the proposals of Peace [from Congress] could not be more humiliating to this Country."[13]

What passed for restraint and obedience on one side of the Atlantic was regarded as insult and treason on the other. Englishmen denounced indiscriminately the "seditious manifestoes" and the "threats hissed out by the Congress"; all its petitions and resolves seemed to be written "in a stile more becoming the haughty courts of Versailles and Madrid." No matter how dignified and moderate its proceedings, they could win but little approval in Great Britain. The very fact that the Continental Congress represented "not the opposition of a Mob but of the first and best people in all the Colonies" made it, in English eyes, doubly menacing to British authority. Americans had created a rival to Parliament which derived its authority not from the King or Parliament, but from the people of America. England could not yield to the demands of this illegal assembly without being humiliated in the eyes of all Europe and without sacrificing its sovereignty, as Englishmen conceived it, over the colonies.

Although the radicals had been obliged to yield to Dickinson's pleas that the door be kept open for reconciliation, they did not lose sight of the necessity of effecting a revolution in the minds of the American people. In the opinion of radicals both in and out of the Continental Congress, Americans must be groomed to step forward as a free people fighting for liberty against intolerable tyranny. Therefore, while conservatives were anxiously awaiting Great Britain's answer to Dickinson's petition, the radicals were engaged in laying the foundations of the Declaration of Independence and destroying one by one the ties that bound the colonists to the mother country.

[13] *Public Advertiser*, December 13, 1775.

Before Americans could be brought to think of independence, it was necessary that they be convinced it was futile to rely upon either the English Whigs or the English people as a whole to save them from tyranny. So long as the colonists believed themselves to be supported by powerful allies in the mother country, they would be apt to continue to make their goal the rights of Englishmen within the British Empire. Although Americans had been told by the patriot leaders that they had active friends in Great Britain and that there were millions of Whigs throughout the British Empire who would rally to their cause, the tone of patriot propaganda abruptly changed after 1774. The American radicals were now convinced that the English Whigs were an impotent minority which could do nothing to stem the advance of tyranny. It was fatal for the cause of American liberty, they decided, to lean upon such weak reeds: the struggle must be waged by "American Virtue — for . . . there is none left in England." [14] The English Whigs, they discovered, were not true friends of liberty — their only ambition was to get into office and "therefore they bellowed away in favour of the Rights and Privileges of their distant Brethren." [15] The radicals declared that it made little difference to Americans whether the Whigs or Tories were in office in England because when the Whigs came to power they would immediately cast off their pretense of friendship for Americans, and, like the Tories, seek their pound of flesh from the colonies. Even if the Whigs were what they appeared to be — well-meaning and benevolent defenders of liberty — no reliance ought to be placed in them because they were clearly helpless to prevent the triumph of tyranny in the British Empire: "If they are not able to stop the progress of despotism in Britain, where they reside," the patriots pointed out, "we may not imagine they can restore the liberties of America." [16]

The technique of detraction employed by the patriots is well exemplified in the case of Lord Dartmouth. Lord Dartmouth, who had become Secretary of State for the Colonies upon the resignation of Lord Hillsborough in 1772, was a man of impregnable piety.

---

[14] *The Remembrancer, or Impartial Repository of Public Events*, London, 1775, Second Edition, I, 44.

[15] *Pennsylvania Chronicle*, November 27, 1769. *Pennsylvania Evening Post*, February 13, 1769.

[16] *American Archives*, Fourth Series, V, 855.

Not a chink was to be found in his armor of righteousness; he was, indeed, a Methodist of such devoutness and evangelical fervor that the King's advisers feared to admit him to the royal closet lest he undermine the King's adherence to the High Church. As a humanitarian and philanthropist, he was one of the few members of the English Ministry during the early reign of George III worthy of giving his name to an American college. But his piety did not endear him to the American radicals; on the contrary, they feared him more than they did Lord North himself. It was easy to picture Lord North as a "MONSTEROUS MURDERER" and boon companion of the Devil but Lord Dartmouth could not be classed among the cutthroats and rakehells that were popularly supposed to make up the English Ministry. He was living evidence that not all the British aristocracy was corrupt — that there was a remnant of righteousness left in England to which Americans might cling. The patriots feared the brand of soothing syrup dispensed by Dartmouth; they much preferred the bluster and ill temper of Lord Hillsborough to the prayers and pious ejaculations of Lord Dartmouth. His bedside manner seemed likely to lull American patriotism into sound slumber, in preparation, the Whigs feared, for the shackling of the colonies.

Dartmouth was in fact a sincere friend of the colonies and wished devoutly to inject sweetness and light into British colonial policy. He could do little, however, to persuade his more forthright colleagues that armies and fleets were not the best means of reasoning with Americans; and he found little encouragement for his efforts among American patriots. For the radicals had determined to blast Dartmouth's reputation in the colonies in order to prepare Americans for the day when they must stand alone against Great Britain. Dartmouth was pictured therefore as a well-meaning but incompetent weakling whom Lord North twisted around his finger at pleasure; while Dartmouth was at his prayers or singing Methodist psalms, it was said, Lord North was concocting with his henchmen new oppressions for America.[17] A befuddled, bungling Methodist — however pure his morals — would never, it was clear, preserve Americans from British tyranny.

To blacken the mother country deeper in American eyes, colonial propagandists trumpeted all the corruption of English politics. Parliament, they declared, was composed of "rogues and Scoun-

[17] James Burd to Edward Shippen, August 21, 1774, Shippen MSS., Historical Society of Pennsylvania.

drels" who were "bought and sold like sheep in the markets." So great was its "scandalous prostitution" that Parliament seemed to be "no more to the minister than the footman is to the gentleman. They equally wear the master's livery, and obey every direction." Even "a Couple of Negroes through the Mediation of Money and an active Broker," said a South Carolinian in England, might become members of Parliament. John Adams declared that if Americans were ruled by Parliament they would "not only be slaves — but the most abject sort of slaves to the worst sort of masters!" [18] A Parliament which had persecuted and excluded John Wilkes seemed unlikely to do Americans justice. Petitions were of no avail in turning the wrath of these corrupt representatives of the British people; "Parliament has knowingly and deliberately trampled on the Liberties of America," it was said, " — and from such Men nothing is to be expected but continued Injuries.[19] It is then evident if we have Relief it must come from some other Quarter; it must result from the Union and determined Resolution of the Colonies; they must force their Unjust Oppressors to comply with the Dictates of Reason." [20]

By remaining within the empire, the propagandists warned, Americans would see their property used "to glut the avarice of half a million of swag-bellied pensioners." British ministers clamored for a colonial revenue in order to buy up more votes in Parliament and to give bigger and better sinecures to their henchmen; and they were so eager for money that they were prepared "to dig up the very foundations of Pandaemonium, if they thought there were either gold or diamonds to be found in that soil." [21] The British ruling class had given itself up to high living and in order to pander to its vices it was necessary "to drain off wealth, as their patterns, the debauched *Romans*," did from their colonies. Every shilling squeezed from the colonies, Americans were told, went to "*tyrants and debauchees*" and was spent upon vices that would have made Nero blush.[22] It seemed impossible that so much corruption and

[18] *New York Journal or General Advertiser*, February 22, 1776. *Pennsylvania Evening Post*, August 29, 1775. *The South Carolina Historical and Genealogical Magazine*, 1901, II, 148.
[19] *Boston Gazette*, October 11, 1773.
[20] *Virginia Gazette* (Purdie), March 17, 1775. *Boston Gazette*, December 23, 1771.
[21] Burgh, II, 275.
[22] *Pennsylvania Journal and Weekly Advertiser*, January 20, 1773. *American Archives*, Fourth Series, V, 87, 494, 855.

luxury could fail to bring the empire down in ruins about the heads of the people. Yet while tyranny threatened to fasten itself upon the mother country and colonies, the English aristocracy amused itself at the horse races at Newmarket, at Covent Garden, riding to the hounds on their country estates, swilling port and frolicking with mistresses — in other words, piddling while Rome burned. Britain, it was believed in the colonies, had lost its virtue through imperialism. The desire to seize "the golden groves of Asia, to sparkle in the public eye with jewels torn from the brows of weeping Nabobs, or to riot on the spoils of plundered provinces" had transformed Englishmen from honest patriots to oppressors of the weak and defenseless.[23] They were willing to sacrifice their liberties if only they might be permitted to grind money out of the helpless peoples of the East. As a result, the only champions of liberty left in England seemed to be a handful of horsy peers whose liberalism appeared chiefly to be owing to the fact that they were out of office.

The English people were pronounced to be no less corrupt than their Parliament and aristocratic leaders. Men who allowed themselves to be trampled upon by a despotic, unrighteous government were not the true descendants of Pym and Hampden: "Was their Great Grand Fathers to start up from their Graves," exclaimed a colonist, "with what amasement . . . would they behold their Sons so degenerate & turned so Superalatively wicked, Cruel, & Ungenerous."[24] Had a spark of the old love of liberty still burned in England, the people themselves would have purged "those dens of thieves the Lds and Commons." But the people made no effort to smash the government that oppressed them; neither their own nor the colonists' grievances spurred them to action. They appeared rather to have become "a great tame beast, which fetches and carries for any minister." Every Englishman seemed to have his price; the common people were degenerate, gin-soaked, and sullenly mutinous; and the minority of honest men in the kingdom looked forward to the speedy downfall of their country.[25]

With England falling victim to "debt . . . corruption, and every

[23] Duché, 15.

[24] James Burd to Edward Shippen, August 8, 1774, Shippen MSS., Historical Society of Pennsylvania.

[25] *Principles and Acts of the Revolution*, edited by H. Niles, 23–24. *Boston Gazette*, October 11, 1773. Stephen Sayre to Ezra Stiles, July 20, 1772, Ezra Stiles MSS., Yale University Library.

abomination," there seemed little hope that "wisdom and justice will ever again govern her." Why, then, it was asked, ought Americans to be "whining about a connexion with these depraved People" and calling Great Britain "home" and "the mother country"; they could not do worse if they joined the "Afghan Tartars" and placed themselves under their sovereignty.[26]

One of the strongest arguments for independence was that the vice and corruption of "the rotten island" of Great Britain would eventually spread to America and overwhelm the virtue of the people. "It is impossible for one part of an Empire to be in a corrupt State without endangering the other," Americans pointed out; the longer they remained within the British Empire, the greater was the danger of contamination. The mother country, it seemed, had fallen victim to a highly infectious disease; and Americans would be foolhardy to remain under the same roof in a hopeless effort to nurse her through an illness which bore every sign of being fatal. For the colonies to stay, said Benjamin Franklin, "seems like . . . coupling and binding together the dead and the living." There could be no benefit to America, declared the Whigs, in protracting this unnatural union to "such a prodigious mass of corruption." [27]

Thus the America of 1775 was made to appear tied to a bankrupt, rotting state, that sought to keep itself alive by sucking the strength from its colonies. To retain the connection appeared likely to involve America in the doom of Great Britain; the best that Americans could look forward to, if they remained in the empire, was giving the mother country a decent burial. But prudence seemed to dictate that the colonies leave Great Britain to molder alone. The mother country was overpopulated; its commerce had reached its zenith; and it was now on the downward path that every nation must sooner or later tread. Alexander Hamilton, later to make his reputation by introducing much of the financial machinery of the British government into the United States, calculated that it would take Great Britain at least one hundred and twenty years to pay its public debt provided the country remained at peace.[28] But Britain, it was well

[26] *The Lee Papers,* I, 318.
[27] James Bowdoin to Samuel Adams, December 9, 1775, Adams MSS., New York Public Library. *The Lee Papers,* I, 98, 225. *The Writings of Benjamin Franklin,* VI, 311–312. *The Correspondence of Ralph Izard,* 26.
[28] *The Works of Alexander Hamilton,* I, 146, 149–150.

known, could scarcely look forward to a generation of peace. Hamilton believed that the next war would mark the end of England; even if victorious, her national debt would be so great that the people would be crushed beneath its weight. It behooved Americans to get out from under this impending avalanche of taxes. It was better to cut the moorings now than to remain lashed to this rotten old hulk, certain to go down with all hands in the next war.

Since the radicals believed that British rule would go down in blood, they urged Americans to face the rigors of war with confidence in ultimate victory. "We must excite by Policy," said John Adams, "that kind of exalted Courage, which is ever victorious by sea and land — which is irresistible." [29] The outcome of the battles of Lexington and Bunker Hill spoke louder than any amount of propaganda in giving Americans self-reliance and courage.

With some exaggeration, the Whigs pictured Lexington as an overwhelming rout of the flower of the British army: "The Sight of our Troops under Arms," declared a patriot, "threw them into a Panic, from which they did not recover in a Flight of 20 miles." It was well known that the Americans had been forced to retreat at Bunker Hill only because they ran short of ammunition; so long as they continued to fire, they mowed down the attacking British. Thus the conviction was established that the British lion had become so decrepit that no American need fear to thrust his head in its mouth: "The teeth are harmless, the claws are impotent," it was said, "and this British Lion, who has frightened our children here will, we are persuaded, turn out nothing but a Scottish Ass from the Isle of Bute." [30]

Vast numbers of Americans were believed prepared to spring to arms against Great Britain. "A tremendous band of yeomanry," four hundred thousand strong, was forecast by optimistic patriots; Charles Lee estimated that the colonies would hurl one hundred thousand men upon the British army within three months of the outbreak of war. Many Massachusetts Whigs believed that the Bay Colony alone could dispose of any invading force that the British could bring up: but if the other colonies joined in the struggle, victory would be ensured and "some Cromwell would soon

[29] *Warren-Adams Letters*, Massachusetts Historical Society Collections, LXXIII, Boston, 1925, I, 140.
[30] *Morning Chronicle and London Advertiser*, February 27, 1775.

arise, and trample under his feet our enemies." [31] Besides the fighting men of America, there were the hardly less redoubtable fighting women: the "virtuous matrons, useful wives, industrious daughters" who would rise up in defense of liberty. A hostile British army would be met by these Amazons, predicted the Whigs, who, "with their ladles and broomsticks, would knock them all on the head before they got half way through." [32]

American marksmanship was expected to take a heavy toll of British troops. Britons, unlike Americans, were not trained from childhood to handle a gun and the British army did little to teach them the art; indeed, Charles Lee declared that British regulars were "almost as ignorant in the use of a musket, as they are of the ancient Catepults." [33] One American rifleman, it was calculated, was the equal of five British regulars — a not incredible ratio if, as claimed, an American sharpshooter could pick off a man's nose at one hundred and fifty yards. And in truth these hardened frontiersmen were no mean antagonist: in August 1775, there marched into Fredericktown, Maryland, "a formidable company of upwards of one hundred and thirty men, from the mountains and backwoods, painted like *Indians*, armed with tomahawks and rifles, dressed in hunting shirts and moccasins," every man of them able to march and fight for days on a diet of water and parched corn.[34] Here were at least a hundred good reasons for the patriots' warning: "General Gage, take care of your nose." [35] Besides, Americans expected to be joined by a host of Indian allies, eager to take British scalps. "Gentlemen of the guards, take care of your toupees," British officers were cautioned; "if once your heads should fall under hands of these merciless hair-dressers, you must never appear in a side-box again." [36]

Americans rejoiced in some hardened Indian fighters who had seen service in the Seven Years' War; and these gentry might be counted upon to make British regulars, as they had Indian braves,

[31] Charles Lee, *Strictures on a Pamphlet entitled a Friendly Address*, Philadelphia, 1774, 12. *A Letter to Lord George Germain*, London, 1776, 17. Quincy, 132.
[32] David Humphrey, *Life of Israel Putnam*, Boston, 1788, 43. *Massachusetts Spy*, December 1, 1775.
[33] *Rivington's New York Gazetteer*, January 9, 1775. Charles Lee, 12.
[34] *American Archives*, Fourth Series, III, 2.
[35] *Virginia Gazette* (Purdie), July 14, 1775.
[36] *A Letter to Lord George Germain*, London, 1776, 32.

bite the dust. There were, for example, General Putnam, "a rough, fiery genius," and George Washington, whose brilliance in the last war afforded the best promise of military leadership in the struggle against Great Britain. These men, it was said, were eminently qualified to command "a set of virtuous Provincials" and Americans "would face any danger with these illustrious heroes to lead them.[37] Much favor was shown in Congress to Charles Lee, late of the British army, "a great sloven, wretchedly profane" and eccentric man whose pen was certainly mightier than his sword.[38] He was reputed in certain circles in England to be "Junius," but no one, after his performance in the American Revolutionary War, claimed that he was another Hannibal.

The very extent of the colonies was believed to make impossible any conquest by the British army. Although the British might gain a foothold, they could not hold down the country if the American army adopted the Indian method of fighting. "I think it will be best to let all our Enemies land without opposition," said a colonial strategist, "and we can *bush fight* them and cut off their Officers very easily, and in this way we can subdue them with very little loss." [39] Alexander Hamilton advised Americans to avoid a pitched battle: "It will be better policy," he said, "to harass and exhaust the soldiery by frequent skirmishes and incursions." [40] "It is in vain, it is delirium, it is frenzy," declared a Bostonian, "to think of dragooning Three Millions of English People out of their Liberties, at the Distance of 3000 Miles." [41] "In the arts of the bush, and in skirmishing fight," Americans were assured, "we stand unrivaled"; it seemed probable that if America "with Roman intrepidity" realized the true strength of her position, she might "bid defiance to the conjoined efforts of all Europe." "All the ships in the world," said Charles Lee, "would be too few to transport force sufficient to conquer three millions of people unanimously determined to sacrifice everything to liberty." [42] If worst came to worst, the colo-

---

[37] *Newport Mercury*, August 14, 1775. *The Remembrancer*, London, 1775, Second Edition, I, 10.

[38] *Proceedings of the Massachusetts Historical Society*, Boston, 1860, IV, 81, 82.

[39] *Boston Evening Post*, December 6, 1773. *Massachusetts Spy*, December 8, 1775.

[40] *The Works of Alexander Hamilton*, I, 166.

[41] *Public Advertiser*, April 29, 1775. *Massachusetts Spy*, December 8, 1775. Humphrey, 42. *Principles and Acts of the Revolution*, 111.

[42] *Massachusetts Spy*, December 29, 1775.

nists might make a strategic retreat to the interior and hold out for ages against their enemies. In this spirit, the Continental Congress addressed itself to the people of Great Britain: "Admit that your Fleets could destroy our Towns, and ravage our Sea-Coasts; these are inconsiderable Objects, Things of no Moment to Men, whose Bosoms glow with the Ardor of Liberty. We can retire beyond the Reach of your Navy, and, without any sensible Diminution of the Necessaries of Life, enjoy a Luxury, which from that Period you will want – the Luxury of being Free." Rather than submit to tyranny, the colonists swore that they would "brouse with the goats on the mountain shrubs" and, if need be, cross the Mississippi itself.[43]

Some Englishmen dreaded lest Americans, cutting the ties with civilization in their retreat into the interior of the continent, become transformed into "Hordes of English Tartars, pouring down an irresistible Cavalry on the unfortified Frontiers."[44] Others, however, ridiculed the notion that the colonists could "live like Indians, without Indian constitutions" – after a few weeks in the wilderness they would be ready to return home and become dutiful subjects. But Dr. Johnson would have welcomed the exodus of the Whigs to the west – it meant, he remarked, that "good houses" would be left to "wiser men."[45]

The superior morale of Americans was widely regarded as the best guarantee of victory over the British army. Americans were fighting for freedom and in defense of their homes; the British were slaves and were attempting to impose slavery upon a free people. In this conflict, the colonists might be expected to reach new heights of self-sacrificing idealism: "There is a certain enthusiasm in liberty," said the Whigs, "that makes human nature rise above itself in acts of bravery and heroism."[46] New Englanders were certain, as always, that "the Glory of God is on our side and will fight for us, and this makes us as bold as lions."[47] "The PEOPLE of the AMERICAN WORLD are Millions strong," exclaimed a patriot, "countless Legions compose their united ARMY of FREEMEN – whose intrepid Souls sparkle with LIBERTY, and their Hearts are steeled with Courage." Nothing could stand before the "HERCULEAN

[43] Letters of William Lee, 108, note.
[44] Tucker, An Humble Appeal, 28.
[45] Gazetteer and New Daily Advertiser, November 15, 1765. Johnson, Taxation No Tyranny, 7, 12.
[46] Alexander Hamilton, The Farmer Refuted, New York, 163.
[47] Boston Gazette, July 17, 1775.

ARM *of this* NEW WORLD"; half a million fierce Whigs, spring-ing like one man to arms, would form a phalanx *"before whose blazing Shields* none can stand." [48]

Certainly, the sight of this resolute yeomanry was expected to strike terror in the British army, which, colonial propagandists de-clared, was composed of "the most debauched Weavers 'prentices, the scum of the Irish Roman Catholics, who desert upon every occasion, and a few, very few Scotch, who are not strong enough to carry packs." [49] The British troops stationed in Philadelphia in 1774 were said to be largely invalids and hospitalized rakes who could not march to Boston "were they to have the plunder of the town for their asking." Like everything else in Great Britain, the British army, Americans were told, was rotten with decay — indeed, the rot had penetrated so deeply that British soldiers seemed to be "more like the frog eaters of France, than the hale, lusty Englishmen, nurtured by beef and Sir John Barleycorn." [50] Charles Lee declared that British regulars were good for nothing except parading in Hyde Park or Wimbledon Common — and in the field their smartness in maneuver only made them better targets. It was recalled that the British troops that served in America during the French and In-dian Wars were resplendent in braid and gilt, their hair was finely powdered, and they looked dashing in the ballroom — "but fatal ex-perience taught us, that they knew not how to fight." It was only after they had taken lessons from the American frontiersmen that they won victories over the French and Indians. [51] But even since the Seven Years' War, the quality of British fighting men had deteriorated. Instead of hardening themselves for battle and "seek-ing for glory in the blood stained field," British officers sought only to "captivate the softer sex, and triumph over virtue." [52] The great-est victories of the British army had been won in the boudoir. As "impudent ravishers" and masters of the art of seduction, British officers had no peers; but as fighting men they were believed to fall far short of their American antagonists.

As for the Hessian and Hanoverian mercenaries, it seemed rea-

[48] *Newport Mercury*, January 10, 1774.
[49] Charles Lee, 11.
[50] *Newport Mercury*, August 14, 1775. *Massachusetts Spy*, November 17, 1775. Collections of the New York Historical Society, *The Deane Papers*, New York, 1887, I, 26.
[51] Charles Lee, 11.
[52] *Principles and Acts of the Revolution*, 26.

sonable to suppose that they could be induced to desert as fast as they were brought over: the British government was merely giving free transportation to some very desirable settlers. Even British officers and men might be persuaded, once in America, "to quit the diabolical Service of Tyrants." [53] And as long as a British soldier could be made drunk for a penny's worth of rum, the prospects of breaking up the British army by wholesale desertions were excellent.[54]

The conviction of American impregnability was firmly fixed in the colonies by 1775: tell Americans that British veterans would fly before "an undisciplined multitude of New England squirrel-hunters," said a Tory, "and they will swallow it without a hiccough." [55]

Even the American birth rate was pressed into service to prove the invincibility of the colonies. Franklin calculated that the population of the colonies doubled itself every twenty years by natural means; and, indeed, the vast number of children amazed even travelers accustomed to viewing the wonders of the world. Children swarmed everywhere: "like ants" or "like broods of Ducks in a pond." In the size of families, it was observed, even "Irishmen are nothing to the Yankeys and Buckskins in that Way," although it was thought that the Yankees' custom of bundling gave them an advantage over the less resourceful Irish. Even the beauties of Virginia were found to be "great Breeders." An Englishman who visited the colonies in 1768 concluded that the fruitfulness of Americans endangered the empire. "The good people are marrying one another as if they had not a day to live," he remarked. "I alledge it to be a plot against the State, and the ladies (who are all politicians in America) are determined to raise young Rebels to fight against old England." [56]

Many colonists drew from this generative prowess the conclusion that time was working in their favor. Because America's growth

---

[53] *South Carolina Gazette*, December 26, 1774. *Rivington's New York Gazetteer*, January 19, 1776. *Virginia Gazette* (Purdie), February 3, 1775.

[54] *Reflections on the Rise, Progress and Probable Consequence of the Present Contentions with the Colonies*, Edinburgh, 1776, 51.

[55] Jonathan Sewall, "A Cure for the Spleen," *Magazine of History*, 1922, 38.

[56] Kapp, 63. *Gazetteer and New Daily Advertiser*, July 20, 1769. *The Francis Letters*, I, 90. *Public Advertiser*, January 9, 1770. N. D. Mereness, *Travels in the American Colonies*, New York, 1916, 406. *American Historical Review*, October 1921, XXVI, 84.

was inevitable, it seemed better to wait "till the gentle course of nature shall bring us to maturity and independence than by a premature, doubtful, and dangerous struggle to hazard the ruin of the whole British Empire." [57] Franklin warned the impetuous Boston Whigs that "by a premature Struggle we may be crippled and kept down another Age" and urged them to recognize that "every Incroachment on Rights, is not worth a Rebellion." By waiting until Great Britain became involved in war, the colonies might procure the redress of all their grievances with the threat of withholding aid from the mother country: "Our great Security lies, I think," said Franklin, "in our growing Strength both in Numbers and Wealth; that creates an increasing Ability of assisting this Nation in its Wars, which will make us more respectable, our Friendship more valued, and our Enmity feared." [58] By begetting children, it was said, Americans were doing more to defend their liberties than all the rioting of the hotheaded Sons of Liberty. This, surely, was revolution made easy: the struggle for liberty became largely a matter of procreation — and if every American did his duty, Great Britain would recognize the futility of contending with these "brave propagating Fellows" in the colonies.[59] It was pointed out in 1775, to prove the hopelessness of Great Britain's position, that "Britain, at the expense of three millions has killed one hundred and fifty Yankees this campaign, which is 20,000 pounds a head. . . . During the same time sixty thousand children have been born in America." [60]

Of greater significance is the fact that the rapid growth of American population helped to instill the conviction in the minds of the colonists that America was destined to become the center of a "Great Empire." It was America's destiny, clearly manifest at least to those who studied statistics, that this continent must ultimately become the center of the British Empire. The anomaly of a continent ruled by an island could not be long perpetuated, it was reasoned, because America's birth rate was rapidly shifting the balance from the Old World to the New. Calculating the growth of American population seems to have been one of the popular American

[57] *The Manuscripts of the Earl of Dartmouth*, Part IV, Appendix, I, 345. *Collections of the Massachusetts Historical Society*, Fourth Series, IV, 362.
[58] *The Works of Benjamin Franklin*, VI, 3–4, 273.
[59] Sewall, "A Cure for the Spleen," *Magazine of History*, 1922, 27. Richard Henry Lee, II, 240–241.
[60] *The Works of Benjamin Franklin*, VI, 430.

indoor sports during the revolutionary period. One American concluded in 1770 that there would be 96,000,000 Americans by 1866; another estimated that the population would reach 1,280,000,000 in 2000 A.D.[61] Thus the course of empire seemed to be moving westward in the stout loins of the American colonists. As early as 1765, Americans were telling Englishmen that the colonies were now ready "for the reception of Your King, Lords, and Commons." "Not many generations may pass away," declared a colonist, "before one of the first Monarchs of the World, on ascending his throne, shall declare with exulting joy, *'Born and educated among you, I glory in the name of* AMERICAN.'" [62] The greatness of America and the decline of Great Britain were believed to be inevitable; neither Americans nor Britons could escape their destiny; and, as a colonist observed, "no conduct on Great Britain's part can put a stop to this building. There is no contending with omnipotence, and the predispositions are so numerous, and so well adapted to the rise of America, that our success is indubitable." America was foreordained to become "the imperial Mistress of the world" and therefore it behooved Englishmen to propitiate the colonists in order that they might share in this glory.[63]

Throughout the revolutionary period, the colonists read in their newspapers that America was "advancing to a MIGHTY Empire" and that "all the POWERS of EARTH and hell combin'd, shall not be able to prevail against it." [64] They were outraged by British colonial policy because they believed that "America must grow — England must perceive it, and yet she neglects to reason properly on the event" — instead, Englishmen "smiled with contemptuous sneer, at these vain chimeras of an American brain." Americans found themselves apostrophized in their newspapers as the chosen people of God whose destiny was to rule the world. "Americans," exclaimed a writer in the *Massachusetts Spy* in 1773, "stand on the greatest continent between the poles, your powers may reach to

[61] Edward Wigglesworth, *Calculations on American Population,* Boston, 1775, 22. *Public Advertiser,* March 31, 1775.

[62] Additional MSS. 35911, British Museum, *Hardwicke Papers,* Letter from North America, November 8, 1765, Library of Congress Transcript. *Boston Gazette,* July 11, 1768. *Pennsylvania Packet or General Advertiser,* July 4, 1774.

[63] Arthur Lee to Samuel Adams, December 24, 1772, Adams MSS., New York Public Library. *Pennsylvania Journal,* August 28, 1768.

[64] *Essex Gazette,* July 21, 1772. *Pennsylvania Journal,* August 28, 1768. *New York Gazette or Weekly Post Boy,* May 22, 1769.

distant empires and you become the arbiter of the world! Surely then, it does not suit with your Roman dignity and more than imperial majesty, to be robbed by piratical plunderers. . . . Shall the island of BRITAIN enslave this great continent of AMERICA, which is more than ninety nine times bigger, and is capable of supporting hundreds of millions of millions of people?" [65]

Almost to the eve of the Declaration of Independence, this American empire was generally conceived of as part of the British Empire. There was a strong expansionist sentiment in the American colonies after the victory over France and Spain in 1763 which appeared strikingly in the writings of Benjamin Franklin, James Otis, and many other patriot leaders. These men believed that mankind could attain no greater felicity than to have Great Britain dominate the earth. "If I have one ambitious wish," exclaimed James Otis, "it is to see Great-Britain at the head of the world, and to see my King, under God, the father of mankind." "I have often viewed with infinite satisfaction the prodigious growth & power of the British Empire," declared Charles Thomson of Philadelphia.[66] This veneration for the British Empire was based upon the belief that it stood for liberty and the rights of man. In the eighteenth century, the best hope of human liberty seemed to lie in extension of the British Constitution; even "the finest writers of the most nations on the continent of Europe" were "enraptured with the beauties of the civil constitution of *Great Britain*." [67]

Benjamin Franklin urged British statesmen ever to bear in mind the rapidly increasing wealth and population of the colonies and to recognize that their growth was the best guarantee of the future glory of the British Empire. He advised Englishmen gracefully to accept the inevitability of American greatness; to make no laws that would cramp American trade and manufactures — for such laws would be swept aside in the irresistible surge of American growth; and to think in terms of an Atlantic world, peopled by Englishmen who,

[65] *Massachusetts Spy*, November 11 and 26, 1773; March 24, 1774. *The Connecticut Courant*, July 6, 1773. *Pennsylvania Packet and General Advertiser*, January 20, 1772. *Boston Gazette*, September 27, 1773. *Pennsylvania Journal*, February 6, August 14, 1766.

[66] Collections of the New York Historical Society, *The Thomson Papers*, New York, 1879, 24. James Otis, Jr., to the Earl of Buchan, July 18, 1768, Otis MSS., Massachusetts Historical Society. James Otis, *Rights of the British Colonies*, Boston, 1763, 21.

[67] *Ibid.*, 13.

whether born in England or in America, possessed equal rights and privileges. Finding themselves treated like free men and on an equal plane with Britons, Franklin predicted that the colonists would exert themselves as they had never done before towards enriching the mother country and extending the British Empire until it would reach "round the whole globe, and awe the world!" [68] In effect, Franklin was appealing to Englishmen to throw off their insularity and to call a new world of liberty into being to redress the balance of the old despotic order.

But few Englishmen caught a vision of this world-wide empire of free men; in 1775, the most enlightened imperialists were on the American side of the Atlantic. It was rather the example of Rome which had captured Englishmen's imagination; the British Empire as conceived by Otis and Franklin appeared to them to be merely another American subterfuge to achieve independence of the mother country. Instead of founding the empire upon liberty and human rights, British imperialists thought almost exclusively in terms of revenue and enforcement of the Laws of Trade, and by their efforts to tax the colonies raised the question "whether the rising empire of America, shall be an empire of slaves or of freemen." [69] As a result, the colonists' enthusiasm for extending the British Empire over the world was gradually diverted into creating in this hemisphere a purely "American Empire" of which liberty would be the cornerstone. Here a new civilization was to be established while Europe sank into slavery. Only through independence, it was contended, could America attain its destiny and become "the arbiter of the world" and "reign, not only Lords of America, but . . . possess, in the utmost security, that dominion of sea throughout the world, which their British ancestors enjoyed before them." Having once freed itself from British control, America could become what Great Britain refused to be: "the Glory of the World, and the Terror of the wicked Oppressors among the Nations." [70]

This faith in America as the "Great Empire" of the future was a mainspring of the revolutionary movement. The Revolution was, in a sense, the result of the reaction of the American continent, with its boundless resources and wealth, upon the American mind.

[68] *The Writings of Benjamin Franklin*, IV, 4.
[69] *Principles and Acts of the Revolution*, 19.
[70] *Boston Gazette*, August 24, 1772. *Newport Mercury*, September 21, 1772. *Connecticut Courant*, June 29, 1773.

A British officer observed in 1775 that it was not the work of demagogues or propagandists but of a people who, feeling themselves "wealthy, populous, and strong; and being impatient of restraint, are struggling to throw off that dependency which is so irksome to them." [71] The maturity of the colonies which gave rise to this feeling of strength and self-confidence was an indispensable ingredient of the revolutionary movement. Where it was absent, the colonies remained loyal. The Nova Scotians, for example, had not come to exult in their own vigor and importance. They did not join the rebellion, but "I dare say if the province was a little better settled," remarked an Englishman, "the spirit of patriotism would blaze out amongst them with as much fury as in the Massachusetts." [72]

Meanwhile, English propagandists were not idle in disparaging the prowess of the colonists and giving the English people a false sense of military invincibility. One of the insuperable obstacles to reconciliation with the colonies was the conviction held by virtually all Englishmen that Americans could not resist the British fleet and army. Isaac Barré, the man who first called Americans "Sons of Liberty," said that he "had not a doubt, but a very small part of our strength, will, at any time, overpower them." Even William Pitt declared that "the Idea of coercing the Colonies as dangerous and difficult in its Operation, he must laugh at." [73] However proficient Americans might be in "hunting down Revenue Officers like wild Beasts," terrorizing royal governors and applying a coat of tar and feathers to Tories, they failed to convince Englishmen that they were lion-hearted warriors. Few doubted that after a British fleet had trained its guns upon Boston or any other colonial seaport the upper class, alarmed for the safety of its property, would suppress the mob and make peace. Some suggested that the colonies could be brought to terms by *withdrawing* the British army: the colonists would then find themselves at the mercy of the Indians and would call back the British redcoats and gladly pay taxes to keep them in America. If the redskins did not do the business, the threat of conquest by European powers certainly would. Without

[71] *The Letters of Captain W. G. Evelyn*, edited by G. D. Scull, Oxford, 1879, 46.

[72] Historical Manuscripts Commission, *Reports on the MSS. of Reginald Rawdon Hastings*, London, 1934, III, 149.

[73] *Parliamentary History*, XVII, 1179.

British protection, even "the Petty States of Genoa or little King-dom of Sweden would run away with them." [74]

Englishmen made the mistake of belittling Americans' courage and strength to such a degree that it was difficult to regard colonial resistance seriously. An American, it was said in many quarters, was an unmitigated coward — "the lowest of Mankind, and almost of a different Species from the English of Britain." [75] Whatever courage the colonists possessed was said to be the result of their rum drink-ing: without rum, New Englanders "could neither fight nor say their prayers" — there were not, indeed, "meaner whimpering wretches in this universe" than sober New Englanders. [76] Nothing was to be feared from the much-heralded American yeomanry: they lived too comfortably at home to make good fighters, and at the first opportunity they would desert to their well-stocked kitchens and fond wives. Instead of hardy pioneers, braving the perils of ocean and wilderness, Americans were pictured as cowards whose ancestors had fled the mother country rather than fight for liberty in England. They had brought with them, however, the germs of levelism and democracy which, sprouting in the soil of the New World, now promised to prostrate that small part of the American army which was not already rendered powerless by faintheartedness. Barbers in the American militia were elected colonels by the soldiers; cobblers became captains; and smiths were made generals. The consequence was that there was no pretense of subordination among this "motley rabble": if an officer gave a com-mand, the privates answered, "I vow, Colonel, do it yourself." [77]

It was not believed that colonial union made impossible the conquest of British America. The colonists, it was presumed, were "united by an Enthusiastic Fit of false Patriotism; — a Fit which necessarily cools in Time." The conflict of interest and manners between the Northern and Southern colonies still appeared to be a strong guarantee of continued American dependence upon the mother country. Certainly, it was not to be expected that Virginians

[74] *The South Carolina Historical and Genealogical Magazine*, 1925, XXVI, 76. Archives of Maryland, XIV, *The Correspondence of Governor Horatio Sharpe*, Baltimore, III, 271. *Gazetteer and New Daily Advertiser*, January 9, 1766.

[75] *The Writings of Benjamin Franklin*, VI, 396.

[76] *Letters on the American Revolution, 1774–1776*, edited by Margaret Wheeler Willard, Boston, 1925, 120.

[77] *Public Advertiser*, January 17, 1775.

and Carolinians would fight New Englanders' battles for them: they were "too wise to be caught in such a mouse-trap." Even if they joined forces with the Saints, they would "leave the pumpkin gentry whom they hold in most sovereign contempt to fight it out as they might, and then swagger at the trick they had played the NON CONS." [78] Some Englishmen judged the Virginians to be no more formidable to the British army than were New Englanders. If the Saints were weakened by too large doses of democracy, the Virginians were "yellow shadows of men," debilitated by dissipation and libertinism. Such weaklings, it was held, would be "far fitter for an engagement with our Covent garden ladies, than with our embattled squadrons." Lions in the boudoir, the Virginians were believed to be lambs on the field of battle. It was predicted that at the first volley they would run for shelter to those "extensive woods which they are too lazy or feeble to cut down." [79]

Englishmen generally overlooked what proved to be one of the Americans' most serious weaknesses during the War of Independence: the conviction that the militia were the guardians of liberty and that a regular standing army was its eternal enemy. Every orator who commemorated the Boston Massacre at the annual celebration glorified the militia and denounced regular armies. "The true strength and safety of every commonwealth or limited monarchy," declared James Lovell in 1771, "is the bravery of its freeholders, its militia. By brave militias they rise to grandeur; and they come to ruin by a mercenary army." This view was carried over into the period of the Revolutionary War with almost fatal consequences to the American war effort. Some patriots even feared that the minutemen ought to be carefully watched lest they become a standing army and establish military tyranny. The war was being fought to defend freedom; and many Americans were unwilling to sacrifice their liberties even temporarily for the sake of military efficiency. In keeping with this spirit, members of Congress continued to conjure up visions of military despotism when the great need of the hour was to prevent the continental army from melting away.

[78] *Gazetteer and New Daily Advertiser*, November 13, 1765. Tucker, *Four Tracts*, 145.
[79] *Pennsylvania Journal*, February 27, 1766. *Gazetteer and New Daily Advertiser*, November 13, 1765.

There was little doubt in Englishmen's minds of the ability of the mother country to win a quick decision over the colonies: the only real difference of opinion was how the knockout blow should be administered. Some maintained that the rebellion could be crushed merely by blockading American ports with the British navy: "Let a few Sloops of War cruize along the Coast, and take every Vessel that peeps out of their Harbours," they urged, and England would find that "the Rage and Fury of their most noisy Dutchified Patriots would instantly be changed into the most abject Petitions for Mercy." If Americans did not make their peace with the mother country, they would fall out among themselves and, shut off from the outside world, begin to cut each other's throats, thus sparing the British army this disagreeable business. "Every common Sailor," it was said, "is able to point out to Government how the vain and misled Americans may be reduced, in a few Months or Weeks, to any Degree of Distress, our Humanity will permit." [80] To hasten their return to reason, it was suggested that the British navy might bombard a few colonial seaports and knock the houses, liberty poles, and liberty trees about the heads of the Sons of Liberty.[81]

But most Englishmen, while not forgetting that their natural element was salt water, were of the opinion that the British army must take a hand in subduing the colonists. Both Howe and Germain believed that the army as well as the navy must be employed: then, it was predicted, Great Britain could deliver "such a Peal of Thunder" as would "shake even the Apalatian Mountains." [82] Whether fought on sea or on land, there was no doubt that it would be a short war. "One tolerable Drubbing," and American resistance would collapse; the Whigs would scurry for cover; and the "indisciplined Rabble" that made up the American army would take to its heels, leaving the way open for British armies to march the length and breadth of the "puny Colonies." At worst, it would be a war of one campaign. A large army was not required for this

[80] *Public Advertiser*, January 26, 1775. *Gazetteer and New Daily Advertiser*, November 15, 1765. *The Address of the People of Great Britain to the Inhabitants of America*, London, 1775, 5.
[81] *St. James's Chronicle*, December 22, 1774. *Public Advertiser*, January 26, 1775.
[82] *Public Advertiser*, January 18, 1775. *The Manuscripts of the Earl of Dartmouth*, II, 388.

parade; five hundred men with whips, it was said, could "make them all dance to the tune of Yankee Doodle." [83] A handful of Englishmen were worth a horde of Americans because "English Mastiffs be not scar'd at the Barking of American Curs." The Earl of Sandwich actually rejoiced at the prospect of a large American army being formed: the more troops the better, he said, because "if they did not run away, they would starve themselves into compliance with our measures." [84]

British military policy was predicated during the early period of the war upon two assumptions: that Americans would run at the sight of British troops and that a large number of loyalists would rise to assist the redcoats in putting down the rebellion. Neither calculation proved correct: Americans did not run and the Tories did not rise. Few errors of judgment have proved more costly to the British Empire.

[83] David Hartley to Benjamin Franklin, November 29, 1774, Franklin MSS., American Philosophical Society.
[84] *Public Advertiser*, April 29, 1774; January 17, 1775.

CHAPTER · NINETEEN

AN APPEAL TO HEAVEN

The Movement Toward Independence

Patrick Henry

I

IT WAS one of the cardinal points in the plans of the radicals that Americans must be familiarized with the idea of independence by slowly stripping Great Britain of her authority. It was far safer to inch the colonies toward revolution than to risk all upon a bold push; even Sam Adams cautioned his friends to "wait till the Fruit is ripe before we gather it." [1] Most of the extremists recognized that it was better to declare a belated independence with a united people than to force an immediate decision and thereby produce disunion. The wisest course of action seemed to be to wait for time and events to do their work rather than to adopt high-pressure methods which were almost certain to alienate the great body of moderate Americans. "America," said John Adams, "is a great, unwieldy body. Its progress must be slow. It is like a large fleet sailing under convoy. The fleetest sailors must wait for the dullest and slowest. Like a coach and six, the swiftest horses must be slackened, and the slowest quickened, that all may keep an even pace." [2] To borrow another metaphor from John Adams, the radicals were attempting to steer "a vast, unwieldy machine," which threatened to crack up at every turn. Moreover, the moderates, particularly John Dickinson, were constantly leaping off the machine and protesting that they would not go a foot farther until they were assured that independence was not just around the corner. It is not surprising, therefore, that the progress of the Whigs toward independence was creaking and laborious.

It was evident to the Tories that the very slowness with which the colonies were moving toward revolution favored the extremists; had progress been more rapid, the people might have paid more heed to their warnings. Instead, the baffled Tories were compelled to stand helplessly by as the course of events brought ever closer the final separation of mother country and colonies and to cry out their

[1] *Warren-Adams Letters,* I, 191.
[2] *Letters of Members of the Continental Congress,* I, 132.

futile warning that Whig policies were leading to a bloody civil war. The Tories were true prophets, but they had little honor in the colonies.

The revolutionary movement was not sustained by propaganda alone — rather, it was carried forward by events from which the propagandists manufactured their stock in trade. From the beginning, time and tide favored the radicals; again and again, their cause was buoyed up by some fortuitous event when it seemed about to sink beneath the weight of public indifference. Certainly, the failure of the Continental Association to coerce the mother country, the virtual collapse of the Whig opposition in England, and the necessity of employing force against Canada to forestall British military action immeasurably strengthened the hands of the radicals. It was because they were quick to extract the utmost advantage from them that these events became important milestones on the road which led to the Declaration of Independence.

American hopes of coercing the British government by economic measures were rudely shattered. Great Britain experienced none of "those *black* and *bitter* Days" as a result of the loss of the colonial market to which the patriots had confidently looked forward. Instead, trade was never brisker: new markets in Spain, Russia, and Turkey were being opened and merchants found less difficulty in getting orders than in filling them. Although this boom was ephemeral, it enabled the English merchants and manufacturers to escape the full force of the Continental Association: they declared that trade with the colonies was "nothing more than a drop in the bucket" and expressed gratification over the fact that the Americans had ceased to order merchandise, "otherwise there must have been disappointment somewhere." [3] Indeed, the boycott was attended with so little distress in England that some Englishmen became convinced there was no necessity of fighting to preserve colonial trade. "Better surely will it be to cut off at once a limb that is of no use," they said, "than to hazard the mortification of the whole body, by endeavouring to preserve it." Instead of a general upheaval in England there were only a few riots of sailors in Liverpool in 1775; and although some American patriots regarded these disturbances as a

[3] *The Virginia Magazine of History and Biography*, January 1901, 234. *Correspondence of Ralph Izard*, 79. Tucker, *An Humble Appeal*, 71, 72, 74. *The Journals and Letters of the late Samuel Curwen*, 35. *The West India Merchant*, London, 1778, 35.

promising beginning toward revolution in the mother country, nothing came of them.[4]

As a result, many English merchants and manufacturers refused to regard the Continental Association as a serious threat to their interests. Also, the memory of the breakup of the Nonimportation Agreement of 1768–1770 served in 1774–1776 to quiet their fears. Given time, it was said, colonial jealousies would likewise wreck the Continental Association. The provinces were believed to be overstocked with British goods; and therefore it could be assumed that American merchants had resorted to another boycott in order to dispose of their surplus merchandise at a handsome profit. When they found their shelves empty, it would be the turn of the British merchants to profiteer: they could then unload their shopworn goods upon the colonies and get what prices they pleased. But above all, American women were still believed to be the allies of England in working for the downfall of the boycott: "When a new piece of dress is in question," it was predicted, "they will almost universally be on the side of England." If Americans intended to win the struggle with the mother country, they must "summon up all their wisdom, and regenerate or create anew all their females." There seemed little doubt that the odds were heavily against the patriots in their commercial war with Great Britain: "What chance has a poor, frail American shopkeeper or merchant of remaining unmoved," it was asked, "when irresistibly called to his *duty* and his *interest* by the all-powerful charms and allurements of the modern beauties of America?"[5]

More significantly, English businessmen saw little hope for preserving colonial commerce except by supporting the Ministry in 1774–1776. The Continental Association seemed to them a stab in the back. Were not they — the best friends the colonists had in the mother country — the first to be sacrificed to achieve the Americans' ends! The Association appeared "only a softer Phrase for their [Americans'] resolving to cheat all their English Creditors" after English wealth had raised American "peddlars and ploughmen to the rank of merchants." By 1774, many merchants had begun to

---

[4] *The Remembrancer*, London, 1775, Second Edition, I, 157–158, 239. Macpherson, 26. *Letters of Richard Champion*, 59.

[5] *Public Ledger*, April 6, 1774. *St. James's Chronicle*, November 27, 1774. *Newport Mercury*, November 7, 1774. *Gazetteer and New Daily Advertiser*, January 20, 1774.

suspect that the ministers were right in charging the colonists were bent upon independence. Any further relaxations of authority over them seemed certain to deprive British merchants and manufacturers of their debts and their monopoly of the colonial market. If the colonists were permitted to go on unchecked, the Acts of Trade and Navigation would be swept aside; Americans would repudiate their debts or pay them in worthless paper money; and English business-men would find that instead of customers they had rivals on the other side of the Atlantic. The merchants could not fail to see that they had a large stake in the maintenance of British authority over America. To come to the aid of the colonies in 1775 as they had in 1765 would mean, they feared, that Americans would "never rest till they have obtained a free trade with all the world." "America," an Englishman exclaimed, "is a *Hen* that lays her *Golden Eggs* for Britain"; and it was clear that this hen could be killed by kindness as well as by ill-treatment.[6]

It was also true that English businessmen began to smell the "*haut gout* of profitable war" even though it was directed against their best customers. They looked to the government to reimburse them for their losses and the government was lavish in its promises. As a result, the merchants sat almost "perfectly satisfied and con-tented" and rejoiced in the rise of the price of stocks, paying little more heed, it was said, to the gathering storm in the colonies than to the carving up of Poland. "Any remarkable highway robbery at Hounslow-heath," said Burke in 1774, "would make more conver-sation than all the disturbances of America . . . this unaccountable neutrality of the people, in their own most important affairs," he continued, "does above all things astonish and perplex me."[7] After vast effort, Burke and the Whigs were able to produce only a few petitions from the merchants and manufacturers protesting against the government's policy. In Yorkshire, Birmingham, and Nottingham, counter petitions in favor of the government were circulated with considerable success. Burke began to consider ways of "separating the sound from the rotten contract-hunting part of

---

[6] *Public Advertiser*, September 12, 1774; January 3, February 28, May 4, 1775. Mein, 6–7. *Morning Chronicle and London Advertiser*, February 17, 1775. *Parliamentary History*, XVIII, 182, 879. *Letters of William Lee*, I, 98–99. Reed, I, 102. *Gazetteer and New Daily Advertiser*, January 7, 1775.

[7] *Correspondence of Edmund Burke*, I, 453, 474; II, 50, 107.

the mercantile interest"; but even his own constituency of Bristol declined to support him.[8]

The failure of the merchants to play the part expected of them by the colonial patriots directly affected the fortunes of the Whigs. The liberal opposition in England was based upon a union of the great Whig landowners and the mercantile classes; when the merchants refused to rise en masse in support of the colonies, the Whig politicians were shorn of their strongest weapon against the government. They found little consolation, too, when they turned to the English public. The people were for the most part solidly behind the Ministry during the early part of the war; "It is a capital mistake of our American friends to expect insurrection here," wrote Samuel Curwen of Philadelphia after he had taken refuge in England.[9] Ralph Izard, another colonial observer in England, estimated that four out of five people in Great Britain were against America: "They imagine," he reported, "that in proportion as we are obliged to pay, they will be exonerated." In supporting the Ministry against the colonies, Izard believed that Parliament was reflecting the popular state of mind: "When you see never more than eighty in Parliament opposing the ministry," he remarked, "you may depend upon it, the measure is not thought a bad one; for corruption does not reach as deep. Many members support the minister who are not supported by him." [10]

The Whigs recognized that the "popular tide" was running strongly against them — as well it might, since, as they pointed out, "national prejudice, pride, false glory, and false arithmetic" were being employed to embitter the English people against the colonists. Burke in 1774 compared the House of Commons to "a dead senseless mass, which had neither sense, soul, or activity, but as it derived them from the minister." [11] Englishmen whose ancestors would have been clamoring for the heads of the ministers, said the Whigs, were now diverting themselves at regattas and horse races, at Vauxhall and the theaters, while Great Britain muddled into a ruinous war. When the Whigs attempted to avert the conflict by presenting the

---

[8] *Ibid.*, II, 2–3, 55–56, 62. *Letters of Richard Champion*, 51. *Parliamentary History*, XVIII, 57.

[9] *Journals and Letters of the late Samuel Curwen*, 35.

[10] *Correspondence of Ralph Izard*, 83, 87.

[11] *Parliamentary History*, XVIII, 57, 449, 749.

petitions of the Continental Congress to Parliament, these state papers were overwhelmingly rejected; and the only answer the Ministry deigned to give the Whigs was, "You want our places." The Whigs found themselves blamed for the American rebellion; it was their factious support of the colonists, the ministers declared, that had encouraged Americans to resist the mother country. Opposition gained the Whigs no honor among the people as a whole; they found that the "poor, giddy, thoughtless people" favored the Ministry and were bent upon crushing the Americans. "Who could have imagined," wrote Lord Camden in 1776, "that the Ministry could have become popular by forcing this country into a destructive war, and advancing the power of the Crown to a state of despotism? And yet, that is the fact; and we of the minority suffer under the odium." [12]

The experienced fox hunters who made up the Whig command perceived that in opposing the American war they were "on the coldest scent, without even the most distant prospect of ever reaching the game." [13] For years, the Whig lords had been eager to quit their futile opposition, retire to their estates, and recruit their strength with port and fox-hunting until the "national delirium" had abated. Then they would be called back to save the country, although, as Horace Walpole observed, most of these Cincinnati "will be found at the hazard-table" instead of at the plow. It was clear in 1775 that for the time being, at least, they could do nothing; "We are not only patriots *out of place*," they lamented, "but patriots *out of the opinion of the public*." They concluded that to attempt to form an opposition under such circumstances would only make matters worse; they would be like "a child pulling against a runaway horse; let him alone and he will stop the sooner." [14] The Whigs decided that there was "no dignity in carrying on a teazing and vexatious sort of debate," without other effect than pelting ministers and "keeping honest gentlemen from their dinners." Rather than expose their true weakness in parliamentary divisions, they preferred to absent themselves from Parliament. Chatham, however, insisted upon staying in the fray: there was, he declared, a distinction between right and wrong, between Whig and Tory. Never-

[12] *Correspondence of Edmund Burke*, I, 346. *Pitt Correspondence*, IV, 401. *Letters of Richard Champion*, 50. Grafton, 279.
[13] *Memoirs of the Marquis of Rockingham*, II, 242–243.
[14] *Ibid.*, II, 215, 242–243, 304, 305.

theless, even he began to fear that the English nation was "the tamest and vilest in Europe." He recommended travel to his friends: "If you leave England for a time," he said, "you are at least sure of a better air; and pretty sure not to meet a more corrupted people, or more contemptible country." Most of the Whig lords, however, were content to travel only as far as their estates; accordingly, in 1776, most of the Rockingham Whigs left their seats in Parliament declaring that "there was no saving a people against their will." [15]

The collapse of the Whig opposition was not wholly owing to the corruptibility of Parliament and the astuteness of the King and his ministers. As a party, the Whigs suffered from serious internal weaknesses. Whig lords were peevish, querulous, and easily discouraged, and they were engaged in perpetual bouts with their digestion and the gout. Burke put on his most soothing manner and attempted to console these ailing peers, urging them to raise themselves from their sickbeds and take the field against the King and Tories. These appeals had little effect; but at the sound of a fox horn the Whigs experienced miraculous cures: at the first blast they cast aside their warming pans and medicines and were off to the hunt. Too, their health was often restored by the sight of a well-laden sideboard. The Marquis of Rockingham once described for the edification of his fellow peers his methods of keeping in trim while subjected to the hardships of the hustings. "I have not suffered in health by the fatigues of body or mind," he wrote triumphantly. "I have had a good quantity of Madeira. On Monday last I was very tolerably drunk by 5 o'clock, and though I went through a variety of ceremonials, such as attending the assembly, supping and drinking with many companies, I walked home about 4 o'clock in the morning after having kept myself in fact continually drunk or elevated for eleven hours. I had a very good night's rest, and was not at all the worse for it next day." [16]

Moreover the Whigs were badly divided. Chatham had little love for Rockingham and he suspected that Burke was willing to play fast and loose with the Navigation Acts to conciliate Americans. On their part, the Whigs distrusted Chatham because he had denounced the Declaratory Act. They well remembered how he as-

---

[15] *Pitt Correspondence*, IV, 70, 224. *Correspondence of Edmund Burke*, I, 346–347.

[16] Historical MSS. Commission, *MSS. of F. J. Davile Filjambe*, Fifteenth Report, London, 1895, Part V, Appendix, 146.

sisted George III to break down the party system in Great Britain, and how in 1766 he had wormed his way into the King's closet, "the least peep into which," said Burke, "intoxicates him and will to the end of his life." Shelburne, Chatham's devoted follower, was nicknamed the "Jesuit of Berkeley Square" and was distrusted as much by the Whigs as by the Tories. Chatham called for union — "for God's sake" — but the Whigs continued to be so split by faction that in 1775 they could hardly be termed an opposition. Even the most reliable methods failed to induce the Whigs to bury their differences. At a supper designed to bring about a union of the Rockinghams and the Graftons, a reserve was apparent which, Burke observed, was not dissipated even by wine circulating "briskly until the sunbeams drove us from it." [17]

In spite of their divisions, most Whigs were agreed that the colonies were the battleground upon which the fate of liberty in Great Britain, and indeed in the world, would be decided. The frontier of English freedom seemed to them to lie in America; "The liberties of America and Great Britain," exclaimed Lord John Cavendish, will be "buried in one grave" — or endure forever.[18] If "government à la Prusse" was established in America, Englishmen would soon hold their liberties only at the pleasure of the Crown. The Whig lords viewed the struggle in the colonies chiefly as a reflection of their traditional contest with the Crown: in their eyes the issue was whether or not free men could successfully resist a monarchy bent upon establishing despotism both in England and in the colonies.

But for all their good will, they were troubled by the thought that the Americans, in their struggle for liberty, might be seeking too much liberty — that "democratic anarchy" was spreading over the colonies and threatening the established order in Great Britain itself. As supporters of parliamentary sovereignty, moreover, they winced under the charge that they were abetting the leveling of "all parliamentary authority at the abject feet of an American banditti." [19] Even Charles James Fox was so sharply stung by this accusation that he pleaded for a distinction between "a friend to revolted America, and a friend to Hancock and Adams." The Whigs

---

[17] *Correspondence of Edmund Burke*, I, 378. *Fitzmaurice*, I, 411. *Memoirs of the Marquis of Rockingham*, II, 194.

[18] *Parliamentary History*, XVIII, 889.

[19] *Gazetteer and New Daily Advertiser*, February 3, 1775. *Memoirs of the Marquis of Rockingham*, II, 242.

defended themselves against the reproach that they were fostering democracy by the moderation of their proposals for reform in England itself. They were careful to stop reform short of interference with the corrupt boroughs they controlled; even Chatham maintained that the rotten boroughs "must be considered as the natural infirmity of the constitution. Like the infirmities of the body, we must bear them with patience, and submit to carry them around with us. The limb is mortified, but amputation might be death." [20] Indeed, they could stomach nothing stronger in the way of reform than Burke's plan of "oeconomical reform" which left the real abuses untouched.

To many Whigs — most notably Chatham — the paramount value of the empire was the strength it gave Great Britain in its life-and-death struggle with Bourbon France. France, Chatham exclaimed, was the eternal enemy; and instead of quarreling with her colonies, England ought to be girding its loins for the next war. An empire of free men, he believed, was more likely to be victorious over France than an empire of sullen, tax-ridden subjects: "Can it be expected that Englishmen will unite heartily in the defence of a government, by which they feel themselves insulted and oppressed?" he demanded. "Restore them to their rights; that is the true way to make them unanimous." Chatham and his devoted follower, Shelburne, predicted that the loss of the American colonies would leave Great Britain an easy prey to a revengeful France. "The sun of Great Britain is set," exclaimed Shelburne, "and we shall no longer be a powerful or respectable people, the moment that the independency of America is agreed to by our government!" [21]

Few of the Whigs had any heart in a war to crush the best customers of English merchants and manufacturers. They regarded the struggle as "that kind of war in which even victory may ruin us"; [22] Englishmen might gain "the dazzling Name of Sovereigns of America" but English merchants and manufacturers would have only red ink on their ledgers. Wars against France and Spain offered prospect of commercial gain — the destruction of European manufactures, the enlargement of the market for British goods, and the conquest of territory — and hence were popular among British merchants.

[20] *Parliamentary History*, XVI, 735; XIX, 646.
[21] *Ibid.*, XVIII, 959; XIX, 850–851. *St. James's Chronicle*, November 15, 1774. *Pitt Correspondence*, IV, 15–16.
[22] *St. James's Chronicle*, June 21, 1774.

But the American war was not one in which businessmen could rejoice: it was "like a family quarrel, where every one flying to law, the whole estate becomes lost in the contest." Shelburne declared that "the commerce of America is the vital stream of this great empire." "You have not a loom nor an Anvil but what is stamped with America," exclaimed Colonel Barré: "it is the main prop of your trade," yet it was to be destroyed in order that the mother country might be spared the humiliation of conciliating her oppressed subject.[23] It would have been far more profitable, said Horace Walpole, for England to have gone on "robbing the Indies" than to have meddled with America where there was nothing to gain and everything to lose. The proper epitaph for the British Empire, suggested the Whigs, ought to be: "I was well, I would be better, I took Physick and died." [24]

Would the Whigs, had they been in power, have been able to preserve the British Empire? Probably no Whig administration called to office after a decade of the misrule of George III and his ministers could have averted the debacle; yet had the Whigs been in power continuously from 1763 to 1776, they might have avoided raising a tempest in the colonies. They were content with the old commercial empire which, while restricting the colonists' economic liberties, tolerated their political rights; and they distrusted the newfangled imperialism of George III. As spokesmen of the business interests of Great Britain, they were disposed to regard the colonists primarily as customers of the mother country. Nothing was to be gained, in their opinion, by dragooning Americans; it was far better that they bought English merchandise of their own free will than at the point of a bayonet. They preferred to extract the colonists' money by means of the old reliable method of commercial monopoly. In view of the vital role normally played by the American colonies in British prosperity, they believed that the British government ought to keep Americans quiet and happy while the merchants and manufacturers went about their business of garnering the wealth of the colonies. "A Shop-keeper will never get the more Custom by beating his Customers," they pointed out: "and what is true of a Shop-keeper, is true of a *Shop-keeping* Nation." Why, asked the Whigs, should Great Britain seek from Americans

[23] *Parliamentary History*, XVII, 1179. *New York Gazette and Weekly Mercury*, March 18, 1776.

[24] David Hartley to Benjamin Franklin, November 29, 1774, Franklin MSS., American Philosophical Society.

"a pitiful Pittance in the Form of a Tax, while we may, with a Good-Will, obtain Millions on Millions by fair Commerce?" In their eyes, the colonists were sheep "not worth shearing" except by British merchants; if politicians attempted to wield the shears they would only "raise a cursed outcry & get but little wool." [25] For this reason, Burke urged that the right of taxing the colonies be held in abeyance and used only in the last resort to coerce them when they proved recalcitrant to the exercise of British authority.

The English Whigs were as firm upholders as were the King's friends of the Declaratory Act and the Acts of Trade and Navigation by which the economic subordination of the American colonies was ensured. With the exception of Chatham and Lord Camden, Whigs and Tories held similar views as to the constitutional position of the colonies; it seemed to both that, if Parliament renounced the right of taxing the colonies, "every principle of unity and subordination in the empire" would be destroyed. As late as 1778, Charles James Fox pronounced the Declaratory Act to be "a wise and necessary measure." The Whigs heartily endorsed the principle that "trying to lessen the power of the House of Commons is always lessening liberty"; and they were determined to maintain the rights of Parliament against all attack — whether from the King or the American colonists. They proposed to defend liberty by strengthening Parliament and weakening the prerogative: "Restore the parliament to its native dignity," Burke exclaimed, "and you will then restore peace in America." [26] Perhaps even some Whigs would have been little averse to parliamentary taxation of the colonies had they not feared that the revenue would pass into the hands of the Crown and be used to make the King despotic throughout the empire.

Despite the similarity of the views of the Whigs and Tories respecting the rights of Great Britain over the colonies, it by no means follows that they would have adopted the same colonial policy. Had the faction led by Rockingham and Burke been kept in power, they would have striven to keep the question of principle and fundamental rights out of the dispute and probably would not have played into the hands of colonial radicals as did the ministers of George III. Nor would they have shown so little concern for

[25] *Ibid. Public Advertiser*, January 15, 1770. Tucker, *Four Tracts*, 140.
[26] Cavendish, II, 15, 16–18, 22. *Memoirs of the Marquis of Rockingham*, II, 133. *Correspondence of Edmund Burke*, I, 323; II, 31, 50, 77. *Parliamentary History*, XVIII, 262, 648.

the sensibilities of the colonists as to lead them to believe that they were to be stripped of all their liberties. The Duke of Grafton, an ardent patron of the turf, as were most of Whig peers, declared that the American colonies were like "a generous steed, who had become a little restive, but might, by the experienced *manège* of a good horseman, be easily brought to a gentle obedience; but when whipped, spurred, and harrassed [sic], by a giddy, wanton rider, became insolent of controul, and disdained the reins." [27] The Whigs, then, would have treated the colonies as a high-spirited race horse; the King and his friends fell into the error of treating them like a beast of burden.

A knowledge of horseflesh, however valuable on the race track, did not particularly qualify the Whigs to undertake the management of a great empire. Burke once said that the colonists must be appeased "by the removal of every cause of discontent. This is the only magic, the only charm, which can draw their affection, which can cement and unite the different members of the empire, and make it act as if inspired by one soul." [28] Neither Burke nor his fellow Whigs were prepared to remove fundamental economic grievances and it may be doubted whether they were capable of meeting the problems of an expanding empire. Sooner or later, the Whigs' refusal to recognize the coming of age of the colonies and their insistence upon maintaining the sovereignty of Parliament in all cases whatsoever would have brought them into conflict with the Americans. George III and his ministers precipitated the Revolution; but the colonial policy of the Whigs was no guarantee that it could have been long averted.[29]

II

MEANWHILE, in the colonies, events were shaping toward invasion of Canada by the American army. The Continental Congress,

[27] *Parliamentary History*, XIX, 806.
[28] *Pennsylvania Gazette*, February 7, 1770.
[29] Namier, 45. G. H. Guttridge, *English Whiggism and the American Revolution*, University of California Publications in History, XXVIII, Berkeley, 1942, 138–144.

recognizing that its most powerful weapon was its pen, set out to bring Canada into the continental union by means of letter writing. But even the most expert phrase turners might well have found themselves at a loss in addressing the Canadians. The colonists had been calling the Canadians "Papists" and "slaves" who, in league with the Indians, would drench the frontier in blood at the command of the British Ministry. It was necessary to make a complete about-face; and Congress executed this maneuver with skill and spirit in its "Address to the Citizens of Quebec" of 1774. Religious toleration was now declared to be a characteristic of men struggling for liberty: "The transcendent nature of freedom, elevates those, who unite in her cause, above all such low-minded infirmities" as bigotry. But Congress cheerfully gave the lie to this principle by declaring in its "Letter to the People of Great Britain" that Roman Catholicism was a religion "that has deluged your island in blood and dispersed impiety, bigotry, persecution, murder, and rebellion through every part of the world." Nevertheless, a warm welcome was assured the Roman Catholic Canadians if they saw fit to unite with the Protestant colonies in a perpetual "social compact, formed on the generous principles of equal liberty" and send delegates to the Continental Congress.[30]

This appeal fell upon barren soil. The Canadians were reluctant to fling themselves into the arms of the Pope haters to the south and their chief grievances against the British government had been removed by the Quebec Act. In 1775 Congress made another attempt to win their support with a letter addressed to "The Oppressed Inhabitants of Canada," in which the Quebec Act was declared to be an intolerable grievance to the Canadians themselves inasmuch as it placed them at the mercy of the British Parliament. There was, however, a note of menace in this message to the Canadians: "As our concern for your welfare entitles us to your friendship," Congress said, "we presume you will not by doing us injury, reduce us to the disagreeable necessity of treating you as enemies." [31] One thousand copies were printed for distribution among the Canadians and Congress anxiously awaited the results of this leaflet raid.

But the Canadians, instead of raising rebellion, continued to raise wheat which they shipped to the West Indies, where there was no

[30] *Journals of the Continental Congress*, I, 106, 112, 113.
[31] *Ibid.*, II, 68, 70.

prejudice against "popish wheat." Thereby they helped to nullify the effect of the Continental Association. It was clear that liberty had to be carried by force of arms to the benighted Canadians. By a vote of six colonies to five, in October 1775 the Continental Congress determined upon an invasion of Canada and thus revealed that the colonies were "not only in a defensive Opposition, but driven to the Extremity of an offensive War." [32]

The chief interest of Americans in Canada was strategic. In May 1775, when Crown Point and Ticonderoga fell to the colonists' surprise attack, Congress determined to retain these strongly fortified positions, justifying its action on the ground that because the British were planning to attack through Canada, the colonies must hold the Hudson River–Lake Champlain waterway. It was merely another step to declare that Americans ought to possess themselves of Canada to prevent the British from using it as a springboard for an invasion of the colonies. With a British army firmly established in Canada, said Robert Morris, "they will soon raise a Nest of Hornets on our backs that will sting us to the quick"; and Richard Henry Lee pointed out that Canada and New York were "the openings thro which America may, by able fencers, receive the worst wounds." [33]

These strategical necessities were clothed in the loftiest idealism by the American patriots in undertaking the conquest of Canada. John Hancock, the president of Congress, declared that American arms would "open a Way for Blessings of Liberty, and the Happiness of well-ordered Government to visit that extensive Dominion." "There was benevolence in the whole plan of this expedition," it was said; the only purpose of Americans was to "kindle up the expiring lamp of liberty among them, to open their eyes to its divine effulgence." Canada and Nova Scotia must be brought into the continental union by force if necessary because "they cannot be happy without being so." [34] Some Americans saw other advantages in the conquest of Canada, the chief being that its loss would give "the *coup de grâce* to the hellish junto" that ruled Great Britain and

[32] *Thomas Wharton to Samuel Wharton*, October 3, 1775, P.R.O., C.O. 5, 134 LC. Seabury, *A View of the Controversy*, 30.

[33] *Letters of Members of the Continental Congress*, I, 416. *Letters of Richard Henry Lee*, I, 168.

[34] *The Lee Papers*, I, 217, 220, 314. Horace W. Smith, *The Life and Correspondence of the Reverend William Smith*, Philadelphia, 1879, I, 554–555. *Letters of Members of the Continental Congress*, I, 263.

open the way for new men and new measures. It also promised to strike at the King himself, for Canada was believed to be dearer to him "than all the other Colonies put together, as it is the only part of the British Empire in which arbitrary power is established by law." [35]

The invasion of Canada revealed to the mother country that no time could be lost in crushing the rebellion. Englishmen now recognized that they were dealing with incendiaries who were seeking to set the empire afire in every hemisphere. From Congress came letters to Canadians and Englishmen urging them to throw off their chains; the next step, exclaimed an alarmed Briton, would be an address to the inhabitants of Bengal telling them to rise up in rebellion against Great Britain because they were denied English liberties. Ireland had been marked out for ruin by Congress when it forbade the sending of flaxseed to that kingdom. Thus Ireland was yet "another victim, devoted by the Congress to the infernal Gods, to render them propitious to sedition and rebellion." It seemed unlikely that Congress would be content until the Irish had risen "to *dethrone* the King, kill Lord North, and *blow up* the parliament." [36]

Thus far, the radical policy of relying mainly upon events to bring the issue of independence before the people was fully vindicated. Disillusionment with English liberalism was widespread; "measures short of war" had been discredited; and the United Colonies had undertaken an armed invasion of part of the British Empire. And there were other evidences that Americans were moving steadily in the direction of independence even though they failed to read the signposts.

The Continental Congress was taking long strides in that direction as it strove to prepare the colonies for the inevitable struggle with Great Britain. On July 15, Congress resolved to relax the Association to permit the importation of military supplies; and in September a secret committee was appointed to take charge of the importation of powder and munitions. In August 1775, Congress rejected Lord North's conciliatory plan. In November, news was received that no answer would be given the "Olive Branch" petition, and the King's proclamation declaring the American colonies

[35] *New York Journal or General Advertiser*, March 7, 1776.
[36] Seabury, *A View of the Controversy*, 28-29. *The Address of the People of Great Britain to the Inhabitants of America*, London, 1775, 52.

in a state of rebellion reached Philadelphia. Congress responded by creating the Committee of Secret Correspondence, later known as the Committee for Foreign Affairs; and in December authorization was given for the construction of an American navy. At the same time, the first steps were taken toward creating independent governments in the colonies: Congress advised both New Hampshire and South Carolina, in the autumn of 1775, to establish governments for the duration of the struggle with Great Britain.

These measures clearly looked toward independence, yet the radicals in the Continental Congress hesitated to pronounce that dread word. They were well aware that the majority of the American people still aspired only to restore colonial liberty under the British Crown. The colonists had been led to believe that their rights could be maintained within the empire; indeed, from 1765 to 1775 the revolutionary movement drew much of its strength from this source. It was apparent even to the extremists that a demand for outright independence would be summarily rejected by the people; only the limited objective of liberty within the empire was acceptable to the masses. No doubt Sam Adams would joyfully have cut the knot between Great Britain and the colonies, but Adams was not typical of the state of mind of American patriots before 1776; and the conservatism of the general public obliged even Adams to champion, at least outwardly, the reform of the empire rather than its dissolution. Independence was termed "a tree of forbidden and accursed fruit, which, if any Colony on this continent should be so mad as to attempt reaching, the rest would have virtue and wisdom enough to draw their swords and hew the traitors into submission, if not into loyalty." [37] In 1770, George Mason of Virginia declared that "there are not five men of sense in America who would accept of independence if it were offered; we know our circumstances too well; we know that our own happiness, our very being, depend upon our being connected with our Mother Country." [38] In 1774 John Adams was complaining that independence was "a Hobgoblin of so frightful Mien, that it would throw a delicate Person into Fits to look it in the Face." Thomas Jefferson said that he would "rather be in dependence on Great

---

[37] *Memoirs of the Historical Society of Pennsylvania*, Philadelphia, 1895, XIV, 491. *Massachusetts Spy*, July 7, 1774. *Letters of Members of the Continental Congress*, I, 406.

[38] *The Virginia Magazine of History and Biography*, January 1934. XLII, 14.

Britain, properly limited, than on any other nation on earth, or than on no nation." [39] But it is significant that he added that rather than submit to taxation by Parliament, he would help sink Great Britain in the Atlantic.

The Tories and conservative Whigs recognized that one of the most deadly weapons in their arsenal of propaganda was the charge that the Continental Congress aimed at independence of the mother country. The radicals therefore moved warily when they reached this dangerous ground, fearful lest a false step plummet them into the quicksand. It was, they insisted, a "Tory trick" to suggest that Congress planned to make the colonies independent. Tories found that "to Hint that the Congress had any thoughts of independency, would endanger a man's life." [40] A few months later, a man's life was equally endangered by denying the necessity of independence.

Nevertheless, it is evident that the radicals, in their reluctance to speak boldly for independence, were overplaying their hand. There could no longer be any doubt of the determination of the British government to crush the rebellion: thirty thousand troops and three major generals had been sent to America and it was rumored that the British government was scouring Europe for mercenaries to hurl against the colonists. Still, the politicians and propagandists failed to rise to the occasion. When confronted with the necessity of declaring independence, their ink turned to water. They were too fearful of offending public opinion; too disposed to trust that events would teach the people the need of independence; too reluctant to act without the certainty of support by the majority. And while they hesitated, the hope of reconciliation was sapping the strength of the revolutionary movement.

There could be little question that the most formidable obstacle to independence had been created by the patriots themselves. In fabricating the myth of George III as a benevolent monarch of stainless soul American propagandists now found that they had wrought too well: the King had become a heroic figure revered by thousands of loyal subjects in British America who fondly expected him to rescue the empire by casting out his wicked ministers and restoring to the colonies their rights and privileges. The King, it is true, had not gone entirely unscathed in the passage at arms

[39] *The Works of Thomas Jefferson*, I, 135.
[40] *New York Journal or General Advertiser*, January 5, 1775, Supplement. Charles Inglis, *Letters of Papinian*, New York, 1779, 52.

between the mother country and colonies, but his prestige had not been seriously impaired. One puritanical patriot, for example, found fault with the King because he attended the theater. "I think his Majesty had no manner of business at the play house," he remarked, "but had been much better in his closet, praying and contriving good answers to the just petitions of America, London and Middlesex." [41] There was a more serious outburst against the King when he gave his approval to the Quebec Act, but it was still the "Pimps and Parasites" who advised him that were held responsible rather than George III himself.[42] Even after the battle of Lexington, George Washington and many other Americans continued to call the British troops the "ministerial troops" and some even spoke of colonial soldiers as "the King's troops." [43] So long as Americans attempted to preserve their liberty within the empire, George was their fairest hope. Before independence could be declared, colonial propagandists had to undo their work and reveal George III in his true colors.

But this in 1775 the colonial patriots found themselves unable to do. Even the most vitriolic pens ran dry when the conduct of the King was brought up for review; beyond a few pinpricks, George suffered little at the hands of his subjects overseas. It was as though American patriots could not bring themselves to demolish their own handiwork. It was fitting, therefore, that the first onslaught upon the King should have been made by Tom Paine — a man who had taken no part in creating the mythical figure of George III.

To Tom Paine, in 1775, the crisis called for bold and immediate action. Although he had been in the colonies for only two years, Paine had tasted the bitter dregs of British "tyranny"; he needed no American to tell him of oppression. As an excise officer in Great Britain, Paine found his salary intolerably inadequate; but when he attempted to organize the excise officers to win a raise in pay, he was dismissed from the service. Branded as an agitator, he came to America in 1774 bearing a letter of introduction from Benjamin Franklin. Never a man to temporize, Paine concluded that the patriots had carried caution too far; by refusing to face the in-

[41] *New York Gazette and Weekly Post Boy*, October 9, 1769.

[42] *Massachusetts Spy*, October 20, 1774. *Collections of the Massachusetts Historical Society*, Fifth Series, Boston, 1888, X, 292. *American Archives*, Fourth Series, II, 369, 429.

[43] *The Writings of George Washington*, III, 486. *The Remembrancer*, London, 1775, Second Edition, 42.

evitable, and speak bluntly to the American people, they were giving the British government an opportunity to nip the rebellion in the bud. " 'Tis not in the power of Britain or of Europe to conquer America," he exclaimed, "if she doth not conquer herself by *delay* and *timidity*." America, he said, had neither "an object or a system" and was "fighting, she scarcely knew for what, and which, if she could have obtained, would have done her no good." [44] As long as Americans deluded themselves with the hope that they could be free and yet remain British subjects, Paine believed that the cause of liberty was doomed. While Americans told each other fairy stories of "Good King George" who would save them at the last moment from the dragon, George was preparing to turn the dragon upon them — Paine, indeed, believed that George III *was* the dragon. The only choice open to Americans, as Paine saw it, was between slavery and independence; nor did he believe that they could defend their liberties by measures short of war. The dispute was no longer one of words or of constitutional principles; the British themselves had decided upon war; and unless Americans hardened themselves to face bullets and cold steel, they had better make the best of slavery. To inspire Americans to fight against the country they had regarded as home — to overcome their squeamishness at killing men whom they called their cousins — it was necessary, Paine judged, to give them something to fight for. That could be only independence. The time for decisive action had come; the floodgates of propaganda must be opened; and the people, hesitating upon the brink of revolution, must be shown what happiness and prosperity awaited them when once they had leaped and found safety.

[44] *Deane Papers*, IV, 93.

CHAPTER   TWENTY

The Declaration of
Independence

In CONGRESS, July 4, 1776.

WITH the publication of *Common Sense* in January 1776, Tom Paine broke the ice that was slowly congealing the revolutionary movement. He called boldly for a declaration of independence on the ground that the events of the nineteenth of April, 1775, had put an end to all possibility of permanent reconciliation. By its own act, he argued, Britain had become an open enemy and no American could hereafter "love, honor, and faithfully serve the power that hath carried fire and sword into the land." But there was good even in the evil wrought by British imperialists: it had hastened the dissolution of a union between England and America which Paine regarded as "repugnant to reason, to the universal order of things; to all examples from former ages." [1] Nature herself had decreed the separation; and Paine urged Americans, instead of whining after the British connection, to accept their destiny by thundering across the Atlantic a declaration of independence that would shake the throne itself.

Common Sense was epochal not merely because it placed the issue of independence for the first time squarely before the American people. It marked as well the first vigorous attack upon the King — the strongest bond of union yet remaining in the British Empire — and likewise the first appeal for an American Republic. One of Paine's principal arguments for independence was that the King was a "hardened, sullen-tempered Pharaoh," "the Royal Brute of Great Britain" whose determination to extirpate liberty throughout his dominions made it impossible for free Americans to remain within the empire.[2] He opened the eyes of thousands of Americans to the realities of British politics. He demolished in *Common Sense* the fiction that there was a distinction between the King and the Ministry and between the King and Parliament. The King, he de-

---

[1] *Selections from the Works of Thomas Paine*, edited by A. W. Peach, New York, 1928, 23.

[2] *Ibid.*, 25.

clared, had joined forces with Parliament in order to strip Americans of their freedom; far from being in the clutches of wicked ministers, George had made the Ministry his cat's-paw. By means of pensions and places, the King had made himself master of the state: "Wherefore, tho' we have been wise enough to shut and lock a door against absolute Monarchy, we at the same time have been foolish enough to put the Crown in possession of the key." [3] As a result, the Crown had "engrossed the Commons" and had so effectively destroyed the only parts of the British Constitution worth preserving that England was hardly better than a European despotism.

After the publication of *Common Sense*, the hottest blasts of patriot propaganda were directed against the King, and the full iniquity of George III was exposed to Americans who had only recently revered him as the best of kings. He was denounced as the evil genius of the British Empire: every oppression perpetrated by the British government during his reign was suddenly laid at his door. The kindest word that could be said for George was that he was either a fool or a villain — "In either case," it was added, "he is no good King." [4] After *Common Sense*, the doctrine of ministerial responsibility — by which Americans had repeatedly saved the King's face — was discredited: the "Royal criminal," it was said, could no longer hide behind the skirts of his ministers; he was revealed as the true malefactor and "the influence of bad Ministers is no better apology for these measures, than the influence of bad company is for a murderer, who expiates his crimes under a gallows." [5] He was denounced as "our damn'd Tyrant of St. James's — a full blooded Nero," and it was said that nurses would soon frighten children into obedience by telling them that "the King will fetch 'em away." [6]

Thus George III became the incarnation of evil as previously he had been the embodiment of every virtue. Both views were distortions: Americans never had a proper perspective of their hapless sovereign. He was neither an innocent young man misled by wicked ministers nor a cunning tyrant determined to stamp out every vestige of liberty in the empire. George III belongs neither

---

[3] *Ibid.*, 8.
[4] *New York Journal or General Advertiser*, January 25, 1776.
[5] *American Archives*, Fourth Series, V, 129, 181.
[6] *Pennsylvania Evening Post*, June 13, 1776. *The Lee Papers*, I, 214.

among the angels nor among the devils: he was rather the incarnation of the average rural Englishman of his day. The most just criticism that may be made of his policy is that it never rose above the level of the country gentlemen of England. If his leadership was not inspired, it was at least founded upon the solid rock of British prejudice. Instead of resisting public opinion, he permitted himself to be carried along by it. But in this critical period of the British Empire what was needed was not a spokesman of the lesser squirearchy but the leadership of a man of imperial vision who rose above the prejudices that hemmed in the mind of the majority of Englishmen. Had George III possessed such vision, he might have saved the British Empire. He lost the empire not so much because he was a tyrant as because his outlook was that of the great majority of his subjects: narrow, insular, and contemptuous of "colonists."

Paine did more than smash the oversized statue of George III: he ripped up monarchy root and branch by pronouncing it to be a form of government condemned by the Almighty and by right reason. He traced the origin of kings to robber barons who owed their rise to "savage manners or pre-eminence in subtility"; and the rule of men who excelled in craft or guile was not, Paine contended, fit for free Americans.[7] Before *Common Sense*, Americans had professed to reverence the British Constitution and had declared that they were defending their own liberties and the rights of the King against the usurpations of Parliament. But Paine's attack upon the principle of monarchism struck at the very foundations of the British Constitution and largely destroyed its sanctity in the eyes of Americans. Its abuses and shortcomings were now laid bare in order to persuade the colonists of the necessity of independence; the beauties which Americans had once beheld in it withered under the blasts of Tom Paine and his fellow propagandists. The British Constitution, it was now said, "gives to some to wallow in luxury to destroy themselves, and forces the greater part to live in poverty. And hence innumerable robberies and executions, which have scarce made their appearance in the Colonies, except imported from the *British* Constitution." It was nothing more than an instrument to make easier the exploitation of the poor by the rich; and it made legislators of men who, "brought up in luxury, pride and ambition,"

[7] *Selections from the Works of Thomas Paine*, 13.

knew nothing of law and right but were expert in tyrannizing over their fellow men.[8]

Common Sense, published anonymously, was at first supposed to be the work of one of the radical leaders in the Continental Congress. Horrified conservatives exclaimed that these extremists had at last shown themselves in their true colors as rebels and republicans. The pamphlet was an alarm bell to all friends of the empire and foes of democracy to unite in resisting the radicals in Congress; those "People of Sense & Property, who before would not believe that there were any Persons of Consequence, either in or out of the Congress, who harboured such Intentions" could no longer doubt the worst when they opened the pages of *Common Sense.* In the long history of seditious literature, declared a Tory, there was hardly a more "artful, insidious, and pernicious" work than this: "I find no COMMON SENSE in this pamphlet, but much UNCOMMON phrenzy," he observed. In the eyes of many outraged readers, it seemed nothing more nor less than an invitation to Americans to imitate "the conduct of a rash, forward stripling, who should call his mother a d——m——d b——ch, swear he had no relation to her, and attempt to knock her down." [9]

Half a dozen Tories and conservative Whigs dived into their closets and emerged with answers to *Common Sense* which, they flattered themselves, proved that Paine was guilty of "declamations against the English constitution that would disgrace a school-boy." Rather than follow Paine down "the dark and untrodden way of Independence and Republicanism," these authors urged Americans to look back to the happy state they were leaving: the bounties, protection, and security afforded by the British Empire and the liberties guaranteed by the British Constitution which made America "the happiest country in the universe." [10] They pointed out that it was still easy to get rich in America and that the common people enjoyed the highest standard of living of any in the world. All these solid advantages would be sacrificed if Americans ran

[8] *American Archives,* Fourth Series, V, 854.

[9] Charles Inglis, *The True Interest of America Impartially Stated,* Philadelphia, 1776, v, vi, preface; 21, 39. *Documents relative to the Colonial History of the State of New Jersey,* New Series, X, 708.

[10] Jonathan Sewall, "A Cure for the Spleen," *Magazine of History,* 1922, 14. Jonathan Boucher, *A Letter from a Virginian to the Members of Congress,* Boston, 1774, 30.

after the will-o'-the-wisp of independence. Deluded by "romantic notions of conquest and empire, ere things are ripe," the Tories predicted that the radicals would destroy the glorious promise of America and put in its stead "Ruin, Horror, and Desolation." [11] They warned that the colonies were not prepared to fight Great Britain: it was a struggle against overwhelming odds which could terminate only in the loss by Americans of all their liberties. The colonies were disunited; they were weakened by controversies over boundaries; and they were unable to create a confederation — therefore, said conservatives, it was idle to talk of resisting British armies. Thus, although the conservatives produced no *Common Sense* of their own, they effectively presented the case against independence to all who would pause and read. They quickly learned, however, that "there is a fascination belonging to the word *Liberty* that beguiles the minds of the vulgar beyond the power of antidote." [12]

The Tories rightly pointed out that Paine was shifting the ground of the dispute between mother country and colonies. The professed purpose of Americans had hitherto been to find "a safe, honourable, and lasting reconciliation with Great Britain"; in beating the drum for independence and republicanism, Paine was flying in the face of all the declarations of the Continental Congress and the colonial assemblies. [13] Unquestionably, the demand for independence represented a revolutionary change in American ideology. For over a decade, Americans had been told that their task was to preserve liberty in the British Empire: England as well as America was to be saved from tyranny. America's destiny, it had been said, was "to arrest the hand of tyranny, and to save even Britannia from shakles." [14] Independence was a retreat from this lofty conception of America's purpose. England — "that rotten old state" — must be left to its fate; beginning as a struggle to make the British Empire safe for liberty, the American revolutionary movement was now diverted into an effort to save liberty in America alone. Instead of acting as a spearhead in the battle for freedom, America became a refuge for "all noble spirits and sons of liberty from all parts

[11] William Smith, *Plain Truth*, Philadelphia, 1776, 7. Inglis, *The True Interest of America Impartially Stated*, 71.

[12] *Colonial Records of North Carolina*, X, 265.

[13] *Pennsylvania Gazette*, February 28, 1776. *Pennsylvania Packet*, March 11, 1776.

[14] *Colonial Records of North Carolina*, X, 51.

of the world." "Hither they may retire from every land of oppression," exclaimed a colonist; "here they may expand and exult; here they may enjoy all the blessings which this terraqueous globe can afford to fallen men." [15]

Americans had been prepared for *Common Sense* by the steady progress of reaction in Europe. With deep misgivings, they had watched liberty in Europe snuffed out. Corsica, after a brave struggle for freedom, had fallen to the French; Poland was being partitioned by its rapacious neighbors; Sweden had become a despotism; and everywhere tyranny seemed in the ascendancy. "The passion of despotism raging a plague, for about seven years past," exclaimed John Dickinson, "has spread with unusual malignity through Europe," until liberty had "by a damn'd conspiracy of Kings and Ministers been totally driven from the other Hemisphere." [16] The extinction of liberty in Europe taught Americans that tyranny, if it were to be thwarted, must be resisted in its beginnings. "Those nations who are now groaning under the iron sceptre of tyranny were once free," said the Reverend Jonathan Mayhew; "so they might probably have remained, by a seasonable precaution against despotic measures. Civil tyranny is usually small in its beginning, like the drop of a bucket, till at length, like a mighty torrent, or the raging waves of the sea, it bears down all before it, and deluges whole countries and empires." [17] Such had been its course in Europe and in Great Britain itself where the Ministry, infected with the absolutism of European courts, was seeking to destroy liberty in the British Empire. England and Ireland had already fallen — only the American colonies remained free.

The conviction that the American continent was the last stronghold of liberty in a world of triumphant tyranny strengthened the resolution of Americans to defend freedom in this hemisphere. "This," exclaimed Charles Lee, "is the last asylum of persecuted liberty. Here, should the machinations and fury of her enemies prevail, that bright goddess must fly off from the face of the earth, and leave not a trace behind." "Every spot of the old world is over-run with oppression," declared Tom Paine. "Freedom hath

[15] Green, 29.
[16] *Memoirs of the Historical Society of Pennsylvania*, Philadelphia, 1895, 494. *The Lee Papers*, I, 122, 134.
[17] Thornton, 50. Charles Lee to Samuel Adams, July 21, 1774, Adams MSS., New York Public Library. *Boston Gazette*, August 8, 1774.

been hunted round the globe. Asia and Africa have long expelled her. . . . Europe regards her like a stranger, and England hath given her warning to depart. O receive the fugitive, and prepare in time an asylum for mankind." [18]

The success of *Common Sense* showed the radicals that they might safely rush in where Tom Paine had not feared to tread. They discovered that they could write the word "independence" without a quaver and that a large number of Americans could bear to look upon it. Thus fortified, they took up their pens and carried on Paine's work of cramming "wholesome truths . . . down the throats of squeamish mortals" and opening American eyes to the unpleasant reality that they must choose between slavery and independence. They were not content, however, to present independence merely as a painful necessity; on the contrary, they painted rosy pictures of the glorious future that awaited Americans after they had cast off the dead hand of Britain. The Tories emphasized the safety and security of remaining with the British Empire and the advantage of doing business within its vast protected market, but the radicals pictured the wealth that awaited Americans when the markets of the world were open to them. Free trade, it was asserted, would enable Americans to attain "a state of eminence and glory, and become the envy and admiration of mankind"; when no longer plundered by the British House of Commons and hampered by British commercial laws, they would find the riches of the world at their feet. By declaring their independence, Americans could resume the westward advance over the Alleghanies — barred now by the Proclamation of 1763 and the Quebec Act — and take possession of lands which would keep them "free from slavery and taxation to all generations." It would keep America out of Europe's wars: no longer, said Franklin, would Englishmen be able to "drag us after them in all the plundering Wars, which their desperate Circumstances, Injustices, and Rapacity, may prompt them to undertake." It would, in short, enable America to achieve her destiny of a "Great Empire" and thereby fulfill the will of God and Nature. The American continent which teemed "with patriots, heroes, and legislators, who are impatient to burst forth into light and importance," would attain its true greatness — to the delight of all "the inhabitants of Heaven" who longed to see "the

[18] *London Magazine*, London, 1775, XLIV, 516. *Selections from the Works of Thomas Paine*, 32.

ark finished, in which all the liberty and true religion of the world are to be deposited." [19]

These glowing prospects of future wealth and grandeur by no means converted all Americans to independence. The Whigs complained that "puling pusillanimous cowards" continued to spread defeatism; and probably a majority of the American people still thought in terms of reconciliation with the mother country and expected Congress to produce a plan of "permanent" union.[20] The Continental Congress was clearly split by the issues raised by *Common Sense:* "We do not treat each other with that decency and respect that was observed heretofore," lamented a member.[21] In January 1776, James Wilson moved that Congress dispel the rumors that it was aiming at separation by publicly denying any intentions of declaring independence. Although the radicals mustered their utmost strength to defeat this proposal, they were unable to do more than win a postponement of discussion. The ideas of John Dickinson, rather than those of Sam Adams, were still in the ascendancy. The disposition of the majority to allow valuable time to slip away while the British government prepared to overwhelm the colonies with military force led Sam Adams to suggest that the confederation be formed by the few resolute colonies that dared defy Great Britain and that the other colonies be left to make peace as they saw fit.

In the spring of 1776, the British government widened the breach between the opponents and advocates of independence by announcing its intention of sending commissioners to the colonies bearing peace overtures. With the murky waters of independence and republicanism rising about their feet, conservatives found in this commission a straw at which to clutch. They would have been disagreeably surprised had they known how reluctantly the British government had agreed to make this eleventh-hour attempt at reconciliation. It was only with the greatest difficulty that George III was persuaded to give his consent. "I am not so fond of the sending Commissioners to examine into the disputes," he said; "this looks so like the Mother Country being more afraid of the continuance of

---

[19] *American Archives,* Fourth Series, V, 87, 131, 213, 856. *The Writings of Benjamin Franklin,* VI, 312. David Ramsay, *The History of the American Revolution,* I, 439. *Green,* 25–26. *The Lee Papers,* I, 260, 325. *Virginia Gazette* (Purdie), March 29, 1776.

[20] *Pennsylvania Evening Post,* February 3, 1776.

[21] *Letters of Members of the Continental Congress,* I, 401.

the dispute than the Colonies and I cannot think it likely to make them reasonable; I do not want to drive them to despair but to Submission, which nothing but feeling the inconvenience of their situation can bring their pride to submit to." Although "a thorough friend to holding out the Olive Branch," George wished first to administer some wholesome and, as he suspected, long-overdue chastisement.[22] Unhappily for George's plans, the Brothers Howe — the admiral and the general, in whose ability to crush the revolt great confidence was placed — declined to undertake the subjugation of the colonies unless they were given authority to enter into peace negotiations. George yielded grudgingly to their ambition of carrying both the sword and the olive branch. They were designated as peace commissioners but, as Americans later learned, they were empowered only to accept the submission of the colonies, not to negotiate a settlement which would guarantee American liberties within the empire.

But until this fact was known, conservatives continued to urge that the question of independence be shelved until after the terms of the commission had been received by Congress. They argued so plausibly for delay that the radicals began to regard the commissioners as more dangerous to the cause of independence than the British army: they were "the wooden horse which is to take those by stratagem whom twelve years of hostility could not reduce."[23] The radicals declared that while the British government sought to confuse and disunite Americans, whole armies were being equipped "to butcher us with the utmost expedition." Those who advocated waiting for the peace terms found themselves exposed to the radicals' deadliest propaganda. They were called "timid, irresolute and double faced," traitors who opened their "mouths wide, and bawled stoutly against every vigorous measure" because they expected the commissioners' pockets to be "well lined with English guineas, patents for places, pensions and titles in abundance." In exchange for British gold, these turncoats were declared to be ready to open negotiations with "men who spill your blood with as little ceremony and reluctance, as a butcher would that of an ox."[24]

---

[22] *The Correspondence of King George the Third*, III, 156, 175.
[23] Reed, I, 173.
[24] *Pennsylvania Evening Post*, March 2, 1776. *Virginia Gazette* (Purdie), April 19, 1776. *Letters of Members of the Continental Congress*, I, 433, 502. *American Archives*, Fourth Series, V, 89, 433. James Read to Edward Shippen, May 18, 1776, Shippen MSS., Historical Society of Pennsylvania.

Had the British government pursued consistently this policy of dividing and bewildering Americans by holding out the prospect of reconciliation, the Declaration of Independence might have been postponed and the rebellion crushed. But the mother country, while holding an olive branch in one hand, brandished a sword in the other. *Common Sense* was without doubt a potent force for independence, but its effect, a patriot observed, was "trifling compared with the effects of the folly, insanity and villainy of the King and his Ministers." [25] The New England fisheries were closed; the shipment of war supplies to the colonies was forbidden; colonial trade was prohibited; and on December 22, 1775, Parliament withdrew British protection and directed the seizure and confiscation of American ships at sea. As Edmund Burke said, this legislation made England appear "like a porcupine, armed all over with acts of parliament, oppressive to trade and America." Certainly these measures helped the radicals to wean Americans from dependence upon the mother country. John Adams declared that the British government, by removing its protection from the colonies, had cast them out of the empire and made them independent "in spite of our supplications and entreaties." [26] He contended that the colonies had owed obedience to the mother country only because it protected them; now that they were no longer protected, they were not obliged to obey. The radicals insisted that to declare independence was merely to proclaim to the world the true situation in which the colonies found themselves by the act of Great Britain; the British government had itself "dissevered the dangerous tie: Execrated will he be by the latest posterity who again joins the fatal cord!" [27]

Of all the acts of "transcendent folly and wickedness" perpetrated by the British Ministry, none did more to convince Americans of the necessity of an immediate declaration of independence than the hiring of foreign mercenaries to help suppress the rebellion in the colonies. Reports were heard in the colonies early in 1776 that the British government was scouring Europe for mercenaries to employ against Americans; it was remarked that twenty thousand Russian mercenaries would be "charming visitors at New

[25] *Pennsylvania Evening Post*, March 7, 1776.
[26] *Letters of Members of the Continental Congress*, I, 406. *Parliamentary History*, XVIII, 769.
[27] *Letters of R. H. Lee*, I, 177. *Pennsylvania Evening Post*, February 3, 1776.

York and civilize that part of America wonderfully." [28] Unable to secure the services of these apostles of sweetness and light because of the refusal of Catherine the Great to permit her subjects to fight on Britain's side, the government turned to the German states for manpower, and thereby revealed to the alarmed colonists that the mother country was an "old stern, encroaching step-dame" who tried to collect all the neighborhood bullies to beat up her children. If Britain called upon Europe to help in the subjugation of the colonies, America must clearly do likewise: France must be made a counterweight to the German states and redress the balance of power upon the American continent. More than any other act of the British government, the hiring of mercenaries opened the eyes of Americans to their own peril and to the impossibility of reconciliation. The patriots declared that it was "the *finishing stroke* to dependence. The man who now talks of reconciliation and reunion, ought to be pelted with stones, by the children, when he walks the streets, as a town fool." [29] The news that Britain had called upon the German princes for aid "wrought wonders" in Philadelphia: "Conversions have been more rapid than ever under Mr. Whitefield" (the evangelist), observed a Philadelphian. Even John Dickinson's faith in the essential goodness of the mother country was momentarily shaken and he was heard to say that he saw no alternative but independence or slavery.[30]

While the British government was thus laying its hand rudely upon the "delicate Chinese vase," the friends of the empire in the colonies were losing their struggle to preserve British sovereignty. In Virginia, many members of the tidewater aristocracy arrayed themselves on the side of reconciliation. From the beginning of the dispute with Great Britain, the great planters had been alarmed by the growing power of the Western radicals allied with younger sons of the lowland families and disaffected elements of the East. The aristocracy had carried on the struggle for colonial rights for generations; but they had never sought complete independence of Great Britain nor had they contemplated an internal revolution which would snatch the reins of authority from their own hands,

[28] Keith Feiling, *The Second Tory Party*, London, 1938.
[29] David Ramsay, *The History of the American Revolution*, I, 427. *Pennsylvania Evening Post*, March 2, 1776.
[30] Edward Shippen to Jasper Yeates, January 19, 1776, Shippen MSS., Historical Society of Pennsylvania.

and even in 1776 they refused to admit that the conflict with Great Britain could be resolved only by American independence. These conservatives, said Charles Lee, were "Namby Pambys" whose "little blood has been suck'd out by musketoes"; and when they were confronted with the necessity of declaring independence, "stammer'd nonsense that wou'd have disgraced the lips of an old Midwife drunk with bohea-Tea and gin." [31] As long as the connection with Great Britain was retained, there remained hope that they would be returned to power with the aid of the royal governor; independence meant, on the other hand, the triumph of radicalism and the rule of a new class of men. Thus the fate of the old families of Virginia seemed to depend upon the continuation of the British connection; once that was severed, Pendletons, Robinsons, Randolphs, Nicholases, Blairs, and Tylers might find their estates and privileges at the mercy of their enemies. [32]

The influence of these Virginia conservatives was undermined by the acts of their friends almost as much as by their foes. Early in 1775, Lord Dunmore, the royal governor of Virginia, removed the powder stored in Williamsburg, and put it aboard a British ship. The patriots demanded its return but Dunmore refused to be moved by threats, despite the fact that he could muster only about forty men, most of them sailors, in defense of the capital. Dunmore's weakness was well known to the patriots; and Patrick Henry had little difficulty in rousing the country and encircling Williamsburg with armed men to prevent the escape of the royal governor to the man-of-war lying at York. Had Dunmore enjoyed the support of an army, fighting might have broken out in Virginia at almost the same time that the New England farmers fell upon the British at Lexington; but even bloodshed could hardly have reacted more disastrously upon the conservative cause than did Dunmore's next move. In his desperation, the royal governor summoned the Negro slaves to his standard by promising them emancipation. To Virginians, this was nothing less than a call for race war. Immediately the patriots proclaimed themselves the champions of white supremacy against the British government, which, they declared, was at the bottom of this "hellish plot." With the blessing of the British Ministry, Dunmore was said to be intriguing with

[31] Charles Lee to R. H. Lee, April 5, 1776, Lee MSS., American Philosophical Society. *The Lee Papers*, II, 3.
[32] C. H. Ambler, *Sectionalism in Virginia*, Chicago, 1910, 5, 22, 27.

the Indians to attack the frontiers and holding nightly meetings with the Negroes "for the glorious purpose of enticing them to cut their masters' throats while they are asleep." [33] The report quickly spread over the Southern colonies that British secret agents were arming slaves and Indians; and it was rumored that the King had promised that every Negro who murdered his master would receive the plantation and all the property which had belonged to his owner. The result was that panic swept the South; trouble-makers among the slaves were rounded up and patrols went through the town streets every night to enforce the strict curfew that had been clamped down on the Negroes. However groundless this alarm may have been, it weakened Southerners' loyalty to the British government, which now stood arraigned as the upholder of emancipation and black domination of the South. No government thus indicted could long retain the support of Southerners. "Hell," exclaimed a Southern patriot, "would be ashamed of such mean and more than brutal attempts to destroy us, and the devil would blush at the impudence of the man who would have the effrontery to recommend a re-union with so barbarous a government." [34]

Despite the blunders of the British government and the royal governors, the Carolina and Georgia patriots encountered a formidable obstacle to the revolutionary cause in the Western settlers and frontiersmen. The memory of the Regulators' War was still fresh and nothing had been done to remove the grievances which had led the backwoodsmen to take up arms in 1770. They feared that in joining the East against the British government they would find themselves duped by "gentlemen of fortune and ambition on the sea coast." The Southern frontier, like Nova Scotia and the West Indies, was too exposed to Indian incursions and had not yet attained sufficient self-confidence to embark upon revolution. Without British protection, the outlying settlements seemed likely to be at the mercy of the Indians. As late as March, 1774, the Georgia Assembly appealed to the Crown to dispatch more troops for the defense of the frontier. Moreover, the quietist sects — largely Ger-

---

[33] Lord Dunmore to Lord Dartmouth, May 1, 15, 1775, P.R.O., C.O. 5, 1553, Library of Congress Transcript. *Virginia Gazette* (Purdie), October 27, 1775. *American Archives*, Fourth Series, III, 10. *Newport Mercury*, July 31, 1775. *Journal of a Lady of Quality*, 199–200.
[34] *New York Gazette and Weekly Mercury*, April 1, 1776.

man in origin — abounded in the Southern back country. These German sectarians shared the Quakers' scruples regarding war; and to these religious convictions they joined a prudent apprehension of being stripped of their lands if they joined the losing side against the King. The exemption of rice from the Association was also a sore point to the Western settlers: with considerable justice, they charged that they were being asked to bear all the sacrifices of the economic struggle with Great Britain while the lowland planters enjoyed business as usual.[35]

In contrast to the Germans, the Irish (as the Scotch-Irish were known) on the frontier were hot for rebellion. Indeed, throughout the colonies it was enough for Irishmen that England was the enemy: "in a contest with Englishmen, Irishmen, like the mettlesome coursers of Phaeton, only require reigning in." When in 1774 the assembly of South Carolina asked the governor to give arms to frontiersmen to defend themselves against the Indians, he refused on the ground that Tories, Crown Officers, and even British regulars might, in the eyes of Irishmen, be regarded as better game than redskins. But, except among these Scotch-Irish, Tory propaganda made alarming headway on the Southern frontier. The Tories declared that the dispute was entirely over tea; and since frontiersmen did not drink tea, they ought not to fight the townspeople's battles. Old-wives tales that their lands had been sold secretly by the Whigs to the Indians, "who were to butcher them all on a fixed day," struck terror among the Germans, who refused to sign the Association or to take any part whatever in resisting the British government.

The Southern Whigs could not remain unconcerned by growing Tory strength in the West: the immense number of slaves, the warlike Indians on the frontier, and the open opposition of many Westerners made it doubtful that South Carolina could long resist attack by a British fleet and army. To combat the Tory propaganda and "enlighten" the Western Germans, the Charleston patriots sent William Henry Drayton to the disaffected region. He had little success, although his oratory left "the Mynheers and their

<hr />

[35] Majorie Louise Daniel, *The Revolutionary Movement in Georgia*, University of Chicago, 1927, Ph.D. Theses (1935), 3–12. *Essays in Honor of William E. Dodd* edited by Avery Craven, Chicago, 1935, 4. David Ramsay, *History of the Revolution in South Carolina*, 65. *New York Gazette and Weekly Mercury*, April 1, 1776.

Frows" with "watry Eyes." The impressionable frontiersmen were ready to shed tears for the patriot cause, but they made no move to support it. The royal governor of South Carolina too shed tears, but with better effect: he had, complained the Whigs, "found out a mode of talking over some of our Statesmen: he wheedles, & assures, & reasons, & cries like anything." Recognizing that "an argument relating to money matters most readily catches a Dutchman's ear," the Whigs refused to allow nonsubscribers to the Association to sell or trade at the Charleston stores; all German wagoners entering Charleston were obliged to carry papers proving that they had signed the Association. When even these measures proved ineffectual, the seaboard Whigs were forced to use violence to crush resistance in the interior.[36]

North Carolina, with its considerable population of Scotch (not Scotch-Irish) settlers and unreconstructed Regulators, offered the best prospects to the British government of armed Tory support. Governor Martin of North Carolina declared in 1775 that, given arms and ammunition, he could raise the royal standard in western North Carolina and hold the region against attack. Early in 1776, a British fleet and army under Clinton appeared off Cape Fear; but it was unable to make a junction with the loyalists. Before British aid could reach them the Tories were overwhelmed at Widow Moore's Creek Bridge — the first important battle between Whigs and Tories in the Revolutionary War. The captured loyalists were imprisoned and their property confiscated but many of the rank and file were fortunate enough to get off with a lecture. "I gave them a full and proper account of every thing concerning the ground of the present war," reported a Whig. "This with three or four gallons of rum, was of infinite service to our cause." [37]

Elsewhere, during the War of American Independence, Westerners generally supported the Revolution and furnished expert marksmen who laid low many a British redcoat. In Pennsylvania, the backwoodsmen, largely Scotch-Irish Presbyterians, were eager for the fray; the western part of New England became even more warlike than Boston; and the Green Mountain Boys gave an ac-

[36] Gibbes, 128-129, 135. *The South Carolina Historical and Genealogical Magazine*, 1926, XVIII, 134-135. *North Carolina History Told by Contemporaries*, edited by Hugh Lefler, Chapel Hill, 1934, 111.
[37] *Colonial Records of North Carolina*, IX, 1157, 1167, 1174. *New York Gazette and Weekly Mercury*, April 1, 1776.

count of themselves that General Burgoyne, for one, found it difficult to forget.

Meanwhile the conservative bloc in the Continental Congress remained adamant in its opposition to independence. Nevertheless, Congress adopted retaliatory measures against the British which went far toward making independence inevitable. In March 1776, Congress authorized the issuance of letters of marque and reprisal against British shipping; and in April 1776 American ports were opened to the ships of all nations except Great Britain. Moreover, patriot blood was being spilled as fighting against British armies broke out on all fronts. Canada was unsuccessfully invaded by American troops under Montgomery and Arnold; the British were forced to evacuate Boston; and American seaports were laid waste by the British navy. It was clear that the colonies were in a state of undeclared war against Great Britain both on sea and on land; and it was becoming increasingly apparent that the struggle could not be waged successfully until the royal governments which still existed in some of the colonies had been overthrown. On May 10, 1776, therefore, Congress advised the conventions and assemblies throughout America to establish governments whose authority was derived from the people instead of from the King. In the preamble to this resolution (adopted May 15), it was declared to be "necessary that the exercise of every kind of authority under the said crown should be totally suppressed." The radicals rightly believed that this measure destroyed the last formidable obstacle to a declaration of independence; all that remained was the mere formality of proclaiming the true state of the relations that had come to exist between the former colonies and Great Britain.

This would have been more apparent to Americans had they known what was going on behind the doors of Congress. Unknown to the people at large, the secret Committee of Correspondence which had been appointed to handle foreign affairs had already sent out feelers for a French alliance. On December 12, 1775, the committee asked Arthur Lee, then in London, to learn the attitude of foreign powers towards the colonies. In February 1776, there was open discussion of a foreign alliance; and in March the committee dispatched Silas Deane to sound out Vergennes, the French minister.

The radicals were in general agreed upon the necessity of foreign alliances; but they were divided over the question whether foreign alliances or a declaration of independence ought to be made first

Many patriots feared to burn the bridges behind them without having made sure of European aid. Even Patrick Henry advised caution: before declaring independence, he said, the Continental Congress ought to feel carefully "the pulse of France and Spain." [38] On the other hand, Alexander Hamilton and Richard Henry Lee argued that France was certain to support the colonies in their struggle with Great Britain if they declared their independence. France, they pointed out, burned for revenge upon Great Britain; and all Europe was so weary of British bullying that it wished "the haughty empress of the main reduced to a more humble deportment." [39] Only delay in declaring independence could wreck the prospect of a European coalition against Britain. It might require a year in which to consummiate a formal alliance with France and Spain; and during that interval British diplomacy would be given an opportunity to drive a wedge between America and her friends upon the European continent. The age was so corrupt, Richard Henry Lee warned, that European nations disposed of "Men & Countries like live stock on a farm," selling whole populations to the highest bidder. There was danger, therefore, that France and Spain might be induced to assist Great Britain to crush the American revolt in exchange for a promise of partition of the American continent. Thus, while Americans were "most dutifully whining after" the British connection and permitting their fears of independence to tie their hands, they might find that their European allies had agreed with England "to share the plunder of America." [40]

Some conservatives feared foreign alliances even more than they did a declaration of independence. Calling in the aid of foreign powers meant not only the end of all hope of maintaining the empire but the unleashing of the dogs of war upon the mother country and so making reconciliation forever impossible. Great Britain might be defeated and overrun by the Bourbons, thus destroying one of the bulwarks of freedom in the world.[41] If Great Britain were conquered, and "sunk in the vast Ocean of her own Misconduct," liberty might be overwhelmed in the New World. "Do

[38] *The Lee Papers*, II, 1–3.
[39] *Boston Evening Post*, February 3, 1776. *The Works of Alexander Hamilton*, I, 169.
[40] *Letters of R. H. Lee*, I, 177–178. *Virginia Gazette* (Purdie), March 29, 1776.
[41] Thomas Bradbury Chandler, *The Ass; or the Serpent*, Boston, 1768, preface.

ye feel no remorse for the ruin of the British empire, the scourge of tyrants, the protector of nations and our sacred religion?" asked a pamphleteer.[42] An independent America, allied with France and Spain, might fall a victim to the very powers which she had joined and become "subject to the Will of some despotic Prince, and be of less Importance than it was whilst in the Hands of the Savages." The North American continent, without British protection, would become a football of contending European powers and become "another Poland" to be divided by aggressor European states; and "mixing the virtuous cause of these Colonies with the ambitious views of France and Spain" was certain to hasten this disaster. No European despotism, above all none with colonial possessions, could be expected to assist the rise of an independent republic in the Western Hemisphere. The greatest danger to American liberty came not from Great Britain but from the Catholic, despotic powers of Europe into whose arms Americans were about to fling themselves.[43] The radicals answered that France and Spain could be trusted to withdraw from the colonies after independence had been achieved and that if Great Britain met with destruction as a result of the loss of her empire, it was her own fault. "If she is ruined," they declared, "it is because she is ripe for ruin, and God's judgments must come upon her; in which case we ought to be disunited."[44] The radicals prevailed and, as is well known, the Declaration of Independence was made before France had formally declared herself in alliance with the United States.

In the final analysis, the question of independence was decided not in the Continental Congress but in the states where the issue was threshed out in popular assemblies and meetings. Both conservatives and radicals in Congress appealed to the people outside to voice their wishes; and the people's answer had much to do with the final decision. It was soon made clear that the militant minority that was rapidly coming to dominate the states through committees and revolutionary conventions had little patience with the irresolution displayed by Congress upon the subject of independence. Congress, indeed, was in danger of finding itself left in the wake of

[42] William Smith, 105. Nicholas, 9.

[43] *Pennsylvania Gazette*, April 3, 1776. *The Address of the People of Great Britain to the Inhabitants of America*, London, 1775, 6. William Smith, 29-30. Kapp, 55.

[44] Green, 18. Edward Shippen to Jasper Yeates, January 19, 1776, Shippen MSS., Historical Society of Pennsylvania.

public opinion in some states: "The People are now ahead of you," wrote Joseph Hawley of Massachusetts to Sam Adams, "and the only way to prevent discord and dissension is to strike while the iron is hot. The Peoples blood is too Hot to admit of delays — All will be in confusion if independence is not declared immediately. The Tories take courage and Many Whiggs begin to be chagrined — the Speech in Many parts is what is our Congress about? they are *dozing* or amusing themselves or waiting to have a Treaty with Commissioners which will end in our destruction." Hawley predicted that unless Congress acted swiftly "a Great Mobb" of citizens and soldiers would descend upon Philadelphia to purge Congress and set up a dictator.[45] Virginians were so fiery in the cause, declared Elbridge Gerry, that if Congress did not want to be anticipated by them in making a declaration of independence, it would have to send some Congressmen to Virginia to throw cold water on these red-hot patriots. New Englanders were heard to say, "We must rebel some time or other, and we had better rebel now than at any time to come; if we put it off for ten or twenty years, and let them go on as they have begun, they will get a strong Party among us, and plague us a great deal more than they can now." [46] Time, in other words, seemed to be on the side of the British government and despotism.

A declaration of independence was believed essential to stamping out the growing Tory menace. Although the Tories had begun to flee in 1775 and America seemed in "a fair way of being disgorged of all those filthy, grovelling vermin," those that remained took courage from the divided counsels of the Whigs.[47] Some of them so far recovered from their terror as to grow saucy toward the patriots and taunted them with the charge that they feared to call down the wrath of Great Britain by declaring independence. Early in 1776, General Charles Lee ordered the Tories on Long Island to swear an oath to take up arms if called upon by Congress. Isaac Sears was dispatched to administer the oaths. He met with considerable opposition, however, and reported that when he "tendered the oath to four of the grate Torries," they swallowed it "as hard

[45] Joseph Hawley to Samuel Adams, April 1, 1776, Adams MSS., New York Public Library.

[46] *Old Family Letters*, edited by Alexander Biddle, Philadelphia, 1892, 140. *Letters of Members of the Continental Congress*, I, 438. *The Lee Papers*, I, 380, 426.

[47] *Virginia Gazette* (Purdie), September 22, 1775.

as if it was a four pound shot, that they were trying to git down." [48]
Lee was reprimanded by Congress for exceeding his authority and
the Tories took new heart, which served to confirm the radicals'
opinion that a declaration of independence was the only way of
giving "that many headed Monster the Tory Faction" a fatal wound
by confiscating the estates of wealthy loyalists. It was observed that
the Tories, recognizing this danger, hung their heads at the mention
of independence. "I wish," said a New Englander, "it may not be
long before some are hung by them." [49]

From a mere handful of "oligarchs" in 1765, the Tories had become a powerful minority that included members of all ranks and
classes but was particularly well represented in the Northern colonies by the upper class of merchants, landowners, and lawyers. Not
all Tories were aristocrats; nor were all Whigs "Ragamuffins"; yet
a large proportion of the gentry north of Mason and Dixon's line
were openly Tories or secret sympathizers with the mother country.
Among the upper class, Toryism came dangerously near being
fashionable. In New York City, for example, of the 102 members
of the New York Chamber of Commerce, 54 were Tories, 17 were
neutral, and 21 were Whigs. In New Jersey, eight out of twelve
members of the Council were Tories, as were many of the wealthy
merchants and landowners. When the Tories left Boston, it appeared as though the Harvard alumni were pulling up stakes in
a body. In Virginia, on the other hand, the aristocrats were staunchly
Whig and the Tories were chiefly the Scotch factors and merchants of Norfolk. And in the Carolinas, Toryism flourished largely
in the western counties where frontiersmen took the side of King
and Parliament against the eastern Whigs. [50]

The Tories who were driven into exile were a mere handful
in comparison to the multitude of trimmers and timid souls who
found discretion wiser than active opposition to the Whigs. These
fair-weather Tories were outwardly Whigs until the approach
of a British army made the countryside safe for Toryism. New
York and Pennsylvania harbored so many hot-and-cold Tories that
John Adams declared that "if New England on one side and Virginia on the other had not kept them in awe, they would have

[48] The Lee Papers, I, 359.
[49] Richard Derby, Junior, to Samuel Adams, January 19, 1775, Adams MSS.
[50] Quarterly Journal of the New York State Historical Association, October
1932, XIII, 378.

joined the British." [51] During the early period of the war, the British government relied upon the American loyalists to do a large part of the fighting; but comparatively few Tories sprang to arms. In general, the Tories preferred to sit on the fence, fearful lest by taking sides they would jeopardize their property. Only the most courageous of the loyalists were open Tories, but even they suffered from their inability to unite in defense of their ideals. The Whigs realized that if they did not stand together they would hang together; the Tories, on the other hand, "saw and shuddered at the gathering storm, but durst not attempt to dispel it, lest it should burst on their own heads." Individual Tories hoped that whatever happened to others, they would escape; not until too late did they see that they would go down together once the Whigs gained the upper hand. [52]

Many of the upper-class Tories were highly cultured pillars of society who put the eighteenth-century ideal of "order and decency" above the rights of man. Like the later American Federalists, they believed that America ought to be ruled by the wise, the good, and the rich — by which they meant, of course, themselves. They loved England and sought to create islands of English manners and ideals in a vast sea of farmers and frontiersmen. They wished well to America — so well, indeed, that they wanted to transplant English institutions, society, and culture to the New World under the firm conviction that America could attain no greater felicity.

The Tories denied that all the virtue was on the side of the Whigs: "The Politician who stuns you with harangues of his own angelic purity," said Daniel Dulany, now turned Tory, "is as certainly an errant imposter as the woman who unceasingly prates of her own chastity, and is no better than she should be." [53] Despite the Whigs' practice of putting into the mouths of Tories doctrines which made them appear to be supporters of the "villainous System of Revenues & Domination, and the "infernal doctrine of arbitrary power," not many of them wholeheartedly approved of the meas-

[51] *Works of John Adams*, X, 63. Lord Dunmore to Lord Dartmouth, June 25, 1775, P.R.O., C.O. 5, 1535, Library of Congress Transcript. *Letters of Captain W. G. Evelyn*, edited by G. D. Scull, 51.
[52] *Rivington's New York Gazetteer*, December 22, 1774. *The Correspondence of General Thomas Gage*, I, 363.
[53] *Correspondence of "First Citizen," Charles Carroll of Carrollton and "Antilon," Daniel Dulany, Junior*, edited by E. S. Riley, Baltimore, 1902, 35.

ures of the British government.[54] Far from being the abettors of
British tyranny, the Tories were the first to suffer by it; they deplored Parliament's insistence upon taxing the colonies because they,
like the Whigs, were upholders of colonial liberties, and recognized
that some middle ground must be found between the absolute
authority of Parliament and complete independence. As Governor
Tryon of New York said, "Oceans of Blood may be spilt but in
my opinion America will never receive parliamentary taxation. I
do not meet with any of the Inhabitants who shew the smallest
inclination to draw the Sword in support of that principle." [55]

Up to 1776, there was no unbridgeable gulf between the views of
the Whigs and Tories as to the rights and liberties of the colonies
in the British Empire. Both professed to aim at reconciliation; and
both opposed taxation by Parliament. There was, however, a wide
difference between them regarding the methods to be used to defend American liberty and in their attitude towards the mother
country. The Tories believed that the colonies ought not to go beyond petitions and remonstrances when contesting British authority;
they insisted that nothing was to be gained by spitting in the
mother country's face and calling her names which should not be
heard outside the kennel. Unlike the radicals, they feared the
mother country's military might: "Great Britain," they said, was
not "an old, wrinkled, withered, worn-out hag, whom every jacka-
napes that truants along the streets may insult with impunity," but
"a vigorous matron, just approaching a green old age." [56] They
looked upon her not as a harsh stepmother but as "a fostering
parent" who was sorely tempted by colonial unruliness to apply
the birch to her offspring. Nor did the Tories make a practice, as
did many of the Whigs, of habitually believing the worst of the
British government. They never surrendered their hope that the
dispute might be settled by peaceful means and that "both countries, supporting and supported by each other, might rise to eminence and glory, and be the admiration of mankind till time shall
be no more." [57] To the end, they inveighed against the narrow
provincialism of which many Whigs were guilty: "Remember that

[54] *Massachusetts Spy*, March 9, 1775.
[55] *Documents relative to the Colonial History of the State of New York*,
VIII, 604.
[56] Eddis, *Letters From America*, 94. Seabury, *A View of the Controversy*, 32.
[57] Inglis, *The True Interest of America Impartially Stated*, 35.

not this, or any other province is your country, but the whole British empire," they reminded Americans.[58]

With Great Britain clearly preparing to crush the revolt by every means in her power and with the fair prospect of despoiling the Tories beckoning Americans, the appeal to the people demanded by the conservatives in the Continental Congress proved a boomerang to the cause of reconciliation. As John Adams said, "Every Post and every Day rolls in upon Us Independence like a Torrent." One of the principal sources of this demand for independence was the American army, where it was observed as early as 1775 that the soldiers did not pray for the King. This spirit began to take possession of the provincial congresses, county conventions, and town meetings, which hastened to add their voices to the clamor. In April 1776, Judge William Henry Drayton of South Carolina declared that Americans were absolved from all allegiance to the King of Great Britain; and the North Carolina Provincial Congress directed its delegates in the Continental Congress to vote for independence and foreign alliances. But the greatest triumph of the radical cause came on May 15, 1776, when the Virginia Convention unanimously instructed its delegates to cast their vote for independence and the "UNION FLAG of the American states" was raised over the capital at Williamsburg.[59]

The last-ditch opposition to independence came from the Middle colonies, where the people were yet unreconciled to shoving off into uncharted waters. The delegates of these colonies in the Continental Congress delighted in tripping up the radicals; "The Proprietary Colonies do certainly obstruct and perplex the American Machine," lamented Richard Henry Lee as he observed the halting progress towards independence. The "feeble politicks" of these colonies repeatedly threatened to disrupt the American union. When Congress urged the Maryland Council of Safety to seize Governor Eden, the Council refused and roundly declared that Congress was attempting to encroach upon colonial rights and make itself dictator of the continent. For this display of bad temper, President John Hancock of the Continental Congress pointedly snubbed the Maryland delegates, but they continued to toss monkey wrenches into the radicals' machinery. Maryland, observed John

[58] Rivington's New York Gazetteer, November 18, 1773.
[59] Principles and Acts of the Revolution in America, edited by H. Niles, 111. Virginia Gazette (Purdie), May 17, 1776.

Adams, was "so eccentric a Colony — sometimes so hot, sometimes so cold," that he wished "it could exchange Places with Hallifax." [60]

From the moment that independence had loomed upon the horizon, the Middle colonies had desperately attempted to arrest its progress. In November 1775, the New Jersey Assembly appointed a committee to draft a petition to the King, whereupon Congress declared that it was "dangerous to the liberties and welfare of America" if any colony petitioned separately. Congress put John Dickinson at the head of a committee and dispatched it to New Jersey to persuade the assembly not to break the ranks. Dickinson and his colleagues were able to quash the petition but the New Jersey Legislature shortly thereafter assured Governor Franklin that it knew of "no sentiments of independency that are, by men of consequence, openly avowed." The Pennsylvania Assembly followed up this action by instructing the Pennsylvania delegates in Congress "utterly to reject" any attempt to separate the mother country and colonies. New Jersey followed suit and Maryland imposed much the same restrictions upon her delegates.[61]

To the radicals in the Continental Congress, Pennsylvania proved the worst stumbling block of all. As late as May, 1776, the advocates of reconciliation carried the elections in Philadelphia and the merchants refused to join the planters of Maryland and Virginia in making a contract to supply the Farmers-General of France with tobacco on the ground that it would raise a barrier to peace between the mother country and colonies. The radicals railed at the "damned Aristocracy" and the "perverse drivelling knot of Quakers" whose domination of the province throttled support for the revolutionary cause: Pennsylvania, they said, was showing "the moderation of a Spaniel dog, that grows more fond in proportion to the ill usuage he received," and Charles Lee recommended that the members of the Pennsylvania Assembly, as punishment for their "damn'd trick of adjourning and procrastinating," be turned out of the Statehouse and sent to Germantown to make stockings for the army — an occupation, he remarked, "manly enough for 'em." [62]

[60] *American Archives*, Fourth Series, V, 983, 1010. *Letters of Members of the Continental Congress*, I, 442, 461.

[61] *Ibid.*, I, 460. *Documents relative to the Colonial History of the State of New Jersey*, New Series, X, 690–691.

[62] *The Lee Papers*, I, 143, 227, 476. *Report on the MSS. of Mrs. Stopford-Sackville*, II, 22. *Memoirs of the Historical Society of Pennsylvania*, Philadelphia, 1895, XIV, 281. Alexander Graydon, *Memoirs of a Life chiefly passed*

With many of the delegates from the Middle colonies striving to dam the flood, Congress yielded slowly to the "torrent of Independence." On June 7, 1776, Richard Henry Lee introduced a resolution as he had been directed by the Virginia Convention, to the effect that the "united Colonies are, and of right ought to be, free and independent States," and that foreign alliances and a plan of confederation ought to be created. Largely because the delegates from Pennsylvania, New Jersey, New York, and Delaware had no authority to enter into this resolution, it was decided to postpone the question of independence until July 1. The Middle colonies, it was expected, would use this interval to put themselves on record in favor of independence or at least to remove the restrictions upon their delegates which prevented them from voting for such a declaration. In Pennsylvania, the radicals found it necessary to carry out a *coup d'état* to put the province in line: a Provincial Conference dispossessed the assembly of its authority and on June 24 declared that the province was ready to join the other colonies in declaring independence. Delaware and New Jersey freed their delegates from the restrictions that had hitherto tied their hands; and the Maryland delegation was likewise empowered to vote for independence. By July 1, 1776, Pennsylvania was the only state a majority of whose delegates opposed independence; but with the struggle going steadily against them and a backfire springing up in Pennsylvania itself, Robert Morris and John Dickinson, the old guard of the Pennsylvania delegation, absented themselves from Congress on July 2, 1776, and thereby permitted an almost unanimous vote by the states — although not by the delegates themselves — in favor of independence. Because the vote of a state was determined by a majority of its delegates, evidences of dissent in Congress were not revealed to the people. New York, however, having failed to instruct its delegates, voted neither aye nor nay on July 2. On July 4, when the Declaration of Independence was adopted, New York still declined to vote; and it was not until July 15 that the New Yorkers formally threw in their lot with the rebellious states.

The Declaration of Independence, as drawn up by Thomas Jefferson, was the final proof — if Englishmen needed any further proof — that the doctrines of John Locke could be made to serve the purposes of revolutionists everywhere. Many years later, Jeffer-

---

in Pennsylvania, 117. *American Archives*, Fourth Series, V, 800. *Virginia Gazette* (Purdie), March 17, 1775.

son said that the Declaration was intended to be "an expression of the American mind"; "I know only that I turned to neither book nor pamphlet while writing it," he said. "I did not consider it as any part of my charge to invent new ideas altogether, and to offer no sentiment which had ever been expressed before." The American mind of 1776 was saturated with John Locke. The Declaration frequently repeats even the phraseology of the philosopher of the "glorious revolution"; and it applies to the dispute between Great Britain and the colonies his compact theory of government and his insistence upon the right of revolution when the existing government has become destructive of the ends for which all governments are instituted. In the final analysis, the separation of Great Britain and the colonies is justified by the natural rights of man which Locke had emphasized rather than upon the narrower rights of British subjects: the colonists had originally become members of the British Empire by their own free will — they withdrew because the King had invaded the inalienable rights which they retained from the state of nature.

The Declaration of Independence submitted "Facts . . . to a candid world" and was written out of "decent respect to the opinions of mankind." This might be held to imply that the Declaration was written chiefly for foreign consumption and that Jefferson's primary purpose was to lay the cause of the United States before the tribunal of world opinion. The character of the "Facts" contained in it militates against this view. It is the iniquity of the King which is held to be the principal, if not the only cause of Americans' withdrawal from the empire. Parliamentary tyranny — against which the colonists had inveighed for a decade — is almost entirely forgotten. "The history of the present King of Great Britain is a history of repeated injuries and usurpations, all having in direct object the establishment of an absolute Tyranny over these States," Jefferson declared; and under twenty-eight headings the crimes of George III are enumerated. It is clear that Jefferson's purpose in portraying the King as the root of all evil in the empire was to convince the vast numbers of Americans who were still unreconciled to independence that their last hope had failed them. Jefferson saw that the overstuffed figure of George III which the patriots had created with their own hands was the last obstacle to independence. The job that Tom Paine had begun in *Common Sense* Jefferson intended to finish in the Declaration of Independence.

While demolishing the reputation of George III and the monar-
chial ideal itself, Jefferson gave his countrymen a new goal toward
which to strive: a republican system of government in which human rights would take precedence over property and privilege. No
one who read the Declaration could fail to see that an experiment
in human relations was being made and that the new order which it
established was to be chiefly for the benefit of the common man.
Equality and liberty — government by the consent of the governed
— were the ideals now held up to men. Here, surely, the common
man was given something to fight for and, if need be, to die for.
The war aims of the Revolution were now complete: the struggle
against Great Britain was to be waged for independence; for the
liberty of the individual; and for the creation of a society in which
men were free and equal.

Independence was proclaimed as the portentous shadow of British
military might again fell upon the American states. Although the
British army had been forced to evacuate Boston in March 1776, on
July 3 — the day before the Declaration of Independence was
adopted by the Continental Congress — Sir William Howe, at the
head of a formidable force, seized Staten Island and began to prepare to drive the American army from Long Island and New York
City. The Declaration had come just in time. In the days ahead that
were to try men's souls, only the loftiest ideals and most stirring
phrases could sustain Americans in their struggle for freedom.

CHAPTER   TWENTY-ONE

The American Revolution
As a Democratic Movement

Independence Hall

PHILADELPHIA

I

THE Declaration of Independence represented not merely the triumph of Whigs over Tories but the victory of the radical wing of the Whig Party over the conservative wing. Conservative patriots had opposed independence hardly less vehemently than had the Tories and with hardly less effectiveness. What chiefly distinguished the Tories from the conservative Whigs was that the Tories staunchly refused to accept independence after it had been declared, whereas the Whigs, after a sharp struggle with their consciences, threw in their lot with the rebels. Although the revolutionary movement had taken what seemed to them a wrong turning, they remained loyal to the cause of American liberty. To take a conspicuous example, although John Dickinson had sacrificed his popularity by leading the fight against independence, he declared that he would dedicate his life to "the defence and happiness of those unkind Countrymen whom I cannot forbear to esteem as fellow Citizens amidst their Fury against me." [1] And thereupon he enlisted as a private in the American army. It is also true that many conservatives refused to surrender their hopes of reconciliation even after the Declaration of Independence; in the Middle colonies, independence was often spoken of as a strategic move designed to put the colonies in a better bargaining position. It was widely believed that Americans could walk back into the empire as easily as they had walked out. Some months after the Declaration, Richard Henry Lee asked in exasperation: "Shall we never cease to be teased with the Bugbear Reconciliation, or must we hang for ever on the hagger'd breast of G. Britain?" [2]

Whatever their hopes of restoring British sovereignty, the conservative Whigs were determined to prevent the revolutionary movement from becoming a social upheaval. In general, this was

[1] *The Thomson Papers*, 29, 31.
[2] Richard Henry Lee to Samuel Adams, July 29, 1776, Adams MSS., New York Public Library.

true of American revolutionaries; radical as regards American rights against Great Britain, they had no wish to usher in democracy in the United States. They were not making war upon the principle of aristocracy and they had no more intention than had the Tories of destroying the tradition of upper-class leadership in the colonies. Although they hoped to turn the Tories out of office, they did not propose to open these lush pastures to the common herd. They did believe, however, that the common people, if properly bridled and reined, might be made allies in the work of freeing the colonies from British rule and that they — the gentry — might reap the benefits without interference. They expected, in other words, to achieve a "safe and sane" revolution of gentlemen, by gentlemen, and for gentlemen. They conceived that the American Revolution was to be a revolution of limited liability from the point of view of the upper classes and that it was to be modeled upon the "glorious revolution" of 1688 which had redounded largely to the advantage of the aristocracy.

Many Virginia planters certainly did not intend that the revolutionary movement should break its leash and run with that mongrel, democracy. The rights of property, they insisted, must be kept uppermost and the rights of gentlemen ought never to be subordinated to the rights of man. "Is it right," they said, "that men of *birth* and *fortune*, in every government that is free, should be invested with power, and enjoy higher honours than the people? If it were otherwise, their privileges would be less, and they would not enjoy an equal degree of liberty with the people." [3] "We are not contending," said another Southern aristocrat, "that our rabble, or all unqualified persons, shall have the right of voting, or not be taxed; but that the freeholders and electors, whose right accrues to them from the common law, or from charter, shall not be deprived of that right." [4]

Like the conservative Whigs, the Tories dreaded the effect of revolutionary ideals upon the common people; but unlike the Whigs they did not believe that if revolution broke out in America it could be kept under control by its upper-class sympathizers. They held a catastrophic theory of revolutions: the plebeians would inevitably turn against the aristocracy and overwhelm all gentlemen, whether Whig or Tory. The Tories placed no trust in the "giddy-

[3] *Virginia Gazette* (Rind's), June 9, 1768.
[4] *Ibid.*, March 31, 1768.

headed multitude": they held the common people to be "damned villains," "like the Mobility in all Countries, perfect Machines, wound up by any Hand who might first take the Winch."[5] They suspected that the "loud unlettered orators of the republican tribe" whom the conservative Whigs expected to use for their own purposes would soon set the people to robbing the rich and pulling down the well-born. "I have seen the same trick practised in the Play-house," remarked a Tory; "where a set of wretches with a view of plunder, have given the alarm of fire; and while the terrified spectators were scampering over one another's heads, those villains have made a large collection of earrings, watches &c. before the cheat could be discovered."[6] They deplored that any "crack-brained zealot for democracy" should be listened to in America where the people already enjoyed "the best, the most beautiful political fabric which the sun ever beheld."[7] Edward Biddle of Philadelphia declared that he "sickened" at the thought of "thirteen unconnected petty democracies; if we are to be independent," he exclaimed, "let us, in the name of God, at once have an empire, and place Washington at the head of it."[8] "God forbid," they prayed, "that we should ever be so miserable as to sink into a Republick" — yet they believed that the Whigs were headed directly for this slough of despond.[9] For this reason, the Tories came to believe that they were holding the front line against democracy which, if victorious in America, might sweep across the Atlantic and overwhelm Great Britain itself. But they made little effort to save the people from the Whigs: for the most part, they were content to enjoy that last gratification of doomed aristocrats — damning the people roundly over their port and Madeira.

The menace of colonial democracy caused the Tories' love for the mother country to grow visibly fonder. Great Britain was the sheet anchor of colonial conservatism; the British government had repeatedly intervened in the colonies to save the aristocracy from the common people; and the Tories believed that, despite the unkind cuts of British imperialists, the authority of the mother country was still their best security against the rising tide of democracy.

[5] Peter Oliver, *Origin and Progress of the American Rebellion*, 1781, Egerton MSS., Gay Transcripts, Mass. Hist. Soc., 90.
[6] *Rivington's New York Gazetteer*, August 11, 1774.
[7] Inglis, *The True Interest of America Impartially Stated*, 52–54.
[8] Graydon, 301.
[9] *New York Gazette and Weekly Mercury*, April 23, 1770.

They concluded that it would be safer both for liberty and for property to be under the authority of the British Parliament and "subject to all the duties and taxes which they might think fit to impose, than to be under the government of the *American sons of liberty*, without paying any duties or taxes at all." If obliged to choose between "two of the greatest of human evils, the arbitrary conduct of a Prince: to the tyranny of an insolent and aspiring demagogue," the Tories regarded the despotism of a prince as the lesser evil.[10]

Tory fears that the Revolution would lead to a democratic upheaval were not altogether without foundation; certainly some Americans regarded the principles of the Declaration of Independence as presaging a new social and political order. They were not content with the mere name of republic; in their eyes, the Revolution was a struggle not only against British tyranny but against those aristocrats at home who longed for the power exercised by "Turkish Bashaws, French Grandees, and the Romish Clergy."[11] They were resolved to sweep away all "Foreign or Domestic Oligarchy" in America and to establish a society in which every citizen would enjoy equal rights and receive his "just share of the wealth."[12] There was growing insistence that the doctrine of no taxation without representation be applied in America itself as well as against Great Britain; and some even decried all government as "a combination among a few to oppress the many." Evidences of class hostility multiplied as the revolutionary movement progressed. As early as 1773, it was observed that "both employers and the employed no longer live together with any thing like attachment and cordiality on either side: and the labouring classes instead of regarding the rich as their guardians, patrons, and benefactors, now look on them as so many over-grown colossuses whom it is no demerit in them to wrong."[13] Even titles were called in question. Charles Lee denounced the practice of using such "tinsel epithets" as "his Excellency and His Honour, The Honourable President of the Honourable Congress, or the Honourable Convention." "This fulsome nauseating cant," said Lee, "may be well enough adapted

[10] *New York Gazette and Weekly Mercury*, June 25, 1770.
[11] *New York Gazette or Weekly Post Boy*, January 29, 1770.
[12] *Pennsylvania Evening Post*, April 30, 1776.
[13] Boucher, *A View of the Causes and Consequences of the American Revolution*, 309.

to barbarous monarchies; or to gratify the adulterated pride of the *Magnifici* in pompous Aristocracies, but in a great free manly equal Commonwealth it is quite abominable."[14] Some Americans began to demand that all institutions be subjected to the test of reason. There was, as one radical put it, "a great deal of contemptible, but superstitiously worshipped rubbish, both in Church and State, which has been swept down to us from heathenism and popery, by the great net of time. It is now high time to examine the net, cull out the good fishes, and cast the bad away!"[15]

The demand that the revolution be directed against abuses at home as well as tyranny abroad was strengthened by the efforts of many American merchants to pile up fortunes during the war at the expense of the people. Profiteering was rife; the price of many necessities soared beyond the reach of the common people; and the merchants grew rich by speculation and cornering commodities. "If affairs continue any time in their present condition," exclaimed a Philadelphian in 1776, "they (the great Whig merchants) will have the whole wealth of the province in their hands, and then the people will be nearly in the condition that the East India Company reduced the poor natives of Bengal to."[16] When refugees from Boston and Charlestown began to stream into Connecticut, they found themselves at the mercy of landlords who promptly doubled their rents. To the patriots, these profiteers were "the rankest Tories of America." Did Americans "flee from the rage of Fire and Violence of bloody Men," it was asked, "to be plundered" by exploiters who called themselves Whigs but who in all but name were Tories? It was believed that the Tories opposed independence because it would mean that "their visions of golden mountains, and millions of acres of tenanted soil, will all vanish, and themselves remain in the despised rank of their honest and contented neighbours."[17] Americans did not propose to allow Whig profiteers and speculators to despoil their fellow citizens behind the screen of patriotism.

Resentment against these profiteers was particularly strong among the mechanics and laborers of the towns who were pinched more severely than any other class by their exactions. The town workers

---

[14] *The Lee Papers*, II, 178.
[15] *American Archives*, Fourth Series, V, 1157.
[16] *Pennsylvania Evening Post*, April 30, 1776.
[17] *Pennsylvania Gazette*, March 6, 1776. *New York Gazette and Weekly Mercury*, March 4, 1776.

were the first to recognize that while Americans were engaged in defending their liberties from tyrants overseas they were in danger of losing their liberties to monopolists at home. In their eyes, the greatest threat to American freedom was that wealth would be concentrated in the hands of a few and that American farmers and workers, victorious against the British and Tories, might find themselves under the heel of new masters. The profiteers, they declared, were as great enemies of revolutionary ideals as were the Tories and they merited no better treatment; unless they were struck down, it seemed certain that the common people of America would shed their blood merely in order to exchange the rule of one oligarchy for that of another no less oppressive and self-seeking.[18]

The town artisans were also the chief sufferers by the property requirements placed upon the suffrage in the new state constitutions. Few of them possessed sufficient property to qualify as voters and so they remained an unrepresented group, keenly aware that the Revolution had passed them by. In vain they demanded the recognition of their "inalienable Right" to ratify all laws enacted by the assembly and to pass upon the proposed state constitutions, and protested against the system whereby in politics a workingman was no better than "a Jew or a Turk." [19] When they declared that "*every man in the country* who manifests a disposition *to venture his all for the defence of its Liberty*, should have *a voice in its Councils*," their voices were drowned out by their opponents' denunciations of "this cursed spirit of levelling." [20] The conservatives who held the reins were determined not to trust themselves on a runaway democracy; on the contrary, they recognized that it was "time the Tradesmen were checked. They take too much upon them. They ought not to intermeddle in State Affairs. They ought to be kept low. They will become too powerful." [21] These measures were taken in time; although the town workers grew increasingly restive and radical in their demands for reform, they were unable to break the grip of the aristocracy.

While kicking against the pricks of Old England, conservative patriots had never overlooked the menace of New England; and the

---

[18] *New York Journal or General Advertiser*, January 4, March 7, 1776. *New York Gazette and Weekly Mercury*, April 8, June 10 and 17, 1776.

[19] C. H. Lincoln, *The Revolutionary Movement in Pennsylvania*, 80, note.

[20] *Pennsylvania Packet*, April 29, 1776.

[21] *Pennsylvania Gazette*, September 22, 1772.

Declaration of Independence by no means extinguished their fear of New England levelism. Particularly dreaded were the New England soldiers, the most democratic element in that hotbed of democracy. It was suspected that these men spread subversive ideas wherever they went, thereby causing Americans to become social revolutionaries instead of God-fearing patriots whose energies were wholly taken up in combating British tyranny. Southern gentlemen who frowned upon democracy and all its works considered the New England army to be a horrible example of the effects of the popular delusion that one man was as good as another. There were, they pointed out, too many officers in proportion to men in the regiments and the pay of officers and men was too nearly equal. New Englanders, on their part, warmly defended their equalitarianism and branded Southerners' demands that the pay of officers be raised and that of privates lowered as "incompatible with freedom." [22] The absence of gentlemen in the New England army was also distressing to conservatives: some even looked upon the minutemen with apprehension because they were "composed of people of the smallest property, and perhaps of the least virtue" — and might therefore be tempted to turn their arms against the landowning gentry. Although these skittish Whigs found a few men of good family and "decent breeding" among the higher ranks in the New England army, they reported that "anything above the condition of a clown, in the regiments we came in contact with, was truly a rarity." As for General Artemas Ward, a New Englander who had risen to high command in the continental army, he was held to be merely "a drivelling deacon." [23]

Despite these misgivings, the democratic movement achieved its greatest triumph during the Revolution not in New England but in Pennsylvania. The common people of that state had long been under the domination of a Quaker oligarchy; and this protracted repression of the democratic forces led to a violent upheaval in which aristocratic rule was swept away. The Pennsylvania Constitution of 1776 — the product of the victory of western farmers and Philadelphia artisans over the eastern ruling · class — was the high-water mark of radicalism during the American Revolution.

[22] Joseph Hawley to Samuel Adams, November 12, 1775, Adams MSS.. New York Public Library.
[23] Graydon, 154. *The Writings of George Washington*, III, 49. *American Archives*, Fourth Series, VI, 219.

Drawn up by Tom Paine and Benjamin Franklin, it provided for manhood suffrage; a unicameral legislature, elected annually; complete religious freedom; and a plural executive so hedged and constrained by constitutional limitations that it could never aspire to seize authority from the all-powerful assembly. This constitution gave no protection to the "opulent minority" whose interests loomed so large in the minds of the framers of the Federal Constitution of 1787. The majority ruled in Pennsylvania under the constitution of 1776 and the privileged class was stripped of its power as the center of gravity shifted from the polite and genteel of Philadelphia to the rough Scotch-Irish farmers of the west and the plebeians of the metropolis. "It is a fact," said Franklin in 1784, "that the Irish emigrants and their children are now in possession of the government of Pennsylvania, by their majority in the Assembly, as well as of a great part of the territory; and I remember the first ship that brought them over."

The Pennsylvania Constitution of 1776 realized the worst fears of the Tories and conservative Whigs; throughout the Revolutionary War, it stood as a dire warning of what happened when a revolutionary movement got out of the control of gentlemen. William Hooper of North Carolina, in deploring the fondness of his fellow citizens for the Pennsylvania Constitution, declared it deserved "more Imprecations than the Devil and all his Angels." He pronounced it to be "the motley mixture of limited monarchy, and an execrable democracy — a Beast without a head. The Mob made a second branch of Legislation — Laws subjected to their revisal in order to refine them, a Washing in ordure by way of purification" — with the result that "Taverns and dram shops" were made "the councils to which the laws of this State are to be referred for approbation before they possess a binding Influence." [24] With the "Mobility" firmly in the saddle in Pennsylvania, the upper classes did not find the journey so easy and pleasant as when they had been the riders instead of the ridden. "Fiery Independents" seemed to be gathering all the fruits of the Revolution and crowding their betters out of political office. In this new order, exclaimed the conservatives, the people of Pennsylvania were divided "into those that plunder and those that are plundered." In Pennsylvania, at least, the Revolution had become what conservatives most dreaded: a social convulsion in which "the most insignificant"

[24] *Colonial Records of North Carolina*, X, 819.

Americans lorded it "with impunity and without discretion over the most respectable characters" — in short, the rule of "the worst over the best." [25]

What upper-class Americans found most alarming in the Pennsylvania Constitution was that it towered "like another Babel, to the skies," a beacon for the discontented and oppressed all over America. Certainly, to the democrats, the frame of government created by Franklin and Paine in Pennsylvania was a hope achieved and a challenge to fresh efforts to make the United States safe for democracy. Sam Adams in Massachusetts raised his voice for a unicameral legislature modeled upon that of Pennsylvania; a bicameral legislature, he declared, aped the British Parliament — which ought to damn it in the eyes of all true Americans. But it is significant that a bicameral legislature was adopted in Massachusetts and in most of the other states on the ground that it was necessary to check the power of the people and protect property and vested interests by means of an upper house.

Until the end of the War of Independence, conservatives generally succeeded in stemming the democratic tide and in keeping the revolutionary movement from being directed primarily against the privileged class. Their confidence that they had embarked upon a revolution of limited liability was little shaken before 1782. It was not until after the Peace of Paris when Americans put away their arms and vigorously sought to apply the ideals for which they had fought to conditions at home that the conservative patriots saw that the Tories had been true prophets. The forces unleashed by the Revolution could not long remain under the control of Whigs who aspired to step into the shoes of the former Tory aristocrats and to rule the masses in the name of the rich, the wise, and the good. The "principles of '76" were a powerful solvent upon the old aristocratic society that the Whig leaders hoped to perpetuate in the United States. Many years later, Harrison Gray Otis wrote to a friend of revolutionary days: "You and I did not imagine, when the first war with Britain was over, that revolution was just begun."

It has not yet ended.

[25] *Pennsylvania Magazine of History and Biography*, 1895, IX, 196. Diary of James Allen, entry of March 6, 1776, MS. Historical Society of Pennsylvania. Graydon, 305.

BIBLIOGRAPHY

MANUSCRIPTS

Samuel Adams MSS, New York Public Library
Bancroft Collection, New York Public Library
Belknap MSS, Massachusetts Historical Society
Bernard MSS, Harvard University Library
Chalmers MSS, Harvard University Library
Clifford MSS, Historical Society of Pennsylvania
Committee of Correspondence Papers, New York Public Library
Egerton MSS, British Museum
Franklin MSS, American Philosophical Society
Hardwicke MSS, Library of Congress Transcript
Hollis MSS, Massachusetts Historical Society
House of Lords MSS
Hutchinson Correspondence, Massachusetts Archives
Hutchinson MSS, New York Public Library
Sir William Johnson MSS, Library of Congress
Lamb MSS, New York Public Library
Livingston MSS, New York Public Library
Penn MSS, Historical Society of Pennsylvania
Shippen MSS, Historical Society of Pennsylvania
William Smith MSS, New York Public Library
Ezra Stiles MSS, Yale University Library
Samuel Wharton MSS, Historical Society of Pennsylvania
Israel Williams MSS, Massachusetts Historical Society

NEWSPAPERS AND MAGAZINES

Boston Gazette
Boston Evening Post
Boston News Letter
Essex Gazette
Gazetteer and New Daily Advertiser (London)
General Evening Post (London)
London Chronicle
The London Magazine
Maryland Gazette
Massachusetts Spy (Boston)
Morning Chronicle and London Advertiser
Morning Post and Daily Advertiser (London)
The New London Gazette
Newport Mercury
New York Gazette and Weekly Mercury
New York Gazette or Weekly Post Boy
New York Mercury
Pennsylvania Chronicle
Pennsylvania Evening Post
Pennsylvania Journal and Weekly Advertiser

The Political Register (London)
Providence Gazette and Country Journal
Public Advertiser (London)
Rivington's New York Gazetteer
St. James's Chronicle (London)
The Scots Magazine (Edinburgh)
South Carolina Gazette
Virginia Gazette (Purdie and Dixon)
Virginia Gazette (Rind's)

CONTEMPORARY PAMPHLETS

Abingdon, Earl of. *Thoughts on the Letter of Edmund Burke, Esq. to the Sheriffs of Bristol on the Affairs of America.* Oxford, 1777.

Almon, John. *A Collection of Interesting, Authentic Papers . . . . from 1764 to 1775.* London, 1777.

Bancroft, Edward. *Remarks on the Review of the Controversy Between Great Britain and her Colonies.* London, 1769.

Boucher, Jonathan. *A Letter from a Virginian to the Members of the Congress.* Boston, 1774.

————*A View of the Causes and Consequences of the American Revolution.* London, 1797.

Burgh, James. *Political Disquisitions.* London, 1774.

Cartwright, John. *American Independence, the Interest and Glory of Great Britain.* Philadelphia, 1776.

Chandler, Thomas B. *A Friendly Address.* New York, 1774.

Chauncey, Charles. *A Discourse on "The Good News from a Far Country."* Boston, 1766.

Cooper, The Reverend Samuel. *A Sermon Preached Before His Excellency Thomas Pownall.* Boston, 1759.

Crowley, Thomas. *Letters and Dissertations on Various Subjects.* London, 1776.

Dickinson, John. *Letters from a Farmer in Pennsylvania.* Philadelphia, 1768.

————*A New Essay on the Constitutional Power of Great Britain over the Colonies in America.* Philadelphia, 1774.

————*The Regulations Respecting the British Colonies on the Continent of America Considered.* London, 1765.

Drayton, William Henry. *A Letter from the Freemen of South Carolina.* Charleston, 1774.

Duche, The Reverend Jacob. ~~The Duty of Standing Fast in Our Spiritual and~~ *Temporal Liberties.* Philadelphia, 1775.

Dulany, Daniel. *Considerations on the Propriety of Imposing Taxes on the British Colonies.* London, 1766.

Dummer, Jeremiah. *Defence of the New England Charters.* London, 1765.

Eddis, William. *Letters from America.* London, 1792.

Estwick, Samuel. *A Letter to the Reverend Josiah Tucker, D.D.* London, 1776.

Fletcher, J. *American Patriotism further Confronted with Reason, Scripture and the Constitution.* London, 1777.

Fothergill, John. *Considerations Relative to the North American Colonies.* London, 1765.

Galloway, Joseph. *Historical and Political Reflections.* London, 1780.

Green, Jacob. *Observations on the Reconciliation of Great Britain and the Colonies.* Philadelphia, 1776.

Hopkins, Stephen. *The Rights of the Colonies Examined.* Providence, 1765.

————*The Grievances of the American Colonies Candidly Examined.* 1766 (English edition of *The Rights of the Colonies Examined*).

Howard, Martin. *A Letter from a Gentleman at Halifax to His Friend in Rhode Island.* Newport, 1765.

Jenyns, Soame. *The Objections to the Taxation of Our American Colonies by the Legislature of Great Britain Briefly Consider'd.* London, 1765.

Johnson, Samuel. *Taxation no Tyranny.* London, 1775.

Johnson, The Reverend Samuel. *A Short Vindication of the Society for the Propagation of the Gospel.* Boston, 1763.

Knox, William. *The Controversy Reviewed.* London, 1769.

Lathrop, John. *Innocent Blood Crying to God from the Streets of Boston.* Boston, 1771.

Lee, Charles. *Strictures on a Pamphlet Entitled a Friendly Address.* Philadelphia, 1774.

Leigh, Sir Egerton. *Considerations on Certain Political Transactions.* London, 1774.

Leonard, Daniel. *The Origins of the American Contest with Great Britain.* New York, 1775.

Lyttelton, Thomas. *A Letter to the Earl of Chatham on the Quebec Mill.* London, 1774.

Macaulay, Catherine. *Observations on a Pamphlet Entitled, Thoughts on the Causes of the Present Discontents.* London, 1770.

Macpherson, James. *The Rights of Great Britain Asserted.* London, 1776.

McCulloh, Henry. *Miscellaneous Representations Relative to Our Concerns in America.* London, 1761.

Maseres, Francis. *Considerations on the Expediency of Admitting Representatives from the American Colonies into the British House of Commons.* London, 1770.

Mayhew, Jonathan. *Observations on the Character and Conduct of the Society for the Propagation of the Gospel in Foreign Parts.* Boston, 1763.

————*Popish Idolatry.* Boston, 1765.

————*Remarks on an Anonymous Tract.* Boston, 1764.

————*The Snare Broken.* Boston, 1766.

Mein, John. *Sagittarius's Letters and Political Speculations.* Boston, 1775.

Otis, James. *Considerations on Behalf of the Colonies.* London, 1765.

————*Rights of the British Colonies.* Boston, 1765.

Pinto, M. de. *Letters on the American Troubles.* London, 1776.

Price, Richard. *Observations on the Nature of Civil Liberty.* London, 1776.

Priestley, Joseph. *The Present State of Liberty in Great Britain and the American Colonies.* London, 1769.

Pulteney, William. *Thought on the Present State of Affairs with America.* London, 1778.

Ramsay, Allan. *Thoughts on the Origin and Nature of Government.* London, 1766.

Ray, Nicholas. *The Importance of the Colonies of North America.* London, 1766.

Robinson, Matthew. *Considerations on the Measures Carrying on with Respect to the British Colonies in North America.* London, 1774.

Seabury, The Reverend Samuel. *The Congress Canvassed.* New York, 1774.

————*Free Thoughts on the Proceedings of the Congress.* New York, 1774.

————*A View of the Controversy Between Great Britain and her Colonies.* New York, 1774.

Steele, Joshua. *An Account of a Late Conference on the Occurrences in America.* London, 1766.

Thacher, Oxenbridge. *The Sentiments of a British American.* Boston, 1764.

Tucker, Josiah. *Four Tracts*. Gloucester, 1774.
————*An Humble Address*. Gloucester, 1775.
Wesley, John. *A Calm Address to Our American Colonies*. London, 1775.
Whately, Thomas. *Considerations on the Trade and Finances of the Kingdom, a Collection of Tracts*. 2 vols. London, 1767.
Wilkins, Isaac. *Short Advice to the Counties of New York*. New York, 1774.
Williamson, Hugh. *The Plain Dealer*. Philadelphia, 1764.

ANONYMOUS CONTEMPORARY PAMPHLETS

The Address of the People of Great Britain to the Inhabitants of America. London, 1775.
The American Alarm. By a British Bostonian. Boston, 1773.
An Appeal to the Justice and Interest of the People of Great Britain in the Present Dispute with America. By an Old Member of Parliament. London, 1776.
An Appeal to the Public. London, 1774.
An Application of Political Rules to Great Britain, Ireland and America. London, 1766.
The Claim of the Colonies to Exemption Considered. London, 1765.
A Collection of Scarce and Interesting Tracts. London, 1767.
The Conduct of the Late Administration Examined. London, 1767.
Considerations upon the Rights of the Colonies. New York, 1766.
Considerations Relative to the North American Colonies. London, 1765.
The Constitutional Right of the Legislature of Great Britain to Tax the British Colonies in America Impartially Stated. London, 1768.
The Crisis, or a Full Defence of the Colonies. London, 1766.
Good Humour, or, a Way with the Colonies. London, 1766.
The Importance of the British Plantations in America to this Kingdom. London, 1739.
Independency, or the Object of the Congress in America. London, 1776.
The Interests of the Merchants and Manufacturers of Great Britain in the Present Contest with the Colonies Stated and Considered. London, 1774.
The Justice and Necessity of Taxing the American Colonies Demonstrated. London, 1766.
The Late Occurrences in North America and the Policy of Great Britain Considered. London, 1766.
A Letter from an Officer Retired to His Son in Parliament. London, 1776.
A Letter to Lord George Germain. London, 1776.
A Letter to a Member of Parliament. London, 1765.
The Necessity of Repealing the American Stamp Act Demonstrated. London, 1766.
A New and Impartial Collection of Interesting Letters. London, 1767.
The Other Side of the Question. By a Citizen. New York, 1774.
A Plain and Seasonable Address to the Freeholders of Great Britain on the Present Posture of Affairs in America. London, 1766.
The Political Controversy. London, 1762.
The Present State of the Nation. London, 1768.
Reflections on the American Contest. London, 1776.
Reflections upon Representation in Parliament. London, 1776.
The Regulations Lately Made Concerning the Colonies and the Taxes Imposed upon Them, Considered. London, 1765.
Some Important Observations. Newport, 1766.

The Trade and Navigation of Great Britain Considered. London, 1790.
The True Interest of Great Britain, with Respect to her American Colonies Stated and Impartially Considered. London, 1766.
Two Papers on the Subject of Taxing the British Colonies in America. London, 1767.

CONTEMPORARY HISTORIES AND MEMOIRS

Curwen, Samuel. *Journal and Letters of the Late Samuel Curwen.* New York, 1842.
Drayton, John. *Memoirs of the American Revolution.* Charleston, 1821.
Fithian, P. V. *The Journal and Letters of Phillip Vickers Fithian.* Edited by J. R. Williams. Princeton, 1934.
The Francis Letters. Edited by Beata Francis and Eliza Kearny. London, 1901.
Grafton, August Henry, 3rd Duke of. *Autobiography and Political Correspondence of August Henry, Third Duke of Grafton.* Edited by Sir William Anson. London, 1898.
Graydon, Alexander. *Memoirs of a Life chiefly passed in Pennsylvania.* Philadelphia, 1846.
Hutchinson, Thomas. *The History of the Colony and Province of Massachusetts Bay.* 3 vols. Cambridge, 1936.
Jones, Thomas. *History of New York During the Revolutionary War.* New York, 1874.
Macfarlane, Robert. *History of the Reign of George III.* London, 1770.
Maury, Ann. *Memoirs of a Huguenot Family.* New York, 1872.
The Montressor Journals. New York, 1882.
Peters, The Reverend Samuel. *The General History of Connecticut.* New York, 1877.
Ramsay, David. *The History of the American Revolution.* 2 vols. Trenton, 1816.
————*The History of the Revolution in South Carolina.* Trenton, 1875.
Rockingham, Charles Watson-Wentworth, 2nd Marquis of. *Memoirs of the Marquis of Rockingham.* Edited by George Thomas, Earl of Albemarle. 2 vols. London, 1852.
Rowe, John. *Diary.* Edited by Anne Rowe Cunningham. Boston, 1903.
Stiles, Ezra. *The Literary Diary of Ezra Stiles.* Edited by F. B. Dexter, 2 vols. New York, 1901.
Walpole, Horace. *Memoirs of the Reign of King George the Third.* New York, 1894.

COLLECTED WORKS AND HISTORICAL COLLECTIONS

Adams, John. *The Works of John Adams.* Edited by C. F. Adams. 10 vols. Boston, 1850.
Adams, Samuel. *The Writings of Samuel Adams.* Edited by H. A. Cushing. 4 vols. New York, 1904-1908.
American Archives. Edited by Peter Force. Washington, 1837.
American Antiquarian Society. Proceedings of the American Antiquarian Society.
The Barrington-Bernard Correspondence. Edited by Edward Channing and A. C. Coolidge. Harvard Historical Studies, XVII.
Beloff, Max. *The Debate on the American Revolution.* London, 1949.
Biddle, Alexander, ed. *Old Family Letters.* Philadelphia, 1892.
The Burd Papers. Edited by Lewis Burd Walker. Philadelphia, 1897.
Burke, Edmund. *The Correspondence of Edmund Burke.* 4 vols. London, 1844.
————*The Works of Edmund Burke.* 12 vols. Boston, 1880.

Carroll, B. R., ed. *Historical Collections of South Carolina.* 2 vols. Charleston, 1836.

Cobber, William, ed. *Parliamentary History of England.* 36 vols. London, 1806-1820.

Continental Congress, *Journals of the Continental Congress, 1774-1789.* 34 vols. Washington, 1904-1937.

Continental Congress. *Letters of the Members of the Continental Congress.* Edited by E. C. Burnett. 8 vols. Washington, 1921-1938.

The Writings of John Dickinson. Edited by P. L. Ford. 2 vols. Philadelphia, 1895.

Dorson, Richard M., ed. *American Rebels: Narratives of the Patriots,* New York, 1953.

Evelyn, W. G. *Letters of Captain W. G. Evelyn.* Edited by G. P. Scull. Oxford, 1879.

Fitch Papers. Hartford, 1920. Collections of the Connecticut Historical Society, XVIII.

Franklin, Benjamin. *The Writings of Benjamin Franklin.* Edited by A. H. Smyth. 10 vols. New York, 1906.

————*Benjamin Franklin's Letters to the Press.* Edited by V. W. Crane. Chapel Hill, 1950.

Gage, Thomas. *Correspondence of General Thomas Gage.* 2 vols. Edited by C. E. Carter. New Haven, 1931-1933.

George III. *The Correspondence of King George the Third.* Edited by Sir John Fortescue. 6 vols. London, 1927-1928.

Gibbs, R. W., ed. *Documentary History of the American Revolution.* New York, 1885.

The Grenville Papers. Edited by William James Smith. London, 1852-1853.

Hamilton, Alexander. *The Works of Alexander Hamilton.* Edited by Henry Cabot Lodge. 12 vols. New York, 1904.

Hamilton, S. M., ed. *Letters to George Washington.* Boston, 1901.

Hutchinson-Oliver Letters. Boston, 1774.

The Ingersoll Papers. New Haven, 1918. Collections of the New Haven Historical Society.

Izard, Ralph. *The Correspondence of Ralph Izard.* New York, 1844.

Jefferson, Thomas. *The Papers of Thomas Jefferson.* Edited by Julian P. Boyd. Princeton, 1950——

————*The Writings of Thomas Jefferson.* Edited by Paul Leicester Ford. 10 vols. New York, 1894.

Kimball, Gertrude S., ed. *The Correspondence of the Colonial Governors of Rhode Island.* 2 vols. Boston, 1903.

Lee, Charles. *The Charles Lee Papers.* 4 vols. New York, 1872. Collections of the New York Historical Society.

Lee, Henry. *Letters of Richard Henry Lee.* Edited by J. C. Ballagh. 2 vols. New York, 1911.

Lee, William. *Letters of William Lee.* Edited by W. C. Ford. 3 vols. Brooklyn, 1891.

Letters and Papers Relating Chiefly to the Provincial History of Pennsylvania. Philadelphia, 1855.

Massachusetts State Papers. Edited by Alden Bradford. Boston, 1815.

Murray, James. *Letters of James Murray, Loyalist.* Boston, 1911.

Morison, Samuel Eliot. *Sources and Documents Illustrating the American Revolution.* Oxford, 1948.

O'Callaghan, E. B., ed. *Documents Relative to the Colonial History of the State of New York.* Edited by E. B. O'Callaghan. 15 vols. Albany, 1853-1887.
Paine, Thomas. *Selections from the Works of Thomas Paine.* Edited by A. W. Peach. New York, 1928.
Pitt, William. *The Correspondence of William Pitt.* Edited by G. S. Kimball. 2 vols. New York, 1906.
Rodney, Caesar, *et al. Letters to and from Caesar Rodney.* Edited by George H. Ryder. Philadelphia, 1833.
The Sandwich Papers. London, 1932. Publications of the Navy Records Society, LXIX.
Sharpe, Horatio. *The Correspondence of Governor Horatio Sharpe.* 2 vols. Baltimore, 1888-1890.
Stock, F. L., ed. *Proceedings and Debates of the British Parliament Respecting North America.* 3 vols. Washington, 1937.
Warren-Adams Letters. 2 vols. Boston, 1917-1925.
Washington, George. *The Writings of George Washington.* Edited by J. C. Fitzgerald. 39 vols. Washington, 1931-1944.
Wharton, Francis, ed. *The Revolutionary Diplomatic Correspondence of the United States.* 6 vols. Washington, 1889.

BIOGRAPHIES

Adams, Charles Francis. *Life of John Adams.* 2 vols. Philadelphia, 1871.
Alden, John. *General Gage in America.* Baton Rouge, 1948.
————*General Charles Lee: Patriot or Traitor?* Baton Rouge, 1951.
————*John Stuart and the Southern Colonial Frontier.* Ann Arbor, 1944.
Allan, H. S. *John Hancock, Patriot in Purple.* New York, 1948.
Baldwin, E. H. *Joseph Galloway, the Loyalist Politician.* Philadelphia, 1902.
Beardsley, E. E. *Life and Correspondence of the Right Reverend Samuel Seabury.* Boston, 1881.
Bowen, Catherine Drinker. *John Adams and the American Revolution.* Boston, 1950.
Bradford, Alden. *Memoirs of the Life and Writings of the Reverend Jonathan Mayhew.* Boston, 1838.
Brant, Irving. *James Madison: The Virginia Revolutionist.* Indianapolis, 1941.
Campbell, John Lord. *The Lives of the Lord Chancellors.* 10 vols. New York, 1875.
Chinard, Gilbert. *Honest John Adams.* Boston, 1933.
————*Thomas Jefferson, the Apostle of Americanism.* Boston, 1929.
Conway, M. D. *Life of Thomas Paine.* 2 vols. New York, 1862.
Crane, Verner W. *Benjamin Franklin—Englishman and American.* Providence, 1936.
Cranston, Maurice. *John Locke.* New York, 1957.
Van Doren, Carl. *Benjamin Franklin.* New York, 1938.
Fitzmaurice, Lord. *Life of William, Earl of Shelburne.* 2 vols. London, 1875.
Forbes, Esther. *Paul Revere and the World He Lived in.* Boston, 1942.
Ford, P. L. *The True George Washington.* Philadelphia, 1896.
Freeman, Douglas Southall. *George Washington: A Biography.* Vols. I & II. New York, 1948.
Frothingham, Richard, Jr. *The Life and Times of Joseph Warren.* Boston, 1865.
Gipson, L. H. *Jared Ingersol: A Study in American Loyalism in Relation to British Colonial Government.* New Haven, 1920.
Goss, E. H. *The Life of Colonel Paul Revere.* 2 vols. Boston, 1891.
Harley, Lewis R. *The Life of Charles Thomson.* Philadelphia, 1906.
Harris, George. *The Life of Lord Chancellor Hardwicke.* 3 vols. London, 1847.

Henry, William Wirt. *Patrick Henry: Life, Correspondence and Speeches.* 3 vols. New York, 1891.

Hill, Helen D. *George Mason, Constitutionalist.* Cambridge, Mass., 1938.

Hosmer, J. K. *The Life of Thomas Hutchinson.* Boston, 1896.

Humphrey, David. *The Life of Israel Putnam.* Boston, 1898.

Hunt, Gaillard. *James Madison.* New York, 1902.

Kapp, Friedrich. *The Life of John Kalb.* New York, 1884.

Lee, Richard Henry. *Life of Arthur Lee.* 2 vols. Boston, 1829.

————*Memoir of the Life of Richard Henry Lee.* 2 vols. Philadelphia, 1825.

Livingston, E. B. *The Livingstons of Livingston Manor.* New York, 1910.

Lossing, B. J. *The Life and Times of Philip Schuyler.* New York, 1860.

Lucas, Reginald. *Lord North.* London, 1913.

Malone, Dumas. *Jefferson the Virginian.* Boston, 1948.

Mayo, Lawrence Shaw. *John Wentworth.* Cambridge, Mass., 1921.

Miller, John C. *Sam Adams, Pioneer in Propaganda.* Boston, 1936.

Reed, William B. *The Life and Correspondence of Joseph Reed.* 2 vols. Philadelphia, 1847.

Rives, W. C. *James Madison.* 3 vols. Boston, 1859-1868.

Rowland, Kate M. *The Life and Correspondence of George Mason.* 2 vols. New York, 1892.

Schutz, J. A. *Thomas Pownall, British Defender of American Liberty.* Glendale, California, 1951.

Sedgwick, Theodore. *A Memoir of the Life of William Livingston.* New York, 1844.

Stephenson, N. W., and W. H. Dunn. *George Washington.* 2 vols. New York, 1940.

Stillé, C. J. *The Life and Times of John Dickinson.* Philadelphia, 1891.

Trevelyan, Sir George Otto. *Early History of Charles James Fox.* London, 1908.

Trumbull, Jonathan. *The Life of Jonathan Trumbull.* Boston, 1919.

Tuckerman, Bayard. *Life of General Philip Schuyler.* New York, 1903.

Tudor, William. *The Life of James Otis of Massachusetts.* Boston, 1864.

Tunstall, Brian. *William Pitt.* London, 1938.

Wallace, P. A. W. *The Muhlenbergs of Pennsylvania.* Philadelphia, 1949.

Wells, W. V. *The Life and Public Service of Samuel Adams.* 3 vols. Cambridge, Mass., 1866.

Williams, Basil. *William Pitt, Earl of Chatham.* 2 vols. London, 1913.

Yarborough, M. C. *John Horne Tooke.* New York, 1912.

Yorke, Philip C. *The Life and Correspondence of Philip York, Earl of Hardwicke.* 2 vols. Cambridge, 1913.

GENERAL HISTORIES AND MONOGRAPHS

Abbott, Wilber C. *New York in the American Revolution.* New York, 1929.

Abernethy, Thomas P. *Western Lands and the American Revolution.* Charlottesville, Virginia, 1937.

Adams, James Truslow. *Revolutionary New England.* Boston, 1923.

Adams, Randolph G. *Political Ideas of the American Revolution.* Durham, North Carolina, 1922.

Alvord, Clarence W. *The Mississippi Valley in British Politics.* 2 vols. Cleveland, 1917.

Ambler, C. H. *Sectionalism in Virginia.* Chicago, 1910.

Andrews, Charles M. *The Colonial Background of the American Revolution.* New Haven, 1924.

————*The Colonial Period of American History.* 4 vols. New Haven, 1934-1938.

Baldwin, Alice. *The New England Clergy and the American Revolution.* Durham, North Carolina, 1928.

Bancroft, George. *History of the United States.* 10 vols. Boston, 1874.

Beard, Charles and Mary. *The Making of American Civilization.* 2 vols. New York, 1930.

Becker, Carl L. *The Declaration of Independence.* New York, 1922.

————*The Eve of the Revolution.* New Haven, 1921.

————*The Making of Political Parties in the Province of New York.* Madison, Wisconsin, 1909.

————*The Spirit of Seventy-Six.* Washington, 1927.

Beer, George L. *British Colonial Policy, 1754-1765.* New York, 1907.

————*The Old Colonial System.* 2 vols. New York, 1912.

————*The Origins of the British Colonial System.* New York, 1908.

Belcher, Henry. *The First American Civil War.* London, 1911.

Bemis, S. F. *The Diplomacy of the American Revolution.* New York, 1935.

Bining, A. C. *Pennsylvania Iron Manufacture in the Eighteenth Century.* Harrisburg, 1938.

Bridenbaugh, Carl. *Cities in Revolt.* New York, 1958.

————*Cities in the Wilderness.* New York, 1938.

Brown, Robert E. *Charles Beard and the Constitution: A Critical Analysis of "An Economic Interpretation of the Constitution."* Princeton, 1956.

————*Middle-Class Democracy and the Revolution in Massachusetts.* Cornell, 1955.

Buck, Philip W. *The Politics of Mercantilism.* New York, 1942.

Burnett, Edmund C. *The Continental Congress.* New York, 1941.

Butterfield, Herbert. *George III and the Historians.* London, 1957.

Channing, Edward. *A History of the United States.* 6 vols. New York, 1927.

Coupland, Edward. *The American Revolution and the British Empire.* London, 1930.

————*The Quebec Act.* Oxford, 1925.

Cross, Arthur Lynn. *The Anglican Episcopate and the American Colonies.* New York, 1902.

Crowl, Philip A. *Maryland during and after the Revolution: A Political and Economic Struggle.* Baltimore, 1943.

Davidson, Philip G. *Propaganda and the American Revolution.* Chapel Hill, North Carolina, 1941.

Degler, Carl N. *Out of Our Past: The Forces that Shaped Modern America.* New York, 1959.

DeMond, E. O. *The Loyalists in North Carolina.* Durham, North Carolina, 1940.

Dewey, Davis Rich. *Financial History of the United States.* New York, 1931.

Dickerson, Oliver M. *American Colonial Government.* Cleveland, 1912.

————*The Navigation Acts and the American Revolution.* Philadelphia, 1951.

Dorn, Walter L. *Competition for Empire.* New York, 1940.

Douglass, Elisha P. *Rebels and Democrats: The Struggle for Equal Political Rights and Majority Rule during the American Revolution.* Chapel Hill, North Carolina, 1955.

Doyle, James A. *The English Colonies in America.* New York, 1882.

Eckenrode, H. J. *The Revolution in Virginia.* Boston, 1916.

Edwards, G. W. *New York as an Eighteenth Century Municipality.* 2 vols. New York, 1917.
Egerton, H. J. *The Causes and Character of the American Revolution.* Oxford, 1923.
Feiling, Keith. *The Second Tory Party.* London, 1938.
Fiske, John. *The American Revolution.* 2 vols. Boston, 1891.
Flick, A. C. *Loyalism in New York.* New York, 1901.
French, Allen. *The First Year of the American Revolution.* Boston, 1934.
————*General Gage's Informers.* Ann Arbor, 1932.
Friedenwald, Herbert. *The Declaration of Independence.* New York, 1904.
Frothingham, Richard. *The Rise of the Republic of the United States.* Boston, 1910.
Gipson, Lawrence H. *The Coming of the Revolution, 1763-1775.* New York, 1954.
Greene, Evarts B. *Provincial America.* New York, 1905.
————*The Provincial Governor.* New York, 1898.
————*The Revolutionary Generation.* New York, 1943.
Guttridge, G. H. *English Whiggism and the American Revolution.* Berkeley, 1942.
Hacker, Louis M. "The First American Revolution," *Columbia University Quarterly*, Vol. XXVII (September 1935).
Handlin, Oscar and Mary F. "Radicals and Conservatives in Massachusetts after Independence," *New England Quarterly*, Vol. XVII (1944).
Harper, Lawrence A. *The English Navigation Laws.* New York, 1939.
Hewers, George R. T. *Traits of the Tea Party.* New York, 1835.
Hinkhouse, Fred J. *The Preliminaries of the American Revolution as Seen in the English Press.* New York, 1926.
Hotblack, Kate. *Chatham's Colonial Policy.* London, 1917.
Jameson, J. Franklin. *The American Revolution Considered as a Social Movement.* Princeton, 1926.
Jensen, Merrill. *The Articles of Confederation: An Interpretation of the Social-Constitutional History of the American Revolution, 1774-1781.* Madison, 1948.
Jones, E. Alfred. *The Loyalists of New Jersey.* Newark, 1927.
Kenyon, Cecilia M. "Men of Little Faith: The Anti-Federalists on the Nature of Representative Government," *William and Mary Quarterly*, 3rd Series, Vol. XII (1955).
Labaree, Leonard Woods. *Conservatism in Early American History.* New York, 1948.
————*Royal Government in America.* New Haven, 1930.
Lincoln, C. H. *The Revolutionary Movement in Pennsylvania.* Philadelphia, 1901.
Mark, Irving. *Agrarian Conflicts in New York.* New York, 1940.
McIlwain, Charles H. *The American Revolution.* New York, 1923.
McKinley, A. E. *The Suffrage Franchise in the English Colonies in America.* Philadelphia, 1905.
Morgan, Edmund S. "The American Revolution: Revisions in Need of Revising," *William and Mary Quarterly*, 3rd Series, Vol. XIV (1957).
————*The Birth of the Republic, 1763-1789.* Chicago, 1956.
Morgan, Edmund S. and Helen M. *The Stamp Act Crisis: Prologue to Revolution.* Chapel Hill, North Carolina, 1953.
Namier, Sir Lewis. *England in the Age of the American Revolution.* London, 1930.
————*The Structure of Politics at the Accession of George III.* London, 1929.

Nettels, Curtis P. *George Washington and American Independence.* Boston, 1951.
————*The Roots of American Civilization.* New York, 1938.
Nevins, Allan. *The American States during and after the Revolution, 1775-1789.* New York, 1924.
Osgood, H. L. (edited by Dixon Ryan Fox). *The American Colonies in the Eighteenth Century.* 2 vols. New York, 1924.
Pargellis, Stanley M. *Lord Loudon in North America.* New Haven, 1933.
Parkman, Francis. *A Half-Century of Conflict.* Boston, 1929.
————*Montcalm and Wolfe.* 2 vols. Boston, 1927.
Pitman, F. W. *The Development of the British West Indies.* New Haven, 1917.
Rossiter, Clinton. *Seedtime of the Republic: The Origin of the American Tradition of Political Liberty.* New York, 1953.
Savelle, Max. *Seeds of Liberty: The Genesis of the American Mind.* New York, 1948.
Schlesinger, Arthur M. *The Colonial Merchants and the American Revolution.* New York, 1918.
————*New Viewpoints in American History.* New York, 1926.
Schuyler, R. L. *Parliament and the British Empire.* New York, 1929.
Singleton, Esther. *Social New York Under the Georges.* New York, 1902.
Smith, Adam. *The Wealth of Nations.* New York, 1937.
Thayer, Theodore G. *Pennsylvania Politics and the Growth of Democracy, 1740-1776.* Harrisburg, 1953.
Thornton, John W. *The Pulpit of the American Revolution.* Boston, 1860.
Tolles, Frederick. "The American Revolution Considered as a Social Movement: A Re-evaluation," *American Historical Review,* Vol. LX (1954).
Trevelyan, Sir George. *The American Revolution.* 4 vols. New York, 1899-1913.
Van Tyne, Claude H. *The Causes of the War of Independence.* Boston, 1922.
————*The Loyalists in the American Revolution.* New York, 1902.
————*The War of Independence.* Boston, 1929.
Winstanley, D. A. *Lord Chatham and the Whig Opposition.* Cambridge, 1912.
————*Personal and Party Government.* Cambridge, 1910.
Wright, Benjamin F., Jr. *American Interpretations of Natural Law.* Cambridge, Mass., 1931.
Wright, L. B. *The Atlantic Frontier: Colonial American Civilization, 1607-1763.* New York, 1947.

INDEX

Great Barrington, Mass., 371
Great Britain, in 1763, 3; trade of,
with colonies, 8–9; financial position after Seven Years' War, 81–82,
89; colonial relations, 208–211, 218–
220, 242–243, 275–276, 285–294, 437–
444; virtual representation in, 212–
215; upholds Mutiny Act, 240–241;
Dickinson petitions, 420–422; colonial propaganda against, 424–428;
Americans foresee decline of, 435.
See also British Empire
Great Commoner. *See* Pitt, William
Great Palladium, 5
Green Mountain Boys, 318, 481–482
Grenville, George, 6, 38, 104, 129, 131,
150, 156, 162, 185, 220, 240, 257, 266,
289, 345; quoted on requisitions, 49;
First Lord of the Treasury, 82-83; attempts to suppress smuggling, 84–
86; taxes molasses, 95; proposes Sugar
Act, 100–101; introduces Stamp Act,
109–116, 157; Rockingham succeeds,
117; loses colonial support, 119;
on external and internal taxes, 181;
King dislikes, 235; and Townshend
duties, 243, 250; denounces Dickinson, 261
Greyhound, ship, 350
Guadeloupe, 70

HALIFAX, accepts Stamp Act, 141
Hamilton, Alexander, 427–428, 483;
quoted on tradition, 29; his doctrine
of George III, 182, 184; and child
labor, 275; on taxation, 291; on
Quebec Act, 373–374; on impend-
ing war, 430
Hampden, John, 426
Hancock, John, 130–131, 135, 203, 219,
272, 307, 385, 489; celebrates repeal
of Stamp Act, 159; upholds Dickin-
son, 260; smuggles wine, 288; quoted
on Tea Act, 341–342; at Boston Tea
Party, 347–348; Massacre Day orator,
395; arrest ordered, 407, 408; on
invasion of Canada, 458
Hancock family, fortune of, 90
Hanover, House of, 182, 201
Hanoverians, 432–433
Harvard College, 193, 272
Hats, restriction on export of, 20–21
Hawley, Joseph, 485

Heart and Hand Fire Company, 137
Hearts of Oak, 136
Henry VIII, 221, 294
Henry, Patrick, 42, 76, 139, 169, 175,
374, 478; opposes stamp tax, 122–
126; at Continental Congress, 381;
quoted on need to fight, 392; on
foreign alliance, 483
Hessians, 432–433
Hewes, George, 347, 348
Hillsborough, Lord, 76, 316, 424;
quoted on colonies, 206; Secretary
of State for Colonies, 261; com-
poses British Circular Letter, 261–
264; opposes Townshend duties,
277; controls colonial policy, 279,
281
Hollis, Thomas, 191
Hood, Zachariah, 132, 144
Hooper, William, 504
Howe, Adm. Sir Richard, 475
Howe, Gen. Sir William, 441, 475;
seizes Staten Island, 493
Hughes, John, 114; stamp master,
135–136, 137; quoted on Stamp Act,
152; on Calvinists, 195–196; advocates representation, 227
Huguenots, 53
Husbands, Harmon, 321
Huske, John, 104
Hutchinson, Anne, 348
Hutchinson, Peggy, 346
Hutchinson, Thomas, 58–59, 117, 266,
317, 362; fears Sugar Act, 104; denounced as oligarch, 134–135; quoted
on anti-imperialism, 163; on *Gaspee*
affair, 327; Franklin acquires letters
of, 330–334; upholds Tea Act, 346–
347, 348; on Boston Port Act, 359

IMPERIALISM, 7–8, 18; British, American attitude toward, 3–4
Independence, war of, 440; causes,
24–25, 30–31, 126, 167–168, 216–217,
252, 437–438; early British indifference to, 219; role of press in,
288–293; and Nonimportation
Agreement, 315–317; preparations,
398–402, 416–417, 428–432, 446–447,
459–461, 482–486; Lexington and
Concord, 407–411; British Whigs
and, 499–456; Paine and, 467–473;
colonial opposition to, 477–481,

view of, 439–440; soldiers dreaded,
502–503
New England Confederation, 366
New Hampshire, resists stamp master,
133
New Hampshire Grants, 318
New Jersey, outbreaks against lawyers
in, 56; resists stamp masters, 133–
134
New Lights, 188
New York, 54; Assembly, 40, 248, 255–
257; patroon system, 56; smuggling,
83, 340; resents Stamp Act, 112,
117–118, 142–143, 159–160; Church
of England in, 193; class struggle
in, 298–306; reaction to Boston
Port Bill, 363–364; British loyalty
in, 404–405; reaction to Lexington
in, 415–416
Newcastle, Duke of, 37–38, 66, 67,
154
Newfoundland, 73
Newport, supports Boston against
Port Act, 362
Newspapers, 64; influence in colonies,
288–293
Nonconsumption Agreement, 385–
387
Nonimportation Agreement, 279, 287,
304, 381; consummated, 269–270;
women aid, 270–271; menaced by
British troops, 294; merchants lose
control of, 298; enforcement, 308;
collapse, 309–311, 315–316; at Continental Congress, 385–387, 406,
447
North, Lord, 89, 182, 185, 247, 311,
325, 344, 362, 398, 421, 424, 459;
quoted on requisitions, 66; resents
Boston Tea Party, 225, 256; Chancellor of Exchequer, 277; disap-
proves repeal of Townshend duties,
278; controls colonial policy, 279;
refuses to repeal tea duty, 280–281;
upholds tea tax, 337–339, 342–343,
345; and Boston Port Act, 358–359;
attempts reform of Massachusetts
Constitution, 369–376; attempts appeasement, 402; Conciliatory Propositions, 405–407
North Briton, 305
North Carolina, at Continental Congress, 381. See also Carolinas

Northern Thane. See Bute, Earl of
Nova Scotia, 31, 438, 458

Ogden, speaker of New Jersey As-
sembly, 138–139
Oligarchy, in American colonies, 57,
59–60; planter, in Virginia, 122, 125;
hatred of colonial, 134–135. See also
Conservatives; Tories
"Olive Branch" petition, 459
Oliver, Andrew, stamp master for
Massachusetts Bay, 132, 135; Frank-
lin acquires letters of, 330–334
Oliver, Peter, 171, 334
Otis, Harrison Gray, 505
Otis, James, 46, 126, 145, 153, 211;
leader of popular party, 59; quoted
on customs officers, 83; opposes
Stamp Act, 122, 137, 159; on co-
lonial assemblies, 179; on virtual
representation, 214–215; his views
on imperial federation, 225–226; on
Mutiny Act, 238–239; on Town-
shend duties, 255, 268; on hopes for
Britain, 436

Paine, Thomas, 171, 492; quoted on
court influence, 66-67; upholds
American freedom, 462–463, 467–
473; draws up Pennsylvania Con-
stitution, 504, 505
Paper money, issue of, as legal tender
forbidden, 18–20
Parliament, colonial resistance to, 38–
39; American conception of, 176,
178–180; George III distinct from,
181–185; British view of supremacy
of, 216–218
Parson's Cause, 41, 122, 124
Partridge, Richard, 99
Party System, British, under George
III, 67–68
Patroon system, 56
Paxton, Charles, Commissioner of
Customs, 266
Paxton Boys, 62
Peace of Paris, 25, 71–74, 505
Penn, Gov. John, 22
Penn family, 62
Pennsylvania, and Seven Years' War,
40, 43; Scotch-Irish and Germans in,
53, 504; suffrage in, 55; sectionalism
in, 61–64; resists Stamp Act, 135–